Lecture Notes in Computer Science

Lecture Notes in Computer Science

Vol. 49: Interactive Systems. Proceedings 1976. Edited by A. Blaser and C. Hackl. VI, 380 pages. 1976.

Vol. 50: A. C. Hartmann, A Concurrent Pascal Compiler for Minicomputers. VI, 119 pages. 1977.

Vol. 51: B. S. Garbow, Matrix Eigensystem Routines – Eispack Guide Extension. VIII, 343 pages. 1977.

Vol. 52: Automata, Languages and Programming. Fourth Colloquium, University of Turku, July 1977. Edited by A. Salomaa and M. Steinby. X, 569 pages. 1977.

Vol. 53: Mathematical Foundations of Computer Science. Proceedings 1977. Edited by J. Gruska. XII, 608 pages. 1977.

Vol. 54: Design and Implementation of Programming Languages. Proceedings 1976. Edited by J. H. Williams and D. A. Fisher. X, 496 pages. 1977.

Vol. 55: A. Gerbier, Mes premières constructions de programmes. XII, 256 pages. 1977.

Vol. 56: Fundamentals of Computation Theory. Proceedings 1977. Edited by M. Karpiński. XII, 542 pages. 1977.

Vol. 57: Portability of Numerical Software. Proceedings 1976. Edited by W. Cowell. VIII, 539 pages. 1977.

Vol. 58: M. J. O'Donnell, Computing in Systems Described by Equations. XIV, 111 pages. 1977.

Vol. 59: E. Hill, Jr., A Comparative Study of Very Large Data Bases. X, 140 pages. 1978.

Vol. 60: Operating Systems, An Advanced Course. Edited by R. Bayer, R. M. Graham, and G. Seegmüller. X, 593 pages. 1978.

Vol. 61: The Vienna Development Method: The Meta-Language. Edited by D. Bjørner and C. B. Jones. XVIII, 382 pages. 1978.

Vol. 62: Automata, Languages and Programming. Proceedings 1978. Edited by G. Ausiello and C. Böhm. VIII, 508 pages. 1978.

Vol. 63: Natural Language Communication with Computers. Edited by Leonard Bolc. VI, 292 pages. 1978.

Vol. 64: Mathematical Foundations of Computer Science. Proceedings 1978. Edited by J. Winkowski. X, 551 pages. 1978.

Vol. 65: Information Systems Methodology, Proceedings, 1978. Edited by G. Bracchi and P. C. Lockemann. XII, 696 pages. 1978.

Vol. 66: N. D. Jones and S. S. Muchnick, TEMPO: A Unified Treatment of Binding Time and Parameter Passing Concepts in Programming Languages. IX, 118 pages. 1978.

Vol. 67: Theoretical Computer Science, 4th GI Conference, Aachen, March 1979. Edited by K. Weihrauch. VII, 324 pages. 1979.

Vol. 68: D. Harel, First-Order Dynamic Logic. X, 133 pages. 1979.

Vol. 69: Program Construction. International Summer School. Edited by F. L. Bauer and M. Broy. VII, 651 pages. 1979.

Vol. 70: Semantics of Concurrent Computation. Proceedings 1979. Edited by G. Kahn. VI, 368 pages. 1979.

Vol. 71: Automata, Languages and Programming. Proceedings 1979. Edited by H. A. Maurer. IX, 684 pages. 1979.

Vol. 72: Symbolic and Algebraic Computation. Proceedings 1979. Edited by E. W. Ng. XV, 557 pages. 1979.

Vol. 73: Graph-Grammars and Their Application to Computer Science and Biology. Proceedings 1978. Edited by V. Claus, H. Ehrig and G. Rozenberg. VII, 477 pages. 1979.

Vol. 74: Mathematical Foundations of Computer Science. Proceedings 1979. Edited by J. Bečvář. IX, 580 pages. 1979.

Vol. 75: Mathematical Studies of Information Processing. Proceedings 1978. Edited by E. K. Blum, M. Paul and S. Takasu. VIII, 629 pages. 1979.

Vol. 76: Codes for Boundary-Value Problems in Ordinary Differential Equations. Proceedings 1978. Edited by B. Childs et al. VIII, 388 pages. 1979.

Vol. 77: G. V. Bochmann, Architecture of Distributed Computer Systems. VIII, 238 pages. 1979.

Vol. 78: M. Gordon, R. Milner and C. Wadsworth, Edinburgh LCF. VIII, 159 pages. 1979.

Vol. 79: Language Design and Programming Methodology. Proceedings, 1979. Edited by J. Tobias. IX, 255 pages. 1980.

Vol. 80: Pictorial Information Systems. Edited by S. K. Chang and K. S. Fu. IX, 445 pages. 1980.

Vol. 81: Data Base Techniques for Pictorial Applications. Proceedings, 1979. Edited by A. Blaser. XI, 599 pages. 1980.

Vol. 82: J. G. Sanderson, A Relational Theory of Computing. VI, 147 pages. 1980.

Vol. 83: International Symposium Programming. Proceedings, 1980. Edited by B. Robinet. VII, 341 pages. 1980.

Vol. 84: Net Theory and Applications. Proceedings, 1979. Edited by W. Brauer. XIII, 537 Seiten. 1980.

Vol. 85: Automata, Languages and Programming. Proceedings, 1980. Edited by J. de Bakker and J. van Leeuwen. VIII, 671 pages. 1980.

Vol. 86: Abstract Software Specifications. Proceedings, 1979. Edited by D. Bjørner. XIII, 567 pages. 1980

Vol. 87: 5th Conference on Automated Deduction. Proceedings, 1980. Edited by W. Bibel and R. Kowalski. VII, 385 pages. 1980.

Vol. 88: Mathematical Foundations of Computer Science 1980. Proceedings, 1980. Edited by P. Dembiński. VIII, 723 pages. 1980.

Vol. 89: Computer Aided Design - Modelling, Systems Engineering, CAD-Systems. Proceedings, 1980. Edited by J. Encarnacao. XIV, 461 pages. 1980.

Vol. 90: D. M. Sandford, Using Sophisticated Models in Resolution Theorem Proving.
XI, 239 pages. 1980

Vol. 91: D. Wood, Grammar and L Forms: An Introduction. IX, 314 pages. 1980.

Vol. 92: R. Milner, A Calculus of Communication Systems. VI, 171 pages. 1980.

Vol. 93: A. Nijholt, Context-Free Grammars: Covers, Normal Forms, and Parsing. VII, 253 pages. 1980.

Vol. 94: Semantics-Directed Compiler Generation. Proceedings, 1980. Edited by N. D. Jones. V, 489 pages. 1980.

Vol. 95: Ch. D. Marlin, Coroutines. XII, 246 pages. 1980.

Vol. 96: J. L. Peterson, Computer Programs for Spelling Correction: VI, 213 pages. 1980.

Vol. 97: S. Osaki and T. Nishio, Reliability Evaluation of Some Fault-Tolerant Computer Architectures. VI, 129 pages. 1980.

Vol. 98: Towards a Formal Description of Ada. Edited by D. Bjørner and O. N. Oest. XIV, 630 pages. 1980.

Vol. 99: I. Guessarian, Algebraic Semantics. XI, 158 pages. 1981.

Vol. 100: Graphtheoretic Concepts in Computer Science. Edited by H. Noltemeier. X, 403 pages. 1981.

Vol. 101: A. Thayse, Boolean Calculus of Differences. VII, 144 pages. 1981.

Vol. 102: J. H. Davenport, On the Integration of Algebraic Functions. 1–197 pages. 1981.

Vol. 103: H. Ledgard, A. Singer, J. Whiteside, Directions in Human Factors of Interactive Systems. VI, 190 pages. 1981.

Vol. 104: Theoretical Computer Science. Ed. by P. Deussen. VII, 261 pages. 1981.

Vol. 105: B. W. Lampson, M. Paul, H. J. Siegert, Distributed Systems – Architecture and Implementation. XIII, 510 pages. 1981.

Vol. 106: The Programming Language Ada. Reference Manual. X, 243 pages. 1981.

Lecture Notes in Computer Science

Edited by G. Goos and J. Hartmanis

158

Foundations of Computation Theory

Proceedings of the 1983 International FCT-Conference
Borgholm, Sweden, August 21–27, 1983

EATCS

Edited by Marek Karpinski

Springer-Verlag
Berlin Heidelberg New York Tokyo 1983

Editor

Marek Karpinski
Computer Science Department, University of Bonn
Wegelerstr. 6, D-5300 Bonn 1, West-Germany

AMS Subject Classifications (1980): 03 B 25, 03 D 05, 03 F 60, 10 A 30, 10 N 05, 58 B 05, 60 C 05, 68 C 25, 68 D 05, 68 E 10, 68 F 20, 94 C 99
CR Subject Classifications (1982): C.2, E.2, E.3, E.4, F.2, F.3, F.4, G.2.1

ISBN 3-540-12689-9 Springer-Verlag Berlin Heidelberg New York Tokyo
ISBN 0-387-12689-9 Springer-Verlag New York Heidelberg Berlin Tokyo

Printed in Germany

Printing and binding: Beltz Offsetdruck, Hemsbach/Bergstr.
2145/3140-543210

CONFERENCE COMMITTEES

PROGRAM COMMITTEE

K.R. Apt (Paris), G. Ausiello (Rome), A.J. Blikle (Warsaw), E. Börger (Dortmund), W. Brauer (Hamburg), M. Broy (Munich), L. Budach (Berlin), R. Burstall (Edinburgh), P. van Emde Boas (Amsterdam), F. Gecseg (Szeged), J. Gruska (Bratislava), M.A. Harrison (Berkeley), J. Hartmanis (Ithaca), K. Indermark (Aachen), M. Karpinski (Bonn), D. Kozen (Yorktown Heights), J. van Leeuwen (Utrecht), L. Lovasz (Budapest), A. Mazurkiewicz (Warsaw), G.L. Miller (Cambridge Mass.), P. Mosses (Aarhus), B. Nordström (Gothenburg), M. Paterson (Warwick), A. Salomaa (Turku), C.P. Schnorr (Frankfurt), J.W. Thatcher (Yorktown Heights)

PROGRAM COMMITTEE CHAIRMAN

Prof. Marek Karpinski
Computer Science Department
University of Bonn
Wegelerstr. 6
D-53oo Bonn 1
W.Germany

ORGANIZING COMMITTEE

E. Sandewall (Chairman)
A. Lingas
J. Maluszynski

ORGANIZING SECRETARY

Lillemor Wallgren

PROGRAM SECRETARY

Mariele Knepper

The International Conference on "Foundations of Computation Theory - 1983" follows thematically the series of the international FCT-conferences founded in 1977 in Poznan-Kornik, Poland. The program of the conference, including invited lectures and selected contributions, falls into eight categories:

* Constructive Mathematics in Models of Computation and Programming
* Abstract Calculi and Denotational Semantics
* Theory of Machines, Computations, and Languages
* Nondeterminism, Concurrency, and Distributed Computing
* Abstract Algebras, Logics, and Combinatorics in Computation Theory
* General Computability and Decidability
* Computational and Arithmetic Complexity
* Analysis of Algorithms and Feasible Computing

ORGANIZED BY:

The Department of Computer and Information Science, Linköping University and Institute of Technology

WITH THE COOPERATION OF:

The Departments of Computer Science and Mathematics, University of Bonn

UNDER THE AUSPICES OF:

The Royal Swedish Academy of Engineering Sciences
The European Association for Theoretical Computer Science
Gesellschaft für Informatik e.V., Bonn
The Swedish Society for Information Processing

PREFACE

The papers in this Volume constitute the proceedings of the 1983 International Conference on "Foundations of Computation Theory", FCT '83, held at Borgholm, Sweden, August 21-27. The Conference is to follow thematically the series of the international FCT-conferences initiated in 1977 in Poznan-Kornik, Poland. The Conference was organized by the University of Linköping with the cooperation of University of Bonn under the auspices of the European Association for Theoretical Computer Science, the Royal Swedish Academy of Engineering Sciences, Gesellschaft für Informatik, e.V., Bonn, and the Swedish Society for Information Processing.

The Swedish Board for Technical Development (STU) provided the financial support that made this Conference possible.

The Proceedings contain the texts of the addresses given by the invitation of the International Program Committee falling into one of the two categories:
- invited addresses, and - (selected) contributions.

The 34 papers (- shorter communications) were selected on April 7 and 8, 1983 at the Program Selection Committee Meeting in Bonn from the large number of papers submitted to the organizers in response to the Call for Papers. The International Program Committee consisted of: K.R. Apt (Paris), G. Ausiello (Rome), A.J. Blikle (Warsaw), E. Börger (Dortmund), W. Brauer (Hamburg), M. Broy (Munich), L. Budach (Berlin), R. Burstall (Edinburgh), P. van Emde Boas (Amsterdam), F. Gecseg (Szeged), J. Gruska (Bratislava), M.A. Harrison (Berkeley), J. Hartmanis (Ithaca), K. Indermark (Aachen), M. Karpinski (Bonn), D. Kozen (Yorktown Heights), J. van Leeuwen (Utrecht), L. Lovasz (Budapest), A. Mazurkiewicz (Warsaw), G.L. Miller (Cambridge, Mass.), P. Mosses (Aarhus), B. Nordström (Gothenburg), M. Paterson (Warwick), A. Salomaa (Turku), C.P. Schnorr (Frankfurt), J.W. Thatcher (Yorktown Heights).

My thanks, at this place, go to the members of this Committee (which I have had pleasure to chair) as well as to all subreferees for the FCT '83 (see the separate page) for all their efforts and time they invested in reading submitted papers.

The definite decision to organize the "Foundations of Computation Theory - 1983" Conference in Sweden was made in late November, 1982. That it really took place in 1983 is due to initiative and continuing support and encouragement of Professor Erik Sandewall of Linköping University, who served also as Conference Organizing Chairman, as well as my colleagues A. Lingas, and J. Maluszynski from the Organizing Committee. The extraordinary short time for preparation of the Conference added another difficulty factor to its Program and Organizing Committees. The extent of their success is to be measured by this LNCS-Volume.

The Committee owe special debt to Professor K.H. Böhling for his continuing support while making the Program of the Conference in Bonn.

I am deeply indebted to Mariele Knepper whose outstanding work as the Program Secretary was genuine source of support to all of us, and decisive for the smooth work of the FCT-Program Committee - as it was. I wish to thank R. Verbeek for running all the computer programs for the April's Program Committee Meeting in Bonn. Our thanks go to Lillemor Wallgren, The Organizing Secretary, for the masterful way she handled all the complex organizational matters of her secretariate.

Finally, I wish to thank the many persons, too numerous, perhaps, to name for the enthusiastic support of the idea of this FCT-Conference. They all contributed not only to the success of the Conference in its present shape - but to its very existence in this year in the first place - as well.

June 1983

Marek Karpinski

Referees of FCT'83

Aalbersberg, I.J.
Abramsky, S.
Alexi, W.
Anderson, S.
Apt, K.R.
Arnold, A.
Ausiello, G.
Back, R.J.R.
Backhouse, R.
Bartha, M.
Bednarczyk, M.
Berghammer, R.
Bergman, M.
Bergstra, J.A.
Best, E.
Blikle, A.J.
Bloom, S.L.
Boehm, A.P.W.
Boerger, E.
Brauer, W.
Broy, M.
Burstall, R.
Chrzastowski-Wachtel, P.
Chytil, M.P.
Coffman, E.G. (Jr.)
Coleman, D.
Constable, R.
Costa, G.
Courcelle, B.
Crasemann
Curien, J.L.
Curien, P.J.
Czaja, L.
Damm, W.
Darlington, J.
de Roever, W.P.
Delgado Kloos, C.
Delporte, C.
Dembinski, P.
Denning, P.J.
Dosch, W.
Duris, P.
Dybjer, P.
Engelfriet, J.
Esik, Z.
Fagin, R.
Fehr, E.
Fiby, R.
Fich, F.E.
Fle, M.P.
Fortune, S.
Ganzinger, H.
Gecseg, F.
Gerth, R.
Gnatz, R.
Goltz, U.
Gruska, J.
Guessarian, I.
Hangel, E.
Harrison, M.A.
Hartmanis, J.
Hennessy, M.
Horejs, J.
Horvath, G.
Ibarra, O.H.
Imreh, B.
Indermark, K.
Janicki, R.
Janssens, D.
Jantzen, M.
Jochum, G.
Josko, B.
Karpinski, M.
Kelemenova, A.
Kemp, R.
Kennaway, R.
Kintala, C.M.R.
Klaeren, H.A.
Kleijn, H.
Klein, H.-J.
Klop, J.W.
Korec, I.
Kott, L.
Kozen, D.
Krause,
Kreczmar, A.
Kroeger, F.
Kuiper, R.
Kupka, J.
Kwasowiec, W.
Lange, K.J.
Langmaack, H.
Leighton, F.T.
Leszczylowski, J.
Lippe, W.-M.
Lipski, W. Jr.
Lovasz, L.
Lub, B.E.
Martel, C.U.
Matzner, T.A.
Mazurkiewicz, A.
Meseguer, J.
Meyer, J.-J.Ch.
Michael, J.
Miller, G.L.
Milner, R.
Moeller, B.
Mosses, P.
Muchnick, S.S.
Munro, J.
Mycroft, A.
Nickl, F.
Nijhold, A.
Nissim, F.
Niwinski, D.
Nordstroem, B.
Novotny, M.
Obermeier, R.
Ochranova, R.
Odlyzko, A.
Olderog, E.-R.
Oslowska, E.
Overmars, M.H.
Padawitz, P.
Park, D.
Paterson, M.
Pepper, P.
Petersson, K.
Pettorossi, A.
Poigne, A.
Privara, I.
Reiser, A.
Reisig, W.
Rinnooy Kan, A.H.G.
Ritchie, R.W.
Rudnicki, P.
Ruzicka, P.
Rydeheard, D.E.
Rytter, W.
Salomaa, A.
Schmidt, G.
Schnorr, C.P.
Schoett, O.
Schroeter, N.
Shields, M.W.
Shmoys, D.B.
Smith, J.
Smyth, M.B.
Stirling, C.
Stougie, L.
Streicher, T.
Strong, H.R.
Talcott, C.
Tarlecki, A.
Thatcher, J.W.
Thomas, W.
Thompson, C.
Tiuryn, J.
Torenvliet, L.
Townley, J.
Tucker, J.V.
Turan, G.
Turjan, G.
Urzyczyn. P.
Valk, R.
van der Wall, R.W.
van Emde Boas, P.
van Leeuwen, J.
Vazirani, V.
Vidal-Naquet, G.
Viragh, J.
Vitanyi, P.M.B.
Vogel, H.
Waldinger, R.
Wiedermann, J.
Winkowski, J.
Wirsing, M.
Woessner, H.

Foundations of Computation Theory

FCT '83

August 21-27, 1983

Borgholm, Sweden

TABLE OF CONTENTS

Experiments, Powerdomains and Fully Abstract Models for Applicative Multiprogramming

Samson Abramsky
Department of Computer Science and Statistics
Queen Mary College
Mile End Road
London E1 4NS

1. Introduction

Consider a computer system with a number of input devices (e.g. keyboards) and a number of output devices (e.g. visual displays, printers). Users of the system interact with it by supplying inputs and observing outputs. For each input device, the values successively input on it form a sequence (in time); similarly, the values produced on each output device form a sequence. It is natural to abstract the behaviours of such a system as a function from the sequences of values supplied on each of its inputs to the sequences of values produced on its outputs. Because of unpredictable time dependencies, arising either from the internal operations of the system, or from the need for it to respond to input values on different devices in the order in which they arise, the system may be non-deterministic, i.e. it computes a relation or multi-valued function over sequences of values.

How can structure be imposed on the behaviour of systems of this type? The approach taken here, following [DeNH82], is that structure is relative to the discriminations we, as observers or experimenters on the system, are prepared to admit. The more powerful the experiments we can perform, the finer the structure that will be imposed.

In particular, we show that, if only finite experiments are admissible, the classical powerdomain constructions [Plo76, Smy78] capture exactly the discriminations which can be made; they are fully abstract in the sense of Milner [Mil73]. This extends results obtained in [Hen81] for the simpler case of functions over flat (or "discrete") domains, and shows exactly which operational notions of indistinguishability these powerdomain constructions do embody. We then consider how, as the programming language and the class of admissible experiments are varied, the notions of equivalence change. For lack of space, all proofs are omitted.

2. Experiments and Preorders

In this section, we firstly consider an abstract framework for formulating notions of operational equivalence, and then specialise it to systems which compute over sequences of values. Our approach is based on [DeNH82], with some variations partly suggested by [KH80].

2.1

We assume the following sets:

P - processes, ranged over by p
T - tests, ranged over by t
C - computations, ranged over by c

Since processes are non-deterministic, they are represented by sets of computations:

Comp : $P \to 2^C$

The act of testing is formalised as a relation between computations and tests:

passes $\subseteq$ C×T.

On this basis, we define two important relations between processes and tests:

$$p \text{ may } t \equiv \exists c \in Comp(p)\ c \text{ passes } t$$
$$p \text{ must } t \equiv \forall c \in Comp(p)\ c \text{ passes } t.$$

We can now define three operational preorders on P, which express various notions of "satisfying more experiments (or assertions)":

(i) $p \sqsubseteq_1 p' \equiv \forall t\ p \text{ may } t \Rightarrow p' \text{ may } t$

(ii) $p \sqsubseteq_2 p' \equiv \forall t\ p \text{ must } t \Rightarrow p' \text{ must } t$

(iii) $p \sqsubseteq_3 p' \equiv p \sqsubseteq_1 p'\ \&\ p \sqsubseteq_2 p'$.

For further discussion of the rationale for these preorders, see [DeNH82].

2.2

We now apply this abstract framework to processes which intermittently produce output (at present we are not considering input).

Our formulation is still somewhat abstract. P remains unanalysed. We assume a set D of atomic data values, ranged over by d.

$D_\tau = D \cup \{\tau\}$,

where $\tau \notin D$. D_τ is ranged over by μ.

We assume familiarity with the following standard notions on sequence domains (cf. [Kah74], [Niv79]): for X a countable, non-empty set

$X^\infty = X^* \cup X^\omega$

the set of finite and infinite sequences over X, ordered by the prefix (initial subsequence) relation $\leq$, is a countably algebraic, consistently complete partial order. It is the order-completion of X^*. Also, for $Y \subseteq X$,

$\_\pi Y : X^\infty \to X^\infty$ ("projection" onto a sub-alphabet)

is the function obtained from the assignment on X:

$x\pi Y \mapsto$ | $\langle x \rangle$ if $x \in Y$
| $\langle\rangle$ otherwise

as the unique homomorphic extension to X^* (the free monoid on X), and then the unique continuous extension to X^∞.

We now assume a D_τ-indexed family of <u>transition relations</u>,

$$\xrightarrow{\mu}$$

on P.

$$\longrightarrow \; = \; \cup \overset{\mu}{\longrightarrow}$$

Here

$$p \overset{\mu}{\longrightarrow} p'$$

means that process p can take a single computational step, changing state to become process p'; if $\mu=\tau$, no output is produced on that step, while if $\mu=d\in D$, output d is produced.

$$C^{fin} = \{p_0\mu_0\ldots p_{n-1}\mu_{n-1}p_n \mid n\geq 0 \;\&\; \forall i<n \; p_i \overset{\mu_i}{\longrightarrow} p_{i+1} \;\&\; p_n \notin \text{dom} \longrightarrow\}.$$

$$C^{inf} = \{\langle p_i\mu_i\rangle_{i\in N} \mid \forall i \; p_i \overset{\mu_i}{\longrightarrow} p_{i+1}\}.$$

$$C = C^{fin} \cup C^{inf}.$$

$$\text{Comp}(p) = \{c\in C \mid c_0=p\}.$$

$T \subseteq 2^{D^{\infty}}$ (We are parameterising on the choice of T)

$$\ell : C \to D^{\infty}$$

$$\begin{aligned}\ell(c) &= \dagger\; (\mu_0\ldots\mu_{n-1})^{\pi}D \quad \text{for } c = p_0\mu_0\ldots p_{n-1}\mu_{n-1}p_n \in C^{fin}\\ &= \dagger\; \langle\mu_i\rangle_{i\in N}{}^{\pi}D \quad \text{for } c = \langle p_i\mu_i\rangle_{i\in N} \in C^{inf}.\end{aligned}$$

c **passes** t $\equiv \exists s\in t \; s\leq\ell(c)$.

As we have now specified P, T, C, Comp and **passes**, the definitions of the three preorders follow as in 2.1.

Our notion of a computation passing a test is that at some stage in the computation, the output produced matches one of the sequences in the test set. If the sequence matched is finite, the computation may subsequently produce more output; if the sequence is infinite, this possibility does not arise. We allow tests to be <u>sets</u> of sequences because of non-determinism; in particular, if tests comprised single values only, the **must** relation, and hence $\sqsubseteq_2$, would be vacuous.

3. An Applicative Programming Language and its Operational Semantics

<u>3.1</u>

We now give internal structure to P, the set of processes, by specifying an applicative programming language, incorporating non-deterministic choice and stream processing. The language comprises: first-order (non-deterministic) recursion equations ([Niv80]); arithmetic primitives like those of PCF [Plo77]; and Kahn's stream processing primitives [Kah74].

We assume familiarity with the following standard concepts of universal algebra (e.g. [ADJ78]): **ranked alphabet, term, word algebra.**

Notation Given a ranked alphabet Σ, and a set of variables X, $T_\Sigma(X)$ is the Σ-word algebra over X.

Our language is specified, firstly, by a ranked alphabet Σ of base function symbols:

Σ_0 = {ZERO, Ω}
Σ_1 = {SUCC, PRED, HD, TL}
Σ_2 = {OR, CONS}
Σ_3 = {IF}
$\Sigma_n = \emptyset$, n>3.

For simplicity, we assume a fixed set of user-defined function symbols,

$\Phi = \{F_1,\ldots,F_m\}$

each of the same arity k, and a fixed set of variables

$X = \{x_1,\ldots,x_k\}$.

We now have the following sets:

Terms (ranged over by T) - $T_{\Sigma\cup\Phi}(X)$

Closed Terms (also ranged over by T) - $T_{\Sigma\cup\Phi}$

Declarations (ranged over by D)
- all m-tuples $\langle F_1(x_1,\ldots,x_k) = T_1,\ldots,F_m(x_1,\ldots,x_k) = T_m\rangle$ where $D_i = T_i$, $1 \leq i \leq m$.

Programs (ranged over by P)
- pairs ⟨D,T⟩, D a declaration and T a closed term.

This completes our description of the syntax of the language.

3.2 Operational Semantics

N_T, N^∞ are as in 2.2. We now specify an N_T-indexed family of transition relations over P. The relations are defined axiomatically, in the style of Plotkin [Plo82].

Notation
(i) Since in all cases

$$\langle D,T\rangle \overset{\mu}{--\!\!\rightarrow} \langle D',T'\rangle$$

will imply D = D', we shall omit the declaration components of programs in the following axioms, simply writing

$$T \overset{\mu}{--\!\!\rightarrow} T'$$

(ii) For terms $T, T_1,\ldots,T_k$
$T[T_1,\ldots,T_k]$
denotes the result of substituting each T_i for x_i in T; see [ADJ78].

(I) $F_i(T_1,\ldots,T_k) \xrightarrow{\tau} D_i[T_1,\ldots,T_k]$

(II) $\mathrm{ZERO} \xrightarrow{0} \Omega$

(III) (i) $T \xrightarrow{\tau} T' \Rightarrow \mathrm{SUCC}(T) \xrightarrow{\tau} \mathrm{SUCC}(T')$

(ii) $T \xrightarrow{n} T' \Rightarrow \mathrm{SUCC}(T) \xrightarrow{n+1} \Omega$

(IV) (i) $T \xrightarrow{\tau} T' \Rightarrow \mathrm{PRED}(T) \xrightarrow{\tau} \mathrm{PRED}(T')$

(ii) $T \xrightarrow{0} T' \Rightarrow \mathrm{PRED}(T) \xrightarrow{\tau} \Omega$

(iii) $T \xrightarrow{n+1} T' \Rightarrow \mathrm{PRED}(T) \xrightarrow{n} \Omega$

(V) (i) $T \xrightarrow{\tau} T' \Rightarrow \mathrm{HD}(T) \xrightarrow{\tau} \mathrm{HD}(T')$

(ii) $T \xrightarrow{n} T' \Rightarrow \mathrm{HD}(T) \xrightarrow{n} \Omega$

(VI) (i) $T \xrightarrow{\tau} T' \Rightarrow \mathrm{TL}(T) \xrightarrow{\tau} \mathrm{TL}(T')$

(ii) $T \xrightarrow{n} T' \Rightarrow \mathrm{TL}(T) \xrightarrow{\tau} T'$

(VII) (i) $T_1 \xrightarrow{\tau} T_1' \Rightarrow \mathrm{CONS}(T_1,T_2) \xrightarrow{\tau} \mathrm{CONS}(T_1',T_2)$

(ii) $T_1 \xrightarrow{n} T_1' \Rightarrow \mathrm{CONS}(T_1,T_2) \xrightarrow{n} T_2$

(VIII) (i) $\mathrm{OR}(T_1,T_2) \xrightarrow{\tau} T_1$

(ii) $\mathrm{OR}(T_1,T_2) \xrightarrow{\tau} T_2$

(IX) (i) $T \xrightarrow{\tau} T' \Rightarrow \mathrm{IF}(T,T_1,T_2) \xrightarrow{\tau} \mathrm{IF}(T',T_1,T_2)$

(ii) $T \xrightarrow{0} T' \Rightarrow \mathrm{IF}(T,T_1,T_2) \xrightarrow{\tau} T_1$

(iii) $T \xrightarrow{n+1} T' \Rightarrow \mathrm{IF}(T,T_1,T_2) \xrightarrow{\tau} T_2$

Notes

1. To avoid having multiple sorts, all operations work on streams, and conditional tests for zero. For a denotational view of the operators, see section 4.4.

2. Ω corresponds to NIL in Milner's CCS [Mil80]; as we shall see, it denotes the least elements in our semantic domains, and hence can be pressed into double service as the "underdefined process", with no special treatment via a divergence predicate as in [deNH82] being necessary.

3. The idea of giving operational semantics to an applicative stream processing language via labelled transition relations, with the labels carrying the output, is due to Broy [Bro82]; however, he uses a combination of reduction (for atomic values) and output, and his language and semantics differ in a number of other respects from the above.

The transition relation on P defined above fits exactly into the framework established in 2.2. We thus immediately obtain definitions of the preorders $\sqsubseteq_i$, i=1,2,3 on programs in our language.

We now give an operational semantics for programs:

Definition
$OP : Programs \rightarrow 2^{N^\infty}$

$OP[P] = \{\ell(c) \mid c \in Comp(P)\}$

3.3

We now fix T, for the remainder of this paper, to be the set of all finite sets of finite elements of N^∞, i.e. all finite subsets of N^*. T is ranged over by A.

We define three relations on $2^{N^\infty}-\emptyset$ (which is ranged over by X,Y):

Definition
(i) $X \sqsubseteq_U Y \equiv \forall x \in X\ \exists y \in Y\ x \leq y$
(ii) $X \sqsubseteq_S Y \equiv \forall y \in Y\ \exists x \in X\ x \leq y$
(iii) $X \sqsubseteq_{EM} Y \equiv X \sqsubseteq_U Y\ \&\ X \sqsubseteq_S Y.$

For an important analysis of (ii) and (iii) in the case that $X \in T$ see [Smy78]. The subscript "U" stands for "Upwards", since one can think of (i) and (ii) as dual, "upwards" and "downwards" conditions. "S" abbreviates Smyth, and "EM" Egli-Milner.

Definition (Smyth)
(i) $X \sqsubseteq_U Y \equiv \forall A \in T\ A \sqsubseteq_U X \Rightarrow A \sqsubseteq_U Y$
(ii) $X \sqsubseteq_S Y \equiv \forall A \in T\ A \sqsubseteq_S X \Rightarrow A \sqsubseteq_S Y$
(iii) $X \sqsubseteq_{EM} Y \equiv \forall A \in T\ A \sqsubseteq_{EM} X \Rightarrow A \sqsubseteq_{EM} Y.$

All the six relations defined above are preorders.

Definition
For $i \in \{1,2,3,U,S,EM\}$
$\simeq_i$ is the equivalence relation associated with preorder $\sqsubseteq_i$.

We now draw some simple consequences of the definitions.

Proposition 1 P must A $\Leftrightarrow$ A $\sqsubseteq_S$ OP[P].

Proposition 2
(i) $A' \subseteq A\ \&\ A \sqsubseteq_U X \Rightarrow A' \sqsubseteq_U X$
(ii) $A \subseteq A'\ \&\ A \sqsubseteq_S X \Rightarrow A' \sqsubseteq_S X.$

Proposition 3
$X \sqsubseteq_{EM} Y \Leftrightarrow X \sqsubseteq_U Y \ \& \ X \sqsubseteq_S Y$.

Proposition 4
(i) $P \sqsubseteq_1 P' \Leftrightarrow OP[P] \sqsubseteq_U OP[P']$
(ii) $P \sqsubseteq_2 P' \Leftrightarrow OP[P] \sqsubseteq_S OP[P']$
(iii) $P \sqsubseteq_3 P' \Leftrightarrow OP[P] \sqsubseteq_{EM} OP[P']$

4. Powerdomains and Denotational Semantics

4.1 Powerdomains

We shall use two characterisations of powerdomains in what follows. Let D be a strongly algebraic cpo (i.e. SFP-object - see [Plo76,Smy78]). Then for $i \in \{U,S,EM\}$, $P_i[D]$ is given, up to isomorphism, in either of the two following ways:

(I) $P_i[D] = (F[D]/\approx_i, \sqsubseteq_i/\approx_i)$

Here F[D] is the set of finitely generable subsets of D (see below); these are preordered by $\sqsubseteq_i$. Smyth [Smy78] proved that this preorder is a predomain, i.e. the poset obtained by factoring via $\approx_i$ is complete and has the (equivalence classes of) finite sets of finite elements of D as a basis of finite elements.

(II) $P_i[D] = (\{X^*_i \mid X \in 2^D - \emptyset\}, \sqsubseteq_i)$

Here $\_^*_i$ is a closure operator on (arbitrary) subsets of D, to be described below. Plotkin [Plo76] proved that restricting to the closed subsets, and ordering directly by $\sqsubseteq_i$, gives a domain, with the (closures of) finite sets of finite elements of D as a basis.

The isomorphism between (I) and (II) is given by

$[X]_i \to X^*_i$.

X^*_i is the $\subseteq$-maximal element of its equivalence class. X^*_i is finitely generated, even if X is not. (Actually, Plotkin only worked with $P_{EM}[]$, and Smyth with $P_{EM}[]$ and $P_S[]$, but the extension of these results is straightforward.)

A generating tree T is a finitary tree, all of whose branches are infinite, whose nodes are labelled with elements of D, such that if n is an ancestor of n', label(n)<label(n'). T then generates the set of lubs of the chains labelling its branches. X is **finitely generable** if it is generated by some tree.

Notation We will use i to range over the sets {1,2,3} and {U,S,EM}. Moreover, in a sentence containing mixed uses of i, e.g. 'P_i' and '$\sqsubseteq_i$', we intend the following fixed correspondence:
(1,U) (2,S) (3,EM).

4.2 Closure Operators

The operators $\_^*_i$ mentioned in the previous section can be factored into a topological closure operator, common to all three powerdomains, composed with operators specific to each. We shall call the closure operator Cl, and defer its characterisation.

<u>Definition</u> For any domain D, and $X \subseteq D$:
(Left Closure) $LC(X) = \{d \in D \mid \exists x \in X\ d \leq x\}$
(Right Closure) $RC(X) = \{d \in D \mid \exists x \in X\ x \leq d\}$
(Convex Closure) $Con(X) = \{d \in D \mid \exists x, y \in X\ x \leq d \leq y\}$

<u>Proposition</u>
(i) $\_^{*}_{U} = LC \circ Cl$

(ii) (Smyth) $\_^{*}_{S} = RC \circ Cl$

(iii) (Plotkin) $\_^{*}_{EM} = Con \circ Cl$

<u>Proposition</u>
(i) $LC = LC \circ Con$; $RC = RC \circ Con$

(ii) $\_^{*}_{U} = LC \circ \_^{*}_{EM}$; $\_^{*}_{S} = RC \circ \_^{*}_{EM}$

(iii) $LC : P_{EM}[D] \to P_{U}[D]$; $RC : P_{EM}[D] \to P_{S}[D]$ are continuous.

It remains to describe Cl. We shall provide an explicit characterisation of it for the case of sequence domains, which somewhat sharpens that in [Plo76], and clarifies the relationship with Nivat's work on ∞-languages [Niv79]. We begin with some definitions. X is a non-empty subset of N^{∞}.

Prefix Closure:
<u>Definition</u> $Pref(X) = LC(X) \cap N^{*}$.

Adherence [Niv79]:
<u>Definition</u> $Adh(X) = \{s \in N^{\omega} \mid Pref(\{s\}) \subseteq Pref(X)\}$

Inherence
<u>Definition</u> $Inh(X) = \{s \in N^{*} \mid card\{n \mid s\langle n\rangle \in Pref(X)\} = \infty\}$

<u>Proposition</u> X is finitely generated $\Leftrightarrow$ $Inh(X) \subseteq Con(X)$.

<u>Theorem</u> $Cl(X) = X \cup Adh(X) \cup Inh(X)$.

<u>Remark</u> Nivat's closure operator is $X \cup Adh(X)$; since he works with finite alphabets, his sets are always finitely generated. Our result sharpens Plotkin's in that it applies to non-f.g. sets, and characterises Cl rather than $\_^{*}_{EM}$. It factorises the finiteness constraints of Cl into two "dimensions"; finitary <u>breadth</u> (i.e. bounded non-determinism), given by Inh, and finitary <u>length</u> (infinite behaviour determined by the finite), given by Adh.

4.3 Functions on Powerdomains

The following results were established in [Plo76,Smy78]:

<u>Pointwise extension</u>
given continuous $f : D_1 \times \ldots \times D_n \to E$

$f^{\dagger}_{i} : P_i[D_1] \times \ldots \times P_i[D_n] \to P_i[E]$

defined by

$f^{\dagger}_{i}(X_1, \ldots, X_n) = \{f(x_1, \ldots, x_n) \mid x_i \in X_i\}^{*}_{i}$

is continuous.

Union

$\uplus_i : P_i[D]^2 \to P_i[D]$

$X \uplus_i Y = (X \cup Y)^*{}_i$

is continuous.

4.4 Denotational Semantics

Definition

$succ, pred, hd, tl : \mathbb{N}^\infty \to \mathbb{N}^\infty$
$succ(\langle\rangle) = pred(\langle\rangle) = hd(\langle\rangle) = tl(\langle\rangle) = \langle\rangle$
$succ(\langle n\rangle s) = \langle n+1\rangle$
$pred(\langle 0\rangle s) = \langle\rangle \quad pred(\langle n+1\rangle s) = \langle n\rangle$
$hd(\langle n\rangle s) = \langle n\rangle \quad tl(\langle n\rangle s) = s$

$cons : (\mathbb{N}^\infty)^2 \to \mathbb{N}^\infty$
$cons(\langle\rangle, y) = \langle\rangle \quad cons(\langle n\rangle s, y) = \langle n\rangle y$

$if : (\mathbb{N}^\infty)^3 \to \mathbb{N}^\infty$
$if(\langle\rangle, y, z) = \langle\rangle \quad if(\langle 0\rangle s, y, z) = y \quad if(\langle n+1\rangle s, y, z) = z$

Proposition

succ, pred, hd, tl, cons, if are all continuous.

Definition

We now define three continuous Σ-algebras ([ADJ78]), A_i, $i \in \{U,S,EM\}$:

$Carrier(A_i) = P_i[\mathbb{N}^\infty]$

$F^{A_i} = f^\dagger{}_i$ for $F \in \{SUCC, PRED, HD, TL, CONS, IF\}$

$ZERO^{A_i} = \{\langle 0\rangle\}^*{}_i$

$\Omega^{A_i} = \{\langle\rangle\}^*{}_i$

$OR^{A_i} = \uplus_i$

Since $OR \in \Sigma$, we can treat programs as deterministic recursive program schemes (i.e. the non-determinism is handled in the interpretation, not at the syntactic level), and all the algebraic theory of [ADJ78,Gue81,Niv80] applies. We then immediately get three denotational semantics

$M_i : Programs \to A_i$

The reader is referred to [Gue81], Chapter 4, for details.

Proposition

(i) $LC: A_{EM} \to A_U$, $RC: A_{EM} \to A_S$ are continuous Σ-homomorphisms.

(ii) $M_U = LC \circ M_{EM}$; $M_S = RC \circ M_{EM}$.

5. Full Abstraction

Definition (Milner). Given an operational preorder $\sqsubseteq$ on programs, and a denotational semantics M, then M is **fully abstract with respect to** $\sqsubseteq$ iff for all programs P, P'

$P \sqsubseteq P' \Leftrightarrow M[P] \leq M[P']$.

Definition Given $P = \langle D,T\rangle$, $P_n = \langle D,T_n\rangle$ is obtained from P by performing n parallel-outermost substitutions of function variables in T according to D, and then replacing all occurrences of function variables by Ω (See [Gue81]).

Fact $M_i[P] = \bigsqcup \langle M_i[P_n]\rangle_{n\in N}$

Lemma 1 OP[P] is a l.u.b. (in the predomain $(F[N^\infty], \sqsubseteq_{EM})$) of $\langle OP[P_n]\rangle_{n\in N}$.

Lemma 2 $\forall n\ M_{EM}[P_n] = OP[P_n]^*_{EM} \simeq_{EM} OP[P_n]$.

Lemma 3 X is a l.u.b. of $\langle X_n\rangle_{n\in N}$ in $(F[D], \sqsubseteq_{EM})$
$\Rightarrow X^*_{EM} = \bigsqcup \langle (X_n)^*_{EM}\rangle_{n\in N}$.

From these three lemmas, we have:

Lemma 4 $OP[P] \simeq_i M_i[P]$

Theorem (Full Abstraction)
M_i is fully abstract with respect to $\sqsubseteq_i$, i=U,S,EM.

Programs with input

We now extend the above concepts to programs with input. The syntax of programs with input is obtained simply by lifting the restriction that T be closed in $P = \langle D,T\rangle$. In keeping with our notion of finite experiments, we extend the operational preorders to programs with input as follows:

$\langle D,T\rangle \sqsubseteq_i \langle D',T'\rangle \equiv$ for all closed terms $T_1,\ldots,T_k$
$\langle D,T[T_1,\ldots,T_k]\rangle \sqsubseteq_i \langle D',T'[T_1,\ldots,T_k]\rangle$.

The denotational semantics is extended to programs with input in the usual way, by interpreting the main program term T as a **derived operator** ([ADJ78]), i.e. a function, rather than a value. Thus

M_i : Programs $\rightarrow [P_i[N^\infty]^k \rightarrow P_i[N^\infty]]$.

Theorem
Full Abstraction extends to programs with input.

6. Hierarchies of languages and tests

The results of the previous sections have pointed in the direction of a relativisation of semantics. Rather than a single, "absolute" account of meaning, we have studied three operational preorders, based on a common notion of finite experiment, but on different notions of "relevant information". We now extend the scope of these results in a number of directions. We consider a hierarchy of languages, and a hierarchy of tests, which include the particular language and test-set we have studied so far. A useful common denominator is provided by a third hierarchy, of subsets of 2^{N^∞}. We can measure the strength of a language, in terms of the sets it can be used to define; and the strength of a class of tests, in terms of the sets it can be used to distinguish. What we find is that increases in the power of a language are only detectable modulo a sufficiently powerful class of tests; and conversely, the extra discriminations made possible by increasing the power of tests require a language capable of generating sufficiently rich sets for such discriminations to be pertinent. Thus we can conclude that it is pointless incorporating a facility for "unbounded nondeterminism" (resp. "strong infinite computation") in

our language, unless we are prepared to countenance experiments involving infinite sets of sequences (resp. sets containing infinite sequences). Conversely, allowing such experiments only has point if the language has sufficient power. Interestingly, the downwards preorder is <u>not</u> strengthened by allowing infinite sequences in test sets, while the upwards preorder is not strengthened by allowing infinite test sets. This exposes a new aspect of the duality between the two notions of approximation.
We define four subsets of 2^{N^∞}:

<u>Definition</u>

$S_0 = \{X \in 2^{N^\infty} \mid X = Cl(X)\}$

$S_1 = \{X \in 2^{N^\infty} \mid X = X \cup Adh(X)\}$

$S_2 = \{X \in 2^{N^\infty} \mid X \text{ is finitely generated}\}$

$S_3 = 2^{N^\infty}$

Clearly, we have:

$$S_0 \subseteq S_1 \subseteq S_3$$
$$S_0 \subseteq S_2 \subseteq S_3$$

Moreover, the inclusions are strict, and S_1 and S_2 are incomparable, for:

$\{\langle n\rangle \mid n \in \mathbf{N}\} \in S_1 - S_2$

$1^* \in S_2 - S_1$

$\mathbf{N}^+ \in S_3 - (S_1 \cup S_2)$

We now define four languages and their operational semantics:

<u>Definition</u>

1. L_0 has syntax and transition relations as in Sec. 3. The operational semantics is given by:

   $OP_0[P] = X \cup Adh(X)$
   where $X = OP[P] \cap \mathbf{N}^*$
   (here OP is the operational semantics defined in Sec. 3)

2. L_1 is the language defined in Section 3, with operational semantics $OP_1 = OP$.

3. L_2 is the language of section 3, augmented with the constant symbol ?, and with the transition relations augmented by the schema:

   $$(X)\quad \forall n \in \mathbf{N}\ ?\ \overset{n}{\longrightarrow}\ \Omega.$$

   (Thus ? is an applicative analogue of Apt and Plotkin's "random assignment" [AP80]). Based on this revised transition relation, the operational semantics OP_2 is defined in the same way as OP_0.

4. L_3 has the same syntax and transition relation as L_2; its operational semantics OP_3 is defined as for OP_1.

Definition

Given a language L with operational semantics OP_L:

$$Def(L) = \{X \in 2^{N^\infty} \mid \exists P \in L\ OP_L[p] = X\}.$$

We then have:

Proposition

$$Def(L_i) \subseteq S_i \quad i=0,1,2,3$$

We recall that T comprises the finite sets of finite elements. This suggests two dimensions along which the requirements of finiteness can be relaxed. Accordingly, we define:

$T_1 = \{X \subseteq N^\infty \mid X \text{is finite}\}$

$T_2 = 2^{N^*}$

$T_3 = 2^{N^\infty}$

We now relativise our preorders to a given test set. Since the earlier definitions were parameterised on T, the modifications are immediate.

Theorem

(1) $X \simeq_i Cl(X)$ mod T for i=U,S,EM

(2) $X \simeq_U X \cup Inh(X)$ mod T_3; $X \not\simeq_U X \cup Adh(X)$ mod T_1

(3) $X \simeq_S X \cup Adh(X)$ mod T_3; $X \not\simeq_S X \cup Inh(X)$ mod T_2

(4) $X \simeq_i Y$ mod $T_3 \Leftrightarrow C_i(X) = C_i(Y)$
where $C_U = LC$, $C_S = RC$, $C_{EM} = Con$.

Interpretation

(1) If test set T is used, all languages collapse to L_0; conversely, if language L_0 is used, all test sets determine the same equivalences.
(2) The upwards equivalence is insensitive to breadth-finitariness, regardless of which test set is used, but can distinguish length-finitariness at T_1.
(3) Dually, the downwards equivalence is insensitive to length-finitariness, regardless of which test set is used, but can distinguish breadth-finitariness at T_2.
(4) For language L_3 and test set T_3, the equivalences are exact to within their characteristic closures. In particular, the Egli-Milner equivalence essentially performs an exact comparison on the sets generated by programs under the operational semantics. At this point in the hierarchy, accurate order-theoretic powerdomains are apparently not available (see e.g. [Niv80]). An exact semantics can, however, be given using categorical powerdomains [Abr82].

Acknowledgements

I would like to thank Manfred Broy, Matthew Hennessy and Tom Maibaum for some stimulating discussions.

References

[Abr82] Abramsky, S.
"On Semantic Foundations for Applicative Multiprogramming",
To appear in ICALP '83, Also QMC CSL Report Number 321, 1982.

[AP80] Apt, K. and Plotkin, G.D. "Countable Non-determinism and Random Assignment" Technical Report, Edinburgh University, 1982.

[ADJ78] Goguen, J. Thatcher, J. Wagner, E.G. and Wright, J.B. "Initial Algebra Semantics and Continuous Algebras", JACM (1977).

[Bro82] Broy, M. "Fixed Point Theory for Communication and Concurrency", Technical University of Munich, 1982.

[DeNH82] DeNicola, R. and Hennessy, M. "Testing Equivalences for Processes", Technical Report CSR-123-82, Edinburgh University, 1982.

[Gue] Guessarian I. Algebraic Semantics, Springer LNCS 99, 1981.

[Hen81] Hennessy M. "Powerdomains and Nondeterministic Recursive Definitions", Springer LNCS 137, 1982.

[Kah74] Kahn G. "The Semantics of a Simple Language for Parallel Programming", IFIP Congress 74, 1974.

[KH80] Kennaway, J.K. and Hoare, C.A.R. "A Theory of Nondeterminism", ICALP 80, Springer LNCS 85, 1980.

[Mil73] Milner R.
"Processes: A Mathematical Model for Computing Agents",
in Logic Colloquium '73, ed. Rose H.E. and Shepherdson J.C.,
North Holland 1975.

[Mil80] Milner R. A Calculus of Communicating Systems,
Springer LNCS 92, 1980.

[Niv79] Nivat, M.
"Infinite words, infinite trees, infinite computations",
in Foundations of Computer Science III Part 2,
ed. de Bakker and van Leeuwen, Mathematical Centre Tracts 109,
Amsterdam 1979.

[Niv80] Nivat M. "Nondeterministic Programs: an Algebraic Overview", IFIP Congress 80, 1980.

[Plo76] Plotkin G.D. "A Powerdomain Construction", SIAM Journal on Computing 1976.

[Plo77] Plotkin G.D. "LCF Considered as a Programming Language", Theoretical Computer Science 1977.

[Plo82] Plotkin G.D. "An Operational Semantics for CSP", Technical Report, Edinburgh University, 1982.

[Smy78] Smyth M.J. "Powerdomains", JCSS 1978.

DETERMINISTIC DYNAMIC LOGIC OF RECURSIVE PROGRAMS IS WEAKER THAN DYNAMIC LOGIC

Piotr Berman
Department of Computer Science
Pennsylvania State University
University Park, PA 16802 U.S.A.

INTRODUCTION. This paper proves that there is a formula, called ROOT of dynamic logic of recursive programs (DL) such that ROOT has no equivalent formula of dynamic logic of deterministic recursive programs (DrecDL). This extends the recent result of [BHT], where a similar theorem was proven for deterministic **while**-programs (the formula used there is the same). Since the recursion is known to substantially increase the power of deterministic programs, the result is perhaps surprising, and shows further limitations of determinism.

The strategy of the proof is similar to the one in [BHT], where the problem was reduced to maze-threading by automata. These automata were basicly the same as the JAG-s in [CR]. Some of new techniques were inspired by [CR] and by [BRT]. Our automata, unlike the JAG-s, are no longer finite but they are supplied with a push-down store, where we can keep elements of a finite alphabet and of the structure, over which the computation is being performed.

The part of proof technique due to [BRT] is the choice of the basic underlying structure, later called in this paper Adian's structure. In [A] there is a of existence of an infinite group with two generators, f and g such that each element of this group is of the order 701 (701 is arbitrarily chosen from a larger family of constants). The structure used in this paper has Adian's group as its universe and left multiplication by s and t as its two unary functions. [BRT] provides a proof of the same theorem as [BHT], unfortunately the proof is incomplete.

DYNAMIC LOGIC *Dynamic logic* (cf. [P] and [HMP]) of a set of programs is formed in a similar fashion as the first-order logic. The difference is that it has additional way of creating well formed formulae (wff's): for each wff p and each program α from our set there is another wff $<\alpha>p$.

The semantics of this new construct is dependent on the semantics of programs. In general, the semantics of a formula p is the relation

$$(W,\sigma)\models p$$

which means that in the structure W and for valuation $\sigma\in W^{Var}$ (set of all the mappings from variables into the domain of W) the formula p is true. On the other hand the semantics the semantics of a program α is its input-output relation

$$M^W(\alpha)\subset W^{Var}\times W^{Var}$$

Given the semantics of programs we define the semantics of dynamic formulae as follows:

$$(W,\sigma)\models<\alpha>p \text{ iff } \exists\sigma_0 \ (\sigma,\sigma_0)\in M^W(\alpha)\& (W,\sigma_0)\models p$$

When the above rule is added to the standard rules of the first-order logic we have the complete definition of the semantics of the dynamic logic.

The formula ROOT which is discussed in this paper is the following sentence

$$\exists x \ \forall y \ <(x:=s(x) \cup x:=t(x))^*> x=y$$

which means that all the elements can be derived from a single one by applying two unary function. Binary tree provides here a good intuition. It is easy to see that ROOT has no first-order equivalent: although there are infinite models of ROOT, all of them are countable, what would contradict the Skolem-Loewenheim theorem.

Regular programs are program expressions built from program primitives, brackets(used as **begin** and **end**) and three operations: ; (composition), $\cup$ (union) and *. The program primitives are *assignments* of the form $x:=t$ where x is a variable and t is a variable, and *conditions* of the form p? where p is a quantifier free first-order formula. The semantics of regular program is defined by the following five rules:

i. $(\sigma_1,\sigma_2) \in M_W(x:=t)$ iff $(W,\sigma_1) \models t=\sigma_2(x)$ and for $y \neq x$ we have $\sigma_1(y)=\sigma_2(y)$

ii. $(\sigma_1,\sigma_2) \in M_W(p?)$ iff $\sigma_1=\sigma_2$ and $(W,\sigma_1) \models p$

iii. $M_W(\alpha;\beta) = M_W(\alpha) \circ M_W(\beta)$

iv. $M_W(\alpha \cup \beta) = M_W(\alpha) \cup M_W(\beta)$

v. $M_W(\alpha^*)$ is the reflexive transitive closure of $M_W(\alpha)$

As deterministic regular programs we use **while**-programs, which are a subset of regular programs. Namely, the constructs of $\cup$ and * can appear there only in limited context:

$(p?;alpha) \cup (\neg p?;\beta)$ which is denoted as **if** p **then** α **else** β **fi**

$(p?;\alpha)^*;\neg p?$ which is denoted as **while** p **do** α**od**

It is easy to verify that input-output relation of a **while** program is a function. To describe recursive programs we need to add to our language another class of identifiers $P_0, P_1 \cdots$ for procedures, and another class of program primitives - calls. Calls are of the form **call**$P_i(\vec{t},\vec{x})$ where $\vec{t}$ is the list of the nonmutable parameters (which are terms) and $\vec{x}$ is the list of mutable parameters (variables only).

A recursive program is a system of procedures of the form $P_i(\vec{z};\vec{x})\vec{y}$ body where $\vec{z}$, $\vec{x}$, $\vec{y}$ are disjoint lists of variables without repetitions - $\vec{z}$ is the list of the nonmutable parameters, $\vec{x}$ is the list of mutable parameters, and $\vec{y}$ is the list of local variables; the body is a deterministic regular program which can use calls as its primitives. The parameters of a procedure are called *formal*, while parameters of a call of a procedure are called *actual*.

The semantics of recursive program is defined as in [BMT]. The most succint way of defining semantics is the fixed-point method. Assume that we treat procedures like ordinary regular programs and that we have a way of transforming an input-output relation of a procedure into the input-output relation of a call of this procedure. Then the rules iii, iv and v define the input-output relation of a procedure that uses such calls. Say that a recursive program α consists of procedures $P_0,...,P_k$. According to what we just stated, if we use input-output relations $B_0,...,B_k$ to define the semantics of calls of the corresponding procedures, it yields some $C_0, \ldots, C_k$ as the input-output relations of $P_0,...,P_k$. More formally, if we denote the set of vectors of input-output relations as $\mathbf{B}^{k+1}$ then program α defines a transformation

$$T_\alpha : \mathbf{B}^{k+1} \to \mathbf{B}^{k+1}$$

The choice of $\vec{B} = (B_0,...,B_k)$ as the set of input-output relations for the procedures of α is consistent if $T_\alpha(\vec{B}) = \vec{B}$. In other words $\vec{B}$ must be a fixed point of T_α. A more careful analysis shows that the least fixed point of T_α is the most natural choice for the definition of semantics. By convention, the mainline of α is P_0 and $M_W(\alpha)$ is the first element of the least fixed point of T_α.

PUSH-DOWN AUTOMATA. We don't have enough space to describe formally the way we derive the input-output relation of a recursive call from the relation (or function, since we deal with deterministic case) of the corresponding procedure. The intuition, however, is simple. In a call we specify nonmutable and mutable parameters. This call should perform auxiliary computation of the called procedure, and afterwards change the values of the mutable parameters accordingly. To perform the auxiliary computation, we need to substitute the values of formal parameters of the called procedure by the corresponding values of actual parameters of the call. After the auxiliary computation is finished we restore the values of variables as they were before and we change the values of the actual mutable parameters according to the final values of corresponding formal parameters.

It is easy to see that if a push-down automaton can perform the auxiliary computation, than it can perform the entire call: initially it pushes on its stack the values of all nonmutable variables of the call that may be changed by the auxiliary computation, next it performs the auxiliary computation, lastly it sets the resulting values of mutable variables and restores the values of nonmutable ones, popping the latter from its stack.

Let us notice that each procedure may be called in more than one place in the recursive program, therefore it may be ambiguous what the automaton should do after it have finished with computing a call. This is not a problem, however, since the automaton can push on its stack the relevant information before it executes a call, so afterwards it can pop this information and chose the next step accordingly. To code this information the automaton can use letters from a finite alphabet. This is an argument that we can replace every deterministic recursive program by an automaton with the identical input-output function, an automaton with final control, finite number of registers and the stack. The input which influences the transitions of the automaton consists of letters of the stack alphabet, if such a letters is on the top of the stack and the results of tests on the values of the registers. The transition from programs to automata is fully described in [B].

THE MAIN THEOREM. No formula of Dynamic Logic of deterministic recursive programs is equivalent to ROOT.

The proof reduces the problem to the fact that every push-down automaton walking on Adian structure inspects only finite fragment of it, moreover the size of this fragment is bounded by a constant dependent on the automaton (and not dependent on the initial valuation).

Indeed, the latter implies that for any push-down automaton its input-output relation in Adian's structure can be described by a first-order formula. What is important, it also implies that such a formula describes the input-output relation in any structure that is elementary equivalent to the original one (the detailed argument is contained in [BHT]). Thus for every formula of DrecDL has a first-order translation which is equivalent in all structures elementary equivalent to Adian's structure. Assume that p is a formula of DrecDL which is equivalent to ROOT. Let p' be such a translation, **A** be Adian's structure and **B** be an uncountable structure elementary equivalent to **A**. Then

$$\mathbf{A}\models \mathrm{ROOT} \text{ iff } \mathbf{A}\models p \text{ iff } \mathbf{A}\models p' \text{ iff } \mathbf{B}\models p' \text{ iff } \mathbf{B}\models p \text{ iff } \mathbf{B}\models \mathrm{ROOT}$$

contradiction, because ROOT is true in **A** and false in any uncountable structure.

THE MAIN LEMMA. The current goal is to prove that for any push-down automaton A there is a constant that limits the number of elements of Adian's structure that A can inspect in a single computation, regardless the initial content of its registers.

We will present detailed proof for the case of a finite automaton, i.e. automaton without push-down (Theorem 1 in this section), next will be extensive draft for the case of context-free automaton (Theorem 2), when only letters (but not elements of the structure) can be stored in the push-down. The proof of the general case (Theorem 3) is only suggested because of space consideration, however it doesn't differ substantially from the context-free case. The details of all proofs are contained in [B].

We will consider automata in a certain normal form, to which any automaton computing in structures with the signature $<s,t,=>$ can be reduced. They correspond to programs with assignments exclusively of the form $x:=s(x)$, $x:=t(x)$ and $x:=y$ and conditions of the form $x=y$. The assignments are called moves, and the ones of the form $x:=y$ are called jumps. The conditions will be called tests, the registers heads. It will be convenient to denote heads by bold letters and to avoid brackets for unary functions.

The idea of the proof is too reduce the problem to the case of finite automaton with a single head. Since tests (if there are any) provide in this case only one answer - false - and the control has, say, q different states, after at most q steps automaton will start to repeat its sequence of steps periodically, and if it will keep walking after $701 \cdot q$ steps, it will only inspect the same vertices again and again.

The generalization of this case forms the base step of induction. The critical point in our induction is the choice of the induction parameter. This parameter will be called Level of Cooperation - LC - and will characterize finite fragments of computation of an automaton.

It will be convenient to define first the complement of cooperation - separability. For better intuitions, the definition will be described in informal way, the heads being viewed as similar to people.

Imagine, that at step m of a computation the heads can form a certain number of different clubs, and each head must belong to exactly one. Afterwards heads can change their membership in only one situation: after a jump of the form fBx:=**y** the head **x** must switch to the club of **y**. Assume now that we follow the history of clubs formed at step m up to step n, $n>m$. These clubs are said to be separated up to step n iff for each test performed between step m and n (inclusively) the heads checked are on the same vertex only if they are in the same club.

Now we can define separability of the computation of a given automaton A in a graph H, with initial placement of heads σ, between steps m and n. By definition, this number is not less than k iff there exists a system of clubs formed at step m and separated up to step n such that after step $n-1$ there are k nonempty clubs. In other words, separability is the maximal value of such k.

Finally, the level of cooperation, LC(A,H,σ,m,n), is the difference between the number of heads of A and separability. It is easy to notice, that the initially discussed case was that of LC equal to zero. Thus it was really the base case of induction on LC.

However, to express the hypothesis of this induction precisely, we need still another definition. It will be based on another characteristic of the part of computation of A in G, with initial placement σ, between steps m and n. The latter will be named path($A,G,\sigma,m,n,\mathbf{x}$) and will denote the path traversed by A between steps m and n, the final vertex of which is occupied by the head $\mathbf{x}$. The parameter of induction will be defined as a set of such paths.

We will frequently use the notion of path, LC and other characteristics of a fragment of computation. All this notions depend on the automaton, the graph and the initial valuation. It will simplify reading if in all places when this parameters are A, G and σ we will skip them from the list. For example, instead of path($A,G,\sigma,m,n,\mathbf{x}$) we will write path($m,n,\mathbf{x}$).

Now we again view s and t as elements of Adian's group (the generators), moreover we recall the convention that e denotes the neutral element. From this point of view, a path in the graph, i.e. a sequence of moves along s arcs and t arcs is an element of Adian's group; the empty path and a loop are both identified with e.

The definition of path is recursive.

$$\text{path}(m,m,\mathbf{x})=e$$

For $n \geq m$ path($m,n+1,\mathbf{x}$) is defined according to what was performed at step n.

$$\text{path}(m,n+1,\mathbf{x}) = \begin{cases} \text{s}\cdot\text{path}(m,n,\mathbf{x}) & \text{if this step is } \mathbf{x}{:=}\text{s}\,\mathbf{x} \\ \text{t}\cdot\text{path}(m,n,\mathbf{x}) & \text{if this step is } \mathbf{x}{:=}\text{t}\,\mathbf{x} \\ \text{path}(m,n,\mathbf{y}) & \text{if this step is } \mathbf{x}{:=}\mathbf{y} \\ \text{path}(m,n,\mathbf{x}) & \text{otherwise} \end{cases}$$

Symbol $\cdot$ denotes here the operation of Adian's group. Note that above we used the shorthand convention concerning A,G and σ.

$$\text{PATH}(A,k) = \{\text{path}(A,G,\sigma,m,n,\mathbf{x}) \mid \text{LC}(A,G,\sigma,m,n) \leq k\}$$
$$\text{PATH}(A) = \bigcup_{k} \text{PATH}(A,k)$$

LEMMA 1. For every finite automaton A and integer k the set PATH(A,k) is finite.

THEOREM 1 For every finite automaton A the set PATH(A) is finite.

Proof of Theorem. It follows immediately from the lemma. Indeed, every finite automaton has finite number of heads, let it be h. By definition, the level of cooperation in any fragment of a computation of this automaton cannot exceed h. Thus PATH(A) = PATH(A,h), which, by Lemma 1 is finite.

Proof of Lemma 1. By induction on k.

BASE CASE. Assume that in the computation of A which started from head placement σ the level of cooperation between steps m and n - LC(m,n) - is zero, i.e. the separability is equal to the number of heads. That means that each head of A can join at step m a different club, and these clubs remain separated and nonempty up to step n. Thus tests performed between steps m and n have trivial results, i.e. they yield answer true iff they are of the form $\mathbf{x}{=}\mathbf{x}$?. Therefore between step m and n the new state of control is functionally dependent on the previous state - the results of tests are uniquely determined. Thus the paths generated in this fragment of computation depend only on the initial state of control. Moreover, the sequence of steps must end or cycle after at most q steps, where q is the number of control states. If for an initial state the computation stops within q steps the number of different paths generated in such computation is obviously less than q.

When the state of control repeats itself during given sequence of steps, it doesn't necessarily mean that the computation loops forever: the loop can be broken after a nontrivial test; the point is that the level of cooperation will be then greater than zero, thus it cannot happen within the discussed fragment of computation. However, if a cycle of steps will be repeated 701 times, each initial position will be leftmultiplied by the same value. Since every element of Adian's group is of the order 701, the positions of heads will be same as before. Thus although a single cycle of step doesn't imply that the entire computation looped, 701 consecutive cycles does.

In the above reasoning we used the fact that the position of each variable is multiplied in each cycle by the same element of the group. This is true, because within level of cooperation zero no jumps may be performed, since the first jump would make empty the club of **x**.

INDUCTIVE STEP. Now we assume that for every A the set PATH(A,k) is finite. There are two observations important for the inductive step of the proof.

Observation 1. For any A,σ,m,n, LC($m,n+1$)≤LC(m,n)+1.

Indeed, it is easy to check that each step can diminish separability (and thus increase LC) by at most one. Let us consider any system of clubs formed at step m and separated up to step n. The one of two cases when the separability decreases is when step n is a jump of the form **x=y?** where **x** and **y** are from different clubs. Then we can join this two clubs so the resulting system, with the number of elements less by one is separated up to step n+1. The other case is when this jump is **x:=y** and the club of **x** becames empty.

Observation 2. For any computation, if step n follows m then for each head **x** and its place u at the beginning of step n the following holds

u = path($m,n,$**x**)·w

where w is a place of one of heads at the beginning of step m. Moreover, if at step m a system of clubs was founded, and it remained separated up to step n, then w is a place of a head which belongs to the same club at step m as **x** at step n.

It can be checked easily by induction.

Let us consider fragment of computation of A from step m to n such that LC is equal to $k+1$. We will compute a constant c such that for any such fragment either $n-m$ will be smaller than c or there are two different steps m_1 and m_2 in this fragment, such that the state of control and the position of each head are identical. This is equivalent to the fact that PATH($A,k+1$) is finite. Indeed, if we assume that such a c exists, than all paths generated in a fragment of computation with LC≤$k+1$ are generated in the first c steps of this fragment (by observation 2, path is the relation between the current position and the initial one), thus PATH($A,k+1$)⊂s,t^c. Conversely, if PATH($A,k+1$) has, say p elements, then it is easy to check that any fragment of computation of A with LC≤$k+1$ inspects at most $p\cdot h$ vertices and thus c is no greater than $(ph)^h q$.

As the first step toward computing c we will show that it suffices to find another constant d satisfying a weaker condition. Namely, for any fragment of computation of A with LC≤$k+1$ either the length of this fragment is smaller than d or there are two steps in this fragment, m_1 and m_2 such that the sequences of computation starting at these steps are equal (i.e. steps m_1+l and m_2+l are identical for any l).

Indeed, assume that such d exists and that a fragment is longer than d. Then the steps in this fragment are performed cyclicly, with the first cycle completed no later than at d-th step of the fragment. Such a cycle is equivalent to a strightline program which can be easily reduced to the base case (by taking certain repetition of a cycle instead of the cycle itself we can eliminate jumps).

Next, we define step numbers $m=m_0,m_1,...,m_j=n$ such that for $i=1,...,j$ $m_{i-1}\le m_i$ and m_i is the minimum of n and the smallest m' such that $\mathrm{LC}(m_{i-1},m')=k+1$. According to the first observation, these numbers exist.

Assume that for LC$\le k$ the role of c is played by c'. Than it will be sufficient to show that there is d' such that either the discussed fragment has less than $c'\cdot d'$ steps, or there is $i\le j$ such that $m_i-m_{i-1}>c'$, or there are $i',i''\le d'$ such that the sequences of computation starting at steps $m_{i'}$ and $m_{i''}$ are identical. It is obvious that $d\le c'd'$.

To see that we note that if m_i-m_{i-1} is greater than c', than by inductive hypothesis we can find in this subfragment two steps with identical placements of heads and state of control. Thus if for an $i\le d'$ we have $m_i-m_{i-1}\ge c'$ then the desired pair of steps exists. If, on the other hand all subintervals are short, then the desired pair of steps will consist of two ends of subinterval, and the total length of d' subintervals is limited by $c'\cdot d'$.

To find d', we need to find such a finite characteristic of the configuration of A at step m_i that fully predicts further sequence of steps. The number of all possible values of these characteristic will be our d'. We will define such a characteristic in stages. At the last stage we will use the special properties of the placement of heads after step of the form m_i, which is characterized by the fact that at this step the level of cooperation of a subinterval of the computation increases.

Let us consider first an obvious characteristic, that fully predicts the further sequence of steps. It is the current state of control together with all positions of heads. Of course, the number of possible values of it is infinite.

Next, let us observe that instead of head positions we can keep relative positions. For heads **x** and **y** with positions u and w correspondingly, the position of **x** in relation to **y** is $u\cdot w^{-1}$. Thus **x** and **y** are in the same place iff their relative positions are both e (the position of **y** in relation to **x** is inverse to that of **x** in relation to **y**). It is obvious how to update them after each step, e.g. after step $\mathbf{x}:=s\mathbf{x}$ we should multiply $u\cdot w^{-1}$ by s from the left, and $w\cdot u^{-1}$ by s^{-1} from the right. Again, the number of possible values of this characteristic is infinite.

Now we can start to define the actual characteristic. The idea is that we need not to keep all the relative positions, because some of them are irrelevant for the computation. Therefore we will find which relative positions are irrelevant and we will replace them by ∞.

As the preliminary step, we describe how for arbitrary fragment of computation, say from step m to n, construct the 'maximal' system of clubs, such that it is founded at step m and separated up to step n. Initially the clubs are singletons of heads. Next, if this system contains a pair that is not separated up to step n, we join them together and try again. Eventually, we will get a system which is separated up to n and which is a refinement of any other with such property. Let us call it 'the maximal system for m and n.

Let us return to the previously discussed m and n. Let us first consider the maximal system for m and n and next the maximal system for m_{i-1} and m_i, $i<j$. It is easy to see, that at step m_i both system have identical clubs: it is easy to see that the second system is refinement of the second - since it is another system of clubs separated between m_{i-1} and m_i - and that both have at step m_i exactly $h-k-1$ elements.

Now let us replace in our second characteristic all relative positions of heads belonging to different clubs by ∞. The latter is updated only after jumps of the form **x**:=**y**. This characteristic is surely sufficient, because whenever **x** and **y** are tested, they can't be in the same place when their relative position is marked ∞, since heads from different clubs never are.

To conclude the proof of INDUCTIVE STEP we need to show a finite set such it contains all possible relative positions of heads from the same club at that for steps $m_1,...,m_{j-1}$. If this set has, say, $p-1$ elements, the number of different characteristics is limited by $q \cdot p^{h(h-1)/2}$, since for each of $h(h-1)2$ pair of heads we keep one of $p-1$ relative positions, if they are from the same club, or ∞, if they aren't.

To show this, we need to return to the general construction of the maximal system of separated clubs. Let us consider the relative head positions at step m_i and the system of one-element clubs founded at step m_{i-1}. For each step m', such that $m_{i-1} \leq m' \leq m_i$ and heads from different clubs are compared and are in the same place, we should join this clubs together. Assume now that one-element clubs, to which **x** and **y** belong at step m_i were joined because their members occupied the same position at step m'. Let us call this position w.

We will analyze, what under this assumption we can say about the relative position of **x** and **y**. Because step m_i increases LC, it cannot be of the form **x**:=s**y** or **x**:=t**y**. That means that the paths of **x** and **y** were already generated at previous step, i.e path(m',$m_{i-1,\mathbf{x}}$) = path(m',$m_{i-1}-1$,**x**) and same for **y**, and since LC(m',$m_{i-1}-1$)$\leq k$, these paths belong to PATH(A,k). Thus the positions of **x** and **y** at step m_i are of the form u·w and v·w where u,v $\in$ PATH(A,k), and their relative positions are $u \cdot v^{-1}$ and $v \cdot u^{-1}$. Of course, the number of such relatioships is limited by $2|\mathrm{PATH}(A,k)|^2$, since we take into account all pairs from PATH(A,k), the factor of 2 represents here the fact that we count converse positions as different.

By the very construction of the maximal system of clubs we know that for each two elements of a club he have a chain of such relationships joining them together. It is easy to see that the position of **x** in relation to **z** is the position of **x** in relation to **y** multiplied by the position of **y** in relation to **z**. Since any of separated clubs at step m_i has at most $k+1$ elements, every relationship of elements of one club can be described as a multiplication of k relationships from the previous paragraph. Thus the set of all such relationships has at most $2(|\mathrm{PATH}(A,k)|^2)^h$ elements

This concludes the proof of Lemma 1.

In the proof of the result concerning context-free automata, we will also use a parameter of induction that limitates the level of cooperation. However, in the inductive assumption we also need to restrict the usage of push-down store. Therefore we will use modified notions of LC and PATH, let us call them LC^{cf} and PATH^{cf}. For the computation of automaton A, starting from head placement σ let us denote the depth of the push-down at step m as $\delta(m)$. In fact, it is rather $\delta(A,G,\sigma,m,n)$, but as before we skip the always repeating parameters A,G and σ. The same comment concerns LC^{cf} and PATH^{cf}.

$LC^{cf}(m,n)=k$ iff $LC(m,n)=k$ and
for every $m \le m' \le n$, $\delta(m') \ge \delta(m)$
$PATH^{cf}(A,k) = \{path(m,n,x) \mid LC^{cf}(m,n) \le k\}$

Now we are ready to formulate

LEMMA 2. For every context-free automaton A and integer k the set $PATH^{cf}(A,k)$ is finite.

THEOREM 2. For every context-free automaton A the set PATH(A) is finite.

Proof of the Theorem. It follows immediately from the Lemma. Indeed, every context-free automaton has finite number of heads and starts computation with empty push-down - $\delta(A,1)$ is always zero. Thus every path$(1,n) \in PATH^{cf}(A,h)$, where h is the number of heads. It is easy to see that every path of the form path(m,n,x) can, for certain head y, be represented as $w \cdot u^{-1}$, where w = path$(1,n,x)$ and u = path$(1,m,y)$. Thus $|PATH(A)| \le |PATH^{cf}(A,h)|^2$.

Proof of Lemma 2. Before we start the induction, we will make two observations.

Observation 1. Assumptions. Consider a fragment of computation of a context-free automaton A from step m to n which starts with a head placement σ and such that the push-down depth is never in this fragment smaller than at the initial step m. Consider also step m' from this fragment. For both steps m and m' consider the maximal system of clubs, formed at this step and separated up to step n. Assume that levels of cooperation $LC^{cf}(m,n)$ and $LC^{cf}(m',n)$ are both equal to k. For both m and m' the following characteristic is the same: the relative positions of heads from the same club, the state of control and the top symbol on the push-down.

Claim. For any l such that $LCcxf(m,m'+l) \le k$ the above characteristic is equal for $m+l$ and $m'+l$.

The Observation 1 is based on two facts: first is that Adian's structure is fully symmetric, so there is no way to distinguish two configurations with identical relative positions; second is that since descendents of the members of different clubs cannot meet one another before step n, their relative position don't influence the computation.

Then it is easy to see that between steps m and m' the content of the push-down at step m is not used, with the exclusion of the top element. Thus the sequence of computation from step m to m' depends exclusively on the value of our characteristic at step m. Since at step m' we have the same value of this characteristic, the sequence of computation between steps m' and $m'+l$ is also the same. Thus for any n between m' and $m'+l$ we know that $\delta(n) \ge \delta(m') \ge \delta(m)$. A simple induction shows that our observation is true.

We will describe the situation from Observation 1 as follows : to stress the fact that throughout this fragment of the computation the push-down depth was no smaller than at its beginning.

Observation 2. To prove Lemma 2 it suffices to show the following: for any context-free A there is d such that if in a computation of A in G the following inequality holds for steps m and $m+l$:

$$\delta(m+l) \ge \delta(m)+d$$

then for certain $m \le m_1 < m_2 \le m+l$ the automaton A makes a nondecreasing loop between steps m_1 and m_2.

Indeed, assume that the above is true and replace A by its modified version A', which works identically as A with one difference: it keeps only d symbols on the push-down. One can see that with our assumption A and A' are equivalent: all symbols on the push-down, that are deleted by A' are never used later in the computation of A. If at step m' the automaton A' deleted from the push-down a symbol written at step m, then the depth at step m' exceeds the depth at step m by d, and thus we know that A makes somewhere between m and m' a nondecreasing loop. According to the first observation, starting from step m' the depth will never be as small as at step m.

Now we know that A is equivalent to the finite automaton A', so we can apply Lemma 1.

Thus we will inductively prove the following: for any A and k there is d such that for any σ, m, n such that $LC^{cf}(m,n) \le k$ and $\delta(n) \ge \delta(m)+d$ the automaton A makes a nondecreasing loop between steps m_1 and m_2, where $m \le m_1 \le m_2 \le n$.

BASE CASE. For $k=0$ we can show that $d=qt$, where q is the number of states of control of A and t the number of symbols of the push-down alphabet, fulfills the above requirements. For an arbitrary fragment of computation of A such that $LC^{cf}(m,n)=0$ and $\delta(n) \ge \delta(m)+d$ we can exhibit required m_1 and m_2. Let for $i=0,\ldots,d$ m_i denote the largest $m' \le n$ such that $\delta(m')=\delta(n)-i$. It is easy to see that these numbers exist in the interval $<m,n>$. Since there are $qt+1$ of them, and only qt different characteristics at level 0, it is possible to find amoung them the desired pair.

INDUCTIVE STEP. Assume that in the case of $LC^{cf} \le k$ we have found the desired d. Let A' be again A modified in such a way that it keeps only top d elements of push-down. By same reasoning as before we know that A' can simulate faithfully all parts of computation of A which generate terms from $PATH^{cf}(A,k)$. By Theorem 1 it implies that $PATH^{cf}(A,k)$ is finite. The proof that $PATH^{cf}(A,k)$ is finite too is based on the following

Observation 3. Consider a fragment of computation of A, such that $LC^{cf}(m,n)=k+1$ and $LC^{cf}(m,n-1)=k$. Then at step m the relative positions of members of the same club are of the form $u_1 \cdot w_1^{-1} \cdots u_k \cdot w_k^{-1}$, where u's and w's belong to $PATH^{cf}(A,k)$.

A proposition similar to this is the inductive step of the proof of Lemma 1. The argument now is not very different than before, nevertheless the more complicated inductive hypothesis necessitates more careful analysis of the situation. If we have Observation 3 proven, we can calculate the number of distinguishable configurations of A at steps of the above form and apply this number similarly like qt in the BASE CASE.

Now we will consider the case of push-down automaton, i.e. an automaton with the control enhanced by the push-down store, in which we can store symbols from a finite alphabet and vertices of the graph (perhaps it would be better to say that we store identifiers of vertices, but that point of view is unnecessarily complicated). This kind of automaton can perform these new types of steps: send one of the current head positions to the push-down, set new position of a head as the current top element of the push-down. For the proof convenience, we don't compare the top of push-down with any of variables. However, as before the transition of the control state and the selection of the next step depend on the top element of the push-down store, if the latter belongs to the finite alphabet.

The proof in the case of push-down automata is surprisingly similar to the one for context-free automaton. The biggest difficulty was to find the suitable definitions for club membership and for separability. The following property of the notion of club is to be preserved: whenever a sequence of steps implies that two positions are in the same weakly connected component of the structure, then these two position must belong to members of the same club. Since there is a possibility to first store a position of a head and next assign this position to another head, we need to extend the 'privilege' to the positions inserted to the push-down during the discussed fragment of computation. As in the case of the context-free automata we will denote the push-down depth as $\delta(m)$. This time the notion of club will be meaningful only for such parts of computation, say from step m to step n, that for $m \leq m' \leq n$ we have $\delta(m) \leq \delta(m')$.

Assume that at step m we founded a system of clubs, such that each head is in only one club. At the first step of discussed fragment, i.e. at step m, only heads are members of clubs. Later on the membership can change only according to the following rules:
-after the jump **x**:=**y** the head **x** must join the club of **y**;
-after the position of **x** is sent to the push-down, it must belong to the same club as **x**;
-after the vertex from the top of the push-down became the new position of **x**, **x** must join the club of this vertex;
-after each step the clubs are disjoint.

One remark - if the same vertex appears more than once in the store, each occurrence is regarded as a separated entity (so different occurrences can belong to different clubs and the clubs still can be disjoint).

Different notion of clubs requires changes in the definition of separability (and thus also level of cooperation. The important property of separability which we want to preserve is that the separability of subfragment of a computation cannot be smaller than the separability of entire fragment.

Therefore now we define separability between m and n as the **minimum** for $m \leq m' \leq n$ of **maximums** for all systems of clubs founded at m' and separated up to n of the numbers of nonempty clubs at step n. One shall note that the entries stored before step m are members of no club. Thus it is really essential that they are never used in the discussed part of computation. Otherwise, i.e. when for certain step between m and n the push-down depth is smaller than at step m, the notion of separability, and the subsequent notion of level of cooperation are meaningless.

Again, the level of cooperation, $\mathrm{LC}^{rec}(A,G,\sigma,m,n)$, is the difference between the number of heads of A and separability. Similarly, $\mathrm{PATH}^{rec}(A,k)$ is the set of all path(A,G,σ,m,n) such that $\mathrm{LC}^{rec}(A,G,\sigma,m,n) \leq k$.

Now we can formulate

LEMMA 3. For every A and k the set $\mathrm{PATH}^{rec}(A,k)$ is finite.

THEOREM 3. For every A the set PATH(A) is finite.

Proof of the Theorem. The proof is identical to that of Theorem 2.

Careful analysis reveals that the properties of our definitions that were important for the proof of Lemma 2 are preserved.

REFERENCES

[A] Adian S.I. Burnside's Problem and Identities in Groups, Springer Ergebnise der mathematik und ihre Grenzgebiete 95 (1979)

[B] Berman P. Expressive Power in Dynamic Logic and Maze Threading, technical report of Dep. of Comp. Sc., Penn. St. Univ., 1983

[BHT] Berman P., Halpern J.Y., Tiuryn J. DDL is Weaker Than DL, Proc. of ICALP 1982, Lect. Not. in Comp. Sc., Vol. 140

[BRT] DDL is weaker than DL, Rept. of Karaganda University, 1981 (in Russian)

[CR] S.A. Cook, C.W. Rackoff, Space Lower Bounds for Maze Threadability on Restricted Machines, SIAM J. Comput.,Vol. 9, August 1980

[H] Harel D. First-Order dynamic Logic, Lect. Not. in Comp. Sc., Vol. 68

[HMP] D. Harel, A.R. Meyer and V.R. Pratt Computability and Completeness in Logics of Programs, Proc. of the Ninth STOC, May 1977

[HPS] D. Harel, A. Pnuelli, J. Stavi, A Complete Axiomatic System for Proving Deductions about Recursive Program, Proc. of The Ninth STOC, May 1977

[P] Pratt, V.R. Semantical consideration on Floyd-Hoare Logic, Proc. of 17th Symp. on Found. of Comp. Sc. Houston, Texas, 1976

Reversal-Bounded and Visit-Bounded Realtime Computations

Andreas Brandstädt and Klaus Wagner
Section of Mathematics
Friedrich-Schiller University Jena
German Democratic Republic

Abstract. First it is dealt with the class RBQ (also sometimes called BNP) of all languages acceptable in linear time by reversal-bounded nondeterministic multitape Turing machines.
It has been shown (see /2/) that the RBQ languages can already be accepted by nondeterministic realtime machines having only three pushdown stores and working with at most one reversal per pushdown store. We show that these three pushdown stores can be replaced by two checking stacks each making at most two reversals. In this result "two" cannot be replaced by "one" because of a recent result by HULL (see /7/).
The class RBQ is known to be closed under intersection and the AFL operations except for Kleene star. It is conjectured that RBQ is not closed under Kleene star (see /3/). We show that the least intersection closed AFL containing RBQ (or, equivalently, the least intersection closed semi-AFL containing the set PAL*) coincides with the class VBQ of all languages acceptable in linear time by visit-bounded nondeterministic multitape Turing machines. Furthermore, the VBQ languages can already be accepted by nondeterministic realtime machines having only three pushdown stores and working with at most 3 visits (or, equivalently, having only two checking stacks and working with at most 4 visits). These results cannot be improved unless RBQ = VBQ.

0. Introduction

In 1970 BOOK and GREIBACH showed that the class Q of all languages acceptable in linear time by multitape Turing machines coincides

with the class of all languages acceptable in realtime by two-tape Turing machines - the tapes being actually a pushdown store and a checking stack - or, equivalently, by three-tape machines where all tapes are actually pushdowns.
In 1974 BOOK, NIVAT and PATERSON showed that for reversal-bounded Turing machines a similar result holds true: the class RBQ of languages acceptable in linear time by multitape Turing machines with a constant-bounded number of reversals coincides with the class of languages acceptable in realtime by machines with three pushdown (checking stack) tapes each of them making only 1 reversal.
The questions remained open whether two stores making one reversal are sufficient and whether RBQ is closed under Kleene star.
A recent result of HULL (/7/) shows that two 1-reversal bounded stores are not sufficient.
In section 2 we investigate reversal-bounded acceptors with two checking stack tapes showing that already a reversal bound 2 on both tapes or 1 on one tape and 3 on the other yield the whole class RBQ.
In section 3 similar results are derived for visit-bounded computations.
In section 4 the least intersection closed AFL containing RBQ is characterized in terms of visit-bounded computations, and the language $PAL^* =_{Df} \{ww^R : w \in \{0,1\}^*\}^*$ turns out to be a generator for the least intersection closed AFL containing RBQ using only the semi-AFL operations and intersection. Thus, for the problem whether RBQ is closed under Kleene star, PAL^* is a hardest language, i.e. RBQ is closed under Kleene star iff PAL^* RBQ.

1. Notions

Let $\mathbb{N}$ denote the set of all natural numbers.
For our machine models we use a one-way read-only input tape and three types of working tapes: Turing (T), pushdown (PD) and checking stack (CS) tapes. A checking stack tape is essentially a Turing tape whose head, after its first reversal, can never change the content of any tape square, i.e. it can only read the tape content which has been written up to this moment (for a formal definition of these notions see e.g. /4/).
We investigate reversal and visit bounded computations of nondetermi-

nistic machines having such tapes. The reversal complexity for a tape is given by the number of steps in which the head alters its direction (from left to right or from right to left). The visit complexity of a tape is given by the maximum number of steps in which the head visits a certain tape square, the maximum taken over all visited tape squares (for a formal definition see e.g. /5/).

Because we can have reversal bounds on one tape and visit bounds on another and furthermore the bounds can be different we give the kind of complexity restriction separately for each tape in our denotation of complexity classes: The class

$1\text{-}k_1X_1\text{-}Y_1(g_1)\text{-} \ldots \text{-}k_mX_m\text{-}Y_m(g_m)\text{-NTIME}(f)$ for

$k_1,\ldots,k_m \in \mathbb{N}$ (the number of tapes with the same complexity restriction – $k_i = 1$ can be omitted)

$X_1,\ldots,X_m \in \{T, PD, CS\}$ (indicates the type of the tape)

$Y_1,\ldots,Y_m \in \{REV, VIS\}$ (indicates the kind of complexity restriction)

$g_1,\ldots,g_m, f$ – bounding functions

denotes the class of all languages accepted by f-time bounded nondeterministic machines with a one-way read-only input tape and (for $i = 1,\ldots,m$) k_i working tapes of type X_i on which the resource Y_i is bounded by g_i.

For instance: 1-CS-REV(1)-CS-REV(3)-NTIME(n) is the class of all languages acceptable by nondeterministic machines with a one-way read-only input tape and two chacking stack tapes working in realtime where one tape is 1-reversal bounded and the other is 3-reversal bounded.

Instead of k_i we also use the prefix "multi" which indicates an arbitrary number of tapes.

Instead of single bounding functions we also use classes $\mathfrak{F}$ of bounding functions where $\Phi(\mathfrak{F}) = \bigcup_{f \in \mathfrak{F}} \Phi(f)$, for any complexity measure Φ. Frequently used examples are const $= \{\lambda n(c) : c \in \mathbb{N}\}$ and lin $= \{\lambda n(c \cdot n) : c \in \mathbb{N}\}$.

The result of BOOK and GREIBACH (/1/) can be expressed as

$$Q =_{Df} \text{1-multiT-NTIME(lin)} \underset{/1/}{=} \text{1-3PD-NTIME(n)} \underset{/1/}{=} \text{1-CS-PD-NTIME(n)}.$$

The result by BOOK, NIVAT and PATERSON mentioned above can be expressed as

RBQ $=_{Df}$ 1-multiT-REV(const)-NTIME(lin)
$\underset{/2/}{=}$ 1-3PD-REV(1)-NTIME(n)

The result by HULL (/7/) can be expressed as 1-2PD-REV(1)-NTIME(n)$\subset$ $\subset$ RBQ or, which is the same, 1-2CS-REV(1)-NTIME(n) $\subset$ RBQ.

2. Reversal-Bounded Realtime Acceptors

Let $\mathcal{L}_1 \wedge \mathcal{L}_2 \wedge \ldots \wedge \mathcal{L}_k =_{Df} \{L_1 \cap L_2 \cap \ldots \cap L_k : L_i \in \mathcal{L}_i \text{ for } i=1,\ldots,k\}$ and $\bigwedge_k = \underbrace{\mathcal{L} \wedge \mathcal{L} \wedge \ldots \wedge \mathcal{L}}_{k \text{ times}}$. Let further e denote the empty word.

A homomorphism h : $\Sigma^* \longrightarrow \Sigma^*$ is nonerasing iff h(x) $\neq$ e for all $x \in \Sigma$.

For a family $\mathcal{L}$ of languages, let

H($\mathcal{L}$) $=_{Df}$ {h(L) : L$\in\mathcal{L}$ and h a nonerasing homomorphism}

<u>Theorem 1:</u> RBQ = 1-CS-REV(3)-CS-REV(1)-NTIME(n).

Proof: Since RBQ = 1-3PD-REV(1)-NTIME(n) =
= H($\bigwedge_3$ 1-PD-REV(1)-NTIME(n)) and since
1-CS-REV(1)-CS-REV(3)-NTIME(n) is closed under nonerasing homomorphisms it is sufficient to prove
$\bigwedge_3$ 1-PD-REV(1)-NTIME(n) $\subseteq$ 1-CS-REV(3)-CS-REV(1)-NTIME(n).

We use a special variant of the simulation method developed in /1/ and /2/. In order to meet the reversal bound 1 on one tape it is important 1) to simulate successively the psuhing phases of the three pushdown stores and

2) to simulate the popping phases successively in the converse order.

Each of these phases requires a special input copy which coincides with the real input.

Both tapes will contain seven blocks $B_1,\ldots,B_7$ which serve as input copies. Block B_i has the shape

$$u_{1,j+1} * u_{1,j+2} * u_{1,j+3} * u_{1,j+4}$$
$$v^R_{1,j+1} * v^R_{1,j+2} * v^R_{1,j+3} * v^R_{1,j+4}$$
$$u_{2,j+1} * u_{2,j+2} * u_{2,j+3} * u_{2,j+4}$$
$$v^R_{2,j+1} * v^R_{2,j+2} * v^R_{2,j+3} * v^R_{2,j+4}$$

$$u_{3,j+1} * u_{3,j+2} * u_{3,j+3} * u_{3,j+4}$$
$$v^R_{3,j+1} * v^R_{3,j+2} * v^R_{3,j+3} * v^R_{3,j+4}$$
$$u_{4,j+1} * u_{4,j+2} * u_{4,j+3} * u_{4,j+4}$$
$$v^R_{4,j+1} * v^R_{4,j+2} * v^R_{4,j+3} * v^R_{4,j+4}$$

where $j = 4(i-1)$.

The words $u_{i,l}$ and $v_{i,l}$ will be nondeterministic guesses of the i-th quarter of the input word w. It will be tested during the simulation that all these guesses are correct, i.e. that $u_{i,l}$ and $v_{i,l}$ coincide with the i-th quarter of the input w for all $l = 1,\dots,28$.
Tape 1 has 11 tracks. The last three tracks serve for storing the real input. Therefore the head of tape 1 will move in every step. The input head will move in every 28-th step (the input length is assumed to be divisible by 28 - for other input length only slight modifications are necessary). The simulating machine works in four distinct phases as follows:

Phase 1 (Guessing blocks $B_1,\dots,B_7$):

On both tapes the heads write the guessed blocks $B_1,\dots,B_7$ from left to right **(see Figure 1)**.
Simultaneously the words w_1, w_2^{-1}, w_3 are written in the last three tracks of tape 1. The word w_1 is the first quarter of the real input intermixed with blanks (27 blanks, 1 input symbol). The word $w_2(w_3)$ is a nondeterministic guess of the second (third) quarter of the real input intermixed with blanks.

Phase 2 (Simulation of the three realtime one - reversal bounded pushdown automata computations):

By I_1, I_2, I_3 let us denote the maximum content of the pushdown stores of M when working on input w. We assume that special markers are inserted into the input copies to indicate the input head position when the popping phase is started for the first, second and third pushdown store, respectively.
The head on tape 1 moves to the left and reads $v_{1,28}\ v_{2,27}\ v_{3,26}\ v_{4,25}$ as an input copy in order to simulate the pushing phase of the first pushdown store where I_1 is written. Reading the marker for the start of the popping phase of I_1 the head moves to the right end of B_6 and reads a corresponding input copy contained in B_6 for the pushing phase of I_2 and similarly for I_3.
Thus after the simulation of the pushing phases the head on tape 1

Figure 1

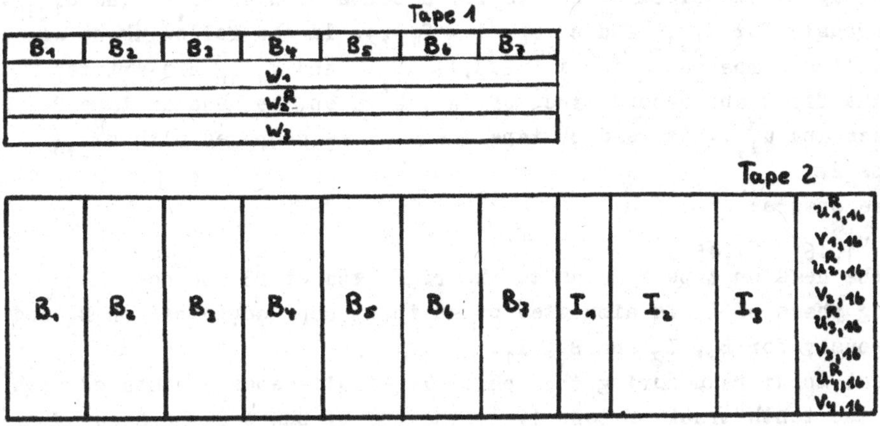

Figure 2

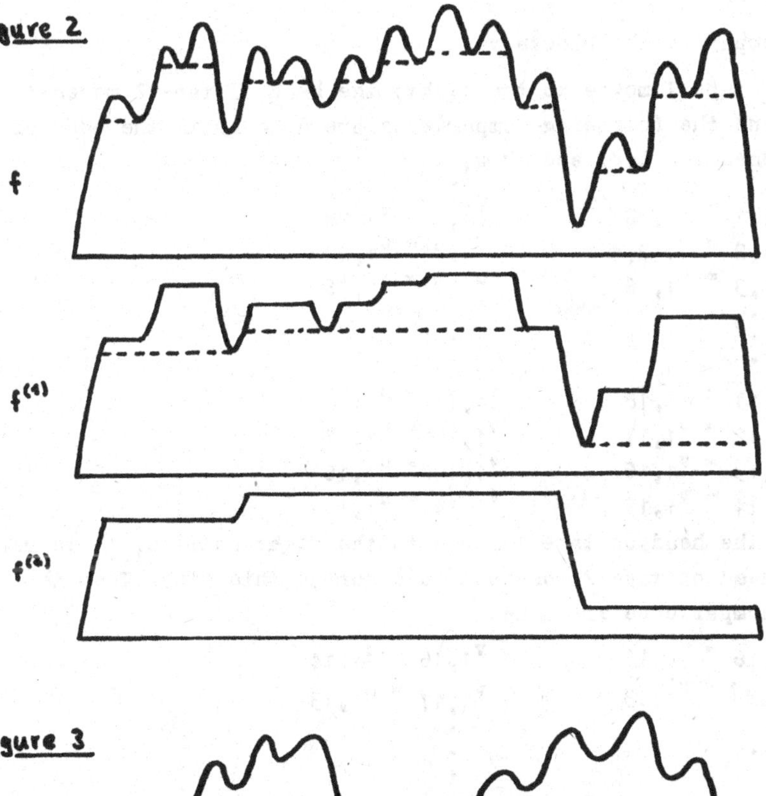

Figure 3

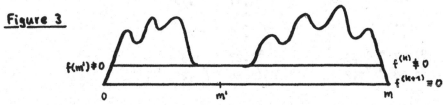

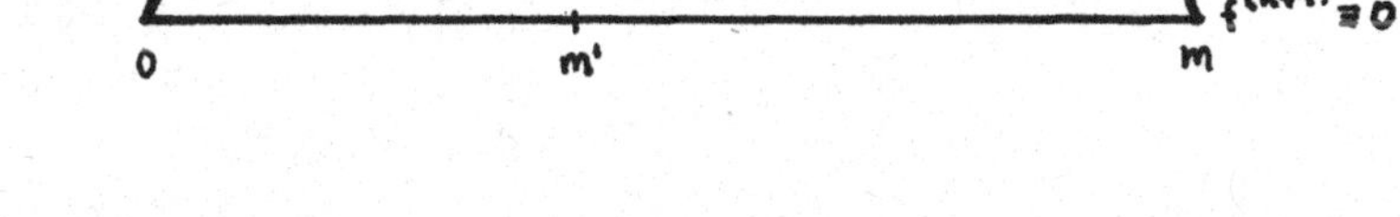

has reached the right and of B_4. The head on tape 2 is still moving to the right. The block B_4 serves for a comparison of $v_{1,16}$ and $u_{1,15}$. (Analogously for $v_{i,16}$ and $u_{i,15}$, $i = 2,3,4$. In the following we do not mention comparisons for $i = 2,3,4$.) $u^R_{1,16}$ and $v_{1,16}$ are written into the first and second track of tape 2. Then the head on tape 2 reverses and $u^R_{1,15}$ is read on tape 1 and it is compared with $v^R_{1,16}$ on tape 2.

Thus we ensure:

(1) $v_{1,16} = u_{1,15}$.

Then the head on tape 1 moves to the right end of B3 and now the popping phase of I_3 is simulated by an input copy contained in B_3 and analogously for B_2, I_2 and B_1, I_1.

The real input read during this phase is simultaneously compared with w_2 on the tenth track of tape 1. At the end of phase 2 the head of tape 1 is at the left and of B_1 and the head of tape 2 is at the right end of B_7.

Phase 3 (Comparing the blocks):

The head of tape 1 moves to the right, the head of tape 2 moves to the left, and the following comparisons are done until the head of tape 1 reaches the left end of $u_{1,15}$:

(2)
$$\begin{array}{ll}
u_{1,1} = v_{1,28} & v_{1,1} = u_{1,28} \\
u_{1,2} = v_{1,27} & v_{1,2} = u_{1,27} \\
u_{1,3} = v_{1,26} & v_{1,3} = u_{1,26} \\
\vdots & \vdots \\
u_{1,11} = v_{1,18} & v_{1,11} = u_{1,18} \\
u_{1,12} = v_{1,17} & v_{1,12} = u_{1,17} \\
u_{1,13} = v_{1,16} & v_{1,13} = u_{1,16} \\
u_{1,14} = v_{1,15} & v_{1,14} = u_{1,15}
\end{array}$$

After this the head on tape 1 moves to the right until $u_{1,16}$ is reached. The head on tape 2 does not move during this time. Then the following comparisons are done:

(3)
$$\begin{array}{ll}
u_{1,16} = v_{1,14} & v_{1,16} = u_{1,14} \\
u_{1,17} = v_{1,13} & v_{1,17} = u_{1,13} \\
\vdots & \vdots \\
u_{1,27} = v_{1,3} & v_{1,27} = u_{1,3} \\
u_{1,28} = v_{1,2} & v_{1,28} = u_{1,2}
\end{array}$$

The real input read during this phase is simultaneously compared with w_3 on the eleventh track of tape 1.
At the end of phase 3 the head on tape 1 has reached the right end of the tape and the head on tape 2 has reached the right end of $u_{1,1}$.

Phase 4 (Comparing the real input with one of the input copies):

The head on tape 1 moves to the left and the head on tape 2 also moves to the left, but with "lower speed". Thus w_1 is compared with $u_{1,1}$, w_2^R is compared with $v_{2,1}^R$, w_3 is compared with $u_{3,1}$, and the real input read during this phase is compared with $v_{4,1}^R$.
The simulating machine accepts the input iff the three simulated machines accept and all comarisons during the whole simulation have been successful. Now we still have to see whether the coincidences of all input copies have already been checked:

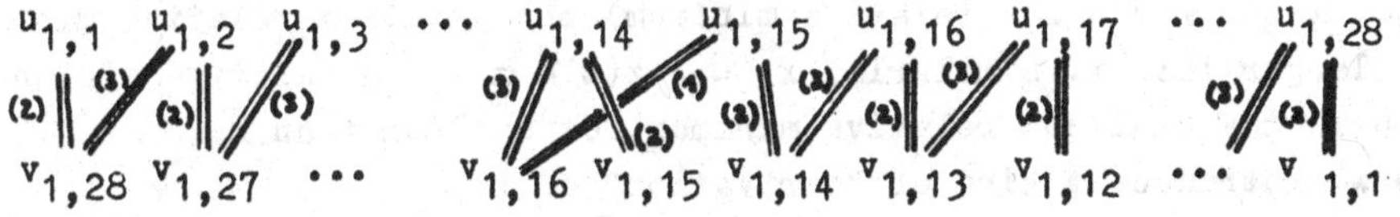

Thus the simulating machine (having two checking stack tapes) works in quasi-realtime, and it is obvious that only 3(1) reversals have been made on tape 1(2).
Using lemma 2.1 of /2/ and a simulation similar to that in the above proof one can show

<u>Corollary 1:</u> 1. 1-multiCS-NTIME(lin) = 1-2CS-NTIME(n)
2. 1-multiCS-VIS(const)-NTIME(lin) = 1-CS-REV(3)-CS-VIS(const)-NTIME(n).

<u>Theorem 2:</u> RBQ = 1-2CS-REV(2)-NTIME(n).
<u>Proof.</u> By a slight modification of the simulation given above.
<u>Open problem:</u> Is 1-CS-REV(1)-CS-REV(2)-NTIME(n) properly included in RBQ?

3. Visit-Bounded Realtime Accpetors

For reversal-bounded realtime acceptors a restriction to a fixed number of tapes and a fixed number of reversals is possible, namely three tapes with reversal 1 or two tapes with reversal 2 are sufficient. We show that a similar property is valid also for visit-bounded realtime acceptors. This will lead to a characterization of the least intersection closed AFL containing RBQ.

We start with some technical preliminaries needed for the reduction of the visit bound.

Clearly, a visit-bounded Turing tape can be simulated by two pushdown stores with the same visit bound.

A function $f : \{0,1,\dots,m\} \to \mathbb{N}$, $m \in \mathbb{N}$, is called a <u>pushdown growth function</u> iff

$f(0) = f(m) = 0$ and $|f(x) - f(x+1)| \leq 1$.

For $z \in \{0,1,\dots,m\}$, z is called a relative minimum of f iff either $f(z) = 0$ or there are $i,i' \in \mathbb{N}$ with the property:

$$f(z) = f(z-1) = \dots = f(z-i) < f(z-i-1) \quad \text{and}$$
$$f(z) = f(z+1) = \dots = f(z+i') < f(z+i'+1) \ .$$

For $x \in \{0,1,\dots,m\}$ we denote by

$x_0 = \nu z(z \leq x \wedge z \text{ a relative minimum})$ the greatest relative minimum not larger than x. Similarly, $x_1 = \mu z(z \geq x \wedge z \text{ a relative minimum})$ denotes the smallest relative minimum not smaller than x.

Now we introduce a kind of "derivation" of f:

$$f'(x) =_{Df} \begin{cases} f(x_0) \text{ if } f(x) > f(x_0) \geq f(x_1) \\ f(x_1) \text{ if } f(x) > f(x_1) > f(x_0) \\ f(x) \ \text{ otherwise} \end{cases}$$

(For a similar construction cf. /8/).

Furthermore

$$f^0 =_{Df} f \ , \ f^{(k+1)} =_{Df} f^{(k)'} .$$

The idea behind this construction is to cut off simultaneously "simple mountains" from the function f. An example is shown in Figure 2.

We define

$$\text{degree } (f) = \begin{cases} 0 \text{ if } f \equiv 0 \\ \mu k \ (f^{(k)} \equiv 0 \wedge f^{(k-1)} \not\equiv 0) \text{ otherwise.} \end{cases}$$

We investigate now the relation between visit and degree bounds. This is useful because a pushdown store with a growth function whose degree is constant-bounded admits a simulation by a constant number of pushdown stores whose visit is bounded by 3. The number of these pushdown stores is bounded by the degree of the original growth function.

<u>Lemma 1:</u> If degree (f) = k then there are pairwise disjoint intervals $[x_1,y_1],\dots,[x_k,y_k] \subseteq \{0,\dots,m\}$ and a $z \in \mathbb{N}$ with the property:

for all $i \in \{1,\dots,k\}$,

$$f(u) = z \text{ for } u \in [x_i,y_i]$$

$f(x_i-1) \neq z$ and $f(y_i+1) \neq z$.

(We actually have 2k-1 such intervals. However, to prove Theorem 3 it will be sufficient to prove the existence of k such intervals.)

Proof: (induction on k)

For k=1 the assertion is trivial.

Let us assume that the assertion is true for degree k, and let degree (f) =k+1, i.e. $f^{(k)} \not\equiv 0$ and $f^{(k+1)} \equiv 0$. Then for $f^{(k)}$ there is a $m' \in \{1,\ldots,m-1\}$ with $f(m') > 0$ and m' is a relative minimum of f.

Figure 3 shows an example for such a situation.

For $g_1(x) =_{Df} f(x) - f(m')$, $g_1 : \{0,\ldots,m'\} \to \mathbb{N}$ and $g_2(x) =_{Df} f(x+m') - f(m')$, $g_2 : \{0,\ldots,m-m'\} \to \mathbb{N}$, degree $(g_1) =$ = degree (g_2) = k.

Without loss of generality let us assume that

$\max_{0 \leq n \leq m'} g_1(n) \leq \max_{0 \leq n \leq m-m'} g_2(n)$. Because of degree (g_1) = k there are pairwise disjoint $[x_1, y_1], \ldots, [x_k, y_k] \subseteq \{0,\ldots,m'\}$ and a $z \in \mathbb{N}$ with the property: for all $i \in \{1,\ldots,k\}$

$g_1(n) = z$ for all $n \in [x_i, y_i]$

$g_1(x_i-1) \neq z$ and $g_1(y_i+1) \neq z$.

Furthermore, there is an interval $[x', y'] \subseteq \{0,\ldots,m-m'\}$ such that $g_2(n) = z$ for all $n \in [x',y']$,

$g_2(x'-1) \neq z$ and $g_2(y'+1) \neq z$.

Defining $x_{k+1} = x' + m'$ and $y_{k+1} = y' + m'$ we obtain intervals $[x_1,y_1],\ldots,[x_k, y_k],[x_{k+1},y_{k+1}]$ such that for all $i \in \{1,\ldots,k+1\}$

$f(n) = z' =_{Df} z + f(m')$ for all $n \in [x_i, y_i]$,

$f(x_i-1) \neq z'$ and $f(y_i+1) \neq z'$.

Corollary 2: If a pushdown store is visit-bounded by k, then its growth function has a degree not larger than k.

Theorem 3: 1-mPD-VIS(k)-NTIME(t) $\subseteq$ 1-(k·m)PD-VIS(3)-NTIME(lin t).

Proof: Let M be a 1-mPD-machine working in time t and visit k. Every pushdown store of M will be simulated by k pushdown stores of a machine M' working in time lin t and visit 3.

Let f denote the pushdown growth function of a pushdown store of M. From Corollary 2 we have degree (f) $\leq$ k. The i-th pushdown store simulates the work on "simple mountains" which are out off during the i-th derivation of f.

Before simulating a new "simple mountain" M' pushs down in a nondeterministic manner as many auxiliary symbols as necessary to obtain a new maximum pushdown store height (see Figure 4).

Figure 4:

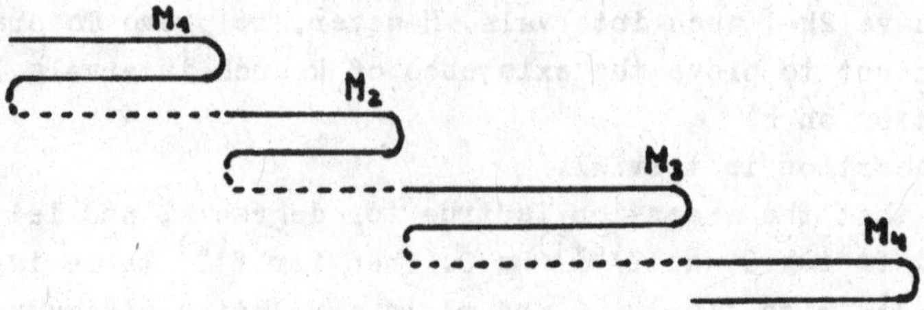

Thus the visit bound 3 is ensured and the time may increase by at most a constant factor.

Corollary 3: VBQ $=_{Df}$ 1-multiT-VIS(const)-NTIME(lin)
= 1-multiPD-VIS(3)-NTIME(lin)

(The notation VBQ is an abbreviation from "visit-dounded Q" similarly to RBQ.)

Theorem 4: VBQ = 1-multiPD-VIS(3)-NTIME(n).

Proof: This theorem is an immediate consequence from Lemma 2.1 of /2/ where it is shown that three additional 1-reversal bounded (and thus 2-visit bounded) pushdown stores ensure realtime on 1-multiPD-machines.

Theorem 5: VBQ = 1-PD-VIS(3)-2PD-REV(1)-NTIME(n).

Proof: The proof follows the idea of the proof of Lemma 3.2 in /2/.

Theorem 6: VBQ = 1-CS-REV(3)-CS-VIS(4)-NTIME(n).

This theorem can be shown in a similar way as Theorem 2 using a slight modification of the proof of Theorem 1.

4. The least intersection closed AFL containing RBQ

It is an open problem whether RBQ is closed under Kleene star, but RBQ is closed under the remaining AFL operations and intersection, and in /3/ it has been conjectured that the language $PAL^* = \{ww^R : w \in \{0,1\}^*\}^*$ is not contained in RBQ.

On the other hand the class VBQ is easily seen to be an intersection closed AFL, and PAL^* can even be accepted by a nondeterministic pushdown automaton (checking stack automaton) which works in linear time and with visit bound 3 (4):

$PAL^* \in$ 1-PD-VIS(3)-NTIME(lin)

($PAL^* \in$ 1-CS-VIS(4)-NTIME(lin)).

By standard methods of AFL theory it can be shown that the language PAL^* is a generator of VBQ with respect to the following operations: nonerasing homomorphisms (eh), inverse homomorphisms (h^{-1}), intersections with regular sets ($\wedge_R$) and intersections ($\cap$) (Γ denotes the closure operator).

Theorem 7: VBQ = $\Gamma_{eh,h^{-1},\wedge_R,\cap}(PAL^*)$

(the least intersection closed semi-AFL genrated by PAL^*). The proof uses the fact that every VBQ language can be accepted by a nondeterministic multipushdown machine in realtime whose pushdown stores work in the special manner described by Figure 4 (see the proof of Theorem 3).

Corollary 4: VBQ = $\Gamma_{AFL,\cap}(PAL)$ = $\Gamma_{AFL,\cap}(RBQ)$

(the least intersection closed AFL containing RBQ).

Note that in /3/ the following characterizatipn of $\Gamma_{AFL,\cap}(RBQ)$ is given: A language is in $\Gamma_{AFL,\cap}(RBQ)$ iff it can be accepted in realtime by a nondeterministic Turing machine with 3 pushdown tapes which operates in such a way that in every computation each pushdown store makes at most one reversal between the times it is empty. This corresponds to our result $\Gamma_{AFL,\cap}(RBQ) =$ 1-3PD-VIS(3)-NTIME(n).

Corollary 5: RBQ = VBQ iff $PAL^* \in$ RBQ.

Thus PAL^* is "inclusion-complete" for the problem RBQ $\overset{?}{\subseteq}$ VBQ .

5. Representations and Summary

It has been mentioned in /1/ and /2/ that the simulation results for the classes Q and RBQ, resp., admit representations by means of nonerasing homomorphisms and intersections of languages

Q = H(CF $\wedge$ CF $\wedge$ CF) (/1/)

= H(CF $\wedge$ LIN $\wedge$ LIN) (/2/)

RBQ = H(LIN $\wedge$ LIN $\wedge$ LIN) (/2/)

A similar representation is possible also for VBQ.

Theorem 8: VBQ = H($LIN^* \wedge$ LIN $\wedge$ LIN).

Proof: (Sketch) It is not hard to see that

1-PD-VIS(3)-NTIME(Lin) = eh($LIN^* \wedge$ REG).

By standard methods we obtain

VBQ = 1-PD-VIS(3)-2PD-VIS(1)-NTIME(n)

$\subseteq$ H(1-PD-VIS(3)-NTIME(n) $\wedge$ 1-PD-REV(1)-NTIME(n) $\wedge$ 1-PD-REV(1)-NTIME(n))

$\subseteq$ H(H(LIN* $\wedge$ REG) $\wedge$ LIN $\wedge$ LIN)

H(LIN* $\wedge$ REG $\wedge$ LIN $\wedge$ LIN)

H(LIN* $\wedge$ LIN $\wedge$ LIN).

<u>Summary of the results:</u>

(1) RBQ $=_{Df}$ 1-multiT-REV(const)-NTIME(lin)

$=_{/2/}$ 1-3PD-REV(1)-NTIME(n)

= 1-3PD-VIS(2)-NTIME(n)

= 1-CS-REV(1)-CS-REV(3)-NTIME(n)

= 1-2CS-REV(2)-NTIME(n)

= 1-2CS-VIS(3)-NTIME(n)

= $\Gamma_{eh,h^{-1},\wedge_R,\cap}$ (PAL).

$=_{/2/}$ H(LIN $\wedge$ LIN $\wedge$ LIN)

(2) VBQ $=_{Df}$ 1-multiT-VIS(const)-NTIME(lin)

= 1-PD-VIS(3)-2PD-REV(1)-NTIME(n)

= 1-CS-VIS(4)-CS-REV(3)-NTIME(n)

= $\Gamma_{eh,h^{-1},\wedge_R,\cap}$ (PAL*)

= $\Gamma_{AFL,\cap}$ (PAL)

= $\Gamma_{AFL,\cap}$ (RBQ)

= H(LIN* $\wedge$ LIN $\wedge$ LIN)

(3) 1-2CS-VIS(1)-NTIME(n) = REG (the class of regular languages)

1-2CS-VIS(2)-NTIME(n) = H(LIN $\wedge$ LIN) (Hull's class)

1-2CS-VIS(3)-NTIME(n) = RBQ

1-2CS-VIS(4)-NTIME(n) = VBQ

(and for all k $\geq$ 4

1-2CS-VIS(k)-NTIME(n) = VBQ) .

<u>References:</u>

/1/ Book, R.V., Greibach, S.A., Quasi-Realtime Languages, Math. Syst. Theory 4(1970), 97-111

/2/ Book, R.V., Nivat, M., Paterson, M., Reversal-Bounded Acceptors and Intersections of Linear Languages, SIAM J. Computing 3(1974), 283-295

/3/ Book, R.V., Nivat, M., Linear Languages and the Intersection Closures of Classes of Languages, SIAM J. Computing 7(1978),

167-177

/4/ Ginsburg, S., Algebraic and automata theoretic properties of formal languages, North-Holland 1975

/5/ Greibach, S.A., One way finite visit autbmata, Theor. Comp. Science 6 (1978), 175-221

/6/ Greibach, S.A., Checking automata and one-way stack languages, J. Comp. Syst. Sci. 3 (1969), 196-217

/7/ Hull, R.B., Containments between intersection families of linear and reset langugges, Ph. D. thesis 1979

/8/ Wechsung, G., The oscillation complexity and a hierarchie of context-free languages (extended abstract), Fundamentals of Computation Theory FCT '79, Akademie-Verlag Berlin 1979, 508-515

Input-Driven Languages are Recognized in $\log n$ Space

by

Burchard von Braunmühl
Rutger Verbeek

University of Bonn

Introduction

Since the famous algorithm of Lewis, Hartmanis and Stearns [LSH 65] many attempts have been made to determine the exact lower and upper space bounds for the recognition of context-free languages. It is quite unprobable that the $\log^2 n$ upper bound can be improved for general CFLs, since every improvement would improve the bound for the deterministic simulation of nondeterministic Turing machines [Su 75]. But even for deterministic CFLs no better space bound than $\log^2 n$ is known. Only the simultaneous time-space bound for DCFLs is much better than in the general case: using a black pebbling strategy for the computation graphs of deterministic pushdown automata Cook [Co 79] has shown, that DCFLs can be recognized using $\log n$ pebbles (i.e. in $\log^2 n$ space) and polynomial time simultaneously; this strategy was improved by the authors [BV 8o], [BCMV 83] and shown to be almost optimal (as pebbling strategy) [Ve 81], [Ve 83]. On the other hand several important subclasses of DCFLs are known to be recognized in $\log n$ space: Dyck sets [RS 72], bracket languages [Me 75] and leftmost Szilard languages [Ig 77]. All these examples are included in the class of input driven languages [Me 8o], which is already known to require a bit less than $\log^2 n$ space: according to Mehlhorn [Me 8o] there is a black pebbling strategy with $(\log n/\log\log n)^2$ pebbles where every pebble requires only $O(\log\log n)$ space.

In this paper we shall present a $\log n$ space algorithm for the recognition of input driven languages. Our algorithm uses a black and white pebbling strategy [CS 76] of the computation graphs, where the fact is important, that the structure of the computation graph of an input driven PDA can be computed by a counter automaton (and hence in $\log n$ space). The pebbles are distributed on the graph in such a way that their position needs not to be stored but can be recomputed. In this way our algorithm uses $O(\log n)$ pebbles, where each pebble requires only bounded space. Our approach gives a simple prove for the space complexity of a great subclass of DCFLs. In terms of pebbling complexity the strategy is optimal: it pebbles every n-node computation graph using $O(\log n)$ pebbles in n steps and there are computation graphs which require $\Omega(\log n)$ black and white pebbles [Ve 83].

Since our aim is to prove a space bound for some DCFLs, we shall describe the algorithm directly as simulation algorithm for input driven PDAs rather than as black and white pebble game.

There are some other classes of DCFLs that are contained in DSPACE(log n): counter languages (where the space bound is obvious), the languages recognized by finite minimal stacking PDAs [Ig 78] (which can be proved via a simple black pebbling strategy with a finite number of pebbles) and the two sided Dyck sets [LZ 77] which is the only known example of a non input driven DCFL in DSPACE(log n), for which the space bound is not obvious.

We call a (deterministic or nondeterministic) real-time pushdown automaton (pda) "input driven", if it reacts to an input symbol always with a push (the stack grows) or always with a pop (the stack falls). The moves of the stack are controlled only by the actual input symbol. The sequence of push and pop, i.e. the graph of stack height function $h(t)$ $(1 \leq t \leq n)$ is encoded in the input and is readable from it.

Definition

A real-time pushdown automaton (pda) is denoted by

$$P = (\Sigma, \Gamma, Q, \#, q_o, Q_f, \delta)$$

where Σ, Γ, Q are finite disjoint sets, $\# \in \Gamma$, $Q_f \subseteq Q$, $q_o \in Q$, δ a finite subset of $Q \times \Gamma \times \Sigma \times Q \times \Gamma^*$.

P is input driven, if Σ is the disjoint union of $\Sigma_o, \Sigma_1, \Sigma_2$ and $\delta \subseteq \bigcup_{i=o}^{2} Q \times \Gamma \times \Sigma_i \times Q \times \Gamma^i$ ($x \in \Sigma_o$ means pop, $x \in \Sigma_2$ means push).

A language $L \subseteq \Sigma^*$ is input driven, if it is recognized by some input driven pda.

A configuration is a pair (q,W) containing the state q and the content of the pushdown store W. For every $w \in \Sigma^*$, $q,q' \in Q$, $X \in \Gamma$, $W,W' \in \Gamma^*$, we define $\vdash_w$ inductively by

$(q,WX) \vdash_e (q,WX)$,

$(q,WX) \vdash_{wx} (q',W')$ iff there are $W_1,W_2 \in \Gamma^*$, $Y \in \Gamma$, $q_1 \in Q$, such that $(q,WX) \vdash_w (q_1,W_1Y)$, $(q_1,Y,x,q',W_2) \in \delta$ and $W' = W_1W_2$.

If $x_1 \ldots x_n$ is the input word, we define the stack height at time t by

$h(t) = |W|$ if $(q,X) \vdash_{x_1 \ldots x_t} (q',W)$ for $1 \leq t \leq n+1$.

($x_i x_{i-1}$ is the empty word).

In the following we consider languages of nondeterministic realtime input driven pda's.

The principle of the simulation

Let be $w = a_1 \ldots a_n$ the input of our input driven pda M and let be $v = a_i \ldots a_{k-1}$ a subword of w, such that in a computation of M applied to w, the stack height at time t_i (i.e. reading the input symbol a_i) is the same as at time t_k and never lower in between. Because the graph $h(t)$ depends on the input only, each computation on w produces the same graph. So following definition makes sense: The table T_v of v is a relation out of $(Q \times \Gamma)^2$ with $(q,A,q',A') \in T_v$ iff holds: if at time t_i M is in state q and the stack top symbol is A then at time t_k M reaches state q' reading stack top A'.
To find the result of the computation of M on w, we compute T_w.

Let us consider the directed, acyclic computation graph G of M computing w. The nodes are the points $(t,h(t))$ of the "graph" of h. $(t,h(t)) \to (t',h(t'))$ is a (directed) edge of G iff $t' = t+1$ or $(h(t+1) > h(t)$ and t' is the next time after t with $h(t) = h(t'))$.
That means an edge lies on the curve $h(t)$ (i.e. on the shape of the computation graph) or is cutting a mountain of the curve horizontaly. In the second case a table corresponds to this edge. The idea is determining the tables on the peaks of our push-pop mountain range, then going down the left and right flanks and in each step computing the table.

Corresponding the actual horizontal edge from the pda-relation δ and the last computed table (on the next level). In the bottom of a valley we compose the meeting tables to one table.

This is a special black and white pebbling strategy. This pebble game on graphs is played as follows: you may place a white pebble or remove a black pebble everywhere at any time and you may place a black pebble or remove a white pebble only if all predecessors are pebbled (black or white) (or no predecessor exists). On our computation graph G the game starts without any pebble. The goal is: the node $(n,h(n)) = (n,o)$ has a black pebble and no other node is pebbled. To come to this goal you can choose a black pebbling strategy beginning with node $(1,h(1))$ ending with node $(n,h(n))$ or you may prefer a white pebbling strategy working in the opposite direction. The table idea is a mixed strategy with black and white pebbles. We are putting white pebbles on the peaks and on the left flanks of the mountains and black pebbles on the right flanks and on the bottom of the valleys. Each table corresponds to a pair of a white and a black pebble lying on the nodes of the corresponding horizontal edge.

Since our aim is to save space and time we must not remember too many tables at a time. Thus we have to develop divide-and-conquer strategy of logarithmical depth: We can't handle parts of the mountain range with different starting and ending height. So we don't divide the mountain range into halves, but we cut a part out of it (with one bottom level) getting an inside and outside area of rather equal expansion. Hence we have intervals with a gap (the inside part cutted out). We want to attend to two points:

1) the inner interval and the rest interval should be of an expansion of equal order,

2) no interval should have more than one gap.

We will proceed in the following way:

Let $I = (i,k)$ be the interval under consideration and $g = (g_1,g_2)$ its gap. (If (i,k) doesn't contain a gap, we state an empty gap $(g_1 = g_2)$ in the position $(i-2k)/3$ (the end of the medium third of (i,k)).

We take the larger of the two intervals (i,g_1) and (g_2,k), and divide it into halves. Let (l,r) be the inner half, i.e. the half next to a gap. Then we search for the first point t in (l,r) of lowest stack height. Going horizontally left and right until we cut (not only touch) the shape of the graph we come to the points bt and at resp. of the same height h as t. So we have three new intervals: (bt,t), (t,at) (one of these with gap (g_1,g_2)) and the rest interval (i,k) with gap (bt,at). Because bt and at cannot lie in (l,r), and $\frac{1}{4}|I| \leq |(l,r)| \leq \frac{3}{4}|I|$ $[|I| = k-i-(g_2-g_1)]$ the length of the two intervals with gap is at most $\frac{3}{4}|(i,k)|$. The third interval without gap may be larger. But in the next division this interval falls into three intervals with at most $\frac{2}{3}$ length. So after two divisions of some interval I each of the 9 possible resulting intervals has length at most $\frac{2}{3}|I|$. After $2 \cdot \log_{3/2}(n) \leq 3{,}5 \cdot \log(n)$ successive divisions the resulting intervals have length ≤ 2. Moreover an interval contains never more than one gap. If interval I is of length ≤ 2 we obtain the table for I directly from the pda-relation δ and the table for the gap of I.

Now we give a recursive description to specify our idea. Then an interative implementation follows to state the costs in terms of time and space on a Turing machine.

We define a function procedure:
the input is an interval (i,k) and a gap $G = (g_1,g_2,TG)$ where g_1,g_2 are the limits of the gap and TG is the table corresponding to the interval (g_1,g_2).

The procedure returns the table for the interval (i,k).

```
Function  T(i,k,G);
Begin
  if  (k-i)-(g2-g1) > 2  (i.e. the interval is too big)
    then
      (bt,t,at) := Suc(i,k,G);
      if  bt ≤ g1  and  g2 ≤ t  (i.e. G  is a gap in  [bt,t])
        then  Gl := G;            Gr := Gap(t,at)
        else  Gl := Gap(bt,t);  Gr := G
      fi
      G := (bt,at, T(bt,t,Gl) o T(t,at,Gr));
      T := T(i,k,G)
    else  T := F(i,k,G)
  fi
end;
```

The functions Suc, Gap, F are defined below.
If T,T' are tables, then $T \circ T'$ is the table defined by:
$(qAq'A') \in T \circ T'$ iff $(qApB) \in T$ and $(pBq'A') \in T'$ for some p and B.
Function $Suc(i,k,G)$ returns the limits bt,t,at of the new double interval.

```
Function  Suc(i,k,G)
Begin
  if  g1-i ≥ k-g2  then  l := (i+g1)/2;  r = g1
                   else  l := g2       ;  r = (k+g2)/2
  fi
      t   := first point with lowest stack height  h(t)  in  (l,r)
      bt  := max {t' < t | h(t') < h(t)} + 1
      at  := min {t' > t | h(t') < h(t)  - 1
      Suc := (bt,t,at)
end;
```

Function $Gap(i,k)$ provides for an interval (i,k) without gap an interval (i,k) with an empty gap in the position $(i+2k)/3$. An empty gap has the form (i,i,Id), where Id is the identity-table.

<u>Function Gap(i,k)</u>

<u>Begin</u> $j := \lfloor (i+2k)/3 \rfloor$; Gap := (i,k,(j,j,Id)) <u>end</u>

Function F(i,k,G) is applicable to small intervals. It computes the table of interval (i,k) from the table for G and the relation δ of the PDA.

<u>Algorithm I</u>

First we describe an algorithm, that remembers the limits of the intervals and works in space $O(\log^2 n)$ and time $O(n \cdot \log n)$. Later we forget the limits of the intervals and remember only the tables and some information which of the intervals is considered next, which leads to algorithm II and works on space $O(\log n)$ in time $O(n^2)$.

In a list B we store elements of the form

(i,j,k) L R, where $i,j,k \in (1,n+1)$; $L,R \in POT(Q \times \Gamma \times Q \times \Gamma) \cup \{-,+\}$

and of the form

(i,j,k)/, where $i,j,k \in (1, n+1)$.

Elements of the first kind represent double-intervals (bt,t,at) being considered, where L,R are the tables of the left respectively right interval (if they are already determined) and + marks the part of the double-interval just being considered.

(e.g. (i,j,k)-+ means: the interval (j,k) is just being considered,
(i,j,k)+T means: T is the table for (j,k) and (i,j) is being considered).
The elements of the second kind are double-intervals whose tables are already determined; the last of them is the gap in the smallest interval under consideration, this and its table are stored as G and T.
The algorithm works as follows: Initially the interval I is (1,n+1), B contains (1, n+1, n+1) as bottom, G and T are empty. If the length of $I \setminus G$ is greater than 2, (bt,t,at) are determined using G (as described above).
If $G = \emptyset$ or if G is contained in (bt,t) the new I is (bt,t) and (bt,t,at)+- is stored in B, otherwise I := (t,at) and (bt,t,at)-+ is stored.

If $|I \setminus G| \leq 2$ we determine the table for I using the table T (which is the table for G). I is a part of E(B), which is the last element of B of the form (i,j,k)LR; I is the left part of E(B) if L=+, otherwise the right part. Now we can delete all later elements on B, since they have been used only for determining the table of I.
We have to consider two cases:

1. If the table of the other part of E(B) is already determined, we can combine these tables; the combination yields the table for (i,k). In this case E(B)

is replaced by (i,j,k) / ; the new gap G is (i,k), its table is stored as T. Finally the new I is determined from the next element of the form (i,j,k)LR below (i.e. (i,j) if L=+, (j,k) if R=+).

2. If the table of the other part is not yet determined (i.e. marked by -), this is the next interval I; the table of the old I is stored instead of the old +. The new I does not contain a gap; thus G and T are empty.

In this way we proceed until the table of the first interval I = (1,n+1) is determined. Then we can see from this table, whether the input $x_1 \ldots x_n$ is accepted or not.

The following flowchart gives the full algorithm I.

i_l, i_r, g_l, g_r denote the limits of the actual interval I and the actual gap G.

E(B) is the uppermost element of B of the form (i,j,k) LR.

$$f(I,G,T) := \begin{cases} \{q\ X\ y'\ Y \mid (q,X) \underset{x_{i_l} \ldots x_{i_r - 1}}{\vdash\!\!\!-\!\!\!-} (q', WY) \text{ for a } W\} \\ \qquad \text{if } G = \emptyset, \text{ where } W = \varepsilon \text{ if } i_r \le n \\ \{q\ X\ q'\ Y \mid (q,X) \underset{x_{i_l} \ldots x_{g_l - 1}}{\vdash\!\!\!-\!\!\!-} (p, WZ),\ p\ Z\ p'\ Z' \in T, \\ (p', WZ') \underset{x_{g_r} \ldots x_{i_r - 1}}{\vdash\!\!\!-\!\!\!-} (q', VY) \text{ for some } V,W,Z,Z',p,p'\} \\ \qquad \text{if } G \ne \emptyset, \text{ where } V = \varepsilon \text{ if } i_r \le n \end{cases}$$

$$bt(I,t) := \max\{t' \mid i_l - 1 \le t' < t \text{ and } h(t') < h(t)\} + 1$$

$$at(I,t) := \min\{t' \mid t < t' \le i_r \text{ and } h(t') < h(t)\} - 1$$

$$low(i,j) := \min\{k \mid h(k) \le h(k') \text{ for all } k',\ i \le k' < j\}$$

$$LP(I,G) := \begin{cases} low\left(\frac{2i_l + i_r}{3}, \frac{i_l + 2i_r}{3}\right) & \text{if } G = \emptyset \\ low\left(\frac{i_l + g_l}{2}, g_l - 1\right) & \text{if } G \ne \emptyset \text{ and } g_l - i_l \ge i_r - g_r \\ low\left(g_r, \frac{g_r + i_r}{2}\right) & \text{otherwise.} \end{cases}$$

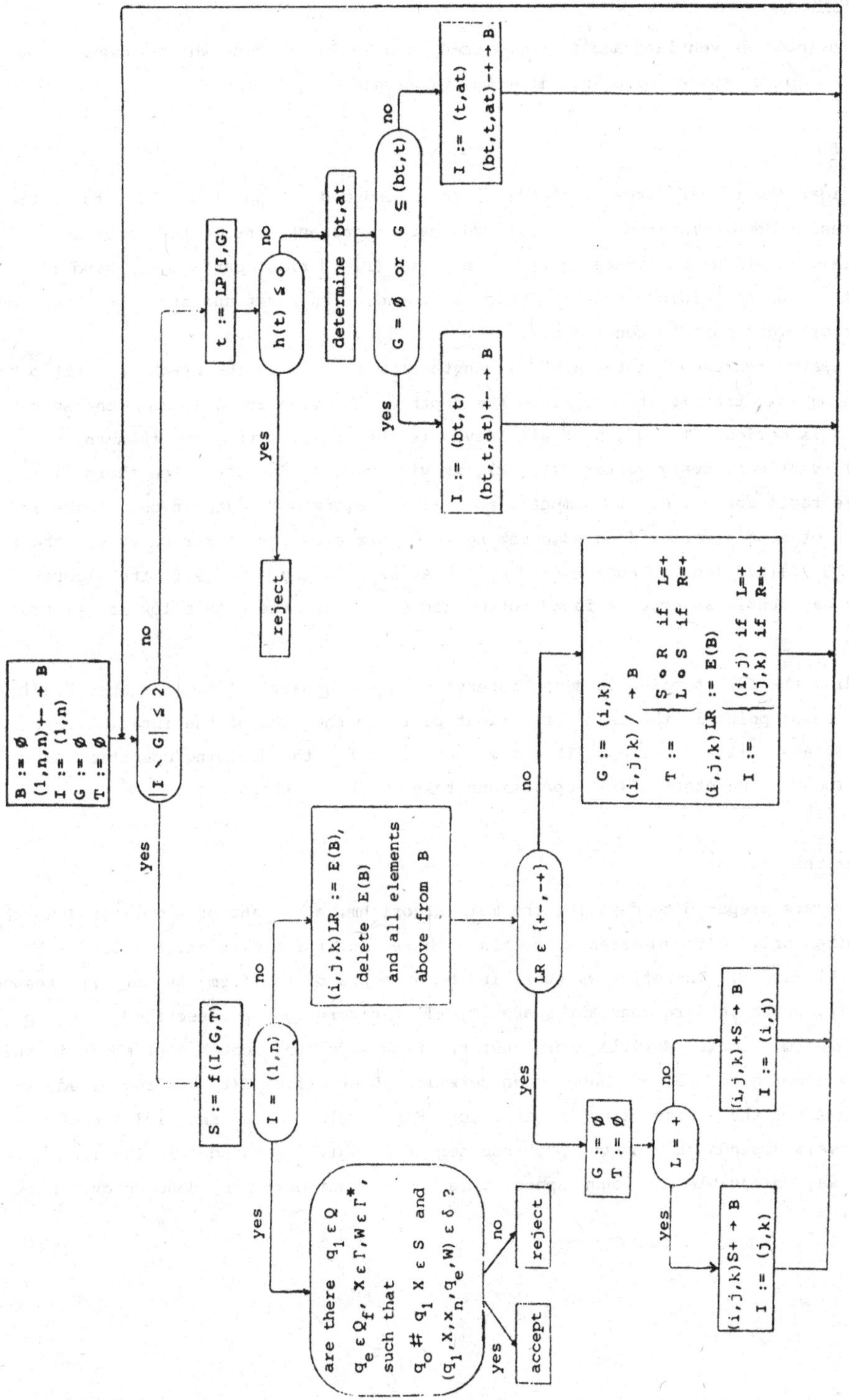
B := Ø
(1,n,n)+- → B
I := (1,n)
G := Ø
T := Ø
|I \ G| ≤ 2
yes
no
S := f(I,G,T)
t := LP(I,G)
h(t) ≤ o
yes
no
reject
determine bt,at
G = Ø or G ⊆ (bt,t)
yes
no
I := (bt,t)
(bt,t,at)+- → B
I := (t,at)
(bt,t,at)-+ → B
I = (1,n)
yes
no
are there q1 ε Ω
qe ε Ωf, X ε Γ, W ε Γ*,
such that
qo # q1 X ε S and
(q1,X,xn,qe,W) ε δ ?
yes
no
accept
reject
(i,j,k)LR := E(B),
delete E(B)
and all elements
above from B
LR ε {+-,-+}
yes
no
G := Ø
T := Ø
L = +
yes
no
(i,j,k)S+ → B
I := (j,k)
(i,j,k)+S → B
I := (i,j)
G := (i,k)
(i,j,k) / → B
T := S o R if L=+
L o S if R=+
(i,j,k)LR := E(B)
I := (i,j) if L=+
(j,k) if R=+

Theorem 1

Every input driven language is recognized on a Turing machine which random access input tape on space $O(\log^2 n)$ in time $O(n \cdot \log n)$.

Proof

Consider the ternary tree of the "intervals" induced by the algorithm. Its vertices represent double-intervals (i,j,k) and each represents one of the three possible "intervals" to be considered next (left part (i,j), right part (j,k) and the rest of the containing interval, which is found at the next ancestor, in which the left or right part is considered).

The leaves represent "intervals" of length at most 2. On the stack B just one path on that tree is stored. Since the depth of the tree is $O(\log n)$, the space bound is obvious. The union of all leaves is the interval $(1,n+1)$ thus the tree has $O(n)$ vertices. Every vertex (i,j,k) is visited 4 times, after the third visit the whole table for (i,k) is computed and (i,k) becomes the gap in one of the inner parts of some ancestor (the edge coming from this ancestor is marked by +); the third son is visited (on the edge marked by /). After visiting some leaf, the algorithm goes back until an edge is found not marked by / and the path below is deleted from B.

Finding the lowest point in some "interval" $I \setminus G$ costs $|I \setminus G|$ steps. Finding the lowest point in the left part, right part and the rest of the interval cost together also $|I \setminus G|$ steps. Thus the whole cost for the dividing operations are $O(n \cdot \log n)$. The other $O(n)$ operations take $O(\log n)$ steps each. □

Algorithm II

Now we are prepared to describe the main algorithm, a variant of algorithm I which requires only $O(\log n)$ space. In this case we cannot remember all the limits (i,j,k) in B. Therefore we store in B elements of the form LR or /, respectively, which require constant space. Recall the ternary tree described in the proof of theorem 1 above. We will store just the path (i.e. the sequence of edges in this tree) leading to the node under consideration. Every time E(B) is requested, we reconstruct the limits using the function E(B) below. Since the division of the intervals depends only on the push-pop sequence (which is encoded in the input) in a way computable on $\log n$ space, this reconstruction can be done in our space limit.

Function E(B) (returns the limits of the last double-interval not completely determined)

```
begin  j := 2;
       I := (1,n);
       G := Ø;
       Z := (1,n,n);
       while  B(j) ≠ Ø  do
       begin  t := LP(I,G);
              determine new  bt,  at  from  I,G  and  t;
              if  B(j) = /  then  G := (bt,at)
              else begin  Z := (bt,t,at);
                          if  B(j) = +R  then  I := (bt,t)
                                         else  I := (t,at)  fi;
                          if  B(j) ∉ {+-,-+}  then  G := Ø  fi
                     end;
              fi;
              j := j+1
       end;
       E := Z
end
```

Lemma

Function E(B) determines the limits of the last double interval not completely determined. On a Turing machine E(B) takes time $O(n\cdot\log n)$ and space $O(\log n)$; using a random-access input tape, it takes time $O(n)$.

Proof

During the simulation algorithms I and II change only the top of B. Hence the limits of the intervals corresponding to elements of B depend only on elements below. Furthermore it is sufficient to know E(B) and G for the computation of the next interval.

1. $B(j) \in \{+-,-+\}$: the new I is the interval marked by + and contains the old G.
2. $B(j) \in \{+R,L+\}$, $L,R \neq -$: the part of the corresponding double-interval, that contains the gap, has been determined, the other part becomes I and thus $G=\emptyset$.
3. $B(j) = /$: both parts of the corresponding double-interval have been determined and become now the new gap for I.

Each of the $O(\log n)$ calls of $LP(I,G)$ takes $O(n)$ moves on a Turing input tape and $O(|I \setminus G|)$ moves on a random-access input tape. Thus the time costs on an ordinary Turing machine are $O(n \cdot \log n)$.
Since the length of $|I \setminus G|$ corresponding to $B(j)$ is exponentially decreasing in j, their sum is $O(n)$. Thus the time bound for random-access input follows.
The space bound is obvious.

□

Theorem 2

On a Turing machine algorithm II works on tape $O(\log n)$ in time $O(n^2 \cdot \log n)$.

Proof

Since B contains $O(\log n)$ elements of constant length (depending on the size of the simulated pda), the space bound is obvious. Procedure E(B) is called $O(n)$ times. Any other operation takes at most $O(n)$ steps. Since there are $O(n)$ other operations, the time bound follows from the lemma.

□

Turing machines with random-access input use only $O(n^2)$ time. Also for ordinary Turing machines the time bound can be decreased to n^2 with following modification of algorithm II: The table for some $(I \setminus G)$ is determined, when $|I \setminus G| \leq \log n$. This can be done on space $O(\log n)$ in time $O(\log^2 n)$. Then E(G) is called only $O(n/\log n)$ times, since every subtree of the tree induced by the algorithm contains at least one leaf representing an "interval" $I \setminus G$ of length at least $\frac{\log n}{3}$ (and thus the tree has $O(n/\log n)$ vertices).

References

[BCMV 83] B.v.Braunmühl, S.A. Cook, K. Mehlhorn, R. Verbeek:
The recognition of deterministic CFLs in small time and space, submitted for publication.

[BV 8o] B.v. Braunmühl, R. Verbeek:
A recognition algorithm for DCFLs optimal in time and space, Proc. 21th FOCS, pp. 411-42o.

[Co 79] S.A. Cook:
Deterministic CFLs are accepted simultaneously in polynomial time and log squared tape, Proc. 11th ACM-STOC, pp. 338-345.

[CS 76] S.A. Cook, R. Sethi:
Storage requirements for deterministic polynomial time recognizable languages. JCSS 13, 25-37.

[Ig 77] Y. Igarashi:
The tape complexity of some classes of Szilard languages, SIAM 3. Comp. 6, pp. 46o-466.

[Ig 78] Y. Igarashi:
Tape bounds for some subclasses of deterministic context-free languages, Inf. Contr. 37, 321-333.

[LSH 65] P.M. Lewis, R.E. Stearns, J. Hartmanis:
Memory bounds for the recognition of context-free and context-sensitive languages,
Proc. 6th IEEE-SWAT, pp. 191-212.

[LZ 77] R. Lipton, Y. Zalcstein:
Word problem solvable in log-space,
JACM 24, 522-526.

[Me 75] K. Mehlhorn:
Bracket languages are recognizable in logarithmic space,
Technical report, FB 1o. Universität Saarbrücken.

[Me 8o] K. Mehlhorn:
Pebbling mountain ranges and its application to DCFL-recognition,
Proc. 7th ICALP, pp. 422-432.

[PH 7o] M.S. Paterson, C.E. Hewitt:
Comparative schematology,
project MAC, Conf. on concurrent systems and parallel computation, pp. 1o9-127.

[RS 72] R.W. Ritchie, F.N. Springsteel:
Language recognition by marking automata,
Inf. Contr. 2o, 313-33o.

[Su 75] I.H. Sudborough:
On tape bounded complexity classes and multi-head finite automata,
JCSS 1o, 177-192.

[Ve 81] R. Verbeek:
Time-space tradeoffs for general recursion,
22nd IEEE-FOCS, pp. 228-234.

[Ve 83] R. Verbeek:
Complexity of pushdown computations,
Institut für Informatik der Universität Bonn.

HOW TO SEARCH IN HISTORY

BERNARD CHAZELLE
Computer Science Department
Brown University
Providence, RI 02912

Abstract

This paper considers the problem of granting a dynamic data structure the capability of remembering the situation it held at previous times. We present a new scheme for recording a history of h updates over an ordered set S of n objects, which allows fast neighbor computation at any time in the history. This scheme requires $O(n+h)$ space and $O(\log n \log h)$ query response-time, which saves a factor of $\log n$ space over previous structures. Aside from its improved performance, the novelty of our method is to allow the set S to be only partially ordered with respect to queries and the time-measure to be multi-dimensional. The generality of our method makes it useful to a number of problems in three-dimensional geometry. For example, we are able to give fast algorithms for locating a point in a 3d-complex, using linear space, or for finding which of n given points is closest to a query plane. Using a simpler, yet conceptually similar technique, we show that with only $O(n^2)$ preprocessing, we can determine in $O(\log^2 n)$ time which of n given points in E^3 is closest to an arbitrary query point.

1. Introduction

This paper considers the problem of searching in the past. We make this problem very general by making virtually no assumption on the time-measure, i.e. the time θ will not necessarily be sequential but possibly multidimensional. Let $S = \{v_1, \ldots, v_n\}$ be a set of n objects provided with a total order. Depending on the value of a parameter θ (the time) each object is either *active* or *inactive*, so that we can define the ordered set $S(\theta)$ of active objects for any value of θ in some range Θ. The collection of all distinct sets $S(\theta)$ is called a *history*, and is assumed to be of finite "size" h. We define a *query* on the history as a pair (q, θ), where q is an object (not necessarily in S) with the following property: for any $v \in S(\theta)$, either $q \leq v$ or $q > v$, but q *cannot* be compared with any v not in $S(\theta)$. It is possible to define the *neighbor* of q, denoted $n(q, \theta)$, as the largest object v in $S(\theta)$ such that $v \leq q$. By convention, if no such object exists, the neighbor of q is denoted $-\infty$. The main purpose of this paper is to construct a data structure that allows the efficient computation of $n(q, \theta)$.

We present a data structure that requires $O(n+h)$ storage and allows the computation of $n(q, \theta)$ in $O(\log n \log h)$ time. This result has several applications in geometric searching. For example, we are able to give an $O(n)$ space, $O(\log^2 n)$ query time algorithm for locating a point in an n-vertex partition of the space whose faces can be *ordered* along some direction. This can be applied to the complex formed by n hyperplanes, which leads to an $O(n^3)$ space, $O(\log^2 n)$ query time algorithm. This also allows us to determine which of n given points in E^3 is closest to a query plane with the same time and space complexity. Using a slightly different technique, we show that with only $O(n^2)$ preprocessing, we can determine, in $O(\log^2 n)$ time, which of n given points is closest to an arbitrary query point. This result improves the best solution previously known by a factor of $n^3 \log n$.

The general problem of searching in the past has been previously studied by Dobkin and Munro in [DM], who described a method for computing, in time $O(\log n \log h)$, the *rank* of any object at any given time, i.e. the number of objects that preceded it at that time. One remarkable feature of their method is to avoid recording the "state of the universe" at all times, which would take $O(nh)$ space. Instead, they use a clever tree structure to limit the storage requirement to $O(n + h \log n)$. The query time of their algorithm was subsequently reduced to $O(\log(h + n))$ by Overmars [O], who also considered methods for testing membership in the past. All previous work, however, has assumed that the time was one-dimensional (a fairly reasonable assumption from a human perspective...) and has never dealt with neighbor computation. But perhaps the most fundamental assumption, imposed on us by our geometric applications, is that **inactive objects can never be used.** Without this requirement a number of very efficient solutions could be derived quite easily. For example, assuming that the time is one-dimensional, as observed by Overmars in [O] we can view the life periods of each object as vertical intervals in the Euclidean plane, whereby the ordered list $v_1, \ldots, v_n$ is spread along the X-axis and the time corresponds to the Y-axis. Since the problem essentially reduces to finding the vertical segment immediately to the left of a query point, we can introduce horizontal segments to subdivide the plane into regions with common "answers". This is the *adjacency-map* of [LiP] to which we refer the reader for details. With this structure in hand, it suffices to locate the query in the subdivision, which we can do using the optimal planar point location algorithms of [LT,K]. This leads to an $O(n + h)$ space, $O(\log(n + h))$ query time algorithm. However, this relies on the Euclidean nature of the map and assumes that inactive objects can indeed be effectively used in the neighbor computation. It is therefore unacceptable for our purposes.

2. The Canal-Tree

2.1. The Basic Ideas

Let's first assume that the time is real, i.e. $\Theta = \Re$. We introduce a new data structure, T, which we called a *canal-tree*. T is a complete binary tree with n leaves, the i-th from the left corresponding to v_i. Since T is essentially a static tree, it should probably be stored in an array so as to avoid the use of pointers. Similarly, assigning objects to the leaves, and not to the internal nodes as well, may not lead to the most efficient implementation. Simplicity will, however, dictate our choice in the matter, and we will avoid overburdening our exposition with issues of implementation optimization.

Let's first describe a tentative data structure, which we will use as a stepping-stone for constructing the *canal-tree*. Ideally, we would like to keep in each node v of T a pointer to a list, $L(v)$, which gives a chronological account of all the largest active objects in the interval spanned by the left subtree rooted at v. More precisely, let z be the left son of v and let $I(z)$ be the interval $[i, j]$ such that the leaves of the subtree rooted at node z are from left to right $\{v_i, \ldots, v_j\}$. Let $v_{i_1}, \ldots, v_{i_k}$ be the list, in chronological order, of the largest objects in $S(\theta)$ during the history, with indices in $I(z)$, and let θ_j be the time corresponding to v_{i_j}'s promotion. $L(v)$ is simply the list of pairs $\{(\theta_1, v_{i_1}), \ldots, (\theta_k, v_{i_k})\}$. We define the θ-entry of $L(v)$ as the pair (θ_j, v_{i_j}) such that $\theta_j \leq \theta < \theta_{j+1}$ (for consistency, we may assume that θ_1 is always 0). It is clear that by traversing T in inorder each internal node v can be uniquely associated with an interval (v_i, v_{i+1}); we can therefore extend the concept of neighbor to v itself, and define $n(v, \theta)$ as the largest object v_l in $S(\theta)$, with $l \in I(z)$. Answering a query (q, θ) can now be easily described. Starting at the root of T, we find $n(root, \theta)$ in $O(\log h)$ time, by performing a simple a binary search in $L(root)$. If $q = n(root, \theta)$, we are clearly finished; otherwise if $q > n(root, \theta)$, we keep $n(root, \theta)$ as a potential candidate and we iterate on the right son of the root, and if $q < n(root, \theta)$, we blithely branch to the left. This type of binary search is fairly standard and we may omit the details. Unfortunately the overall scheme is wasteful in its use of space, as it is not difficult to show that it may entail the use of $O(n + h \log n)$ storage.

The *canal-tree* is a simple modification of the tree described above. Here we avoid duplicates by recording events only once: let $z_1, \ldots, z_p$ be the list of internal nodes, on the path from v_i to the root, that appear *after* v_i in inorder. Informally, $z_1, \ldots, z_p$ are the nodes encountered after each rightward move on the way up from v_i to the root. Let w_i denote the right son of z_i. Suppose now that an insertion or a deletion of v_i takes place at time θ, and consider the largest index j such that $I(w_1), \ldots, I(w_{j-1})$ are all free of active objects at θ. It is clear that whether v_i is inserted or deleted, the only nodes of T which witness a change in neighbor are precisely $z_1, \ldots, z_j$. The main feature of the canal-tree, however, will be to record the event in $L(z_j)$, only. It will result from this restriction that, since only one update is necessary per operation, the total space needed to store the lists $L(v)$ will be $O(n + h)$. We will use the remainder of this section to describe the update operations and show that the canal-tree still allows efficient searching.

Before proceeding, let's give an image to help visualize the workings of the canal-tree and also justify its name. Figure 1 illustrates the canal-like structure of T: let $S(\theta) = \{v_{i_1}, v_{i_2}, \ldots, v_{i_k}\}$ be, as usual, the list of objects active at time θ, in left-to-right order. We introduce the *canal* of v_{i_j} as the path from v_{i_j} to a node z_j, defined iteratively as follows: z_k is a *pseudo-root*, situated right on top of the usual root. In the general case, z_{i_j} is the first point of contact with the canal of $v_{i_{j+1}}$. We will refer to v_{i_j} (resp. z_j) as the *source* (resp. *sink*) of the canal, which itself will be denoted $C(v_{i_j})$. Let v (resp. w) be the left (resp. right) son of the root. We observe that when the objects in $I(w)$ are not all inactive, the root is the sink of the canal whose source is the largest active element in $I(v)$. We can now state the basic requirement of the canal-tree: for all j; $1 \le j \le k$, the index i_j should appear in the θ-entry of $L(z_j)$, paired of course with the value of θ when v_{i_j} was last activated. In other words, $L(z_j)$ should contain a pair of the form (θ^*, v_{i_j}); $\theta^* \le \theta$. With this new, more economical scheme, it is clear that the lists $L(v)$, considered individually, may give us erroneous information about current neighbors. To allow for proper use of these lists, we must include in them the times θ at which the current information ceases to reflect reality. More precisely, each list $L(v)$ will be a sequence of the form

$$\{(\theta_1, v_{i_1}), \theta_1^{(end)}, \ldots, (\theta_k, v_{i_k}), \theta_k^{(end)}\},$$

whereby $\theta_j^{(end)}$ signifies that v_{i_j} should not be relied upon as an indicator of $n(v, \theta)$ for θ; $\theta_j^{(end)} < \theta \le \theta_{j+1}$. By "not to be relied upon", we mean that although the information may be occasionally correct, we should never use it, for it may not always be so. Note that we will often have $\theta_j^{(end)} = \theta_{j+1}$, in which case we should simply omit $\theta_j^{(end)}$ from the list, altogether. For convenience, we will refer to $\theta^{(end)}$ as an *info-unavail* flag. To summarize, we state the fundamental property of the canal-tree:

Fact. At any time $\theta \in \Theta$, the θ-entry of any internal node v of T is of the form (θ^*, v_i) (with $\theta^* \le \theta$) if v is a currently a sink, or is an *info-unavail* flag, otherwise.

Let $[op, \text{i}, \theta]$ be a shorthand for "apply operation op (activate or deactivate) to v_i at time θ". We can represent the history of S as a sequence of triplets $[op, \text{i}, \theta]$, ordered with respect to θ. Setting up T simply involves going through each instruction of the history in turn, updating the lists $L(v)$ accordingly. We will assume that, initially, all the lists $L(v)$ are empty.

2.2. Setting Up the Canal-Tree

We are now ready to give a description of the algorithms for activating and deactivating an object, respectively.

I. Activating an Object

Informally, activating v_i at time θ involves tracing down the path from the root to v_i and determining the last canal visited. Let v_j be the source of this canal, and z be the last node visited on the canal. There are basically two cases to consider (Fig.2):

1. Suppose that $i < j$ (Fig.2-a). Let w denote the left son of z. Since z is the first canal node on the path from v_i to the root, none of the objects in $I(w)$ is active at time θ, therefore we have $n(z,\theta) = v_i$ and $n(v,\theta) \neq v_i$, for all the ancestors v of z. Furthermore, the global inactivity of $I(w)$ prior to θ shows that all the θ-entries in the subtree rooted at w are ***info-unavail*** flags, and should remain so. Therefore, the only updating required consists of appending (θ, v_i) to the end of $L(z)$.
2. Suppose that $i > j$ (Fig.2-b). Let w denote the right son of z, and u be the sink of $C(v_j)$. We must introduce a new canal, $C(v_i)$, with u for sink, and we must move the sink of $C(v_j)$ down to z. This involves appending (θ, v_i) and (θ, v_j) to the lists $L(u)$ and $L(z)$, respectively. Since no sink is either destroyed or created, no ***info-unavail*** flag has to be added.

Note that in both cases, finding the relevant nodes u, w, z mentioned above is straighforward. To do so, we simply have to traverse the tree from the pseudo-root towards v_i, using a standard binary search, and stopping at the first node encountered that is not on a canal. To be able to do this as well as the updating described above, it suffices to keep track, at all times, of the most recent sink visited from which we left a canal. Since this involves only checking whether the current node v is a sink towards whose source we are heading, a simply look at the last item of $L(v)$ suffices, therefore activating v_i requires only $O(\log n)$ operations.

II. Deactivating an Object

Let z be the sink of $C(v_i)$ and let w be the left son of z (Fig.3). If $I(w)$ is entirely inactive right after θ, the only action to take is clearly to append an ***info-unavail*** flag to the end of $L(z)$. Otherwise, the only active objects in $I(w)$ can only be of the form v_l for $l < i$ (see iterative definition of the canal-tree). Let j be the largest such index l. Note that the sink, u, of the canal $C(v_j)$ is the last sink encountered in a downward traversal of $C(v_i)$. Once we have found this node, we only have to append (θ, v_j) to the end of $L(z)$ as well as include an ***info-unavail*** flag at the end of $L(u)$.

There again, finding all the appropriate nodes u, w, z can be done easily by walking down the tree, and keeping record of 1) the most recent sink visited from which we left a canal (e.g. z), 2) the most recent sink visited (e.g. u). Since both pieces of information can be updated in constant time at each node v visited, by simply looking at the last item in $L(v)$, the algorithm requires $O(\log n)$ operations. We can finally conclude:

Lemma 1. The canal-tree can be constructed in $O(n + h \log n)$ time and $O(n + h)$ space.

2.3. Computing Neighbors

We can now show how to use T for computing the neighbor of a query (q, θ). Starting at the pseudo-root, we retrieve the corresponding θ-entry and terminate if it gives us an *info-unavail* flag. This would, indeed, signify that all the objects were inactive at θ, so $-\infty$ should be our answer. If, instead, the θ-entry is a pair (θ^*, v_i), we start the iterative part of the search. Informally, we follow the current canal always trying to branch left to the first canal $C(v_j)$ with $q \leq v_j$. More precisely, we need to keep track of two variables: 1) *cur*, the index of the current canal traversed, 2) *last*, the index of the last sink visited to whose canal we did not branch. Initially, *cur* $= i$ and *last* $= -\infty$. At the generic step, let $C(v_k)$ be the current canal, F be the θ-entry of the current node v, and w be the next node after v on $C(v_k)$. If F is an *info-unavail* flag, we simply proceed to the next node towards v_k, and iterate. Assume now that F is of the form (θ^*, v_t), in which case w must be the right son of v. If $q = v_t$, we return v_t and stop. If $q < v_t$, we set *cur* $= t$ and branch left, otherwise we set *last* $= t$ and proceed to the right. When we eventually reach a leaf of T, we return the current value of *last*. Since computing each θ-entry takes $O(\log h)$ operations, the entire search requires $O(\log n \log h)$ time. We conclude:

Theorem 2. It is possible to record a history of h events involving n objects in $O(n + h)$ space, so that retrieving any neighbor information can be done in $O(\log n \log h)$ time.

2.4. Generalizing to Multidimensional Parameters

The key to the method described above was to be able to produce a snapshot of the canal-tree, at any time, very efficiently. Unfortunately, this is not always easy, in particular when the parameter θ is multidimensional. In that case, we may no longer be able to arrange the sink in a linear list to reflect the chronological sequence of events. We observe, however, that since the use of canal-trees makes the whole problem totally local, i.e. comes down to allowing fast sink retrieval at each node, we can formulate a model in which efficient search in history is always possible by means of canal-trees. Let $\theta \in \Re^d$ $(d > 1)$. Let $T(\theta)$ be a snapshot of the canal-tree T at time θ. We define $J(v)$ to be the set of distinct values of the sinks, for all $\theta \in \Theta$. Assume that there exists a data structure $DS(J(v))$ that organizes the elements of the set $J(v)$ in such a way that we can compute the sink-value of $T(\theta)$ at v, in time $O(Q(h))$. In this model, it is clearly possible to adapt the algorithm described earlier so as to compute the neighbor of any query (q, θ) in time $O(Q(h) \log n)$. We will show in the next section how this result can be used to derive new algorithms for several of geometric problems.

3. Geometric Applications

We will apply the previous ideas to point location problems: for the sake of illustration, let's start with the problem of locating a point in a planar subdivision. Although this problem has already been given several optimal solutions [LT,K], we will for the sake of illustration show how to use canal trees to produce a very simple near-optimal algorithm:

3.1. Planar Point Location

Let $S = \{s_1, \ldots, s_n\}$ be the segments of a straight-line subdivision of the plane. We can obtain a total order on S by topologically sorting the relation $\preceq$, defined as follows: $s_i \preceq s_j$ whenever there exists a line parallel to the X-axis that intersects s_i (resp. s_j) in p (resp. q), with $p \leq q$ with respect to the X-coordinate. We precompute this partial order by sweeping a horizontal line L downwards, maintaining the current order of the intersections with L in a dynamic balanced search tree. The line L starts at the highest vertex of G and proceeds to visit each vertex of G in turn in descending Y-order. If the current vertex is the upper end of a segment, this segment is inserted into the tree, otherwise it is deleted. This method is very standard [BO], so we may omit the details. The next step is to embed the partial order in a total order, which simply requires a topological sort. We are now ready to set up a canal tree T on the following basis: θ is the Y-coordinate of the line L, and $S(\theta)$ is the set of segments that intersect L when positioned at $y = \theta$. Since an event in the history corresponds to the promotion or demotion of an edge, we have $h = 2n$. Finally, comparing a query point against an object simply involves computing the relative position of a point with respect to a line, therefore we have the following result.

Theorem 3. It is possible to use a canal-tree to solve the planar point location problem in $O(n)$ space and $O(\log^2 n)$ time.

This method is akin to Lee and Preparata's algorithm [LP]; it shows that the latter is a particular instance of a general searching technique to which canal-trees are especially tailored. The basic difference with their algorithm is that we do away with the actual computation of "geometric chains". Instead, our method relies on the topological (rather than geometrical) nature of the problem, and thus, reduces the geometric part of the algorithm to its simplest expression. This has the effect of granting the algorithm great conceptual simplicity. Also, the basic generality of the method makes it directly applicable to other problems as well. The algorithm can be used, for example, to compute the horizontal neighbors of a query point, given a set of n pairwise disjoint segments. This involves reporting the first segment to the right and to the left of the query point that intersect a horizontal line passing through it.

3.2. Spatial Point Location

Using a more general method, Dobkin and Lipton [DL] have shown how to solve the point location problem in higher dimensions. Assume that the regions are defined by n arbitrary hyperplanes in d-dimensional Euclidean space, i.e. the regions form a d-dim complex. Dobkin and Lipton's method requires $O(n^{2^d-1})$ space and $O(2^d \log n)$ time per query. The purpose of this section is to show how point location problems in general can be viewed as history retrieval problems, for which canal-trees can be used. We will illustrate our point by presenting an improved algorithm for searching a three-dimensional complex.

Let P be a convex 3d-complex, i.e. a partition of the three-dimensional space into polyhedra. We will assume that either all the polyhedra are convex (think for example of a Voronoi diagram in 3d) or exactly one is non-convex. In the latter case we will assume that P is a convex partition of a convex polyhedron to which we adjoin the outside, unbounded polyhedron. We define the *cap* of any convex polyhedron of P as the subset of its faces looking to the right inward, i.e. faces whose inward-directed normal vector has a positive X-coordinate. From our assumptions on P, it easily follows that the cap of a polyhedron Q is a connected set of faces whose projection on the YZ-plane coincides with the projection of Q (Fig.4).

We define the following order among caps: $C \preceq C'$ if there exist two points $(x, y, z) \in C$ and $(x', y, z) \in C'$ with $x \leq x'$. Whenever it is possible to find a direction for the X-axis such that this order is embeddable in a total order, we say that the complex P is *acyclic*. Unfortunately, complexes are often non-acyclic as suggested by Fig.5. It is however always possible to refine the complex so as to make it acyclic [F] so we will assume from now on that P is acyclic. This refinement typically involves splitting faces, therefore usually causes the introduction of new vertices. Let $S = \{C_1, \ldots, C_m\}$ be the set of caps given in an order that embeds the partial order. We let n denote the actual size of the partition, which up to within a constant factor, can be taken to be the number of vertices in S.

For the sake of clarity, we will first describe a method for locating a point in P that is slightly wasteful of space. With this background it will then be easy to proceed with the description of a linear space algorithm. The underlying search structure T will be a canal-tree defined over the m caps, with the left-to-right order of the leaves corresponding to the order of the caps. We attach an additional search structure to each leaf, so that once the neighboring cap of a query point has been found, we can refine that piece of information and obtain its actual neighboring face. Since the projection of a cap on the YZ-plane is a planar graph, we can use any optimal planar point location algorithm for that purpose (e.g. [K]). This requires an amount of space linear in the size of caps, so it does not affect the asymptotic space complexity of the whole data structure.

Let L be any line parallel to the X-axis; we say that the cap C_i is ***right-visible*** with respect to a subset of caps, W, if there exists a position of L for which the intersection of C_i and L is a point with maximum X-coordinate among all intersections between W and L. Let r be the pseudo-root of the underlying tree structure T. We define $J(r)$ as the set of all caps C_i in S that are at right-visible with respect to S. $J(root)$ is defined in a similar manner with respect to the set $\{C_1, \ldots, C_{\lceil m/2 \rceil}\}$. In general, for any internal node v, the set $J(v)$ contains all the caps in $I(z)$ that are right-visible with respect to $I(z)$, where z is the left son of v. Since a query (q, θ) is now a point (x, y, z), with $q = x$ and $\theta = (y, z)$, let's define $L(\theta)$ as the line parallel to the X-axis that passes through (x, y, z). The ***neighbor*** of (q, θ) in $I(z)$ is defined as the cap $C_i \in I(z)$ that intersects $L(\theta)$ at the point with largest X-coordinate. If there is no such point, the neighbor is taken to be $-\infty$, as usual. Since we have organized each cap with a planar point location structure, it is easy to retrieve in $O(\log n)$ operations the face of the cap C_i that intersects $L(\theta)$. The next step is to organize $J(v)$ into a data structure, $DS(J(v))$, which allows us to compute the neighbor of (q, θ) in $I(v)$ very efficiently.

I. A Tentative Solution

For the sake of clarity we will, in a first stage, drop the compaction feature of canal-trees, i.e. the requirement that an object be stored in its corresponding sink and only there. This simplification implies that each node v contains, at all times, the proper information to ensure correct branching. We can regard the problem of branching at node v as a generalized planar point location problem. Indeed, let $C_i, \ldots, C_j$ be the caps of $I(z)$ in increasing order (recall that z is the left son of v). Assign a different color to each cap and project their **boundaries** on the YZ-plane. We obtain a set of convex polygons, which we next fill with their respective color, applying the painter's algorithm (i.e. in the order $C_i, \ldots, C_j$) so as to resolve conflicts. This produces a subdivision, $K(v)$, of the plane into polygons $t_1, \ldots, t_q$, each part t_l emanating from a cap $C_{f(l)}$. It is important to note that $K(v)$ contains the projection of the boundaries of the caps (cap-projections, for short) and none of the edges within the interior. Finding the rightmost intersection of L with $\{C_i, \ldots, C_j\}$ clearly reduces to locating the region t_l that contains the point (y, z), and reporting the cap $C_{f(l)}$. From that information, we can next turn to the planar point location structure stored at the leaf $C_{f(l)}$, and retrieve the intersecting face in $O(\log n)$ time.

The choice of caps, rather than faces, as our basic objects is motivated by the following, crucial fact: $K(v)$ consists of cycles (cap projections) no pair of which are strictly intersecting. This implies, in particular, that each edge in the caps of $I(z)$ contributes at most one edge in $K(v)$, therefore storing $K(v)$ takes $O(V)$ storage, where V is the number of vertices in all the caps of $I(z)$. To prove the former claim, it suffices to show that each edge u of $K(v)$ is the projection of a whole edge e of some cap C_k and not just some sub-part of it. Let Q be the polyhedron whose cap is C_k, and let f_1 and f_2 be the two faces of Q adjacent to e, with $f_1 \preceq f_2$. Since some part of C_k in the neighborhood of e is visible, the cap containing f_2 is not in $I(v)$, and for that reason, neither is any face that could prevent a point of e from being visible. This shows that the entire edge e is visible, which proves our claim. We should still be aware that $K(v)$ may not be a collection of disjoint cap projections. It may, indeed, contain projections embedded into one another (Fig.6).

To summarize, our tentative solution consists of associating to v a data structure $DS(J(v)) = K(v)$, preprocessed for optimal point location [K]. With each face of $K(v)$ we associate a pointer to the corresponding cap as as to be able to retrieve the point $n(v,\theta) \bigcap L(\theta)$. This scheme will clearly provide an $O(\log^2 n)$ search time while requiring $O(n \log n)$ space.

II. An Improved Solution

Let's now use the compaction feature of canal-trees in order to reduce the space requirement to $O(n)$. Consider any point of a subdivision $K(w)$. This point corresponds uniquely to a point M on some cap C. The basic principle of a canal-tree stipulates that M should be "stored" at the highest node v where it is right-visible with respect to $I(z)$, where z is the left son of v. Of course, M will be stored implicitly by keeping in v the set of all the points of C sharing the same property. To save space, we will actually only keep the projection of this set on the YZ-plane with a pointer to the cap C. This projection forms a polygon which has a convex boundary and possibly convex holes. Caps will thus be conceptually partitioned into parts with common sinks. To visualize this partitioning, just consider each subdivision $K(v)$ as defined in the tentative solution, and decompose the corresponding caps into the parts induced by the subdivision. This defines new caps whose projections will now be pairwise disjoint. This will grant caps the nice property of being either totally visible or totally invisible from the right at any given node of T. The idea is now to store each new cap at the highest node from which it is right-visible. The *holes* thus left in lower levels will correspond to the *info-unavail* elements of the canal-tree. Let's be more specific and detail the operations for, say, the pseudo-root: consider $K(r)$ and $K(v)$, where v is the root, i.e. the unique son of the pseudo-root r. If $K(r)$ and $K(v)$ share a common edge, they share the entire cycle containing it: we will then delete this cycle from $K(v)$ and attach a flag *info-unavail* to the new face thus created (resulting from merging the two faces inside and outside the cycle). After we have iterated on this process, we next take care of those caps which contain points right-visible in $I(v)$ and points that are not right-visible in $I(v)$ but that are right-visible in I(left son of v). In $K(r)$, these caps have a cap-projection with holes in them; these holes being the projections of caps in I(right son of v). We must then add the cycles corresponding to these holes into $K(v)$. Note that 1) the face right outside these holes will have already been marked *info-unavail*, and 2) the added cycles will not strictly intersect with the cycles already in $K(v)$. As usual each (new) cap will be preprocessed for planar point location. Since the overall process adds duplicates of each cap-projection at most once, the total space needed is $O(n)$. The neighbor search can now proceed as specified in Section 2.3. This involves performing a planar point location at each node visited during the search, branching left if we land in a face marked *info-unavail*, otherwise branching according to the newly computed result. We leave out the details which were given in Section 2.3. Once again we associate with each face of the new subdivisions a pointer to the unique cap they correspond to. We have avoided dealing about the time complexity of the preprocessing altogether, for it is extremely dependent on the form of the input. We conclude.

Theorem 4. It is possible to preprocess an acyclic 3d-complex with $O(n)$ vertices so that locating any point can be done in $O(\log^2 n)$ time, using $O(n)$ storage.

Let's make a few comments on this result. The reason why we chose caps and not faces as our basic objects comes from the fact that projecting sets of right-visible faces on the YZ-plane can often entail a quadratic blow-up. Think of two sets of parallel strips, one vertical and the other horizontal. Another difficulty comes from the fact that there are in general many total orders to embed a given partial order and that consequently little can be assumed on the relative position of consecutive faces besides the known order between comparable ones.

As an example, consider the convex 3d-complex formed by n hyperplanes. It is easy to show that this complex is always acyclic. To see this, consider the directed graph G induced by $\preceq$. It is clearly acyclic since no path from any cap C of a polyhedron Q can lead to a cap outside the unbounded convex polyhedron R, where R is defined as the intersection of the halfspaces containing Q and bounded by the faces of C. We may then embed the relation $\preceq$ in a total order, and to do so, we proceed as follows: for each polyhedron Q set an arc from its cap C to the cap containing each of Q's faces that are not in C. This gives us a directed acyclic graph, H, whose transitive closure is precisely G. We avoid computing G explicitly but, instead, simply number each cap by performing a topological sort on H.

Corollary: Given a subdivision of E^3 by n hyperplanes, it is possible to determine which region contains a query point in $O(\log^2 n)$ time, using $O(n^3)$ storage.

This result has a number of immediate corollaries. One of them is, of course, the existence of an $O(n^3)$ space algorithm for determining, in $O(\log^2 n)$ time, whether a given test point lies on any of n arbitrary planes in three-dimensional space. A simple duality argument shows that the same result applies to n arbitrary points to be tested for containment in a query plane. Using the fact that our algorithm returns "neighbors" and not only region names, we can also prove that

Theorem 5. It is possible to arrange n points in E^3, using $O(n^3)$ storage, so that the closest point to a query plane can be determined in $O(\log^2 n)$ time.

Proof: Let's map any point $p:(x,y,z)$ of E^3 to the plane $f(p): Z = xX + yY + z$. Since all the points of the plane $P: \alpha X + \beta Y + \gamma Z + \epsilon = 0$ will then be mapped to planes which all pass through the point $(\frac{\alpha}{\gamma}, \frac{\beta}{\gamma}, -\frac{\epsilon}{\gamma})$, it is consistent, conversely, to map P to the point $f(P): (\frac{\alpha}{\gamma}, \frac{\beta}{\gamma}, -\frac{\epsilon}{\gamma})$. In this way, the vertical distance between points and planes in invariant under the mapping. More precisely, let q be the projection of the point $p\,(x,y,z)$ on the plane P, parallel to the Z-axis; similarly, let t be the projection of the point $f(P)$ on the plane $f(p)$. We easily check that $p_z - q_z = t_z - f(P)_z = z + \frac{\alpha x + \beta y + \epsilon}{\gamma}$. Since the orthogonal distance from p to P is proportional to the quantity $p_z - q_z$, it suffices to organize the dual set as in Theorem 5 (substituting Z for X) to be able to report the closest point to a query plane in $O(\log^2 n)$ time and $O(n^3 \log n)$ preprocessing. ∎

3.3. Computing Nearest-Neighbors in 3d.

Some of the ideas developed above can also be used to improve on the best algorithms known for computing the closest neighbor of a query point in three dimensions [DL,Y]. The problem is that of preprocessing a set S of n points $\{p_1, \ldots, p_n\}$ in E^3, so that for any test point q, the index m such that $[\forall\, i\, (1 \leq i \leq n) \mid d(q, p_m) \leq d(q, p_i)]$ can be determined very effectively. Let $P(n)$, $S(n)$, and $Q(n)$ be respectively the preprocessing time, storage, and query time of a solution to this problem. The solution given in [DL] for the two-dimensional version of this problem can be generalized to E^3. It consists of solving a point location problem in the complex created by the $n(n-1)/2$ bisecting planes. This can be done in $Q(n) = O(\log n)$ time, but the price to pay is a tremendously large $S(n) = O(n^{14})$ storage requirement. This can be improved by using the point location algorithm described above, which leads to $S(n) = O(n^6)$ and $Q(n) = O(\log^2 n)$. This does not, however, constitute an improvement over the method proposed by Yao [Y], whose complexity is $P(n) = S(n) = O(n^5 \log n)$ and $Q(n) = O(\log^2 n)$.

We show here how the basic idea of nested binary search used throughout in this paper can be used to extend Shamos's scheme for 2d-closest-point problems [SH], and produce a substantial saving in storage. We next describe a nearest-neighbor algorithm, quite simple conceptually, with the following features: $S(n) = P(n) = O(n^2)$ and $Q(n) = O(\log^2 n)$.

Let $V(S)$ denote the Voronoi diagram of S. In [SE] Seidel describes an optimal method for computing convex hulls in E^{2d}. Using a duality argument it is possible to adapt Seidel's algorithm for 4d-convex hulls so as to compute $V(S)$ in $O(n^2)$ time [SE]. In the following we will denote by $f_S(i,j)$ the face of $V(S)$ supported by the bisector between p_i and p_j. Suppose now that the points $p_1, \ldots, p_n$ appear X-sorted in this order. As usual, our underlying search structure, T, is a complete binary tree over the n objects, here in left-to-right order, $p_1, \ldots, p_n$. Let v be an internal node of T and let w_1 (resp. w_2) be the left (resp. right) son of v. We define $J(v)$ to be the set of faces in the Voronoi diagram of $I(v)$, whose corresponding points lie in $I(w_1)$ and $I(w_2)$. More precisely, we have

$$J(v) = \{f_{I(v)}(i,j) \mid i \in I(w_1) \textit{ and } j \in I(w_2)\}.$$

Recall that $I(v)$ is the set of points p_i that appear at the leaves of the subtree rooted at v. We next prove the following fact.

Lemma 6. Any line L parallel to the X-axis intersects one and only one face of $J(v)$.

Proof: Let L intersect the face $f_{I(v)}(i,j)$; $i \in I(w_1)$, $j \in I(w_2)$. Since the vector normal to $f_{I(v)}(i,j)$, p_ip_j, has positive X-coordinate, the nearest neighbor of a point traveling along L in ascending X-order will be successively p_i then p_j, when crossing the face $f_{I(v)}(i,j)$. This shows that L can intersect at most one face in $J(v)$. On the other hand, for any point position of L, the traveling point will start from $x = -\infty$ with its nearest neighbor in $I(w_1)$, eventually to end up having its nearest neighbor in $I(w_2)$. This shows that L always intersects at least one face of $J(v)$, which completes the proof. ∎

It follows from Lemma 6 that the projection of $J(v)$ on the YZ-plane is a planar graph and that the projections of no two faces can intersect strictly. We can thus preprocess this graph for efficient searching. This will allow us to determine, in $O(\log n)$ time, which face of $J(v)$ intersects the line L passing through the query point, from which we can decide where to branch in the tree T. We will thus keep in v a pointer to a data structure $DS(J(v))$, which will be essentially a planar point location structure, as described in [K].

Since Kirkpatrick's algorithm requires only linear preprocessing time, given the clockwise order of the edges around each vertex, and since we can compute $J(v)$ from $V(I(v))$ by a simple depth-first search, both $P(n)$ and $Q(n)$ satisfy the relation: $R(1) = 1$ and $R(n) = 2R(n/2) + O(n^2)$, whence $R(n) = O(n^2)$. Note that, in general, keeping the adjacencies vertex/edge sorted is not a problem, since the degree of a vertex in a 3d Voronoi diagram is 4, barring singularities (i.e. more than four points on a common sphere).

Theorem 7. It is possible to preprocess n points in $O(n^2)$ time and space, so that any near-neighbor query can be answered in $O(\log^2 n)$ time.

5. Further Research

All the algorithms given here have an $O(\log^2 n)$ query response-time, and it seems that $O(\log n)$ can be achieved only at the price of a formidable blow-up in space complexity [DL]. Can this observation be confirmed by lower bounds, or can an additional structure (e.g. layered structure [W]) be grafted to the algorithms so as to perform only one binary search per query, while preserving the same asymptotic space complexity?

REFERENCES

[BO] Bentley, J.L., Ottmann,T. *Algorithms for reporting and counting geometric intersections*, IEEE Trans. Comp., vol. C–28, pp. 643-647, 1979.

[DL] Dobkin, D.P., Lipton ,R.J. *Multidimensional searching problems*, SIAM Journal on Computing, 5, pp. 181-186, 1976.

[DM] Dobkin, D.P., Munro, J.I. *Efficient uses of the past*, Proc. 21st Annual FOCS Symp., pp. 200-206, 1980.

[F] Fuchs, H., Kedem, Z.M., Naylor, B. *On visible surface generation by a priori tree structures*, Computer Graphics, 14, pp. 124-133, 1980.

[K] Kirkpatrick, D.G. *Optimal search in planar subdivisions*, University of British Columb Tech. Report 81-13, 1981.

[LP] Lee, D.T., Preparata, F.P. *Location of a point in a planar subdivision and its applications*, SIAM Journal on Computing, 6, pp. 594-606, 1977.

[LiP] Lipsky, W., Preparata, F.P. *Segments, rectangles, contours*, J. Algorithms, 2, pp. 63-76, 1981.

[LT] Lipton, R.J., Tarjan, R.E. *Applications of a planar separator theorem*, Proc. 18th Annual FOCS Symp., pp.162-170, 1977.

[O] Overmars, M.H. *Searching in the past I*, University of Utrecht, The Netherlands Report RUU-CS-81-7, 1981.

[SE] Seidel, R. *A convex hull algorithm optimal for point sets in even dimensions*, Master's Thesis, Tech. Report 81-14, Univ. British Columbia, Vancouver, Canada, 1981.

[SH] Shamos, M.I. *Geometric complexity*, Proc. 7th ACM SIGACT Symposium, 1975, pp. 224-233.

[W] Willard, D.E. *New data structures for orthogonal queries*, To appear in SIAM J. Comp.

[Y] Yao, A.C. *On the preprocessing cost in multidimensional search*, IBM San Jose Research Center, Tech. Rep., to appear.

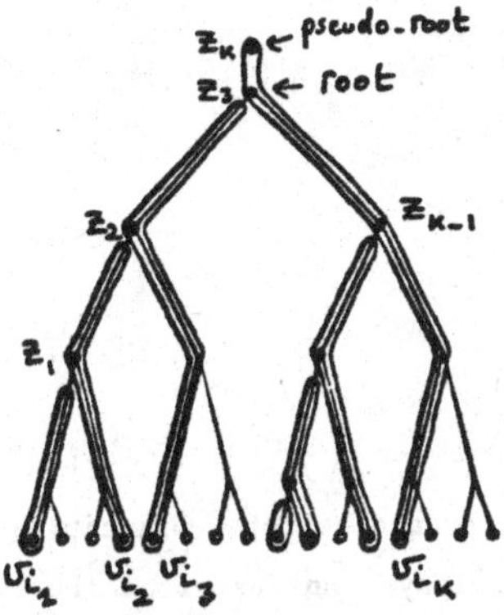

Figure 1

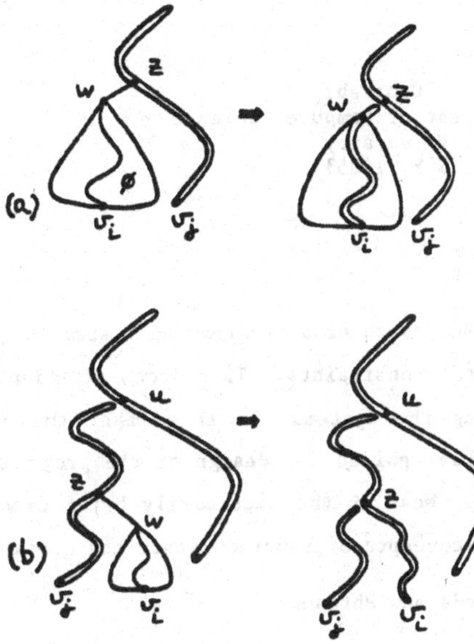

Figure 2

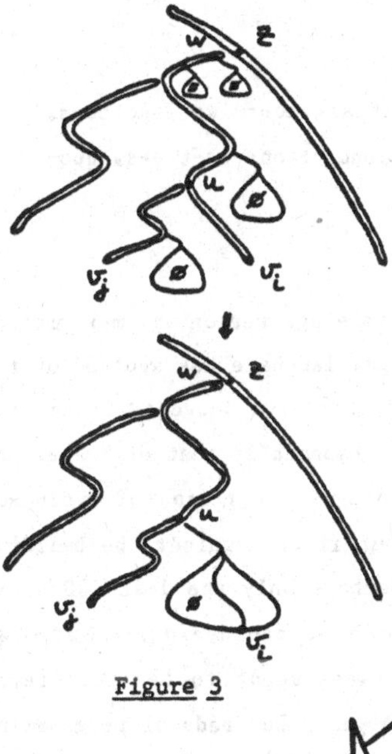

Figure 3

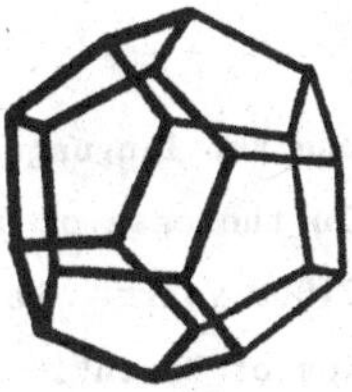

Figure 4

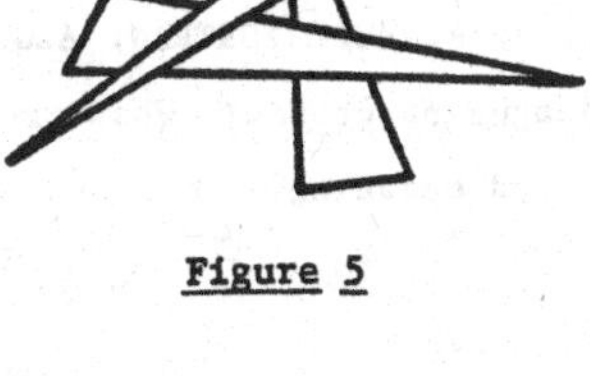

Figure 5

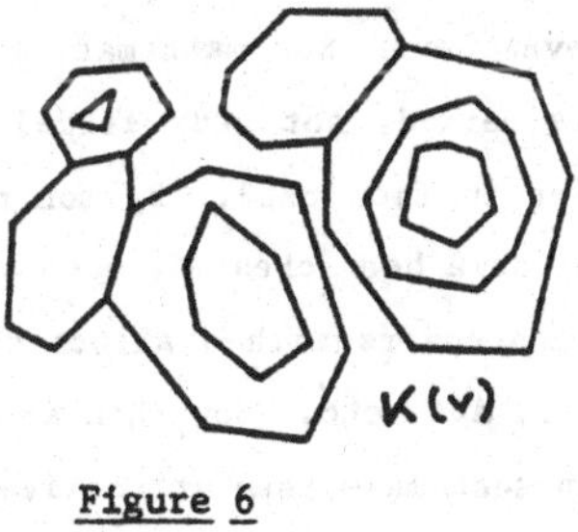

Figure 6

CONSTRUCTIVE MATHEMATICS AS A PROGRAMMING LOGIC I: SOME PRINCIPLES OF THEORY

Robert L. Constable
Department of Computer Science
Cornell University
Ithaca, N.Y. 14853

Abstract

The design of a programming system is guided by certain beliefs, principles and practical constraints. These considerations are not always manifest from the rules defining the system. In this paper the author discusses some of the principles which have guided the design of the programming logics built at Cornell in the last decade. Most of the necessarily brief discussion concerns type theory with stress on the concepts of function space and quotient types.

Key Words and Phrases:

automated logic, combinators, Edinburgh LCF, partial recursive functions, programming languages and logics, PL/CV, PRL, propositions-as-types, quotient types, strong intensionality, type theory.

I. Introduction

How do we choose the languages in which to express exact reasoning, mathematics and programming? In the case of logic and mathematics, language has evolved over a period of perhaps 2,000 years. We know enough to say that such language is not the "God-given expression of Truth". Indeed human genius, especially that of Frege, has played a major role. In the case of programming languages the period of evolution is shorter. It might appear dramatically shorter, but if we consider the building of relatively rigorous and symbolic language, then perhaps only the last 100 years are relevant even for mathematics and logic. Although we can learn a great deal from this period, not many formal languages from it were meant to be used; fewer still were in fact used. By contrast in the past 40 years hundreds of programming languages have been created, each vying for prominence. Among these a few dozen are serious contenders with distinct characteristics, e.g. FORTRAN, ALGOL (60, W, 68), LISP, PL/I, ADA, etc. How then are these languages chosen? What are the principles of design that make them attractive, usable and enduring?

This work was supported in part by NSF grants MCS-80-03349 and MCS-81-04018.

There have been studies which attempt to sort out the principles behind such languages [32]. But not many deep principles have emerged. We can classify languages based on their control structures and make illuminating comparisons [9,28]. We can discuss procedure calling mechanisms and other features of implementation. With more modern languages we can compare type structures and mechanisms for achieving modularity and protection.

While these differences among programming languages are fascinating and while their study may contribute to better designs and implementations, such differences do not reveal deep principles of language value. The deeper principles emerge at the level of programming logic.† Such logics must take a position about the structure of the universe in which we compute, about what is real and what actions are possible, about what is expressible and what is true. It will happen that these deeper principles determine other aspects of language structure and sometimes obviate the need for explanations in terms of implementation or syntactic style. For instance, principles about the nature of type equality may dictate that the equality relation is not decidable. This would rule out certain approaches to syntactic type checking.

I do not claim to know the principles that determine a programming logic's value. I am not even confident that we will ever be able to coherently state any, but I know from our work on programming logics at Cornell since 1971 that certain experiences and ideas emerged as significant and have shaped the systems we built. I will describe some of these ideas, formulating them as principles, and discuss their consequences. In particular I want to examine the decisions we made in designing the two versions of type theory we have used at Cornell, V3 [13] and PRL [2]. Since these theories are both closely related to Per Martin-Löf's well-known type theories, I will phrase my discussion in terms of them, using M-L75 for [29] and M-L82 for [30], and M-L when it doesn't matter which. For details of these systems, refer to the cited literature. (We use ML to denote the widely used programming language part of Edinburgh LCF [24].) First let me put the Cornell work in context.

---

†As programming languages become richer, and as their definitions become more formal, the distinction between a programming <u>language</u> and a programming <u>logic</u> may disappear. A theory such as M-L82 [30] is indistinguishable from the applicative programming language described by Nordstrom [31]; the theories V3 [13] and PRL [2] are as much programming languages as they are logics. So these remarks apply to such "third generation" programming languages as well.

Our work on programming logics goes back to 1970, when we suggested [8] using formal constructive mathematics as a programming language and investigated some of the theoretical issues. This program was explained more thoroughly in a series of lectures entitled "Constructive Mathematics as a Programming Language" given at Saarbrücken, Advanced Course on Programming in 1974. Here the connections to so called "program verification" were also explored. In 1975 we began the design of a working system which we then called a programming logic. This was reported in the book A Programming Logic with Mike O'Donnell [15]. We incorporated procedural programs into a constructive weak second-order logic and provided a proof checking system which employed several efficient decision procedures for subsets of the logic [16]. As we tried to treat data types and some version of constructive set theory, we encountered the work of Per Martin-Löf [29] which fit extremely well with our plans (see P1, P6) and with the principles we had isolated. We incorporated our ideas with his and with various notions from Edinburgh LCF into a programming logic V3 [13]. At the same time we were joined by Joseph L. Bates who had several significant ideas for greatly improving the applicability of these methods in a modern computing environment [1]. We proceeded to design a new and more grand system [3] with the acronym PRL, for Program Refinement Logic. We designed an "ultimate PRL" system and an initial core system [2]. Since 1980 Bates has led the implementation of the system, and together we have been experimenting with it and progressing toward the "ultimate" system.

II. Principles

P1: The first principle of our work has been that the logic of programming should itself be computational and thus self-contained. The principles of computation are as fundamental as any other and can be axiomatized directly. We see no theoretical or practical limits unique to computational explanations and no need for non-computational ones. So Occam's razor can prune away those systems of reasoning based on Platonic conceptions of truth or on classical set theory and its models of computability.

There are numerous systems of reasoning with purely computational meaning such as Skolem's quantifier free logic [37], Intuitionistic logic, Bishop's constructive analysis [5], Russian constructive logic, etc. Among these, Bishop's style of constructive reasoning seems to capture the core of all of the sufficiently rich computational logics. It indeed describes the computational core of classical mathematics. Based on Bishop's writings [5,6] we could and did imagine doing mathematics inside a programming logic. When we began, it seemed that a language like Algol 68 possessed the right concepts and that its "theory of data types" might be adequate to describe the mathematical types.† In retrospect such a view is not so terribly wrong, but we began our detailed work with a much simpler theory which focused first on elementary data types and procedural programs. As we said in [15], "...the programming logic does not fit the classical pattern of partial or total correctness because commands themselves are treated like statements; the predicate calculus is based on a block structured constructive natural deduction system..."

P2: All objects come with a type. One decision that comes early in the design of a logic or language is whether types are specified with objects or as properties of a universal collection of objects. If one focuses on the nature of computer memory or on the development of recursive function theory, it is tempting to think of a single universe of "constructive objects" from which types arise by classifying these objects. This is the approach of Lisp. One sees it in the logics of Fefermann [22] and recently in the programming language Russell [20]. This principle is also at work in set theory where one starts with a collection of individuals and builds a cumulative hierarchy of sets over them.

We argue that the clearest conception is that by saying how to build objects one is in fact specifying a type. So objects come with their types. This is similar to Bertrand Russell's conception [33] (belying the name of the programming language [20])and to the Algol 68 conception and to the M-L conception.

P3: Products and unions are basic. The nature of pairing is fundamental (although we know that in set theory it is reducible) as is a notion of uniting. Our treatment of unions is dictated by a deeper principle, that is propositions as types (P6).

P4: Functions are effectively computable and total. The notion that functions are effectively computable follows from P1; that they are total we take as a basic principle. The recursive function theory notion of a partial function can be derived from this concept in several ways. The notion of an algorithm or rule we take as "categorical" like that of type. It is a concept which is manifest in specific types. So there are rules for computing functions from A to B, but the same underlying rule may also compute from A' to B.

---

†In 1975 we considered using a subset of Algol 68 as the basis for our programming logic, but there wasn't sufficient local expertise to cope with the complexity of defining and implementing the subset. There was such expertise for PL/I. But we did use Algol 68 like notation in [15].

We classify a function to be in type $A \rightarrow B$ if the inputs are from A and the outputs are in B regardless of what types are used along the way in determining this value.

P5: <u>The structure of functions is discernible</u>. According to Frege functions arise by abstraction from certain linguistic forms. This principle is followed in M-L82 where the canonical form of a function is $(\lambda x)b$. All functions are determined by forms or expressions of the range type. This view is unlike that of Curry [17,18] who thinks of functions as built from primitive functions by application.

From Frege's and Martin-Löf's standpoint, the structure of functions is primarily a linguistic matter. Computation is also primarily a linguistic matter. One is thus led to the notion that equality of functions is extensional since other aspects are not internal to mathematics.

Technically it is not easy to adopt another view of functions. For example, in order to analyze the structure of f in $A \rightarrow B$ one would be forced to consider component functions g which might have arbitrary type (lying arbitrarily high in the hierarchy of universes as well). Nevertheless we have felt that there are sufficient benefits to explore the possibility of building a usable theory in which functions have discernible structure.

The principal reason that our type theories have provided a means to analyze the structure of functions is that we have encountered informal arguments about program structure which are powerful and necessary to a programming logic [12]. Other ways of capturing such arguments (see for example [10]) seem very cumbersome. We would like to deal with the issue at a fundamental level in hopes of finding a powerful solution.

It is not obvious how to analyze the structure of functions as mathematical objects when they are presented as λ-terms because these terms involve the inherently linguistic notion of a <u>variable</u> in an essential way. The λ-terms suggest an analysis of descriptions but not of functions. However, the <u>combinator</u> form of a function involves only the concept of function and application and does suggest a means of analysis. To follow this line of thought requires that we define a certain <u>combinatorial basis</u> for the function spaces $A \rightarrow B$ and $\Pi x \in A.B$. This is a collection of basic functions, called <u>combinators</u>, from which all other functions can be built by <u>application</u>; such is the style of the theory of combinators [18,36]. Here is an informal account of how this can be done in the context of M-L82. Details of a related theory can be found in [12,13].

For any universe U_i and $A\epsilon U_i$, $B\epsilon \Pi x\epsilon A.U_i$, $C\epsilon \Pi x\epsilon A.(\Pi y\epsilon B(x).U_i)$ there is a function

$$S_i \ \epsilon \Pi A\epsilon U_i.\Pi B\epsilon(\Pi x\epsilon A.U_i).\Pi C\epsilon(\Pi x\epsilon A.(\Pi y\epsilon B(x).U_i))$$
$$.\Pi f\epsilon(\Pi x\epsilon A.(\Pi y\epsilon B(x).C(x)(y))).\Pi g\epsilon(\Pi x\epsilon A.B(x)).\Pi x\epsilon A.C(x)(g(x))$$

so that

$$S_i \ ABC \ \epsilon \ \Pi f\epsilon(\Pi x\epsilon A.(\Pi y\epsilon B(x).C(x)(y))).$$
$$\Pi g\epsilon(\Pi x\epsilon A.B(x)).(\Pi x\epsilon A.C(x)(g(x))).$$

The computation rule defining S_i ABC f g is S_i ABC f g = $\lambda x.f(x)(g(x))$. For convenience we write S_i ABC as S_{ABC}, making it clearer that S_{ABC} is a typed version of the S combinator. We can do the same for the K combinator so that K_i AB ϵ $\Pi x\epsilon A.(\Pi y\epsilon B(x).A)$, and K_i AB a = $\lambda x.a$.

Given these combinators as well as those of level U_i derived from the other constants of the theory such as pairing, (a,b), selection, E, induction, R, etc.; we can define for any f ϵ $\Pi x\epsilon A.B$ in any U_i whose definition, f, does not involve notions beyond U_j, a combinator form, say $Comb_j(f)$, equal to f. We need a form, level(f), which discovers the maximum level, j, used in building f.

These combinator forms can be analyzed inside the theory. For example, given (S_{ABC} f)g we can build in operations <u>op</u> and <u>arg</u> to decompose it, e.g.

op (S_{ABC} f)g = (S_{ABC} f) and
arg(S_{ABC} f)g = g.

We also must build in operations <u>optype</u> and <u>argtype</u> which compute the type of (S_{ABC} f) and g from that of (S_{ABC} f)g. There must be versions of these functions which work for each level n.

Actually using S and K combinators or anything very similar is totally infeasible because they encode the structure of functions in a form too primitive to use. The size of a combinator for a λ-term, say $\lambda x.b$, built from S and K and the constants might be quadratic in the size of $\lambda x.b$ (depending on the abstraction algorithm). But there are combinators which allow a much more intelligible description. One such I call the <u>L-combinator</u>. Using it there is a translation of λ-terms of length n to combinators in which the combinator is no more than log(n) times as large. The form of the combinator is L_A where A is a list of addresses of "locations" in the operand which are to be identified by L_A. For example, given p ϵ N $\rightarrow$ N $\rightarrow$ N $\times$ N such that p(x,y) = (x,y), the function $\lambda x.p(x,s(x))$ has the form $L_{\{1.1,1.2\}}.p(I())(s())$ where the argument "holes" have addresses 1.1 and 1.2 respectively. Such combinator forms are very similar to λ-terms (λx becomes L_A for A a list of occurrences of x), but L_A can be more easily treated as an operator.

In building a theory in which the structure of functions can be analyzed, it is important to provide a simple treatment of extensional equality as well, because it is a far more commonly needed equality than the intensional equality required to support the structural analysis. One way to insure a sufficiently simple treatment of extensional equality is to provide it as atomic, along side of the intensional equality. This requires distinguishing the function space with one equality from that with the other. For example $A \Rightarrow B$ and $\forall x \epsilon A.B$ can be used for the intensional space and $A \rightarrow B$ and $\Pi x \epsilon A.B$ for the extensional.

P6: Propositions are types. Since 1975 with PL/CV we were treating proofs as objects, and we were aware of the Edinburgh LCF scheme for manipulating proofs as objects. Therefore when we read in Stenlund [36] and Martin-Löf [29] of the propositions-as-types principle, we were prepared to accept it completely. Indeed, we now see this as a basic principle of semantics; not as a semantic theorem to be used to interpret the logical operators, but as a principle to organize the entire theory. Revealing the role of this principle was one of the major accomplishments of M-L, and we have followed Martin-Löf's example. Although this notion appears also in deBruijn's AUTOMATH [19] and in Scott's "Constructive Validity" paper [35] and can be traced back to Curry and Feys [17] and Howard [26], we were not struck by its fundamental nature and its proper place in organizing concepts until reading [29].

P7: Type structure is discernible. For reasons similar to those that justify the view that the structure of functions is discernible, we claim that the structure of types is discernible as well. This is especially important in light of the propositions-as-types principle since we want to express inside our theories various algorithms for deciding simple classes of propositions. These algorithms work on the structure of propositions (see [12]).

Since type equality in M-L82 respects structure, our ideas here are close to Martin-Löf's. However in V3 for example, we are able to determine for any type whether and how it is built from the basic constructors, and we are able to argue by induction over the "structured part" of the type universes. These capabilities can be consistently added to M-L82 by rules of the following sort (as above these "rules" only suggest a set of concepts using the M-L82 format, they are not definitively integrated into M-L82 to extend it).

First there is a form to decide the outer structure of a type in any universe, although only the form for the first universe is shown here.

$$\frac{x \in U_0 \quad \begin{matrix}(z \in U_0)\\ C\ type\end{matrix} \quad \begin{matrix}(k=1,\dots,9)\\ e_k \in C(x/z)\end{matrix} \quad \begin{matrix}(j \in N)\\ e_1 \in C(x/z)\end{matrix}}{typecase\ (x,\ e_1,\ \dots,\ e_9) \in C(x/z)}$$

There is a rule insuring functionality of typecase in all of its arguments, e.g.

$$\frac{x = x'\ in\ U_0 \quad \begin{matrix}(k = 1,\ \dots,\ 9)\\ e_k = e_k' \in C(x/z)\end{matrix}}{typecase\ (x,\ e_1,\ \dots,\ e_q) = typecase\ (x',\ e_1',\ \dots,\ e_9') \in C(x/z)}$$

There are eight rules for reducing typecase such as

$$\begin{aligned} typecase\ (N_i,\ e_1,\dots,e_9) &= e_1(i/j)\\ typecase\ (N,\ e_1,\dots,e_9) &= e_2\\ typecase\ (A\times B,\ e_1,\dots,e_9) &= e_3\\ typecase\ (A+B,\ e_1,\dots,e_9) &= e_4\\ typecase\ (A\to B,\ e_1,\dots,e_9) &= e_5\\ typecase\ (\Sigma x\in A.B,\ e_1,\dots,e_9) &= e_6\\ typecase\ (\Pi x\in A.B,\ e_1,\dots,e_9) &= e_7\\ typecase\ (Wx\in A.B,\ e_1,\dots,e_9) &= e_8 \end{aligned}$$

Using these rules we can define functions $U_0 \to N_2$ which decide whether a type has a certain structure. For example isprod = $\lambda x.typecase(x,\ 0_2,\ 0_2,\ 1_2,\ 0_2,\ \dots,\ 0_2)$ has value 1_2 iff x is a product type, A×B. Notice that $typecase(x,\ 0_2,\ \dots,\ 0_2,\ 1_2)$ will equal 1_2 iff x is not one of the atomic types or structured types.

There are also functions to decompose the structured types. These provide what we call <u>strong intensionality</u>.

$$\frac{x \in U_i}{\begin{matrix}left(x) \in U_i\\ right(x) \in U_i\end{matrix}} \qquad \frac{x = x' \in U_i}{\begin{matrix}left(x) = left(x') \in U_i\\ right(x) = right(x') \in U_i\end{matrix}}$$

We then need axioms to define left, right such as

$$\frac{A \in U_i \quad B \in U_i}{\begin{matrix}left(A\times B) = A\\ right(A\times B) = B\end{matrix}} \qquad \frac{x \in U_0 \quad typecase(x,\ 0_2,\ 0_2,\ 1_2,\ \dots,\ 0_2) = 1_2 \in N_2}{x = left(x) \times right(x)}$$

for each of the binary operators, x, +, →.

We also need forms for analyzing the structure of types built from families of types.

$$\frac{x \in U_0 \quad typecase(x,\ 0_2,\ \dots,\ 0_2,\ 1_2,\ 0_2,\ 0_2) = 1_2 \in N_2}{\begin{matrix}index(x) \in U_0\\ fam(x) \in \Pi y\in index(x).U_0\end{matrix}}$$

$$x = \Pi z\in index(x).fam(x)(z)$$

We also have rules such as

$$\frac{A \in U_i \quad \begin{matrix}(x \in A)\\ B \in U_i\end{matrix}}{\begin{matrix}\text{index}(\Sigma x\epsilon A.B) = A\\ \text{fam}(\Sigma x\epsilon A.B) = \lambda x.B\end{matrix}}$$

P8: Equality information is not needed in constructing objects. We knew from [15] that we did not need the information from equality assertions to execute proofs, and we learned from Bates [1] that one did not need this information to extract executable code from proofs. This led us to accept readily the M-L treatment of equality. But we did not recognize this as a basic principle until after studying M-L. We still considered the possibility in V3 [13] of storing with equality assertions the algorithms for deciding them.

Accepting this principle bears heavily on one of the features of our type theories, the use of quotient types, discussed in the next section.

III. Features of Cornell Type Theories

F1: Quotient types are very useful. A type is determined not only by a method of construction but by a criterion of equality on the objects constructed (this notion too can be found in Frege and is prominent in Bishop's writings). The type can be changed by changing either the method or the notion of equality. However, it appears not to be essential to build in a capability to express this latter change. It can be reflected by pairing a type, say A, with a notion of equivalence on A, say E. However economical such a scheme is, it is not natural and it cuts off such types from the other type forming operations. A common example illustrates these issues.

Consider Bishop's definition of a real number as a Cauchy convergent sequence of rationals [5], letting Q denote the rationals,

$$(1)\quad R = \Sigma x{:}N\to Q.\Pi(n,m){:}Z^{+}.(|x(n) - x(m)| \leq 1/m + 1/n).$$

He defines two real numbers to be equal, E(x,y), iff

$$(2)\quad \Pi n\epsilon Z^{+}.(|x(n) - y(n)| \leq 2/n).$$

We take the real numbers, $\mathbb{R}$, to be the quotient type of (1) with (2) written $\mathbb{R}$ = R/E. Then the equality relation on the type $\mathbb{R}$, $=_{\mathbb{R}}$, is E.

When we want to define the functions from $\mathbb{R}$ to $\mathbb{R}$ we simply take $\mathbb{R} \to \mathbb{R}$ and by the nature of equality on any type, it is known that these functions respect E.

The concept of a real can be defined without quotients. We take R as the reals. Then we can define the functions from $\mathbf{R}$ to $\mathbf{R}$, say $\mathbf{F}(\mathbf{R},\mathbf{R})$ following Bishop's notation, as $\{f\in R\to R \mid \forall(x,y)\in R.(E(x,y) \Rightarrow E(f(x),f(y)))\}$. But now we not only need to build another apparatus for function spaces, but we must carry around certain information which is not necessary in computing reals. In those cases where the information is needed the quotient construct cannot be used.

Here is a suggestive account of quotient types in the setting of M-L (also see [13]).

(1) $$\frac{A\ \text{type} \qquad \begin{array}{c}(x\in A,\ y\in A)\\ R\ \text{type}\end{array}}{A/R\ \text{type}}$$

(2) $$\frac{A\in U_n \qquad \begin{array}{c}(x\in A,\ y\in A)\\ R\in U_n\end{array}}{A/R\in U_n}$$

Call A/R the <u>Quotient</u> of A by R

(3) $$\frac{A_1 = A_2 \qquad \begin{array}{c}(x\in A,\ y\in A)\\ R_1 \Leftrightarrow R_2\end{array}}{A_1/R_1 = A_2/R_2}$$

(4) $$\frac{a\in A \qquad \begin{array}{c}(x\in A,\ y\in A)\\ R\ \text{type}\end{array}}{a\in A/R}$$

(5) $$\frac{a_1\in A \quad a_2\in A \quad e\in R(a_1/x,\ a_2/y)}{r\in(a_1 =_{A/R} a_2)}$$

So $a_1 =_{A/R} a_2$ iff $R^*(a_1/x,\ a_2/y)$ where R^* is the reflexive, transitive, symmetric closure of R (since for all types we have $a =_A a$ and $a =_A b$ iff $b =_A a$ and $a =_A b$ and $b =_A c$ implies $a =_A c$).

(6) $$\frac{\begin{array}{c}(w\in A)\\ B\ \text{type}\end{array} \qquad \begin{array}{c}(x\in A,\ y\in A,\ e\in R)\\ B(x/w) = B(y/w)\end{array} \qquad z\in A/R}{B(z/w)\ \text{type}}$$

(7) $$\frac{\begin{array}{c}(z\in A/R)\\ B\ \text{type}\end{array} \qquad \begin{array}{c}(w\in A)\\ b\in B\end{array} \qquad \begin{array}{c}(x\in A,\ y\in A,\ w\in R)\\ b(x/w) = b(y/w)\in B\end{array} \qquad z\in A/R}{b(z/w)\in B}$$

Ideally the conclusions of (6) and (7) would have the form "$z\in A/R \vdash B(z/w)$ type" and "$z\in A/R \vdash b(z/w)\in B$" but the M-L82 style does not keep track of assumptions in the sequent style.

F2: The least number operator allows information hiding. There is a relatively straightforward way to build the theory of partial recursive functions inside M-L82. For example, the (small) partial functions $N \to N$ can be defined as those functions from subtypes of N into N, say $f \in ((\Sigma x \in N.T(x)) \to N)$ for $T \in N \to U_1$. Then the μ-recursive functions can be defined as an inductive subset (see [10] for details). The least number operator, μ, is applied only when we know it succeeds, say we have a proof of $\exists y \in N.f(x,y)=0$. So then $\mu y.(f(x,y)=0)$ can be defined "primitive recursively" from the proof information. One inconvenience of this approach is that partial recursive functions carry their domain information around explicitly. This information does not determine the value of the function, but it is necessary in defining it.

Type theory would be more convenient if it were possible to systematically suppress proof information when it was not needed to determine other objects. In the core of recursive function theory at least, this would be possible by introducing an unbounded search operator which could be used when it is known that the search terminates but which does not require the termination proof for its computation. Here is a simple way to accomplish this, again expressed in M-L82 (without all the details).

First, in order to restrict information available to the search operator, we modify the subtype concept. Instead of taking $\{x:A \mid B\}$ to mean $\Sigma x \in A.B$ we introduce a new type by these rules

$$\frac{A \text{ type} \quad \overset{(x\in A)}{B \text{ type}}}{\{x:A \mid B\} \text{ type}} \qquad\qquad \frac{A_1 = A_2 \quad \overset{(x\in A_1)}{B_1 \Leftrightarrow B_2}}{\{x:A_1 \mid B_1\} = \{x:A_2 \mid B_2\}}$$

$$\frac{a\in A \quad \overset{(x\in A)}{B \text{ type}} \quad b\in B(a/x)}{a\in\{x:A \mid B\}}$$

We think of $\{x:A \mid B\}$ as $\Sigma x \in A.B$ without information about the second component. (An alternative approach to hiding information is to regard $\{x:A \mid B\}$ as merely a notational convention signifying a restricted way to use $\Sigma x \in A.B$. One might use $Ux \in A.B$ as a convention when the first component should be ignored.)

The μ-operator allows us to use this type under the following circumstances. Suppose $R \in A \to N \to N_2$ so that for every $x \in A$, $n \in N$, $R(x,n) = 0_2$ or $R(x,n) = 1_2$. Then given $x \in \{y:A \mid \exists n:N.(n>k \,\&\, R(y,n)=0_2)\}$, the μ-operator $\mu>k.(R(x,n) = 0_2)$ defines a unique number without recourse to any information about the proof of $\exists n:N.(n>k \,\&\, R(y,n)=0_2)$ except that it exists. These observatons are codified in the following rule:

$$\frac{\begin{matrix}(x\epsilon A,\ n\epsilon N) & & \\ R\epsilon N_2 & k\epsilon N & x\epsilon\{y:A \mid \exists n:N.(n>k\&R = 0_2)\}\end{matrix}}{\mu n>k.(R=0_2) \in N}$$

We need an axiom that μ- is functional, i.e. if $R_1 = R_2$ then $\mu n>k.(R_1=0_2) = \mu n>k.(R_2=0_2)$, and we need a computation rule for μ which is this:

$$\begin{aligned}&\text{if } R(k+1/n) = 0_2 \text{ then } \mu n>k.(R=0_2) = k+1\\ &\text{otherwise } \mu n>k.(R=0_2) = \mu n>k+1.(R=0_2).\end{aligned}$$

IV. Conclusion

Constructive type theory has contributed to our understanding of programming languages and logics; it also suggests a wide range of problems, from the very theoretical to the very practical. The preceding brief discussion was intended to reveal the dynamics of the subject and raise some of the theoretical issues, especially those dealing with information hiding.

Acknowledgements

I want to thank Joseph Bates for his perceptive comments on a draft of this paper and Stuart Allen for many stimulating discussions about type theory. Joe Bates and I are finishing a description of the type theory used in Nu-PRL, the document is tentatively titled "The Nearly Ultimate PRL" and will describe how type theory is used as a refinement style programming logic.

I also thank Donette Isenbarger for her careful and patient preparation of this document under the pressure of a deadline.

References

[1] Bates, J.L., A Logic for Correct Program Development, Ph.D. Thesis, Department of Computer Science, Cornell University, 1979.

[2] Bates, J.L. and R.L. Constable, "Proofs as Programs", Dept. of Computer Science Technical Report, TR 82-530, Cornell University, Ithaca, NY, 1982.

[3] Bates J. and R.L. Constable, "Definition of Micro-PRL", Technical Report TR 82-492, Computer Science Department, Cornell University, October 1981.

[4] Beeson, M., "Formalizing Constructive Mathematics: Why and How?", Constructive Mathematics (ed., F. Richman), Lecture Notes in Computer Science, Springer-

Verlag, NY, 1981, 146-190.

[5] Bishop, E., Foundations of Constructive Analysis, McGraw Hill, NY, 1967, 370 pp.

[6] Bishop, Errett, "Mathematics as a Numerical Language", Intuitionism and Proof Theory, ed. by Myhill, J. et al., North-Holland, Amsterdam, 1970, 53-71.

[7] Boyer, R.S. and J.S. Moore, A Computational Logic, Academic Press, NY, 1979, 397 pp.

[8] Constable, Robert L., "Constructive Mathematics and Automatic Program Writers", Proc. of IFIP Congress, Ljubljana, 1971, pp 229-233.

[9] Constable, Robert L. and David Gries, "On Classes of Program Schemata", SIAM J. Comput., 1:1, March 1972, pp. 66-118.

[10] Constable, Robert L., "Mathematics As Programming", Proc. of Workshop on Logics of Programs, Lecture Notes in Computer Science, 1983.

[11] Constable, Robert L., "Partial Functions in Constructive Formal Theories", Proc. of 6th G.I. Conference, Lecture Notes in Computer Science, Vol. 135. Springer-Verlag, 1983.

[12] Constable, Robert L., "Intensional Analysis of Functions and Types", University of Edinburgh, Dept. of Computer Science Internal Report, CSR-118-82, June, 1982, pp. 74.

[13] Constable, Robert L. and D. Zlatin, "Report on the Type Theory (V3) of the Programming Logic PL/CV3", Logics of Programs, Lecture Notes in Computer Science, Vol. 131, Springer-Verlag, NY, 1982, pp. 72-93.

[14] Constable, R.L., "Programs and Types", Proc. of 21st Ann. Symp. on Found. of Comp. Science, IEEE, NY, 1980, pp 118-128.

[15] Constable, Robert L. and M.J. O'Donnell, A Programming Logic, Winthrop, Cambridge, 1978.

[16] Constable, Robert L., S.D. Johnson and C.D. Eichenlaub, Introduction to the PL/CV2 Programming Logic, Lecture Notes in Computer Science, Vol. 135, Springer-Verlag, NY, 1982.

[17] Curry, H.B. and R. Feys, Combinatory Logic, North-Holland, Amsterdam, 1968.

[18] Curry, H.B., J.R. Hindley, and J.P. Seldin, Combinatory Logic, Volume II, North-Holland Publ. Co., Amsterdam, 1972.

[19] deBruijn, N.G., "A Survey of the Project AUTOMATH", Essays on Combinatory Logic, Lambda Calculus and Formalism, (eds. J.P. Seldin and J.R. Hindley), Academic Press, NY, 1980, 589-606.

[20] Donahue, J., and A.J. Demers, "Revised Report on Russell", Department of Computer Science Technical Report, TR 79-389, Cornell University, September 1979.

[21] Dummett, Michael, Frege Philosophy of Language, Duckworth, Oxford, 1973.

[22] Feferman, S., "Constructive Theories of Functions and Classes", Logic Colloquium '78, North-Holland, Amsterdam, 1979, pp. 159-224.

[23] Fraenkel, A.A., and Y. Bar-Hillel, Foundations of Set Theory, North-Holland Publ. Co., Amsterdam, 1958.

[24] Gordon, M., R. Milner and C. Wadsworth, Edinburgh LCF: A Mechanized Logic of Computation, Lecture Notes in Computer Science, Vol. 78, Springer-Verlag, 1979.

[25] Gries, David, The Science of Programming, Springer-Verlag, 1982.

[26] Howard, W.A., "The Formulas-As-Types Notion of Construction" in Essays on Combinatory Logic, Lambda Calculus and Formalism, (eds., J.P. Seldin and J.R. Hindley), Academic Press, NY, 1980.

[27] Krafft, Dean B., "AVID: A System for the Interactive Development of Verifiable Correct Programs", Ph.D. Thesis, Cornell University, Ithaca, NY, August 1981.

[28] Luckham, D.C., M.R. Park, and M.S. Paterson, "On Formalized Computer Programs", JCSS, 4, 1970, pp. 220-249.

[29] Martin-Löf, Per, "An Intuitionistic Theory of Types: Predicative Part", Logic Colloquium, 1973, (eds. H.E. Rose and J.C. Shepherdson), North-Holland, Amsterdam, 1975, 73-118.

[30] Martin-Löf, Per, "Constructive Mathematics and Computer Programming", 6th International Congress for Logic, Method and Phil. of Science, North-Holland, Amsterdam, 1982.

[31] Nordstrom, B., "Programming in Constructive Set Theory: Some Examples", Proc. 1981 Conf. on Functional Prog. Lang. and Computer Archi, Portsmouth, 1981, 141-153.

[32] Pratt, Terrence W., Programming Languages: Design and Implementation, Prentice-Hall, Englewood Cliffs, 1975, 530p.

[33] Russell, B., "Mathematical Logic as Based on a Theory of Types", Am. J. of Math., 30, 1908, pp. 222-262.

[34] Scott, Dana, "Data Types as Lattices", SIAM Journal on Computing, Vol. 5, No. 3, September, 1976.

[35] Scott, Dana, "Constructive Validity", Symposium on Automatic Demonstration, Lecture Notes in Mathematics, 125, Springer-Verlag, 1970, 237-275.

[36] Stenlund, S., Combinators, Lambda-terms, and Proof-Theory, D. Reidel, Dordrecht, 1972, 183 pp.

[37] Skolem, T., "Begründung der elementären Arithmetik durch die rekurrierende Denkweise ohne Anwendung scheinbarer Varanderlichen mit unendlichen Ausdehnunggsbereich, Videnskapsselskapets Skrifter 1, Math-Naturv K16, 1924, 3-38, (also in From Frege to Gödel, p. 302-333 and in Skolem's Selected Works in Logic ed., J.E. Fenstad, Oslo, 1970).

[38] Teitelbaum, R. and T. Reps, ''The Cornell Program Synthesizer: A Syntax-Directed Programming Environment'', CACM, 24:9, September 1981, 563-573.

The Classification of Problems which have Fast Parallel Algorithms

Stephen A. Cook*
Department of Computer Science
University of Toronto
Toronto, Canada M5S 1A4

1. Introduction

In this paper we are concerned with the class of functions computable very rapidly (in time polynomial in log n) by a parallel computer with a feasible (i.e. polynomial) number of processors. This class, now commonly called *NC* ([Co], [DC], [Ru3]) was first identified and characterized by Pippenger [P]. Since then, the class has been shown to include a large and interesting variety of problems. Our task here is to give examples of these problems and classify them according to the methods applicable for demonstrating their inclusion in *NC*.

A great many formal parallel computer models have appeared in the literature (see [Co] and [Vi] for surveys). One common kind is the shared memory computer, in which a number of processors work together synchronously and communicate with a common random access memory. In the event of read or write conflicts in this shared memory several conventions are possible. The particular variation we mention here is the SIMDAG introduced in [Go1] in which both read and write conflicts are allowed, and the lowest numbered processor succeeds in the case of a write conflict. One reason for favoring these conventions is that the circuitry needed to implement them seems not to be substantially more complicated than that needed to implement a machine which disallows read and write conflicts. A more important reason is that the complexity classes defined in terms of SIMDAG time have nice characterizations in terms of the alternation depth required on circuits [CSV] or alternating Turing machines [RT] (see Proposition 6 below).

At the present time no large scale general purpose parallel computers have been built. Although the shared memory model seems like a good way to go (see [Sc1]), the arbitrariness in the detailed definition makes it unappealing for an enduring mathematical theory. A more attractive model for such a theory is uniform Boolean circuit families [Bo]. It seems that all real computers will be built from circuits, and the circuit complexity of Boolean functions is an appealing mathematical subject that has been studied since Shannon [Sh]. Also, the complexity classes defined in terms of circuit families have a precise characterization in terms of alternating Turing machines [Ru3]. Fortunately, the parallel class *NC* remains the same whether uniform circuit

* The author is grateful to the Killam Foundation of Canada for support.

families or shared memory computers are used to define it, although the subclasses NC^k may be different.

In this paper we will present the following sequence of class inclusions (where *FP* is the class of functions computable in deterministic polynomial time):

$$NC^1 \subseteq FL \subseteq NL^* \subseteq \begin{matrix} CFL^* \subseteq AC^1 \\ DET \end{matrix} \subseteq NC^2 \subseteq NC \subseteq FP$$

In section 2, uniform circuit families and the classes NC^k are defined. In section 3, examples in the fundamental class NC^1 are given and the notion of NC^1 reduction is introduced. In section 4 the classes *FL*, NL^*, CFL^* and AC^1 are defined with examples, and the parallel greedy algorithm is explained. In section 5 the class *DET* of problems reducible to computing integer determinants is introduced with examples. In section 6, examples of problems in *FP* which are likely not in *NC* because they are complete for *FP* are given. In section 7 the classes random NC^k are defined with examples. Finally, in section 8 some general remarks and open questions are presented.

2. Uniform Circuit Families

A *(Boolean) circuit* α with n inputs and m outputs is a finite directed acyclic graph with nodes (called ***gates***) labelled as follows. The circuit α has n "input nodes" with indegree zero labelled $x_1,...,x_n$, respectively. All other nodes of indegree zero are labelled either 0 or 1. All nodes of indegree one are labelled $\neg$. All other nodes have indegree two and are labelled either $\wedge$ or $\vee$. Exactly m nodes are labelled output nodes and have labels $y_1,...,y_m$, respectively. Every input node has at least one path from it to some output node. We use $c(\alpha)$, complexity of α, to denote the number of nodes of α, and $d(\alpha)$, depth of α, to denote the length of the longest path from some input to some output.

If α has n inputs and m outputs, then α computes a function $f:\{0,1\}^n \to \{0,1\}^m$ in the obvious way. In general, we are interested in computing partial functions $f:\{0,1\}^* \to \{0,1\}^*$. For example, the function "directed graph transitive closure" is defined on bit strings of the form $\{0,1\}^{n^2}$, and when these are taken to designate the n rows of the $n \times n$ adjacency matrix of an n-node digraph G, the value of the function is the n^2-bit string representing the adjacency matrix of the transitive closure of G. This function can be computed by a family $<\alpha_n>$ of circuits, where α_n has n^2 inputs and n^2 outputs and computes the restriction of the function to $\{0,1\}^{n^2}$.

In general a *circuit family* is a sequence $<\alpha_n>$, where α_n is a circuit with $g(n)$ inputs, and $g(n)$ is monotone strictly increasing and $g(n) = n^{O(1)}$. The family $<\alpha_n>$ computes a partial function $f:\{0,1\}^* \to \{0,1\}^*$ in the way indicated above. (For all n, f is defined on all strings of length $g(n)$, but not defined on strings whose lengths are not in the range of g).

In this paper we restrict our attention to "uniform" circuit families. A common definition of uniform (called U_{BC} in [Ru3]) is that the description of α_n can be generated in space $O(\log n)$ by a deterministic Turing machine. However, I prefer the definition introduced by Ruzzo [Ru3] called U_{E^*}, which will be discussed below. We adopt this definition of uniform in the following

Definition. NC^k is the set of all functions f computable by a uniform circuit family $<\alpha_n>$ with $c(\alpha_n) = n^{O(1)}$ and $d(\alpha) = O(\log^k n)$. $NC = \bigcup_k NC^k$.

(We have taken the liberty of generalizing NC^k to include functions instead of just sets, as is usually done). It is worth noting that NC remains the same when any of the standard shared memory computer models are used to define it.

Ruzzo [Ru3] proved that NC^k remains the same no matter which of the two definitions of uniform (U_{E^*} or U_{BC}) are used, provided $k \geq 2$. For NC^1 however, there may be a difference. I prefer U_{E^*}, because then NC^1 can be characterized as precisely the set of functions computable by an alternating Turing machine (ATM) in time $O(\log n)$.

We will not define ATM's here (see [CKS] and [Ru2]) because the majority of the results presented here can be understood without understanding them. However, we should explain that our ATM's compute functions instead of recognizing sets. The set A_f associated with the function f is $\{<x,i> \mid$ the ith bit of $f(x)$ is $1\}$. Then we say that an ATM computes f iff it recognizes A_f. Note that f is in NC^k iff (the characteristic function of) A_f is in NC^k.

Proposition 1. (Ruzzo [Ru3]). For all $k \geq 1$, f is in NC^k iff f is computed by some ATM in time $O(\log^k n)$ and space $O(\log n)$.

The above proposition is useful, but suppose we wish to show that f is in NC^k by exhibiting an appropriate circuit family $<\alpha_n>$ computing f, according to our definition of NC^k. Then as mentioned above, for $k \geq 2$ a sufficient uniformity condition is that the description of α_n be generated by some deterministic Turing machine in space $O(\log n)$, given n in unary as input. However, for $k=1$, the condition U_{E^*} must be met, which demands that the so-called "extended connection language" [Ru3] for $<\alpha_n>$ can be recognized by an ATM in time $O(\log n)$. A sufficient condition for this is that some deterministic Turing machine, given n in binary, a gate number g, a path $p \in \{L,R\}^*$ of length $O(\log n)$, and a parameter y, can determine in space $\sqrt{\log n}$ whether y describes the gate reached in α_n by tracing the path p back towards the inputs from gate g. Since a Turing machine which is allowed space up to the square root of its input length is very powerful, there is usually no difficulty in verifying this condition for families $<\alpha_n>$ which are intuitively uniform.

3. The Class NC^1, and NC^1 Reducibility

Recall that NC^1 consists of all functions computable by a uniform circuit family of depth $O(\log n)$, where n is the number of input bits (the polynomial size bound is redundant in this case). Examples of functions in NC^1 are: the sum or product of 2 integers of n bits each, the sum of n integers of n bits each, integer or Boolean matrix multiplication, and sorting n integers of n bits each. Circuits for these functions are described in [Sa], [BCP], and [MP].

Integer division is not known to be in NC^1. The smallest depth known for a log space uniform family of polynomial size circuits for division is $O(\log n\ (\log\log n)^2)$ [Re2]. If the uniformity condition is relaxed somewhat, the depth can be reduced to $O(\log n \log^* n)$ [BCH].

In the study of sequential time complexity, polynomial time reducibility (in its two forms "Cook" and "Karp" [GJ]) has become standard, and in the study of space complexity log space reducibility (usually in its "Karp" or many-one form) is used [JL]. In the study of parallel computation, it seems to me that NC^1 reducibility is appropriate, and partly because we are studying functions instead of sets, the "Cook" (or "Turing") version is most useful.

Definition. A function f is NC^1 reducible to g (written $f \leq g$) iff there is a U_E-uniform family of circuits $\langle \alpha_n \rangle$ for computing f, where $d(\alpha_n) = O(\log n)$, and α_n is allowed to have *oracle nodes* for g. An oracle node for g is a node with some sequence $\langle y_1,\dots,y_r \rangle$ of input edges and a sequence $\langle z_1,\dots,z_s \rangle$ of output edges whose values satisfy $\langle z_1,\dots,z_s \rangle = g(\langle y_1,\dots,y_r \rangle)$. For the purpose of defining depth in α_n, this oracle node counts as depth $\lceil \log(r) \rceil$.

A similar definition for the case of sets is found in [W]. It is not hard to check that $\leq$ is transitive and reflexive. The *closure* S^* of a class S of functions (under $\leq$) consists of all functions f such that $f \leq g$ for some g in S. The class S is *closed* iff $S = S^*$.

Proposition 2. The class NC^k is closed under $\leq$ for all $k \geq 1$.

Proof. Suppose $f \leq g$ and $g \in NC^k$. Suppose $\langle \alpha_n \rangle$ realizes the reduction $f \leq g$, and $\langle \beta_n \rangle$ computes g in NC^k. Then a family $\langle \gamma_n \rangle$ for computing f in NC^k can be constructed by letting γ_n be α_n with each oracle node for g_m replaced by β_m. To check for example, that $d(\gamma_n) = O(\log^k n)$, consider any path p in γ_n and suppose p hits instances $\beta_{m_1}, \beta_{m_2}, \dots$ of circuits substituted for oracle nodes in α_n. Then the length of p is at most $\Sigma d(\beta_{m_j}) + O(\log n) = O(\Sigma \log^k m_j) + O(\log n) = O(\log^k n)$, where the last bound follows since $\Sigma \log m_j = O(\log n)$. The uniformity of $\langle \gamma_n \rangle$ can be proved from the uniformity of $\langle \alpha_n \rangle$ and $\langle \beta_n \rangle$.

Definition. A function f is *hard* (or *NC^1 hard*) for the class S iff $g \leq f$ for all g in S. Further, f is *complete* (or *NC^1 complete*) for S iff f is hard for S and $f \in S$.

4. Other Classes and the Parallel Greedy Algorithm

Let FL be the class of functions computable in space $O(\log n)$ on a deterministic Turing machine, where the output is placed on a special write-only tape which does not participate in the space bound. Then one can show FL is closed under $\leq$ by a proof similar to that of Proposition 1, using the simulation of depth-bounded circuits by space-bounded Turing machines given in [Bo]. This shows $NC^1 \subset FL$.

Two examples of problems in FL not known to be in NC^1 are (1) undirected graph acyclicity [Co], and (2) the Boolean formula value problem [Ly]. The first is NC^1 complete for FL by an adaptation of a proof in [Ho]. It would be interesting to know whether the second is complete.

Let NL be the class of sets accepted by a nondeterministic machine in space $O(\log n)$. Examples of sets complete for NL are the (directed) graph accessibility problem, k-connectivity, and unsatisfiability of 2-DNF Boolean formulas [JJS].

Let NL^* be the closure of NL (as a class of 0−1 functions) under $\leq$. Of course every problem complete for NL is also complete for NL^*. Examples of problems complete for NL^* which are more naturally expressed as functions than sets are transitive closure of a Boolean matrix (i.e. directed graph transitive closure), and the shortest path problem for graphs with positive edge weights expressed in unary notation. Examples of problems in NL^* but not necessarily complete are computing a topological sort of a directed acyclic graph [Ru1] and the following application of the "parallel greedy algorithm".

Proposition 3. The problem of finding a minimum spanning forest for an n-node undirected graph with n-bit positive integer weights is in NL^* (and hence in NC^2).

The proof is a parallel version of the sequential greedy algorithm (see [PS], for example). Let $G = (V,E)$ be the input graph, and for any set $E' \subseteq E$ of edges let rank(E') be the number of edges in a spanning forest for $G(E')$, the graph spanned by E'. Then rank(E') is the number of vertices in $G(E')$ minus the number of connected components in $G(E')$. The number of components in $G(E')$ can be computed in NL^* by computing the transitive closure of $G(E')$ in NL^* and using this to count in NC^1 the number of vertices i in $G(E')$ which are not connected to any vertex j in $G(E')$ with $j<i$. The parallel greedy algorithm proceeds by first sorting in NC^1 the edges $\{e_1, e_2, \ldots, e_r\} = E$ of G according to increasing weight and then outputting each edge e_i which satisfies the condition:

$$\text{rank}(e_1,\ldots,e_i) > \text{rank}(e_1,\ldots,e_{i-1}).$$

The fact that these edges form a minimum weight spanning forest follows from Proposition 4 below, and from the fact that the rank function defined above satisfies the matroid axioms in a matroid whose bases are the spanning forests of G.

Note that $NL^* \subseteq NC^2$ by [Bo].

Proposition 4. (Parallel greedy algorithm). Let E be a finite set with a positive weight associated with each element of E, and suppose $\{e_1, \ldots, e_r\}$ is a list of the elements of E in increasing order of weight. Suppose a function rank(E') is defined on the subsets of E which satisfies the matroid axioms. Then the set $B = \{e_i \mid \text{rank}(e_1,\ldots,e_i) > \text{rank}(e_1,\ldots,e_{i-1})\}$ is a matroid base of minimum total weight.

The proof is similar to the justification of the sequential greedy algorithm [PS]. This Proposition is an abstraction of the method described in [BGH] for finding a column basis for a matrix. The method yields a fast parallel algorithm whenever the rank function can be computed quickly in parallel.

The class *LOGCFL* consists of all sets log space reducible to the class *CFL* of context free languages. (Here A is ***log space reducible*** to B iff there is some log space computable function f such that for all x, $x \in A$ iff $f(x) \in B$). Sudborough [Su] characterized *LOGCFL* as those sets accepted by a nondeterministic auxiliary pushdown machine in log space and polynomial time. From this, it follows that $NL \subseteq LOGCFL$. Ruzzo [Ru2] further characterized *LOGCFL* as those sets accepted by an ATM in log space and polynomial tree size, and proved $LOGCFL \subseteq NC^2$.

Besides context-free languages and members of *NL*, the class *LOGCFL* contains the monotone planar circuit value problem [DC], bounded valence subtree isomorphism [Ru3], and basic dynamic programming problems [Go1]. The latter are more naturally expressed as functions, and so it seems that the natural class to consider is CFL^* (the closure of *CFL* under $\leq$).

Proposition 5. $LOGCFL \subseteq CFL^*$.

Proof. An inspection of Sudborough's proof [Su] that every set accepted by a nondeterministic auxiliary pushdown machine in log space and polynomial time is log space reducible to *CFL* shows that the reduction is via an NC^1 computable function. Hence $LOGCFL = NC^1CFL$, and the proposition follows.

The above inclusion is proper, not only because CFL^* contains functions other than 0–1 functions, but because apparently *LOGCFL* is not closed under complementation. For example, the complement of the graph accessibility problem does not appear to be in *LOGCFL*.

An example of a dynamic programming problem in CFL^* is computing the minimum cost order of multiplying a string of n matrices (see [AHU] for a dynamic programming solution to the problem and [Go1] for the method of putting such problems into CFL^*).

It turns out that all functions in CFL^* can be solved on a SIMDAG (see the Introduction) in time $O(\log n)$. To state a more general form of this result we introduce the following terminology.

Definition: AC^k, for $k = 1,2,...$, is the class of all functions computable by an ATM in space $O(\log n)$ and alternation depth $O(\log^k n)$.

Proposition 6. (Ruzzo and Tompa [RT]). AC^k is the class of all functions computable on a SIMDAG in $O(\log^k n)$ time with $n^{O(1)}$ processors.

A similar characterization of "nonuniform AC^k" in terms of circuits with unbounded fan-in for "and" and "or" appears in [CSV]. In fact, AC^k itself has a characterization analogous to that of NC^k in Proposition 1. Namely, AC^k consists of those functions computable by uniform circuit families in $O(\log^k n)$ depth and $n^{O(1)}$ size [CRT], where "and" and "or" gates are allowed unbounded fan-in and negations have been pushed to the leaves. A suitable definition of *uniform* for such a circuit family $<\alpha_n>$ is that the "direct connection language" for the family (which includes all triples $<n,u,v>$ such that node u is an input to node v in α_n, together with node labelling information) have nondeterministic space complexity $O(\log n)$.

By Proposition 1 of [Ru3] it follows that $AC^k \subseteq NC^{k+1}$. One way to see this using unbounded fan-in circuits is that each "or" gate or "and" gate has fan-in $n^{O(1)}$ and hence can be replaced by a tree of depth $O(\log n)$ of fan-in two gates. In particular, $AC^1 \subseteq NC^2$.

Ruzzo [Ru2] showed $LOGCFL \subseteq AC^1$. Since AC^1 is closed under $\leq$ (as can be seen from the unbounded fan-in circuit characterization), we have

Proposition 7: $CFL^* \subseteq AC^1$

By putting Propositions 6 and 7 together we obtain

Corollary 1. All problems described so far are solvable by SIMDAG's in $O(\log n)$ time with $n^{O(1)}$ processors. This applies in particular to context-free language recognition and finding a minimum spanning forest in an undirected graph ([AS], [Re1]).

5. The class DET

Let *intdet* be the problem of computing $\det(A)$ given an $n \times n$ matrix of n-bit integers, and let *matpow* be the problem of computing the powers $A^1, A^2, \ldots, A^n$, given such an A. Since integer matrix multiplication is in NC^1 it is easy to see that *matpow* is in NC^2 (see [BCP]). Csanky [Cs] was the first to give an argument which shows *intdet* is in NC^2, and recently Berkowitz [Be] gives an alternative argument which also shows clearly that *intdet* $\leq$ *matpow* (recall $\leq$ means "is NC^1 reducible to"). (The germ of another argument showing this reduction appears in [Co]). Since many problems in NC^2 are reducible to *intdet*, we make the following

Definition: $DET = \{intdet\}^* = \{f \mid f \leq intdet\}$.

It is clear that the problem "iterated integer product" (given n-bit integers $a_1, a_2, \ldots, a_n$ compute their product $a_1 a_2 \ldots a_n$) is in DET by computing the determinant of the matrix with $a_1, \ldots, a_n$ on the diagonal and zeroes elsewhere. From this it follows that integer division is in DET (see [Hv] or [BCH]).

A large class of problems in DET comes from the following:

Proposition 8. $NL^* \subseteq DET$.

Proof. It suffices to show that the graph accessibility problem is reducible to *intdet*, since the former is complete for NL. Let A be the adjacency matrix of an n-node digraph G and assume A has zeroes on the diagonal. Then the i,j-th element of A^k, where A is treated as an integer matrix, is the number of paths of length k from i to j in G. For any ε with $0 < \varepsilon < ||A||$ (the norm of A) we have, setting $M = I - \varepsilon A$,

$$M^{-1} = (I - \varepsilon A)^{-1} = I + \varepsilon A + (\varepsilon A)^2 + \cdots$$

Therefore, the i,j-th element of M^{-1} is nonzero iff there is a path from i to j in G. Since $M^{-1} = \mathrm{adj}(M)/\det(M)$, and we can take $\varepsilon = \frac{1}{n}$ (since $||A|| < n$), we have, multiplying M by $\frac{1}{\varepsilon}$,

$$\exists \text{ path in } G \text{ from } 1 \text{ to } n \quad \text{iff} \quad \det((nI - A)[n \mid 1]) \neq 0,$$

where $[n \mid 1]$ indicates the deletion of the n-th row and first column.

Proposition 9: The following problems are complete for DET:

(1) *intdet* (integer determinant)

(2) *matpow* (matrix powering)

(3) *itmatprod* (iterated matrix product)
Input : n $n \times n$ matrices with n-bit integer entries
Output: Their product

(4) *matinv* (integer matrix inverse)
Input : $n \times n$ matrix A with n-bit integer entries
Output: A^{-1} in the form <adj(A),det(A)>, where all entries are integers with $n^2 + \lceil \log_2 n \rceil + 1$ bits.

Proof.

(a) *intdet* $\leq$ *matpow*: (see [Be]).

(b) *matpow* $\leq$ *matinv*: Let N be the $n^2 \times n^2$ matrix consisting of $n \times n$ blocks which are all zero except for $n-1$ copies of A above the diagonal of zero blocks. Then $N^n = 0$ and $(I-N)^{-1} = I+N+N^2+\ldots+N^{n-1} =$

$$\begin{bmatrix} I & A & A^2 & \cdots & A^{n-1} \\ 0 & I & A & \cdots & A^{n-2} \\ & & & & \\ 0 & & & & I \end{bmatrix}$$

(Joachim von zur Gathen pointed out this argument to me.)

(c) *matinv* $\leq$ *intdet*: All entries of adj(A) are determinants of minors of A with appropriate sign.

(d) *matpow* $\leq$ *itmatprod*: Obvious.

(e) *itmatprod* $\leq$ *matpow*: Let $A_1,\ldots,A_n$ be $n \times n$ matrices, and let B be an $(n^2+n) \times (n^2+n)$ matrix consisting of $n \times n$ blocks which are all zero except for $A_1,\ldots,A_n$ appearing above the diagonal of zero blocks. Then B^n has the product $A_1 A_2 \ldots A_n$ in the upper right corner.

This completes the proof of Proposition 9. Clearly the inverse of matrices over the rationals (expressed as integer pairs <numerator, denominator>) and solutions of nonsingular systems of linear equations over the rationals are also in *DET*. It is not clear that these problems are complete for *DET* (unless they are artificially formulated) because although the determinant of an integer matrix can be expressed as a quotient of integers using solutions to these problems, I do not see how to reduce integer division to them.

One can add many other problems to *DET*. The method in [Be] actually shows how to compute the coefficients of the characteristic polynomial det($\lambda I-A$) given an oracle for matrix powering, so this problem is in *DET* (and complete). This shows how to compute the coefficients of a polynomial $(x-a_1)(x-a_2)\ldots(x-a_n)$ in *DET*, so the Lagrange interpolation polynomials are in *DET*. Hence polynomial interpolation over the rationals is in *DET*. This allows us solve all the problems listed in Proposition 9 in *DET* even when the matrix entries are polynomials with a fixed number of variables (or rational functions) over the integers or rationals by polynomial evaluation and interpolation. Hence by [BCP] the problems of computing the stochastic closure of a matrix and simulating a log n space-bounded probabilistic Turing machine are in *DET*.

Another source of problems in *DET* is [BGH] and [vzG] in which algebraic reductions to computing determinants are given. From these we can conclude, for example, that computing the greatest common divisor of n univariate polynomials over the rationals is in *DET*. Also according to [IMR] computing the rank of a matrix over the rationals can be reduced to computing characteristic polynomials, so this problem is in *DET*. In [BGH] it is shown how to find a column basis for a matrix (using the parallel greedy algorithm: see Proposition 4) once the rank can be computed, and show how this can be used to find a general solution to a singular system of linear equations. Hence this problem is in *DET*, in case the ground field is the rationals.

6. Problems NC^1 complete for FP

Let *FP* be the set of all functions computable in polynomial time. Since at present we cannot prove $FP \neq NC^1$ the best way to indicate that a problem in *FP* is probably not in *NC* is to prove it is complete for *FP* (such arguments are usually stated with respect to log space reducibility, but in fact the proof usually show that NC^1 reducibility applies as well. If F is NC^1 complete for *FP* and f is in *NC*, then $FP = NC$, an unlikely result.

Examples of problems complete for *FP* are the circuit value problem [La] (either monotone or planar [Go2]), linear programming ([K] and [DLR]), and maximum network flow (with capacities given in binary notation) [GSS]. See [JL] for several others. Here is one new one:

Proposition 10. Finding the lexicographically first maximal clique in an undirected graph is NC^1 complete for *FP*.

Proof. We show how to reduce the monotone circuit value problem to the above problem. Given a monotone Boolean circuit α (with each input assigned 0 or 1) we construct a graph G such that each gate v of α is associated with nodes v' and v'' of G. This will be done in such a way that the lexicographically first clique C of G includes v' iff the value $\nu(v)$ of v in α is 1, and C includes v'' iff $\nu(v) = 0$. We assume that the gates and inputs of α are ordered topologically with the inputs first and the output last. If the gates and inputs are ordered $\langle v_1, v_2, \ldots, v_k \rangle$ then the nodes of G are ordered $\langle v_1', v_1'', v_2', v_2'', \ldots, v_k' v_k'' \rangle$, except the order of (v_i', v_i'') may be reversed. If v is an input labelled 1 then v' is adjacent to all preceding nodes and v'' is adjacent to no preceding nodes. If v is an input labelled 0 then these conditions are reversed, except v' and v'' are never adjacent. If v is an "and" gate with inputs

u and w, then v' is adjacent to all preceding nodes except u'' and w'', and v'' is adjacent to all preceding nodes except v'. If v is an "or" gate, then v'' precedes v', v'' is adjacent to all preceding nodes except u' and w', and v' is adjacent to all preceding nodes except v''.

7. Random *NC*

The class *BPP* [Gi] can be defined as the class of all sets recognizable in polynomial time by a probabilistic Turing machine with error probability at most $\frac{1}{4}$. Similarly one can define *RNC* (random *NC*) to be the class of functions computable by probabilistic circuits in polylog depth and polynomial time. More precisely, a function f is in RNC^k iff it is computed by a uniform family $<\alpha_n>$ of probabilistic circuits with bitwise error probability at most $\frac{1}{4}$, where $d(\alpha_n) = O(\log^k n)$ and $c(\alpha_n) = n^{O(1)}$. Here a ***probabilistic circuit*** is a Boolean circuit with ordinary inputs x and "coin tossing" inputs y. The probability that a particular output bit v is 1 is defined to be the fraction of input strings y such that the value of v is 1 when α_n has inputs (x,y). If each bit of $f(x)$ is computed correctly with probability at least $\frac{3}{4}$, then one can arrange many circuits in parallel each computing the same bit, and a majority vote can be taken to obtain a reliable value. Thus if f is in RNC^k under the above definition, then for each l some other uniform family $<\beta_n>$ of probabilistic circuits with polynomial size and the same depth bounds computes all bits of f correctly with the probability of one or more errors at most 2^{-n^l}.

If f is in RNC^k, then using the techniques of [A] one can show that f is in "nonuniform NC^k", that is, NC^k with the uniformity restriction removed.

It is of course not clear whether *RNC* is a subclass of *NC*, or even of *FP*, although certainly $RNC \subseteq BPP$. Since it seems unlikely that $FP \subseteq RNC$, a proof that f is hard for *FP* (under NC^1, NC^k, RNC^k, or log space reducibility) is a strong indication that f is not in *RNC*. (Equivalently a proof that f is in *RNC* is a strong indication that f is not hard for *FP*).

A number of problems in RNC^2 appear in [BGH] (see also [vzG]). Examples are finding the rank of a matrix (and solving possibly singular systems of linear equations) over a finite field, and finding the size of a maximum matching in a bipartite graph (or an arbitrary undirected graph [F]). These methods are extended in [F] to show that the size of the maximum flow in a network with edge capacities expressed in unary is in RNC^2. (When edge capacities are expressed in binary the problem is complete for *FP* [GSS]). In [Sc2] it is shown that testing the singularity of a matrix of polynomials in many variables is in RNC^2. Recently it has been shown [MC] that the abelian permutation group membership problem is in RNC^3.

8. Conclusion and Open Questions

I have noticed three generalizations concerning parallel complexity classes:

(1) Most natural problems in $DSPACE((\log n)^{O(1)})$ are in NC.

(2) Most natural problems in NC are in NC^2.

(3) Most natural problems in NC^2 are in CFL^* or DET.

The apparent exceptions to the above provide us with the challenge of either making them fit the generalizations or providing an explanation. A possible exception to (1) is the problem of determining whether two groups, presented by their multiplication tables, are isomorphic. A possible exception to (2) is the problem of finding a *maximal* matching in a bipartite graph (shown to be in NC^3 in [Le]). A possible exception to (3) is the shortest path problem when edges have positive integer weights presented in binary notation (known to be in NC^2 by min-plus matrix powering [AHU]).

These generalizations are largely concerned with whether certain of the inclusions listed in the Introduction are proper:

$$NC^1 \subseteq FL \subseteq NL^* \subseteq \begin{matrix} CFL^* \subseteq AC^1 \\ DET \end{matrix} \subseteq NC^2 \subseteq NC \subseteq \begin{matrix} DSPACE((\log n)^{O(1)}) \\ FP \end{matrix}$$

Natural examples complete for each of the above classes (suggesting that the inclusion immediately to the left of the class might be proper) are known, with the exceptions of AC^1, NC^2, NC, and $DSPACE((\log n)^{O(1)})$. There is provably no complete problem for this last class, and there is none either for NC unless $NC = NC^k$ for some k. An intriguing open question is to find natural complete problems for AC^1 and NC^2, or anything natural in AC^1 not known to be in CFL^*. (The word "natural" precludes having "$\log^2 n$" appear in the statement of a problem. Of course the circuit value problem for circuits of depth at most $\log^2 n$ is complete for NC^2).

It would be interesting to show that DET and CFL^* are comparable. It seems unlikely that $DET \subseteq AC^1$ (and hence unlikely that $DET \subseteq CFL^*$) since integer matrix powering is in DET, and if A^n is computed by repeated squaring then $\log n$ stages are required and each stage requires unbounded alternation depth by [FSS].

The question of whether $DET = NC^2$ has an interesting algebraic analog (see [Va] and [VSBR]).

Of course it would require a breakthrough in complexity theory to prove $NC^1 \neq FP$, and hence a breakthrough to prove any two of the above classes are unequal (excluding $DSPACE((\log n)^{O(1)})$).

It would be nice to show that the problems in RNC mentioned in Section 7 are in NC. Among the interesting problems in FP not known to either complete for FP or in (random) NC are integer greatest common divisors, computing $a^b \bmod c$ (a,b,c positive integers presented in binary), and finding a maximum matching in a bipartite graph (the *size* of the matching can be computed in RNC^2).

Acknowledgements: My thanks to Patrick Dymond for helpful discussions, Larry Ruzzo for circulating a list of NC^2 problems, and to Paul Beame and Jim Hoover for a careful reading of the manuscript.

References

[A] Adleman, L. Two theorems on random polynomial time, *Proc. 19th IEEE FOCS* (1978), 75-83.

[AHU] Aho, A.V., Hopcroft, J.E. and Ullman, J.D. *The Design and Analysis of Computer Algorithms*, Addison-Wesley, Reading, Mass. (1974).

[AS] Awerbuch, B. and Shiloach, Y. New connectivity and MSF algorithms for Ultracomputer and PRAM. Preprint, IBM-Israel Scientific Center, Technion, Haifa (1983).

[BCH] Beame, P.W., Cook, S.A. and Hoover, H.J. Small depth circuits for integer products, powers, and division. Preprint (1983).

[Be] Berkowitz, S.J. On computing the determinant in small parallel time using a small number of processors. Preprint (1982).

[Bo] Borodin, A. On relating time and space to size and depth, *SIAM J. Comput.* 6(1977), 733-744.

[BCP] Borodin, A., Cook, S.A. and Pippenger, N. Parallel computation for well-endowed rings and space-bounded probabilistic machines. Technical Report 162/83, Department of Computer Science, University of Toronto (1983).

[BGH] Borodin, A., von zur Gathen, J. and Hopcroft, J. Fast parallel matrix and GCD computations, *Proc. 23rd IEEE FOCS* (1982), 65-71.

[CKS] Chandra, A.K., Kozen, D.C. and Stockmeyer, L.J. Alternation, *J. ACM* 28, 1(Jan. 1981), 114-133.

[CSV] Chandra, A.K., Stockmeyer, L.J. and Vishkin, U. Complexity theory for unbounded fan-in parallelism, *Proc. 23rd IEEE FOCS* (1982), 1-13.

[Co] Cook, S.A. Towards a complexity theory of synchronous parallel computation, *L'Enseignement Mathematique XXVII* (1981), 99-124.

[CRT] Cook, S.A., Ruzzo, W.L. and Tompa, M. "Oral theorem" (1983).

[Cs] Csanky, L. Fast parallel matrix inversion algorithms, *SIAM J. Comput.* 5(1976), 618-623.

[DLR] Dobkin, D., Lipton, R.J. and Reiss, S. Linear programming is log-space hard for P, *Information Processing Letters* 8(1979), 96-97.

[DC] Dymond, P.W. and Cook, S.A. Hardware Complexity and Parallel Computation, *Proc. 21st IEEE FOCS* (1980), 360-372.

[F] Feather, T. M.Sc. thesis, Department of Computer Science, University of Toronto. To appear.

[FSS] Furst, M., Saxe, J., Sipser, M. Parity, circuits, and the polynomial- time hierarchy, *Proc. 22nd IEEE FOCS* (1981), 260-270.

[GJ] Garey, M.R. and Johnson, D.S. *Computers and Intractability: A Guide to the Theory of NP-Completeness*, W.H. Freeman, San Francisco (1979).

[vzG] von zur Gathen, J. Parallel algorithms for algebraic problems, *Proc. 15th ACM STOC* (1983), 17-23.

[Gi] Gill, J. Computational complexity of probabilistic Turing machines, *SIAM J. Comput.* 6(1977), 675-695.

[Go1] Goldschlager, L.M. Synchronous Parallel Computation, Ph.D. Thesis, University of Toronto (1977). See also *Proc. 10th ACM STOC* (1978), 89-94 and *J. ACM* 29, 4(Oct. 1982), 1073-1086.

[Go2] Goldschlager, L.M. The monotone and planar circuit value problems are log space complete for P, *SIGACT News* 9, 2(summer 1977), 25-29.

[GSS] Goldschlager, L.M., Shaw, R.A. and Staples, J. The maximum flow problem is log space complete for P, *Theoretical Computer Science* 21(1982), 105-111.

[Ho] Hong, J.W. On some space complexity problems about the set of assignments satisfying a boolean formula, *Proc. 12th ACM STOC* (1980), 310-317.

[Hv] Hoover, H.J. Some Topics in Circuit Complexity, M.Sc. Thesis, University of Toronto, Department of Computer Science (1979). Also available as Department of Computer Science Technical Report 139/80.

[IMR] Ibarra, O.H., Moran, S. and Rosier, L.E. A note on the parallel complexity of computing the rank of order n matrices, *Information Processing Letters* 11(1980), 162.

[JJS] Ja' Ja', J. and Simon, J. Parallel algorithms in graph theory: planarity testing, *SIAM J. Comput.* 11(1982), 314-328.

[JL] Jones, N.D. and Laaser, W.T. Complete problems for deterministic polynomial time, *Theoretical Computer Science* 3(1977), 105-117.

[K] Khachian, L.G. A polynomial time algorithm for linear programming, *Doklady Akad. Nauk SSSR*, 244, 5(1979), 1093-96. Translated in *Soviet Math. Doklady*, 20, 191-194.

[La] Ladner, R.E. The circuit value problem is log space complete for P, *SIGACT News* 7, 1(1975), 18-20.

[Le] Lev., G. Size bounds and parallel algorithms for networks, Doctoral Thesis, Report CST-8-80, Dept. of Computer Science, University of Edinburgh (1980).

[Ly] Lynch, N. Log space recognition and translation of parenthesis languages, *J. ACM* 24, 4(Oct. 1977), 583-590.

[MC] McKenzie, P. and Cook, S.A. Parallel complexity of the Abelian permutation group membership problem. Extended abstract (1983).

[MP] Muller, D.E. and Preparata, F.P. Bounds to complexities of networks for sorting and switching, *J. ACM* 22, 2(April 1975), 195-201.

[P] Pippenger, N. On simultaneous resource bounds (preliminary version), *Proc. 20th IEEE FOCS* (1979), 307-311.

[PS] Papadimitriou, C.H. and Steiglitz, K. *Combinatorial Optimization: Algorithms and Complexity*, Prentice-Hall, Englewood Cliffs, NJ (1982).

[P] Pippenger, N. On simultaneous resource bounds (preliminary version), *Proc. 20th IEEE FOCS* (1979), 307-311.

[Re1] Reif, J.H. Symmetric complementation, *Proc. 14th ACM STOC* (1982), 201-214.

[Re2] Reif, J.H. Logarithmic depth circuits for algebraic functions, TR-35-82, Aiken Computation Laboratory, Harvard University (Nov. 1982).

[Ru1] Ruzzo, W.L. Unpublished list of problems in NC^2 (1980).

[Ru2] Ruzzo, W.L. Tree-size bounded alternation, *Journal of Computer and System Sciences* 21, 2(Oct. 1980), 218-235.

[Ru3] Ruzzo, W.L. On uniform circuit complexity, *Journal of Computer and System Sciences* 22, 3(June 1981), 365-383.

[RT] Ruzzo, W.L. and Tompa, M. Unpublished result (1982). See Stockmeyer, L. and Viskin, U. Simulation of parallel random access machines by circuits, Report RC-9362, IBM Research, Yorktown Heights, NY.

[Sa] Savage, J.E. *The Complexity of Computing*, Wiley, New York (1976).

[Sc1] Schwartz, J.T. Ultracomputers, *ACM Trans. on Prog. Languages and Systems* 2, 4(Oct. 1980), 484-521.

[Sc2] Schwartz, J.T. Probabilistic algorithms for verification of polynomial identifies, *J. ACM* 27, 4(Oct. 1980), 701-717.

[Sh] Shannon, C.E. The synthesis of two terminal switching circuits, *BSTJ* 28(1949), 59-98.

A FAIR CALCULUS OF COMMUNICATING SYSTEMS*

Gerardo Costa** and Colin Stirling
Dept. of Computer Science
Edinburgh University, U.K.

Abstract We contrast a two level operational approach to fairness with a single level approach. The latter involves presenting a set of rules which generate all and only the fair execution sequences of a concurrent language. This we do for a subset of Milner's CCS.

Introduction

An accepted constraint on models of parallel systems is that they imply nothing about the relative speeds of the concurrent components. On the other hand, it is desirable that they also imply that each component always eventually proceeds (unless it has deadlocked or terminated). Such models reflect the principle of fairness [Pa, M2].

Complications arise if a component cannot always proceed autonomously: other components may prevent it from proceeding (for instance, because of mutual exclusion) or it may not be able to proceed without interacting (for example, communicating) with other components. In such situations different notions of fairness may be distinguished [LPS,P]. These situations do not arise in this paper.

Fairness has been examined from disparate viewpoints. Examples include [Pa,AO,P, GPSS,OL,M2,H]. Here we are concerned with an operational approach, the problem of defining and generating the fair execution sequences of a concurrent language. One solution is to invoke two semantic levels. One level prescribes the finite and infinite execution sequences without regard to their fairness whilst the other filters out the unfair ones. The first level is given via a set of generative rules whereas the second is encoded as a definition of fair (or unfair) execution sequence. Those sequences generated by the rules which fail to be fair according to the second level are discounted. ([LPS] offers a general method for doing this.)

A neater solution, a single level approach, is simply to offer rules which generate just the fair sequences. A second semantic level is then unnecessary. This requires there to be rules for the concurrent operator which ensure that both components eventually proceed if they can. But, at the same time, the rules should not prejudge the relative speeds of the components: no unwanted synchrony should be enforced. Plotkin does this for a concurrent guarded command language using random assignment [P]. He defines the parallel operator in terms of a set of auxiliary parallel operators $|^n$, $|_n$ for each natural number n. The rules for $|^n$ ensure that the left component proceeds no more than n+1 steps: each time it makes a move the superscript is reduced

* This work was supported by an SERC grant
** On leave from Istituto di Matematica, Universita di Genova, Italy.

[Su] Sudborough, I.H. On the tape complexity of deterministic context-free languages, *J. ACM* 25, 3(July 1978), 405-414.

[Va] Valiant, L.G. Completeness classes in algebra, *Proc. 11th ACM STOC* (1979), 249-261.

[VSBR] Valiant, L.G., Skyum, S., Berkowitz, S. and Rackoff, C. Fast parallel computation on polynomials using few processors. Preprint. Preliminary version in *Springer Lecture Notes in Computer Science*, 118(1981), 132-139.

[Vi] Vishkin, U. Synchronous parallel computation - a survey. Preprint, Courant Institute, New York University (1983).

[W] Wilson, C. Preprint (1982).

by 1 until it reaches 0. At this point it makes a move and then a random choice is made as to the maximum number of steps the right hand component may move via the operator $|_n$. Plotkin shows that the set of execution sequences generated by his rules coincide with a two level approach [ibid]. This method is not without problems. The auxiliary parallel operators simulate a fair parallel operator rather than describe it because of the involvement of predictive choice [M2]. This forcing of choice in advance has the consequence that under some definitions of program equivalence the parallel operator is not associative [CS2]. In this paper we offer an alternative single level approach.

Standard operational semantics are based upon rules which show how programs may proceed in a single step. Single step, here, is tied to some notion of atomic action - for instance, an assignment or an evaluation of a boolean in the case of an imperative language. Given this, it is difficult to see how one can offer rules for a parallel operator which explicitly ensure that both components proceed (if they can) without, at the same time, enforcing (a version of strict) synchrony. A central feature of our approach, which, in part, overcomes this, is to offer rules for sequences of single steps. In the case of rules for the parallel operator we make use of a finite merge operator: if two components can each proceed a sequence of steps then in parallel they can proceed any sequence which is a merge of the component sequences. Our definition of merge allows for communication. Unfortunately, this simple-minded approach does not, by itself, generate all the fair sequences. A (very weak) form of synchrony is still presupposed. To overcome this we give rules which involve two transition relations. One gives rise to all execution sequences without regard to fairness: the other gives rise only to the fair sequences. The trick is that the fair relation is defined using the other relation. It is this which provides the flexibility required to generate all the fair sequences. We show that a two level approach and our approach agree upon the set of fair execution sequences.

The language we use is Milner's CCS without value passing, restriction and renaming [M1]. The last feature is omitted merely for convenience: it can be accommodated without problem. The other pair require refinement of our tools. In particular, restriction not only introduces those complications, mentioned earlier, which arise if a component cannot always proceed autonomously, but also requires an explicit use of labelling in the rules. Here labelling is only needed for the definition of fairness. We shall consider restriction and the different definitions of fairness which may arise because of it elsewhere. Our approach also appears to work for the concurrent guarded command language which Plotkin uses. We compare his approach with ours in [CS2]. Our method, therefore, seems to be robust enough to deal with concurrent languages based on communication and those based on shared variables.

In section 1 we describe CCS and define the set of fair execution sequences using a two level method. (Familiarity with CCS is not required.) In section 2 we offer our calculus and show that the fair relation gives rise to the set of fair execution sequences as defined in section 1. Proofs are omitted: they appear in the more comprehensive version [CS1].

1. The Two Level Approach

The two level method of characterizing fair execution sequences is illustrated for Milner's CCS without renaming, restriction and value passing [M1]. Expressions of the language stand for processes. The semantics of a process is its behaviour, a behaviour determined by the rules of the calculus.

The Language

Let Act = $\Delta \cup \bar{\Delta}$ be a set of atomic actions where $\bar{\Delta}$ is a set of co-actions disjoint from Δ and in bijection with it. The bijection is $\bar{}$: $\bar{a} \in \bar{\Delta}$ stands for the co-action of $a \in \Delta$. Using $\bar{}$ for the inverse means a is also the co-action of $\bar{a}$. The calculus allows synchronization of co-actions. The set of single moves is Move = Act $\cup \{\tau\} \cup \{(a\bar{a})$: a and $\bar{a}$ are co-actions$\}$: τ stands for a silent (or internal) action and $(a\bar{a})$ for a (handshake) communication. We assume throughout that $(a\bar{a})$ is an unordered pair. Milner uses τ to represent a communication: we don't for reasons explained below. We let a,b,c range over Act; m,n over Move; and we let X,Y,Z be process variables. The syntax of the language is:

$$E ::= X \mid NIL \mid a\,E \mid \tau\,E \mid E+E \mid fix\ X.E \mid E|E$$

NIL is the nullary process which does nothing; + represents nondeterministic choice; $|$ concurrency; and fix recursion. A restriction on the language is that in the expression fix X.E X is guarded in E: that is, every free occurrence of X in E is within a subexpression g F of E where $g \in$ Act $\cup \{\tau\}$.

Rules and Derivations

The behaviour of a process E is determined by the following rules where $E \xrightarrow{m} F$ means E becomes F by performing the move m:

Move $\quad g\,E \xrightarrow{g} E \quad g \in Act \cup \{\tau\}$

+R $\quad \dfrac{E \xrightarrow{m} E'}{E+F \xrightarrow{m} E'} \qquad$ +L $\quad \dfrac{F \xrightarrow{m} F'}{E+F \xrightarrow{m} F'}$

fix $\quad \dfrac{E[fix\ X.E/X] \xrightarrow{m} E'}{fix\ X.E \xrightarrow{m} E'} \quad$ where $[\cdot/.]$ denotes substitution

$|$R $\quad \dfrac{E \xrightarrow{m} E'}{E|F \xrightarrow{m} E'|F} \qquad |$L $\quad \dfrac{F \xrightarrow{m} F'}{E|F \xrightarrow{m} E|F'} \qquad |$Com $\quad \dfrac{E \xrightarrow{a} E' \quad F \xrightarrow{\bar{a}} F'}{E|F \xrightarrow{(a\bar{a})} E'|F'}$

For an explanation of the rules see [M1]. However, two points are worth mentioning here. First, situations arise where the + rules do not allow choice: a E + NIL can only move to E by performing a. Secondly, the $|$ rules do not compel communication: a NIL$|\bar{a}$ NIL can move to NIL$|\bar{a}$ NIL by performing a and to a NIL$|$NIL by performing $\bar{a}$ as well as to NIL|NIL by performing ($a\bar{a}$).

A derivation is any sequence $E_0 \xrightarrow{m_1} E_1 \xrightarrow{m_2} \ldots$. An execution sequence is a maximal derivation. We let h,k,l range over finite sequences of moves. If $E_0 \xrightarrow{m_1} E_1 \xrightarrow{m_2} \ldots \xrightarrow{m_n} E_n$ we write $E_0 \xrightarrow{h} E_n$ where $h = m_1 m_2 \ldots m_n \in$ Move*. Example derivations are:

i. (a NIL + $\bar{b}$ τ NIL)| b NIL $\xrightarrow{(\bar{b}b)}$ τ NIL|NIL $\xrightarrow{\tau}$ NIL|NIL

ii. fix X.aX|fix X.aX $\xrightarrow{a}$ fix X.aX|fix X.aX $\xrightarrow{a}$ fix X.aX|fix X.aX

iii. ((fix X.aX|fix Y.bY)|fix Z.$\bar{a}$Z)|fix X.$\bar{b}$X $\xrightarrow{(a\bar{a})}$ ((fix X.ax|fix Y.bY)|fix Z.$\bar{a}$Z)| fix X.$\bar{b}$X

The first of these is also an execution sequence. Example ii is ambiguous: it is left undetermined which fix X.aX makes an a move at each step. Example iii is ambiguous in Milner's calculus where τ is used for a communication. It is essential to the discussion of fairness to know which subprocesses contribute to a move. Ambiguities are dissolved if the proof of the derivation is included. (For example, the proof of each move of example ii either uses the |R or the |L rule, thus, showing which side of the | a comes from.) But we have found it simpler to use a labelling and to use ($a\bar{a}$) for a communication. For any expression E and g ∈ Act ∪ {τ} distinct occurences of g in E receive different labels. This unique labelling is preserved by substitution: variable occurrences are also labelled (except for X in the binder fix X) and substituted expressions inherit the label of the variable occurrences they replace. Moreover, it is preserved by derivation: if E has a unique labelling and $E \xrightarrow{m} F$ then so has F. The labelling is only required for fairness. The calculus is unaffected because we assume that ($a_s \bar{a}_r$) is a communication and X_s can be bound to fix X irrespective of the labels r and s. The machinery for labelling is given in [CS1] and the following unicity lemma is a consequence of it:

Lemma 1.1 if $E \xrightarrow{m} G$ and $E \xrightarrow{m} H$ then G = H.

The concatenation of h,k ∈ Move* is denoted by hk. Their merge h ⊗ k is inductively defined as a subset of Move* where ε stands for the empty sequence:

mh ⊗ nk = {ml|l ∈ h ⊗ nk} ∪ {nl|l ∈ mh ⊗ k} ∪ {(mn)l|l ∈ h ⊗ k and m,n are co-actions}
ε ⊗ h = h = h ⊗ ε

We now state some lemmas about CCS. The first two are trivial. The second two are proved by induction on the lengths of h_i and h. Because of the labelling h_1, h_2, F_1 and F_2 of Lemma 1.5 are uniquely determined. Lemma 1.6 is proved by induction on the structure of E.

Lemma 1.2 if h ≠ ε then $E_1 + E_2 \xrightarrow{h} F$ iff $E_1 \xrightarrow{h} F$ or $E_2 \xrightarrow{h} F$.

Lemma 1.3 if h ≠ ε then fix X.E $\xrightarrow{h}$ F iff E[fix X.E/X] $\xrightarrow{h}$ F.

Lemma 1.4 (Synthesis of |)
If $E_i \xrightarrow{h_i} F_i$, i=1 and 2, then $E_1|E_2 \xrightarrow{h} F_1|F_2$ ∀h ∈ $h_1 \otimes h_2$.

Lemma 1.5 (Analysis of |)

If $E_1|E_2 \xrightarrow{h} F$ then $\exists h_1 h_2 F_1 F_2 . h \in h_1 \otimes h_2$ and $E_i \xrightarrow{h_i} F_i$ i=1,2 and $F = F_1|F_2$.

Lemma 1.6 fix X.E $\xrightarrow{m}$ G iff E $\xrightarrow{m}$ F and G = F[fix X.E/X].

Liveness and Immediacy

A process is live just in case it can make a move: a E is live whereas NIL + NIL is not. Alternatively, E is live if its set of immediate (or possible) moves is non-empty. This is made precise by defining inductively the set of immediate moves of E, Im(E):

$$\mathrm{Im(NIL)} = \mathrm{Im(X)} = \emptyset \qquad \mathrm{Im(E+F)} = \mathrm{Im(E)} \cup \mathrm{Im(F)}$$

$$\mathrm{Im(g\ E)} = \{g\} \quad g \in \mathrm{Act} \cup \{\tau\} \qquad \mathrm{Im(fix\ X.E)} = \mathrm{Im(E)}$$

$$\mathrm{Im(E|F)} = \mathrm{Im(E)} \cup \mathrm{Im(F)} \cup \{(a\bar{a}) : a \in \mathrm{Im(E)} \wedge \bar{a} \in \mathrm{Im(F)}\}$$

Lemma 1.6 justifies the definition of Im(fix X.E). We define Live(E) as Im(E) ≠ ∅ and Dead(E) as ¬ Live(E). (Note that Live(E) is decidable, for any E, because Im(E) is effective.) A corollary of the following lemma is that Dead(E) just in case E can not make a move. Hence, a finite maximal derivation - a finite execution sequence - always ends in a process which is dead.

Lemma 1.7 m ∈ Im(E) iff ∃F.E $\xrightarrow{m}$ F.

And from Lemma 1.1 we know that here F is unique.

The rules of the calculus imply that an immediate move loses its immediacy either by actually happening or because another move happens which is an alternative to it. For example, b loses its immediacy because it is an alternative to a in a E + b F $\xrightarrow{a}$ E and a and $\bar{a}$ lose theirs in $\bar{a}$ E|a F $\xrightarrow{(\bar{a}a)}$ E|F because they are alternatives to the move $(\bar{a}a)$. Despite this we have defined Im(F + G) and Im(F|G) using set union even though this means that, in general, Im(E) will contain mutually exclusive moves. The trick is that when E $\xrightarrow{h}$ F, Im(E) ∩ Im(F) only includes those moves in Im(E) which could still happen when E has become F: the moves in Im(E) which are alternative to those in h have disappeared. Once the immediacy of a move is lost it is never regained. (Note that these comments and the three lemmas below depend upon the labelling.) This is proved in Lemmas 1.8 and 1.9. Lemma 1.10 is a corollary of 1.9. These last two lemmas are important to the discussion of fairness in the next section.

Lemma 1.8 if E $\xrightarrow{h}$ F and $h = m_1 \ldots m_n$ then $\mathrm{Im(F)} \cap \{m_1, \ldots, m_n\} = \emptyset$.

Lemma 1.9 if E $\xrightarrow{h}$ F $\xrightarrow{k}$ G then Im(E) ∩ Im(G) ⊆ Im(E) ∩ Im(F).

Lemma 1.10 if E $\xrightarrow{h}$ F $\xrightarrow{k}$ G and Im(G) ∩ Im(F) = ∅ then Im(E) ∩ Im(G) = ∅ .

Fairness

A desirable constraint on an execution sequence of a process involving concurrent live subprocesses is that they proceed: each such subprocess eventually moves. But the rules of the calculus fail to enforce this fairness condition. An example is the sequence $E \xrightarrow{a} E \xrightarrow{a} \ldots \xrightarrow{a} E \xrightarrow{a} \ldots$ where E is fix X.aX|b NIL. The live subprocess b NIL fails to make a move: the (occurrence of the) move b remains immediate (or possible). More generally, an execution sequence γ is unfair if (an occurrence of) a move becomes immediate and remains so throughout the rest of γ. Clearly, then, any immediate move arising in γ must eventually lose its immediacy for γ to be fair. In the derivation $E \xrightarrow{h} F$ the immediate moves of E, Im(E), have lost their immediacy whenever $Im(E) \cap Im(F) = \emptyset$. Lemma 1.11 says there is always such a derivation from E when it is live. Here the labelling is essential: if E is $a_r\ b_s$ NIL|b_t NIL and $E \xrightarrow{a_r b_t} F = b_s$ NIL|NIL then $Im(E) \cap Im(F) = \emptyset$. Without labels this would not be true.

Lemma 1.11 $\exists h,F.\ E \xrightarrow{h} F$ and $Im(E) \cap Im(F) = \emptyset$.

This motivates the following definition of fair execution sequence:

Definition 1.12 Let $\gamma = E_1 \xrightarrow{m_1} E_2 \xrightarrow{m_2} \ldots E_n \xrightarrow{m_n} ..$ be an execution sequence then:

i) γ is fair at i if $\exists j \geq i \forall k \geq j\ \ Im(E_i) \cap Im(E_k) = \emptyset$

ii) γ is fair if $\forall i\ \gamma$ is fair at i

As a result of Lemma 1.9 clause i) of this definition is equivalent to i'):

i') γ is fair at i if $\exists j \geq i. Im(E_i) \cap Im(E_j) = \emptyset$

(This shows that no distinction is to be made here between so-called weak and strong fairness.) A consequence of the definition is that a finite execution sequence is fair because, as we have seen, it must end in a dead process, a process F where $Im(F)=\emptyset$.

Armed with this definition the unfair execution sequences can be disallowed by fiat. This is tantamount to an additional semantic level over and above the rules of the calculus, a filter which precludes the unfair sequences. A theoretically neater solution is to adjust the rules of the calculus so that only the fair sequences are derivable.

2. A Single Level Approach

Unfair sequences are derivable because of the |R and |L rules above. In effect, a use of either of these rules in a derivation involves an enforced delay of one or other of the subprocesses E,F in E|F. And from small enforced delays lengthier delays can grow without limit: if either E or F has an infinite behaviour then there is nothing in the rules to force the other to proceed (when it is live).

A method of controlling the length of delay is to simulate a finite delay restriction using random assignment. Plotkin introduces a subsidiary set of parallel operators $|^n$, $|_n$ in the case of a guarded command language {P}: the rules for $|^n$ ensure that the left subprocess proceeds for (at most) $n+1$ moves; a choice is then made as to the maximum number of moves that the right process can make via the operator $|_n$. This method is not entirely free of problems. It is more a simulation than a description because finite delay is achieved by attributing predictive choice [M2]. This forcing of choice in advance has the consequence that under some definitions of program equivalence the parallel operator is not associative [CS2].

Towards a Fair Calculus

An alternative method is to give rules for | which ensure that both subprocesses proceed if they are live. An example rule is:

$$\frac{E \xrightarrow{m} E' \quad F \xrightarrow{m'} F'}{E|F \xrightarrow{h} E'|F'} \quad \text{for any } h \in m \otimes m'$$

But this rule imposes a strong form of synchrony: it completely prejudges the relative speed of movement of each concurrent live subprocess. An attempt to loosen this synchrony is to formalize $\xrightarrow{h}$ as the basic transition relation:

$$\frac{E \xrightarrow{h} E' \quad F \xrightarrow{h'} F'}{E|F \xrightarrow{k} E'|F'} \quad \text{for any } k \in h \otimes h' \text{ where } h \text{ and } h' \text{ are not } \varepsilon$$

Both subprocesses are forced to proceed without prejudice to their relative rates. Unfortunately, this rule (even if complemented by rules to cover the case when one of the subprocesses is not live) still imposes a weak form of synchrony which prevents the derivation of certain fair infinite sequences [CS1]. A further weakening is necessary. Our solution suggested by Matthew Hennessy is to formalize a calculus with two transition relations $\overset{h}{\Rightarrow}$ and $\overset{h}{\dashrightarrow}$, $h \in Move^+$. The necessary weakening results from their interaction. $E \overset{h}{\Rightarrow} F$ is always a fair derivation (or fair step) in the sense that $Im(E) \cap Im(F) = \emptyset$ - c.f. Definition 1.12 part i'. On the other hand $E \overset{h}{\dashrightarrow} F$ is a potentially unfair derivation, or better a derivation without regard to fairness. In fact $\overset{h}{\dashrightarrow}$ is formalized to coincide with $\xrightarrow{h}$ $(h \neq \varepsilon)$ of the previous section. (This is not the only option.)

The Rules

We assume the same method of labelling as in section 1. As before the rules of the calculus do not depend upon the labelling although, again as before, the discussion of fairness does. (The situation is different when restriction is included in the language: a labelled calculus is then necessary.) The calculus consists of two kinds of rules U (potentially unfair) and F (fair) rules. The merge operator $\otimes$ is as before. The boxed rules are redundant because of lemma 2.4 below and the remaining rules. They are included to show that all possibilities are covered: but we assume they are not part of the calculus.

U-Rules		F-rules	
UMove	$g\ E \xrightarrow{g} E$ $g \in Act \cup \{\tau\}$	FMove	$g\ E \xRightarrow{g} E$ $g \in Act \cup \{\tau\}$

U+R $\dfrac{E \xrightarrow{h} E'}{E+F \xrightarrow{h} E'}$ F+R $\dfrac{E \xRightarrow{h} E'}{E+F \xRightarrow{h} E'}$

U+L $\dfrac{F \xrightarrow{h} F'}{E+F \xrightarrow{h} F'}$ F+L $\dfrac{F \xRightarrow{h} F'}{E+F \xRightarrow{h} F'}$

Ufix $\dfrac{E[fix\ X.E/X] \xrightarrow{h} E'}{fix\ X.E \xrightarrow{h} E'}$ Ffix $\dfrac{E[fix\ X.E/X] \xRightarrow{h} E'}{fix\ X.E \xRightarrow{h} E'}$

U|R $\dfrac{E \xrightarrow{h} E'}{E|F \xrightarrow{h} E'|F}$ F|R $\dfrac{E \xRightarrow{h} E' \quad Dead(F)}{E|F \xRightarrow{h} E'|F}$

U|L $\dfrac{F \xrightarrow{h} F'}{E|F \xrightarrow{h} E|F'}$ F|L $\dfrac{F \xRightarrow{h} F' \quad Dead(E)}{E|F \xRightarrow{h} E|F'}$

U| $\dfrac{E \xrightarrow{h} E' \quad F \xrightarrow{h'} F'}{E|F \xrightarrow{k} E'|F'}$ for any $k \in h \otimes h'$ F| $\dfrac{E \xRightarrow{h} E' \quad F \xRightarrow{h'} F'}{E|F \xRightarrow{k} E'|F'}$ for any $k \in h \otimes h'$

Utrans $\dfrac{E \xrightarrow{h} E' \quad E' \xrightarrow{k} F}{E \xrightarrow{hk} F}$ ⌐‾‾‾‾‾‾‾‾‾‾‾‾‾‾‾‾‾‾‾¬
Ftrans $\dfrac{E \xRightarrow{h} E' \quad E' \xRightarrow{k} F}{E \xRightarrow{hk} F}$
⌐‾‾‾‾‾‾‾‾‾‾‾‾‾‾‾‾‾‾‾‾‾‾‾‾‾‾‾‾‾‾‾‾‾‾‾¬

U|1 $\dfrac{E \xRightarrow{h} E' \quad F \xrightarrow{h'} F'}{E|F \xrightarrow{k} E'|F'}$ for any $k \in h \otimes h'$

U|2 $\dfrac{E \xrightarrow{h} E' \quad F \xRightarrow{h'} F'}{E|F \xrightarrow{k} E'|F'}$ for any $k \in h \otimes h'$
⌐‾‾‾‾‾‾‾‾‾‾‾‾‾‾‾‾‾‾‾‾‾‾‾‾‾‾‾‾‾‾‾‾‾‾‾¬

Ftrans1 $\dfrac{E \xRightarrow{h} E' \quad E' \xrightarrow{k} F}{E \xRightarrow{hk} F}$

Frans2 $\dfrac{E \xrightarrow{h} E' \quad E' \xRightarrow{k} F}{E \xRightarrow{hk} F}$

Some example derivations are now given.   In examples i,ii and iii the underlying arrow shows that the two moves above it can be made in a single step using the trans rules. The alternative arrows of example vi represent different derivation possibilities.

i. a b NIL $\xrightarrow{a}$ b NIL $\xrightarrow{b}$ NIL
$\overset{ab}{\text{-------->}}$

ii. a b NIL $\xRightarrow{a}$ b NIL $\xrightarrow{b}$ NIL
$\overset{ab}{\longrightarrow}$

iii. a b NIL $\xrightarrow{a}$ b NIL $\xRightarrow{b}$ NIL
$\overset{ab}{\longrightarrow}$

iv. a E|NIL $\xRightarrow{a}$ E|NIL

v. a E|b F $\xrightarrow{a}$ E|b F   but   a E|b F $\xRightarrow{a}\!\!\!\!\!/$ E|b F

vi. a b NIL|c d NIL $\overset{ac}{\xRightarrow{\quad}}$ b NIL|d NIL $\xRightarrow{bd}$ NIL|NIL
$\overset{acd}{\xRightarrow{\quad}}$ b NIL|NIL $\xRightarrow{b}$ NIL|NIL

vii. a b NIL|c d NIL $\overset{cdab}{\xRightarrow{\quad\quad}}$ NIL|NIL

There are two kinds of rules: those only involving a single type of transition relation and those involving both. $\Rightarrow$ depends on $\dashrightarrow$ because of the two fair trans rules whereas $\dashrightarrow$ is 'self-contained'. In fact, theorem 2.3 shows that the set of rules only involving $\dashrightarrow$ formalizes the transitive closure of the calculus of the previous section.

The move rules are similar to the previous calculus as shown by examples i,ii and iii. $g\ E \stackrel{g}{\Rightarrow} E$ is a fair derivation because $Im(g\ E) \cap Im(E) = \emptyset$. We let $g\ E \stackrel{g}{\dashrightarrow} E$ also be a derivation because, as noted, our aim is that $\stackrel{h}{\dashrightarrow}$ and $\stackrel{h}{\rightarrow}$ ($h \neq \varepsilon$) coincide. The fair and potentially unfair + and fix rules are transitive closure correlates of the previous calculus - c.f. lemmas 1.2 and 1.3. The U|R and U|L rules have potentially unfair consequents because they do not force the subprocesses to proceed. These two rules distinguish the two transition relations. Their fair correlates F|R and F|L can only be applied if one of the subprocesses is dead as in example iv. This means that $\Rightarrow$ is more restrictive than $\dashrightarrow$ as is shown by example v: the calculus does not allow as a derivation $a\ E|b\ F \stackrel{a}{\Rightarrow} E|b\ F$. Uses of the other parallel rules are contained in examples vi and vii. Note that either transition relation could be used for any of the moves. These examples bring out some of the possibilities allowed by the merge operator : for instance, vii can be inferred as follows

$$\text{F}|\ \frac{\text{Ftrans 2}\ \dfrac{a\ b\ NIL \stackrel{a}{\dashrightarrow} b\ NIL \stackrel{b}{\Rightarrow} NIL}{a\ b\ NIL \stackrel{ab}{\Longrightarrow} NIL} \qquad \dfrac{c\ d\ NIL \stackrel{c}{\Rightarrow} d\ NIL \stackrel{d}{\dashrightarrow} NIL}{c\ d\ NIL \stackrel{cd}{\Longrightarrow} NIL}\ \text{Ftrans 1}}{a\ b\ NIL\ |\ c\ d\ NIL \stackrel{cdab}{\Longrightarrow} NIL|NIL}$$

An alternative conclusion here would be $a\ b\ NIL|c\ d\ NIL \stackrel{acdb}{\Longrightarrow} NIL|NIL$: both cdab and acdb belong to $ab \otimes cd$.

The trans rules formalize explicitly transitive closure. The Utrans rule is clear: example i is an instance of its use. It is the other two trans rules which are central to the calculus. They allow fair derivations to be inferred from a mixture of fair and potentially unfair derivations. Given the connections between $\stackrel{h}{\Rightarrow}$, $\stackrel{h}{\dashrightarrow}$ and $\stackrel{h}{\rightarrow}$ Ftrans 1 is justified by lemma 1.9: $Im(E) \cap Im(F) \subseteq Im(E) \cap Im(E')$ when $E \stackrel{h}{\Rightarrow} E' \stackrel{k}{\dashrightarrow} F$: because $E \stackrel{h}{\Rightarrow} E'$ then $Im(E) \cap Im(E') = \emptyset$. The fair consequent, therefore, follows. Example ii illustrates its use. Similarly, Ftrans2 is justified by lemma 1.10. If $Im(E') \cap Im(F) = \emptyset$ and $E \stackrel{h}{\dashrightarrow} E' \stackrel{k}{\Rightarrow} F$ then $Im(E) \cap Im(F) = \emptyset$. This means that $E \stackrel{hk}{\Longrightarrow} F$. Example iii illustrates this.

The boxed rules are redundant because $\stackrel{h}{\Rightarrow}$ is contained in $\stackrel{h}{\dashrightarrow}$ (lemma 2.4): that is, whenever $E \stackrel{h}{\Rightarrow} E'$ then $E \stackrel{h}{\dashrightarrow} E'$. Consequently, U| makes U|1 and U|2 unnecessary. Similarly, either Ftrans 1 or Ftrans 2 makes Ftrans redundant.

Connections between $\stackrel{h}{\rightarrow}$, $\stackrel{h}{\dashrightarrow}$ and $\stackrel{h}{\Rightarrow}$

Theorem 2.3 says that when $h \neq \varepsilon$ $\stackrel{h}{\rightarrow}$ and $\stackrel{h}{\dashrightarrow}$ coincide. One half of this result is given by lemma 2.2. Its proof is by induction on the depth of the inference of (the derivation) $E \stackrel{h}{\dashrightarrow} F$. The other half directly follows from lemma 2.1 (whose proof is obvious) and the UTrans rule.

Lemma 2.1 $E \overset{m}{\longrightarrow} F$ iff $E \overset{m}{\dashrightarrow} F$.

Lemma 2.2 if $E \overset{h}{\dashrightarrow} F$ then $E \overset{h}{\longrightarrow} F$.

Theorem 2.3 if $h \neq \varepsilon$ then $E \overset{h}{\longrightarrow} F$ iff $E \overset{h}{\dashrightarrow} F$

Lemma 2.4 (whose proof is obvious) says that $\overset{h}{\Longrightarrow}$ is a subset of $\overset{h}{\dashrightarrow}$. An obvious corollary, given lemma 2.2, is that $\overset{h}{\Longrightarrow}$ is also contained in $\overset{h}{\longrightarrow}$. Recall that a live process can always make a fair sequence of moves (lemma 1.11). Lemma 2.5 is the correlate of this for the fair relation $\overset{h}{\Longrightarrow}$. This result follows from lemma 1.11 and lemma 2.6 below.

Lemma 2.4 if $E \overset{h}{\Longrightarrow} F$ then $E \overset{h}{\dashrightarrow} F$.

Lemma 2.5 if Live(E) then $\exists F,h.\ E \overset{h}{\Longrightarrow} F$.

We now come to the main result of the paper that $\overset{h}{\Longrightarrow}$ characterizes fairness.

The Main Result

Recall that the definition of Im(E) did not appeal to the rules of the calculus. This means that it can be carried over to the present calculus. The situation is different in the case of the definition of fairness only because of its appeal to single moves. However both $\overset{h}{\dashrightarrow}$ and $\overset{h}{\Longrightarrow}$ are contained in $\overset{h}{\longrightarrow}$, and $E \overset{h}{\longrightarrow} F$ means that if $h = m_1 \ldots m_i$ then $\exists E_1 \ldots E_{i-1} (E \overset{m_1}{\longrightarrow} E_1 \overset{m_2}{\longrightarrow} \ldots \overset{m_{i-1}}{\longrightarrow} E_{i-1} \overset{m_i}{\longrightarrow} F)$. Moreover, by lemma 1.1 , we know that each of these E_is is uniquely determined. Consequently, associated with $E \overset{h}{\Longrightarrow} F$ or $E \overset{h}{\dashrightarrow} F$ is a unique derivation $E \overset{m_1}{\longrightarrow} \ldots \overset{m_i}{\longrightarrow} F$. More generally, associated with each execution sequence γ involving $\Longrightarrow$ and $\dashrightarrow$ there is a unique sequence γ' involving $\overset{m}{\longrightarrow}$, $m \in$ Move. Consequently, we can say that <u>an execution sequence arising from the present calculus is fair if its associated sequence is.</u>

An execution sequence involving only the transition $\Longrightarrow$ is fair. This is part ii of theorem 2.8. The proof follows from lemma 2.7 and the properties of Im (notably lemma 1.10). The other half of the theorem states the converse result. More precisely, it says that given any fair execution sequence γ' using $\overset{m}{\longrightarrow}$, $m \in$ Move, we can then construct an execution sequence γ involving only $\Longrightarrow$ whose associated sequence is γ'. The construction is straightforward from lemma 2.6. Pictorially:

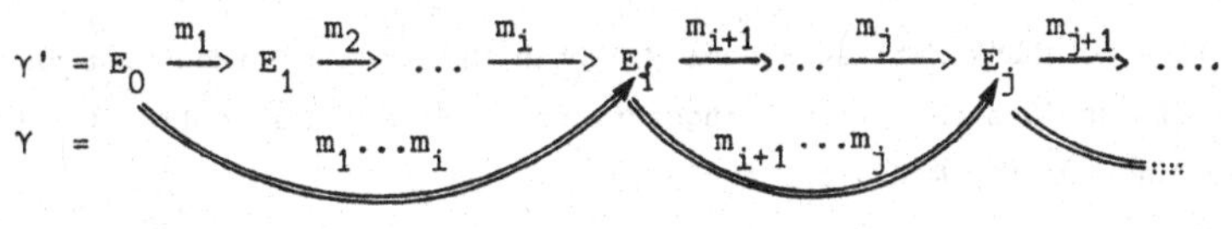
γ' = E0 —m1—> E1 —m2—> ... —mi—> Ei —mi+1—>... —mj—> Ej —mj+1—> ....
γ =
m1...mi
mi+1...mj

where $Im(E_0) \cap Im(E_i) = \emptyset$, $Im(E_i) \cap Im(E_j) = \emptyset$ and etc.

The proofs of the following two lemmas are by induction on the depths of the inferences of the derivations. (In the case of lemma 2.6 the depth of the inference of

$E \xrightarrow{h} F$ is the sum of the depths of the inferences of the single moves.)

Lemma 2.6 if $E \xrightarrow{h} F$ and $Im(E) \cap Im(F) = \emptyset$ then $E \overset{h}{\Longrightarrow} F$ or Dead(E).

Lemma 2.7 if $E \overset{h}{\Longrightarrow} F$ then $Im(E) \cap Im(F) = \emptyset$.

Theorem 2.8 (the fairness theorem).

i. if $E_1 \xrightarrow{m_1} E_2 \xrightarrow{m_2} \ldots E_i \xrightarrow{m_i} \ldots$ is a fair execution sequence then $\exists j_1 \ldots j_k \ldots$ such that $E_{j_1} = E_1 \overset{h_1}{\Longrightarrow} E_{j_2} \overset{h_2}{\Longrightarrow} \ldots$ and $h_i = m_{j_i} \ldots m_{j_{i+1}-1}$

ii. Any execution sequence $E_1 \overset{h_1}{\Longrightarrow} E_2 \Rightarrow \ldots \overset{h_{i-1}}{\Longrightarrow} E_i \overset{h_i}{\Longrightarrow} \ldots$ is fair.

This theorem shows that the set of all and only the fair sequences can be generated using the rules of the calculus.

Conclusion

We have contrasted a two level operational approach to fairness with a single level approach. The latter involves presenting a set of rules which generate all and only the fair execution sequences of a concurrent language. This we have done for a subset of Milner's CCS. (In a more comprehensive version of this paper we give more details together with proofs of the lemmas and theorems [CS1].) The method presented here is, however, more general. In later work we shall consider a more interesting subset of CCS, a subset which allows distinctions to be made between different notions of fairness. Moreover, the method appears to work for a concurrent guarded command language [CS2].

A task ahead of us is to consider what kind of equivalences can be deduced from our CCS rules. In particular, we wish to contrast 'fair equivalences' with standard ones as presented in [M1]. We hope that this work will connect up with Milner's approach to fairness [M2,H].

A second area of development is to connect our method with a tense logical approach. Fairness can be clearly expressed in tense logic [GPSS]. However, when analysing concurrent programs it is standard practice to assume fairness as an additional tense logical axiom. This attitude is akin to the two level method. We hope to develop tense logics where (formulas expressing) fairness can be derived rather than assumed.

Acknowledgements

We would like to thank Matthew Hennessy, Robin Milner and Gordon Plotkin for many illuminating discussions and helpful suggestions. We would also like to thank Eleanor Kerse and Dorothy McKie for typing.

References

[AO] K. Apt and E. Olderog. 'Proof rules dealing with fairness'. Bericht Nr. 8104, Inst. für Informatik und Praktische Mathematik, Kiel University (1981).

[CS1] G. Costa and C. Stirling. 'A fair calculus of communicating systems'. To appear.

[CS2] G. Costa and C. Stirling. 'Fair rules for a concurrent guarded command language'. In preparation.

[GPSS] D. Gabbay, A. Pnueli, S. Shelah and J. Stavi. 'On the temporal analysis of fairness'. Proc. 7th ACM POPL, Las Vegas (1980).

[H] M. Hennessy. 'Axiomatising finite delay operators'. Technical Report CSR-124-82, Dept. of Computer Science, Edinburgh University (1982).

[LPS] D. Lehmann, A. Pnueli and J. Stavi. 'Impartiality, justice and fairness: the ethics of concurrent termination'. LNCS 115, pp. 264-77, Springer-Verlag (1981).

[M1] R. Milner. 'A Calculus of Communicating Systems'. LNCS 92, Springer-Verlag (1980).

[M2] R. Milner. 'A finite delay operator in synchronous CCS'. Technical Report CSR-116-82, Dept. of Computer Science, Edinburgh University (1982).

[OL] S. Owicki and L. Lamport. 'Proving liveness properties of concurrent programs'. Technical Report, SRI International (1980).

[Pa] D. Park. 'On the semantics of fair parallelism'. LNCS 86, pp. 504-26, Springer-Verlag (1980).

[P] G. Plotkin. 'A powerdomain for countable non-determinism'. LNCS 140, pp. 418-28, Springer-Verlag (1982).

TWO WAY FINITE STATE GENERATORS[1)]

Karel Culik II[2)] and Emmerich Welzl[3)]

INTRODUCTION

A problem for chain code picture languages posed by Maurer, Rozenberg, and Welzl [MRW], motivated the investigation of a device which we call nondeterministic two-way finite state generator. It has a writing head with a finite control and an (initially blank) two-way infinite working tape. At each step it writes a symbol into the current cell and moves in either direction. It has no reading capacity which means that that the action depends only on the current state of the finite control. Concerning the writing there are different interpretations some of them are the following: (1) the generator simply overwrites the current symbol under the writing head, (2) every cell contains an initially empty set of symbols (subset of a finite alphabet) and the generator adds a symbol to the set under the writing head (i.e. if the symbol is already in the set, the contents of the cell remains unchanged) and (3) the set of output symbols has a priority hierarchy and if the generator tries to write a symbol a of higher priority than the symbol b at the current position on the tape, then it overwrites this symbol b by a; otherwise it leaves the symbol of higher priority on the tape.

In the next Section we give a formal definition of nondeterministic two-way finite state generators and the three mentioned output interpretations. Then we show for cases (2) and (3) above that the generated languages are regular, i.e. two-way finite state generators generate the same as one-way finite state generators (right-linear grammars, respectively). This corresponds to the result for acceptors, see Sheperdson, [S] for a proof that two-way finite automata accept the same languages as one-way finite automata (a proof is also presented in Harrison, [H]). However, the authors do not see how to carry over the result for acceptors to generators, while the implication in the other direction is not too difficult to show.

DEFINITIONS

A <u>two-way finite state generator</u> is a tuple $G=(Q,\delta,d,q_0,q_f,\Sigma,\mathrm{INT})$ where

(i) Q is a finite nonempty set of <u>states</u>

(ii) $\delta: Q \to 2^Q$ is a <u>transition function</u>, which gives the set of possible next states.

---

1) This work has been done during the first author's visit at the IIG.

2) Department of Computer Science, Univeristy of Waterloo, Waterloo, Canada.

3) Institutes for Information Processing, IIG, Technical University of Graz and Austrian Computer Society, Graz, Austria.

(iii) d: $Q \to 2^{\{-1,0,1\}}$ is a <u>direction function</u>, which indicates whether - being in a state $q \in Q$ - the writing head can move to the right ($1 \in d(q)$), to the left ($-1 \in d(q)$) or can remain in the same position ($0 \in d(q)$) next.

(iv) $q_0 \in Q$: an <u>initial state</u>

(v) $q_f \in Q$: an <u>accepting state</u>

(vi) Σ: a finite <u>output alphabet</u> and, finally,

(vii) INT: $Q^+ \to \Sigma$ an <u>interpretation function</u>.

Using (i)-(v) we define the computations of G, the language generated by G will then be defined using (vi) and (vii).

Computations of a generator G will be described by strings over $(Q\times\mathbb{Z})$[1], where $(q,k) \in Q\times\mathbb{Z}$ stands for "current state: q" and "current position on the tape: k". The <u>move relations</u> $\vdash$ of the computation of a two-way finite state generator is defined as follows: Let $c \in (Q\times\mathbb{Z})^*$, $(q,k) \in Q\times\mathbb{Z}$. Then

$$c(q,k) \vdash c(q,k)(q',k+i)$$

if $q' \in \delta(q)$, $i \in d(q)$. As usual, $\vdash^*$ denotes the reflexive transitive closure of $\vdash$. The set of <u>valid computations</u> of G is defined as

$$\text{comp}(G)=\{c \in (Q\times\mathbb{Z})^* \mid c=(q_0,0)c'(q_f,k) \text{ for some } c',k,(q_0,0) \vdash^* c\}$$

For a valid computation $c \in (Q\times\mathbb{Z})^+$ the <u>leftmost</u> (<u>rightmost</u>) <u>visited position by</u> c, shortly <u>lm</u>(c) (<u>rm</u>(c)), is defined as the minimal (maximal) k, such that c can be written as $c=c_1(q,k)c_2$ for some $c_1,c_2 \in (Q\times\mathbb{Z})^*$, $(q,k) \in (Q\times\mathbb{Z})$.

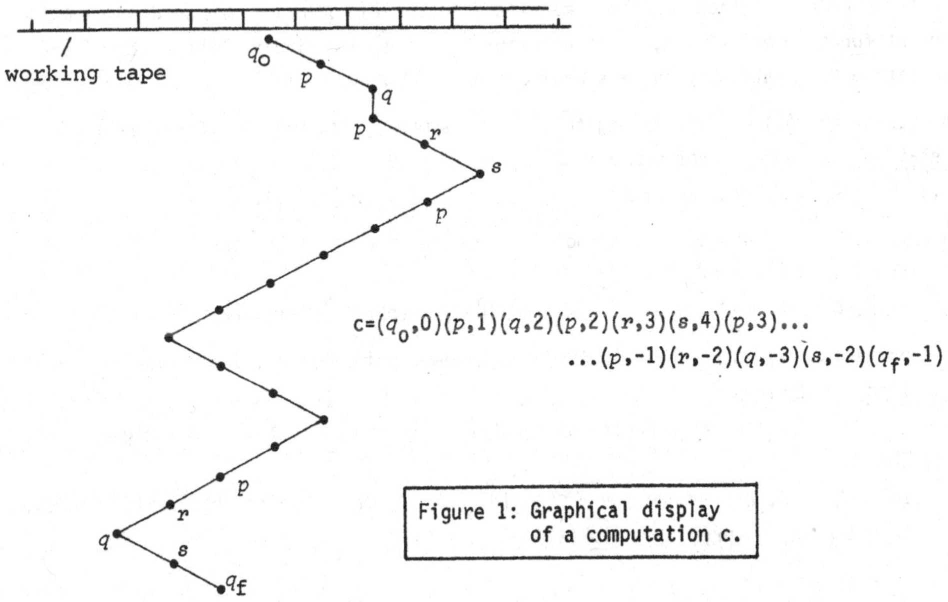

Figure 1: Graphical display of a computation c.

1) $\mathbb{Z}$ denotes the set of integers.

In order to support the reader's intuition for some of the proofs, we sometimes give a graphical display of computations. Figure 1 gives an example of such a representation.

Consider a valid computation. Then at a certain position on the tape, the writing head passes by potentially several times with different states. Let us call this sequence of "passes" the history of this position during the computation. We can describe this history with a string over Q, simply catenating the current state to this string, whenever the writing head passes this position. In order to examine the history of a particular position on the tape, we define for all integers k the history-k-homomorphism $h_k : (Q\times\mathbb{Z})^* \to Q^*$, where for $(q,i) \in (Q\times\mathbb{Z})$

$$h_k(q,i) = \begin{cases} q & \text{if } i=k \\ \lambda & \text{if } i\neq k \end{cases}$$ [1]

In order to specify how a generator defines a language we use the interpretation function INT : $Q^+ \to \Sigma$ which usually will be fixed for a whole class of generators. Intuitively, the interpretation maps the history of every individual cell into the final output symbol written in this cell.

The word generated by some computation c is defined as

$$\underline{\text{word}}(c)=\text{INT}(h_i(c))\text{INT}(h_{i+1}(c))\ldots\text{INT}(h_{j-1}(c))\text{INT}(h_j(c))$$

where $i=\underline{\text{lm}}(c)$ and $j=\underline{\text{rm}}(c)$.

The language defined by a two-way finite state generator G is

$$\underline{\text{lang}}(G)=\{\underline{\text{word}}(c) \mid c \in \underline{\text{comp}}(G)\}.$$

The three interpretation functions mentioned in the introduction can be defined using a print function pr : $Q \to \Delta$, Δ an alphabet, meaning intuitively : the writing head in state $q \in Q$ wants to print a symbol $a \in \Delta$.

Interpretation (1) of overwriting the current symbol in the cell (overwrite-interpretation) is formally defined by:

(1') $\text{INT}_1: Q^+ \to \Sigma$, $\Sigma=\Delta$, where for $w \in Q^*$, $q \in Q$, $\text{INT}_1(wq)=\text{pr}(q)$.

Interpretation (2) of adding a symbol to the current contents of the cell (set-interpretation) is defined by:

(2') $\text{INT}_2: Q^+ \to \Sigma$, $\Sigma=2^\Delta$, where for $w \in Q^+$, $\text{INT}_2(w)=\{\text{pr}(q) \mid q \in \underline{\text{alph}}(w)\}$.[2]

Interpretation (3) where the symbol of the highest priority survives (priority-interpretation) is defined by:

Let $\Delta=(a_1,a_2,\ldots a_n)$ be an ordering of Δ, where $1\leq i<j\leq n$ means that a_j has higher priority than a_i.

(3') $\text{INT}_3: Q^+ \to \Sigma$, $\Sigma=\Delta$, where for $w \in Q^+$ $\text{INT}_3(w)=a_i$, with i being the greatest index, such that $a_i \in \{\text{pr}(q) \mid q \in \underline{\text{alph}}(w)\}$.

---

1) λ denotes the empty string.

2) alph(w) denotes the set of symbols which occur in w .

SET- AND PRIORITY-INTERPRETATIONS YIELD REGULAR LANGUAGES

In what follows (except for our last Corollary) we consider only two-way finite state generators with set-interpretation. More specifically, we consider the output alphabet always to be the set of nonempty subsets of the set of states Q, and $INT_\alpha : Q^+ \to 2^Q$, where for $w \in Q^+$, $INT_\alpha(w)=$alph(w). Additionally, we will put some restrictions on the direction function: A two-way finite state generator $G=(Q,\delta,d,q_0,q_f,\Sigma,INT)$ is called direction deterministic if (i) $|d(q)|=1$[1] for all $q \in Q$ and if (ii) for some $q,q_1,q_2 \in Q$, $q \in \delta(q_1)$ and $q \in \delta(q_2)$ then $d(q_1)=d(q_2)$. This means that if the device is in some state q, then the direction of the next move (see(i)) and the direction of the move before (see(ii)) is determined.

We will show that the languages generated by these special generators are always regular. It turns out that the languages obtained by (direction-nondeterministic) generators with general set-interpretation and priority-interpretation can be obtained as homomorphic images of the languages of our special generators treated in the sequel. This will also solve the regularity problem for these interpretations.

From now on let $G=(Q,\delta,d,q_0,q_f,\Sigma,INT_\alpha)$, $\Sigma=2^Q$, be a direction-deterministic two-way finite state generator. Then for some word $x \in \Sigma^+$ we define

$$\text{left}(x)=\{c \in \text{comp}(G)\,|\,\text{word}(c)=xy \text{ for some } y \in \Sigma^*\}.$$

and

$$\text{right}(x)=\{c \in \text{comp}(G)\,|\,\text{word}(c)=yx \text{ for some } y \in \Sigma^*\}.$$

Thus left(x) (right(x)) describes the set of valid computations of G which generate a word with prefix (suffix) x.

Additionally, we need the following notions.

$$\text{lcut}(x)=\{h_k(c) \in Q^*\,|\,c \in \text{left}(x),\ k=\text{lm}(c)+|x|-1\}$$

and

$$\text{rcut}(x)=\{h_k(c) \in Q^*\,|\,c \in \text{right}(x),\ k=\text{rm}(c)-|x|+1\}.$$

Informally, lcut(x) (rcut(x)) contains for all computations in left(x) (right(x)) the history of the position on the tape which carries the last (first) symbol of x.

Observation 1: Let $x,y \in \Sigma^*$, $a \in \Sigma$. Then

$$xay \in \text{lang}(G) \quad \text{iff} \quad \text{lcut}(xa) \cap \text{rcut}(ay) \neq \emptyset.$$

The easy proof of this observation is omitted. Note, however, that the assertion only holds because we consider deterministic direction functions.

In general there are infinitely many different sets lcut(x), $x \in \Sigma^*$. Our goal is to find a simple description, simple(w), of the words w in lcut(x) (and rcut(x)) for $x \in \Sigma^+$ such that (i) we still have a relation:

$$xay \in \text{lang}(G) \text{ iff simple(lcut}(xa) \cap \text{simple(rcut}(ay) \neq \emptyset$$

1) For a set A, |A| denotes the cardmality of A.

and (ii) $\{$simple(lcut(x))$\mid x \in \Sigma^+\}$=$\{$simple(rcut(x))$\mid x \in \Sigma^+\}$ is a finite set. These conditions will be sufficient for regularity of lang(G) due to results on right congruence relations as treated in Nerode, [N].

For a word $w \in \Sigma^+$ the simple description of w, simple(w) for short, is a 4-tuple

$$\text{simple}(w)=(p,q,\{u \in Q^2 \mid \#_u(w)=1\},\{u \in Q^2 \mid \#_u(w)\geq 2\})^{1)}$$

where $p \in Q$ is the first symbol of w and $q \in Q$ is the last symbol of w. For a language $S \subseteq Q^+$ we define simple(S)=$\{$simple(w)$\mid w \in S\}$.

Observation 2: (a) Let $v,w \in Q^+$. If simple(v)=simple(w) then $\text{INT}_\alpha(v)=\text{INT}_\alpha(w)$. (b) Let $x,y \in \Sigma^+$. If simple(lcut(x))=simple(lcut(y)) $\neq \emptyset$ then the last symbol of x and y are the same.

Condition (ii) clearly is satisfied by simple. To show (i) we need some lemmas.

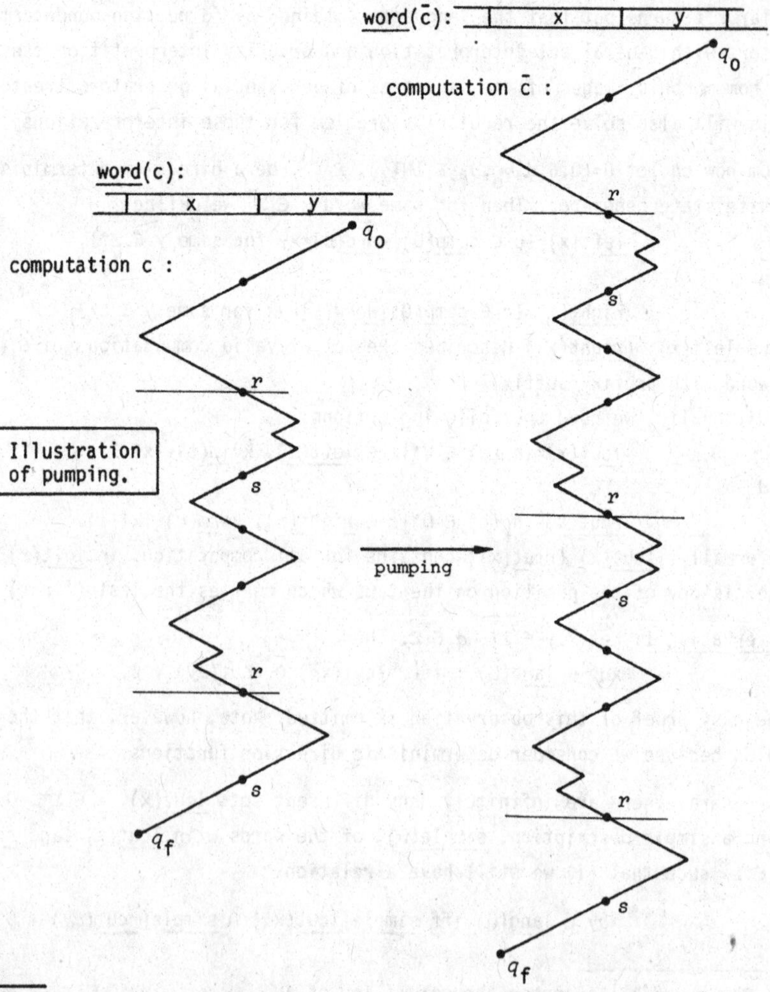

Figure 2: Illustration of pumping.

1) $\#_u(w)$ denotes the number of occurences of the word u as subword in w.

Lemma 3 (pumping): Let $x \in \Sigma^+$ and let $t=(p,q,S_1,S_2)$ be a simple description in simple(lcut(x)). Then for all positive integers m there are words $w_m \in$ lcut(x) such that (a) simple(w_m)=(p,q,S_1',S_2'), where $S_1' \cup S_2'=S_1 \cup S_2$, and (b) for all $u \in S_2$: $\#_u(w_m)\geq m$.

Proof: Let $w \in$ lcut(x), such that simple(w)=(p,q,S_1,S_2). If S_2 is empty, then w satisfies the assertion of the Lemma for all positive integers. If $S_2 \neq \emptyset$, let $w=q_1,q_2\ldots q_n, q_1=p, q_n=q, q_i \in Q, 1\leq i\leq n$. We consider a computation $c \in$ comp(G) such that word(c)=xy for some $y \in \Sigma^*$, and $h_k(c)=w$, for $k=$lm$(c)+|x|-1$. The computation c can be written as

$$c=e_0(q_1,k)e_1(q_2,k)e_2\ldots\ldots e_{n-1}(q_n,k)e_n,$$

where $e_i \in (Q\times(\mathbf{Z}\setminus\{k\}))^*$. Let $u=rs \in S_2, r,s \in Q$. Consequently,

$$c=f_1(r,k)e_i(s,k)f_2(r,k)f_3$$

for some $f_1,f_2,f_3 \in (Q\times\mathbf{Z})^*$, $1\leq i\leq n-1$. Then for

$$\bar{c}=f_1((r,k)e_i(s,k)f_2)^m(r,k)f_3$$

it is easily seen that (i) $\bar{c}$ is still in comp(G), (ii) word($\bar{c}$)=word(c), i.e. $\bar{c} \in$ left(x), (iii) $\#_u(h_k(\bar{c}))\geq m$, (iv) $\#_v(h_k(\bar{c}))\geq\#_v(h_k(c))$ for all $v \in S_1 \cup S_2$, and (v) $\text{sub}_2(h_k(c))=\text{sub}_2(h_k(\bar{c}))$[1]. Figure 2 gives an illustration of the idea of this pumping. We apply this mechanism iteratively for all $u \in S_2$ to get a computation c' for which $h_k(c')$ is the required w_m in lcut(x). □

In the following lemma we need a so-called transformation-k-homomorphism $t_k : (Q\times\mathbf{Z})^* \rightarrow (Q\times\mathbf{Z})$, for $k \in \mathbf{Z}$, where for $(q,i) \in Q\times\mathbf{Z}$, $t_k(q,i)=(q,i+k)$.

Observation 4: Let $c_0(p,k)c_1(q,k)c_2$ and $d_0(p,l)d_1(q,l)d_2$ be valid computations. Then $c_0(p,k)t_{(k-l)}(d_1)(q,k)c_2$ is a valid computation.

Lemma 5 (composing): Let $x,y \in \Sigma^*$, $a \in \Sigma$. Let $w_1 \in$ lcut(xa) and $w_2 \in$ rcut(ay), such that the first (resp. last) symbol of w_1 and w_2 are the same, $\text{sub}_2(w_1)=\text{sub}_2(w_2)$ and for all $u \in Q^2$, $\#_u(w_1)\geq\#_u(w_2)$. Then $w_1 \in$ rcut(ay).

Proof: We start by giving the intuitive idea of the proof (consult Figure 3 for illustration). Step 1: Choose a computation c which generates a word with prefix xa and which has the history w_1 for the cell containing the last symbol a in xa. Step 2: Analogously, choose a computation d which generates a word with suffix ay and which has the history w_2 for the cell containing the first symbol a in ay. Step 3: Omit the right parts (=right of the parts which generate the prefix xa) of c and omit the left parts (=left of the parts which generate the suffix ay) of d. Step 4: Try to compose the remaining parts of c and d such that we get a computation c' for xay and with the history w_1 for the cell containing the a (between x and y). This will show that $w_1 \in$ rcut(ay).

---

1) $\text{sub}_2(w)$ denotes the set of subwords of length 2 of w.

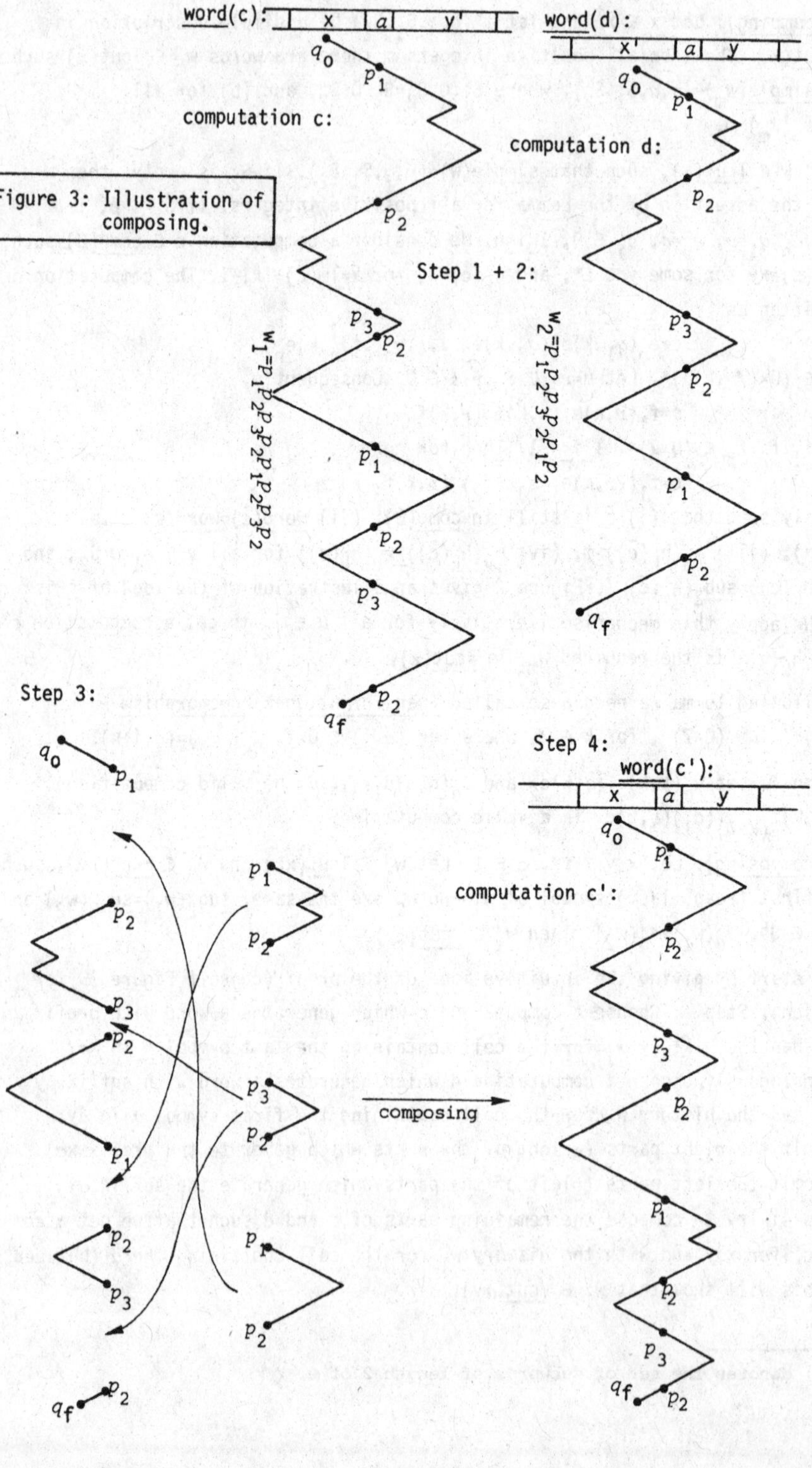

Figure 3: Illustration of composing.

Formally, let $c \in \underline{left}(xa)$, such that $h_k(c)=w_1$, $k=\underline{lm}(c)+|xa|-1$ and let $d \in \underline{right}(ay)$, such that $h_1(d)=w_2$, $l=\underline{rm}(c)-|ay|+1$. Again we write

$$c=e_0(q_1,k)e_1(q_2,k)\ldots e_{n-1}(q_n,k)\ e_n,$$

where $e_i \in (Q\times(\mathbb{Z}\setminus\{k\}))^*$, $0\le i\le n$ and $w_1=q_1,q_2\ldots{}_n$, and

$$d=f_0(p_1,l)f_1(p_2,l)\ldots f_{m-1}(p_m,l)f_m$$

where $f_i \in (Q\times(\mathbb{Z}\setminus\{l\}))^*$ $0\le i\le m$ and $w_2=p_1,p_2\ldots p_m$.

Case 1: $k\ge 0$, i.e. the first symbol $(q_0,0)$ of c contributes to xa in $xay'=\underline{word}(c)$. The intuitive idea is to leave unchanged the (q,k)-parts and e_i-parts in c which contribute to the prefix xa of $\underline{word}(c)$, and to replace the other e_i-parts appropriately by f_j-parts of d, such that we get a computation c' with $\underline{word}(c')=xay$.

We set

$$c'=e_0'(q_1,k)e_1'(q_2,k)\ldots e_{n-1}'(q_n,k)e_n'$$

where(i) $e_0'=e_0$; (ii) If $e_i \in (Q\times\{g \in \mathbb{Z}|g<k\})^*$, $1\le i\le n$ then $e_i'=e_i$;
(iii) If $e_i \in (Q\times\{g \in \mathbb{Z}|g>k\})^*$, $1\le i\le n$ then f_j is chosen, such that $q_i=q_j$ (and $q_{i+1}=p_{j+1}$ if $i \neq n$) and set $e_i'=t_{(k-l)}(f_j)$. Moreover, use every $f_j \in (Q\times\{g \in \mathbb{Z}|g>l\})^*$ at least once for a replacement. This is possible since $\#_u(w_1)\ge\#_u(w_2)$ for all $u \in Q^2$. We get $c' \in \underline{comp}(G)$, $h_k(c')=h_k(c)=w_1$, $\underline{word}(c')=xay$ and consequently, $w_1 \in \underline{rcut}(ay)$. This completes the argument for Case 1.

Case 2: $k<0$, is similar and left to the reader. □

Lemma 6: Let $x,y \in \Sigma^*$, $a \in \Sigma$. Then

$$xay \in \underline{lang}(G) \text{ iff } \underline{simple}(\underline{lcut}(xa)) \cap \underline{simple}(\underline{rcut}(ay)) \neq \emptyset$$

Proof: (⇒) This is trivial, because of Observation 1. (⇐) If $\underline{simple}(\underline{lcut}(xa)) \cap \underline{simple}(\underline{rcut}(ay)) \neq \emptyset$ then there is $w_1 \in \underline{lcut}(xa)$ and $w_2 \in \underline{rcut}(ay)$, such that $\underline{simple}(w_1)=\underline{simple}(w_2)$. Lemma 3 guarantees the existence of a word $w_1' \in \underline{lcut}(xa)$, for which Lemma 5 holds in the sense that $w_1' \in \underline{rcut}(ay)$. Consequently, $\underline{lcut}(xa) \cap \underline{rcut}(ay) \neq \emptyset$, which implies that $xay \in \underline{lang}(G)$ (see Observation 1). □

In order to prove our theorem, we need the following Proposition due to Nerode, [N].

Proposition 7: Let L be a language over some alphabet Σ. Define R_L, the right congruence relation induced by L, as follows:

$$(x,y) \in R_L \quad \text{iff} \quad \text{for all } z \in \Sigma^*$$
$$[xz \in L \quad \text{iff} \quad yz \in L].$$

Let $E(R_L)=\{[x]=\{y|(x,y) \in R_L\}|x \in \Sigma^*\}$ be the set of equivalence classes induced by R_L. Then L is regular iff $E(R_L)$ is finite.

Theorem 8: For a direction deterministic two-way finite state generator $G=(Q,\delta,d,q_0,q_f,\Sigma,INT_\alpha),\Sigma=2^Q$, the generated language $\underline{lang}(G)$ is regular.

Proof: Let $L=\text{lang}(G)$ and let R_L be the right congruence relation induced by L. Lemma 6 and Observation 2(b) imply that if for $x,y \in \Sigma^+$, $\underline{simple}(\underline{lcut}(x))=\underline{simple}(\underline{lcut}(y))$ then $(x,y) \in R_L$. Let $E'=\{\{y|\underline{simple}(\underline{lcut}(y)=\underline{simple}(\underline{lcut}(x))\}|x \in \Sigma^*\}$ be the set of equivavalence classes induced by simple lcut . Then $E(R_L)$ consists of unions of sets in E'. Since E' is a finite set, $E(R_L)$ is a finite set, which completes the argument. □

Finally, we carry over this result for INT_α to set-and priority-interpretation.

Corollary 9: Let $G=(Q,\delta,d,q_0,q_f,\Sigma,INT)$ be a two-way finite state generator. Then (i) if INT is a set-interpretation and (ii) if INT is a priority interpretation, then lang(G) is a regular language.

Proof: The reduction from direction-nondeterministic to direction deterministic generators is quite a standard one and hence, we omit it here. Thus let $L'=\text{lang}(G')\subseteq(2^Q)^*$ be the regular language generated by $G'=(Q,\delta,d,q_0,q_f,2^Q,INT_\alpha)$.

(i) For $w \in Q^+$, $INT_2(w)=\{pr(q)|q \in \text{alph}(w)\}$ for some print function $pr : Q \to \Delta$, Δ a finite alphabet. We define a homomorphism: $h_2 : (2^Q)^* \to (2^\Delta)^*$, where for $S \in 2^Q$, $h_2(S)=\{pr(q)|q \in S\}$. Then $\text{lang}(G)=h_2(L')$, which is a regular language since the family of regular languages is closed under homomorhphism.

(ii) Let $\Delta=(a_1,a_2...a_n)$ be the priority hierarchy of the alphabet Δ and let $pr : Q \to \Delta$ be the output function for INT_3. For $w \in Q^+$, $INT_3(w)=a_i$, where i is the greatest index such that $a_i \in \{pr(q)|q \in \text{alph}(w)\}$. We define a homomorphism $h_3 : (2^Q)^* \to \Delta^*$, where for $S \in 2^Q$, $h_3(S)=a_i$, with i being the greatest index such that $a_i \in \{pr(q)|q \in S\}$. We conclude as above that $\text{lang}(G)=h_3(L')$ is regular.

□

CONCLUSION

As already indicated in the beginning, the result presented can be used to solve the regularity problem for OI-interpretations of regular chain code picture languages (see Welzl, [W] for more details). This application is also the reason for choosing set-and priority interpretation for this presentation. Overwrite-interpretation which also yields regularity will be treated in a forthcoming more detailed paper. There we will also give nontrivial examples of interpretations which generate even non-contextfree languages.

Acknowledgement:

The authors are grateful to J. Albert for discussion of this material.

References:

[MRW] H. Maurer, G. Rozenberg and E. Welzl, "Chain code picture languages", to appear in Lecture Notes in Computer Science.

[H] M.A. Harrison, Introduction to Formal Language Theory, Addison Wesley (1978).

[N] A. Nerode, "Linear automation transformations", Proceedings of the American Mathematical Society 9 (1958) 541-544.

[S] J. Sheperdson, "The reductions of two-way automata to one-way automata", IBM Journal of Research and Development 3 (1959) 198-200.

[W] E. Welzl, "Regular picture languages: Optimality and OI-interpretations", in preparation.

A COMPLETE SET OF AXIOMS FOR
A THEORY OF COMMUNICATING SEQUENTIAL PROCESSES

Rocco de Nicola*
Department of Computer Science
University of Edinburgh

Abstract

In [9] an abstract version of Hoare's CSP is defined and a denotational semantics based on the possible failures of processes is given for it. This semantics induces a natural preorder on processes. We define formally this preorder and prove that it can be characterized as the smallest relation satisfying a particular set of axioms. The characterization will shed lights on problems arising from the way divergence and underspecification are handled.

1. Introduction

Research on denotational semantics, beginning with the pioneering work of Scott and Strachey, has shown that a relatively small number of basic semantic contructions can be used to adequately model the meanings of sequential, deterministic programs [16]. There have been various attempts [12], [15] to generalize the Scott-Strachey approach to cover languages with primitives for parallelism, nondeterminism and communication but the mathematics involved gets immediately complicated. Moreover, in some cases the mathematical objects used to denote the meanings of programs do not completely respect operational intuitions.

More recently a new approach to the semantics of parallelism has been developed beginning with Milner's work on CCS [6], [10]. In this approach the semantics of a system is given by considering the actions it can accomplish and its possible configurations after the various actions. The calculus is based on a few operators corresponding to intuitive ideas of systems behavior and its semantics is based purely upon operational definitions. No prior decision on what aspect to ignore is made. In [3] it has been shown that depending on the "operationally" defined congruence relation chosen it is possible to get various different mathematical models for the calculus and so various different denotational semantics. Moreover from the notion of congruence it is possible to infer nice algebraic laws describing the interactions between the various operators.

Since its appearance, CSP, [7], has played the role of a test language for every proposed theory of concurrency, by providing very interesting control structure. Various formal semantics for CSP have been proposed. The so-called **trace semantics** [8] is suitable for reasoning about potential communication sequences but insensitive to deadlock. The **B-semantics** [4] gives the semantics in two steps: first every process of a system is given an individual semantics, and then the semantics of the system is obtained by a binding operator **B** which takes into account the concurrent interactions among the various processes. Moreover other more operational directions have been followed: [14] gives a structured operational semantics for CSP and [1] gives its semantics by translation into CCS.

In [9], to define a mathematical model for CSP a new approach, basically denotational but

---

*On leave from Istituto di Elaborazione della Informazione, Pisa (Italy).

having strong connections with operational behaviours, has been taken. Following the lead of CCS, a notion of process based on the elementary concepts of event and transition is introduced. Starting from a set of events (the elementary processes) a number of combinators are introduced which allow processes to be built from smaller ones. The meanings of the various processes is then specified by postulating that two processes are identical if and only if they cannot be distinguished by observing their behaviour in finite environments.

Their semantics is given by associating to every process a so-called refusal set. Each refusal set consists of a set of failures. A failure is a pair <s,V>, where s is a finite sequence of visible actions in which the process may have been engaged up to a certain moment and V is a set of actions the process is able to reject on the next step. The semantics of the various combinators is given by defining the transformations they induce on the domain of refusal sets.

The association of a process with a refusal set is not one-to-one; the same refusal set can be associated to more than one process. A notion of congruence is then introduced as follows: two processes are congruent if and only if they happen to have the same refusal set as denotation.

The congruence obtained in this way and the refusal set model itself present striking similarities with one of the behavioral equivalences which has been defined for CCS starting from its standard operational semantics, and the mathematical model it induces [3]. It is tempting to try to understand the relation between the two seemingly very different approaches. This paper starts investigations in this direction. The congruence on processes induced by the denotational model (the refusal set model) is characterized algebraically and a sound and complete set of axioms is defined to form the basis of the theory. This allows a deeper understanding of the model and sheds some light on problems connected with the choices for the denotation of some particular processes. In particular it appears that considering divergent and underspecified processes as the ones with the maximum of nondeterminism, though appealing, causes serious problems when operating upon them.

The remainder of the paper is organized as follows. In §2 the syntax of a version of the language for a Theory of Communicating Sequential Processes (not containing recursively defined processes) is introduced; the refusal set model is then presented and used to give the semantics of the language; finally, a preorder for processes (the one naturally induced by the denotational semantics) is defined. In §3 it is proved that the preorder can be characterized as the smallest relation satisfying a particular set of axioms; the complete set of axioms is defined and proved consistent, and other axioms, useful for a better understanding of the model and for later proofs, are derived. §4 is completely dedicated to discussing the existence of normal forms for processes and to presenting the proof of the completeness theorem. In the final section the results are discussed, problems arising from the way divergence and underspecification are handled are presented, possible changes to the model are suggested and relations with other models are pointed out. Due to lack of space some proofs will be omitted; they will appear in an extended version of the paper.

2. The language and its semantics

In this section we review the definition of the various operators of a Theory for Communicating Sequential Processes (TCSP) and their denotational semantics. All the operators are described in [9] where their definition and their use are motivated. Only a subset of the operators in [9] is considered; the reasons for the exclusion of some of them (e.g.

rec x. _) will be discussed later. We start by giving an informal description of the various operators:

1. **Inaction.** Stop represents the process which never does anything

2. **Undefined.** CHAOS represents the wholly arbitrary process which can exhibit every possible behaviour; it is the most nondeterministic process.

3. **Action.** If A is a set of elementary actions, $a \in A$ and P is a process then $a \rightarrow P$ represents the process which can perform the action a and then behave like P.

4. **External Choice.** If P and Q are processes then $P \Box Q$ is a process having the actions of both P and Q. The environment (the other processes interacting with it), will resolve the choice as to which subprocess is in fact used.

5. **Internal Choice.** If P and Q are processes then $P \sqcap Q$ is the process representing their nondeterministic composition. $P \sqcap Q$ behaves like P or Q and the environment has no control over the choice.

6. **Parallel Composition.** If P and Q are processes then $P \| Q$ is a process. It can perform a particular action only if both P and Q can perform it together. This gives a very tight form of parallelism.

7. **Hiding.** If P is a process and a is an elementary action then P/a is a process which behaves exactly the same as P apart from the fact that all the actions a are invisible to the environment. These actions can occur without the environment having any control over them.

The behaviour of processes built using the above operators is specified by associating a refusal set to every process. A refusal set gives the means of observing the traces a process can execute and at the same time the elementary actions it will be able to refuse to execute after every single trace. A refusal set F is a subset of $POW(A^* \times POW(A))$, (where POW(S) denotes the set of subsets of S) which satisfies the following conditions:

1. $\langle s, V\rangle \in F \Longrightarrow V$ is finite.

2. $\langle \varepsilon, \{\,\}\rangle \in F$, where ε represents the empty string and $\{\,\}$ the empty set.

3. $\langle st, \{\,\}\rangle \in F \Longrightarrow \langle s, \{\,\}\rangle \in F$.

4. $V \subseteq W$ *and* $\langle s, W\rangle \in F \Longrightarrow \langle s, V\rangle \in F$.

5. Let $U = \{a \mid \langle sa, \{\,\}\rangle \in F\}$ and let W be a finite subset of $(A - U)$, then $\langle s, V\rangle \in F \Longrightarrow \langle s, (V \cup W)\rangle \in F$.

We are now ready to present the syntax and the semantics of TCSP. The set of finite processes ranged over by P, Q, R ... is defined by the following BNF-like notation:

$$P ::= Stop \mid CHAOS \mid a \rightarrow P \mid P_1 \sqcap P_2 \mid P_1 \Box P_2 \mid P_1 \| P_2 \mid P/a.$$

In the sequel $\sum \{P_i \mid i \in I\}$ will be used to denote $P_{i_1} \Box \ldots \Box P_{i_n}$ where $I = \{i_1, \ldots, i_n\}$. If $I = \{\,\}$ then it will denote Stop. $\prod \{P_i \mid i \in I\}$ will be used to denote $P_{i_1} \sqcap \ldots \sqcap P_{i_n}$ where $I = \{i_1, \ldots, i_n\}$ is not empty. The absence of brackets will be justified by axioms to be introduced; both $\Box$ and $\sqcap$ will in fact be proved associative. The precedence of the operators is given by: $/a \;>\; a\rightarrow \;>\; \| \;>\; \sqcap \;>\; \Box$.

The semantic function $[\![\;]\!]$ is defined by structural induction in denotational style:

$$[\![Stop]\!] = \{\langle \varepsilon, V\rangle \mid V \subseteq A\}$$

$[\![\text{CHAOS}]\!] = \{ \langle s, V\rangle \mid s \in A^* \text{ and } V \subseteq A \}$

$[\![a \rightarrow P]\!] = \{\langle \epsilon, V\rangle \mid V \subseteq A-\{a\} \} \cup \{ \langle as, W\rangle \mid \langle s, W\rangle \in [\![P]\!] \}$

$[\![P \square Q]\!] = \{\langle \epsilon, V\rangle \mid \langle \epsilon, V\rangle \in [\![P]\!] \cap [\![Q]\!]\} \cup \{ \langle s, W\rangle \mid s \in A^+ \text{ and } \langle s, W\rangle \in [\![P]\!] \cup [\![Q]\!] \}$

$[\![P \sqcap Q]\!] = [\![P]\!] \cup [\![Q]\!]$

$[\![P \| Q]\!] = \{ \langle s, V \cup W\rangle \mid \langle s, V\rangle \in [\![P]\!] \text{ and } \langle s, W\rangle \in [\![Q]\!] \}$

$[\![P/a]\!] = \{ \langle s/a, V\rangle \mid \langle s, V \cup \{a\}\rangle \in [\![P]\!] \} \cup$

$\{ \langle (s/a)t, V\rangle \mid \langle t, V\rangle \in \text{CHAOS if } \forall n \ \langle sa^n, \{ \}\rangle \in [\![P]\!] \}$

where s/b is formed from s by removing all occurrences of b.

Note, however, that in the definition of the semantics of P/a the second member of the union is present just in case CHAOS is a subprocess of P and P can offer a sequence of a's and then behaves like CHAOS.

Associated with every failure set we have the following

Definition 1: $\text{Init}(P) = \{ a \mid \langle a, \{ \}\rangle \in [\![P]\!] \}$

Definition 2: $\text{Traces}(P) = \{ s \mid \langle s, \{ \}\rangle \in [\![P]\!] \}$

Definition 3: $\text{Refusals}(P) = \{ V \mid \langle \epsilon, V\rangle \in [\![P]\!] \}$

The proposed semantics for processes of TCSP immediately suggests a natural equivalence between them:

$$P \approx Q \quad \text{if and only if} \quad [\![P]\!] = [\![Q]\!]$$

In the sequel we break the natural equivalence induced by the denotational semantics into two preorders, relations which are reflexive and transitive. We find this more natural for describing the relationship between CHAOS and the other processes and for discussing divergence and underspecification. An equivalence is generated by a preorder in a natural way ($\approx = \sqsubseteq \cap \sqsupseteq$).

We have

$$P \sqsubseteq Q \quad \text{if and only if} \quad [\![P]\!] \supseteq [\![Q]\!]$$

meaning intuitively that P is considered less defined than Q when P behaves more nondeterministically than Q; i.e. the external environment can control the progression of P in a smaller number of circumstances.

It is well known that, because of the way the semantic function $[\![\ ]\!]$ has been defined, $P \sqsubseteq Q$ implies $\mathbb{C}[P] \sqsubseteq \mathbb{C}[Q]$ for every context $\mathbb{C}[\ ]$; i.e. $\sqsubseteq$ is a precongruence on TCSP.

Proposition 4: $\sqsubseteq$ is preserved by all the operators in TCSP.

3. The axiom system

In this section we examine the axiom system corresponding to the preorder defined in the previous section. For every operator in the language we have a corresponding set of axioms. We have, moreover, some axioms showing the interrelationships between certain pairs of operators. The basic axioms are given in Table 1. Most of them are given in term of " = " and they are intended to be read in conjunction with the rules:

$X = Y$ implies $X \sqsubseteq Y$ and $Y \sqsubseteq X$

$X \sqsubseteq Y$ *and* $Y \sqsubseteq X$ implies $X = Y$

Some of the axioms were stated in [9], others have been worked out by stressing the similarities with the models in [3] and [10]; in fact some of them are reminiscent of the ones in [3], in spite of the very different set of operators we started with.

If A is the set of axioms C1, E1-E4, I1-I4, D1-D4, H1-H6, PC1-PC5 we have:

Proposition 5: The set of axioms A is <u>sound</u> for $\underset{\sim}{\sqsubseteq}$, i.e. if $P \sqsubseteq Q$ ($P = Q$) is an instance of an axiom from A then $P \underset{\sim}{\sqsubseteq} Q$ ($P \approx Q$).

<u>Proof</u> The proof consists of determining the refusal sets of P and Q, whatever they are, and comparing them. We will just sketch the proof of some axioms which are not stated in [6].

H5 $(a \rightarrow X \,\square\, Y)/a = X/a \sqcap (X \,\square\, Y)/a$

We assume H4, it is then enough to prove

$(a \rightarrow X \,\square\, Y)/a = (X \sqcap (X \,\square\, Y))/a$

$[\![a \rightarrow X \square Y]\!] = \{ \langle \varepsilon, W\rangle \mid \langle \varepsilon, W\rangle \in [\![Y]\!] \text{ and } a \notin W \} \cup \{ \langle as, T\rangle \mid \langle s, T\rangle \in [\![X]\!] \} \cup$
$\{ \langle bt, V\rangle \mid \langle bt, V\rangle \in [\![Y]\!] \}$

$[\![X \sqcap (X \square Y]\!] = \{ \langle s, T\rangle \mid \langle s, T\rangle \in [\![X]\!] \cup \{ \langle bt, V\rangle \mid \langle bt, V\rangle \in [\![Y]\!] \}$

and so we have

$[\![lhs]\!] = [\![rhs]\!] = \{ \langle as/a, T\rangle \mid \langle as, T\rangle \in [\![X]\!] \text{ and } a \in T \} \cup$
$\{ \langle bt/a, V\rangle \mid \langle bt, V\rangle \in [\![Y]\!] \text{ and } a \in V \}$

PC2 $(P \square CHAOS) \| Q = \sum\{ a_k \rightarrow CHAOS \mid k \in I \cap J \} \sqcap \{ \sum b_j \rightarrow Q_j \mid j \in J \}$

where P and Q are as in Table 1

We have $[\![P \square CHAOS]\!] = \{ \langle \varepsilon, V\rangle \mid V \subseteq A\text{-}Init(P) \} \cup \{ \langle s, W\rangle \mid s \in A^+, W \subseteq A \}$

$[\![P \| CHAOS]\!] = \{ \langle s, W\rangle \mid s \in traces(P), W \subseteq A \}$

$[\![lhs]\!] = \{ \langle \varepsilon, V\rangle \mid V \subseteq A\text{-}Init(P) \text{ or } V \subseteq A\text{-}Init(Q) \} \cup$
$\{ \langle s, W\rangle \mid s \in A^+ \text{ and } s \in traces(Q) \text{ and } W \subseteq A \}$

$[\![rhs]\!] = \{ \langle \varepsilon, V\rangle \mid V \subseteq A\text{-}(Init(P) \cap A\text{-}Init(Q)) \} \cup$
$\{ \langle s, W\rangle \mid s \in A^+ \text{ and } s \in traces(Q) \text{ and } W \subseteq A \}$

The result follows from $V \subseteq (A\text{-}(Init(P) \cap A\text{-}Init(Q)) \iff V \subseteq A\text{-}Init(P) \text{ or } V \subseteq A\text{-}Init(Q)$ □

From the axioms in Table 1 we can derive many more axioms which will prove very useful in the sequel during the proof of the completeness theorem. Moreover they give more indication of the behaviour of the various operators. A list of derivable axioms is given below.

DER1 $X \sqcap CHAOS = CHAOS$

DER2 $(X \sqcap Y) \square X = (X \square Y) \sqcap X$

DER3 $X \sqcap Y = X \sqcap Y \sqcap (X \square Y)$

DER4 $X \square Y = X \square Y \square (X \sqcap Y)$

DER5 $X \sqcap (X \square Y \square Z) = X \sqcap (X \square Y) \sqcap (X \square Y \square Z)$

DER6 $X \square (X \sqcap Y \sqcap Z) = X \square (X \sqcap Y) \square (X \sqcap Y \sqcap Z)$

DER7 $(a \rightarrow X_1 \square Y) \sqcap (a \rightarrow X_2 \square Z) = (a \rightarrow X_1 \square a \rightarrow X_2 \square Y) \sqcap (a \rightarrow X_1 \square a \rightarrow X_2 \square Z)$

Undefined

C1 $\quad \mathrm{CHAOS} \sqsubseteq X$

External Choice

E1 $\quad X \Box X = X$

E2 $\quad X \Box Y = Y \Box X$

E3 $\quad X \Box (Y \Box Z) = (X \Box Y) \Box Z$

E4 $\quad X \Box \mathrm{Stop} = X$

Internal Choice

I1 $\quad X \sqcap X = X$

I2 $\quad X \sqcap Y = Y \sqcap X$

I3 $\quad X \sqcap (Y \sqcap Z) = (X \sqcap Y) \sqcap Z$

I4 $\quad X \sqcap Y \sqsubseteq X$

Distributive Laws

D1 $\quad X \sqcap (Y \Box Z) = (X \sqcap Y) \Box (X \sqcap Z)$

D2 $\quad X \Box (Y \sqcap Z) = (X \Box Y) \sqcap (X \Box Z)$

D3 $\quad (a \to X) \sqcap (a \to Y) = a \to (X \sqcap Y)$

D4 $\quad (a \to X) \Box (a \to Y) = a \to (X \sqcap Y)$

Hiding

H1 $\quad \mathrm{Stop}/a = \mathrm{Stop}$

H2 $\quad \mathrm{CHAOS}/a = \mathrm{CHAOS}$

H3 $\quad (X/a)/b = (X/b)/a$

H4 $\quad (X \sqcap Y)/a = X/a \sqcap Y/a$

H5 $\quad (a \to P \Box Q)/a = P/a \sqcap (P \Box Q)/a$

H6 $\quad \sum\{(b_i \to X_i)/a \mid i \in I\} = \sum\{b_i \to X_i/a \mid i \in I\}$ if $\forall i\ b_i \neq a$

Parallel Composition

If $P = \sum\{a_i \to P_i \mid i \in I\}$ and $Q = \sum\{b_j \to Q_j \mid j \in J\}$ then:

PC1 $\quad P \| Q = \sum\{a_k \to (P_k \| Q_k) \mid k \in I \cap J\}$

PC2 $\quad (P \Box \mathrm{CHAOS}) \| Q = \sum\{a_k \to \mathrm{CHAOS} \mid k \in I \cap J\} \sqcap \sum\{b_j \to Q_j \mid j \in J\}$

PC3 $\quad P \| (Q \Box \mathrm{CHAOS}) = \sum\{a_k \to \mathrm{CHAOS} \mid k \in I \cap J\} \sqcap \sum\{a_i \to P_i \mid i \in I\}$

PC4 $\quad (P \Box \mathrm{CHAOS}) \| (Q \Box \mathrm{CHAOS}) = \sum\{a_k \to \mathrm{CHAOS} \mid k \in I \cap J\} \Box \mathrm{CHAOS}$

PC5 $\quad (X \sqcap Y) \| Z = (X \| Z) \sqcap (Y \| Z)$

Table 1: The Axiom System

DER8 $a \rightarrow \Pi\{ X_i \mid i \in I \} = \Pi\{ a \rightarrow X_i \mid i \in I \}$

DER9 $X \sqcap Y \sqsubseteq X \square Y$

DER10 $a \rightarrow X \square CHAOS = a \rightarrow CHAOS \square CHAOS$

DER11 $(\sum\{a_i \rightarrow X_i \mid i \in I\} \square CHAOS = (\sum\{a_i \rightarrow CHAOS \mid i \in I\} \square CHAOS$

DER12 $CHAOS \| a \rightarrow P = Stop \sqcap a \rightarrow (P \| CHAOS)$

DER10 and DER12 deserve some comments. They in fact shed lights on difficulties of refusal sets in modelling the operational intuitions of the interaction between the fully undefined process (CHAOS) and other completely specified ones.

DER10, in fact, says that a finite process P in alternative with CHAOS presents the same behaviour of an agent that behaves like CHAOS in every circumstance apart from the fact that it will always accept the experiment a if proposed by the environment. For example when considering an underspecified process the only actions which will be taken into account will be its initial ones.

DER12, on the contrary, shows that the behaviour of the process resulting from the parallel composition of any process with the process CHAOS, is modeled in such a way that it does not take into account the possibility of divergence, i. e. of computing forever without offering any communication to the environment. This possibility should be taken into account since the process CHAOS can be used to model infinite chattering (infinite internal message exchange, without offering any external communication). We have in fact the axiom CHAOS/a = CHAOS. This problem is even more evident if we consider the general language including recursively defined terms. We have in this case that P = rec x. $a \rightarrow x$ implies P/a = CHAOS.

These difficulties in coping with CHAOS prevented us from axiomatizing the operator |||, an operator used in [9] to model the interleaving of the action of two processes (if P and Q are processes then P|||Q can perform the interleaving of the sequences of actions the single processes P or Q can perform). While we have found an axiomatization which allowed us to remove all the occurrences of the operators || and /a from all the processes, we have not been able to find a process expressed only in term of $\square$, $\sqcap$, $a \rightarrow$, CHAOS and Stop with the same denotation as P|||CHAOS, i. e. another process which can be denotated by a failure set which has the same traces as CHAOS but can refuse only the actions P can refuse.

These problems seem to suggest that, though appealing, it may be inappropriate to model divergent or unguarded processes as those with the maximum of nondeterminism. A process is unguarded [10] if it is defined recursively and a bound variable is not prefixed by any elementary action in the recursion body, e. g. P = rec x. $a \rightarrow Stop \square x$ is unguarded while Q = rec x. $a \rightarrow x$ is guarded. In the last section we will discuss possible ways of avoiding these deficiences.

4. The completeness theorem

This section is entirely dedicated to proving that the set of axioms in Table 1 completely characterizes the preorder $\underset{\sim}{\sqsubset}$. The proof rests heavily on the existence of <u>normal forms</u> for processes.

If $\mathbb{L}$ is a set of sets let $A(\mathbb{L}) = \{ X \mid X \in L$ for some $L \in \mathbb{L} \}$. $\mathbb{L}$ is said to be <u>saturated</u> if for every $K \subseteq A(\mathbb{L})$, $K \supseteq L$ for some $L \in \mathbb{L}$ implies $K \in \mathbb{L}$. For example $\{ \{a\}, \{a, b\} \}$ is saturated whereas $\mathbb{L}_1 = \{ \{a\}, \{b\} \}$ is not because $\exists$ K_1 such that $K_1 \subseteq A(\mathbb{L}_1)$ and $K_1 \supseteq \{a\}$ but $K_1 \notin \mathbb{L}_1$.

Saturated sets are used in the following definition of normal form. Through the rest of the paper we use " ⊑ " to denote the least TCSP-precongruence generated by the axioms A. The related congruence is denoted by " = ".

Definition 6: P is in <u>normal form</u> if it is of the form:

$\sqcap \{ \sum \{ a \to P(a) \mid a \in L \} \mid L \in \mathbf{L} \}$ [□CHAOS]

where [□CHAOS] denotes that CHAOS is an optional summand. $\mathbf{L}$ is a nonempty saturated set, P(a) are in normal form and moreover if CHAOS is a summand then for all $a \in A(\mathbf{L})$ we have that P(a) is CHAOS.

Some examples will clarify this definition. In the examples for a belonging to A, a→Stop is denoted by a for simplicity.

1. a→(b□c)□CHAOS is not in normal form because P(a) is different from CHAOS
2. $(a_1 \to b) \sqcap (a_2 \to c)$ is not in normal form because $\{(a_1), (a_2)\}$ is not saturated, i.e. there is no subterm corresponding to the set (a_1, a_2), the corresponding normal form is $a_1 \to b \sqcap a_2 \to c \sqcap (a_1 \to b \square a_2 \to c)$.
3. a→b⊓(a→c□d→b) is not in normal form because for every normal form we have that if a→P and a→Q are summands of the normal form then P is syntactically identical to Q. The corresponding normal form is a→(b⊓c) ⊓ (a→(b⊓c) □ d→b).
4. Stop and Stop□CHAOS are in normal form.

It is possible to prove that every process can be reduced to an equivalent one which is in <u>normal form</u> by using axioms from A

Proposition 7: For every P ∈ TCSP there exists a normal form <u>nf</u> such that P = <u>nf</u>(P).

We will use <u>normal forms</u> to prove the completeness theorem. First we define orderings on them.

Definition 8: If n and m are normal forms and

$n = \sqcap \{ \sum \{ a \to n(a) \mid a \in L \} \mid L \in \mathbf{L}(n) \}$ [□CHAOS]

$m = \sqcap \{ \sum \{ b \to m(b) \mid b \in L \} \mid L \in \mathbf{L}(m) \}$ [□CHAOS] then

$n < m$ if

1. for all $M \in \mathbf{L}(m)$ there exists $N \in \mathbf{L}(n)$ such that $M \supseteq N$
2. if CHAOS is not a summand of n then it is not a summand of m and $\mathbf{L}(n) \supseteq \mathbf{L}(m)$.

This order is able to compare normal forms at the topmost level only. We define now a new preorder, ≪, which extends < recursively to compare normal forms at all levels.

Definition 9: If n and m are as in the previous definition then

$n \ll m$ if

1. $n < m$ and
2. $n(a) \ll m(a)$ whenever both are defined.

Lemma 10: If m and n are normal forms and CHAOS is not a summand of n then $n \sqsubseteq m$ implies $Init(n) \supseteq Init(m)$.

<u>Proof</u> Suppose ∃a ∈ A such that a ∉ Init(n). Then we have <a,( )> ∈ ⟦m⟧ and

$\langle a,(\,)\rangle \notin [\![n]\!]$ which contradicts $[\![n]\!] \supseteq [\![m]\!]$. □

Lemma 11: If n and m are normal forms then $n \sqsubseteq m$ implies $n < m$.

<u>Proof</u>

1. Suppose there exists $M_0 \in \mathbb{L}(m)$ such that for all $N \in \mathbb{L}(n)$ there exists $a \in A$ such that $a \in N$ and $a \notin M_0$. If we choose $X = \{\, a \mid a \notin M_0$ *and* $a \in A(\mathbb{L}(n))\}$ we have that $\langle \epsilon, X\rangle \in [\![m]\!]$ while $\langle \epsilon, X\rangle \notin [\![m]\!]$, which contradicts $[\![n]\!] \supseteq [\![m]\!]$.

2. Suppose CHAOS is not a summand of n. Then we have to prove

   a. CHAOS is not a summand of m and

   b. $\mathbb{L}(n) \supseteq \mathbb{L}(m)$

a. Suppose CHAOS is a summand of m, then $\forall a \in A$ such that $a \notin Init(n)$ we have $\langle a,(\,)\rangle \in [\![m]\!]$ while $\langle a,(\,)\rangle \notin [\![n]\!]$

b. From the previous lemma we have $A(\mathbb{L}(n)) \supseteq A(\mathbb{L}(m))$. Moreover $\mathbb{L}(n)$ is saturated so in order to prove the claim it is sufficient to show that $M \in \mathbb{L}(m)$ implies that there exists $N \in \mathbb{L}(n)$ such that $M \supseteq N$. The proof is now similar to the one for case 1. □

Lemma 12: If n and m are normal forms then $n \sqsubseteq m$ implies $n(a) \sqsubseteq m(a)$ whenever both exist.

<u>Proof</u> If CHAOS is a summand of n then $n(a)$ = CHAOS and the claim is verified by C1. Suppose CHAOS is not a summand of n and suppose there exists $a \in A$ such that $[\![n(a)]\!] \subseteq [\![m(a)]\!]$. If we choose $A = \{\, \langle as, V\rangle \mid \langle s, V\rangle \in [\![m(a)]\!]\,\}$ and $B = \{\langle at, W\rangle \mid \langle t, W\rangle \in [\![n(a)]\!]\}$ we have $A \in [\![m]\!]$ implies $B \in [\![n]\!]$ and moreover $A \not\subseteq B$. Now since for every normal form r of the form $(a \to P \square R) \sqcap (a \to Q \square S) \sqcap T$ we have that P is syntactically identical to Q, $A \not\subseteq B$ implies $[\![m]\!] \not\subseteq [\![n]\!]$. □

Lemma 13: If n and m are normal forms then $n \sqsubseteq m$ implies $n \ll m$.

<u>Proof</u> From the previous lemma we can assume $n(a) \sqsubseteq m(a)$ whenever both are defined. By induction we have $n(a) \ll m(a)$; the result then follows from lemma 11. □

Lemma 14: If n and m are normal forms then $n \ll m$ implies $n \sqsubseteq m$.

<u>Proof</u> By induction we may assume that $n(a) \sqsubseteq m(a)$ whenever both are defined. We have to distinguish two cases:

1. CHAOS is a summand of n.

Because of Lemma 11 and of axioms I2, I3 we have

$$m = \sqcap\{\, (\textstyle\sum\{a \to m(a) \mid a \in M_1\}) \;\square\; (\sum\{b \to m(b) \mid b \in M_2\}) \mid M_1 \in \mathbb{L}(n) - \mathbb{K}\,\} \;[\square \text{CHAOS}]$$

where $\mathbb{K} = \{\, V \mid V \in \mathbb{L}(n)$ *and* not $\exists M \in \mathbb{L}(m)$ such that $V \subseteq M\,\}$

$$m \sqsupseteq \sqcap\{\, (\textstyle\sum\{a \to m(a) \mid a \in M_1\}) \square \text{CHAOS} \mid M_1 \in \mathbb{L}(n) - \mathbb{K}\,\} \;[\square \text{CHAOS}] \qquad \text{by C1}$$

$$\sqsupseteq \sqcap\{\, (\textstyle\sum\{a \to n(a) \mid a \in M_1\}) \mid M_1 \in \mathbb{L}(n) - \mathbb{K}\,\} \sqcap$$

$$\sqcap\{\, (\textstyle\sum\{b \to n(b) \mid b \in K\}) \mid K \in \mathbb{K}\} \;[\square \text{CHAOS}]$$

since $m(a) \sqsupseteq n(a)$ by induction and by I4.

$$= \sqcap\{\, (\textstyle\sum\{a \to n(a) \mid a \in N\}) \mid N \in \mathbb{L}(n)\,\} \sqcup \text{CHAOS} \qquad \text{by I2, I3}$$

$= n$

2. CHAOS is not a summand of n. In this case we have that CHAOS is not a summand of m as well and by lemma 11 and l1. l2 we have

$$n = \prod\{ (\sum\{a \rightarrow n(a) \mid a \in L\}) \mid L \in \mathbb{L}(m) \} \sqcap$$

$$\prod\{ (\sum\{b \rightarrow n(b) \mid b \in K\}) \mid K \in \mathbb{L}(n) - \mathbb{L}(m) \}$$

$$\sqsubseteq \prod\{ (\sum\{a \rightarrow m(a) \mid a \in L\}) \mid L \in \mathbb{L}(m) \} \sqcap$$

$$\prod\{ (\sum\{b \rightarrow n(b) \mid b \in K\}) \mid K \in \mathbb{L}(n) - \mathbb{L}(m) \}$$

because $n(a) \sqsubseteq m(a)$ by induction

$$\sqsubseteq \prod\{ (\sum\{a \rightarrow m(a) \mid a \in L\}) \mid L \in \mathbb{L}(m) \} \qquad \text{by 14}$$

$= m$

We are now ready to state the main theorems.

Theorem 15: For every P, Q ∈ TCSP $P \underset{\sim}{\sqsubseteq} Q$ implies $P \sqsubseteq Q$.

Proof It follows directly from the existence of normal forms for P and Q (prop. 7) and from lemma 13 and lemma 14. □

Theorem 16: $\underset{\sim}{\sqsubseteq}$ is the least precongruence on TCSP generated by the axioms A.

Proof Follows from the fact that $\underset{\sim}{\sqsubseteq}$ is a precongruence (prop. 4), the set of axioms A is sound (prop. 5) and from the previous theorem. □

5. Discussion

In the previous sections we have shown that a natural precongruence on communicating processes, the one induced by the denotational semantics, can be characterized algebraically. A set of algebraic laws describing the behaviour of processes has been introduced and has been proved consistent and complete with respect to the denotational precongruence.

This work has already given some side-results. It has allowed to explore the relationship between the language of a Theory of Communicating Sequential Processes (TCSP) and Milner's CCS as determined by one of the behavioural equivalence of [3] (OCCS). This result can be obtained in spite of the very different set of operators and the very different approaches taken in giving their semantics. In the case of OCCS the semantics is in fact given in a purely operational way by starting from a transition based semantics [13] and introducing a notion of equivalence for processes by considering the tabulations of the possible effects of the interaction between a set of observers and the processes. For lack of space we just sketch the main results.

By passing to normal forms in both calculi it is possible to define two functions:

1. tr: TCSP → OCCS

2. rt: OCCS → TCSP

where tr is an <u>injective</u> function from TCSP normal forms to OCCS normal forms and rt is a surjective function from OCCS normal forms to TCSP normal forms and moreover rt(tr(P)) = P and tr(rt(Q)) = Q' where Q' is equivalent to Q but not necessarily congruent to it. The asymmetry of the two functions is mainly determined by the different stress put on internal non-controllable decisions, and it seems to suggest that CCS has more expressive power than TCSP.

Unfortunately all this works only for finite, completely specified, non-divergent processes (in the case of TCSP, for processes which do not have the agent CHAOS as a subprocess). The problem probably lies in the way CHAOS is handled by the refusal set model. Some of the theorems derived in §3 strongly suggest this.

Similar problems prevented the extension of the axiom system to infinite, recursively defined processes. The way CHAOS is denoted and the way its interaction with other processes is modeled causes problems when trying to define head normal forms for infinite terms as in [3] or when trying to prove that the complete partial order formed by the refusal sets ordered by reverse set inclusion is algebraic [5]. In this case the main difficulties lie in the fact that the refusal sets of all the finite approximations of infinite processes are infinite.

To try to overcome these difficulties two approaches can be tried out:

1. Define an operational semantics for TCSP and immerse it in the general setting of [3], by defining a notion of observation and making clear choices about how to handle divergence.

2. Change the denotational model, using the Representation Trees of [3] instead of the refusal set model and once again choosing carefully the denotation for CHAOS.

The first approach is very promising; it is possible to prove that for finite processes the equivalence induced by the denotational semantics via refusal sets can easily be obtained by an operationally defined one, and [3] has shown the feasibility of a generalization of the axiom system to infinite terms by just adding the axiom rec x. P = P[rec x. P/x]. The second approach has already been attempted in [11], but the problem of the denotation of CHAOS has been left unsolved.

The questions to be answered before choosing one approach or the other are: is there a unique mathematical concept of process which can be frozen in a denotational model? Or is it not better to take an operational approach which gives the possibility of postponing the decision and makes clear the choice of the mathematical model, by defining an operationally based congruence relation?

After writing the paper we learnt about a third attempt [2]. Along the same lines of [3] a process Ω with a denotation different from the one for CHAOS is introduced and the possibility of divergence and the inability to diverge are distinguished. Many of the previous difficulties are overcome but the problem of underspecified and unguarded recursive processes are left unsolved.

Acknowledgements

Tha author would like to thank G. Costa, M. Hennessy, M. Millington and D. Sannella for many useful discussions, and S. Brookes for comments on a first draft. The work has been supported in part by a grant from the Italian Research Council (C.N.R.) and by a scholarship from the University of Edinburgh.

6. References

LNCS n denotes Lecture Notes in Computer Science Volume n, Springer-Verlag

[1] Astesiano, E. and Zucca, E. Semantics of CSP via translation into CCS. Proc. MFCS 1982, LNCS 116, 1982.

[2] Brookes, S. D. A Model for Communicating Sequential Processes. Ph. D. thesis, University of Oxford, 1983.

[3] De Nicola, R. and Hennessy, M. Testing equivalences for processes. Technical Report CSR-123-82, University of Edinburgh. To appear in Proc. ICALP '83.

[4] Francez, N., Hoare, C. A. R., Lehmann, D. J. and De Roever, W. P. Semantics of non-determinism, concurrency and communication. JCSS, Vol. 19, No. 3, 1979.

[5] Guessarian, I, Algebraic Semantics, LNCS 99, 1981.

[6] Hennessy, M., Milner, R. On Observing Nondeterminism and Concurrency, LNCS 85, pp. 299-309, 1980.

[7] Hoare, C. A. R. Communicating Sequential Processes, CACM Vol. 21, No. 8, 1978.

[8] Hoare, C. A. R. A Model for Communicating Sequential Processes. Technical Monograph Prg-22, Computing Laboratory, University of Oxford, 1982.

[9] Hoare, C. A. R., Brookes, S. D., and Roscoe, A. D. A Theory of Communicating Sequential Processes, Technical Monograph Prg-16, Computing Laboratory, University of Oxford, 1981.

[10] Milne, G. The representation of Communication and Concurrency, Internal Report, Computer Sciencce Departement, California Institute of Technology, 1980.

[10] Milner, R. A Calculus of Communicating Systems, LNCS 92, 1980.

[11] Olderog, E. R. and Hoare, C. A. R. Specification-Oriented Semantics for Communicating Processes, Unpublished Draft, Oxford University Computing Laboratory, 1982. To appear in Proc. ICALP '83.

[12] Plotkin, G. A Powerdomain Constuction, SIAM J. on Computing, No. 5, pp. 452-486, 1976.

[13] Plotkin, G. A Structural Approach to Operational Semantics, Lecture notes, Aarhus University, 1981.

[14] Plotkin, G. An Operational Semantics for CSP, Internal Report, University of Edinburgh, CSR-114-82. To appear in Proc. IFIP WG 2.2 Working Conference on Formal Description of Programming Concepts II, North-Holland 198?.

[15] Smyth, M. B. Power Domains, JCSS, Vol. 2, pp. 23-36, 1978.

[16] Stoy, J. Denotational Semantics: The Scott-Strachey Approach to Programming Language Theory, MIT Press, 1977

The Consensus Problem in Unreliable Distributed Systems (A Brief Survey)†

Michael J. Fischer
Yale University
New Haven, Connecticut

Abstract

Agreement problems involve a system of processes, some of which may be faulty. A fundamental problem of fault-tolerant distributed computing is for the reliable processes to reach a consensus. We survey the considerable literature on this problem that has developed over the past few years and give an informal overview of the major theoretical results in the area.

1. Agreement Problems

To achieve reliability in distributed systems, protocols are needed which enable the system as a whole to continue to function despite the failure of a limited number of components. These protocols, as well as many other distributed computing problems, requires cooperation among the processes. Fundamental to such cooperation is the problem of agreeing on a piece of data upon which the computation depends. For example, the data managers in a distributed database system need to agree on whether to commit or abort a given transaction [20, 26]. In a replicated file system, the nodes might need to agree on where the file copies are supposed to reside [19, 30]. In a flight control system for an airplane [35], the engine control module and the flight surface control module need to agree on whether to continue or abort a landing in progress. The key point here is not *what* the processes are agreeing on but the fact that they must all come to the *same* conclusion.

An obvious approach to achieving agreement is for the processes to vote and agree on the majority value. In the absence of faults, this works fine, but in a close election, the vote of one faulty process can swing the outcome. Since distinct reliable processes might receive conflicting votes from a faulty process, they might also reach conflicting conclusions about the outcome of the election and hence fail to reach agreement. Davies and Wakerly [2] realized this difficulty and proposed a multistage voting scheme to overcome the problem.

---

†This work was supported in part by the Office of Naval Research under Contract N00014-82-K-0154, and by the National Science Foundation under Grant MCS-8116678.

A simple form of the problem is to achieve consensus on a single bit. Assume a fixed number of processors, some of which are initially faulty or may fail during the execution of the protocol. Each processor i has an initial bit x_i. The *consensus* problem is for the non-faulty processes to agree on a bit y, called the *consensus value.* More precisely, we want a protocol such that each reliable process i eventually terminates with a bit y_i, and $y_i = y$ for all i.

y in general will depend in some way on the initial bits x_i. In the absence of such a requirement, the problem becomes trivial, for each process can simply choose $y_i = 0$. Some dependency requirements that have been studied, in order of increasing strength, are:

1. (non-triviality): For each $y \in \{0, 1\}$, there is some initial vector x_i and some admissible execution of the protocol in which y is the consensus value. (The qualification "admissible" allows for additional restrictions, such as bounds on the number of faulty processes, on the kinds of computations we are willing to consider.)
2. (weak unanimity): If $x_i = x \in \{0, 1\}$ for all i, then $y = x$, provided that no failures actually occur during the execution of the protocol.
3. (strong unanimity): If $x_i = x \in \{0, 1\}$ for all i, then $y = x$.

Two other closely related problems have been studied extensively in the literature. The *interactive consistency* problem is like the consensus problem except that the goal of the protocol is for the non-faulty processes to agree on a vector **y**, called the *consensus vector.* Again, we add dependency requirements:

1. (weak): for each j, $\mathbf{y}_j = x_j$ if j is non-faulty, provided that no failures actually occur during the execution of the protocol.
2. (strong): for each j, $\mathbf{y}_j = x_j$ if j is non-faulty.

Finally, in the *generals* problem or *reliable broadcast* problem, one assumes a distinguished processor (the "general" or "transmitter") which is trying to send its initial bit x to all the others. As before, all the reliable processes have to reach consensus on a bit, and we add dependency requirements:

1. (weak): $y = x$ if no failures occur during the execution of the protocol.
2. (strong): $y = x$ if the general is non-faulty.

Without further qualification, any reference to one of these problems will refer to the version with the strong dependency requirement.

2. Models of Computation

The kinds of solutions that can be obtained to agreement problems depend heavily on the assumptions made about the model of computation and the kinds of faults to which it is prone. Throughout this paper, we will assume a fixed number n of processes. A protocol is said to be *t-resilient* if it operates correctly as long as no more than t processes fail before or during execution.

We consider two kinds of processor faults. A *crash* occurs when a process stops all activity. Up to the point of the crash, it operates correctly and after that it is completely inactive. A protocol that can tolerate up to t crashed processes is said to be *t-crash resilient*. We do not concern ourselves with the problem of repairing a faulty process and reintegrating it into the system, although that of course is a crucial problem in the practical implementation of any of these ideas [28].

A more disruptive kind of failure is the so-called *Byzantine failure*[1] in which no assumptions are made about the behavior of a faulty process. In particular, it can send messages when it is not supposed to, make conflicting claims to other processes, act dead for awhile and then revive itself, etc. A protocol that can tolerate up to t processes which exhibit Byzantine failures is said to be *t-Byzantine resilient* and is sometimes called a *Byzantine* protocol. The problem of finding a t-Byzantine resilient protocol for the (weak) generals problem is called the *(weak) Byzantine generals* problem.

To show that a protocol is Byzantine resilient, one has to consider all possible faulty behaviors, including those in which the failed processes act maliciously against the protocol. This doesn't mean that Byzantine protocols are only appropriate in adversary situations. The folklore is full of stories in which systems failed in bizarre and unexpected ways, and in the absence of good ways of characterizing the kinds of failures that occur in practice, protecting against Byzantine failures is a conservative approach to reliable systems design.

We assume the message system to be completely reliable and that only processes are subject to failure. We also assume that any process can reliably determine the sender of any message it receives, and any message so delivered arrives intact and without errors. Unless stated otherwise, we assume the network is a completely connected graph.

Of course, in real systems, communication links as well as processors are subject to failure. However, a link failure can be identified with the failure of one of the processors at its two ends, so a t-resilient protocol automatically tolerates up to t process and link failures. Nevertheless, this may give an overly pessimistic view of the reliability of the system. Reischuk [32] greatly refines the fault assumptions, enabling him to obtain more informative results on the actual behaviors of the systems.

A crucial assumption concerns whether or not the failure of a process to send an expected message can be detected. If so, then the expectant receiver gains the valuable knowledge that the sender is faulty. In a model with accurate clocks and bounds on message transit times, such detection is possible through the use of timeouts. (Cf. [21].) Also, detection is automatic in a synchronous model in which the processes run in lock step and messages sent at one step are

---

[1]The terminology comes from [25], in which a fable is recounted concerning a problem of military communications in times of old.

received at the next. However, detection is impossible in a fully asynchronous model in which no assumptions are made about relative step times or message delays, for there is no way to tell whether the sender has failed or is just running very slowly. This turns out to have a profound effect on the solvability of agreement problems.

We use the terms *synchronous* and *asynchronous* to distinguish between these two extreme cases, while remaining fully cognizant of the fact that synchronous message behavior can be achieved in systems with weaker assumptions than full synchrony. For our purposes, we will assume that a synchronous computation proceeds in a sequence of *rounds*. In each round, every process first sends as many messages as it wishes to other processes, and then it receives the messages sent to it by other processes. Thus, messages received during a round cannot affect the messages sent during the same round.

One further significant assumption is whether or not the model supports signatures. We assume that the author of a signed message can be reliably determined by anyone holding the message, regardless of where the message came from and regardless of anything that the faulty processes might have done. In other words, signatures cannot be forged by faulty processes, so if C receives a message from B signed by A, then C knows that A really sent the message and that it was not fabricated by B. Signatures, too, have a profound effect on the solvability of agreement problems. We sometimes use *authenticated* to refer to a protocol using signed messages.

Digital signatures can be implemented using cryptographic techniques [3, 4, 27, 33], or if one is willing to assume that faulty processes are not malevolent, simple signature schemes which are not cryptographically secure can be used instead. All that we require is that it be unlikely for a faulty process to generate a valid signature of some other process. Note that no special techniques are needed to implement signatures if only crashes (and not Byzantine failures) are considered, for then no incorrect messages are ever sent.

The practicality of agreement protocols depends heavily on their computational complexity. Some factors that might be important are the amount of *time* needed to complete the protocol, the amount of *message traffic* generated, or the amount of *memory* needed by the participants. All of these quantities are in general dependent on which faults actually occur and when. A reasonable assumption in many situations is that faults happen rarely, so it is acceptable to spend considerable resources handling them, but one wants the normal case to be handled quite efficiently. Note however that in a very large system, the probability of at least one fault is high, and the expected number of faults grows linearly with the size of the system.

We measure time in terms of the number of rounds of message exchange that take place. Thus, we assume every process can potentially exchange messages with every other in a single unit of time. Just how realistic this notion of time is depends highly on the structure of the message system and on the reasonableness of the assumption that a process can really send or receive n messages in a single time step. We measure message traffic variously as the total number of messages sent, the total number of bits in those messages, or the number of signatures (in the case of an authenticated protocol).

3. Relations Among Agreement Problems

The three agreement problems are closely related. The generals problem is a special case of the interactive consistency problem in which only one process's initial value is of interest, so a protocol achieving interactive consistency also solves the generals problem. Conversely, n copies of a protocol for the generals problem can be run in parallel to solve the interactive consistency problem.

The consensus problem appears to be slightly weaker than the other two. An interactive consistency algorithm can be modified to solve the consensus problem by just having each process choose as its consensus value the majority value in the consensus vector. This works as long as fewer than 1/2 of the processes are faulty.

Using a consensus algorithm to solve either of the other two problems, however, seems to require an additional round of information exchange. For example, the general's problem can be solved as follows:

Algorithm I

1. The general sends its value to each of the other processes.
2. All of the processes together run a consensus algorithm using as initial values the bits received from the general at the first step. (The general of course uses its own bit.)

This solves the generals problem since if the general is reliable, then all of the processes receive the same value in step 1. By the strong unanimity condition, this value will be chosen as the consensus value. In any case, agreement is reached. The extra cost is one additional round of 1-bit messages in step 1. Thus, we have proved:

Theorem 1. Given a t-resilient solution to the consensus problem, there is a t-resilient solution to the generals problem which uses one more "round" of message exchange and sends n−1 additional messages of 1-bit each.

Many solutions to the generals problem have the general structure of Algorithm I and thus appear to have embedded within them solutions to the consensus problem, seemingly obviating the need for Algorithm I and the extra round of messages. However, the embedded consensus algorithm does not necessarily solve the full consensus problem, for the case in which the general is reliable yet the x_i's are not all the same can never arise when the x_i's are obtained from the general on the first step.

Similar remarks apply to the corresponding weak versions of these problems. In fact, a weak Byzantine generals algorithm solves the weak consistency problem directly (without first using it to solve the interactive consistency problem), for if all the initial values are the same and no process is faulty, then it suffices to simply agree on the general's value. There is not, however, any readily apparent way to use a solution to any of the weak versions of the agreement problem to solve any of the strong ones. In fact, for a slightly different "approximate" agreement problem, Lamport [22] shows that the weak version has a solution whereas the strong one does not.

4. Solvability of Agreement Problems

Perhaps the most basic question to ask of a proposed agreement problem is whether or not it has a solution at all. By the previous discussion and Theorem 1 the consensus problem and the interactive consistency problem have t-resilient solutions iff the generals problem does, so we will restrict attention to the latter problem in this section.

Consider first the synchronous case. With signatures, Pease, Shostak, and Lamport [25, 29] give a t-resilient solution for any t.

Theorem 2. There is a t-resilient authenticated synchronous protocol which solves the strong (weak) Byzantine generals problem.

Briefly, the protocol consists of t+1 rounds. In the first round, the general sends a signed message with its value to each other process. At each round thereafter, each process adds its signature to each valid message received from the previous round and sends it to all processes whose signature does not already appear on the message. A message received during round k is *valid* if it bears exactly k distinct signatures, the first of which is the general's. Let V_i be the set of values contained in all the valid messages received by i through the end of round t+1. If V_i is a singleton, then that value is chosen as the consensus value. Otherwise, a fixed constant NIL is chosen.

To prove agreement, we argue that if i and j are both reliable, then $V_i = V_j$. There are two cases to consider. If the general is reliable, then both V_i and V_j consist solely of the general's value, since no other value ever appears in a valid message. Otherwise, consider the message M from which i first learned of v. M consists of v followed by a list of distinct signatures m_1, ..., m_k, the first of which is the general's, and $k \leq t+1$. If $k < t+1$ and process j does not already know about v, then j learns of v from i on the next round. If $k = t+1$, then m_1, ..., m_t are all faulty or else i would have learned of v earlier. But then m_{t+1} is reliable, so j learns of v at the same round as i. Correctness of the protocol easily follows.

Without signatures, there is a solution if and only if the fraction of faulty processes is not too large.

Theorem 3. There is a t-resilient synchronous protocol without authentication which solves the strong (weak) Byzantine generals problem iff $t/n < 1/3$.

The impossibility argument for $t/n \geq 1/3$ appears in [25, 29] for the strong case and in [22] for the weak case of the problem. Protocols demonstrating the solvability of both problems for $t/n < 1/3$ appear in [25, 29]. Various protocols have since appeared with additional desirable properties, some of which will be discussed later in this paper.

In the fully asynchronous case, there is no solution. In fact, Fischer, Lynch, and Paterson [18] show that the problem remains unsolvable even with much weaker requirements:

Theorem 4. In a fully asynchronous environment, there is no 1-crash resilient solution to the consensus problem, even when only the non-triviality condition is required.

The proof is by contradiction. In general outline, one assumes the existence of such a protocol. The protocol is *committed* to the eventual consensus value at a certain point in time if thereafter only the one value is a possible outcome, no matter how processes are scheduled or how messages are delivered. One shows that at least for some initial configuration, the outcome is not already committed. Starting from there, one constructs an infinite computation such that the system forever stays uncommitted, contradicting the assumed correctness of the protocol. The details get somewhat involved since it is necessary to insure that the infinite computation results from a "fair" schedule. The interested reader is referred to [18].

Returning to the Byzantine generals problem in a synchronous environment, we consider weaker connectivity assumptions on the network which nonetheless permit a solution. With signatures, Lamport et al. [25] show that the Byzantine Generals problem can be solved in any network in which the reliable processes are connected. Without signatures, they show that a solution is possible in a 3t-"regular" graph. Dolev [5, 6] extends this latter result to completely characterize the networks in which the problem is solvable:

Theorem 5. Consider a synchronous network with connectivity k having n processors, t of which may be faulty. Then the Byzantine generals problem is solvable without authentication iff $t/n < 1/3$ and $t/k < 1/2$.

Three recent unpublished results deserve brief mention, all of which extend the asynchronous model slightly in order to avoid the assumptions of Theorem 4. Ben-Or [1] allows randomized algorithms and shows that crash-resilient consensus is achievable with probability 1 when $t/n < 1/2$, and Byzantine-resilient consensus is achievable with probability 1 when $t/n < 1/5$. Rabin [31] uses randomized algorithms with an initial random "deal" and signatures to achieve certain agreement with an expected number of rounds that is only 4, independent of n and t, so long as $t/n < 1/4$. Finally, Dolev, Dwork, and Stockmeyer [7] distinguish among the different kinds of asynchrony in the model of [18] to get tighter conditions on when consensus protocols are and are not possible.

5. Complexity Results

5.1. Upper Bounds

The t-resilient Byzantine generals algorithms of [25, 29] take time t+1 and send a number of message bits that is exponential in t. The first algorithm to use only a polynomial number of message bits was found by Dolev and Strong [12] and subsequently improved by Fischer, Fowler, and Lynch [16]. The still stronger result below is from [8].

Theorem 6. Let $t/n < 1/3$. There is a t-resilient solution without authentication to the Byzantine generals problem which uses $2t + 3$ rounds of information exchange and $O(nt + t^3 \log t)$ message bits.

It remains an open problem if there is any unauthenticated algorithm which simultaneously achieves fewer than $2t + 3$ rounds and uses only polynomially many message bits.

With authentication, and counting number of messages instead of message bits, we get:

Theorem 7.

(a) There is a t-resilient authenticated solution to the Byzantine generals problem which uses t+1 rounds and sends O(nt) messages;

(b) There is a t-resilient authenticated solution to the Byzantine generals problem which uses O(t) rounds and sends only $O(n+t^2)$ messages.

Part (a) was shown by Dolev and Strong [15], and part (b) was shown by Dolev and Reischuk [10].

For practical applications, these bounds are not very encouraging, especially the t+1 bound on the number of rounds. As we shall see, this bound cannot be improved in the worst case that t faults actually occur. However, Dolev, Reischuk and Strong [11, 14] have looked at the question of whether Byzantine generals solutions exist which stop early when fewer faults occur. The answer depends on whether synchronization upon termination is also required.

For definiteness, we say that a process *halts within* r rounds if it is non-faulty and it chooses its consensus value and enters a stopping state before sending or receiving any round r+1 messages. It *halts in* round r if it halts within r rounds but does not halt within r−1 rounds. An agreement protocol *terminates* when all reliable processes have halted. If it terminates, we say it reaches *immediate* agreement if all reliable processes halt in the same round, and it reaches *eventual* agreement otherwise. Thus, immediate agreement serves to synchronize the processes as well as enabling them to agree on a value. Note that all of the protocols discussed previously achieve immediate agreement since all processes choose their consensus value in the last round.

The following theorem is from [11]:

Theorem 8. Let $t/n < 1/3$. There is a t-resilient protocol without authentication which solves the Byzantine generals problem and reaches eventual agreement within $\min(2t + 3, 2f + 5)$ rounds, where $f \leq t$ is the actual number of faults.

The same paper also contains a more refined protocol which stops even earlier when t is only about $\sqrt{n}$.

If one assumes processes can fail only by crashing, then Lamport and Fischer show that these bounds can be improved [23].

Theorem 9. There is a t-crash resilient protocol (without authentication) which solves the generals problem and reaches eventual agreement by the end of round f+2, where $f \leq t$ is the actual number of crashes.

We give the protocol and sketch its proof. There are only four possible messages — 0, 1, NIL, and ϕ. 0, 1 are the two possible initial values of the general, ϕ means "I don't know", and NIL is a default consensus value which is chosen when crashes prevent the reliable processes from discovering the general's value.

Algorithm II

A. Round 1: Process 1 (the general) sends its value to every process.

B. Round r, $1 < r \leq t+1$: Each process does the following:

1. If it received a value $v \in \{0, 1, NIL\}$ from any process in round r−1, then it:
   - takes v as its consensus value;
   - sends v to every process;
   - halts.
2. Otherwise, if it received ϕ during round r−1 from every process not known to have crashed before the beginning of that round, then it:
   - takes NIL as its consensus value;
   - sends NIL to every process;
   - halts.

   (It knows a process has crashed if it failed to receive an expected message from it during the previous round.)
3. Otherwise, it sends ϕ to every process.

C. End of Round t+1: Each process that has not halted does the following:

1. If it received a value $v \in \{0, 1, NIL\}$ from any process during round t+1, then it takes v as its consensus value and halts.
2. Otherwise, it chooses NIL as its consensus value and halts.

Correctness of the algorithm follows readily from the following facts. Recall that a crashed process is not considered to be halted.

1. If some process halts at step B1 or B2 during round r and chooses value v, then

every other process which halts at step B1 or B2 during round r also chooses v.

2. If some process halts at step B1 or B2 during round r and chooses value v, then every reliable process which has not already halted will choose v and halt at step B1 in round r+1 (if $r < t+1$) or at step C1 in round t+1 (if $r = t+1$).
3. If no process crashes or halts during round $r > 1$, then ϕ is the only message sent during that round.
4. If any process terminates at step C2 in round t+1, then all reliable processes do.

Moreover, if fewer than k processes crash in the first k rounds, then the protocol terminates within k+1 rounds; hence if there are at most f crashes, then the protocol terminates within f+2 rounds.

A more elaborate protocol with similar abstract properties but which is quite possibly more efficient in practice appears in [34].

5.2. Lower Bounds

All of the protocols above use t+1 rounds in the worst case. Fischer and Lynch [17] present a proof that t+1 rounds are necessary for achieving interactive consistency without signatures and hence also for solving the unauthenticated Byzantine generals problem. Several people have extended this result in one way or another. DeMillo, Lynch, and Merritt [3, 27] and independently Dolev and Strong [12, 15] show that the t+1 lower bound holds for authenticated solutions to the Byzantine generals problem. Lamport and Fischer [23], by a similar proof, show that the same bound holds assuming that the protocol is only crash resilient and solves the weak consensus problem, but they did not consider the authenticated case. We summarize these results below.

Theorem 10. Assume $t \leq n-2$.

(a) Every t-resilient protocol without signatures for the weak consensus problem uses at least t+1 rounds of message exchange in the worst case.

(b) Every t-resilient authenticated protocol for the Byzantine generals problem uses at least t+1 rounds of message exchange in the worst case.

We note that the weak consensus problem has not been explicitly studied with signed messages, but we conjecture that the same bound will still hold.

We sketch the basic structure underlying these proofs, although much more is involved in really making them go through. For two distinct computations S and T, define $S \sim T$ if S and T "look" the same to some reliable process p, that is, p receives the same messages and behaves exactly the same in both S and T. Hence, p chooses the same consensus value in each, which must be the consensus value for both S and T. Now, the proof proceeds by assuming at most t rounds and then constructing a sequence of t-round computations $S_0, S_1, ..., S_k$ such that S_0 has consensus value 0, S_k has consensus value 1, and $S_{i-1} \sim S_i$ for $1 \leq i \leq k$. This results in a contradiction. The constructions need one faulty process per round; hence, they cannot be used to find computations of more than t rounds.

Dolev and Strong [14] show that t+1 rounds are needed in a t-resilient immediate Byzantine generals protocol even when the actual number of failures is less. These theorems also appear without proofs in [11].

> **Theorem 11.** Let $t \leq n-2$, and let P be a t-resilient (authenticated) protocol solving the Byzantine generals problem which always reaches immediate agreement. Then it is possible for P to run for at least t+1 rounds even when there are no faults.

In the case of eventual agreement, they prove the following:

> **Theorem 12.** Let P be a t-resilient (authenticated) protocol solving the Byzantine generals problem which reaches eventual agreement, and let $f < t$. Then it is possible for P to run for at least f+2 rounds with only f faults.

We conjecture that this can be extended to t-crash resiliant generals protocols, which would then show the optimality of 9.

Finally, we look at lower bounds on the number of messages and signatures needed. Dolev and Reischuk [10] show:

> **Theorem 13.** The total number of messages and signatures in any t-resilient (authenticated) Byzantine generals solution is $\Omega(nt)$.

Theorem 6 shows that this bound is tight when n is large relative to t. If one counts only messages, then they show

> **Theorem 14.** The total number of messages in any t-resilient (authenticated) Byzantine generals solutions is $\Omega(n + t^2))$.

Theorem 7, part (b) shows this bound "best possible" for authenticated algorithms.

6. Applications of Agreement Protocols

The abstract versions of agreement problems considered in this survey are not general enough to be directly applicable to many practical situations. We mention here some extensions and applications of these problems.

First of all, one often wants to reach agreement on a value from a larger domain than just {0, 1}. If the domain has v elements, then one can encode the elements in binary and run $\lceil \log_2 v \rceil$ copies of the agreement protocol, one for each bit, but more efficient algorithms might be possible. In applications such as clock synchronization, the domain of values can be taken to be the real numbers, and only approximate agreement is needed. Lamport and Melliar-Smith [24] studies the clock synchronization problem, and Dolev, Lynch, and Pinter [9] look at the abstract approximate agreement problem.

A difficult part of implementing these algorithms is building message systems which actually have the reliability and synchronization properties that were assumed in the models. Real distributed systems are quasi-asynchronous, and to avoid the difficulties of Theorem 4 one must make reasonable timing assumptions and make effective use of clocks and timeouts. Lamport [21] gives some insights as to how this can be done.

Finally, we should mention the papers by Dolev and Strong [13] and Mohan, Strong, and Finkelstein [28] that describe serious attempts to apply agreement protocols to real problems of distributed databases.

7. Acknowledgement

The author is grateful for Ming Kao for help in assembling the bibliography and to Paul Hudak for many helpful comments on an early draft of this paper.

References

1. Ben-Or, M. "Another Advantage of Free Choice: Completely Asynchronous Agreement Protocols." *Proc. 2nd ACM Symposium on Principles of Distributed Computing*, 1983. To appear.

2. Davies, D. and Wakerly, J. F. "Synchronization and Matching in Redundant Systems." *IEEE Trans. on Computers C-27*, 6 (June 1978), 531-539.

3. DeMillo, R. A., Lynch, N. A., and Merritt, M. J. "Cryptographic Protocols." *Proc. 14th ACM Symposium on Theory of Computing*, 1982, pp. 383-400.

4. Diffie, W. and Hellman, M. "New Directions in Cryptography." *IEEE Trans. on Information Theory IT-22* (1976), 644-654.

5. Dolev, D. "Unanimity in an Unknown and Unreliable Environment." *Proc. 22nd IEEE Symposium on Foundations of Computer Science*, 1981, pp. 159-168.

6. Dolev, D. "The Byzantine Generals Strike Again." *J. Algorithms 3*, 1 (1982), 14-30.

7. Dolev, D., Dwork, C., and Stockmeyer, L. On the Minimal Synchronism Needed for Distributed Consensus. Manuscript.

8. Dolev, D., Fischer, M. J., Fower, R., Lynch, N. A., and Strong, H. R. "An Efficient Byzantine Agreement Without Authentication." *Information and Control* (to appear). See also IBM Research Report RJ3428 (1982).

9. Dolev, D., Lynch, N. A., and Pinter, S. Reaching Approximate Agreement in the Presence of Faults. Manuscript.

10. Dolev, D., and Reischuk, R. "Bounds on Information Exchange for Byzantine Agreement." *Proc. ACM SIGACT-SIGOPS Symposium on Principles of Distributed Computing*, 1982, pp. 132-140.

11. Dolev, D., Reischuk, R., and Strong, H. R. "'Eventual' is Earlier Than 'Immediate'." *23rd IEEE Symposium on Foundations of Computer Science*, 1982, pp. 196-203.

12. Dolev, D., and Strong, H. R. "Polynomial Algorithms for Multiple Processor Agremment." *Proc. 14th ACM Symposium on Theory of Computing*, 1982, pp. 401-407.

13. Dolev, D., and Strong, H. R. "Distributed Commit with Bounded Waiting." *Proc. Second Symposium on Reliability in Distributed Software and Database System*, Pittsburgh, July, 1982.

14. Dolev, D., and Strong, H. R. "Requirements for Agreement in a Distributed System." *Proc. Second International Symposium on Distributed Data Bases*, Berlin, Sept., 1982.

15. Dolev, D., and Strong, H. R. "Authenticated Algorithms for Byzantine Agreement." *SIAM J. Comput.* (to appear). See also IBM Research Report RJ3416 (1982).

16. Fischer, M. J., Fowler, R. J., and Lynch, N. A. "A Simple and Efficient Byzantine Generals Algorithm." *Proc. Second IEEE Symposium on Reliability in Distributed Software and Database Systems*, Pittsburgh, 1982, pp. 46-52.

17. Fischer, M. J., and Lynch, N. A. "A Lower Bound for the Time to Assure Interactive Consistency." *Inf. Proc. Lett. 14*, 4 (1982), 183-186.

18. Fischer, M. J., Lynch, N. A., and Paterson, M. S. "Impossibility of Distributed Consensus with One Faulty Process." *Proc. Second ACM Symposium on Principles of Database Systems*, March, 1983.

19. Gifford, D. K. Weighted Voting for Replicated Data. Tech. Rept. CSL-79-14, XEROX Palo Alto Reserach Center, Sept., 1979.

20. Gray, J. A Discussion of Distributed Systems. Research Report RJ2699, IBM, Sept., 1979.

21. Lamport, L. "Using Time Instead of Timeout for Fault-Tolerant Distributed Systems." *ACM Trans. on Programming Lang. and Systems* (to appear). See also technical report, Computer Science Laboratory, SRI International (June 1981).

22. Lamport, L. "The Weak Byzantine Generals Problem." *J. ACM 30*, 3 (July 1983). To appear.

23. Lamport, L. and Fischer, M. J. Byzantine Generals and Transaction Commit Protocols. Manuscript.

24. Lamport, L., and Melliar-Smith, P.M. Synchronizing Clocks in the Presence of Faults. Computer Science Laboratory, SRI International, March, 1982.

25. Lamport, L., Shostak, R.., and Pease, M. "The Byzantine Generals Problem." *ACM Trans. on Programming Lang. and Systems 4*, 3 (July 1982), 382-401.

26. Lindsay, B. G., et al. Notes on Distributed Databases. Research Report RJ2571, IBM, July, 1979.

27. Merritt, M. J. Cryptographic Protocols. Tech. Rept. GIT-ICS-83/06, School of Inf. & Comp. Sci., Georgia Institute of Techonology, Feb., 1983.

28. Mohan, C., Strong, H. R., and Finkelstein, S. Method for Distributed Transaction Commit and Recovery Using Byzantine Agreement within Clusters of Processors. Research Report RJ3882, IBM, 1983.

29. Pease, M., Shostak, R., and Lamport, L. "Reaching Agreement in the Presence of Faults." *J. ACM 27*, 2 (1980), 228-234.

30. Popek, G., et al. "LOCUS: A Network Transparent, High Reliability Distributed System." *Proc. 8th ACM Symposium on Operating Systems Principles*, Dec., 1981, pp. 169-177.

31. Rabin, M. Randomized Byzantine Generals. Manuscript.

32. Reischuk, R. A New Solution for the Byzantine Generals Problem. Research Report RJ3673, IBM, Nov., 1982.

33. Rivest, R., Shamir, A., and Adleman, L. "A Method for Obtaining Digital Signatures and Public-Key Cryptosystems." *Comm. ACM 21*, 2 (Feb. 1978), 120-126.

34. Schneider, F. B., Gries, D., and Schlichting, R. D. Fast Reliable Broadcasts. Computer Science Technical Report TR 82-519, Cornell University, Sept., 1982.

35. Wensley, J. H., et al. "SIFT: Design and Analysis of a Fault-Tolerant Computer for Aircraft Control." *Proc. IEEE 66*, 10 (Oct. 1978), 1240-1255.

METHODS IN THE ANALYSIS OF ALGORITHMS :

EVALUATIONS OF A RECURSIVE PARTITIONING PROCESS

Philippe FLAJOLET

INRIA, Rocquencourt

78150, Le Chesnay (France)

Abstract : *We show how the analysis of a large number of algorithms used for sorting, searching, retrieving multidimensional data, accessing external files, factoring polynomials, implementing communication protocols... reduce to the study of a simple recursive partitioning process. We present systematic methods for obtaining from the structural definitions of characteristic parameters of the process corresponding average values in either exact or asymptotic form through the use of generating functions.*

Analyzing algorithms is an activity that is often of practical value : it helps building a precise *classification* of alternative solutions to a common algorithmic problem (Are bubblesort or heapsort faster than quicksort ?), permits to select amongst proposed *optimizations* those whose gain is not offset by higher overhead costs (Is it worth using "median-of-three" rule to select partitioning elements in quicksort ?) and allows *tuning* some of the design parameters to a particular utilization (When should we stop recursively sorting small subfiles in a recursive sorting algorithm ?). It is also a surprising fact that in a large number of cases algorithmic analyses lead to interesting mathematical developments usually related to advanced methods of *combinatorial analysis* in the phase of counting characteristic configurations and *asymptotic analysis* used to replace complex expressions of costs by their asymptotic equivalents, normally of a much simpler form.

Knuth's books provide an excellent illustration of the interplay between algorithimic analysis ; for instance [Kn73p381] contains a complete description of the costs of the main sorting methods on a particular, but typical, machine model : with the notable exception of balanced tree structures (heaps, AVL trees, 2-3 trees) for which fully adequate mathematical tools are still lacking, the complexity of each main sorting method presented is precisely characterized through a complete mathematical analysis.

Similar analyses together with a discussion of their relevance and the methodology for carrying them out also appear in [Kn71], [Se82], [FS81]. However, many of the analyses are often one-shot : one sets up in each particular case recurrence equations to be solved using techniques from the calculus of finite differences, or the algebra of formal power series. As discussed in [FS81], when analyzing structurally complex programs there arises instead the need of more general evaluation methodologies that relate the structure of programs to their (average-case) complexity behaviours.

The present paper is in the lines of [FS81] and some preliminary investigations in [FS82] : we introduce a *recursive partitioning process* of a simple yet very general nature. This process models a wide class of algorithms including : radix searching methods (tries), radix sorting, dynamic hashing schemes, multidimensional radix techinques, and such seemingly unrelated applications as polynomial factorization and communication protocols. We discuss general methods for translating in various situations the structural definitions of characteristic parameters (height, path length, number of partitioning stages...) to exact and asymptotic expressions for their expected values. An important intermediary stage is a unified framework for obtaining *generating functions* of these expected values. After a brief survey of corresponding asymptotic methods, we conclude by applications to the analysis of several algorithms in the classes previously mentioned.

Apart from basic results that appear in [Kn73] and [TP78], several of the results mentioned here have been obtained in collaboration with D. Sotteau (algebraic methods) [FSo82], C. Puech [FP83], N. Saheb [FSa82], J-M. Steyeart [FSt82] and by M. Regnier [Re83].

I - THE BASIC PARTITIONING PROCESS ; VARIANTS AND APPLICATIONS

The simplest form of the recursive partitioning process we are considering here is as follows : one starts with a fixed set of individuals G ; in the first stage each individual in G flips a coin and individuals are partitioned in two groups G_H and G_T representing respectively the group of "heads" and the group of "tails". These subgroups are themselves partitioned recursively by a new flipping of coins, G_H giving rise to G_{HH} and G_{HT}... . The partitioning of subgroups continues until subgroups of cardinality at most 1 have been individuated.

```
procedure partition (G:set) ;
   begin
      if card(G)≤1 then halt ;
       G_H:=∅ ; G_T:=∅ ;
      for each g in G do
         if flip=head then G_H:=G_H∪{g} else G_T:=G_T∪{g} ;
      partition (G_H) ;
      partition (G_T)
   end ;
```

The succession of splittings corresponding to a particular sequence of flippings is naturally described by a tree : G is put at the root of the tree, G_H and G_T are drawn as left and right sons of the root respectively..., and groups of size 0 or 1 are represented as leaves (see Figure 1).

A number of variants of this process are obtained by changing

- the terminating condition to "card(G)≤b" for some fixed constant b ;
- the splitting policy, using various types of unbiased/biased coins/dice.
- the arrival policy, occasionally allowing the initial population to admit newcomers in the course of the partitioning process.

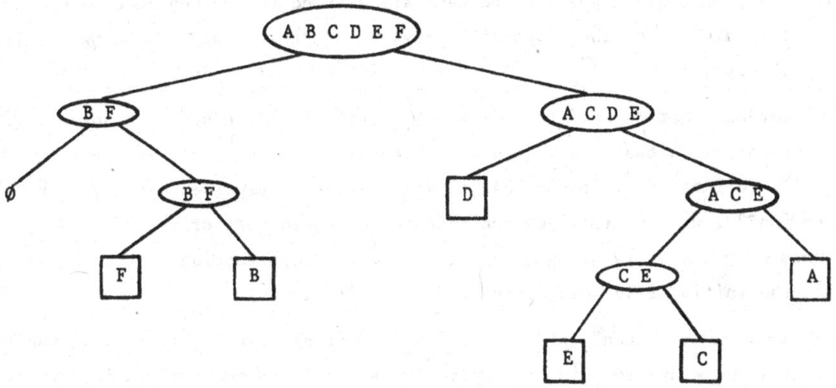

Firuge 1 : A recursive partitionning tree on the set {A,B,C,D,E,F}. Terminating subgroups are represented by squares.

We briefly describe the way this process models several algorithmic applications.

I.1 - Digital searching and sorting

Tries are tree structures associated to finite sets of strings over some fixed alphabet (see for instance [Kn73], [AHU83], [Se83]). Assuming for simplicity the alphabet to be binary, the set ω is partitioned into two subsets depending on the values of the most significant bit of its elements : those starting with a 0 are placed in the first subset ω_0 ; those starting with a 1 are placed in the second subset ω_1;we then proceed according to the second most significant bit... . The construction of a trie associated to a set ω of binary strings is therefore isomorphic to the execution of the previous partitioning procedure if we interpret 0 as heads, 1 as tails and assume that individuals have predetermined a sufficiently long sequence of flippings. For instance the tree of Figure 1 would correspond to the set ω={A,B,C,D,E,F} where A=111... ; B=011..., C=1101... ; D=10... ; etc... .

Tries are an attractive alternative to binary search trees with which they have many similarities. They have the further advantage of allowing set-theoretic operations like union, intersection, symmetric difference to be performed easily and efficiently (see [TP78]).

Two different types of statistical assymptions are usually made to analyze trie structures :

(i) the infinite key model : there keys are assumed to be infinitely long binary sequences formed from independently uniformly distributed {0;1} bits.

(ii) the finite key model : there keys are assumed to be idependently drawn from the universe of the 2^s possible keys of length s (each key being equally likely).

From methods that we describe below will result that the somewhat unrealistic model (i) is in most situations a good approximation of model (ii), also giving expressions simpler to interpret. Statistics (i) and (ii) are described mor fully in [TP78]. From [Kn73], we know for instance that the expected cost of a search in a trie formed with n keys is O(log n) and the expected construction cost of the trie (which puts the initial file into sorted order) is O(n log n).

Radix exchange sort [Kn73,p125] is a way of sorting binary strings avoiding the additional storage due to pointers implied by a construction of the trie structure. As such it bears the same relation to tries as quicksort does to standard binary search trees, and most of the relevant parameters can be expressed in terms of trie parameters.

I.2 - Tries as indexes and dynamic hashing schemes

Files on some external storage device can also be accessed through indexes organized as tries. Let b represent the page capacity measured in the maximum number of records a page can hold (page capacity may vary from a few hundred to a few tenths of thousand bytes depending on the installation). We can start building a trie as in I.1 but stop the partitioning a soon as subsets of size at most b are obtained. These "small" subsets are stored in disk pages while the remaining part of the tree is kept in core. When the trie structure is built on hashed values of keys (instead of actual key bits) to ensure uniformity of bit values, one obtains exactly Larson's *Dynamic Hashing* method [La78] . This method is also closely related to Litwin's Virtual Hashing [Li78]. *Extendible Hashing* of [FNPS79] uses a further strategy to page the index if it is too large to fit in core (the paging is in the form an array imbedding).

These access methods are useful in practice since in most situations they guarantee quasi-direct access to disk files in about 1 to 4 disk accesses irrespective of file sizes.

I.3 - Multidimensional tries (k-d-tries)

These are used [Ri76] to represent sets of *multidimensional records*, that is records from some universe

$$D = D_1 \times D_2 \times \ldots \times D_k$$

(each D_j is called an attribute domain or a field) where each D_j is encoded as a binary string which, again as a first approximation, may be considered as infinite. A k-d-trie is nothing but the trie formed on records by taking in sequence the first bit of attribute 1, the first bit of attribute 2,... ; then cyclically again the second bit of attributes 1,2,... ; etc... . Like their comparison-based counterparts known as k-d-trees, k-d-tries are useful for answering *partial match queries*, that is queries that only specify some attribute values of records to be retrieved. A partial match search in such a structure proceeds through a regular succession of one-way and two-way branching in the tree depending on whether corresponding bit values are specified or not in the query. From the analysis in [FP83], there results that k-d-tries asymptotically outperform k-d-trees, the cost of partial match in a file of size n with a proportion of s/k specified attributes being $O(n^{1-s/k})$.

I.4 - Communication protocols

The basic partitioning procedure may be viewed as a way of allocating resources to some contending indivuduals. In a decentralized ntework, several users have access to a common channel which they use to broadcast information and on which collisions that occur have to be resolved. Basically, when a collision occurs, colliding senders separate themselves into two groups (using a stochastic decision procedure). Members of the first group first recursively resolve their conflicts and broadcast, and members of the second group wait until the channel is free to transmit. The Capetanakis-Tsybakov-Vvedenskaya protocol is essentially based on the observation that such a way of resolving collisions can be implemented in a fully decentralized manner (see [Ma81]). The main problem in the analytic techniques involved is the fact that arrivals may be continuous in some versions of the protocol.

I.5 - Polynomial factorization

Some recent developments of Berlekamp's Factorization algorithm for polynomials over a finite field due to Cantor, Zassenhauss [CZ81] and Lazard [La81] are based on an iterative construction of primitive idempotents. The construction is a refinement process that can be shown equivalent to the generation of a partition tree with biased probabilities on splittings.

I.6 - Simulation algorithms

Many other algorithms can also be described and analyzed in terms of trie structures, even though no explicit trie construction takes place (radix exchange sort previously mentioned is an example of such a situation). An interesting illustration is the von Neumann-Knuth-Yao algorithm for generating "exactly" an exponentially distributed variate. It is shown in [FSa82] that such an algorithm generates k bits of this distribution in an expected number of

$$k + 5.679... + O(1)$$

elementary coin flippings. Compared to a general result by [KY76] on generating biased distributions, this shows the algorithm to be optimal up to a fixed constant term.

II - ALGEBRAIC METHODS

Many of the characteristic parameters of the algorithms we have just mentioned are expressible in terms of classical parameters of the corresponding partition tree (equivalent trie). In this section, we show how to determine quasi-automatically generating functions of expected values of inductively defined parameters. More precisely, let $\pi(\omega)$ be a parameter of the partition tree (number of nodes, path length, height...) associated to ω. We let

$$\overline{\pi}_n = \text{Expectation}(\pi(\omega)):|\omega|=n) \qquad (1)$$

for some statistics on n-sets of sequences (e-g the finite of infinite key model). Our goal is to relate the structural definition of π to the form of a *generating function*

$$\pi(z) = \sum_{n\geq 0} \overline{\pi}_n \rho_n z^n \qquad (2)$$

for some reference sequence ρ_n, independent of π but adequately chosen in accordance with the statistical model chosen. For instance under the *finite key model*, with keys of a fixed length s, we take

$$\rho_n = \binom{2^s}{n} ; \qquad (3)$$

in other words since the number of n-sulsets of keys is given by the binomial expression (3), (2) is nothing but the *ordinary generating fonction* of the *cumulated values* of π over all n-sets of keys of length n. Under the *infinite key model* we shall take

$$\rho_n = \frac{1}{n!} ,$$

so that (2) is the *exponential generating function* of the expected values of π over all n-sets of infinite binary sequences.

2.1 - The finite model

A convenient way of obtaining generating functions under this model is through the use of *multivariate* polynomials that represent an *encoding* of the possible keys in the set $\mathcal{B}^{(s)} = \{0 ; 1\}^s$ of all binary sequences of some fixed length s, which has cardinality 2^s. We also set $\mathcal{P}^{(s)} = \mathbb{P}(\mathcal{B}^{(s)})$, the power set of $\mathcal{B}^{(s)}$. The number of n-subsets of $\mathcal{B}^{(s)}$ is thus given by the binomial coefficient (3).

(i) We represent each element $u \in \mathcal{B}^{(s)}$ by a corresponding variable x_u.

(ii) An element ω of $\mathcal{P}^{(s)}$, $\omega = \{u_1, u_2, \ldots, u_n\}$, is represented by the product

$$\text{rep}\ (\omega) = x_{u_1} x_{u_2} \ldots x_{u_n}$$

(iii) A family F of elements of $P^{(s)}$ is then represented by the *sum*

$$\text{rep}(F) = \sum_{\omega \in F} \text{rep}(\omega).$$

For instance when s = 2, $F = P^{(2)}$ is represented by the polynomial

$$1+x_{00}+x_{01}+x_{10}+x_{11}+x_{00}x_{01}+x_{00}x_{10}+x_{00}x_{11}+x_{01}x_{10}$$
$$+x_{01}x_{11}+x_{10}x_{11}+x_{00}x_{01}x_{10}+x_{00}x_{01}x_{11}$$
$$+x_{00}x_{10}x_{11}+x_{01}x_{10}x_{11}+x_{00}x_{01}x_{10}x_{11}$$

which appears to be equal to :

$$(1+x_{00})\ (1+x_{01})\ (1+x_{10})\ (1+x_{11}).$$

Similarly, a multiset on $P^{(s)}$, defined by a valuation μ on elements of $P^{(s)}$

$$M = \sum_{\omega \in P^{(s)}} \mu(\omega)\ .\ \omega$$

is represented by the polynomial $$M^{(s)}(X) = \sum_{\omega \in P^{(s)}} \mu(\omega)\ \text{rep}(\omega). \qquad (4)$$

In order to express recurrences based on the size s of binary sequences we introduce the functions :

$$\sigma_0 : B^{(s)} \to B^{(s+1)} \quad ; \quad \sigma_1 : B^{(s)} \to B^{(s+1)}$$

defined by :

$$\sigma_0(u) = \underline{0}u \quad ; \quad \sigma_1(u) = \underline{1}u$$

with normal extension to sets and multisets.

For β in $B^{(s)}$ with s>0, we introduce the dual operations $\beta/0$, $\beta/1$ by :

$$\beta/0 = \{u\} \text{ if } \omega = 0u,\ \beta/0 = \emptyset \text{ if } \omega = 1u$$

$$\beta/1 = \ u \ \text{ if } \omega = 1u,\ \omega/1 = \emptyset \text{ if } \ = 0u,$$

with extensions to sets ; for $\omega \in P^{(s)}$, we have $\omega/0 = \sum_{\beta \in \omega} \beta/0 \qquad \omega/1 = \sum_{\beta \in \omega} \beta/1$

so that $\omega = \sigma_0(\omega/0) + \sigma_1(\omega/1)$.

The σ operations are applied to generating polynomials interpreting these polynomials as multisets. For instance $\sigma_1(1+2x_{00}+4x_{01}x_{10}) = 1+2x_{100}+4x_{101}x_{110}$.

In the sequel, we adhere to the notational conventions of (4), representing valuations on the $P^{(s)}$ by lower case letter, corresponding multisets by script letters and associated generating polynomials by capital letters. Whenever convenient, we also identify multisetsand generating polynomials that encode them.

<u>Lemma 1</u> : *Let* $v^{(s)}$, $w^{(s)}$ *be two valuations on* $P^{(s)}$. *The valuations on* $P^{(s)}$, $P^{(s+1)}$ *defined by*

$$a^{(s)}(\omega) = v^{(s)}(\omega) + w^{(s)}(\omega)$$

$$b^{(s)}(\bar{\omega}) = v^{(s)}(\omega/0) + w^{(s)}(\omega/0)$$

have corresponding generating polynomials : $A^{(s)}(X) = V^{(s)}(X) + W^{(s)}(X)$

$$B^{(s+1)}(X) = \sigma_0(V^{(s)}(X)) \cdot \sigma_1(W^{(s)}(X)).$$

In particular since $P^{(s)}$ is the multiset that corresponds to the constant valuation $p(\omega) = 1$, we have

$$p(\omega) = p(\omega/0) \cdot p(\omega/1)$$

whence the recurrence $\quad P^{(s+1)}(X) = \sigma_0(P^{(s)}(X)) \cdot \sigma_1(P^{(z)}(X))$

with $\quad P^{(0)}(X) = 1 + x_\varepsilon$

(ε denoting the empty sequence). Thus by recurrence the expected result :

$$P^{(s)}(X) = \prod_{u \in B^{(s)}} (1+x_u) \qquad (5)$$

As a consequence of Lemma 1, if $\quad a^{(s+1)}(\omega) = v^{(s)}(\omega/0) + w^{(s)}(\omega/1) \qquad (6)$

we have

$$a^{(s+1)}(\omega) = v^{(s)}(\omega/0) \cdot p^{(s)}(\omega/1) + p^{(s)}(\omega/0)\, w^{(s)}(\omega/1),$$

so that

$$A^{(s+1)}(X) = \sigma_0(V^{(s)}(X))\sigma_1(P^{(s)}(X)) + \sigma_0(P^{(s)}(X)) \cdot \sigma_1(W^{(s)}(X)). \qquad (7)$$

The power of Lemma 1 and of (6), (7) comes from the fact that most parameters of interest on trees are definable as additive-multiplicative combinations of similar or simpler parameters on subtrees, so that a large number of equations can be written systematically. Also these equations on multivariate generating functions yield more classical generating functions by various sorts of morphisms. Starting again from (3), (4), and denoting by M(x) the polynomial obtained from M(X) by replacing all subscripted variables by the variable x, we see that :

$$[x^n]M^{(s)}(x) = \sum_{\substack{\omega \notin P^{(s)} \\ |\omega|=n}} \mu(\omega)$$

where $|\omega|$ is the number of sequences in ω and $[x^n]\, f(x)$ is the coefficient of x^n in f(x).

Equations obtained in this way are much simpler and can usually be solved by iterating the recurrence on s. We give below a few examples :

1. The univariate generating polynomial of $P^{(s)}$ is from (5)

$$P^{(s)}(x) = (1+x)^{2^s} \qquad (8)$$

and accordingly the number of n-subsets of $B^{(s)}$ is

$$[x^n]\,(1+x)^{2^s} = \binom{2^s}{n}.$$

2. Let $P_k^{(s)}$ be the family of sets whose associated tree has height $\leq k$. Clearly

$$P_0^{(s)} = 1 + \sum_{u \in B^{(s)}} x_u \;;\; P_{k+1}^{(s+1)}(X) = \sigma_0(P_k^{(s)}(X))\, \sigma_1(P_k^{(s)}(X))$$

so that $$P_k^{(s)} = (1+2^{s-k}x)^{2^k} \qquad (9)$$

and the probability that a set of n sequences of length s gives rise to a tree of height $\leq k$ is :

$$2^{n(s-k)} \binom{2^k}{n} \binom{2^s}{n}^{-1}. \qquad (10)$$

3. Similarly if the tree growth is stopped when groups have size $\leq b$, the probability that the height is $\leq k$ for a tree formed with n sequences is

$$\frac{1}{\binom{2^s}{n}} [x^n] \quad B_b^{(2^{s-k})}(x)^{2^k}$$

where $B_b^{(m)}$ is the truncated binomial series :

$$B_b^{(m)}(x) = 1 + \binom{m}{1}x + \binom{m}{2}x + \binom{m}{2}x^2 + \ldots + \binom{m}{b}x^b. \qquad (11)$$

4. The previous examples showed the use of the product rule of Lemma 1. A large number of parameters of interest in applications are defined as additive and multiplicative combinations. The simplest example is the statistics of the total number of nodes in the tree constructed from binary sequences of fixed length. This parameter $no(\omega)$ is defined by the recurrences

$$no^{(0)}(\omega) = |\omega|$$

$$no^{(s+1)}(\omega) = no^{(s)}(\omega\backslash 0) + no^{(s)}(\omega\backslash 1) + 1 - \delta_{|\omega|,0} - \delta_{|\omega|,1} \cdot$$

whence the equations

$$NO^{(s+1)}(x) = 2P^{(s)} NO^{(s)}(x) + P^{(s+1)}(x)-1-2^{s+1}x . \qquad (12)$$

The equation can be solved by iteration and we find

$$NO_n^{(s)} = \binom{2^s}{n}(n+2^s-1) - \sum_{j=1}^{s-1} 2^i \binom{2^s-2^{s-j}}{n} + 2^s \binom{2^s-2^{s-j}}{n-1} \qquad (13)$$

5. Path length is another parameter of interest since it is related to the time necessary for sorting a set of sequences by constructing the associated tree. From the classical inductive definition of path length, we find equations similar to those of part (4) above, and solving one has for the cumulated path length of trees constructed on n binary sequences :

$$LCE_n^{(s)} = \binom{2^s-1}{n-1} 2^s(s+1) - 2^s \sum_{j=0}^{s-1} \binom{2^s-2^{s-j}}{n-1} \qquad (14)$$

2.2 - <u>The infinite key model</u>

For a fixed cardinality n, letting s tend to infinity, one notices that average values of most practical parameters on trees tend to well defined limits. These limiting values coincide with the average values of the corresponding parameters on trees constructed from infinite sequences, under the usual statistic on $\{0:1\}^{\infty}$ (The trees are finite with probability 1). They are also useful as they constitute good approximations to the finite case when $n<<2^s$ and are themselves easier to estimate by the methods of section 3.

For a parameter $\pi^{(s)}$ on $P^{(s)}$, we defined the cumulative values

$$\Pi_n^{(s)} = \sum_{\substack{|\omega|=n \\ \omega\in P^{(s)}}} \pi^{(s)}(\omega) \tag{15}$$

and we are interested in computing the quantities (of which we assume the existence) :

$$\Pi_n^{(\infty)} = \lim_{s\to\infty} \frac{\Pi^{(s)}}{\binom{2^s}{n}} . \tag{16}$$

Lemma 2 : *The average values of parameters corresponding to infinite sequences have exponential generating function given by :*

$$\Pi^{(\infty)}(z) = \sum_{n\geq 0} \Pi_n^{(\infty)} \frac{z^n}{n!} = \lim_{s\to\infty} \Pi^{(s)} \left(\frac{x}{2^s}\right).$$

In particular the exponential generating function of the parameter $p(\omega)\equiv 1$ is e^x and one has

$$e^x = \lim_{s\to\infty} \left(1 + \frac{x}{2^s}\right)^{2^s}$$

in accordance with Lemma 2.

Lemma 2 used in conjuction with Lemma 1 permits a direct calculation of generating functions associated to parameters defined on $P(B^{(\infty)})$ (finite sets of infinite sequences). So that, if :

$$a(\omega) = v(\omega/0) + w(\omega/1) \ ; \ b(\omega) = v(\omega/0) \ . \ w(\omega/0), \tag{17}$$

one has for the associated exponential generating functions :

$$A^{(\infty)}(x) = e^{x/2}\left(V^{(\infty)}\left(\frac{x}{2}\right) + W^{(\infty)}\left(\frac{x}{2}\right)\right) \ ; \ B^{(\infty)}(x) = V^{(\infty)}\left(\frac{x}{2}\right) \ . \ W^{(\infty)}\left(\frac{x}{2}\right). \tag{18}$$

For recursively defined parameters, the translation schemes (17), (18) lead to functional difference equations of the form

$$\phi(x) = a(x)\ \phi\left(\frac{x}{2}\right) + b(x). \tag{19}$$

These can normally be solved by iteration, so that

$$\phi(x) = \sum_{k\geq 0} b(x2^{-k}) \prod_{j=0}^{k-1} a(x2^{-j}) .$$

In the frequent case $a(x) = Ae^{cx}$, (20) further simplifies to

$$\phi(x) = \sum_{k\geq 0} A^k\ b(x2^{-k})\ \exp(c(1-2^{-k})x) \tag{20}$$

whose Taylor coefficient have an explicit form. Some examples follow :

1. The cumulative distribution of height in trees corresponding to Example 3 of the finite case, becomes in the infinite case : $[\frac{x^n}{n!}]\ e_b(\frac{x}{2^k})^{2^k}$

where $$e_b(x) = 1 + \frac{x}{1!} + \frac{x^2}{2!} + \ldots + \frac{x^b}{b!} \tag{21}$$

which agrees with the classical result on occupancy problems in probability theory.

2. External path length leads to the equation $\phi(x) = 2e^{x/2}\phi\ \frac{x}{2} + x(e^x-1)$,

which when solved by (20) (21) leads to the two equivalent forms :

$$LCE_n^{(\infty)} = n \sum_{k\geq 0} (1-(1-2^{-k})^{n-1}) = \sum_{p=2}^{n} \binom{n}{p} \frac{(-1)^p p}{2^{p-1}-1} \tag{22}$$

Example 1 above appears in the analysis of extendible hashing [FS82] ; Example 2 is a classical result [Kn73].

Amongst the several possible extensions of these algebraic methods, we mention :

(i) Translation schemes corresponding to a biased distribution on bits of sequences. For instance, in the infinite case, if p and q are the probabilities of zeros and 1 respectively, then (17) translates into :

$$A^{(\infty)}(x) = e^{qx}\ V^{(\infty)}(px) + e^{px}\ W^{(\infty)}(qx)\ ;\ B^{(\infty)}(x) = V^{(\infty)}(px)\ W^{(\infty)}(qx). \tag{23}$$

For instance if $h_m(\omega)$ is 1 if the height of the tree associated to ω is $\leq m$ and 0 otherwise, we have $$H_m^{(\infty)}(x) = H_{m-1}^{(\infty)}(px)\ H_{m-1}^{(\infty)}(qx)$$

whence $$H_m^{(\infty)}(x) = \prod_{k=0}^{m} (1+p^k q^{m-k} x)^{\binom{m}{k}} \tag{24}$$

This result is used in [FS82] to analyze a polynomial factorization algorithm. The methods extend to alphabets of cardinality larger than 2.

(ii) Extension to functions of several sets of binary sequences : in applications,these occur for instance in algorithms for performing set-theoretic operations (see [TP78] for several examples). Thus using trees to compute the intersection of two sets ω, ω' by the relation :

$$\omega \cap \omega' = \sigma_0(\omega\backslash 0 \cap \omega'\backslash 0) + \sigma_1(\omega\backslash 1 \cap \omega'\backslash 1) \tag{25}$$

with the corresponding computation time :

$$I(\omega,\omega') = I(\omega\backslash 0,\ \omega'\backslash 0) + I(\omega\backslash 1,\omega'\backslash 1)$$
$$+ 1 - \delta_{|\omega|,0} - \delta_{|\omega'|,0} + \delta_{|\omega|,0}\ \delta_{|\omega'|,0}\ ,$$

we find for the bivariate exponential generating fonction of computation times :

$$I^{(\infty)}(x,v) = 2e^{x/2}\, e^{v/2}\, I(\frac{x}{2}, \frac{y}{2}) + (e^{x}-1)\,(e^{y}-1)\ . \qquad (26)$$

This equation can be solved by techniques described above.

(iii) Variances and higher moments can also be derived. With q a formal variable, we have for external path length :

$$q^{e(\omega)} = q^{e(\omega/0)}\, q^{e(\omega/1)}\, q^{|\omega|}\, q^{-\delta_{|\omega|,1}}$$

whence for the bivariate generating function of probabilities the recurrence

$$L^{(s)}(z;q) = (L^{(s-1)}(qz,q))^2 + 2^s q(1-q)z\ldots\ .$$

Similar techniques are used in [FSa82] to derive the distribution of costs in the Von Neumann-Knuth-Yao algorithm.

III - ASYMPTOTIC METHODS

Expressions derived in the previous section under the infinite key model do not show explicitly the asymptotic dependence between n and the expectations of parameters of interest on n-subsets. It appears that these expectations almost invariably involve non trivial periodicities for which special asymptotic methods based on the Mellin integral transform need to be used.

III.1 - Multiplicative valuations

Purely multiplicative valuations on trees lead to generating functions that have product forms. A typical example is *tree height* with equations (9), (11), (21), (24). The saddle point method is well suited to the derivation of limit distributions (whence averages and variances). The starting point is Cauchy's integral form of coefficients of analytic functions :

$$[z^n]\ f(z) = \frac{1}{2i\pi} \int_\Gamma f(z) \frac{dz}{z^{n+1}} \qquad (27)$$

which can be put under the form $\frac{1}{2i\pi} \int_\Gamma e^{h(z)} dz.$

The saddle point heuristic (see [He78]) consists in selecting for Γ a contour that crosses some saddle point of h(z), i.e. a point s such that $h'(s) = 0$.

In the case of integrals of the form (27) with f an entire function depending on a parameter, a circle centered around the origin and crossing the saddle point of smallest modulus leads to good localization properties of the integral (27) ; the main contribution is shown to come from a small fraction of the contour around the saddle-point ; there local expansions are used to approximate the integral.

One proves in this way [FSt82] that the probability π_n^m of having a tree of height $\le m$ with n key when subtrees of size $\le b$ are grouped in a single leaf (page) satisfies :

$$\pi_n^m = e^{-\beta(n)\,2^{-b\delta}}$$

with $$\delta = m - (1 + \frac{1}{b}) \log_2 n \tag{28}$$

and $\beta(n)$ a bounded fluctuating function of n. This formula shows in particular that $\pi_n^m - \pi_n^{m-1}$ has a strong peak around $(1 + \frac{1}{b}) \log_2 n$, with periodicities (in n) appearing in the probability distribution.

III.2 - Additive valuations

Examples of additive valuations have been given when discussing statistics on the number of nodes and external path length. The algebraic paradigm is summarized by equations (19), (20) ; results appear as sums of which (22) is typical. Using thus path length as an illustration, the problem is to approximate sums like

$$S_n = \sum_{k\geq 0} [(1-2^{-k})^n - 1] \ . \tag{29}$$

The classical way of dealing with such sums is first to introduce an exponential approximation, using $(1-a)^n \approx e^{-na}$ valid for small a. Thus one first approximates S_n by :

$$T_n = \sum_{k\geq 0} (e^{-n2^{-k}} - 1) \ . \tag{30}$$

An expression like (30) belongs to the category of *harmonic sums* of the general form

$$F(x) = \sum \alpha_k \ f(\beta_k x) \ . \tag{31}$$

To determine the asymptotic behaviour of (31) for large values of x, following [Kn73], one computes the Mellin transform of F :

$$F^*(s) = \int_0^\infty F(x) \ x^{s-1} \ dx \tag{32}$$

which in this case factorizes as

$$F^*(s) = f^*(s) \sum_{k\geq 0} \alpha_k \ \beta_k^{-s}, \tag{33}$$

i.e. as the product of the Mellin transform of the fundamental function and of a Dirichlet series related to the amplitudes and phases of the harmonics. As is known, the singularities of $F^*(s)$ -which are easy to determine using the factor form (33)- are related to the terms in the asymptotic behaviour of F(x) at 0 and at ∞ : a combination of the Mellin inversion theorem with Cauchy's redisue theorem shows that

$$F(x) = \sum \mathrm{Res}(F^*(s) \ x^{-s}) \ + \text{remainder of smaller order} \tag{34}$$

where the summation is extended to poles of F(s) in a stripe. Equation (34) is based on the inversion theorem for the Mellin transform :

$$F(x) = \frac{1}{2i\pi} \int_{c-i\infty}^{c+i\infty} F^*(s) \ x^{-s} \ ds. \tag{35}$$

In the case of the sum arising in the analysis of path length by (29), (30)

$$T(x) = \sum_{k\geq 0} e^{-x2^{-k}} - 1,$$

one finds :

$$T^*(s) = \frac{\Gamma(s)}{1-2^s} \qquad -1 < \mathrm{Re}(s) < 0.$$

This function has a double pole at $s=0$ and simple poles at $s = \frac{2ik\pi}{\log 2}$, $k \in Z/\{0\}$.

Hence, computing residues in (34), we get [Kn73] :

$$T(x) = -\log_2 x + \frac{1}{2} - \gamma + \frac{1}{\log 2} \sum_{k\neq 0} \Gamma\left(\frac{2ik\pi}{\log 2}\right) e^{-2ik\pi(\log_2 n)} + O(x^{-M}), \text{ any } M>0,$$

the sum being a Fourier series in $\log_2 n$.

Such periodicities are of frequent occurrence in the analysis of algorithm and they have here a clear origin in regularly spaced singularities of functions of the type $(1-2^s)^{-1}$. An alternative derivation, which avoids the exponential approximation is based on the observation that S_n is itself a harmonic sum :

$$S(x) = \sum_k \left(e^{-s\log(1-2^{-k})^{-1}} - 1\right)$$

which can be dealt with by the preceding techniques, leading sometimes to simpler derivations.

Let us last mention that the results of the exponential approximations (30) coincide in a large number of cases with expressions derived by assuming the sequences to be generated by a Poisson process.

IV - APPLICATIONS

As already said, the fist set of results on tries appears in [Kn73, sect. 6.3 and 5.2.2] in relation to trie searching and radix exchange sort (see equation (22)):

Theorem 1 [Kn73]: (i) *The average number of bit inspections of a search in a trie formed with* n *infinite binary keys satisfies*(*)

$$\overline{C}_n = \log_2 n + \frac{\gamma}{\log 2} + \frac{1}{2} + F(\log_2 n) + O\left(\frac{1}{n}\right)$$

(ii) *The average number of bit inspections required by radix exchange sort applied to* n *binary keys is*

$$n\overline{C}_n = n\log_2 n + O(n).$$

Theorem 1 establishes that tries are almost optimal for performing standard (1-dimensional) searching and sorting. In particular, they tend to be better balanced than binary search trees, a fact that results in appreciable differences in the cost of partial match retrievals between multidimensional tries and multidimensional search trees.

(*) Here and in forthcoming theorems F,G,... denote periodic functions with period 1. Mean values of these functions are denoted by $\overline{F}$, $\overline{G}$...

In the case of tries built over an alphabet of cardinality α, statistics on the number of nodes permit for instance to compare the linked (leftmost-child/right-sibling) representation of tries to a fixed branching representation of degree α, and using again results from [Kn73] we can prove

Theorem 2 : *Measured in number of pointers used, the linked representation of tries is more storage efficient as soon as the cardinality of the alphabet* α *is larger than* 6.

L. Trabb Pardo's thesis contains several other analyses along these lines related to the size of various representations of tries and the evaluation of the cost of performing unions and intersections on trie representations of sets.

The next set of analyses is relative to the use of tries as indexes for externally stored files. Statistics on heights discussed in Sections 3,4, above, [FSt82] show :

Theorem 3 : (i) *The average height of a trie of size* n *where subfiles of size at most* b *are stored in page leaves is*

$$(1+\frac{1}{b})\log_2 n + G((1+\frac{1}{b})\log_2 n) + O(1).$$

(ii) *The expected size of the directory in Extendible Hashing for a file of* n *elements is*

$$H((1+\frac{1}{b})\log_2 n)\, n^{1+1/b}(1+O(1))$$

where

$$\hat{H} = \frac{1}{\log 2}(b+1)!^{-1/b}\,\Gamma(1-\frac{1}{b}).$$

This result shows in particular that having small page capacities entails that an Extendible Hashing directory is very likely to blow up for relatively small file cardinalities (for b=10, the directory becomes as large as the file itself when n is near 10^5) so that compromise chaining methods should be used in these situations (see [Re83] for a complete characterization of the parameters of dynamic hashing schemes).

As pointed out in the introduction multidimensional tries (k-d-tries) may be used for partial match retrieval queries. The cost of a partial match search is expressible as an additive combination of costs on subtrees, and using combinations of difference equations and Mellin transform techniques [FPu83] prove :

Theorem 4 : *The cost of a partial match query in a* k-d-*trie of* n *elements with* s *out of* k *attributes specified is*

$$\overline{C}_n = K(\frac{1}{k}\log_2 n)n^{1-s/k} + O(1)$$

where

$$\hat{K} = -\frac{s}{k^2\log_2}\,\Gamma(\frac{s}{k}-1)\sum_{\ell=0}^{k-1}(\delta_1\delta_2\ldots\delta_e)2^{-\ell(1-s/k)}$$

with $\delta_j=1$ *if the* j-*th attribute is specified in the query and* $\delta_j=2$ *otherwise.*

This result is to be compared to the expected cost of a partial match in k-d-tree which has cost

$$O(n^{1-s/k+\theta(s/k)}) \qquad 0 < \theta(u) < 0.07,$$

so that k-d-tries are in this context axymptotically more efficient than k-d-trees. A result similar to Theorem 4 is proved for the grid file access method of [NHS81], the cost being then measured by the number of disk accesses [FPu83]. Other structures proposed in the data base literature for organizing multidimensional records (multiple attribute trees and doubly chained trees) can be analyzed using the finite key models of Section 3.

The tree protocol (under a Poisson model) leads to difference equations of a more complex form due to the occurrence of continuous arrivals. If λ is the arrival rate on the channel, it is shown in [FFH82] that the quantities α_n representing the expected lenght of the collision resolution interval (CRI) when starting with n initial colliders have an exponential generating function that satisfies (compare with (19)) :

$$\alpha(z) = e^{-qz}\,\alpha(\lambda + pz) + e^{-pz}\,\alpha(\lambda + qz) + \beta(z)$$

for some $\beta(z)$ with p+q = 1. Whence :

<u>Theorem 5</u> : *The expected lenght of the* CRI *when* n *transmitters initially collide satisfies*

$$\alpha_n = An + \psi(n).n + o(n)$$

where ψ *is a fluctuating (aperiodic) function.*

Similar methods have been used by the author and P. Mathys to show that ternary branching results in an increased throughput of about 10% compared to binary branching.

The next result is relative to the height of tries formed on strings with a biased probability distribution of bits (α for zeros and β for ones). It models exactly the behaviour of some polynomial factorization algorithms based on the construction of idempotents [FSt82] , and we have :

<u>Theorem 6</u> : (i) *The expected height of a trie formed with* n *keys with biased bits satisfies :*

$$\overline{H}_n(\alpha,\beta) = 2\,\frac{\log_2 n}{\log_2(\alpha^2+\beta^2)^{-1}} + O(1)$$

(ii) *The expected number of idempotemt refinement steps when factoring a polynomial with* n *irreducible factors over* GFp *is*

$$\overline{H}_n\left(\frac{1}{2} + \frac{1}{2p}, \frac{1}{2} - \frac{1}{2p}\right).$$

Lastly we mention the analysis of the von Neumann-Knuth-Yao algorithm [FSa82], which leads to statistics on the length of the leftmost branch, path length.. in tries :

Theorem 7 : *The expected number of coin tossing necessary to generate* n *bits of an exponentially distributed variate satisfies :*

$$\overline{C}(n) = n + \gamma + o(2^{-n})$$

where

$$\gamma = e(2 + \frac{3}{e+1}) - \sum_{k\geq 0} \frac{1}{e^{1/2k}-1} [\frac{e}{4^k} + 1 - e^{1/2k} (1 - \frac{1}{2^k})].$$

REFERENCES

[AHU83] A. Aho, J. Hopcroft, J. Ullman : "Data Structures and Algorithms", Addison Wesley, Reading (1983).

[FFH82] G. Fayolle, P. Flajolet, M. Hofri : "A Functional Equation Arising in the Analysis of a Protocol for a Multiaccess Broadcast Channel", INRIA Research Report n° 131, 36 pages.

[FS81] P. Flajolet, J-M. Steyaert : "A Complexity Calculus for Classes of Recursive Search Programs Over Tree Structures" in 22nd IEEE FOCS Symp., Nashville (1982), pp. 386-393.

[FNPS79] R. Fagin, J. Nievergelt, N. Pippenger, R. Strong : "Extendible Hahing-A Fast Access Method for Dynamic Files", ACM TODS, 4 (1979), pp. 315-344.

[FSa82] P. Flajolet, N. Saheb : "Digital Search Trees and the Complexity of Generating an Exponentially Distributed Variate", in CAAP 82, Lecture Notes in Comp. Sc. (to appear).

[FSo82] P. Flajolet, D. Sotteau : "A Recursive Partitioning Process of Computer Science", in IInd World Conference on Mathematics at the Service of Man, Las Palmas (1982), pp. 25-30.

[FSt82] P. Flajolet, J-M. Steyaert : "A Branching Process Arising in Dynamic Hashing Trie Searching and Polynomial Factorization", ICALP 82, Lectures Notes in Comp. Sc. 140, (1982), pp. 239-251.

[FPu83] P. Flajolet, C. Puech : "Tree Structures for Partial Match Retrieval of Multidimensional Data", submitted for publication (1983).

[He78] P. Henrici : "Applied and Computational Complex Analysis", vol. 2, J. Wiley New York (1978).

[Kn71] D.E. Knuth : "Mathematical Analysis of Algorithms", in IFIP Congress 1971, Ljubljana.

[Kn73] D.E. Knuth : "The Art of Computer Programming", vol. 3, Addison Wesley, Reading (1973).

[La78] P.A. Larson : "Dynamic Hashing", BIT, 18(1978), pp. 184-201.

[Li78] W. Litwin : "Virtual Hashing : A Dynamically Changing Hashing", in Proc. VLDB Conf., Berlin (1978), pp. 517-523.

[Ma80] J.L. Massey : "Collision Resolution Algorithms and Random Access Communication", in Multi-User Communication Systems, CISM Lectures n° 265, G. Longo Ed., Springer Verlag (1980).

[NHS81] J. Nievergelt, H. Hinterberger, K. Sevcik : "The Grid File : An Adaptable Symmetric Multikey File Structure", ETH Report 46 (1981).

[Ri76] R.L. Rivest : "Partial Match Retrieval Algorithms", SIAM J. Comp. 51 (1976), pp. 19-50.

[Re83] M. Regnier : "Evaluation des Performances du Hachage Dynamique", Thesis, University of Paris-Orsay (1983).

[Se82] R. Sedgewick : "Mathematical Analysis of Combinatorial Algorithms", in Probability Theory and Computer Science, G. Louchard, G. Latouche Ed., Academic Press, New York (1982).

[Se83] R. Sedgewick : "Algorithms", Addison-Wesley, Reading (1983).

[TP78] L. Trabb Pardo : "Set Representation and Set Intersection", Stanford Univ. Report CS-78-681 (1978).

SPACE AND REVERSAL COMPLEXITY OF PROBABILISTIC ONE-WAY TURING MACHINES

Rusins Freivalds
Computing Center, Latvian State University, Riga, USSR

Probabilistic 1-way Turing machines are proved to be logarithmically more economical in the sense of space complexity for recognition of specific languages. Languages recognizable in o(log log n) space are proved to be regular. One or two reversals of the head on the work tape of a probabilistic 1-way Turing machine can sometimes be simulated in no less than const.n reversals by a deterministic machine.

1. INTRODUCTION

The problem whether or not probabilistic machines can recognize a language not recognizable by deterministic machines of the same type has arisen in Theoretical Computer Science long ago. If there are no bounds on the computation time or space or on another complexity measure then the answer is negative [8]. If the bounds are maximally tight and the machines are equivalent to finite automata then the answer again is negative: every language recognizable by a finite probabilistic automaton with an isolated cut-point is recognizable also by a finite deterministic automaton [9].

We have been able to prove in a series of papers [3-5] for various types of automata and machines intermediate between finite automata and Turing machines without complexity bounds that probabilistic machines can recognize languages not recognizable by deterministic machines of the same type. In particular, when the considered type of the machines is time-bounded Turing machines, it was proved that probabilistic machines can recognize palindromes in essentially less time than deterministic machines ($n \log n$ versus n^2) [2,3].

In this paper we consider 1-way Turing machines and two complexity measures for them: space and reversals. 1-way Turing machines are formally defined in [7]. They have an input tape with a single head on it capable to move only in one direction and one work tape with one head on it. In the second half of Section 2 we consider also 1-way Turing machines with many work tapes.

Space complexity is the number of squares in the used part of the work tapes. Reversal complexity is the number of times when the head on a work tape changes the direction of its move.

Probabilistic 1-way Turing machines are 1-way Turing machines which can in addition make use at each step of a generator of random numbers with a finite alphabet, yielding its output values with equal probabilities and in accordance with a Bernoulli distribution, i.e. independently of the values yielded at other instants.

We shall say that the probabilistic machine recognizes the language L in space $s(n)$ (or with $r(n)$ reversals, respectively) with probability p if the machine when working on an arbitrary x,

1) stops having used no more than $s(n)$ squares of the work tapes (or having made $r(n)$ reversals, respectively) with probability 1.
2) yields 1 if $x \in L$ and yields 0 if $x \in \overline{L}$ with a probability not less than p.

This definition of the complexity measures for probabilistic machines is a bit nontraditional. Usually it is demanded only that the probability of the following event exceeds p: "the machine stops having not overused the limited space and yields the correct answer". Nevertheless all our probabilistic machines satisfy our more restrictive condition.

2. SPACE COMPLEXITY

All the results in this Section on advantages of probabilistic machines are based on the following lemma.

Let $P_1(l)$ be the number of primes not exceeding $2^{\lceil \log_2 l \rceil}$, $P_2(l, N', N'')$ be the number of primes not exceeding $2^{\lceil \log_2 l \rceil}$ and not dividing $|N'-N''|$, and $P_3(l,n)$ be the maximum of $P_2(l, N', N'')$ over all $N' < 2^n$, $N'' < 2^n$, $N' \neq N''$.

LEMMA 2.1. ([3]) Given any $\varepsilon > 0$, there is a natural number c such that

$$\lim_{n \to \infty} \frac{P_3(cn, n)}{P_1(cn)} < \varepsilon$$

This lemma is, in fact, a simple corollary from Cebisev's theorem on the density of primes (see [1]).

We define a language $S \subset \{0,1,2,3,4,5\}^*$. Let $bin(i)$ denote a string representing i in the binary notation (the first symbol of $bin(i)$ being 1).

We start to describe how the strings in S can be generated. An arbitrary integer k is taken and the following string is considered

$$bin(1)\ \ 2\ bin(2)\ \ 2\ bin(3)\ 2 \ldots 2\ bin(2k).$$

Next, every symbol in the substrings $bin(k+1)$, $bin(k+2)$, ..., $bin(2k)$ is preceded by one arbitrary symbol from $\{3,4\}$. If the obtained string in $\{0,1,2,3,4\}^*$ is denoted by x then the language S contains the string $x5x$. Every string in S is obtained by this procedure.

THEOREM 2.2. (1) Given any $\varepsilon > 0$, there is a logn-space bounded probabilistic 1-way Turing machine which accepts every string in S with probability 1 and rejects every string in S with probability $1-\varepsilon$. (2) Every deterministic 1-way Turing machine recognizing S uses at least const.n space.

PROOF. (1) The head of a string w is its initial fragment up to the symbol 5. The tail of w is the rest of the string.

The probabilistic machine performs the following 11 actions to recognize whether or not the given string w is in S:
1) it checks whether the projection of the head of w to the subalphabet $\{0,1,2\}$ is a string of the form

$$\text{bin}(1)\ 2\ \text{bin}(2)\ 2 \ldots 2\ \text{bin}(2k_1)$$

for an integer k_1;

2) it checks whether the projection of the tail of w to the subalphabet $\{0,1,2\}$ is a string of the form

$$\text{bin}(1)\ 2\ \text{bin}(2)\ 2 \ldots 2\ \text{bin}(2k_2)$$

for an integer k_2;

3) it checks whether $k_1 = k_2$;

4) it counts the number k_3 of the substrings bin(1), bin(2), ..., bin(k_3) in the head of w where no symbols from $\{3,4\}$ are inserted;

5) it checks whether $k_1 = k_3$;

6) it counts the number k_4 of the substrings bin(1), bin(2), ..., bin(k_4) in the tail of w where no symbols from $\{3,4\}$ are inserted;

7) it checks whether $k_2 = k_4$;

8) using the generator of random numbers it generates a string in $\{0,1\}^{c \cdot l}$, where c is the constant from Lemma 2.1, and l is the length of bin($2k_3$). The generated string m ($1 \leq m \leq 2^{c \cdot l}$) is tested for primality. If m is not prime, a new string bin(m) is generated, tested for primality, and so on;

9) it regards the projection y_1 of the head of w to the subalphabet $\{3,4\}$ as binary notation of a number N_1 ($0 \leq N_1 \leq 2^{|y_1|} - 1$) and calculates the remainder m_1 obtained by dividing N_1 to m;

10) it regards the projection y_2 of the tail of w to the subalphabet $\{3,4\}$ as binary notation of a number N_2 ($0 \leq N_2 \leq 2^{|y_2|} - 1$) and calculates the remainder m_2 obtained by dividing N_2 to m;

11) it checks whether $m_1 = m_2$.

The string w is accepted if all the checks result positively. Otherwise w is rejected.

The actions 1) - 11) can be performed in log w space. Lemma 2.1 implies the correctness of the result with the needed probability.

(2) If $w \in S$ then its projection to the subalphabet $\{3,4,5\}$ is of the form y5y, where $y \in \{3,4\}^*$ and $|y| \geq \frac{|w|}{6} - 2 \log_2 |w|$. Let $y' \in \{3,4\}^{|y|}$ be a string different from y. It is obvious that there is a string $w' \in S$ such that its projection to $\{3,4,5\}$ is y'5y'. We denote the set of all $2^{|y|}$ such strings w' by M. Let the machine process two distinct strings in M. We consider the moments when it has just finished to read the heads of the two strings. The content of the work tape squares or the internal state of the machine is to differ in the two cases. Hence there are strings in M such that the length of the used part of the work tape is no less than

$$\frac{1}{2 \log_2 b} \left(\frac{|w|}{6} - 2 \log_2 |w| \right)$$

where b is the cardinality of the work tape alphabet.

The language $\tilde{S}$ is similar to S but it is defined in a more complicate way.

Let the strings $x = x_1x_2 \ldots x_u$ and $y = y_1y_2 \ldots y_v$ in $\{0,1\}^u$ and $\{0,1\}^v$, respectively, be considered, and either $u = v$ or $u + 1 = v$. We use join (x,y) to denote the string $x_1y_1x_2y_2 \ldots$

We define a map $z: \{0,1\}^* \rightarrow \{0,1,2,3,4,5\}^*$. At first, the given $w \in \{0,1\}^*$ is transformed into w', substituting every symbol 0 in w by 3 and every 1 by 4. We denote the total number of symbols in the strings bin(t+1), bin(t+2), ..., bin(2t) by s(t). Let l be an integer such that $s(l-1) < |w| \leq s(l)$. Then z(w) can be obtained from the string

$$\text{bin}(1)\ 2\ \text{bin}(2)\ 2\ \text{bin}(3)\ 2 \ldots 2\ \text{bin}(2l)$$

inserting symbols from $\{3,4,5\}$ so that every symbol in the substrings bin(l+1), bin(l+2), ..., bin(2l) is preceded by one symbol from $\{3,4,5\}$ and the projection of the obtained string to the subalphabet $\{3,4,5\}$ equals the $w'555\ldots$

The language $\tilde{S}$ consists of all possible strings of the form

z(join(bin(1), bin(2))) 6 z(join (bin(2), bin(3))) 6 z(join (bin(3), bin(4)))) 6 ...
... 6 z(join (bin(2k-1), bin(2k))).

THEOREM 2.3. (1) Given any $\varepsilon > 0$, there is a loglogn-space bounded probabilistic 1-way Turing machine which accepts every string in $\tilde{S}$ with probability 1 and rejects every string in $\overline{\tilde{S}}$ with probability $1-\varepsilon$. (2) Every deterministic 1-way Turing machine recognizing S uses at least const.log n space.

PROOF is similar to the proof of Theorem 2.2.

It is possible to extend Theorems 2.2 and 2.3 for "natural" space complexities f(n) between log n and loglog n. On the other hand, the method used above does not permit to construct nonregular languages recognizable by probabilistic 1-way Turing machines in o(loglog n) time. Indeed, Theorem 2.8 below shows that if a language L is recognized by probabilistic 1-way Turing machine with probability $p > 1/2$ in o(loglog n) space then L is regular. The result may seem trivial since Trakhtenbrot [11] and Gill [6] have proved theorems showing that determinization of probabilistic Turing machines increase space complexity no more than exponentially, and it is known from [10] that if a language L is recognized by a deterministic 1-way Turing machine in o(log n) space then L is regular..Unfortunately, the situation is more complicate since no function o(log n) is space constructible by deterministic 1-way Turing machines. Hence the argument by Trakhtenbrot and Gill is not applicable. Our proof is nonconstructive. We do not present an algorithm for determinization of probabilistic 1-way Turing machines.

It will turn out to be essential that we consider 1-way Turing machines with many work tapes in the rest of this Section.

Let s(n) be any function of o(loglog n), and L be a language recognized by a probabilistic 1-way Turing machine TM with probability p in s(n) space. Let x, y, z be strings such that $xz \in L$, $yz \in \overline{L}$. Let n be an integer such that $|x| \leq n$ and $|y| \leq n$. Let $id_1, id_2, \ldots, id_r$ be all possible instaneous descriptions of the content of the work tapes and the internal state of the machine under the condition that no more than s(n) squares are used on every work tape. Let $p_x(id_i)$ denote the probability of the instaneous description being id_i immediately after the reading the last symbol of the string x from the input. Let $q_i(z)$ denote the probability of acceptance of z if the machine starts its reading from the input with the content of work tapes and the internal state corresponding to the description id_i.

LEMMA 2.4.
$$|p_x(id_1) - p_y(id_1)| + |p_x(id_2) - p_y(id_2)| + \ldots + |p_x(id_r) - p_y(id_r)| > 3p - 2.$$

PROOF. $xz \in L$ implies

$$p_x(id_1)\cdot q_1(z) + p_x(id_2)\cdot q_2(z) + p_x(id_3)\cdot q_3(z) + \ldots > p$$

$yz \in \overline{L}$ implies

$$p_y(id_1)\cdot q_1(z) + p_y(id_2)\cdot q_2(z) + p_y(id_3)\cdot q_3(z) + \ldots < 1-p.$$

Subtraction results in

$$(p_x(id_1) - p_y(id_1))\cdot q_1(z) + (p_x(id_2) - p_y(id_2))\cdot q_2(z) + \ldots > 2p-1.$$

For $i \leq r$ we substitute $(p_x(id_i) - p_y(id_i))$ by $|p_x(id_i) - p_y(id_i)|$ and $q_i(z)$ by 1. For $i > r$ we substitute $p_y(id_i)$ by 0, $q_i(z)$ by 1, and $p_x(id_{r+1}) + p_x(id_{r+2}) + \ldots$ by 1-p (since the string x is accepted using no more space than s(n) with probability p).

LEMMA 2.5. Let a set R consist of $\sqrt[3]{n}$ distinct strings the length of which does not exceed n. Then there are strings $v, w \in R$ such that
$$|p_v(id_1) - p_w(id_1)| + |p_v(id_2) - p_w(id_2)| + \ldots + |p_v(id_r) - p_w(id_r)| \leq 3p-2.$$

PROOF. There are no more than $r = (\text{const})^{s(n)}$ instaneous descriptions of the length $\leq s(n)$. The vector $p_x = (p_x(id_1), p_x(id_1), \ldots, p_x(id_r))$ can be interpreted as a point in r-dimensional unit cube. The inequality in the formulation of the Lemma asserts that the points under the question are close in the metrics
$$\rho(p_x, p_y) = |p_x(id_1) - p_y(id_1)| + \ldots + |p_x(id_r) - p_y(id_r)|.$$

Assume the contrary of the Lemma. We take the points corresponding to the $\sqrt[3]{n}$ strings in R and consider them as the centers of the following body

$$\rho(p_x, p_{x_0}) < \frac{3p-2}{2}.$$

It is easy to see that the bodies do not intersect. The volume of each of them is

$$\frac{2^r \left(\frac{3p-2}{2}\right)^r}{r!}$$

All they are situated within an r-dimensional cube, the length of edge of which equals 1 + (3p-2). Hence the total number of the bodies does not exceed

$$(3p-1)^r, r! \,/\, \left(\frac{3p-2}{2}\right)^r \cdot 2^r = 2^{0(r \log r)}.$$

Hence
$$\sqrt[3]{n} < 2^{0(r \log r)}$$

$$\log r \geq \log\log n - \log\log\log n + \text{const}$$

On the other hand,

$$\log r = s(n) = o(\log\log n).$$

Contradiction.

COROLLARY 2.6. Let a language L be recognized by a probabilistic 1-way Turing machine with many work tapes with probability $p>2/3$ in $o(\log\log n)$ space. Let a set R consist of $\sqrt[3]{n}$ distinct strings the length of which does not exceed n. Then there are strings $x,y\in R$ such that $(xz\in L \Leftrightarrow yz\in L)$ holds for every z.

PROOF. Immediately from Lemma 2.4.

LEMMA 2.7. If a language L is recognized by a probabilistic 1-way Turing machine with many work tapes with probability $p>2/3$ in $o(\log\log n)$ space then L is regular.

PROOF. Every language $L\subseteq\Sigma^*$ where Σ is a finite alphabet can be represented by an infinite labelled tree. The edges of the tree correspond to the symbols in Σ, the vertices correspond to the strings, and the labels "0" and "1" at the vertices show whether or not the string is in the language L.

We consider the following equivalence between strings. $x\equiv y$ if and only if $(xz\in L \Leftrightarrow yz\in L)$ holds for every $z\in\Sigma^*$. The language L is regular if and only if there is only finite number of equivalence classes.

Assume from the contrary that the language L satisfy the conditions of the Lemma but it is nonregular. Then there are infinitely many equivalence classes.

An argument based on Konig's lemma for infinite trees shows that for every n there is a route in our tree beginning at the root of the tree such that it contains at least n nonequivalent vertices. We fix an arbitrarily large n and consider the shortest route containing n nonequivalent vertices. We denote the length of this route by m. To put it another way, we consider the shortest string $x_1x_2x_3\ldots x_m$ such that there are n nonequivalent strings in the set $T=\{x_1, x_1x_2, x_1x_2x_3, \ldots, x_1x_2x_3\ldots x_m\}$.

We consider two cases separately,

Case 1. $n^2\geq m$.

Let K be a subset of T consisting of n nonequivalent strings. The length of all strings in K does not exceed m. Hence, by Corollary 2.6, there are two equivalent strings in K. Contradiction.

Case 2. $n^2 < m$.

We will prove the contradiction by showing that $x_1x_2x_3\ldots x_m$ is not the shortest string with at least n nonequivalent strings in the set T.

We fix precisely n strings in T as being pairwise nonequivalent and denote the set of these n strings by K.

Since $n^2<m$, there are two strings $x_1x_2\ldots x_u$ and $x_1x_2\ldots x_ux_{n+1}\ldots x_v$ in K such that:

1) $v-u\geq\sqrt{m-n}$

2) for every w, if $u<w<v$ then the string $x_1x_2 \dots x_w$ is not in K.

Let the set R consist of the strings $x_1x_2 \dots x_{u+1}, x_1x_2 \dots x_{u+2}, \dots, x_1x_2 \dots x_{v-1}$. Corollary 2.6 shows that there are two equivalent strings in R. We denote them by $x_1x_2 \dots x_q$ and $x_1x_2 \dots x_r$ $(q<r)$.

This allows us to show that the string $x_1x_2x_3 \dots x_m$ can be replaced by a shorter string $x_1x_2 \dots x_{q-1}x_qx_{r+1}x_{r+2} \dots x_m$ so that the set of all its initial fragments contains at least n nonequivalent strings. Indeed, we consider the set K' obtained from K by omitting the fragment $x_{q+1}x_{q+2} \dots x_r$ in all the strings (if the fragment is contained there) and prove that the strings in K' also are pairwise nonequivalent.

For instance, let the strings

$$x_1 \dots x_qx_{q+1} \dots x_rx_{r+1} \dots x_t$$

and $x_1 \dots x_qx_{q+1} \dots x_rx_{r+1} \dots x_tx_{t+1} \dots x_s$

be nonequivalent. Hence there is a string z such that

$$x_1 \dots x_qx_{q+1} \dots x_rx_{r+1} \dots x_tz \in L \not\Leftrightarrow$$
$$\not\Leftrightarrow x_1 \dots x_qx_{q+1} \dots x_rx_{r+1} \dots x_tx_{t+1} \dots x_sz \in L.$$

On the other hand,

$$x_1 \dots x_qx_{q+1} \dots x_rx_{r+1} \dots x_tz \in L \Leftrightarrow x_1 \dots x_qx_{r+1} \dots x_tz \in L,$$

and $$x_1 \dots x_qx_{q+1} \dots x_rx_{r+1} \dots x_tx_{t+1} \dots x_sz \in L \Leftrightarrow$$
$$\Leftrightarrow x_1 \dots x_qx_{r+1} \dots x_tx_{t+1} \dots x_sz \in L.$$

Hence

$x_1 \dots x_qx_{r+1} \dots x_tz \in L \not\Leftrightarrow x_1 \dots x_qx_{r+1} \dots x_sz \in L$, and the strings $x_1 \dots x_qx_{r+1} \dots$ $\dots x_t$ and $x_1 \dots x_qx_{r+1} \dots x_tx_{t+1} \dots x_s$ are nonequivalent. Thus, the string $x_1x_2x_3 \dots x_m$ is not the shortest one with the mentioned property. Contradiction.

THEOREM 2.8. If a language L is recognized by a probabilistic 1-way Turing machine with many work tapes with probability $p>1/2$ in $o(\log\log n)$ space then L is regular.

PROOF. This is the first proof in the paper where we use essentially our nontraditional definition of the space complexity for probabilistic machines.

Let there be a "black box" containing a random number generator with two output symbols 0 and 1 such that one of the output symbols is produced with probability no less than $p>1/2$ but we unfortunately do not know which symbol has this probability. It is a simple corollary from the law of large numbers that for arbitrary $p>1/2$ there is a constant d (depending on p) such that d independent experiments suffice to identify the prevailing output symbol with probability 3/4.

Let the given Turing machine have k work tapes. We consider a new machine with kd work tapes. It has d k-typles of tapes, each of them independently simulating the given probabilistic machine. The output of the new machine is obtained from the majority of the outputs of the simulated machines.

The new machine recognizes L in $o(\log\log n)$ space with probability 3/4. Hence, by Lemma 2.7, L is regular.

3. REVERSAL COMPLEXITY

We return to 1-way Turing machines with one work tape only. Reversal complexity for these machines was introduced and first explored by Hartmanis [7]. We prove that probabilistic machines can have advantages in reversal complexity over deterministic ones. To achieve this goal, new high lower bounds of reversal complexity for specific languages are proved.

If x is a string then $|x|_i$ is the number of symbols i in x.

$Q = \{x3y \mid x,y \in \{0,1,2\}^* \ \& \ |x|_0 = |y|_0 \ \& \ |x|_1 = |y|_1 \ \& \ |x|_2 = |y|_2\}$.

THEOREM 3.1. (1) Given any $\varepsilon > 0$, there is a 1-reversal bounded probabilistic 1-way Turing machine which accepts every string in Q with probability 1 and rejects every string in $\overline{Q}$ with probability $1-\varepsilon$. (2) Every deterministic 1-way Turing machine recognizing Q makes at least const.log n reversals. (3) Given any $c>0$, there is a deterministic 1-way Turing machine which recognizes Q making no more than $c \cdot \log n$ reversals.

PROOF. (1) At first, the machine chooses a random i from a set consisting of at least $3/\varepsilon_2$ integers. The work tape is used as a counter to accumulate $1 \cdot |x|_0 + i^1 \cdot |x|_1 + i^2 \cdot |x|_2$ and then to compare it with $1 \cdot |y|_0 + i^1 \cdot |y|_1 + i^2 \cdot |y|_2$. An easy argument involving the properties of Vandermonde determinant shows that if $x3y \in \overline{Q}$ then no more than 2 distinct values of i can make the machine to accept the string.

(2) The proof is similar to the proof of the part (2) of Theorem 3.3 below.

(3) The machine depends on the given c only by appropriate choice of the parameter i. The input string is rewritten on the work tape. Then after every reversal very many symbols are erased. Namely, only every i-th symbol 0, every i-th symbol 1 and every i-th symbol 2 remain not erased. This erasion allows to compare modulo i the number of remaining symbols 0,1,2 in the strings x and y. All the symbols are erased in $\lfloor \log_i |x3y| \rfloor$ reversals.

Next we consider a sequence of languages R_m in $\{0,1,2,3\}^*$. The language R_m consists of all the strings of the form $x_1 2 x_2 2 x_3 2 \ldots 2 x_k 3 x_{k+1} 2 x_{k+2} 2 \ldots 2 x_{2k}$, where $k > 2m$, the integers 2,3,4, ..., 2m+1 do not divide k, $x_1 \in \{0,1\}^*$, $x_2 = mi(x_1)$, $x_1 = x_3 = x_5 = \ldots = x_{2k-1}$, $x_2 = x_4 = x_6 = \ldots = x_{2k}$. (We use $mi(x)$ to denote the mirror reflection of x).

THEOREM 3.2. (1) Given any m, there is a 2-reversal bounded probabilistic 1-way Turing machine which accepts every string in R_m with probability 1 and rejects every string in R_m with probability 1-1/m. (2) Every deterministic 1-way Turing machine recognizing R_m makes at least const.$\sqrt{n}$ reversals. (3) Given any $c>0$ and any natural number m, there is a deterministic 1-way Turing machine which recognizes R_m making no more than $c \cdot \sqrt{n}$ reversals.

PROOF. We use L_r ($r \in \{1,2, \ldots, m\}$) to denote the recognized by the following deterministic 1-way Turing machine with 2 reversals. The conditions $k>2m$ and indivisibility of k is tested using only the internal memory. All the other conditions are tested displaying the input string on the work tape in the following way:

$$\begin{array}{l} \qquad\qquad\qquad\qquad\qquad\qquad\qquad\qquad\qquad x_1 \ * \ x_2 \ * \ldots * \ x_r \\ mi(x_{k+r}) * mi(x_{k+r-1}) * \ldots * mi(x_{2r+1}) * mi(x_{2r}) * mi(x_{2r-1}) * \ldots * mi(x_{r+1}) \end{array}$$

$x_{k+r+1} * x_{k+r+2} * \dots * x_{2k}$

This display allows to compare x_i with $mi(x_j)$ if and only if $i+j \equiv 2r+1 \pmod{2k}$. Obviously, $R_m \subset L_r$.

The probabilistic machine picks a random r and then recognizes the language L_r.

We proceed to prove that $u \neq v$ implies $L_u \cap L_v = R_m$. Indeed, let $z \in L_u \cap L_v$ and s be an arbitrary element of the set $\{0,1, \dots, k-1\}$. Since $z \in L_u$, there is a j such that $x_{2s+1} = mi(x_{2j})$, $2s+1+2j = 2u+1 \pmod{2k}$. Since $z \in L_v$, there is a t (different from s) such that $x_{2t+1} = mi(x_{2j})$, $2t+1+2j = 2v+1 \pmod{2k}$. Thus for $t-s \equiv v-u \pmod{k}$ the following holds $x_{2s+1} = x_{2t+1}$.

Since k and v-u are relatively prime, it can be proved using only elementary properties of congruences (e.g. Theorem 107 in [1]) that the set $\{0,1, \dots, k-1\}$ can be displayed into a sequence $i_1, i_2, \dots, i_k$ such that $i_{l+1} - i_l \equiv v-u \pmod{k}$ for all $l \in \{1,2, \dots, k\}$. Hence all the x_{2i+1} are equal. It follows that all $mi(x_{2j})$ also are equal. $z \in R_m$.

(2) The proof is similar to the proof of the part (2) of Theorem 3.3 below.

(3) The machine depends on the given c only by appropriate choice of the parameter d. When reading the input the machine stores the information on a 6-floor work tape. The first 3 floors are filled until the machine has read the symbol 3, the rest 3 floors are filled afterwards.

When reading x_1 the machine stores it both at the first and the second floor. When the machine reads x_2 the head on the work tape returns and checks whether or not $x_2 = mi(x_1)$. Then one more reversal is made and while reading x_3 the machine checks whether $x_3 = x_1$ and moves the string on the second floor d squares to the right. While reading x_4 (and all the subsequent substrings) the input string is compared with the string on the second floor and at the same time the latter string is moved d squares to the right. This sequence of checks and moves is performed until the string on the second floor is moved off the string on the first floor (This means $k > |x_1|/d$). If this happens then all the rest x_j's (up to the symbol 3) are stored on the third floor without new reversals.

After the input symbol 3 the head returns to the initial square and proceeds to fill the 4th, 5-th and 6-th floors in the same way. When the reading of the input is completed, in the case if there are nonempty strings on the 3-rd and 6-th floors, the machine sweeps through these strings checking whether all the substrings x_{2j+1} and $mi(x_{2j})$ coincide in the first d symbols, the second d symbols, etc.

Let $x \in \{0,1,2,3,4,5\}^*$ $proj_{ij}(x)$ is the string obtained from x by omitting all the symbols not from $\{i,j\}$. We consider the language $T = T_{01} \cup T_{23} \cup T_{45}$, where $T_{ij} = \{ x6y6ij \mid x,y \in \{0,1,2,3,4,5\}^* \ \& \ proj_{ij}(x) = proj_{ij}(y)\}$.

THEOREM 3.3. (1) There is a 1-reversal bounded probabilistic 1-way Turing machine which recognizes T with probability 2/3. (2) Every deterministic 1-way Turing machine recognizing T makes at least const.n reversals. (3) Given any $c > 0$, there is a deterministic 1-way Turing machine which recognizes T making no more than $c \cdot n$ reversals.

Proof. (1) The machine picks a random $i \in \{0,2,4\}$ recognizes whether the input string z is in $T_{i\,i+1}$ and turns special attention to the fragment after the second symbol 6. If this fragment is (i, i+1) and $z \in T_{i\,i+1}$ then z is accepted. If it is (i, i+1) and $z \in \overline{T}_{i\,i+1}$ then z is rejected. If the fragment is of the form (j, j+1) with $j \in \{0,2,4\}$ but it is not equal to (i, i+1) then z is accepted or rejected, both with probability 1/2.

(2) Let $\mathcal{M}$ be a deterministic 1-way Turing machine recognizing T. We note that until a symbol 6 is read from the input the machine is to remember $proj_{01}(x)$, $proj_{23}(x)$ and $proj_{45}(x)$.

Assume from the contrary that $\mathcal{M}$ is making $o(|w|)$ reversals for arbitrary input strings w. We denote the number of internal states of $\mathcal{M}$ by a and the cordinality of the work tape alphabet by b.

Let n be a large integer. Precise order of magnitude of n will be described below. Consider the following finite subset M of the language T. Every string w in M is uniquely determined by the strings

$$v_{01} \in \{0,1\}^n, \quad v_{23} \in \{2,3\}^{n\, 8a \log_2 b}, \quad v_{45} \in \{4,5\}^n.$$

The string w is defined by a procedure as follows. It will turn out that $w = x6y6\alpha \in M$, $proj_{01}(x) = v_{01}$, $proj_{23}(x) = v_{23}$, $proj_{45}(x) = v_{45}$.

Let c(w,i) describe how many time the head crosses the point i on the work tape. Let f(n) be the maximum of c(w,i) over all strings of length $\leq 4n + 4n\, a \log_2 b + 3$ and over all the points. The assumed contrary implies $f(n) = o(n)$.

The string w corresponding to v_{01}, v_{23}, v_{45} begins with v_{01}. We shall use the term "initial zone" to denote the part of the work tape used during the reading of v_{01}. The length of the initial zone does not exceed $a(n + f(n))$.

To define the subsequent symbols of w we look at $\mathcal{M}$ processing the string w. If $\mathcal{M}$ is going to read a symbol from the input and the head of the work tape is in the initial zone then the current symbol is taken from v_{23}. If the head is not in the initial zone then the current symbol is taken from v_{45}. When one of the strings v_{23} or v_{45} is exhausted, the remaining symbols of the other string and the symbol 6 are added to w. Then we again look at processing w. If the head of the work tape is in the initial zone then the current symbol is taken from v_{45}. If the head is not in the initial zone then the current symbol is taken from v_{01}. When one of the strings v_{45} or v_{01} is exhausted, the obtained string w is completed by: 1) the remaining symbols of v_{45}, the string v_{23}, the string 601 (if v_{01} was exhausted), or 2) the remaining symbols of v_{01}, the string v_{23}, the string 645 (if v_{45} was exhausted).

Note that in the case 1) all the symbols 0,1 of the tail of w are read with the head of the work tape not in the initial zone. In the case 2) all the symbols 4,5 of the tail of w are read with the head in the initial zone.

Let $M(v_{01}, v_{45})$ denote the subset of M consisting of all w corresponding to the given v_{01}, v_{45} and all possible v_{23} such that in the head of w the string v_{23} is exhausted before the string v_{45}. Let t(w) denote the length of the head of w up to the last symbol from v_{45}. When $\mathcal{M}$ processes such a string in the period between the reading of (n+1)-th and t-th symbols $n\, 8a \log_2 b$ symbols are read with the head in the initial zone and less than n symbols with the head outside, and the head can use no more than $a f(n) + an$ new squares on the work tape (otherwise $\mathcal{M}$ would get $\geq n$

symbols from v_{23}).

$\mathcal{M}$ is to remember distinct strings $w \in M(v_{01}, v_{45})$ by distinct instaneous descriptions. Hence

$$|M(v_{01}, v_{45})| \leqslant a \cdot 2(an+o(n))\ b^{2(an+o(n))}.$$

In particular, for arbitrary pair (v_{01}, v_{45}) there is a v_{23} such that $w \in M \setminus M(v_{01}, v_{45})$. Let M_1 consist of 2^{2n} such strings, one per every pair (v_{01}, v_{45}).

We cut M_1 into two subsets in accordance with the last symbol of w. The largest subset is denoted by M_2. If the last symbol is 1 (5, respectively), then M_2 is cut into subsets in accordance with $proj_{45}(w)$ ($proj_{01}(w)$, respectively). The largest subset is denoted by M_3. M_3 is cut into subsets in accordance with the crossing sequence (showing the internal states at the crossing moments and the order of crossings) on the pair of end-points of the initial zone. The largest subset is denoted by M_4.

$$|M_4| \geqslant \frac{2^{n-1}}{(2a+1)^{2 \cdot f(n)}}$$

Now we make precise that n should be large enough to ensure this estimate to exceed 2. Hence M_4 contains two distinct strings w_1 and w_2. This allows us to construct a third string $w_3 \in \overline{T}$ such that $\mathcal{M}$ cannot tell it from w_1 nad w_2 and to arrive to contradiction.

(3) Obvious.

REFERENCES

1. Bukhstab A.A. Number theory. Ucpedgiz, 1960 (Russian).

2. Freivalds R. Fast computation by probabilistic Turing machines. - Ucenye Zapiski Latviiskogo Gosudarstvennogo Universiteta, v.233, 1975, 201-205 (Russian).

3. Freivalds R. Probabilistic machines can use less running time. - Information Processing '77, IFIP, North-Holland, 1977, 839-842.

4. Freivalds R. Capabilities of various models of probabilistic one-way automata. - Izvestiya VUZ. Matematika, No.5(228), 1981, 26-34 (Russian).

5. Freivalds R. Probabilistic two-way machines. - Lecture Notes in Computer Science, Springer, v.118, 1981, 33-45.

6. Gill J.T. III. Computational complexity of probabilistic Turing machines. - Proc. 6th ACM Symposium on Theory of Computation, 1974, 91-95.

7. Hartmanis J. Tape-reversal bounded Turing machine computations. - Journal of Computer and System Sciences, v.12, No.5, 1968, 117-135.

8. de Leeuw K., Moore E.F., Shannon C.E. and Shapiro N. Computability by probabilistic machines. - Automata Studies, Princeton University Press, 1956, 183-212.

9. Rabin M.O. Probabilistic automata. - Information and Control, v.6, No.3, 1963, 230-245.

10. Stearns R.E., Hartmanis J. and Lewis P.M. II. Hierarchies of memory limited computations. - Proc. IEEE Symp. on Switching Circuit Theory and Logical Design, 1965, 179-190.

11. Trakhtenbrot B.A. Notes on complexity of computation by probabilistic machines. - Research in Mathematical Logic and Theory of Algorithms, Moscow, Comp.Ctr. Acad.Sci. USSR, 1974 (Russian).

PSEUDORANDOM NUMBER GENERATION AND SPACE COMPLEXITY

Merrick Furst
Department of Computer Science
Carnegie-Mellon University
Pittsburgh, PA 15213

Richard Lipton
Department of Electrical Engineering and Computer Science
Princeton University
Princeton, NJ 08544

Larry Stockmeyer
IBM Research Lab
San Jose, CA 95193

1. INTRODUCTION

Recently, Blum and Micali [3] described a pseudorandom number generator that transforms each m-bit seed to an m^k-bit pseudorandom number, for any integer k. Under the assumption that the discrete logarithm problem cannot be solved by any polynomial-size combinational logic circuit, they show that the pseudorandom numbers generated are good in the sense that no polynomial-size circuit can determine the tth bit given the 1st through $(t-1)^{st}$ bits, with better than 50% accuracy. Yao [12] has shown, under the same assumption about the nonpolynomial complexity of the discrete logarithm problem, that these psuedorandom numbers can be used in place of truly random numbers by any polynomial-time probabilistic Turing machine. Thus, given a time n^k probabilistic Turing machine M and given any $\varepsilon > 0$, a deterministic Turing machine can simulate M by cycling through all seeds of length n^ε, giving a deterministic simulation in time 2^{n^ε}, an improvement over the time 2^{n^k} taken by the obvious simulation. Yao also shows that other problems, for example, integer factorization, can be used instead of the discrete logarithm in the intractability assumption.

The purpose of this paper is to observe that these intractability assumptions have implications toward space complexity. Two implications are that random time T(n) is contained in deterministic space T(n)/log T(n), and checking whether a bipartite graph has a perfect matching can be done in space n^ε for any $\varepsilon > 0$.

2. DEFINITIONS

We assume that the reader is familiar with time and space complexity for Turing machines (see, e.g., [2,7]), combinational circuit complexity (see, e.g., [9]), and probabilistic Turing machines (see, e.g., [5,1]). We consider only probabilistic Turing machines with one-sided error; that is, for rejected inputs the machine rejects with probability 1, and for accepted inputs the machine accepts with probability bounded away from zero.

Definition 1. Let $L \subseteq \{0,1\}^*$ and let $\psi(x,y)$ be a predicate on two binary strings x and y. We say that ψ *defines* L *in random time* T(n) if there is a constant $\eta > 0$ such that for all n and all x of length n:

(1) if $x \notin L$ then there is no y such that $\psi(x,y)$;

(2) if $x \in L$ then $|\{ y \in \{0,1\}^{T(n)} \mid \psi(x,y) \}| / 2^{T(n)} \geq \eta$.

Furthermore, there is a deterministic Turing machine that, when given an x of length n and a y of length at least T(n) on two separate input tapes, computes $\psi(x,y)$ within T(n) steps.

Define RTIME(T(n)) to be the class of languages $L \subseteq \{0,1\}^*$ that are defined by some ψ in random time T(n). Let $\mathcal{R}$ denote the union of RTIME(T(n)) over all polynomials T(n). Let DSPACE(S(n)) (resp., DTIME(T(n))) denote the class of binary languages accepted by deterministic Turing machines in space S(n) (resp., in time T(n)). Let $\mathcal{P}$ denote the union of DTIME(T(n)) over all polynomials T(n).

For our purposes we use the following definition of pseudorandom number generator which differs from the definitions in [3,12].

Definition 2. The function ρ is an *E(m)-expanding pseudorandom number generator (PNG)* if:

(1) $\rho:\{0,1\}^m \to \{0,1\}^{E(m)}$ for all m;

(2) ρ is computable by a deterministic Turing machine in space m and time polynomial in m;

(3) if ψ defines L in random time T(n), then there is an n_0 such that if $x \in L$, $|x| \geq n_0$ and $E(m) \geq T(|x|)$, then there is an $s \in \{0,1\}^m$ such that $\psi(x,\rho(s))$ is true.

We say that *polynomial-expanding PNG's exist* if an E(m)-expanding PNG exists for any polynomial E(m).

Condition (3) means that to determine if $x \in L$, it is sufficient to check whether $\psi(x,\rho(s))$ is true for any $s \in \{0,1\}^m$ where $E(m) \geq T(|x|)$. In condition (2) we assume that the Turing machine produces the output on a write-only output tape; the space used on the output tape is not bounded by m.

It is not known whether polynomial-expanding PNG's exist. However, under any of the following three assumptions, Yao [12] proves that they do exist. We say that a function F(m) is *superpolynomial* if for any polynomial Q(m), F(m) > Q(m) for almost all m.

Assumption A1. Let p be an m-bit prime and let g be a generator of the multiplicative group {1,2,...,p−1} (mod p). Let $L_{p,g}$ be the minimum size of a circuit that when given input y finds the x such that $g^x \equiv y \pmod p$. Let L(m) be the maximum of $L_{p,g}$ over all such p and g. Then L(m) is superpolynomial.

Assumption A2. Let F(m) be the minimum size of any circuit that can factor at least 4/5 of the 2m-bit composite numbers N with two m-bit prime factors. Then F(m) is superpolynomial.

Assumption A3. There is a 1-1, onto function $f:\{0,1\}^* \to \{0,1\}^*$ such that f is computable in polynomial time and linear space, $|f(x)| = |x|$ for all x, and if $B_f(m)$ is the size of the smallest circuit which computes $f^{-1}(y)$ for at least 1/2 of the y's of length m then $B_f(m)$ is superpolynomial.

Theorem 2.1 (A. Yao). If Assumption A1, A2 or A3 holds, then polynomial-expanding PNG's exist.

The new observation here is that the pseudorandom strings can be computed in space m where m is the length of the seed. For Assumption A1 (resp., Assumption A2) the necessary computations are arithmetic operations modulo p (resp., modulo N) and only a fixed constant number of m-bit results need be remembered at any point during the computation. For Assumption A3, the computation requires computing several binary strings of the form $\alpha_i = f(s_i)f^2(s_i)f^3(s_i)\ldots$ where the s_i are taken from disjoint parts of the seed s. The output string is then the exclusive-or of the α_i or shifts of the α_i. Thus, to compute a particular bit of the output, compute the appropriate bit of each α_i (which can be done in linear space since f is computable in linear space) and exclusive-or these bits as they are computed.

Remark. Actually Yao proves a stronger result. The fraction of seeds s such that $\psi(x,\rho(s))$ is very close to the fraction of y's such that $\psi(x,y)$. (For Assumption A1, the PNG must have access to some sequence of primes and generators such that $L_{p,g}$ is superpolynomial.) However, for our results we only need that at least one seed work.

3. RESULTS

Hopcroft, Paul and Valiant [6] have shown that a deterministic T(n) time-bounded Turing machine can be simulated by a deterministic Turing machine in space T(n)/log T(n). Under any of the assumptions A1, A2 or A3 above, this result can be extended to random time-bounded computations.

Theorem 3.1. If an E(m)-expanding PNG ρ exists for $E(m) \geq 2m \log m$, and if the function T(n)/log(T(n)) is space constructible [7], then

$$\mathrm{RTIME}(T(n)) \subseteq \mathrm{DSPACE}(T(n)/\log T(n)).$$

Proof. Let $L \in$ RTIME(T(n)) and let ψ define L in random time T(n). Given an input x of length n, let the seed length m = T(n)/log T(n). For almost all n, $E(m) \geq T(n)$. Evaluate $\psi(x,\rho(s))$ for all $s \in \{0,1\}^m$ and accept iff the result is ever *true*. The computation of $\rho(s)$ can be done in space m = T(n)/log T(n) by condition (2) of Definition 2. Since ψ is computable in deterministic time T(n) (where n is the length of the input x), ψ is computable in deterministic space T(n)/log T(n) by the result of Hopcroft, Paul and Valiant [6] mentioned above. By standard methods (see, for example, [8] or [11]) if two functions are both computable in deterministic space $S(n) \geq \log n$, then their composition is computable in deterministic space S(n). □

Remark. Since Theorem 3.1 needs only a modest expansion of O(m log m) and since the predicate ψ is computable in time O(m log m), there is a fixed constant d such that the assumption of superpolynomial complexity in A1, A2 or A3 can be relaxed to the assumption that L(m), F(m) or $B_f(m)$ is greater than m^d [13].

In a similar vein, a good space bound for any problem in $\mathscr{P}$ would imply a good space bound for any problem in $\mathscr{R}$.

Theorem 3.2. If polynomial-expanding PNG's exist, then

$$(\forall \varepsilon > 0)[\mathscr{P} \subseteq \mathrm{DSPACE}(n^{\varepsilon})] \quad \text{iff} \quad (\forall \varepsilon > 0)[\mathscr{R} \subseteq \mathrm{DSPACE}(n^{\varepsilon})].$$

Proof. The "if" direction is immediate since $\mathscr{P} \subseteq \mathscr{R}$. For "only if", let L $\in$ RTIME(n^k), and let $\varepsilon > 0$ be arbitrary. Choose integer $b \geq k/\varepsilon$, and let ρ be an m^b-expanding PNG. To accept L for inputs of length n, let $m = n^{\varepsilon}$ and proceed as in the proof of Theorem 3.1. The computation of ρ can be done in space $m = n^{\varepsilon}$, and since $\psi \in \mathscr{P}$ the computation of ψ can be done in space n^{ε} by assumption. (Even though the input (x,y) to ψ has length $n+n^k$, we can choose a constant $\delta > 0$ so small that $(n+n^k)^{\delta} \leq n^{\varepsilon}$ for almost all n.) □

Theorem 3.3. Let ψ define L in random polynomial time where ψ is computable in deterministic space n^{ε} for any $\varepsilon > 0$. If polynomial-expanding PNG's exist, then

$$L \in \mathrm{DSPACE}(n^{\varepsilon}) \text{ for any } \varepsilon > 0.$$

Proof. The proof is similar to the two preceding proofs. Both ρ and ψ can be computed in space n^{ε}. □

Remark. In Theorem 3.3, the algorithm that computes ψ in polynomial time and the algorithm that computes ψ in space n^{ε} do not have to be the same algorithm.

We now give an application of Theorem 3.3. Let PER denote the set of square adjacency matrices of bipartite graphs that have a perfect matching. Equivalently, PER is the set of square 0-1 matrices with nonzero permanent.

Corollary 3.4. If polynomial-expanding PNG's exist, then

$$\mathrm{PER} \in \mathrm{DSPACE}(n^{\varepsilon}) \text{ for any } \varepsilon > 0.$$

Proof. The following probabilistic algorithm for accepting PER is due to Lovasz. Let A be the given $n \times n$ 0-1 matrix. Replace each 1 in A by an integer chosen from the uniform distribution on {1,2,...,n}; let A′ be the resulting matrix. Compute the determinant of A′ and accept iff $\det(A') \neq 0$. If perm(A) = 0 then $\det(A') = 0$. For some constant $\eta > 0$, if perm(A) $\neq 0$, then $\det(A') \neq 0$ with probability $> \eta$. Thus, the predicate ψ(A,y) is a determinant computation where the string y specifies the integers to be substituted for the 1's in A. It is implicit in Czanky [4] that the determinant computation can be done in space $(\log n)^d$ for some constant d, which is $o(n^{\varepsilon})$ for any $\varepsilon > 0$. □

Remark. Corollary 3.4 suggests an interesting distiction between problems defined by predicates ψ(x,y) where the string y is read by a two-way head and those where y is read by a one-way head. For time-bounded probabilistic computation there is clearly no difference, but for space-bounded probabilistic computation where the space bound is much less than the length of y, it could matter. The above algorithm for PER needs a two-way head on y since the polylog-space algorithm for the determinant needs to read the entries of the matrix many times. Of course, this is no problem for our deterministic space n^{ε} algorithm. Since the seed s is short enough to be stored, the bits of $\rho(s)$ can be recomputed whenever they are needed in the computation of $\psi(A,\rho(s))$.

Let RTISP(T(n),S(n)) be the class of languages accepted by probabilistic Turing machines that are simultaneously T(n) time-bounded and S(n) space-bounded. By the proof of Savitch's theorem [10], it is known that RTISP(T(n),S(n)) $\subseteq$ DSPACE(S(n) log T(n)). The proof of the following is similar to other proofs above.

Theorem 3.5. If $S(n) \geq (T(n))^{\varepsilon}$ for some $\varepsilon > 0$, if S(n) is space constructible, and if polynomial-expanding PNG's exist, then

$$\text{RTISP}(T(n),S(n)) \subseteq \text{DSPACE}(S(n)).$$

Acknowledgement. We thank Andy Yao for a very helpful discussion about the results of [12].

REFERENCES

1. L. Adleman, Two theorems on random polynomial time, *Proc. 19th IEEE Symp. on Foundations of Computer Science* (1978), 75-83.

2. A. V. Aho, J. E. Hopcroft, and J. D. Ullman, *The Design and Analysis of Computer Algorithms*, Addison-Wesley, Reading, MA, 1974.

3. M. Blum and S. Micali, How to generate cryptographically strong sequences of pseudo random bits, *Proc. 23rd IEEE Symp. on Foundations of Computer Science* (1982), 112-117.

4. L. Csanky, Fast parallel matrix inversion algorithms, *SIAM J. Comput.* 5 (1976), 618-623.

5. J. Gill, Computational complexity of probabilistic Turing machines, *SIAM J. Comput.* 6 (1977), 675-695.

6. J. Hopcroft, W. Paul, and L. Valiant, On time versus space, *J.ACM* 24 (1977), 332-337.

7. J. E. Hopcroft and J. D. Ullman, *Introduction to Automata Theory, Languages and Computation*, Addison-Wesley, Reading, MA, 1979.

8. N. Jones, Space-bounded reducibility among combinatorial problems, *J. Comput. Sys. Sci.* 11 (1975), 68-85.

9. J. E. Savage, *The Complexity of Computing*, John Wiley and Sons, New York, 1976.

10. W. J. Savitch, Relationships between nondeterministic and deterministic tape complexities, *J. Comput. Sys. Sci.* 4 (1970), 177-192.

11. L. J. Stockmeyer and A. R. Meyer, Word problems requiring exponential time, *Proc. 5th ACM Symp. on Theory of Computing* (1973), 1-9.

12. A. Yao, Theory and applications of trapdoor functions, *Proc. 23rd IEEE Symp. on Foundations of Computer Science* (1982), 80-91.

13. A. Yao, personal communication.

RECURRING DOMINOES:
MAKING THE HIGHLY UNDECIDABLE HIGHLY UNDERSTANDABLE
(Preliminary Report)

David Harel

Department of Applied Mathematics
The Weizmann Institute of Science
Rehovot, 76100 ISRAEL

ABSTRACT.

In recent years many diverse logical systems for reasoning about programs have been shown to posses a highly undecidable, viz Π_1^1-complete, validity problem. All such known results are reproved in this paper in a uniform and transparent manner by reductions from recurring domino problems. These are simple variants of the classical unbounded domino (or tiling) problems introduced by Wang and the bounded versions defined by Lewis. While the former are (weakly) undecidable and the latter complete in various complexity classes, the problems in the new class are Σ_1^1-complete.

It is hoped that the paper, which contains also NP-, PSPACE-, Π_1^0- and Π_2^0-hardness results for logical systems, will enhance interest in the appealing medium of domino problems as a useful set of reduction tools for exhibiting "bad behavior".

1. INTRODUCTION

About two decades ago Hao Wang introduced domino problems [W1]. A domino is a 1×1 square tile, fixed in orientation, each of whose edges is associated with some color. In general, a domino problem is a decision problem that asks whether or not it is possible to tile some portion P of the integer grid $G = Z\times Z$ by dominoes of certain types, with perhaps some constraints on the placement of certain dominoes, colors or combinations thereof. The input to such a problem always includes some finite set $T = (d_0,\ldots,d_m)$ of domino types, consisting of the colors on the sides of each; one assumes the existence of an infinite supply of each of the types in T. The general rules of tiling are that each grid point of P be associated with a single domino type from T, and that adjacent edges be monochromatic.

The class of problems introduced by Wang was motivated by ideas appearing in Buchi [Bu]. Problems in this class are characterized by the fact that the portion of G to be tiled is unbounded; it is either G itself, or a quadrant, halfgrid, octant, etc. The constraints in these unbounded domino problems are of finitary nature; some tile is required to appear, say, at the origin, the boundary of the quadrant (if that be the case) is to be colored, say, white, the dominoes occurring, say, along the diagonal are to be in some specified $T' \subseteq T$, etc. All these unbounded problems are undecidable but are co-r.e. . In other words, they are Π_1^0-complete, i.e., they and their complements reside at the base of the arithmetical hierarchy [R].

With the notable exception of the constraint-free versions (e.g. "can T tile G?") which are more difficult [Be], undecidability is established by setting up a straightforward correspondence between tiled rows of the portion P to be tiled and legal configurations of Turing machines (TM's). This is done such that adjacent rows correspond to legal transitions of the machine at hand, and the constraints are used to enforce an initial configuration containing the start state and, say, a blank tape. Given a TM M one can thus construct a set T_M of domino types which can tile P in accordance with a particular unbounded problem iff M halts on empty tape. Unbounded domino problems have been extensively investigated and have been widely used for proving undecidability of subcases of the decision problem for the predicate calculus (cf. [E,GK,G,KMW,L2,LP,W2]).

Another class of domino problems, characterized by bounded portions P of the grid G, appears in work of Lewis [L1]. These bounded domino problems are complete in various complexity classes such as NP and PSPACE, and the hardness direction of these facts is established by similar reductions from TM computations. Bounded dominoes have been used in [L1,LP,E] for exhibiting intractability of certain problems, including the NP-completeness of satisfiability in the propositional calculus.

In [E] van Emde Boas presents strong arguments to the effect that the combinatorical and geometrical simplicity of domino problems renders them an ideal medium for introducing and proving "bad behavior" such as NP-hardness or undecidability. He suggests that they be used as "master reductions" in such lower bound proofs. Indeed, one can easily describe domino problems to a novice, and unless a proof from first principles (i.e., computing machines such as TM's) is required, the proofs by reduction from dominoes are usually easy to present and to comprehend. Thus, domino problems can be regarded as an appealing abstraction capturing the two-dimensional time/space character of computation, but one which is devoid of the details of particular computing machines.

The existence of a third class of useful domino problems has been recently noticed in Harel [H2]. Problems in this class are obtained from unbounded domino problems simply by requiring that a designated domino, color or finitary combination thereof occur infinitely often in the tiling. These recurring domino problems (not to be confused with periodic tilings as in [GK,Be,Ro]) are shown in [H2] to be Σ_1^1-complete, i.e., to reside at the base of the highly undecidable analytical hierarchy [R]. The proof of these facts is similarly based on reductions from TM's but here the correspondence is with infinite computations of nondeterministic TM's (NTM's) which reenter a "signalling situation" infinitely often. As an illustration of the usefulness of recurring dominoes, an easy, almost trivial proof of the known Σ_1^1-hardness of satisfiability in either infinitary logic [K] or first-order (quantificational) dynamic logic [P,HMP] is presented in [H2]. This is actually an extension of the unbounded domino proof of undecidability of the predicate calculus, which in turn can be seen to be an extension of a bounded domino proof of NP-completeness for the propositional calculus (cf. [LP]).

The purpose of the present paper is to reinforce the arguments of [E,H2] by presenting weighty evidence of the usefulness of domino problems, in particular recurring domino problems, for bounding from below the complexity of decision problems in logical systems, especially program-oriented ones such as dynamic and temporal logics.

Many Π_1^1-completeness results for deciding validity in certain programming logics (i.e., Σ_1^1-completeness for satisfiability) have been established in the past few years using various reduction techniques. These systems are quite diverse both in their motivation and applications and in their expressive power. Examples are quantificational dynamic logic, two-dimensional temporal logic, and context-free propositional dynamic logic.

The bulk of the present paper is Section 4 which is devoted to presenting proofs of all these Π_1^1-completeness results by reductions from recurring dominoes. The moral of this unifying exercise is that when dealing with logics of programs "when you have a grid you have it all"; that is, once one has forced candidate models of the formulas at hand to correspond to a managable grid (usually the positive quadrant of G), the rest of a Π_1^1-hardness proof follows effortlessly by reduction from recurring dominoes. The grid-forcing part varies from trivial to quite tricky among the results presented, but in each case (i) the resulting proof is considerably easier and more transparent than the original one, and (ii) the grid-forcing part usually appears buried in the original proof anyway. Section 4 also contains some domino proofs of related PSPACE- and Π_2^0-hardness results, as well as some hitherto unpublished Π_1^1-results.

Section 2 defines the specific domino problems used in the sequel and states their complexity; it then provides some background on the logical systems discussed. Section 3 presents the three-part warm-up proof given in [H2] that the satisfiability/validity problem for the classical languages behaves as in the following table (in which notation of the polynomial-time, arithmetical, and analytical hierarchies has been used to emphasize uniformity):

Formalism	Satisfiability/validity	reduction from
propositional logic	Σ_1^P / Π_1^P	bounded dominoes
predicate logic	Σ_1^0 / Π_1^0	unbounded dominoes
infinitary logic (constructive)	Σ_1^1 / Π_1^1	recurring dominoes

It is hoped that the exposition presented herein will guide intuition as to the possible high undecidability of logical systems introduced in the future and will ease proofs of Π_1^1 (and other lower bound) results by encouraging reductions from domino problems.

2. PRELIMINARIES

2.1 Domino Problems and Their Complexity

The input to a domino problem always includes a finite set $T = \{d_0, \ldots, d_m\}$ of domino types, each of the form $d_i = (\underline{left}_i, \underline{right}_i, \underline{up}_i, \underline{down}_i)$, giving the four colors associated with the sides of d_i. Colors are taken from some denumerable set C. Let $G = Z \times Z$, $G^+ = \mathbb{N} \times \mathbb{N}$, and $G^{++} = \{(i,j) \mid (i,j) \in G^+, \text{ and } i \leq j\}$.

Following are some particular domino problems utilized in the sequel.

Bounded Problems:

B1: Given T and n (in unary); can T tile an $n \times n$ square?

B2: Given T and two colors c_0, c_1; can T tile an $n \times m$ rectangle, for some m, such that the leftmost colors on the bottom and top match c_0 and c_1, respectively?

Unbounded Problems:

U1: Given T; can T tile G?

U2: Given T; can T tile G^+?

∃U: Given T and two colors c_0, c_1; can T tile G^+ such that the sequence of colors on the bottom of the first row is of the form $c_0^n c_1^\omega$ for some n?

Recurring Problems:

R1: Given T; can T tile G such that d_0 occurs in the tiling infinitely often?

R2: Given T; can T tile G^+ such that d_0 occurs in the tiling infinitely often in the first column?

R3: Given T; can T tile G^{++} such that d_0 occurs in the tiling at least once in every column?

We assume familiarity with the hierarchy notation of Rogers [R], and with standard notions of complexity theory. In particular, we shall be using NP and PSPACE to stand for the set of problems decidable by a nondeterministic Turing machine in polynomial time and space, respectively. (By [Sa] the adjective "nondeterministic" is redundant for the latter.) NP is denoted Σ_1^P in the notation of the polynomial-time hierarchy [St], and PSPACE contains that entire hierarchy.

Σ_1^0 is the class of r.e. sets and its complement, Π_1^0, is the class of co-r.e. sets. Π_2^0 consists of all those sets (such as the codes of everywhere-halting TM's) which can be characterized by formulas over $\mathbb{N}$ of the form $\forall x \exists y R$ for recursive R; its complement is Σ_2^0. These classes reside low in the arithmetical hierarchy [R].

The class Σ_1^1 and its complement Π_1^1 reside low in the analytical hierarchy and represent sets characterizable, respectively, by formulas over $\mathbb{N}$ of the forms $\exists f R$ and $\forall f R$ for arithmetical R.

Fact: (i) B1 is NP-complete, cf. [L1,LP,E].

(ii) B2 is PSPACE-complete, [L1,E].

(iii) U1 and U2 are Π_1^0-complete, [Be,Ro].

(iv) ∃U is Σ_2^0-complete, cf. [H2].

(v) R1, R2 and R3 are Σ_1^1-complete, [H2].

For details and discussions of these and other domino problems the reader is referred to van Emde Boas [E] and Harel [H2]. Problems U1 and R1 are not used in the paper and are described in order to exhibit the "cleanest" known unbounded and recurring versions.

2.2. The Logical Systems Considered

The systems considered in the sequel are of propositional and quantificational (first-order) character. We briefly describe each and provide references for details.

1) Propositional calculus, cf. [Me,Sh]:

Closure under $\vee$ and $\neg$ of propositional variables P,Q,... Abbreviations: $\wedge,\supset,\equiv$. Formulas satisfied by truth assignment to propositional variables.

2) Propositional Temporal Logic of Linear Time (TL), cf. [Pn,MP]:

Closure under $\vee,\neg,\Diamond$ and $\bigcirc$ of P,Q,... . Abbreviations: as above, and $\Box = \neg\Diamond\neg$. Formulas satisfied in linear models of order-type ω in which each point supplies a truth assignment for the P,Q,... $\Diamond$ means "eventually", $\bigcirc$ means "at the next instant". Example: $P \wedge \Box\Diamond(Q\supset \bigcirc P)$, "P true now and infinitely often Q implies P at the next instant".

3) Two-Dimensional Temporal Logic (2TL), cf. [HP]:

Closure under $\vee,\neg,\Diamond_i,\bigcirc_i$ for i = 1,2, of P,Q,... . Abbreviations: as above, and $\Box_i = \neg\Diamond_i\neg$. Formulas interpreted is cross-product of two TL models, i.e., in grids G^+, with $\Diamond_i,\bigcirc_i$ indicating process along the two coordinates.
Example: $\Box_1\Diamond_2 P$, "P is true at least once on each column of the grid".

4) Temporal-Spatial Logic (TSL), cf. [RS]:

Closure under $\vee,\neg,\Diamond,\bigcirc$, somewhere and L of P,Q,... . Abbreviations: as in TL, and everywhere = $\neg$somewhere$\neg$. Formulas interpreted in "proper interpretations" of networks of processors, with $\Diamond$ and $\bigcirc$ referring to time, L the (spatial) immediate connection between processors, and somewhere the reflexive transitive closure of L. Proper interpretations have a grid-like structure just as in 2TL.
Example: $P \wedge \Diamond$ L (Q $\vee$ everywhere P), "P true now and here, and eventually the neighboring process satisfies Q or all its connected processes satisfy P".

5) Propositional Dynamic Logic (PDL), cf. [FL,H1]:

Formulas are closure under $\vee$, $\neg$ and $\langle\alpha\rangle$ of P,Q,..., where the programs α are regular expressions (i.e., closure under $\cup$, ;, *) of atomic programs a,b,... and tests p? for formulas p. Abbreviations: as in prop. calc., and $[\alpha] = \neg\langle\alpha\rangle\neg$. Formulas satisfied in structures (W,τ,ρ) with $\tau(P) \subseteq W$ and $\rho(a) \subseteq W\times W$, interpreting propositional variables as true or false in states (= elements of W), and atomic programs as binary relations on states. Regular operators interpreted in standard relational calculus manner. $\langle\alpha\rangle$ means "it is possible to execute α such that".
Example: $P \supset [a^*](R \vee \langle b\cup c^*d\rangle Q)$, "if P is true then any terminating finite sequence of executions of a leads to a state in which either R is true or it is possible to execute either b or some number of c's followed by d and reach a state satisfying Q".

6) PDL With Additional Programs, cf. [HPS]:

Certain single nonregular programs, such as $L_1 = \{a^i ba^i | i \geq 0\}$, denoted $a^\Delta ba^\Delta$, or $L_2 = \{a^{2^i} | i \geq 0\}$ are added to PDL.
Example: $[L_2][a]P$, "P is true at all points along a-paths at distance $2^i + 1$, for $i \in \omega$".

7) Deterministic PDL With Intersection (DPDL + "$\cap$"), cf. [HV]:

PDL interpreted in structures in which $\rho(a)$ is a function, and enriched with the intersection operator on programs; $\rho(\alpha \cap \beta) = \rho(\alpha) \cap \rho(\beta)$.
Example: $\langle a \cap \underline{true}? \rangle \underline{true}$, "there is an effectless execution of a".

8) Inference and Implication in PDL, cf. [MSM]:

A formula of PDL containing a "free" propositional variable Q, and denoted A(Q) is regarded as an axiom scheme, standing for the set A(PDL) of all formulas obtained from it by consistantly substituting arbitrary PDL formulas for Q. A(Q) infers P if P is valid in all structures in which all formulas of A(PDL) are. A(Q) implies P if P is true in any state in which all formulas of A(PDL) are.
Example: $\langle a \rangle Q \supset [a]Q$ infers all formulas true for deterministic a.

9) Global Process Logic, cf. [HKP,S]:

Closure under $\vee, \neg, \langle \alpha \rangle$, first and suf of P,Q,... . Programs are as in PDL.
Abbreviations: as in PDL. Formulas satisfied by paths in structures (W, τ, ρ), where $\tau(P) \subseteq W^*$ and $\rho(a) \subseteq W^*$, interpreting both formulas and programs as paths of states. $\langle \alpha \rangle P$ satisfied in path p if P is satisfied in some path pq with $q \in \rho(\alpha)$. The connective first, for example, is unary and first P is satisfied in p if P is satisfied in the first state of p. A derived operator next is defined so that p satisfies next P if the greatest proper suffix of p satisfies P. For each i a formula L_i can be defined, true in all paths of length i. The operator last is also derived.
Example: $L_0 \wedge \langle a^* \rangle(\underline{last}([b]\underline{next}Q))$, is true in "paths consisting of a single state, in which there is some a^* path, at the end of which each b path is such that the path obtained by truncating the first state satisfies Q".

10) Predicate Calculus (with equality), cf. [Me,Sh]:

Closure under $\vee, \neg, \exists x$ of atomic formulas $P(t_1, \ldots, t_n)$ for terms t_i. Language includes binary predicate "=". Formulas interpreted in first-order structures, "=" interpreted as equality. Abbreviations: as in prop. calc., and $\forall x = \neg \exists x \neg$.

11) Augmented Arithmetic, cf. [Sh]:

Predicate calculus with =,0,1,+,x,< interpreted over $\mathbb{N}$ in the standard way, augmented with extra uninterpreted predicate symbols.

12) Infinitary Logic (constructive version is denoted $L^{CK}_{\omega_1 \omega}$), cf. [K]:

Predicate calculus closed also under disjunctions and conjunctions. In constructive version disjunctions and conjunctions are r.e.

Example: $\bigvee_{i\in\omega} \varphi_i$, where $\varphi_0 = \neg\exists x(x=x)$, $\varphi_1 = \exists x\forall y(x=y)$, $\varphi_2 = \exists x\exists y(\neg x=y \wedge \forall z(x=z \vee y=z))$, etc., is true precisely in finite structures.

13) Quantified Temporal Logic of Linear Time (QTL), cf. [Pn]:

Closure under $\vee,\neg,\diamond,\bigcirc$ and $\exists x$ of atomic formulas as in pred. calc. Abbreviations: as in TL and pred. calc. Formulas satisfied in linear models of order-type ω underlying first-order structures. Each point in time provides values for all variables.
Example: $x=y \supset \diamond\square(P(x) \wedge x=y)$, "if x=y then from some future point on x=y and P is true of x".

14) Quantified Dynamic Logic (QDL), cf. [P,H1]:

Closure under $\vee,\neg,\langle\alpha\rangle,\exists x$ of atomic formulas, where the programs α are regular expressions over assignments $x \leftarrow t$ for term t and tests $\varphi?$ for formula φ. Abbreviations: as in PDL and pred. calc. Formulas satisfied in first-order structures in which states provide values for variables; assignments interpreted in the standard way, and program operations as in PDL.
Example: $x=y \supset [(x \leftarrow f(f(x)))^*]\langle(y \leftarrow f(y))^*\rangle x=y$, is valid, states "every execution of (ff)* corresponds to some execution of f*".

15) Looping in QDL, cf. [H1]:

Predicate loop(α) for α a QDL program states that α contains an infinite computation. Formulas satisfied in QDL structures, * operator interpreted as $*\cup\omega$
Example: loop($(x \leftarrow f(x);P(x)?)^*$), states "for all i, $P(f^i(x))$ is true".

We remark that the rest of the paper presents only the hardness directions of the results. All results are actually completeness results and the upper bounds are usually easy to establish. In particular, Σ_1^1-hard satisfiability problems can be shown to be in Σ_1^1 by appealing to an appropriate version of the Löwenheim-Skolem Theorem, and writing "φ is satisfiable" as "$\exists$ countable structure...", which is Σ_1^1.

3. CLASSICAL SYSTEMS

In all reductions we assume an input set $T = \{d_0,\ldots,d_m\}$ involving colors $C_T = \{c_0,\ldots,c_{k-1}\}$, where w.l.o.g. k is a power of 2. We use propositional or predicate symbols denoted by LEFT, RIGHT, UP, DOWN, indexed by superscripts $1 \leq u \leq \log k$. In propositional logics we might have additional subscripts yielding, for example, $\mathrm{LEFT}^u_{i,j}$, or LEFT^u_i, for $1 \leq i, j \leq n$, and in quantificational (= first-order) logics the predicates are binary or unary, as in $\mathrm{LEFT}^u(x,y)$ or $\mathrm{LEFT}^u(x)$. In general, unsuperscripted symbols stand for the appropriately ordered sets of the log k superscripted ones; e.g., LEFT_i is $(\mathrm{LEFT}^1_i,\ldots,\mathrm{LEFT}^{\log k}_i)$. In this way, indentifying color c_i with the binary representation of i, the colors in C_T are in a fixed one-to-one correspondence with possible truth assignments to such sets. Accordingly, we shall write, say, $\mathrm{RIGHT}_{i,j} = c_\ell$ as an abbreviation of the appropriate conjunction of the $\pm\mathrm{RIGHT}^u_{i,j}$, to indicate that the color on the right hand edge of the domino associated with (i,j) is c_ℓ, or $UP(x,y) = \underline{down}_n$ to mean that the color on the top edge of the domino at (x,y) is that on the bottom of domino d_n in T. To associate dominoes from T with such indices we write, e.g., $LRUD_{i,j} = d_n$ as an abbreviation of $LEFT_{i,j} = \underline{left}_n \wedge RIGHT_{i,j} = \underline{right}_n \wedge UP_{i,j} = \underline{up}_n \wedge DOWN_{i,j} = \underline{down}_n$. Similarly for LRUD(x,y).

<u>Theorem 3.1</u> [C]: Satisfiability in the propositional calculus in NP-hard.

<u>Proof</u> [LP]: Given T and n, construct $P_{T,n}$ as the conjunction of

$$(1)\quad \bigwedge_{i=1}^{n} \bigwedge_{j=1}^{n} \Big(\bigvee_{\ell=0}^{m} LRUD_{i,j} = d_\ell \Big),$$

and

$$(2)\quad \bigwedge_{i=1}^{n-1} \bigwedge_{j=1}^{n} (RIGHT_{i,j} = LEFT_{i+1,j} \wedge UP_{j,i} = DOWN_{j,i+1}).$$

Clearly $P_{T,n}$ is of size a polynomial in $n+m$, and is satisfiable iff T,n satisfies B1. The latter is seen by observing that (1) associates a domino from T with each point of $[1...n] \times [1...n]$, and (2) asserts correct matching of colors. □

<u>Theorem 3.2</u> [Ch,T]: Satisfiability in the predicate calculus is Π_1^0-hard.

<u>Proof</u>: Given T, construct φ_T as the conjunction of

$$(0)\quad \forall x(f(x) \neq z \wedge \forall y(f(x) = f(y) \supset x = y)),$$

$$(1)\quad \forall x \forall y \Big(\bigvee_{\ell=0}^{m} LRUD(x,y) = d_\ell \Big),$$

and

$$(2)\quad \forall x \forall y (RIGHT(x,y) = LEFT(f(x),y) \wedge UP(x,y) = DOWN(x,f(y))).$$

The claim is that φ_T is satisfiable iff T satisfies U2. The <u>if</u> direction is trivial since if a tiling exists φ_T is satisfied in $\mathbb{N}$ with z interpreted as 0 and f as successor. Conversely, the domain of any structure satisfying φ_T must contain, by clause (0), an infinite set S constituting the values of $z, f(z), f(f(z)),...$ The grid G^+ matches $S \times S$, with (i,j) corresponding to $(f^i(z), f^j(z))$. Clause (1) and (2) behave as in Thm. 3.1, yielding a tiling of G^+. □

<u>Theorem 3.3</u> (cf. [K,R]): Satisfiability in constructive infinitary logic is Σ_1^1-hard.

<u>Proof</u> [H2]: Given T, construct φ'_T as the conjunction of φ_T of Thm. 3.2, and

$$(3)\quad \forall x \bigvee_{i\in\omega} (LRUD(z,f^i(x)) = d_0).$$

The claim is that φ'_T is satisfiable iff T satisfies R2. The <u>if</u> direction is as before but now (3) holds by virtue of the recurrence of domino d_0. Conversely, if (3) holds, d_0 occurs arbitrarily high up in the first column $(z, \{f^i(z)\}_{i\in\omega})$ of G^+. □

Theorem 3.4 (cf. [R]): Satisfiability in augmented first-order arithmetic is Σ_1^1-hard.

Proof: There is no need for clause (0) of Thm. 3.2. Given T, construct ψ_T as the conjunction of

(1) $\forall x \forall y (\bigvee_{\ell=0}^{m} \text{LRUD}(x,y) = d_\ell)$,

(2) $\forall x \forall y (\text{RIGHT}(x,y) = \text{LEFT}(x+1,y) \wedge \text{UP}(x,y) = \text{DOWN}(x,y+1))$,

and

(3) $\forall x \exists y (x < y \wedge \text{LRUD}(z,y) = d_0)$.

ψ_T is satisfiable iff T Satisfies R2. □

4. DOMINOE PROOFS OF HARDNESS RESULTS IN LOGICS OF PROGRAMS

The role played by the four conjuncts (0) - (3) in the proofs in the previous section is the connecting thread of all proofs in this one.

While clause (0), which states that "models look like grids", will take on quite diverse forms in the sequel, the general form of (1), (2) and (3) will be

(1) ∀point (point ∈ T)

(2) ∀point (colors match right and above neighbors)

(3) ∀distance ∃point-further-away (point is d_0).

Since in most cases the parenthesized parts are written easily using the abbreviations introduced in Section 3, one really has to specify only how to universally reach all points on the appropriate grid, how to existentially reach points "further away" than the "current" one, and how to reach the neighbors of any "current" point.

We first discuss the quantificational logics QDL and QTL.

Theorem 4.1 ([M], cf. [HMP]): Satisfiability in QDL is Σ_1^1-hard, even for formulas of the form $\forall x <(x \leftarrow f(x))^*> \varphi$ for program-free φ.

Proof: Replace (3) in the proof of Thm. 3.3 by

(3) $\forall x <(x \leftarrow f(x))^*>(\text{LRUD}(z,x) = d_0)$.

Since the program within the <> does not involve z (= the only free variable in φ_T = (0) ∧ (1) ∧ (2)) the final formula ψ_T can be taken to be $\forall x<(x \leftarrow f(x))^*>$ $(\text{LRUD}(z,x) = d_0 \wedge \varphi_T)$. It is satisfiable iff T satisfies R2. □

Theorem 4.2 [H1]: Satisfiability of formulas of the form loop(α), for QDL programs α, is Σ_1^1-hard.

Proof: Given T, let α_T be

$\varphi_T?;\ (x \leftarrow f(x);\ (<(x \leftarrow f(x))^*>(\text{LRUD}(z,x) = d_0))?)^*$, where φ_T is as in the proof of Thm. 3.2. The predicate loop(α_T) is satisfiable iff φ_T is satisfied in a state that admits an infinite computation of $x \leftarrow f(x)$ with d_0 recurring ever higher along the first column of the grid G^+. □

Theorem 4.3: Satisfiability in QTL is Σ_1^1-hard, even for formulas of the form $\Box\Diamond\varphi$ for φ involving only a single $\bigcirc$ (and no $\Box$ or $\Diamond$).

Proof: Given T, construct ψ_T as the conjunction of (0) of the proof of Thm. 3.2, and

(1) $\Box\forall x(\bigvee_{\ell=0}^{m} \mathrm{LRUD}(x) = d_\ell)$,

(2) $\Box\forall x(\mathrm{RIGHT}(x) = \mathrm{LEFT}(f(x)) \wedge \bigwedge_{i=0}^{k-1} (\mathrm{UP}(x) = c_i \supset \bigcirc(\mathrm{DOWN}(x) = c_i)))$,

(3) $\Box\Diamond(\mathrm{LRUD}(x) = d_0)$.

Here the infinite set $z, f(z), f(f(z)),\ldots$ of clause (0) is used only in the horizontal direction; the vertical one is modeled by the temporal axis. The special form is obtained as in Thm. 4.1 and is satisfiable iff T satisfies R2. □

It is possible to prove the Π_2^0-hardness of validity of Hoare [H] partial correctness assertions using the $\exists$U domino problem. To see this note that $\psi\{\alpha\}\varphi$ is $\psi \supset [\alpha]\varphi$ in QDL notation, or $[\psi?;\alpha]\varphi$. The following Theorem thus gives the result.

Theorem 4.4 [HMP]: Satisfiability of formulas of QDL of the form $\langle\alpha\rangle\varphi$ for program-free φ is Σ_2^0-hard, even for test-free α.

Proof: Given T, construct ψ'_T to be the conjunction of φ_T from Thm. 3.2, and

(*) $\mathrm{LRUD}(z,z) = d_0 \wedge \forall x((\mathrm{DOWN}(x,z) = c_0 \supset (\mathrm{DOWN}(f(x),z) = c_0 \vee \mathrm{DOWN}(f(x),z) = c_1)) \wedge (\mathrm{DOWN}(x,z) = c_1 \supset \mathrm{DOWN}(f(x),z) = c_1))$.

Now let ψ_T be

$\langle x \leftarrow z;\ (x \leftarrow f(x))^*\rangle (\mathrm{DOWN}(x,z) = c_0 \wedge \mathrm{DOWN}(f(x),z) = c_1 \wedge \psi'_T)$.

Given that $\mathrm{down}_0 = c_0$, ψ'_T forces the bottom colors on the bottom row of G^+ to be either c_0^ω or $c_0^n c_1^\omega$ for some n. ψ_T then prevents the first possibility and hence is satisfiable iff T satisfies $\exists$U. □

Turning now to the propositional logics PDL, TL and PL, the results here are at times considerably more involved due to the difficulty of forcing models to look like grids.

Theorem 4.5 [HP]: Satisfiability in 2TL is Σ_1^1-hard.

Proof: Given T, construct P_T as the conjunction of

(1) $\Box_1 \Box_2 (\bigvee_{\ell=0}^{m} \mathrm{LRUD} = d_\ell)$,

(2) $\square_1 \square_2 \left(\bigwedge_{i=0}^{k-1} ((\mathrm{RIGHT} = c_i \supset \bigcirc_1(\mathrm{LEFT} = c_i)) \wedge (\mathrm{UP} = c_i \supset \bigcirc_2(\mathrm{DOWN} = c_i)))\right)$,

and

(3) $\square_2 \Diamond_2 (\mathrm{LRUD} = d_0)$.

P_T is satisfiable iff T satisfies R2. □

Theorem 4.6 [RS]: Satisfiability in TSL is Σ_1^1-hard.

Proof: Given T, construct P_T as the conjunction of

(1) $\square$ everywhere $\left(\bigvee_{\ell=0}^{m} \mathrm{LRUD} = d_\ell \right)$,

(2) $\square$ everywhere $\left(\bigwedge_{i=0}^{k-1} ((\mathrm{RIGHT} = c_i \supset \bigcirc(\mathrm{LEFT} = c_i)) \wedge (\mathrm{UP} = c_i \supset \underline{L}(\mathrm{DOWN} = c_i)))\right)$,

(3) everywhere (somewhere($\mathrm{LRUD} = d_0$)).

P_T is satisfiable iff T satisfies R2. □

It is possible to prove that one-dimensional TL is PSPACE-hard using bounded dominoes (without $\bigcirc$ it is NP-complete [SC]):

Theorem 4.7 [SC]: Satisfiability in TL is PSPACE-hard.

Proof: Given T and colors c_0, c_1, construct P_{T,c_0,c_1} as the conjunction of

(1) $\square(Q \supset \bigwedge_{i=1}^{n} \bigvee_{\ell=0}^{m} (\mathrm{LRUD}_i = d_\ell))$,

(2) $\square(Q \supset ((\bigwedge_{i=1}^{n-1} (\mathrm{RIGHT}_i = \mathrm{LEFT}_{i+1}) \wedge \bigwedge_{i=1}^{n} \bigwedge_{j=0}^{k-1} (\mathrm{UP}_i = c_j \supset \bigcirc(\mathrm{DOWN}_i = c_j))))$,

(*) $Q \wedge \square(\neg Q \supset \bigcirc\neg Q) \wedge \mathrm{DOWN}_1 = c_0 \wedge \Diamond(Q \wedge \bigcirc(\neg Q) \wedge \mathrm{UP}_1 = c_1)$

Process along the vertical ($\exists m\ldots$) axis of B2 is achieved with the temporal operators, and the horizontal axis is bounded by n and referred to by $1 \leq i \leq n$. P_{T,c_0,c_1} is thus satisfiable iff (T, c_0, c_1) satisfies B2, since (*) states that the first color on the first row matches c_0 and on some (further) one matches c_1. Throughout Q is forced to be true precisely at the first m vertical points. □

It is possible to use the trick from [MS] to obtain similar transparent domino proofs of PSPACE-hardness for quantified Boolean formulas [MS] and certain systems of modal logic [La]. We omit the details here.

Theorem 4.8 [MSM]: The non-inference and non-implication problems for PDL are Σ_1^1-hard.

Proof: Let $A(Q)$ be

$$(\langle ab\rangle Q \supset [ba]Q) \wedge (\langle ba\rangle Q \supset [ab]Q).$$

Given T, construct P_T as the conjunction of

(0) $[(a\cup b)^*](\langle a\rangle \underline{true} \wedge \langle b\rangle \underline{true})$,

(1) $[(a\cup b)^*](\bigvee_{\ell=0}^{m} LRUD = d_\ell)$,

(2) $[(a\cup b)^*](\bigwedge_{i=0}^{k-1} ((RIGHT = c_i \supset [a](LEFT = c_i)) \wedge (UP = c_i \supset [b](DOWN = c_i))))$,

and

(3) $[b^*]\langle b^*\rangle(LRUD = d_0)$.

Clause (0) forces the existence of a binary a,b tree from any satisfying state. The axiom scheme A(Q) when regarded as the infinite set A(PDL) forces this tree to act, as far as can be detected by PDL formulas, like a grid. Specifically the claims are: (i) A(PDL) infers $\neg P_T$ iff T does not satisfy R2;

(ii) $[(a\cup b)^*]$A(PDL) implies $\neg P_T$ iff T does not satisfy R2.

To see (i), if T satisfies R2 the structure consisting of a quadrant as in Fig. 1, tiled accordingly, satisfies A(PDL) in all states, but satisfies P_T at state s. Conversely, if all states of some structure $\mathfrak{A}$ satisfy A(PDL), and some state s satisfies P_T then the "forward part" of $\mathfrak{A}$ from s [MSM] looks essentially like Fig. 1, by (0) and A(PDL). Clauses (1) - (3) then assert the existence of the required tiling. □

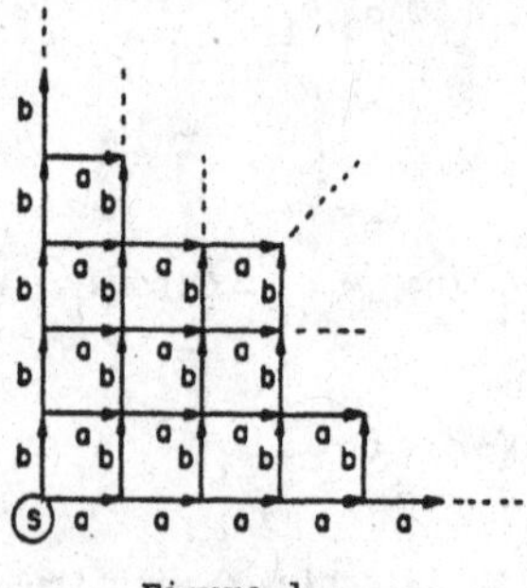

Figure 1.

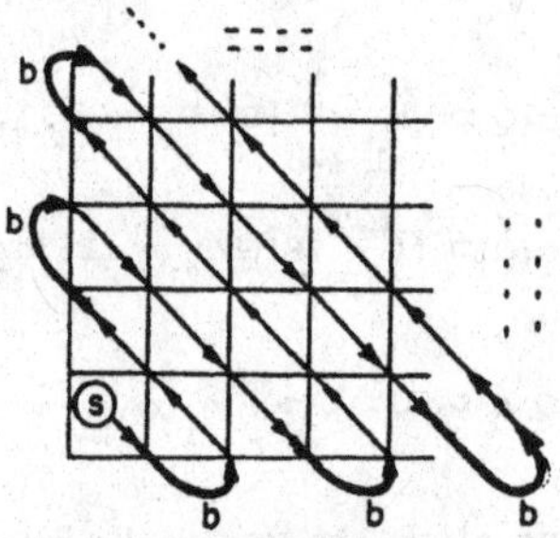

Figure 2.

Remark: Our proof of Theorem 4.8 involves only test-free programs (cf. [MSM, Thm. 4.4]) and can be strengthened as in [MSM, Thms. 4.5, 4.6] to atomic-test-DPDL.

A very similar looking proof can be given for deterministic PDL with intersection:

Theorem 4.9 [HV]: Satisfiability in DPDL + "$\cap$" is Σ_1^1-hard.

Proof [HV]: Construct P_T as the conjunction of (1) - (3) of the previous proof, and,

(0) $[(a\cup b)^*](\langle ab\cap ba\rangle \underline{true})$.

Clause (0) forces the existence of a (possibly cyclic) grid. P_T is thus satisfiable iff T satisfies R2. □

Theorem 4.10 [HPS]: Satisfiability in PDL + $\{a^\Delta ba^\Delta\}$ is Σ_1^1-hard.

Proof: Given T, denoting $a^\Delta ba^\Delta$ by L and a*b by N construct P_T as the conjunction of

$$(0)\quad \langle ab\rangle \underline{true} \wedge [N^*](\langle a^*ab\rangle \underline{true} \wedge [a^*a][L][ab]\underline{false} \wedge [L][aa]\underline{false}),$$

$$(1)\quad [(a\cup b)^*a](\bigvee_{\ell=0}^{m} LRUD = d_\ell),$$

$$(2)\quad [(NN)^*a^*](\bigwedge_{i=0}^{k-1}((RIGHT = c_i \supset [L][a](LEFT = c_i)) \wedge (UP = c_i \supset [L][aa](DOWN = c_i))))$$

$$\wedge [(NN)^*Na^*](\bigwedge_{i=0}^{k-1}((RIGHT = c_i \supset [L][aa](LEFT = c_i)) \wedge (UP = c_i \supset [L][a](DOWN = c_i)))),$$

$$(3)\quad [(NN)^*]\langle (NN)^*\rangle (LRUD = d_0).$$

Clause (0) forces the existence, in any potential model, of an infinite sequence of the form $\sigma = aba^2ba^3b\ldots$. Clause (1) associates dominoes from T with those points of σ that follow a's, and (2) forces the matching of colors, so that σ corresponds to G^+, as illustrated in Fig. 2. Note how neighbors from the right and from above are reached using L. Consequently, P_T is satisfiable iff T satisfies R2. □

Remark: As in the proof in [HPS] it is possible to modify this proof slightly and obtain the result for PDL + $\{a^\Delta b^\Delta, b^\Delta a^\Delta\}$. The question of whether PDL + $\{a^\Delta b^\Delta\}$ is decidable or not is still open, cf. [H2].

Theorem 4.11 [PH]: Satisfiability in PDL + {L}, where $L = \{a^{2^i} \mid i \geq 0\}$, is Σ_1^1-hard.

Sketch of Proof [PH]: Given T, construct P_T as the conjunction of the following formulas, which involve the additional predicate symbols $Q_0,\ldots,Q_6$, and R_0, R_1, R_2.

$$(0)\quad Q_0 \wedge \bigwedge_{i=1}^{6} \neg Q_i$$

$$\wedge [a^*](\langle a\rangle \underline{true} \wedge \bigwedge_{i=0}^{6} (Q_i \supset [a](Q_{(i+1)\bmod 7} \wedge \bigwedge_{\substack{0\le j\le 6 \\ j\ne (i+1)\bmod 7}} \neg Q_j)))$$

$$\wedge [LL](\bigvee_{i=0}^{2} R_i \wedge \bigwedge_{\substack{i\ne j \\ 0\le i,j\le 2}} (R_i \wedge R_j))$$

$$\wedge [LL](R_0 \equiv \bigvee_{i=1,2,4} Q_i)$$

$\wedge\ [La](Q_3 \supset R_1)$

$\wedge\ [LL](\bigwedge_{i=1,2} (R_i \supset [L]\neg R_i))$,

(1) $[LL](\bigvee_{\ell=0}^{m} LRUD = d_\ell)$,

(2) $[LL](\bigwedge_{i=0}^{2} \bigwedge_{j=0}^{k-1} (R_i \supset (RIGHT = c_j \supset [L](R_{(i-1) \bmod 3} \supset LEFT = c_j))$

$\wedge\ (UP = c_j \supset [L](R_{(i+1) \bmod 3} \supset DOWN = c_j))))$,

and

(3) $[L]\langle L\rangle(LRUD = d_0)$.

Here the claim is that P_T is satisfiable iff T satisfies R3. This is rather difficult to see immediately, and the details of the proof will appear in [PH]. However, to get a feeling for it, clause (0) forces points at distances in $\{2^i+2^j \mid i,j \geq 0\}$ to form an octant grid G^{++} as in Fig. 3. There, a parenthesized number is the subscript of that R_i forced to be true at the point. One sees that the element to the right of a point s satisfying R_i satisfies $R_{(i-1) \bmod 3}$ and the one above it $R_{(i+1) \bmod 3}$. Moreover, these are the only two points in G^{++} at distances a power of 2 from s. Thus, from any point in this L^2 grid any execution of L leads either to its neighbors or outside the grid. Clause (3) can be seen to state the recurrence property of R3, and for it to work it is important that d_0 occurs in all columns as in the statement of R3. □

⋮	⋮		⋮		⋮
33 (2)	34 (1)	36 (0)	40 (2)	48 (1)	64 (0)
17 (1)	18 (0)	20 (2)	24 (1)	32 (0)	
9 (0)	10 (2)	12 (1)	16 (0)		
5 (2)	6 (1)	8 (0)			
3 (1)	4 (0)				
2 (0)					

Figure 3.

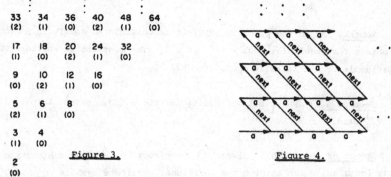

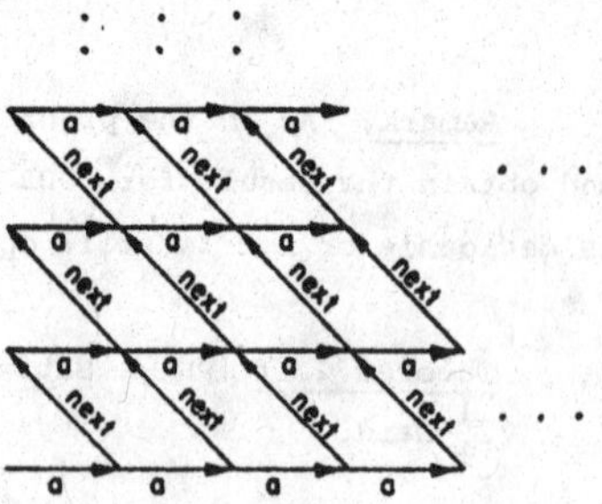

Figure 4.

Remark: It is open whether, e.g., PDL + L, for $L = \{a^{i^2} \mid i \geq 0\}$ or $L = \{a^{i^3} \mid i \geq 0\}$, is undecidable.

Theorem 4.12 [S]: Satisfiability in Global Process Logic is Σ_1^1-hard.

Proof (cf. [S]): Given T, construct P_T as the conjunction of

(0) $L_0 \wedge [a^*]\underline{last}([a]L_1)$,

(1) $[a^*]\underline{last}([a^*](\bigvee_{\ell=0}^{m} LRUD = d_\ell)$,

$$(2)\quad [a^*]\underline{last}([a^*](\bigwedge_{i=0}^{k-1}((RIGHT = c_i \supset [a](LEFT = c_i)) \wedge (UP = c_i \supset [a]\underline{next}(DOWN = c_i))))),$$

$$(3)\quad [a^*]\underline{last}(\langle a^*a\rangle\underline{last}(LRUD = d_0)).$$

Here the claim is that P_T is satisfiable iff T satisfies R2. Clause (0) together with the <> part of (3), forces the existence of an implicit quadrant grid G^+ in which point (i,j) corresponds to the segment $P_{i,j} = (s_i,\ldots,s_{i+j})$ of an infinite path $p = (s_0,s_1,\ldots)$ with $(s_i,s_{i+1}) \in \rho(a)$ for each i. In this way, the right neighbor of $P_{i,j}$ is obtained by an execution of a, and the above neighbor by an execution of a followed by next. Executions of a* followed by last correspond to arbitrary movement up a column; in this way (3) really asserts the recurrence property of R2. See Fig. 4. □

5. CONCLUSIONS AND DISCUSSION

It is hoped that the simplicity and similarity of the proofs in Section 3 and 4 speak for themselves. All lower bounds of NP, PSPACE, Π_1^0, Π_2^0 and Σ_1^1 for satisfiability in logical systems which are known to the author have been provided with such proofs. It seems that domino problems, with their "∃ tiling" format, are a perfect match for satisfiability problems, with their "∃ model" format. It is the third class of domino problems, the recurring ones of [H2], that enable this completion of the picture.

Three general additional points are worth making:

1. Since all domino problems owe their complexity to the correspondence with Turing machine computations, and since this correspondence applies to nondeterministic models just as well ("∃ tiling" corresponds to "∃ computation"), cf. [H2], domino problems can apparently not distinguish between deterministic and nondeterministic classes. Thus, e.g., EXPTIME-hard satisfiability problems, such as that for PDL [FL], do not admit domino proofs, whereas the above mentioned classes all do (PSPACE does by Savitch's Theorem [Sa]).

2. Domino problems are existential in nature and do not seem to extend in any natural way to capture alternation. One additional quantifier can usually be managed, cf. the (relatively cumbersome) formulation of the ∃x∀y format of Σ_2^0 in the proof of Theorem 4.4. Thus, while games are good for alternation, dominoes are good for single existentials. Indeed the EXPTIME-hardness of PDL is proved using EXPTIME = alternating-linear -space, with alternating TM's and as noted above cannot be proved using the kinds of domino problems considered herein.

3. The present paper, and its companion [H2], make the case for viewing Σ_1^1 sets as corresponding to computable finetely-branching trees with an infinite path containing a recurrence. Call these R-trees. It is a well known fact that Σ_1^1 sets correspond to computable possibly infinitely-branching trees containing some infinite path. Call these W-trees. For example, the set of (notations for) recursive ordinals, of well-

founded recursive trees, of terminating computations of programs with unbounded nondeterminism, etc. are all Π_1^1-complete (cf. [R,Cn,AP]).

The correspondence between these views can easily be visualized by traversing a computable infinitely-branching tree with an NTM which at each stage nondeterministically chooses to either move across to a brother or down to a son, signalling when the latter is chosen. Its computation tree is an R-tree with recurring signal iff the initial tree is a W-tree. Conversely, given a computable finitely branching tree with a "signal", an infinitely-branching tree can be constructed with nodes corresponding to signal nodes in the former, and a node's sons corresponding to all possible signalled descendents of the origin node. In particular, the recursive ordinal corresponding to a nonrecurring domino set $T = \{d_0,\dots,d_m\}$ is that associated with the following tree: The root is associated with the 1×1 tiling consisting of d_0. The sons of each node are all possible minimal $n\times n$ extensions of the tiling associated with that node, for any possible n, which contain additional occurrences of d_0. This tree is well-founded iff T does not satisfy R1. (Similar constructions clearly exist for other recurring domino problems).

The (folklore?) observation made here can actually be thought of as an extended form of König's Lemma: well-founded infinitely-branching trees correspond to nonrecurring finitely-branching ones.

6. REFERENCES

[AP] Apt, K.R. and G.D. Plotkin, Countable Nondeterminism and Random Assignment, Manuscript, 1982.

[Be] Berger, R., The Undecidability of the Dominoe Problem, Mem. Amer. Math. Soc. 66 (1966).

[Bn] Buchi, J.R., Turing Machines and the Entscheidungsproblem, Math. Ann. 148 (1962), 201-213.

[Ch] Church, A., A Note on the Entscheidungsproblem, JSL 1 (1936), 101-102.

[Cn] Chandra, A.K., Computable Nondeterministic Functions, 19th FOCS, 127-131, 1978.

[C] Cook, S.A., The Complexity of Theorem Proving Procedures, 3rd STOC, 151-158, 1971.

[E] van Emde Boas, P., Dominoes are Forever, 1st GTI Workshop, Paderborn, 75-95, 1983.

[FL] Fischer, M.J. and R.E. Ladner, Propositional Dynamic Logic of Regular Programs, JCSS 18 (1979), 194-211.

[G] Gurevich, Y., The Decision Problem for Standard Classes, JSL 41 (1976), 460-464.

[GK] Gurevich, Y. and I.O. Koryakov, Remarks on Berger's Paper on the Domino Problem, Siberian Math. J. 13 (1972), 319-321.

[H1] Harel, D., Dynamic Logic, In: Handbook of Philosophical Logic II, Reidel (1983), to appear.

[H2] Harel, D., A Simple Highly Undecidable Domino Problem, Submitted, 1983.

[HKP] Harel, D., D. Kozen and R. Parikh, Process Logic: Expressiveness, Decidability, Completeness, JCSS 25 (1982), 144-170.

[HMP] Harel, D., A. R. Meyer and V.R. Pratt, Computability and Completeness in Logics of Programs, 9th STOC, 261-268, 1977.

[HP] Harel, D. and A. Pnueli, Two Dimensional Temporal Logic, Manuscript, 1982.

[HPS] Harel, D., A. Pnueli and J. Stavi, Propositional Dynamic Logic of Nonregular Programs, JCSS (1983), in press.

[HV] Harel, D. and M. Vardi, PDL with Intersection, In preparation.

[H] Hoare, C.A.R., An Axiomatic Basis for Computer Programming, CACM 12 (1969), 576-580, 583.

[KMW] Kahr, A.S., E.F., Moore and H. Wang, Entscheidungsproblem Reduced to the ∀∃∀ Case, Proc. Nat. Acad. Sci. USA, 48, (1962), 365-377.

[K] Keisler, J., Model Theory for Infinitary Logic, North Holland, 1971.

[La] Ladner, R., The Computational Complexity of Provability in Systems of Modal Propositional Logic, SIAM J. Comp. 6 (1977), 467-480.

[L1] Lewis, H.R., Complexity of Solvable Cases of the Decision Problem for the Predicate Calculus, 19th FOCS, 35-47, 1978.

[L2] Lewis, H.R., Unsolvable Classes of Quantificational Formulas, Addison-Wesley, 1979.

[LP] Lewis, H.R. and C.H. Papadimitriou, Elements of the Theory of Computation, Prentice-Hall, 1981.

[MP] Manna, Z. and A. Pnueli, Verification of Concurrent Programs: Temporal Proof Principles, LNCS 131, Springer, 200-252, 1981.

[Me] Mendelson, E., Introduction to Mathematical Logic, van Nostrand Reinhold, 1964.

[M] Meyer, A.R., Private Communication, 1977.

[MS] Meyer, A.R. and L.J. Stockmeyer, Word Problems Requiring Exponential Time, 5th STOC, 1-9, 1973.

[MSM] Meyer, A.R., R.S. Streett and G. Mirkowska, The Deducibility Problem in Propositional Dynamic Logic, LNCS 125, Springer-Verlag, 12-22, 1981.

[PH] Paterson, M. and D. Harel, In preparation.

[Pn] Pnueli, A., The Temporal Logic of Programs, 18th FOCS, 46-57, 1977.

[P] Pratt, V.R., Semantical Considerations on Floyd-Hoare Logic, 17th FOCS, 109-121, 1976.

[RS] Reif, J.H. and A.P. Sistla, A Multiprocess Network Logic with Temporal and Spatial Modalities, TR-29-82, Harvard, 1982.

[Ro] Robinson, R.M., Undecidability and Nonperiodicity for Tilings of the Plane, Inventiones Math. 12, (1971), 177-209.

[R] Rogers, H., Theory of Recursive Functions and Effective Computability, McGraw-Hill, 1967.

[Sa] Savitch, W.J., Relationships Between Nondeterministic and Deterministic Tape Complexities, JCSS 4 (1970), 177-192.

[Sh] Shoenfield, J.R., Mathematical Logic, Addison-Wesley, 1967.

[SC] Sistla, A.P. and E.M. Clarke, The Complexity of Propositional Linear Temporal Logics, 14th STOC, 159-167, 1982.

[St] Stockmeyer, L.J., The Polynomial Time Hierarchy, TCS 3 (1976), 1-22.

[S] Streett, R.S. Global Process Logic is Π_1^1-Complete, Manuscript, 1982.

[T] Turing, A.M., On Computable Numbers with an Application to the Entscheidungsproblem, Proc. London Math. Soc. 2, 42 (1936-7), 230-265, 43 (1937), 544-546.

[W1] Wang, H., Proving Theorems by Pattern Recognition II, Bell Syst. Tech. J. 40, (1961), 1-41.

[W2] Wang, H., Dominoes and the AEA Case of the Decision Problem, In: Mathematical Theory of Automata, Polytechnic Press, 1963, pp. 23-55.

Propositional Dynamic Logic of Flowcharts

D. Harel and R. Sherman

Department of Applied Mathematics
The Weizmann Institute of Science
Rehovot 76100, Israel

Abstract

Following a suggestion of Pratt, we consider propositional dynamic logic in which programs are nondeterministic finite automata over atomic programs and tests (i.e., flowcharts), rather than regular expressions. While the resulting version of PDL, call it APDL, is clearly equivalent in expressive power to PDL, it is also (in the worst case) exponentially more succinct. In particular, deciding its validity problem by reducing it to that of PDL leads to a double exponential time procedure, although PDL itself is decidable in exponential time.

We present an elementary combined proof of the completeness of a simple axiom system for APDL and decidability of the validity problem in exponential time. The results are thus stronger than those for PDL since PDL can be encoded in APDL with no additional cost, and the proofs simpler, since induction on the structure of programs is virtually eliminated. Our axiom system for APDL relates to the PDL system just as Floyd's proof method for partial correctness relates to Hoare's.

1. Introduction

The propositional version of dynamic logic [FL,P1] is used to reason about the before-after behaviour of programs. In PDL programs are taken to be regular sets of execution sequences represented by regular expressions. An execution sequence is a finite word over an alphabet of atomic programs and tests. The choice of a particular representation for these regular sets clearly has no influence on the expressive power of the language. It is significant, however, in the sense that some representations might be more natural or economical than others. The regular expressions of PDL are natural and often give rise to proofs by induction on their structure. In particular, PDL is known to be decidable in exponential time and to admit a complete axiomatization consisting of a finite set of very natural axiom schemes including one for each of the regular operations on programs. (see [FL,P2,KP,SH,Ha]).

Pratt [P3] raised the question of the behavior of a version of PDL in which programs are represented by flowcharts. A nondeterministic flowchart is simply a finite directed graph with a designated entry node and some exit nodes, whose edges are labelled with atomic programs and tests. Since such a flowchart can clearly be regarded as the transition diagram of a nondeterministic finite automaton, it is immediate that this new version of

PDL, call it APDL, is equivalent in expressive power to the standard version. However, if validity in APDL is decided by translating automata into regular expressions and working in PDL, the translation can cost in the worst case an exponential in the size of the automaton [EZ]. Hence formulas of APDL grow exponentially in length when transformed into PDL formulas, resulting in a double-exponential time decision procedure. Moreover, the axioms of PDL are unfit for APDL unless such a translation is carried out as a preliminary step of each proof.

Pratt [P3] sketched a tableau-like algorithm for deciding APDL in single exponential time, and also indicated, using an algebraic approach, how an axiom system for APDL might be constructed, eliminating the need for translating into PDL.

In this paper we borrow the motivation and some basic ideas of [P3] and provide an elementary combined proof of the two fundamental properties of APDL: exponential-time decidability of the validity problem, and completeness of a simple finitary axiom system. The axiom system is in a sense simpler than that of PDL as it deals globally with the automata rather than with each of the regular operators. The axioms are similar to those given by Wolper [W] for his extended temporal logic. Also, the combined proof itself is a simplification of the similar proof we have given for PDL [SH], as it replaces the three clauses for regular operators in all inductions on the structure of programs by a single clause for an automaton.

Since regular expressions can be translated easily into automata, with no essential growth in size, APDL is a more fundamental formalism than PDL, and the results are thus stronger than those for PDL.

The reader will observe that since APDL relates to PDL as flowcharts do to structured programs, the axiom system for APDL (and our proof of its completeness) relates to that of PDL (and the proof of its completeness) just as Floyd's [F] inductive assertion method for partial correctness relates to Hoare's [Ho] axiomatic system. This point is also hinted at in [P3].

We have used the automata approach presented herein to obtain results for some extensions of APDL (and hence of PDL), which are discussed briefly in Section 4 and which will appear separately. In particular it has been used by the second author and A. Pnueli to prove exponential time decidability for PDL with *loop*, previously known to be decidable only in triple-exponential time [S]. Section 2 contains preliminaries and Section 3 contains the main results.

2. Syntax and Semantics

Definition : A ***finite (nondeterministic) automaton*** over an alphabet Σ is a 4-tuple $\mathcal{F} = \langle Q, q_0, \eta, F \rangle$ where :

Q - is a finite set of states.

$q_0 \in Q$ - is the initial state.

$\eta : Q \times \Sigma \to 2^Q$ - is a transition function assigning a set of states to each state and letter from the alphabet.

$F \subseteq Q$ - is a set of accepting states.

A word $\sigma \in \Sigma^*$, $\sigma = (\sigma_0 \ldots \sigma_{\ell-1})$, is *accepted* by $\mathcal{F}$ if there exists a sequence of states $(q_0, \ldots, q_\ell)$ such that $q_\ell \in F$ and for every i, $0 \leq i < \ell$ $q_{i+1} \in \eta(q_i, \sigma_i)$.

Every finite automaton over the alphabet Σ can be represented as a union of automata of the form (n, i, j, δ) where :

$\overline{n} = \{1, 2, \ldots, n\}$ - is the set of states.

$i \in \overline{n}$ - is the initial state.

$j \in \overline{n}$ - is the final state.

$\delta : \overline{n} \times \overline{n} \to \Sigma$ - is a partial labeling (transition) function.

A word $\sigma \in \Sigma^*$, $\sigma = (\sigma_0 \ldots \sigma_{\ell-1})$, is *accepted* by (n, i, j, δ) if there exists a sequence of states $(i_0, \ldots, i_\ell)$, $i_0 = i$, $i_\ell = j$, $i_k \in \overline{n}$ and $\sigma_{k+1} = \delta(i_k, i_{k+1})$, $0 \leq k < \ell$.

Note that a nondeterministic finite automaton with m states over a finite alphabet Σ, can be represented by a union of at most m automata of the above form each with $n \leq m \cdot |\Sigma|$ states.

APDL is defined over two sets of symbols: Φ_0, the set of *atomic formulas*, and Π_0, the set of *atomic programs*. Φ_0 and Π_0 are, respectively, abstractions of properties of states, and basic instructions such as assignment statements, which tranform one state into another. From these basic alphabets we inductively construct the set Φ of expressions for compound formulas, representing assertions about states, and the set Π of programs representing transformations on states by finite automata.

The following clauses define Φ :

true $\in \Phi$; *false* $\in \Phi$; $\Phi_0 \subseteq \Phi$,

if $p \in \Phi$ and $q \in \Phi$ then $\neg p \in \Phi$ and $(p \vee q) \in \Phi$,

if $p \in \Phi$ and $\alpha \in \Pi$ then $<\alpha>p \in \Phi$.

The following clauses define Π :

$\Pi_0 \subseteq \Pi$,

$\Phi? \subseteq \Pi$, where $\Phi? = \{p? \mid p \in \Phi\}$,

if $\alpha = (n, i, j, \delta)$ is an automaton over the alphabet $\Pi_0 \cup \Phi?$ then $\alpha \in \Pi$.

We use $\wedge$, $\equiv$, $\supset$ as abbreviations in the standard way and, in addition, abbreviate $\neg<\alpha>\neg p$ to $[\alpha]p$.

The semantics of APDL is defined relative to a given *structure* (or *model*) $\mathcal{A} = (W, \tau, \rho)$ where :

W is a set of elements called *states*,

$\tau : \Phi_0 \to 2^W$,

$\rho : \Pi_0 \to 2^{W \times W}$.

Informally the mapping τ assigns to each atomic formula P the set $\tau(P) \subseteq W$ of states in which it is true and ρ assigns to each atomic program a a binary relation with the intended meaning $(s, t) \in \rho(a)$ iff execution of a can lead from state s to state t. Such an $\mathcal{A}$ is called a structure *over* Φ_0 and Π_0. The mappings τ and ρ are extended to supply meanings for the full sets Φ and Π as follows :

$\tau(true) = W;\ \tau(false) = \emptyset,$
$\tau(\neg p) = W - \tau(p),$
$\tau(p \vee q) = \tau(p) \cup \tau(q),$
$\tau(<\alpha>p) = \{s \in W \mid \exists t \in W\,((s,t) \in \rho(\alpha) \wedge t \in \tau(p))\},$
$\rho(p?) = \{(s,s) \mid s \in \tau(p)\},$

$$\rho(n,i,j,\delta) = \{(s,t) \mid \exists k\,((\exists(i_0,\ldots,i_k),\ i_0 = i, i_k = j, \forall \ell\ i_\ell \in \overline{n}) \\ \wedge(\exists(s_0,\ldots,s_k),\ s_0 = s, s_k = t, \forall \ell\ s_\ell \in W) \\ \text{s.t. } (s_\ell, s_{\ell+1}) \in \rho(\delta(i_\ell, i_{\ell+1}))\,\forall \ell, 0 \le \ell < k)\}$$

Actually what the last definition says is that $\rho(n,i,j,\delta)$ is the set of transitions in the model corresponding to transitions from state i to state j in the automaton.

We shall write $A, s \models p$ and say that p *is true in* s or that s *satisfies* p if $s \in \tau(p)$, and omit A when it is clear from the context. We say that p is *valid* if $A, s \models p$ for every structure A and state s and write $\models p$, and that p is *satisfiable* if there exist A and s such that $A, s \models p$. Clearly p is valid iff $\neg p$ is not satisfiable.

Defintion : The *sizes* of a formula p, and a program α, denoted $|p|$ and $|\alpha|$ respectively, are defined as follows :

$|a| = |P| = 1$ for $P \in \Phi_0$, $a \in \Pi_0$

$|\neg q| = |q| + 1$

$|q \vee r| = |q| + |r| + 1$

$|<\alpha>q| = |\alpha| + |q| + 1$

$|q?| = |q| + 1$

$|(n,i,j,\delta)| = n + \Sigma_{(k,\ell)\in V} |\delta(k,\ell)|$
Where : $V = \{(k,\ell) \mid k, \ell \in \overline{n}$ and $\delta(k,\ell)$ is defined$\}$.

It is easy to show that APDL with its special kind of automata is only (in the worst case) quadratically less succinct than a version employing standard nondeterministic automata, by the remark following the definition of automata above. Thus, for our purposes no generality is lost in considering APDL.

3. Decidability and Completeness

The completeness of a simple axiom system for APDL is established, and from the proof it is concluded that the validity of formulas of APDL is decidable deterministically in time which is on the order of an exponential in the size of the input formula. Specifically, validity of p can be tested in deterministic time $2^{c \cdot |p|}$ for some $c > 0$.

The following definition captures a certain notion of the subformula of a formula, and is analogous to the Fischer/Ladner closure of [FL,KP].

Definition : Let p be a formula of APDL; i.e. $p \in \Phi$. The *closure of* p, denoted $CL(p)$, is the smallest set S of formulas containing p and satisfying the following closure rules for all $a \in \Pi_0, (n,i,j,\delta) \in \Pi$, and $q, r \in \Phi$.

$\neg q \in S \Rightarrow q \in S$
$q \vee r \in S \Rightarrow q \in S, r \in S$

$<a>q \in S \Rightarrow q \in S$

$<q?>r \in S \Rightarrow q \in S, r \in S$

$<n,i,j,\delta>q \in S \Rightarrow$ for every $k \in \bar{n}$ such that $\delta(i,k)$ is defined,
$<\delta(i,k)><n,k,j,\delta>q \in S$,
and in addition if $i = j$ then $q \in S$.

It is easy to see that $|CL(p)|$ (i.e. the number of formulas in $CL(p)$) is linear in the length of p; i.e. $|CL(p)| = O(|p|)$.

Let $\neg CL(p)$ be defined as $\{\neg q \mid q \in CL(p)\}$. Denote $CL(p) \cup \neg CL(p)$ by Z We now define certain sets of formulas from Z called *atoms*, which are free of "immediate" inconsistencies. Later we eliminate those which are inconsistent with all others.

Note : In the rest of the section we identify a fromula of the form $\neg\neg q$ with q.

Definition : An *atom for* p (or just *atom* when p is assumed) is a subset A of Z satisfying the following, for every $(n,i,j,\delta) \in \Pi$, $q, r \in \Phi$:

if $q \in Z$ then $q \in A \Leftrightarrow \neg q \notin A$

if $q \vee r \in Z$ then $q \vee r \in A \Leftrightarrow q \in A$ or $r \in A$

if $<q?>r \in Z$ then $<q?>r \in A \Leftrightarrow q \in A$ and $r \in A$

if $<n,i,j,\delta>q \in Z$ then $<n,i,j,\delta>q \in A \Leftrightarrow$
either $i = j$ and $q \in A$
or $<\delta(i,k)><n,k,j,\delta>q \in A$ for some $k \in \bar{n}$

Denote the set of atoms for p by $At(p)$; clearly $|At(p)| \leq 2^{O(|p|)}$.

Let there be given a fixed formula $p \in \Phi$. Since we will be interested only in formulas connected directly with some such given p, we assume, without loss of generality, that Φ_0 and Π_0 consist solely of the atomic formulas and programs appearing in p. A particular finite structure $\mathcal{A} = (W, \tau, \rho)$ is constructed in steps as follows :

$\mathcal{A}_0 = (W_0, \tau_0, \rho_0)$ is defined by

$W_0 = At(p)$,

$\tau_0 : \Phi_0 \to 2^{W_0}$ by $A \in \tau_0(P)$ iff $P \in A$,

$\rho_0 : \Pi_0 \to 2^{W_0 \times W_0}$ by $(A, B) \in \rho_0(a)$ iff

1) there is $<a>q \in A$ such that $q \in B$, and

2) for every $[a]q \in A$ we have $q \in B$

For $i \geq 0$ let $\mathcal{A}_{i+1} = (W_{i+1}, \tau_{i+1}, \rho_{i+1})$ be given by

$W_{i+1} = \{A \mid A \in W_i$ and for every $<\alpha>q \in A$, where $\alpha \in \Pi, q \in \Phi$,
there is $B \in W_i$ such that $(A,B) \in \rho_i(\alpha)$ and $q \in B\}$

$\tau_{i+1}(P) = \tau_i(P) \cap W_{i+1}$, for $P \in \Phi_0$

$\rho_{i+1}(a) = \rho_i(a) \cap (W_{i+1} \times W_{i+1})$, for $a \in \Pi_0$.

Clearly, from the finiteness of $At(p)$ there is some i_0 where the construction closes up; i.e. for every $j > i_0$, $\mathcal{A}_j = \mathcal{A}_{i_0}$. Accordingly we set

$\mathcal{A} = (W, \tau, \rho) = (W_{i_0}, \tau_{i_0}, \rho_{i_0}) = \mathcal{A}_{i_0}$.

Remark : Since $|W_0| \leq 2^{O(|p|)}$, and the computation of $\mathcal{A}_{i+1}$ is clearly polynomial in the size of W_i, it follows that the structure $\mathcal{A}$ can be computed in time exponential in the length of p.

The following lemma connects the two roles played by an atom in W: that of a set of subformulas of p and that of a state in $\mathcal{A}$.

Lemma 1 : For every $A \in W$ and $q \in CL(p)$,

$$q \in A \text{ iff } \mathcal{A}, A \models q$$

Proof : The claim is proved by induction on the structure of q.

$q = Q \in \Phi_0 : Q \in A \Leftrightarrow A \in \tau_0(Q) \Leftrightarrow A \in \tau_0(Q) \cap W \Leftrightarrow A \in \tau(Q) \Leftrightarrow A \models Q.$

$q = \neg r : \neg r \in A \Leftrightarrow r \notin A \Leftrightarrow$ (ind. hyp.) $A \not\models r \Leftrightarrow A \models \neg r.$

$q = r \vee s : r \vee s \in A \Leftrightarrow r \in A \vee s \in A \Leftrightarrow$ (ind. hyp.) $A \models r \vee A \models s \Leftrightarrow A \models r \vee s.$

$q = <\alpha>r$: To prove this we prove the following claim :

For every $A \in W$ and $<\beta>s \in CL(p)$,
$<\beta>s \in A$ iff there is $B \in W$ such that $(A, B) \in \rho(\beta)$ and $s \in B$.

The "only if" direction of the claim is immediate from the construction of the $\mathcal{A}_i$. For the "if" part we proceed as follows :

$\beta \in \Pi_0$: Assume $<b>s \notin A$. By the definition of an atom $\neg<b>s \in A$, i.e., $[b]\neg s \in A$. Now if $(A, B) \in \rho(b)$ then by the definition of ρ we certainly have $(A, B) \in \rho_0(b)$, from which, by the definition of ρ_0 and the fact that $[b]\neg s \in A$ we obtain $\neg s \in B$, or $s \notin B$.

$\beta = u?$: $\exists B((A, B) \in \rho(u?) \wedge s \in B) \Rightarrow ((A, A) \in \rho(u?) \wedge s \in A) \Rightarrow (A \models u \wedge s \in A)$ $\Rightarrow$ (main ind. hyp.) $(u \in A \wedge s \in A) \Rightarrow <u?>s \in A$ by the definition of atoms.

$\beta = (n, i, j, \delta)$: $\exists B((A, B) \in \rho(n, i, j, \delta) \wedge s \in B) \Rightarrow \exists(i_0, \ldots, i_k)$, $i_0 = i$, $i_k = j$, $\exists(A_0, \ldots, A_k)$, $A_0 = A$, $A_k = B$, s.t. $(A_\ell, A_{\ell+1}) \in \rho(\delta(i_\ell, i_{\ell+1}))$ for every ℓ, $0 \leq \ell < k$. We prove that $<n, i, j, \delta>s \in A$ by induction on k.

For $k = 0 : i = j$, $A = B$ then by the definition of atoms $s \in A$ implies $<n, i, i, \delta>s \in A$.

Suppose the claim is true for k. Then for $k + 1$:
$<n, i_0, i_{k+1}, \delta>s \in CL(p)$ implies that $<\delta(i_0, i_1)><n, i_1, i_{k+1}, \delta>s \in CL(p)$ and hence $<n, i_1, i_{k+1}, \delta>s \in CL(p)$. Since $(A_1, A_{k+1}) \in \rho(n, i_1, i_{k+1}, \delta)$, it follows from the inductive hypothesis on k that $<n, i_1, i_{k+1}, \delta>s \in A_1$. Now by $\delta(i_0, i_1) \in \Pi_0 \cup \Phi?$ and the first two cases for β we obtain $<\delta(i_0, i_1)><n, i_1, i_{k+1}, \delta>s \in A_0$ and this implies by the definition of atoms that $<n, i_0, i_{k+1}, \delta>s \in A$.

This completes the proof of the claim.

Back to the main proof : clearly a straightforward argument shows that since $<\alpha>r \in CL(p)$ also $r \in CL(p)$, and so the inductive hypothesis for r can be used, $<\alpha>r \in A \Leftrightarrow$ (by the claim) $\exists B \in W((A, B) \in \rho(\alpha) \wedge r \in B) \Leftrightarrow$ (ind. hyp.) $\exists B \in W((A, B) \in \rho(\alpha) \wedge B \models r)$ $\Leftrightarrow A \models <\alpha>r.$ ∎

We now introduce an axiomatic system for APDL.
Notation : for $k, \ell \in \bar{n}$ we write "$\delta(k,\ell)\downarrow$" for "$\delta(k,\ell)$ is defined".

Axiom schemes :

(A1) All instances of tautologies of the propositional calculus.

(A2) $<\alpha>(p \vee q) \equiv <\alpha>p \vee <\alpha>q$

(A3) $<p?>q \equiv p \wedge q$

(A4) $<n,i,j,\delta>p \equiv \bigvee_{k\in\bar{n},\delta(i,k)\downarrow} <\delta(i,k)><n,k,j,\delta>p$, for $i \neq j$

(A4′) $<n,i,i,\delta>p \equiv p \vee \bigvee_{k\in\bar{n},\delta(i,k)\downarrow} <\delta(i,k)><n,k,i,\delta>p$

(A5) (induction axiom)
$$(\bigwedge_{k,\ell\in\bar{n},\delta(k,\ell)\downarrow}[n,i,k,\delta](p_k \supset [\delta(k,\ell)]p_\ell)) \supset (p_i \supset [n,i,j,\delta]p_j)$$

(A6) $[\alpha](p \supset q) \supset ([\alpha]p \supset [\alpha]q)$

Inference rules :

(R1) Modus Ponens (MP)
$$\frac{p, p \supset q}{q}$$

(R2) Generalization (G)
$$\frac{p}{[\alpha]p}$$

Our axioms (A4) and (A5) are very similar to axioms (G1) and (G2), respectively of Wolper [W, p. 343]. Axiom (A4) states that the possibility of starting at state i and reaching state j with p true is equivalent to that of starting at i and reaching some immediate successor k of i and then from k reaching j with p true. The induction axiom (A5) says that if one has chosen a set $\{p_i\}$ of assertions, and has shown that (i) p_i is true at state i, and (ii) the truth of p_k at some (reachable from i) state k implies the truth of p_ℓ at any successor ℓ of k, then he has in fact established that p_j is true when j is reached. Thus, axiom (A5) formalizes Floyd's inductive assertions method for proving partial correctness; the p_ℓ are the inductive assertions.

It is easy to establish the following two derived rules :

Invariance (I)
$$\frac{\{p_k \supset [\delta(k,\ell)]p_\ell\}_{k,\ell\in\bar{n},\,\delta(k,\ell)\downarrow}}{p_i \supset [n,i,j,\delta]p_j}$$

(apply (G) with $[n,i,k,\delta]$, then (MP) with (A5))

Distribution (D)
$$\frac{p \supset q}{[\alpha]p \supset [\alpha]q}$$

(apply (G) with $[\alpha]$, then (MP) with (A6))

Provability of a formula p in the system is denoted $\vdash p$.

Theorem 1 : The axiom system is sound; i.e., for every $p \in \Phi$, $\vdash p \Rightarrow \models p$.

Proof : It is immediate from the definition of the semantics of APDL that all instances of axioms of the above system are valid and all rules of inference preserve validity. ∎

Definition : For a finite set $A \subset \Phi$,let $\hat{A}$ denote $\bigwedge_{q \in A} q$.
The following lemma shows that non-atoms are provably inconsistent.

Lemma 2 : Let $A \subseteq Z$, such that for $q \in Z$ either $q \in A$ or $\neg q \in A$. If $A \notin At(p)$ then $\vdash \neg\hat{A}$.

Proof : If A does not satisfy the first property of an atom, namely $q \in A \Leftrightarrow \neg q \notin A$ then there will be some $q \in A$ with $\neg q \in A$. One then proves $\neg\hat{A}$ by (A1,MP). Assume, therefore, that $q \in A \Leftrightarrow \neg q \notin A$ for every $q \in Z$. For each of the three remaining properties of an atom it is straightforward to show how a violation causes a provable contradiction. ∎

Corollary 1 : For every $q \in Z$, $E \subseteq At(p)$,

$$\vdash \Big(q \equiv \bigvee_{\substack{A \in At(p) \\ q \in A}} \hat{A}\Big) \qquad (i)$$

$$\vdash \Big(\bigvee_{A \in E} \hat{A} \equiv \bigwedge_{B \in At(p)-E} \neg\hat{B}\Big) \qquad (ii)$$

The Corollary follows from the definition of atoms and Lemma 2. ∎
The following is the main technical lemma needed in the proof, which says that : for every atom A, if $<\alpha>q \in A$ then $\hat{A}$ implies that after every α execution either q is not true or $\hat{C}$ is true for some C, such that $(A, C) \in \rho_0(\alpha)$. It follows that if for every B, s.t. $q \in B$, $(A, B) \notin \rho_0(\alpha)$ then $\neg\hat{A}$ is provable, which justifies the rejection of A from the set of states of the constructed model.

Lemma 3 : Let $A \in At(p)$ and $<\alpha>q \in A$ then :

$$\vdash \hat{A} \supset [\alpha]\Big(\bigvee_{q \notin B} \hat{B} \vee \bigvee_{\substack{q \in C \\ (A,C) \in \rho_0(\alpha)}} \hat{C}\Big).$$

Proof : We prove the claim for the three possible forms of α.

$\alpha \in \Pi_0$: Clearly by Corollary 1(*ii*) it is suffices to show for $a \in \Pi_0$:

$$\vdash \hat{A} \supset [a] \bigwedge_{\substack{q \in B \\ (A,B) \notin \rho_0(a)}} \neg\hat{B},$$

or, using axiom (A2) and the finiteness of $At(p)$, that $\vdash \hat{A} \supset [a]\neg\hat{B}$ for every B such that $q \in B$ and $(A, B) \notin \rho_0(a)$. For such a B, by the definition of ρ_0, it must be the case that there is some $[a]r \in A$ with $\neg r \in B$. Hence $\vdash \hat{A} \supset [a]r$ and $\vdash \hat{B} \supset \neg r$ or $\vdash r \supset \neg\hat{B}$. Using (D) we obtain $\vdash \hat{A} \supset [a]\neg\hat{B}$.

$\alpha = r?$: Tautologically, $\vdash \hat{A} \supset \neg(r \wedge \neg\hat{A})$, thus by axiom (A3) $\vdash \hat{A} \supset \neg <r?> \neg\hat{A}$, or $\vdash \hat{A} \supset [r?]\hat{A}$. Since $<r?>q \in A$, we have $r \in A$ and $q \in A$, thus $(A, A) \in \rho_0(r?)$ and A is a special case of the second part of the required disjunction. Hence weakening the disjunction yields :

$$\vdash \hat{A} \supset [r?]\Big(\bigvee_{q \notin B} \hat{B} \vee \bigvee_{\substack{q \in C \\ (A,C) \in \rho_0(r?)}} \hat{C}\Big).$$

$\alpha = (n, i, j, \delta)$: For each $k \in \bar{n}$ denote by p_k the formula:

$$\bigvee_{<n,k,j,\delta>q \notin B} \hat{B} \vee \bigvee_{\substack{<n,k,j,\delta>q \in C \\ (A,C) \in \rho_0(n,i,k,\delta)}} \hat{C}.$$

We show first that for each $k, \ell \in \bar{n}$ such that $\delta(k, \ell)\downarrow$,

$$\vdash p_k \supset [\delta(k, \ell)]p_\ell.$$

Let B be such that $<n, k, j, \delta>q \notin B$, then by the definition of atoms, for every $\ell \in \bar{n}$ such that $\delta(k, \ell) \downarrow$, $<\delta(k, \ell)><n, \ell, j, \delta>q \notin B$, or $[\delta(k, \ell)] \neg <n, \ell, j, \delta>q \in B$, which implies :

$$\vdash \hat{B} \supset [\delta(k, \ell)] \neg <n, \ell, j, \delta>q$$

and by Corollary 1(i) and (D)

$$\vdash \hat{B} \supset [\delta(k, \ell)] \bigvee_{<n,\ell,j,\delta>q \notin D} \hat{D} \tag{3.1}$$

Let C be such that $<n, k, j, \delta>q \in C$, $(A, C) \in \rho_0(n, i, k, \delta)$ and let $\ell \in \bar{n}$ be such that $\delta(k, \ell) \downarrow$. If $<\delta(k, \ell)><n, \ell, j, \delta>q \notin C$ then as in the previous part :

$$\vdash \hat{C} \supset [\delta(k, \ell)] \bigvee_{<n,\ell,j,\delta>q \notin D} \hat{D} \tag{3.2}$$

If $<\delta(k, \ell)><n, \ell, j, \delta>q \in C$ then by the first two cases for $\delta(k, \ell) \in \Pi_0 \cup \Phi?$ we obtain :

$$\vdash \hat{C} \supset [\delta(k, \ell)]\Big(\bigvee_{<n,\ell,j,\delta>q \notin D} \hat{D} \vee \bigvee_{\substack{<n,\ell,j,\delta>q \in E \\ (C,E) \in \rho_0(\delta(k,\ell))}} \hat{E}\Big) \tag{3.3}$$

If $(A, C) \in \rho_0(n, i, k, \delta)$ and $(C, E) \in \rho_0(\delta(k, \ell))$ then $(A, E) \in \rho_0(n, i, \ell, \delta)$ which together with (3.3) implies :

$$\vdash \hat{C} \supset [\delta(k, \ell)]p_\ell \tag{3.4}$$

As $\bigvee_{<n,\ell,j,\delta>q \notin D} \hat{D}$ is the first disjunct in the definition of p_ℓ, we obtain by weakening from (3.1),(3.2) and (3.4) that for every k, ℓ such that $\delta(k, \ell) \downarrow$:

$$\vdash p_k \supset [\delta(k, \ell)]p_\ell$$

By the invariance rule (I) this implies :

$$\vdash p_i \supset [n, i, j, \delta]p_j \tag{3.5}$$

As $(A,A) \in \rho_0(n,i,i,\delta)$, A is a special case of the second disjunct of p_i, thus :

$$\vdash \hat{A} \supset p_i \tag{3.6}$$

If B is such that $<n,j,j,\delta>q \notin B$ then by the definition of atoms $q \notin B$, thus :

$$\vdash \hat{B} \supset \bigvee_{q \notin D} \hat{D} \tag{3.7}$$

If C is such that $<n,j,j,\delta>q \in C$, $(A,C) \in \rho_0(n,i,j,\delta)$ then:

$$\vdash \hat{C} \supset \Big(\bigvee_{q \notin D} \hat{D} \vee \bigvee_{\substack{q \in E \\ (A,E) \in \rho_0(n,i,j,\delta)}} \hat{E} \Big) \tag{3.8}$$

(3.7) and (3.8) implies :

$$\vdash p_j \supset \Big(\bigvee_{q \notin D} \hat{D} \vee \bigvee_{\substack{q \in E \\ (A,E) \in \rho_0(n,i,j,\delta)}} \hat{E} \Big) \tag{3.9}$$

By (3.5),(3.6),(3.9) and rule (D) we conclude :

$$\vdash \hat{A} \supset [n,i,j,\delta] \Big(\bigvee_{q \notin B} \hat{B} \vee \bigvee_{\substack{q \in C \\ (A,C) \in \rho_0(n,i,j,\delta)}} \hat{C} \Big)$$

∎

We now show that not only non-atoms but even atoms are provably inconsistent, if they are rejected from being states in $\mathcal{A}$.

Lemma 4 : For every $A \in At(p)$, if $A \notin W$ then $\vdash \neg\hat{A}$.

Proof : By induction on the order in which atoms are rejected from W. Assume that for all $B \notin W_i$, $B \in At(p)$, $\vdash \neg\hat{B}$, and let $A \in W_i$, $A \notin W_{i+1}$. (Since $W_0 = At(p)$, the claim clearly holds for $i = 0$). Since $A \notin W_{i+1}$ there must be some $<\alpha>q \in A$ such that for every $B \in W_i$, $(A,B) \in \rho_i(\alpha) \Rightarrow q \notin B$. We can now rewrite the claim in Lemma 3 as :

$$\vdash \hat{A} \supset [\alpha] \Big(\bigvee_{q \notin B} \hat{B} \vee \bigvee_{\substack{q \in C, C \in W_i \\ (A,C) \in \rho_i(\alpha)}} \hat{C} \vee \bigvee_{\substack{q \in D, D \notin W_i \\ (A,D) \in \rho_0(\alpha)}} \hat{D} \Big).$$

For each D in the rightmost disjunct we have $\vdash \neg\hat{D}$ by the inductive hypothesis, and for each C in the middle dijunct we have $q \in C$ and $q \notin C$ by the above remark; hence this disjunction is empty. We are left with $\vdash \hat{A} \supset [\alpha] \bigvee_{q \notin B} \hat{B}$, or $\vdash \hat{A} \supset [\alpha] \bigvee_{\neg q \in B} \hat{B}$, which by Corollary 1($i$) is $\vdash \hat{A} \supset [\alpha] \neg q$, or $\vdash \hat{A} \supset \neg<\alpha>q$. However, since $<\alpha>q \in A$, we have $\vdash \hat{A} \supset <\alpha>q$, from which at once we obtain $\vdash \neg\hat{A}$. ∎

Corollary 2 : p is satisfiable iff $p \in A$ for some $A \in W$.

Proof : One direction is obvious by Lemma 1. Let it be now the case that for every A such that $p \in A$, $A \notin W$. Then by Lemma 4 $\vdash \bigwedge_{p \in A} \neg\hat{A}$, or $\vdash \neg \bigvee_{p \in A} \hat{A}$, which by Corollary 1($i$) yields $\vdash \neg p$. Hence p cannot be satisfiable without violating Theorem 1, the soundness of the axiom system. ∎

Theorem 2 : The axiom system is complete; i.e. for every $p \in \Phi$, $\models p \Rightarrow \vdash p$.

Proof : If $\models p$ then $\neg p$ is not satisfiable, hence for each $A \in W$, $\neg p \notin A$. This means, together with Corollary 1(i), that $\vdash \neg p \equiv \bigvee_{\substack{\neg p \in A \\ A \notin W}} \hat{A}$. But by Lemma 4 $\vdash \neg \bigvee_{A \notin W} \hat{A}$. Hence $\vdash p$ ∎

Theorem 3 : Validity in APDL is decidable in deterministic exponential time.

Proof : By Corollary 2 p is valid if $\neg p \notin A$ for each $A \in W$. As discussed above, the construction of W can be carried out deterministically in time $2^{O(|p|)}$. ∎

4. Extensions of APDL

Some extensions of APDL can be shown to be exponentially decidable and complete by modification of the proofs in Section 3.

(1) Deterministic APDL, DAPDL for short, is syntactically identical to APDL but the structures $\mathcal{A} = (W, \tau, \rho)$ are restricted so that for every $a \in \Pi_0$ if $(s, t) \in \rho(a)$ and $(s, t') \in \rho(a)$ then $t = t'$. To prove that DAPDL is exponentially decidable we change the definition of ρ_0 for $\mathcal{A}_0$ to be : $(A, B) \in \rho_0(a)$ iff for every $<a>q \in Z$, $<a>q \in A$ iff $q \in B$.
The proof of Lemma 1 follows now as for APDL, except that we then have to show that the final structure $\mathcal{A} = (W, \tau, \rho)$ can be "unwinded" into a tree like deterministic structure as in the decidablity proof for DPDL in [BHP].
For a complete axiomatic system the axiom $(<a>p \supset [a]p)$ is added to those of Section 3. Lemma 3 now follows with slight modifications, and the rest of the completeness proof follows exactly the proof for APDL.

(2) APDL with converse (or reverse), CAPDL for short. This version of APDL allows converse programs α^- which have the meaning $\rho(\alpha^-) = \{(s,t) \mid (t,s) \in \rho(\alpha)\}$. Formulas of the form $<(n, i, j, \delta)^->q$ can be translated to $<n, j, i, \delta'>q$ where $\delta'(k, \ell) = (\delta(\ell, k))^-$ for every $\ell, k \in \bar{n}$ such that $\delta(\ell, k)$ is defined. Hence we can translate CAPDL fromulas into formulas such that the only programs that appear with converse are atomic programs (note that $p?^- = p?$). The definition of the structure $\mathcal{A}$ is extended as follows : Π_0' now consists of the atomic programs and reverse atomic programs that appear in p, and the definition of ρ_0' is extended for $b \in \Pi_0'$ by : $(A, B) \in \rho_0'(a)$ iff

(1) there is $<a>q \in A$ s.t. $q \in B$

(2) for every $[a]q \in A$ we have $q \in B$

(3) for every $[a^-]q \in B$ we have $q \in A$.

$(A, B) \in \rho_0'(a^-)$ iff

(1′) there is $<a^->q \in A$ s.t. $q \in B$

(2′) for every $[a^-]q \in A$ we have $q \in B$

(3′) for every $[a]q \in B$ we have $q \in A$.

For the final structure $\mathcal{A}$, ρ is defined by : For $a \in \Pi_0$, $\rho(a) = \rho'(a) \cup \{(s,t) \mid (t,s) \in \rho'(a^-)\}$.
To obtain a complete axiom system for CAPDL we add the axioms $(p \supset [a]<a^->p)$, and $(p \supset [a^-]<a>p)$.

(3) APDL with *loop*, LAPDL, is a version of APDL which allows assertions of the form: "there exists an infinite computation of α from a state s". Formally : for a structure $\mathcal{A} = (W, \tau, \rho)$ formulas of the form $loop(n, i, j, \delta)$ have the meaning :

$$\tau(loop(n,i,j,\delta)) = \{s \mid \exists(i_0, i_1, \ldots), i_0 = i, \forall k \geq 0 \; i_k \in \overline{n} \wedge \\ \exists(s_0, s_1, \ldots), s_0 = s, \forall k \geq 0 \; s_k \in W \wedge \\ (s_k, s_{k+1}) \in \rho(\delta(i_k, i_{k+1})), \forall k \geq 0\}.$$

The corresponding version of PDL, LPDL or PDL$^+$, is discussed in [HP,S]. The best known decision procedure for LPDL is of triple-exponential complexity [S]. No completeness result has been obtained for LPDL. By using the representation of programs as automata and extending the ideas used in this paper, the second author together with A. Pnueli have provided LAPDL with an exponential time decision procedure for validity and a simple complete axiomatic system. Clearly these results, which will appear seperately, imply the corresponding results for LPDL.

References

[BHP] Ben-Ari, M., J. Y. Halpern and A. Pnueli, 1982, Deterministic propositional dynamic logic : finite models, complexity and completeness, *J. Comp. Syst. Sci.* **25**, 402-417.

[EZ] Ehrenfeucht, A. and P. Zeiger, 1976, Complexity measures for regular expressions, *J. Comp. Syst. Sci.* **12**, 2, 134-146.

[F] Floyd, R.W., 1967, Assigning meanings to programs, *19th AMS Symp. Applied Math.* American Math. Society, Providence, R.I. 19-31.

[FL] Fischer, M.J. and R. E. Ladner, 1979, Propositional dynamic logic of regular programs, *J. Comp. Syst. Sci.* **18**, 2 ,194-211.

[Ha] Harel, D., 1983, Dynamic logic, In *Handbook of Philosophical Logic*, Vol. II, Reidel Publishing Company, Holland/USA, in press.

[HP] Harel, D. and V. R. Pratt, 1978, Nondeterminism in logics of programs, *5th AC Symp. on Principles of Programming Languages*, 203-213.

[Ho] Hoare, C. A. R., 1969, An axiomatic basis for computer programing ,*Comm. Assoc. Mach.* **12**, 576-583.

[KP] Kozen, D. and R. Parikh, 1981, An elementary proof of the completeness of PDL, *Theor. Comput. Science* **14**, 113-118.

[P1] Pratt, V. R., 1976, Semantical considerations on Floyd-Hoare logic, *17th IEEE Symp. on Foundations of Computer Science*, 119-121.

[P2] Pratt, V. R., 1979, Models of program logics, *20th IEEE Symp. on Foundations o Computer Science*, 115-122.

[P3] Pratt, V. R., 1981, Using graphs to understand PDL, *Workshop on logics of programs*, (D. Kozen ed.), Lect. Notes in Comput. Sci. 131, Springer-Verlag, New York, 387-396.

[SH] Sherman., R. and D. Harel, 1983, A combined proof of one exponential decidability and completeness for PDL, *1st Int. Workshop on Found. Theoret. Comput. Sci.*, GTI, Paderborn, 221-233.

[S] Streett, R. S., 1983, Propositional dynamic logic of looping and converse is elementarily decidable. *Inf. and Cont.*, in press.

[W] Wolper, P., 1981, Temporal logic can be more expressive, *22nd IEEE Symp. on Foundations of Computer Science*, 340-348.

FAST TRIANGULATION OF SIMPLE POLYGONS

Stefan Hertel
Kurt Mehlhorn

Fachbereich 10
Universität des Saarlandes
D - 6600 Saarbrücken

ABSTRACT

We present a new algorithm for triangulating simple polygons that has four advantages over previous solutions [GJPT, Ch].

a) It is faster: Whilst previous solutions worked in time O(nlogn), the new algorithm only needs time O(n+rlogr) where r is the number of concave angles of the polygon.

b) It works for a larger class of inputs: Whilst previous solutions worked for simple polygons, the new algorithm handles simple polygons with polygonal holes.

c) It does more: Whilst previous solutions only triangulated the interior of a simple polygon, the new algorithm triangulates both the interior and the exterior region.

d) It is simpler: The algorithm is based on the plane-sweep paradigm and is - at least in its O(nlogn) version - very simple.

In addition to the new triangulation algorithm, we present two new applications of triangulation.

a) We show that one can compute the intersection of a convex m-gon Q and a triangulated simple n-gon P in time O(n+m). This improves a result by Shamos [Sh] stating that the intersection of two convex polygons can be computed in time O(n).

b) Given the triangulation of a simple n-gon P, we show how to compute in time O(n) a convex decomposition of P into at most 4·OPT pieces. Here OPT denotes the minimum number of pieces in any convex decomposition. The best factor known so far was 4.333 (Chazelle[Ch]).

O. INTRODUCTION

In computational plane geometry, a powerful new type of algorithm seems to apply to many problems. It sweeps the plane from left to right, in direction of the x-axis, advancing a more or less vertical "cross section" from one point to the next. All processing is done at this moving front the state of which is represented by the "y-structure", while the "x-structure" represents a queue of tasks to be performed.

We tailor the plane-sweep technique as detailed by Nievergelt and Preparata [NP] to the problem of polygon triangulation. Triangulations of the plane are useful in e.g. closest point problems [LP, LT], and polygon triangulations serve for area calculations as well as for solving visibility and internal path problems [Ch], to name just a few applications.

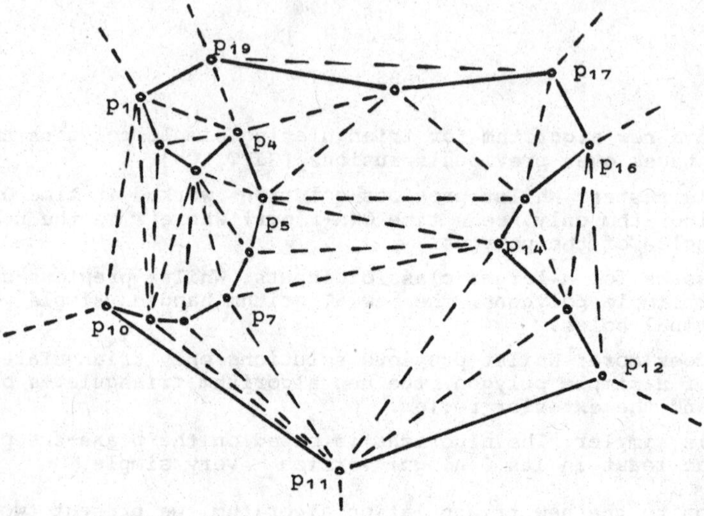

Figure 1. Simple polygon with a possible inner and outer triangulation. Dashed line segments are triangulation edges.

We shall triangulate the plane with respect to arbitrary simple n-gons with r<n concave angles, and we shall give two important applications. Our time O(n + rlogr), space O(n) solution outperforms previous O(nlogn) solutions [GJPT,Ch].

The next section exhibits the necessary basic data structures. Section 2 illustrates the ideas we use by describing a triangulation algorithm that matches the performance of [GJPT] and [Ch]. A few modifications to this algorithm including its data structures allow us to improve the upper bound to O(n + rlogr) in section 3. Within the same time bound, we can also triangulate the region outside the polygon, as shown in section 4. Finally, we give two applications of polygon triangulation.

1. THE BASIC DATA STRUCTURES

Our triangulation algorithm will operate upon four data structures.

Their basic form described here will be modified in later sections as needed. In addition to the x-structure and the y-structure already mentioned we introduce two specific data structures.

The x-structure X

X is a simple queue containing the corners of the polygon yet to be processed, sorted in order of increasing x-coordinate. For simplicity of exposition we assume that all x-coordinates are different. Initially, X contains all n corners. The algorithm removes one point from X at a time, and performs one transition each.

The y-structure Y

The vertical cross section cuts through line segments which partition it into intervals. Intervals inside alternate with intervals outside the polygon, to be referred to as in-intervals and out-intervals, resp. Y describes the cross section, and is very similar to the y-structure in [NP]. It has an entry for each interval, including those that extend to $y = +(-)\infty$; equivalently, an entry for each line segment intersected by the cross section, including two sentinels $+(-)\infty$. A line segment entry is a formula of the form $y = ax + b$ that defines this segment. This allows to find the y-value corresponding to a given x-value in constant time. Y is a dictionary (see [AHU]) that must support the operations FIND, INSERT, DELETE in time O(logk) when it contains k entries, and the operations SUCC and PRED in time O(1), by means of additional pointers. The definition of these 5 operations is slightly modified such that they fit our purpose.

In a left-to-right scan of the plane, each point can be uniquely classified into one of three main categories:

start point:  bend:  end point: 

A start (end) point with its convex angle belonging to the interior of the polygon is called proper, improper otherwise.

The result of the operation FIND(P) depends on the type of point P. For brevity's sake, the exact definitions are not given here. Suffice it to say that such a dictionary can be implemented by any of several kinds of balanced trees.

The p-structure P

P assembles information about parts of the polygon passed already whose triangulation depends on points unseen so far. For any given cross section it contains information about exactly those regions corresponding to in-intervals of this cross section. Specifically, P associates with each line segment s above an in-interval a list L(s), doubly linked by means of NEXT and PREV pointers. L(s) is a chain of corners of the polygon that are connected by either a polygon edge or a triangulation edge, starting with the left endpoint of s. In addition, RM(s) points to the rightmost element of the polygonal chain L(s). A typical cross section with the corresponding structures Y and P is shown in figure 2.

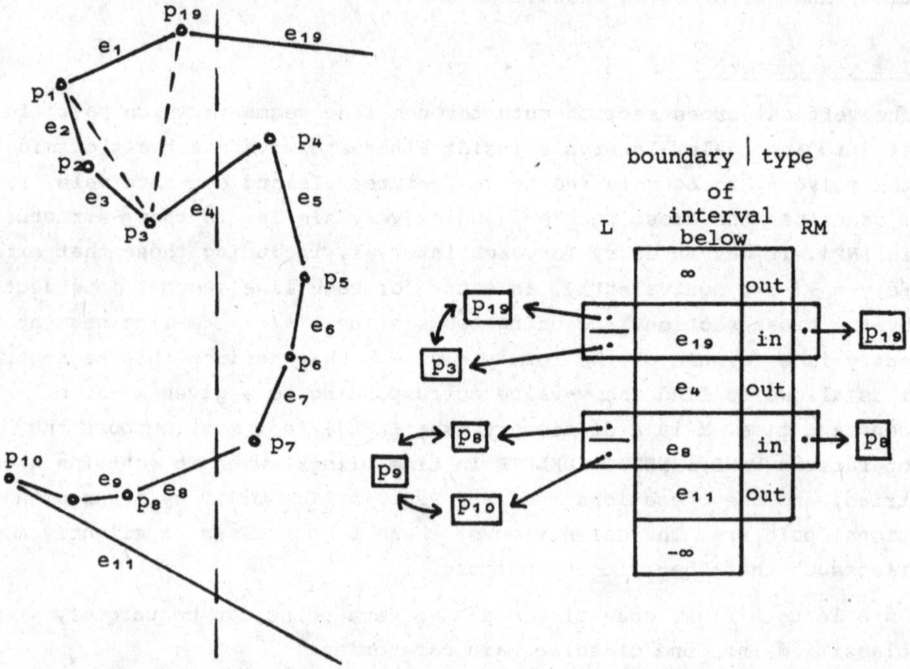

Figure 2. Structure Y-P in a cross section between points p_{19} and p_7. Two triangulation edges have been constructed.

<u>The t-structure T</u>

The output structure T is steadily built up while the plane is swept from left to right. It consists of two lists, a list TRI of triangles and a list EDGES of polygon and triangulation edges. Pointers between the two lists represent triangle-edge adjacencies.

2. THE BASIC ALGORITHM FOR INTERIOR TRIANGULATION

The algorithm that sweeps the plane and constructs triangulation edges has a simple overall structure similar to that of several plane-sweep algorithms. We follow the approach of [NP].

```
procedure SWEEP:
   X  ←  n given points, sorted by increasing x-coordinate
   Y  ←  (∞,out)  ∪ (-∞)
   P  ←  ∅
   TRI  ←  ∅
   EDGES  ←  n polygon edges, given in counterclockwise order
   while  X ≠ ∅  do
                  P  ←  MIN(X)
                  TRANSITION(P)
               od
   end of SWEEP.
```

All the work involved in moving the current cross section across P is performed by procedure TRANSITION. It is invoked exactly n times. Since each invocation will use O(logn) time, this will result in an O(nlogn) algorithm.

TRANSITION handles each of the types of the "next point" P differently. Here we only describe, as an example, the case "improper start" which can be considered to be the most complicated one. "o" denotes concatenation.

case "improper start":

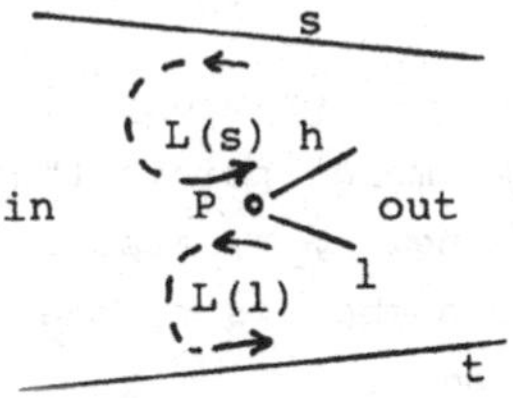


```
  FIND(P) yields the two adjacent
  line segments s and t in whose
  interval [t,s] P lies;
  h  ←  high segment starting at P
  l  ←  low segment starting at P
  Q  ←  RM(s)
  EDGES  ←  EDGES ∪ QP (with pointers set to NIL)
  INSERT((h,out))
  INSERT((l,in))
  RM(s)  ←  P ;  RM(l)  ←  P
  L(l)  ←  P o "remainder of L(s) starting at Q"
  L(s)  ←  "L(s) up to and including Q" o P
  TRIANGULATE(s,"c")
  TRIANGULATE(l,"cc")
  end of case "improper start".
```

TRIANGULATE(e,dir) starts at a point P at one end of a polygonal chain L(e) where e is a polygon edge in the y-structure, and it triangulates "along" L(e) as far as possible. If dir = "cc", P is the head of L(e), and the triangulation proceeds counterclockwise. If dir = "c", P is the tail of L(e), and we triangulate in clockwise direction. The exact description is omitted here but it should be clear that constructing a new triangulation edge and updating the appropriate polygonal chain (also to be referred to as p-chain) as well as T can be done in time O(1). Thus the running time of TRIANGULATE is proportional to the number of new triangulation edges, and the total time spent in TRIANGULATE is O(n). In addition, one call to TRANSITION takes time O(logn), yielding an overall running time of O(nlogn), including the initial sorting.

Extension to polygonal regions

It is easy to see that our algorithm also triangulates polygonal regions, i.e., ring-shaped regions with the circles replaced by simple polygons. A triangulation edge is drawn when the leftmost corner of the interior polygon is encountered - thus, in effect, cutting the polygonal region along this edge and transforming it into a simple polygon. A similar argument holds for regions with several polygonal holes.

3. THE IMPROVED ALGORITHM

We refine our previous algorithm to show that it suffices to consider "not many more" points than the intruding corners, i.e., the corners with in-angle > π, also to be referred to as points with concave angle. If their number is r, the refined algorithm will run in time O(n + rlogr).

Our x-structure X will contain these r intruding corners, and O(r) more points - the proper start and the proper end points. Sorting them according to their x-coordinate requires an effort of O(rlogr).

The y-structure Y now is different from that in the straightforward algorithm in that the current cross section is not any longer simply the "sweeping line", a vertical line right after the point just processed. Instead, a cross section consists of vertical parts that may lag behind the sweeping line, each one of them cutting two polygon edges with an in-interval in-between. A cross section part lagging behind implies points with a convex angle on the extension of the corresponding polygonal chain to the right up to the sweeping line. Note that points after which the number of in-intervals changes - start and end points - are still contained in X. Thus we can justifiably require that the ordering of in-intervals is the same as it would have been with the first algorithm.

Example: After having processed p_7 in figure 1, we could have the situation shown in figure 3.

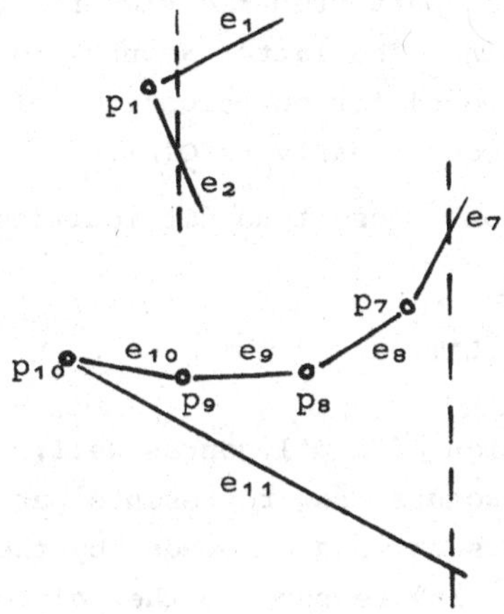

Figure 3. Possible situation after processing p_7 in figure 1. Shown are the cross section parts through the two in-intervals.

To find the location of a new point with respect to the y-structure, we extend some polygonal chains locally, while searching for P in the balanced tree Y. We start at the root and search down the tree. Whenever we encounter an edge e_s, we walk along the main polygon chain to the right, adding new edges to the triangulation, as long as the x-coordinate is smaller than that of P, and proceed, "in parallel", in the same manner with the other end of the polygonal chain of the in-interval adjacent to e_s. Then we can safely add new triangulation edges while searching down the tree Y, as is stated in the following theorem.

Theorem: No triangulation edge drawn from a convex bend intersects an edge we have not seen so far.

All the points processed "on the go" as described above are convex bends. We find each one of them in time O(1) walking along the main polygon chain, and then they are handled like bends in section 2. For an edge starting at a bend, we have to find its successor and its predecessor. INSERTs/DELETEs are not necessary; thus, processing a convex bend takes time O(1) apart from the time spent in TRIANGULATE.

Since the number of in-intervals is bounded by the number of proper start points, Y has at most O(r) entries, and one operation on Y can be implemented to work in O(logr) time. Thus, processing one of the r points in X takes time O(logr) apart from the time for processing convex bends and for triangulating. The latter amounts to a total of O(n), yielding an overall time bound for our algorithm of O(n + rlogr). The space requirement clearly is O(n).

As in section 2, polygonal regions present no difficulties.

4. EXTENSION TO EXTERIOR TRIANGULATION

To triangulate the exterior region of a polygon as well, we expand our data structures. The "p-structure" now represents parts of the plane left of the current cross section and bounded by the current convex hull whose triangulation with respect to the polygon is not finished, yet. The structure H which will be implemented as part of the p-structure is a second output structure; it represents the current state of the convex hull of the polygon.

The main change is in the current cross section. It now consists of vertical parts, each one of them touching two polygon edges (and cutting none) with an in-interval or an out-interval between the two edges. Polygonal chains are also associated with interior out-intervals. Each entry (but for the sentinels $\pm\infty$) in Y now is a double entry for the adjacent in- and out-intervals, respectively. If, during our search for P in Y, we encounter an in-node, we update the in-chain below and the out-chain above; vice versa for an out-node.

The new structure H comprises information about the convex hull of the polygon as seen so far. An h-chain each - similar to the p-chains - is associated with the two fringe intervals. Both h-chains have the very first start point in common; upon processing the very last end point, they are combined to form the convex hull.

<u>Illustration</u>: After processing p_7 in figure 1, we have the situation shown in figure 4.

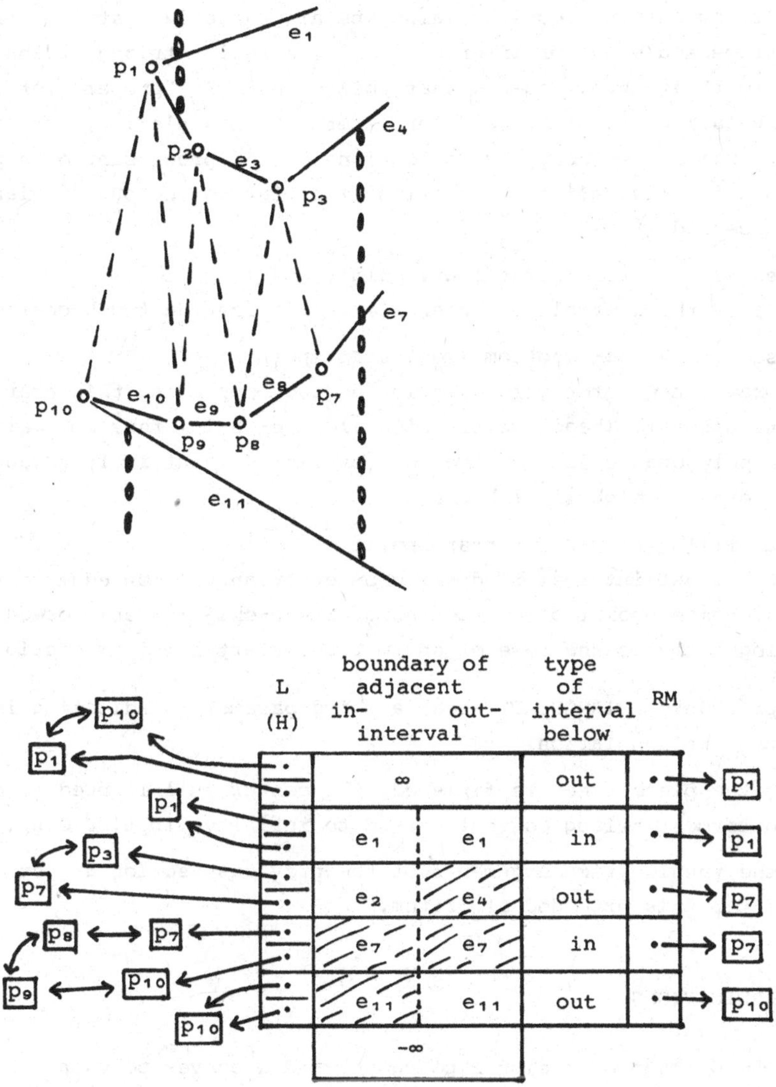

Figure 4. The structure Y-P after processing p_7 in figure 1. h-chains are associated with the top- and the bottom-most out-interval, respectively. Hatched fields are the fields which were updated while searching the lower in-node for p_7.

The triangulation algorithm maintains all these data structures. Points are processed both for interior and for exterior triangulation according to their type. Observe that points that are "proper" for interior triangulation are "improper" for exterior triangulation, and vice versa. As an example, we only give an outline of the processing of a proper start point (as defined in section 1) as far as the outer triangulation is concerned.

Case i) The very first start point
Split the initial out-interval, initialize the two h-chains.

Case ii) A top- (bottom-)most start point
Draw a new outer triangulation edge by appending this start point as new tail (head) to the high (low) h-chain, thus initializing a polygonal chain for the new interior out-interval; triangulate along the high (low) h-chain.

Case iii) An interior start point
Split out-interval by drawing outer triangulation edge to the rightmost point of the corresponding p-chain; then proceed analoguously to the case of an improper start point in section 2.

The procedure TRIANGULATE needs a third parameter indicating inner or outer triangulation.

After the plane-sweep is finished, the convex hull is used to construct the outermost triangles that extend to infinity, in time O(n).

All the running time arguments of the previous section are still valid for this extended algorithm.

5. APPLICATIONS

a) Intersection of a simple polygon P and a convex polygon Q

Shamos [Sh] showed how to compute the intersection of two convex polygons in linear time. We extend his result to

<u>Theorem</u>: Let P be a simple n-gon, and let Q be a convex m-gon. Assume that a triangulation of the plane with respect to P is available. Then $P \cap Q$ can be computed in linear time, i.e., in $O(m+n)$.

<u>Proof</u>(sketch): Let T be a triangulation of P, i.e., a division of the interior and the exterior of P into 2n-2 triangles. Let T be given as described in section 1.

We start with the observation that the intersection has "size" O(n). Note that the triangulation consists of O(n) line segments. Each such line segment can intersect the convex polygon Q in at most 2 points. Hence the total number of intersections between edges of T and edges of Q is O(n).

Let $v_1, \ldots, v_m$ be the vertices of Q. We can certainly find the triangle containing v_1 in time O(n). Also, knowing the triangle containing v_i, we can find all intersections between T and line segment $\overline{v_i v_{i+1}}$ in time $O(s_i+1)$ where s_i is the number of such intersections. Hence the total time needed to find all points of intersection is

$O(m + \Sigma s_i) = O(m+n)$, by the argument above. □

<u>Corollary</u>: Let P be a simple polygon with n vertices and r<n concave angles. Let Q be a convex polygon with m vertices. Then $P \cap Q$ can be computed in time O(n + m + rlogr).

The best solution hitherto known required time O((n+m)log(n+m)), and can be concluded from [BO].

b) Decomposing a simple polygon into few convex parts

Chazelle [Ch] showed how to decompose, in time O(nlogn) and space O(n), a simple n-gon P into fewer than 4.333•OPT convex pieces, without introducing new vertices, where OPT is the minimum number of convex pieces necessary to partition P. His algorithm has two phases. In phase 1 he triangulates P in time O(nlogn), and in phase 2 he constructs a convex decomposition from the triangulation. We already showed how to improve upon phase 1. We can also improve upon phase 2.

<u>Theorem</u>: Let P be a simple n-gon, and let T be an interior triangulation of P. Then a convex decomposition of P with at most 4•OPT pieces can be constructed in time O(n).

<u>Proof</u>(sketch): Observe that OPT ≥ r/2 + 1 since one partitioning edge is necessary for each concave angle. We shall partition P into at most 2r + 1 convex subpolygons.

To do this, scan the n-3 triangulation edges one by one. Drop an edge if it divides two convex angles. Call edge e essential for point p if it cannot be dropped because it divides a concave angle at point p. It is easy to show that not more than two triangulation edges are essential for each point with concave angle. □

REFERENCES

[AHU] A.V.Aho/J.E.Hopcroft/J.D.Ullman: The Design and Analysis of Computer Algorithms, Addison-Wesley Publ. Comp., Reading, Mass., 1974.

[BO] J.L.Bentley/T.A.Ottmann: Algorithms for Reporting and Counting Geometric Intersections, IEEE Trans. on Comp., Vol. C-28, No. 9(1975), pp. 643-647.

[Ch] B.Chazelle: A Theorem on Polygon Cutting with Applications, Proc. 23rd IEEE FOCS Symp. (1982), pp. 339-349.

[GJPT] M.R.Garey/D.S.Johnson/F.P.Preparata/R.E.Tarjan: Triangulating a Simple Polygon, Info. Proc. Letters, Vol. 7(4), June 1978, pp. 175-179.

[LP] D.T.Lee/F.P.Preparata: Location of a Point in a Planar Subdivision and its Applications, SIAM J. Comp., Vol. 6(1977), pp. 594-606.

[LT] R.J.Lipton/R.E.Tarjan: Applications of a Planar Separator Theorem, Proc. 18th IEEE FOCS Symp. (1977), pp. 162-170.

[NP] J.Nievergelt/F.P.Preparata: Plane-Sweep Algorithms for Intersecting Geometric Figures, CACM 25, 10(Oct. 1982), pp. 739-747.

[Sh] M.I.Shamos: Geometric Complexity, Proc. 7th ACM STOC (1975), pp. 224-233.

ON CONTAINMENT PROBLEMS FOR FINITE-TURN LANGUAGES.

(extended abstract)

Yair Itzhaik, Department of Computer Science, Technion - Israel Institute of Technology, Haifa, Israel

&

Amiram Yehudai, Department of Computer Science, School of Mathematical Sciences, Tel-Aviv University, Tel-Aviv, Israel.

1. Introduction

The equivalence problem and the subclass containment problems for deterministic pushdown automata (dpda) have received much attention in recent years. The equivalence problem for dpda's is the problem of deciding for any two dpda's whether the languages accepted by them are the same. The containment problem (dpda, L) is the problem of deciding for an arbitrary dpda M whether there exists a machine in the class L accepting the same language as M.

Many contributions have been made to the equivalence problem by many authors. Although the equivalence problem for general dpda's remains open, it has been shown to be decidable for several subclasses of dpda's [KH, RS, V3, V2, B, TK, OH, OIH2, IY1, GF,U].

On the other hand, there are many subclass containment problems that remain open. However, the equivalence problem and the subclass containment problem are closely related to each other. Friedman and Greibach in [FG] have proved that for any subclass of dpda's L satisfying certain properties, if the containment problem (dpda, L) is decidable, then it is also decidable whether two dpda's at least one of which belongs to L are equivalent. Besides this result, some decidability results for the containment problems have also been otbained. For the class of finite automata, Stearns in [S] proved the decidability of the containment problem (dpda, finite-state automata), which is known as the regularity problem Valiant in [V1] has improved the regularity test to present an exponentially faster algorithm. Greibach in [G2] has shown that it is decidable whether a real-time dpda with empty stack acceptance accepts a linear context-free language.

Oyamaguchi, Inagaki and Honda in [OIH1] and also Itzhaik and Yehudai independently in [IY2] gave a solution to the subclass containment problem (dpda, R_0) where R_0 is the class of real-time dpda's with empty stack acceptance.

In this paper we consider the containment problem (dpda, 1-turn dpda). We shall call this problem the linearity problem for dpda's hereafter. Unfortunately we do not have a solution to this problem in general, but we relate it to the concept of on-line regularity indication. A dpda has the on-line regularity indication property if it knows, at each point in the computation, whether the language accepted from here on is regular. We prove that if a dpda may be simulated by a dpda with the on-line regularity indication, then it may be checked for linearity. Using this reduction we show how to decide linearity for a large subclass of the dpda's.

The techniques we use also serve to provide a better understanding of the behavior of dpda's. We get insight into the structure of the stacking and popping moves of the pushdown store when reading different input words, and also the stack movements of different dpda's while reading the same input word.

The paper is organized as follows. Section 2 contains some preliminary definitions, including the concept of a generative quintet and the jump dpda as a normal form for dpda's. In section 3 we introduce the linearity problem and discuss necessary stack usage through the concept of a necessary quintet. We then show an invariant for all dpda's accepting the same language. In section 4 we sketch the linearity test and prove that it works if the dpda in question may be simulated with the on-line regularity indication. We conclude the section with families of dpda's for which this assumption holds, and get a linearity test for them.

The last two sections deal with the finite-turn property and both use the theorems of section 3. Section 5 contains a finite-turn test for strict deterministic real-time dpda's, and in section 6 we find a reduction result of the containment problems of the general case to those of the es-dpda's [F].

2. Preliminaries

We recall some basic definitions regarding deterministic languages. The empty word over an arbitrary alphabet is denoted by ε, and the length of a word α by $|\alpha|$.

A deterministic pushdown automaton (dpda) is denoted by a 7-tuple $M = (Q,\Sigma,\Gamma,\delta,q_o,Z_o,F)$ where Q, Σ and Γ are respectively finite sets of states, input symbols, and stack symbols; q_o is the initial state; Z_o in Γ is the initial stack symbols; $F \subseteq Q$ is the set of accepting of final states and $\delta: Q\times(\Sigma\ \{\varepsilon\})\times\Gamma\to Q\times\Gamma^*$, the transition function, is a partial function satisfying the determinism condition: if $\delta(q,\varepsilon,A)$ is defined, then for all a in Σ, $\delta(q,a,A)$ is not defined. If the determinism condition is not required, then M is a pushdown automaton (pda).

If $\delta(q,\pi,A) = (q',y)$, we usually write $(q,A) \overset{\pi}{\to} (q',y)$. This transition rule of M has mode (q,A) and input π. If $\pi = \varepsilon$, the transition rule is called an ε-rule.

If the only rule with mode (q,A) is an ε-rule, then (q,A) is an ε-mode, otherwise it is a reading mode. A pair (q,wA), q in Q, A in Γ, w in Γ^* is a configuration with mode (q,A) while (q,ε) is a configuration with mode (q,ε). Configuration $c = (q,w)$ has state q and stack w. The stack height of c is $|c| = |w|$.

$c_s = (q_0,Z_0)$ is the initial configuration of M. A configuration (q,w) $q \in F$, $w \in \Gamma^*$ is said to be accepting configuration. In a dpda that accepts by empty store only (q,ε) $s \in F$ are accepting configurations.

If $(q,A) \overset{\pi}{\rightarrow} (q',y)$ is a transition rule, then we write $(q,wA) \overset{\pi}{\rightarrow} (q',wy)$ for any w in Γ^* and call it a move of M which reads π, and if $\pi = \varepsilon$ we call it an ε-move. A derivation (or an α-derivation) $c \overset{\alpha}{\rightarrow} c'$ is a sequence of such moves through successive configurations where α is the concatenation of the input symbols read by the moves. The language $L(c)$ accepted from a configuration c is $L(c) = \{\alpha \in \Sigma^* | c \overset{\alpha}{\rightarrow} c';\ c'$ is an accepting configuration.$\}$ $L(M) = L(c_s)$ is the language accepted by M. A configuration is reachable if $c_s \overset{\alpha}{\rightarrow} c$ for some α, and live if $L(c) \neq \phi$. Two configurations c and c' are equivalent $(c \equiv c')$, if $L(c) = L(c')$, and two dpda's M and M' are equivalent $(M \equiv M')$, if $L(M) = L(M')$.

$\mathcal{D}$ denotes the class of all dpda's.

For convenience, we assume in this paper that all dpda's are in a normal form such that in each rule $(q,A) \overset{\pi}{\rightarrow} (q',y)$ if $\pi = \varepsilon$, then $y = \varepsilon$, otherwise $|y| \leq 2$. If $y = xB$, then (q',B) is not an ε-mode. Hence, ε-moves always come after erasing move and erase the top symbol. Also we assume that the dpda is loop-free (every input word can be read in a finite number of machine moves) and every accepting mode is a reading mode. This form can be adopted without loss of generality [V1].

The following definitions deal with the moves of the dpda on its stack and are all with respect to some particualr derivation $c \overset{\alpha}{\rightarrow} c'$. c_1 is a stacking (s-) configuration in the derivation if and only if it is not followed subsequently by any configuration of height $\leq |c_1|$. It is a popping (p-) configuration if and only if it is not preceded by any configuration of height $\leq |c_1|$. A derivation is a stacking derivation $(c \uparrow (\alpha)\ c')$ if and only if c is an s-configuration in it, a popping derivation $(c \downarrow (\alpha)\ c')$ if and only if c' is a p-configuration in it.

A dpda makes a turn when it changes from stacking to popping, that is if there is a computation $c_1 \uparrow (\alpha_1)\ c_2 \downarrow (\alpha_2) c_3$ with $|c_1| < |c_2|$ and $|c_2| > |c_3|$. A dpda is n-turn if no computation from the initial configuration (q_0,Z_0) contains more than n turns; it is finite-turn if there is a $k \geq 1$ such that the dpda is k-turn.

For 1-turn dpda's/languages we sometimes use the name linear of deterministic-linear (d-linear) dpda's/languages which is somewhat inaccurate. It is known that linear context-free languages (cfl) are accepted by 1-turn pda's, but it can be shown that the linear cfl's which can be accepted by dpda's properly contain the languages accepted by 1-turn dpda's, and denote the containment problem $(\mathcal{D}, \text{1-turn})$ as the <u>linearity test</u>.

Another family of dpda's is the class $\mathcal{R}$ of <u>realtime</u> dpda's that consists of dpda's with no ε-rules. $\mathcal{D}_0$ $(\mathcal{R}_0)$, the class of <u>strict dpda's (realtime strict dpda's)</u>, contains all dpda's in $\mathcal{D}$ $(\mathcal{R})$ that accept by empty store.

L is a <u>realtime strict deterministic language</u> if $L = L(M)$ for some realtime strict dpda M (similarly for the other families).

The next definition is based on the nature of the main process that a dpda performs on an input word. This process is actually a comparison action between the input subwords. We give here a formalization to this behavior of the dpda in terms of its stack height changes.

<u>Definition:</u> Let $M = (Q,\Sigma,\Gamma,\delta,q_0,Z_0,F)$ be a dpda, c_1 and c_2 configurations of M and $c_1 \overset{\gamma}{\vdash} c_2$, $\gamma \in \Sigma^*$. The quintet $T = (q,q',A,x,y)$ $(A \in \Gamma,\ x,y \in \Gamma^+,\ q,q' \in Q)$ is a <u>generative quintet</u> in $c_1 \overset{\gamma}{\vdash} c_2$ if γ is factored into $\alpha_1,\alpha_2,\alpha_3,\alpha_4,\alpha_5$, $\alpha_i \in \Sigma^*$ $(i=1,2,\ldots 5)$, satisfying the following conditions: $\gamma = \alpha_1\alpha_2\alpha_3\alpha_4\alpha_5$; $\alpha_2,\alpha_4 \in \Sigma^+$ and $c_1 \overset{\alpha_1}{\vdash} (q,xA) \uparrow (\alpha_2)(q,xyA) \downarrow (\alpha_3)(q',xy) \downarrow (\alpha_4)(q',x) \overset{\alpha_5}{\vdash} c_2$ (see Figure 1).

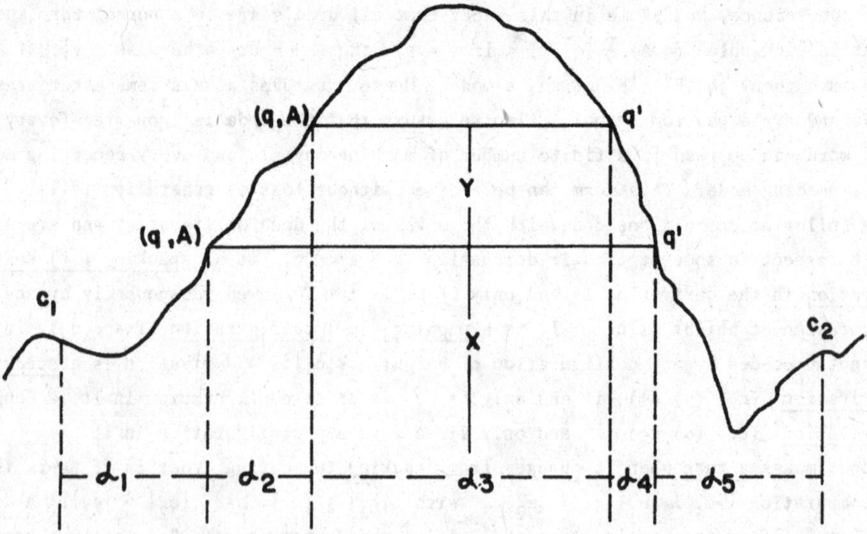

<u>Figure 1:</u> Generative quintet $T = (q,q',A,x,y)$.

It is easy to see that the appearance of a generative quintet in the derivation $c_1 \overset{\gamma}{\vdash} c_2$ with appropriate factorization $\gamma = \alpha_1\alpha_2\alpha_3\alpha_4\alpha_5$ points to an infinite number of derivations $c_1 \xrightarrow{\alpha_1\alpha_2^i\alpha_3\alpha_4^i\alpha_5} c_2$, $i \geq 0$, in which there is a correspondence between

the number of the α_2 and α_4 subwords.
This proposition reminds us of the known pumping lemma, and actually they both deal with the same thing.
It is also clear that in every derivation $c_1 \to c_2$ in which the stack height increases (and then decreases) by more than $|\Gamma||Q|^2$ while reading nonempty input words, the dpda passes through a generative quintet. Generative quintets can be found in various combinations in a derivation and we can define relations between them. For example, if there is a generative quintet T_1 in the derivation $c_1 \overset{\alpha}{\to} c_2$ and a generative quintet T_2 in the derivation $c_2 \overset{\beta}{\to} c_3$, we say that T_2 follows T_1 in $c_1 \xrightarrow{\alpha\beta} c_3$. This relation and others can characterize subclasses of dpda's (new and old ones); for example, in the finite-turn dpda's we can find in each derivation only a bounded number of generative quintets that follow one another. More on the relations between generative quintets may be found in [I].
Next, we are going to define a very useful normal form on dpda's.

Definition: A dpda $M = (Q,\Sigma,\Gamma,\delta,q_o,Z_oF)$ is called jpda if and only if $Q = Q_\varepsilon \cup \overline{Q}_\varepsilon$, $Q_\varepsilon \cap \overline{Q}_\varepsilon = \phi$ and

(a) for every $q \in Q_\varepsilon$ $\exists$ $\psi_q \subseteq \Gamma$ such that

$$\delta(q,\varepsilon,X) = \begin{cases} (q,\varepsilon) & \text{for } X \in \psi_q \text{ and} \\ (p,\varepsilon) & \text{and } p \in \overline{Q}_\varepsilon \text{ for } X \in \Gamma - \psi_q \end{cases};$$

(b) for every q,Y, $q \in \overline{Q}_\varepsilon$, $Y \in \Gamma$, $\delta(q,\varepsilon,Y) = \phi$;

(c) If $\delta(q,a,A) = (p,\gamma)$, then $|\gamma| \leq 2$.

3. Linearity Test

We are trying to find an effective procedure for deciding whether the language accepted by an arbitrary dpda is d-linear.
Testing linearity of a dpda is very easy (see Valiant [V2]), but deciding whether a language is d-linear seems to be very hard, because if we cannot find the 1-turn dpda that accepts the language and we try to prove nonlinearity, we must show that every dpda that accepts the language has at least one derivation with more than one turn. When talking about the connection between a dpda and a language, we must look for the invariant properties of all the machines that accept this language.
Therefore, let us investigate more deeply the nature of the dpda's computation and its influence on the language which that dpda recognizes. To do this we need the notion of necessity of the computation--that means using the stack in a way that must occur (for a particular input segment) in every dpda accepting the language. This notion of necessary usage of the stack is connected to a derivation that passes

through a large number of pairwise inequivalent configurations. We formalize this connection in the following:

Definition: Let $M = (Q,\Sigma,\Gamma,\delta,q_o,Z_o,F)$ be a jpda, a generative quintet $T = (q,q',A,x,y)$ in $c_1 \overset{\gamma}{\to} c_2$ $(q,q' \varepsilon Q,\ A \in \Gamma,\ x,y \in \Gamma^+,\ \gamma \in \Sigma^*$, and c_1,c_2 configurations) is called a necessary quintet in $c_1 \overset{\gamma}{\to} c_2$ if for every $m,n \geq 0$, $m \neq n, (q',xy^n) \not\equiv (q',xy^m)$.

Clearly if $T = (q,q',A,x,y)$ is a necessary quintet in $c_1 \overset{\gamma}{\to} c_2$, then there is a factorization of $\gamma = \alpha_1\alpha_2\alpha_3\alpha_4\alpha_5$ such that for every $n \geq 0 (q,xy^nA) \xrightarrow{\alpha_3} (q',xy^n)$ implying that $(q,xy^n) \not\equiv (q,xy^mA)$ for every $m \neq n$, $m,n \geq 0$ since the same input takes these configurations to inequivalent configurations.

Two of the main theorems of this section relate the appearance of a necessary quintet to computation from equivalent configurations (in the same or other dpda's). These theorems together give sufficient conditions for non-linearity of the language accepted by a given dpda. This condition will be the basis for our linearity test, that is the subject of Section 4.

The proofs of our main results are as important as the results are becauce they provide better understanding of the behavior of the dpda and the necessary usage of the stack, (Proofs will be given in the full paper).

The idea of necessity is related to a "real" usage of the stack. Unlike a regular language which can be recognized by a finite memory, recognition of a deterministic context-free language needs a memory of unbounded number of stack cells. This usage of the stack contains derivations with generative quintets in which there is a comparison between an input word that causes the dpda to add symbols to the stack and an input word that is read in some later stage of the computation and causes these symbols to be erased.

However, there are derivations with a redundant usage of the stack, and the same input word that causes the dpda to write and pop symbols can be accepted by an equivalent dpda that changes only its state during the computation without any usage of the stack.

We relate the concept of necessity (necessary quintet, for example) to a derivation that passes through unbounded number of pairwise inequivalent configurations, because in this case the stack must be used. (If the dpda passes through n pairwise inequivalent configurations, and ℓ is an integer such that $n > |Q||\Gamma|^\ell$, then the dpda must use at least ℓ different cells of the stack in this computation.)

The first theorem claims that the appearance of a necessary quintet in the computation between two configurations implies that between every two respectively equivalent configurations there exists a computation that makes at least one turn.

Theorem 1: Let $M = (Q,\Sigma,\Gamma,\delta,q_o,Z_oF)$ be a jpda, c_1,c_2 configurations and γ an input word.

If $T = (q,q',A,x,y)$ is a necessary quintet in $c_1 \overset{\gamma}{\to} c_2$, <u>then</u>: For every jpda $\bar{M}$ equivalent to M, and for every configuration $\bar{c}_1$ in $\bar{M}$ equivalent to c_1, the following condition holds:
For every natural number $d > 0$ we can find an input word β_d, and a configuration $\bar{c}_2$ equivalent to c_2, such that $c_1 \xrightarrow[M]{\beta_d} c_2$, and in $\bar{c}_1 \xrightarrow{\beta_d} \bar{c}_2$, $\bar{M}$ writes and pops a stack word longer than d.
Theorem 2 gives a sufficient condition for the appearance of a necessary quintet in a given computation.

<u>Theorem 2:</u> Let $M = (Q,\Sigma,\Gamma,\delta,q_0Z_0,F)$ be a jpda; also let c_1,c_2 be configurations and γ an input word such that $c_1 \overset{\gamma}{\to} c_2$. If $T = (q,q',A,x,y)$ is a generative quintet in the computation $c_1 \overset{\gamma}{\to} c_2$, and $(q',x) \not\equiv (q',xy)$, then there exists an integer $n_0 = n_0(q',x,y)$ and input word $\bar{\gamma}$ such that $T_{n_0} = (q,q',A,xy^{n_0},y)$ is a necessary quintet in $c_1 \overset{\bar{\gamma}}{\to} c_2$.

From the two theorems we conclude the next theorem:

<u>Theorem 3:</u> Let $M = (Q,\Sigma,\Gamma,\delta,q_0,Z_0,F)$ be a jpda, c_1,c_2,c_3 configurations of M and $T_1 = (q_1,q_1',A_1,x_1,y_1)$ and $T_2 = (q_2,q_2',Q_2,x_2,y_2)$ are generative quintets in $c_1 \to c_2$ and $c_2 \to c_3$, respectively, such that $(q_1',x_1) \not\equiv (q_1',x_1\,y_1)$ and $(q_2',x_2) \not\equiv (q_2',x_2\,y_2)$. Then the language $L(M)$ is not d-linear

4. <u>Sketch of the Procedure for the Linearity Test.</u>

The linearity test is composed of two partial procedures A and B. We can show that A halts if and only if $L(M)$, the language accepted by the given dpda, is d-linear. We can also prove that if B halts, $L(M)$ is not linear.
We conjecture that the converse is true, and we can prove this for large families of dpda's, and thus obtain decision procedures for linearity of dpda's in these families. So given a dpda M, we apply to M Procedure A and Procedure B in parallel.

<u>Procedure A.</u> This procedure will stop if and only if $L(M)$ is d-linear. We enumerate all the 1-turn dpda's $\{M_i | M_i$ makes at most one turn$\}$, and check for equivalence between M_i and M. The quivalence test is in [OIH2] and [IY2]. If there exists i such that $M_i \equiv M$, the procedure will stop and $L(M)$ is of course d-linear

<u>Procedure B.</u> This partial procedure will stop if and only if the conditions of Theorem 3 exist: there are configurations c_1,c_2,c_3 and $T_1 = (q_1,q_1',A_1,x_1,y_1)$ is a generative quintet in $c_1 \to c_2$ such that $(q_1',x_1) \not\equiv (q_1',x_1y_1)$; and $T_2 = (q_2,q_2',A_2,x_2,y_2)$ is a generative quintet in $c_2 \to c_3$ such that

$(q_2',x_2) \neq (q',x\ y\ )$. If B halts, we know according to Theorem 3 that there is no 1-turn dpda that accepts L(M).

We are going to describe B in therms of a nondeterministic procedure, though it can be very easily transformed to a dterministic one: We guess configurations c_1,c_2 and c_3 and the appropriate generative quintets T_1 and T_2, and then guess the input words that distinguish between (q_1',x_1) and (q_1',x_1y_1) and between (q_2',x_2) and (q_2',x_2y_2). B halts if all the guesses succeed.

As was pointed out, we can only conjecture that B holts for any dpda M accepting a language that cannot be accepted by any 1-turn dpda. To prove this we need to show that for each such M, there must exist a derivation with two necessary quintets following one another. Instead, we can state the contrapositive as follows.

Conjecture: If each derivation of M has at most only one necessary quintet, then there exists a 1-turn dpda that accepts L(M).

We will prove that the conjecture holds if there exists for any given dpda M, a apda M' that acts the same as M and has in every configuration c an indicator whether of not L(c) is a regular language.

Let us define this property of M' more formally.

Definition: A given dpda $M = (Q,\Sigma,\Gamma,\delta,q_o,Z_o,F)$ has an on-line regularity indication property iff there exists a set of modes $S \subseteq Q\times(\Gamma\cup\{\varepsilon\})$ such that for every reachable configuration c, L(c) is regular if and only if the mode of c is in S.

We will show how to transform M' with this property into an equivalent 1-turn dpda $\bar{M}$, and this completes the linearity-test.

If we can build M', then we can actually construct $\bar{M}$, and then check equivalence with M. Using this technique we could prove the linearity test for dpda's from very large families, and in the general case we reduce the problem to that of proving the existence of the dpda M'; so we state and then prove the following theorem:

Theorem 4: Linearity is decidable for a given dpda M if there exists a jpda with on-line regularity indication that accepts L(M).

Proof: We give here an informal proof: To prove that we can decide for a given dpda M if L(M) is d-linear, it is sufficient to prove the conjecture we have stated above. Now, assume that there exists an equivalent jpda M' with an on-line regularity indication and $M' = (Q,\Sigma,\Gamma,\delta,q_o,Z_o,F)$. If each derivation of M has at most only one necessary quintet, so has M' (otherwise it will contradict Theorem 1).

Let us transform M' into an equivalent 1-turn dpda $\bar{M}$. The concept behind the construction of $\bar{M}$ is to make the single downstroke of $\bar{M}$ only when it is really needed. We rely here on the following observations:

(i) if $c \rightarrow c_1$ where L(c) is regular and $|c_1| - |c| > Y$ (Y is a number depending on the parameters of $\bar{M}$ and can be found in [V1]), then we can erase an inner portion of the top segment of Y stack symbols of c_1, and

reduce c_1 to an equivalent configuration c_2.
Therefore, if $\bar{M}$ remembers in its finite state control the Y top stack symbols of M', $\bar{M}$ in simulating M' from configuration c does not have to perform any up-storke move on the stack. (The same concept was used in [IY2].)
(ii) We can easily show (see [I]) that if there is no necessary quintet in the computation from c, then one can simulate the computations from c and perform reductions so that the stack height is bounded by $|c| + Y$. Thus L(c) is regular. Therefore, if L(c) is not regular, there is at least one computation that passes through a necessary quintet.
(iii) Under the assumption that all the derivations of M' have at most only one necessary quintet, we conclude from (ii) that if there is a generative quintet $T = (q,q',A,x,y)$ in the computation $c_0 \to c$ and L(c) is not regular, then $(q',x) \equiv (q',xy)$; and if we are in (q',x), we can return to (q',xy).
Observations (i) - (iii) yield the techniques needed for the simulation. We now sketch these techniques. $\bar{M}$ works in two phases. The first one which we call the non-regular phase is used for simulating M' as long as the configurations visited are non-regular, in which case $\bar{M}$ never reduces its stack. When M' enters a regular configuration, $\bar{M}$ enters its regular phase in which the stack never grows.
To avoid popping the stack in the first phase and increasing it in the regular phase, we handle small changes in the stack (up to Y symbols) in the finite state control.
For computations involving large changes, we do the following:
In the regular phase we must avoid large increases in the size of the stack. We do this by performing "reductions" on the stack as described in (i) above. The non-regular phase is somewhat more complicated to handle. If M' erases a long segment from the stack while reading real input, then we return to a higher and equivalent configuration. This solution applies only if the computation consumed real input, otherwise the same computation will repeat from the higher configuration without advancing the input leading to an infinite loop. We therefore handle a long sequence of ε-moves by simply indicating on the stack that a segment needs to be ε-erased during the second phase, and for now we resume the computation from the mode that would be reached after this sequence of ε-moves (this mode can be computed from the information stored in the finite state control). See Figure 2 for a description of the delayed computations.
A detailed proof will be given in the full text. It is quite long and contains a complicated construction.
We use Theorem 4 in proving the existence of linearity test for various families of dpda's. In [IY3] we introduce these families and discuss their significant role in the deterministic languages. We give there as a result the following theorem:

Theorem 5: Linearity is decidable for proper dpda's, NM and NO dpda's, and NSD dpda's.

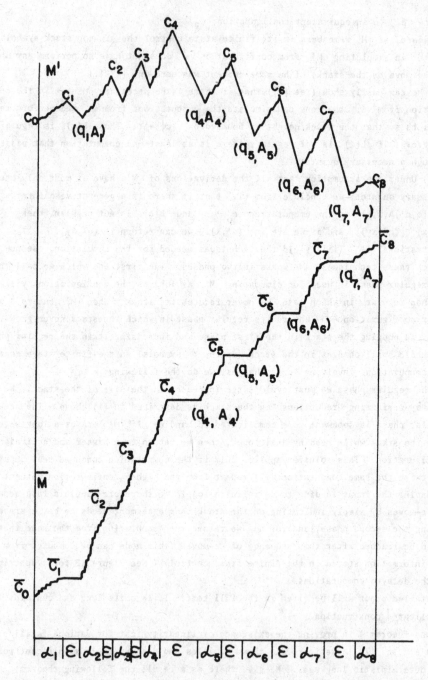

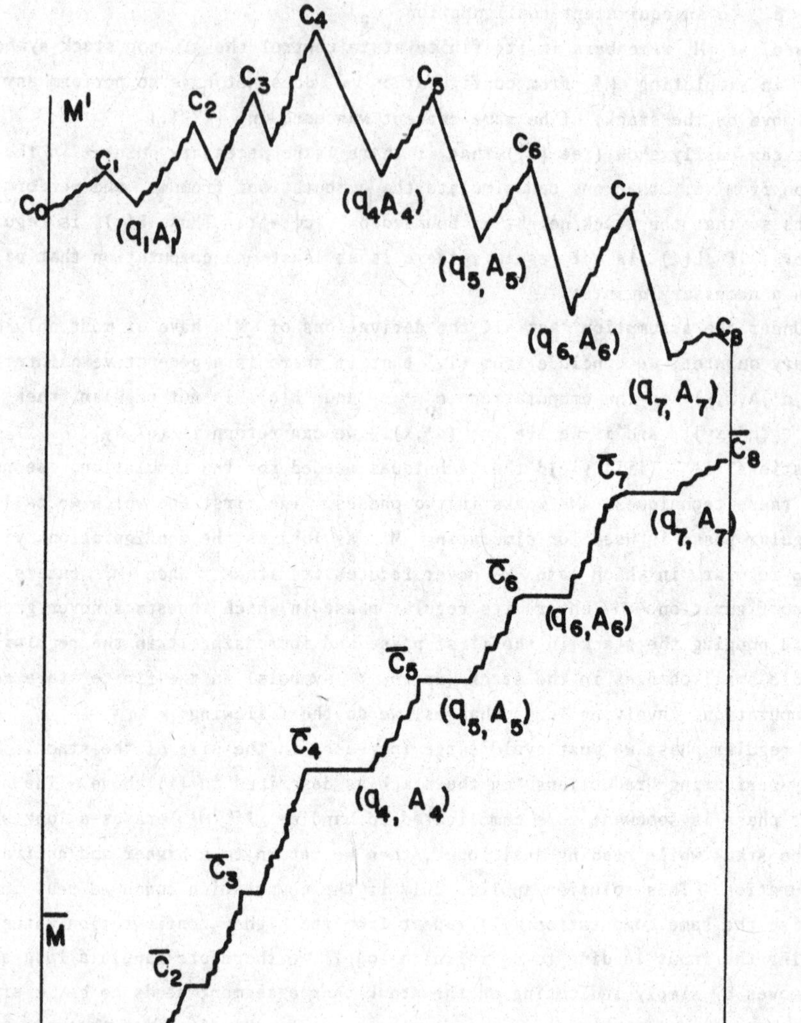

Figure 2: delayed computations of ε-moves

All those families are characterized by the equivalence relations among their configurations during the computation. For example, an NQ dpda is a dpda for which all generative quintets appearing in derivations are necessary quintets, and the NM dpda is a dpda for which all configurations with the same mode in a stacking derivation are pairwise inequivalent.

Proper dpda's were introduced in [U]. We also believe that the above theorem is very close to solving the general problem of deciding linearity for an arbitrary dpda because we conjecture in [IY] that the NSD dpda's accept all the deterministic languages.

5. A finite-turn test for real-time strict dpda's

In this section we prove the decidability of the subclass containment problem (R_o, finite-turn). Specifically, given a real-time strict dpda M one can tell in polynomial time whether or not L(M) can be accepted by a finite-turn dpda. Moreover, if such a finite-turn dpda exists, one can build a real-time strict deterministic n-turn dpda that accepts L(M) with n minimal.

Greibach proved in [G1] that for a given real-time strict dpda M, one can decide in polynomial time if L(M) is a linear language (accepted by some 1-turn pda). Our result contains (as a special case) a test for the existence of 1-turn dpda's that accept L(M) and is done in a completely different way.

Theorem 6: For a given real-time strict dpda M, we can build a real-time strict dpda $\bar{M}$ that accepts L(M), and L(M) is an n-turn/finite-turn deterministic language if and only if $\bar{M}$ is and n-turn/finite turn dpda.

Now, although checking finite turn and n-turn properties for a dpda $\bar{M}$ can be done in polynomial time (see [V2]), we cannot use Theorem 6 for deciding these propeties for the language L(M) in polynomial time because $\bar{M}$ can be exponentially larger than M. Therefore, to establish our second main result, we need a more direct algorithm on M.

Theorem 7: Given a real-time strict dpda M, we can decide in polynomial time if L(M) is an n-turn/finite-turn deterministic language.

Proof: Our algorithm is similar to the one in [V2] for testing the finite-turn property for a given dpda where a new dpda reads one input symbol whenever M makes a turn. But here we have to count only those turns with a downstroke move of more than $|\Gamma||Q|^2$ stack symbols. Details can be found in the full paper. □

6. A reduction result for some subclass containment problems.

In [F] the family of the extended simple machines (ES machines, in short) was defined. It was shown there that the equivalence problem for dpda's is reducible to the equivalence problem for ES machines. Here we give a similar reduction result for some subclass containment problems of the general case (for example, the containment problem ($\mathcal{D}$, finite-turn dpda)) to the appropriate subclass containment problems for ES machines.

An extended simple machine is a single-state dpda with an added feature that allows its read head to remain situated over the same input symbol for more than one move. Thus, such a device can make an unbounded number of moves without advancing the read head. Because these devices possess only one state, no information can be stored in the finite-state control. Therefore, they can althernately be thought of a stateless devices, so there is no necessity for including a state set in the definition.

It was shown in [F] that the family of languages accepted by the ES-dpda's (and ES machine) is properly contained in $\mathcal{D}$. For example, consider the language $L = \{a^n ba^n b\{b \geq 1\} \cup \{a^n ca^n c | n \geq 1\}$. L is certainly accepted by a dpda, but L is not accepted by any ES-dpda. An ES-dpda has no mechanism for "remembering" whether it reads b or c before processing the second segment of a's.

Theorem 10: The finite turn containment problem and the n-turn containment problem and the d-linearity problem for dpda's are reduced to the appropriate subclass containment problems for ES-dpda's

References

[B] C. Beeri, An improvement on Valiant's decision procedure for equivalence of deterministic finite-turn pushdown automata, TCS 3(1976), 305-320.

[C] B. Courcelle, On Jump Deterministic Pushdown Automato, Math Systems Theorey (1977), 87-109.

[F] E.P. Friedman, Equivalence problems for deterministic cfl and monadic recursion schemes JCSS 14 (1977).

[FG] E.P.Friedman and S.A. Greibach, On equivalence and subclass containment problems ofr deterministic context-free languages, Info. Let. 7(1978), 287-290.

[G1] S.A. Greibach, Linearity is polynomially decidable for realtime pushdown store automata, Information and Control, 42(1979), 27-37.

[G2] S.A. Greibach, Jump PDA's and Hierarchies of Context-free languages, SIAM Journal on Computing 3 (1974), 111-127.

[GF] S.A Greibach and E.P. Friedman, Some results on the extended equivalence Problem for dpda's.manuscript 1979.

[GG] S.Ginsburg and S.A. Greibach, Deterministic context-free languages, Information and Control 9(1966), 602 -648.

[I] Y.Itzhaik, Deterministic pushdown automata, Master Thesis, Technion, IIT, June 1978, (In Hebrew).

[IY1] Y.Itzhaik and A. Yehudai, A decision procedure for the euqivalence of two dpta's one of which is linear, proceedings of ICALP 8I, Acre, Lecture Notes in Computer Science No. 115, (1981) Springer-Verlag, 229-237.

[IY2] Y. Itzhaik and A. Yehudai, Checking dterministic languages for the real time strict property, Technical Report, Tel-Aviv University, (1982).

[IY3] Y. Itzahik and A. Yehudai, New families of non real-time dpta's and their decidability results, Accepted to Theoretical Computer Science, 1983.

[KH] A.J. Korenjak and J.E. Hopcroft, Simple Deterministic languages, IEEE 7th Symp. on Switching and Automata Theory Berkeley, California, (1966).

[LP] M. Linna and M.Penttonen, New Proofs for jump dpda's, Math Foundations of Computer Science (1979), 354-362.

[OH] M. Oyamaguchi and N. Honda, The decidability of equivalence for deterministic stateless pushdown Automata, Informaiton and Control 38(1978), 367-376.

[OIH1] M. Oyamaguchi, Y.inagaki and N. Honda, A real-time strictness test for deterministic pushdown automata, Inform. Contr. 47(1980) 1-9.

[OIH2] M.Oyamaguchi, Y. Inagaki and N. Honda, The equivalence problem for two dpda's one which is a finite-turn or one counter machine, JCSS 23(1981) 366-382.

[OIH3] M.Oyamaguchi, Y. Inagaki and N. Honda, On the equivalence problem for two dpda's, one of which is real-time, in "Proceedings IFIP Congress 80, 1980", pp. 52-57.

[RS] D.J. Rosenkrantz and R.E. Stearns, Properties of deterministic top-down grammars, Informaiton and Control 17(1970), 226-255.

[S] R.E. Stearns, A regularity test for pushdown machines, Inform. Contr. 11(1967), 323-340

[TK] K. Taniguchi and T. Kasami, A result on the equivalence problem for deterministic pushdown automata, J. Comp. System Sci. 13(1976), 38-50.

[U] E. Ukkonen, The equivalence problem for some non-real-time deterministic pushdown automata, Proceedings of the 12th STOC Conference (1980) 29-38, also JACM 29 (1982), 1166-1181.

[V1] L.G.Valinat, Regularity and related problems for deterministic pushdown automata, JACM 22 (1975), 1-10.

[V2] L.C.Valiant, The equivalence problem for deterministic finite-turn pushdown automata, Info. Contr. 25, (1974), 123-133.

[V3] L.G. Valiant, Decision procedures for families of deterministic pushdown automata, Ph.D. Dissertation, University of Warwick Computer Centre, Report No. 7, 1973.

ON LANGUAGES GENERATED BY SEMIGROUPS

Ladislav Janiga and Václav Koubek
Charles University
Malostranské náměstí 25
Praha 1
Czechoslovakia

1. Abstract

In this paper we investigate properties of classes of languages generated by semigroups in the following sense:

Let S be a semigroup, s its element, A an alphabet and f a mapping which assignes to each $a \in A$ a finite subset $f(a)$ of S. A word $w = a_1 \dots a_n \in A^+$ belongs to the language generated by S, f, s and A iff the following condition holds:

$$\exists s_1 \in f(a_1) \ \dots \ \exists s_n \in f(a_n) \quad s = s_1 \cdot \dots \cdot s_n .$$

We investigate the languages generated in this sense by certain types of semigroups. It is important to emphasize that we do not consider the empty word, thus all languages are subsets of free semigroups of the form A^+, similarly all homomorphisms we investigate are semigroup homomorphisms only. Since the proofs of our results are based on rather complicated semigroup constructions we sketch them out or omit at all. The detailed proofs are to be presented in [10] .

2. Introduction

The aim of this paper is to present an other way in which formal languages can be characterized. Let us mention three important approaches to characterization of formal languages:

/i/ Characterization of languages by classes of machines which recognize the languages.

/ii/ Characterization via a class of grammars which generate the languages.

/iii/ Characterization by a collection of operations by which the languages can be obtained from a basic class of languages.

Our approach is based on the following idea:

Suppose we are given a class C of objects over which it is possible to effectuate some kind of computation /in the sequel it will be a semigroup together with its operation/. Let us select one object s from C. Now we can, when characterizing some language L, proceed as follows:

/i/ Any word over the alphabet over which we consider L is related with an expression over C.

/ii/ For every word is evaluated the expression and if the resulting object is equal to s then the word is accepted.

This idea is formalized in the following definition:

<u>Definition 1</u>

Let S be a semigroup, let $s \in S$ and let A be an alphabet.

/i/ An assignement is any function f which assignes to every $a \in A$ a finite and nonempty subset $f(a)$ of S.

/ii/ We say that a word $w = a_1 \dots a_n \in A^+$ belongs to the language generated by S,A,f and s /denoted $L(A,S,f,s)$/ iff

$$\exists s_1 \in f(a_1) \ \dots \ \exists s_n \in f(a_n) \quad s_1 \cdot \dots \cdot s_n = s.$$

/iii/ A language L is said to be generated by the semigroup S iff it is of the form $L(A,S,f,s)$ for appropriate A,f and $s \in S$.

<u>Note</u>

Let us denote by P(S) the global of S, i.e. the following set: $\{S' \mid S' \subseteq S \ \& \ S' \text{ is finite}\}$ together with the operation $S_1 \cdot S_2 = \{s_1 \cdot s_2 \mid s_1 \in S_1 \ \& \ s_2 \in S_2\}$. It follows that an assignement f is a function of the form:

$$f : A \to P(S)$$

This function has a unique homomorphism extension $f^+ : A^+ \to P(S)$ and it is easy to see that $L(A,S,f,s) = \{ w \in A^+ \mid s \in f^+(w) \}$.

Definition 1 relates the language $L(A,S,f,s)$ with the following computational process /nondeterministic in its nature/:

input = $w = a_1 \dots a_n$

/1/ for any i select some s_i from the set which is assigned by f to the i-th letter of w,

/2/ compute $s_1 \cdot \dots \cdot s_n = e$,

/3/ if $s = e$ then accept.

As we shall see in the sequel the assumption that the assignement f relates any letter with a finite subset of S only is not restrictive.

Example 1

/i/ Let Z be the additive group of integers. Put $A = \{a,b\}$ and let $f(a) = \{1\}$, $f(b) = \{-1\}$. Then the language $L(A,Z,f,0)$ is equal to $\{w \in A^{+} \mid w$ contain the same number of a's and b's$\}$.

/ii/ The language $L = \{ (ab)^{n} \mid n \geq 1 \}$ is generated by the following semigroup S:

	a	b	c	d	e	f	0
a	0	c	0	e	0	c	0
b	d	0	f	0	d	0	0
c	e	0	c	0	e	0	0
d	0	f	0	d	0	f	0
e	0	c	0	e	0	c	0
f	d	0	f	0	d	0	0
0	0	0	0	0	0	0	0

when $f(a) = \{a\}$, $f(b) = \{b\}$, $L = L(A,S,f,c)$

/iii/ Let G be the group of all rational numbers of the form $2^{i} \cdot 3^{j}$, $i, j \in Z$ with multiplication as the group operation. If we set $f(a) = \{2\}$, $f(b) = \{3\}$, $f(c) = \{2^{-1} \cdot 3^{-1}\}$ then we obtain that the language $L(\{a,b,c\},G,f,1)$ is precisely the set of all words containing the same number of occurences of a's, b's and c's.

The above example shows that semigroups can generate some regular, context-free or even context-sensitive languages. The following theorem states that they can generate all languages:

Theorem 1

For any alphabet A and for any language $L \subseteq A^{+}$ there are a semigroup S, an assignement f and an element $s \in S$ such that:

$L = L(A,S,f,s)$ & $\forall a \in A \ |f(a)| \leq 4$.

The theorem states that any language can be generated by a semigroup and by an assignement which assignes to every letter $a \in A$ at most four elements of the semigroup. Whether this can be improved /e.g. f assigning at most three or two elements/ is unknown. On the other hand one easily obtains the following:

Theorem 2

For any language L of the form $L = L(A,S,f,s)$ we have that $\forall a \in A \ |f(a)| = 1$ iff there is a congruence $\sim$ on A^+ such that L is equal exactly to one class of $\sim$. Moreover if $\sim$ is of a finite index then S can be selected finite.

Since any language can be generated by a semigroup an interesting question arises, the question what kind of languages can be generated by a certain kind of semigroups. For the sake of brevity we introduce the following:

Definition 2

For a class of semigroups $\mathcal{S}$ the symbol $\mathcal{L}(\mathcal{S})$ will stand for the class of all languages which can be generated by some $S \in \mathcal{S}$.

The following theorem characterizes the class of all recursive languages:

Theorem 3

A language $L \subseteq A^+$ is recursive iff there are a semigroup S and the semigroup's presentation $S = \langle s_1,\ldots,s_n;\ R_1,\ldots,R_m,\ldots \rangle$ such that S generates L and the word problem for the presentation is solvable.

3. Closure properties of languages generated by semigroups

In this section we summarize a list of results concerning the closure properties of $\mathcal{L}(\mathcal{S})$ for certain $\mathcal{S}$. We consider the following operations: union, intersection, closure under inverse homomorphisms, closure under one-letter substitution /denoted $\mathcal{C}^C$ for a class $\mathcal{C}$ / and left and right quotients. The properties presented here are easy to prove, the only exeption is the case of union.

/i/ inverse homomorphisms - under this operation is closed any class of the form $\mathcal{L}(\mathcal{S})$,

/ii/ one letter substitution - for any class $\mathcal{L}(\mathcal{S})$ we have $\mathcal{L}(\mathcal{S})^C \subseteq \mathcal{L}(\mathcal{S})$,

/iii/intersection - if $\mathcal{S}$ is closed under finite cartesian products then $\mathcal{L}(\mathcal{S})$ is closed under intersection,

/iv/ concatenation - under this operation are closed e.g. classes $\mathcal{L}(\mathcal{S})$ for $\mathcal{S}$ - the class of all finite semigroups or the class of all J-trivial semigroups /recall that a semigroup S is said to be J-trivial iff distinct elements of S generate distinct two-sided ideals in S/,

/v/ union - if $\mathcal{S}$ is a variety of finite semigroups containing all finite J-trivial semigroups then $\mathcal{L}(\mathcal{S})$ is closed under union,

/vi/ quotients - if $\mathcal{L}(\mathcal{S})$ is closed under union then it is closed under left and right quotients by a word.

Combining these results - /v/ and Theorem 2 we obtain the following important characterization of the class of all regular languages:

Theorem 4

Let $\mathcal{F}$ denote the class of all finite semigroups and let REG denote the class of all regular languages which do not contain the empty word. Then $\mathcal{L}(\mathcal{F})$ = REG.

Note

It is easily verified that all languages which are singletons /and thus all finite languages/ can be generated by J-trivial semi groups. This simple fact will be used in the following section.

4. Relations to varieties of languages

We recall the following /see [5,9] /. A class $\mathcal{S}$ of finite semigroups is said to be a variety if it is closed under finite products, subsemigroups and homomorphic images of semigroups. Denote $L(\mathcal{S}) = \{ L \mid L$ is a language whose syntactic semigroup belongs to $\mathcal{S}\}$. Then $L(\mathcal{S})$ is said to be a +-variety and for $\mathcal{S}_1 \neq \mathcal{S}_2$ we have $L(\mathcal{S}_1) \neq L(\mathcal{S}_2)$. In this section we compare $L(\mathcal{S})$ and $\mathcal{L}(\mathcal{S})$ and we investigate those cases where $\mathcal{L}(\mathcal{S})$ is a +-variety. The following proposition is a basic tool for such a comparison:

Proposition 1

Let L = L(A,S,f,s) and let S(L) denote the syntactic semigroup of L. If S(L) fulfil an identity $\alpha = \beta$ then there is a factor-semigroup S' of S fulfilling $\alpha = \beta$ and generating again L.

From this we immediately obtain:

Corollary 1

If L is a regular language whose syntactic semigroup belongs to a variety $\mathcal{S}$ then L is generated by an other semigroup S' from $\mathcal{S}$. Thus $L(\mathcal{S}) \subseteq \mathcal{L}(\mathcal{S})$.

The following example shows that the inclusion L can be proper:

Example 2 /P.Goralčík/

Let Z_5 be the additive group of integers modulo 5 and let $\mathcal{S}$ be the variety generated by Z_5. Let $A = \{a\}$, $f(a) = \{1,2\}$. Then $L = L(A,Z_5,f,1) = \{a\} \cup \{a^{3+n} \mid n \geq 0\}$. Thus the complement of L w.r.t. A^+ is finite and nonempty. On the other hand we show in the last section that any language generated by a finite group is infinite or empty. Thus $A^+ - L \notin \mathcal{L}(\mathcal{S})$/and clearly $A^+ - L \notin L(\mathcal{S})$/. Since $L(\mathcal{S})$ has to be closed under complements / see [6,9] / we have that $L \in \mathcal{L}(\mathcal{S}) - L(\mathcal{S})$.

Hence we have shown that the syntactic semigroup of a language generated by a semigroup from a variety $\mathcal{S}$ need not to belong to the same variety $\mathcal{S}$. But the converse is true for the following special case:

Proposition 2

Let L be generated by a semigroup from a variety $\mathcal{S}$ and by an assignement f which assignes to every letter exactly one element of the semigroup. Then the syntactic semigroup of L belongs to $\mathcal{S}$.

To describe the relation between $L(\mathcal{S})$ and $\mathcal{L}(\mathcal{S})$ we introduce these notions : for any class of languages $\mathcal{C}$ $B(\mathcal{C})$ will stand for its boolean closure, for a variety $\mathcal{S}$ $P(\mathcal{S})$ will denote the smallest variety containing all semigroups $P(S)$ with $S \in \mathcal{S}$. Combining our results / /ii/ of section 3, Proposition 2/ with those of Straubing [2] we obtain:

Theorem 5

For every variety $\mathcal{S}$ we have that:

$$L(\mathcal{S}) \subseteq \mathcal{L}(\mathcal{S}) = L(\mathcal{S})^C \subseteq B(\mathcal{L}(\mathcal{S})) = L(P(\mathcal{S})).$$

From this theorem we derive that $L(\mathcal{S}) = \mathcal{L}(\mathcal{S})$ if $\mathcal{S} = P(\mathcal{S})$. The varieties $\mathcal{M}$ of monoids for which $\mathcal{M} = P(\mathcal{M})$ were characterized by Pin [1]. Using this characterization we obtain:

Corollary 2

If $\mathcal{S}$ is the variety of all semigroups or if it is a variety of semigroups whose subgroups belong to a commutative variety of groups then $\mathcal{L}(\mathcal{S}) = L(\mathcal{S})$.

Since the characterization of semigroup varieties closed under the operation P seems to be somewhat different from the characterization of such monoid varieties /as shown in [2]/ we can derive that $L(\mathcal{N}) = \mathcal{L}(\mathcal{N})$ where $\mathcal{N}$ stands for the variety of nilpotent semigroups because of the fact that $\mathcal{N} = P(\mathcal{N})$. /Recall that a semigroup S is nilpotent iff there is an integer n with $s_1 \cdot \ldots \cdot s_n = 0$ for every n-tuple of elements of S./

As shown in [1] there is a variety $\mathcal{S}$ with $P(P(\mathcal{S})) \neq P(\mathcal{S})$, thus there is a variety $\mathcal{S}$ such that $\mathcal{L}(\mathcal{S})$ is not a +-variety. Moreover, denoting by J the variety of all J-trivial semigroups we can state that the following holds:

<u>Theorem 6</u>

$\mathcal{L}(J)$ is not a +-variety. Precisely it is not closed under complementation.

<u>Example 3</u>

We know /Theorem 4/ that REG $= \mathcal{L}(\mathcal{F})$. If $\mathcal{A}$ is the variety of all aperiodic semigroups then by the theorem of Myhill we obtain again that REG $= \mathcal{L}(\mathcal{A})$, moreover it follows that REG $= \mathcal{L}(J_1 * D_1)$ where $J_1 * D_1$ consists of all semigroups which divide a semidirect product of finite one-definite semigroup by a finite semilattice.

<u>5 Languages generated by groups</u>

The first result to be mentioned here is the following characterization of the class of all context-free languages which do not contain the empty word /denoted CFL/:

<u>Theorem 7</u> /Chytil and Jančar [3,4] /

The class CFL is exactly the same as the class of all languages generated by free groups.

In this section we shall investigate two questions - what languages are generated by finite groups and how difficult /in the sense of time-complexity/ languages can be generated by finitely presented groups.

Theorem 8

There is no class C of groups generating precisely the class REG.

The proof of this theorem is simple, there are two cases to be distinguished. In the first case the class C contains at least one group having a g with infinite order . In this case $\mathcal{L}(C)$ contains a nonregular language /see Example 1 -/i//. In the second case C contains only those groups whose elements are all of a finite order , i.e $\forall G \in C \forall g \in G \exists i \quad g^i = 1$. In this case $\mathcal{L}(C)$ does not contain finite and nonempty languages. Indeed let L = L(A,G,f,g) and let q be an arbitrary element of f(a) for some a $\in$ A. There is a j with q^j and thus L contains with every word w the whole infinite sequence of words $a^j w$, $a^{2j} w$, ...

Corollary 3

Every language generated by a finite group is empty or infinite.

Proposition 3

Let L be an arbitrary language with a given /recursive/ time complexity. Then there is an other language generated by a finitely presentable group to which L is reducible in linear time.

The proof of this proposition is obtained similarly as the proof of the fact that the word problem for finitely presentable groups is not solvable. 8

Corollary 4

The class of all languages generated by finitely presentable groups has an nonempty intersection with every time-complexity class.

References

Our machinery from the formal languages and semigroup theory is standard, see [5,7,9] .

1 J.E. Pin. Varietés de langages et monoide des parties. Semigroup forum Vol 20 /1980/

2 H.Straubing. Recognizable sets and power sets of finite semigroups. Semigroup forum vol 18 /1979/

3 M.P. Chytil and P. Jančar Personal communications.

4 P.Jančar. Characterization of context-free languages by free groups. Master thesis, Charles University, Prague 1982.

5 G. Lallement. Semigroups and combinatorial applications. John Wiley and sons, N.Y. 1979.

6 S.Eilenberg and M.P. Schützenberger. On pseudovarieties of monoids, Adv. Math. 19 /1979/ 413-448

7 J.E. Hopcroft and J.D. Ullman. Formal languages and their relations to automata. Addison-Wesley 1969.

8 R.C. Lyndon and P.E. Schupp. Combinatorial group theory, Springer Verlag 1977.

9 S. Eilenberg. Automata, languages and machines, Vol B, Ac. Press N.Y. 1976.

10 L. Janiga and Václav Koubek. On languages generated by semigroups and groups - in preparation.

ASPECTS OF PROGRAMS WITH FINITE MODES

H. Langmaack
Institut für Informatik u. Praktische Mathematik
Christian-Albrechts-Universität Kiel
Olshausenstr. 40, D-2300 Kiel

I. Introduction

The phrase "programs with finite modes" came up with the algorithmic language ALGOL68 where the programmer is forced to fully specify all language elements in a program. If necessary he has to do so with the additional help of mode equations. If equations are not needed then we talk about programs with finite modes. Whereas ALGOL68-programs have one fixed interpretation we deal with uninterpreted ALGOL68-like programs with finite modes.

Recently there have appeared several papers [dBCM, Ol2, DJ] which investigate the existence of sound and relatively complete partial correctness proof calculi for sublanguages of full uninterpreted ALGOL68-like languages L_{ss} whose functions and procedures have simple sideeffects only. We give a comprehensive view and demonstrate how equivalence transformations of programs in the style of [Cr, dBCM, La] naturally lead to programs for which sound and relatively complete calculi already exist [Ol1]. This answers Conjecture 1 in [LO] with the proviso that we have to admit more general theories $\mathbb{T}h(I)$ with relation variables and more general expressive power. It is quite interesting that the same transformation technique leads to a proof that L_{ss} has uniformly decidable divergence problems for finite interpretations [La] such that a theorem of [Li] on recursive enumeration of valid Hoare assertions is applicable. [Ol2, DJ] introduce a new proof rule, the so called separation rule. We show that this rule is derivable in our calculus, even exchangable with our relation variable elimination rule.

II. Definitions

We start out from <u>ground modes</u> δ with a special one β for "Boolean" and one γ for "continuation". refδ with $\delta \neq \gamma$ are called reference modes for variables with contents (values) of mode δ and for parameter positions accepting such variables. valδ with $\delta \neq \gamma$ are called value modes for formal value parameters and for parameter positions accepting actual parameters of mode δ, valδ or refδ. These three mode types have mode level 0. We define inductively: If $\mu_1, \ldots, \mu_n, \mu_o$, $n \geq 1$, are modes of level $\nu_1, \ldots, \nu_n, \nu_o$ such that μ_o is no reference nor value mode then $\mu_1, \ldots, \mu_n \rightarrow \mu_o$ is a mode of level $\max\{\nu_1, \ldots, \nu_n, \nu_o\}+1$ and its result mode is μ_o. Modes of level ≥ 1 are called functional; functions never return variables nor value parameters as their results. Name modes are those different from reference or value modes. We find it convenient to require $n \geq 1$ parameters for functional modes to avoid empty parameter lists.

We assume that every mode μ has a countable set Id^{μ} of identifiers x of mode μ. These sets are pairwisely disjoint. Identifiers of reference mode refδ are called variable identifiers y, identifiers of mode välδ are value parameter identifiers v, all others are collectively called function identifiers f. We have special names for the latter ones in case of special modes: (Parameterless) procedure identifier g when its mode is (γ resp.) $\mu_1, \ldots, \mu_n \rightarrow \gamma$ and constant identifier c when it is $\delta \neq \gamma$.

Every full uninterpreted ALGOL68-like programing language L with finite modes is fixed by a so called signature Σ consisting of constants κ of ground mode $\delta \neq \gamma$ and functors φ of mode val$\delta_1, \ldots,$ val$\delta_n \rightarrow \delta_o$ with $\delta_o \neq \gamma$. Functors with result mode β are called relators. Constants and functors are thought to be programming objects given from outside whereas identifiers are deliberately introduced by the programmer.

L has some standard operators with standard interpretation, namely the equal relator = of mode valδ , val$\delta \rightarrow \beta$, Boolean constants true and false of mode β, logical functors $\neg$ of mode val$\beta \rightarrow \beta$, $\wedge$, $\vee$, $\Rightarrow$, $\Leftrightarrow$ of mode valβ, val$\beta \rightarrow \beta$, test of mode val$\beta \rightarrow \gamma$, skip and abort of mode γ abbreviating test true and test false, assignment := of mode refδ, val$\delta \rightarrow \gamma$, composition ; of mode $\gamma, \mu \rightarrow \mu$, non-deterministic choice $\square$ of mode μ, $\mu \rightarrow \mu$, conditional operator if then else fi of mode val$\beta, \mu, \mu \rightarrow \mu$, abstraction <$\lambda$, ..., . > of mode $\mu_1, \ldots, \mu_n, \mu_o \rightarrow (\mu_1, \ldots, \mu_n \rightarrow \mu_o)$, application (, ...,) of mode $(\mu_1, \ldots, \mu_n \rightarrow \mu_o), \mu_1, \ldots, \mu_n \rightarrow \mu_o$, compound block < > of mode $\mu \rightarrow \mu$ and proper block <$\overline{\text{ref}\delta_i}$, $\overline{\text{funct} \Leftarrow}$, > of mode $\overline{\text{ref}\delta_i}, \overline{\mu_j, \mu_j}, \mu_o \rightarrow \mu_o$ with (non-formal) variable and function declarations where μ_j are name modes. Bar $\overline{}$ denotes a finite, non-empty list. We let κ also vary over Boolean constants and φ over equal relator and logical functors.

Uninterpreted programs are built up from <u>expressions</u> s of name mode. When we write s^{μ} then we express that the mode of s is μ.

$$
\begin{array}{lll}
s^{\mu} ::= \kappa^{\delta} \mid \varphi^{\mu} \mid f^{\mu} \mid v^{\underline{val}\delta} \mid y^{\underline{ref}\delta} & & \text{with } \mu=\delta \\
\quad \mid \underline{test}\ s^{\beta} \mid \underline{skip}^{\gamma} \mid \underline{abort}^{\gamma} \mid y^{\underline{ref}\delta} := s^{\delta} & & \text{with } \mu=\gamma \\
\quad \mid s_1^{\gamma};\ s_2^{\mu} \mid s_1^{\mu} \, \square \, s_2^{\mu} & & \\
\quad \mid \underline{if}\ s_o^{\beta}\ \underline{then}\ s_1^{\mu}\ \underline{else}\ s_2^{\mu}\ \underline{fi} & & \\
\quad \mid \langle \lambda x_1^{\mu_1}, \ldots, x_n^{\mu_n} \circ s_o^{\mu_o} \rangle & & \text{with } \mu = \mu_1, \ldots, \mu_n \to \mu_o \\
 & & \text{and } x_i \text{ distinct} \\
\quad \mid s_o^{\mu_1, \ldots, \mu_n \to \mu}(t_1, \ldots, t_n) & & \text{where} \\
 & \text{in case } \mu_i = \underline{ref}\delta_i & t_i \text{ is } y^{\underline{ref}\delta_i} \\
 & \text{in case } \mu_i = \underline{val}\delta_i & t_i \text{ is } s_i^{\delta_i} \\
 & \text{otherwise} & t_i \text{ is } s_i^{\mu_i} \\
\quad \mid \langle s^{\mu} \rangle & & \\
\quad \mid \langle \underline{ref}\delta_i\ y_i^{\underline{ref}\delta_i},\ \underline{funct}\ f_j^{\mu_j} \Leftarrow s_j^{\mu_j},\ s_o^{\mu} \rangle & & \\
 & \text{with } y_i, f_j \text{ distinct} &
\end{array}
$$

<u>Remarks</u>:

<u>1</u>. When a variable $y^{\underline{ref}\delta}$ or a value parameter $v^{\underline{val}\delta}$ is considered as an expression s^{μ} then their modes $\underline{ref}\delta$ resp. $\underline{val}\delta$ are <u>coerced</u> to $\mu = \delta$ [vW].

<u>2</u>. An <u>actual parameter</u> t_i of an application is transmitted <u>by reference</u> if $\mu_i = \underline{ref}\delta_i$, <u>by value</u> if $\mu_i = \underline{val}\delta_i$ or <u>by name</u> otherwise. A call by reference <u>parameter position</u> of mode $\mu_i = \underline{ref}\delta_i$ accepts only variables $y^{\underline{ref}\delta_i}$ as actual parameters, other positions accept beside expressions even variables and value parameters of appropriate mode.

<u>3</u>. Every expression s has so called <u>final subexpressions</u>. In most cases s has exactly one final subexpression, namely s itself. In case $s = s_1; s_2$ the final subexpressions of s are those of s_2, in case $s = s_1 \square s_2$ or $s = \underline{if}\ s_o\ \underline{then}\ s_1\ \underline{else}\ s_2\ \underline{fi}$ those of s_1 and s_2, in case of blocks $s = \langle s_o \rangle$ or $s = \langle \ldots, s_o \rangle$ those of s_o.

An <u>uninterpreted program</u> s is an expression of mode γ without <u>free</u> function or value identifiers. Free variables serve as input-output medium.

A <u>semantics</u> $[\![s]\!]$ of programs is uniquely determined by an <u>interpretation</u> I of the signature Σ with its <u>domains</u> $\mathbf{D}^{\delta} \neq \emptyset$, $\delta \neq \gamma$. We assume that the static scope copy or rewrite rule underlies the semantics of programs as done in [O12] or [DJ] . There is also a denotational or fixed point semantics as presented in [dBCM] with domains naturally extended to discrete complete partial orderings which is an equivalent semantics [Ni]. Two programs s_1, s_2 are called schematically equivalent iff their semantics are equal, $[\![s_1]\!] = [\![s_2]\!]$, for all interpretations I.

III. Equivalence Transformations for Programs

In order to have an easier access to the behaviour of ALGOL68-like programs with finite modes we effectively transform them in several steps into ALGOL60-like programs with procedures.

A program s is in normal form iff

1. abstractions occur only as right-hand sides s" of function declarations;
2. calling expressions s" of applications $s''(t_1,\dots,t_n)$ are function identifiers f or functors φ only;
3. actual parameters s" on name positions of non-functor applications $s_o(\dots,s'',\dots)$ are constants κ, functors φ or identifiers x only.

Lemma 1. Every program s can be transformed into a schematically equivalent one $\tilde{s}$ in normal form.

Proof. We eliminate "critical" subexpresssions s" not fulfilling normal form condition and introduce appropriate function declarations funct $f \Leftarrow s''$. $\diamond$

Global parameters of a function declaration in a program s are identifiers either free in s or declared outside this declaration. A program s without sideeffects is one whose associated normal form program $\tilde{s}$ has no function declaration with global variables. Global "read only parameters" may occur in the form of global value parameters. A program s with simple sideeffects only is one whose global variables in $\tilde{s}$ are totally global, i.e. either free in $\tilde{s}$ or declared outside all function declarations.

Lemma 2. Any program with simple sideeffects only can be transformed into a schematically equivalent one without sideeffects.

Proof. We extend the parameter lists of all function declarations and applications by lists of "all global variables" occurring in the program [O12].◊

Remarks:

1. The authors of [dBCM], [DJ] and [O12] consider proof calculi for special finite mode programs with simple sideeffects only.
2. Programs in [dBCM] have arbitrary abstraction nesting and mode levels, but no function declaration nesting, no local non-formal variables, no reference parameters and no assignments in expressions s" (see proof of Lemma 1).
3. Programs in [DJ] have arbitrary abstraction nesting and mode levels, but no function declaration nesting, no $\delta \neq \gamma$ as result mode, no reference nor value parameters, no local non-formal variables, but assignments to free variables on all abstraction levels.
4. In [O12] programs with nested PASCAL-like procedures and blocks are treated, mode levels are ≤ 2, the only result mode is γ, procedures may have reference and name parameters and simple sideeffects, but no value parameters. Full aliasing is treated, a problem not occurring in [dBCM,DJ] due to language restrictions.

Simple expressions are constants κ, variables y, value parameters v or functor applications $\varphi(\ldots)$ to simple expressions. A normal form program s is called to be in simple form iff every subexpression s' on value position is a simple expression and, moreover, in a function application f(...,s',...) is an atomic simple expression. In an assignment y:=s' we more liberally allow s' to be a constant identifier c or a function application f(...).

Lemma 3. Every normal form program s can be translated into a schematically equivalent one in simple form. No resp. simple sideeffects remain so.

Proof. If a normal form program s is not in simple form then there is at least one "critical" subexpression s' which does not fulfill the conditions above. One of these four cases applies:
a. y:= s' and s' is unequal its final subexpression. Then we erase y:= and place y:= in front of every final subexpression s" in s'.
b. $\varphi(t_1,\ldots,t_n)$ and s' is a non-simple t_i. Then we write $\overline{y_i:=t_i};\varphi(y_1,\ldots$ $\ldots,y_n)$ instead and declare the new variables y_i in the smallest surrounding block (We may assume every abstraction body, every non-abstraction right-hand side of a function declaration and the whole program to be blocks).
c. $f(t_1,\ldots,t_n)$, t_{i_j} are the actual parameters on value positions and s'

is a t_{i_j}, which is not atomic simple. We write $\overline{y_{i_j} := t_{i_j}}$; $f(t'_1,\ldots,t'_n)$ instead of $f(t_1,\ldots,t_n)$ where t_{i_j} have been replaced by y_{i_j} equal t'_{i_j}. Declaration of y_{i_j} as above.

d. if s' then s_1 else s_2 fi or test s' and s' is not simple. Then we write y_1:= s'; if y_1 then s_1 else s_2 fi or y_1:= s; test y_1 instead. Declaration of y_1 as above.

The number of critical subexpressions has obviously decreased (compare [dBCM]). ◇

A simple form program s is in ALGOL60-form iff the following holds: All result modes occurring in s are ground modes and any non-abstraction right-hand side of a function declaration has ground mode. Consequently: If the right-hand side is an abstraction then its result mode is ground.

Lemma 4. Every simple form program s can be translated into a schematically equivalent one in ALGOL60-form. No resp. simple sideeffects remain so.

Proof. We apply the well-known process of decurrying ^{d} to modes, function declarations and expressions. ◇

An ALGOL60-form program s has procedures only iff modes of function identifiers are γ or $\mu_1,\ldots,\mu_n \to \gamma$.

Lemma 5. An ALGOL60-form program s can be translated into a schematically equivalent one with procedures only. No resp. simple sideeffects remain so.

Proof. We apply a process ^{p} of proceduring to modes which leaves refδ, valδ, γ unchanged with δ^p=ref$\delta \to \gamma$, $(\mu_1,\ldots,\mu_n \to \delta)^p = (\mu_1^p,\ldots,\mu_n^p,$ ref$\delta \to \gamma)$ and $(\mu_1,\ldots,\mu_n \to \gamma)^p = \mu_1^p,\ldots,\mu_n^p \to \gamma$. ^{p} is naturally extended to function declarations and expressions. Especially all assignments $y' := f'(t'_1,\ldots,t'_n)$ are replaced by $f'^p(t'^p_1,\ldots,t'^p_n, y')$. ◇

Remark:

All transformations can be done also for ALGOL68-like programs with infinite modes defined by mode equations [Cr].

IV. Partial Correctness

From now on we assume that our programs $s \in L$ have simple sideeffects only, i.e. $s \in L_{ss}$, and due to III., we may further assume that they are in ALGOL60-form with procedures only free of sideeffects. Global parameters are value parameters v or procedure identifiers g only. It is our aim to show up the existence of a sound and relatively complete (in the sense of [Co]) proof calculus for partially correct Hoare assertions {P}s{Q}. P, Q are first order logical formulas ∈LF over Σ and the semantics $[\![P]\!] =_{Df}$ {all states $S|Id \xrightarrow{ref\delta} \mathbb{D}^{\delta}$ which make P true} is uniquely determined by I. It is well defined when a logical formula is valid $\models_I P$ and a Hoare assertation is partially correct $\models_I$ {P}s{Q}, i.e. $[\![s]\!]([\![P]\!]) \subseteq [\![Q]\!]$. The set of valid logical formulas is the theory Th(I). I is called finite iff all $\mathbb{D}^{\delta}$ are finite and all cardinalities $|\mathbb{D}^{\delta}|$, elements $[\![\kappa]\!]$ and functions $[\![\varphi]\!]$ are effectively known. I is called expressive iff for all programs s and P∈LF $[\![s]\!]([\![P]\!])$ can be expressed by $[\![Q]\!]$ with Q∈LF. I is Herbrand definable iff every datum $d \in \mathbb{D}^{\delta}$ can be expressed by a term of constants and functors. I is expressive Herbrand iff it is expressive and (Herbrand definable or finite).

The essential observation in [La] is that

1. name parameters x of procedures can be treated like value parameters v_x the values of which are (finite) relations r,
2. non-formal procedure identifiers g as actual parameters can be handled like variable identifiers y_g for (finite) relations r and
3. formal procedure statements g resp. g(...) behave like non-deterministic assignment statements. So, if we allow
a. to introduce relation variables y_g and v_x [1)] in programs and
b. to form new first order logical formulas $\mathbb{P} \in \mathbb{L}F$ with relation variables and
c. if we accept expressivity with these more general formulas $\mathbb{P}$

then we have arrived by a series of effective equivalence transformations at a set $\mathbb{L}$ of programs $\tilde{s}$ for which a sound and relatively complete proof calculus for partially correct Hoare assertions exists because these programs $\tilde{s}$ have no procedures as parameters [Ol1].

What is the appropriate domain $\mathfrak{R}^{\mu}$ for values r of y_g and v_x if the mode of g or x is a name mode μ equal γ resp. $\mu_1, \ldots, \mu_n \rightarrow \gamma$? W.r.o.g. we may assume that $\mu_1, \ldots, \mu_n$ are ordered:

$$\mu = \underline{ref}\delta_1, \ldots, \underline{ref}\delta_{\tilde{n}}, \underline{val}\delta_{\tilde{n}+1}, \ldots, \underline{val}\delta_{\tilde{\tilde{n}}}, \mu_{\tilde{\tilde{n}}+1}, \ldots, \mu_n \rightarrow \gamma.$$

Since $\tilde{n}$ may be >1 we are necessarily confronted with the sharing

1) Value parameters v behave just like specially used reference parameters y. Treatment of formal and actual value parameters like reference ones requires no sharing between reference and value positions in procedure statements (applications) what can always be assumed w.r.o.g..

or <u>aliasing problem</u>. Consider the interval $[\tilde n]=\{1,\dots,\tilde n\}\subseteq \mathbb{N}$. Let $\mathfrak{T}_{\tilde n}$ be the finite set of <u>sharing classes</u> (congruences) $T\subseteq[\tilde n]^2$ which <u>agree</u> with $\delta_1,\dots,\delta_{\tilde n}$, i.e. if iTi' then $\delta_i=\delta_{i'}$. $\mathfrak{T}_{\tilde n}\subseteq \wp[\tilde n]^2$. In case $\tilde n$ is 0 $[0]$ is $\emptyset$, $[0]^2$ is $\emptyset$, $\wp[0]^2$ is $\{\emptyset\}$ and $\mathfrak{T}_0$ is $\{\emptyset\}$.

Let μ have mode level 0. Then $\mu=\gamma$ and $\mathcal{R}^\mu$ is defined by $\wp\mathfrak{T}_0=\{\emptyset,\{\emptyset\}\}$. $\emptyset$ represents non-termination, $\{\emptyset\}$ termination of a parameterless procedure call. For mode level ≥ 1 we define

$$\mathcal{R}^\mu\subseteq\wp(\mathfrak{T}_{\tilde n}\times(D^{\delta_1}\times\dots\times D^{\delta_{\tilde n}})^2\times D^{\delta_{\tilde n+1}}\times\dots\times D^{\delta_{\tilde{\tilde n}}}\times\mathcal{R}^{\mu_{\tilde{\tilde n}+1}}\times\dots\times\mathcal{R}^{\mu_n})$$

where $\mathcal{R}^\mu$ consists of exactly all those (finite) relations r of $1+\tilde n+n$-tuples $(T,d_1,\dots,d_{\tilde n},d'_1,\dots,d'_{\tilde n},d_{\tilde n+1},\dots,d_{\tilde{\tilde n}},r_{\tilde{\tilde n}+1},\dots,r_n)$ such that iTi' implies $d_i=d_{i'}$ and $d'_i=d'_{i'}$. We say relation r <u>is of mode</u> μ and use the identifiers g in Id^μ both as procedure identifiers of mode μ and as relation variable identifiers of mode <u>ref</u>μ as well as value parameters of mode <u>val</u>μ.

How does the transformation s to $\tilde s$ in [La] look? All procedure statements

$$g(\dots,\tilde g,\dots)$$

with a non-formal actual procedure identifier $\tilde g$ of mode μ are successively replaced by

$<$<u>ref</u>$\mu\ \tilde{\tilde g},\ \tilde{\tilde g}:=\emptyset;$

$W^*_{\tilde g}$:

<u>while</u>*

$\quad\square_{T\in\mathfrak{T}_{\tilde n}}$

$\quad\quad<\overline{\underline{\text{ref}}\,\delta_i y_i},\ \overline{\underline{\text{ref}}\,\delta_i y'_i},\ \overline{\underline{\text{ref}}\,\delta''_j y''_j},\ \overline{\underline{\text{ref}}\,\mu_1 g_1},$

$\quad\quad\overline{y_i}:=?;\ \overline{y'_i}:=\overline{y_i};\ \overline{y''_j}:=?;\ \overline{g_1}:=?;$

$\quad\quad\tilde g(\overline{y'_i},\ \overline{y''_j},\ \overline{g_1});$

$\quad\quad\tilde{\tilde g}:=\tilde{\tilde g}\cup\{(T,\overline{y_i},\ \overline{y'_i},\ \overline{y''_j},\ \overline{g_1})\}>$

<u>end</u>*;

$g(\dots,\tilde{\tilde g},\dots)>$.

$\overline{y_i}$, $\overline{y'_i}$ denote variable lists of length $\tilde n$ which <u>determine</u> sharing class T (new standard constants), i.e. $i=i'$ iff $y_i=y_{i'}$ iff $y'_i=y'_{i'}$ [1]. $\overline{y''_j}, \overline{g_1}$ denote lists of length $\tilde{\tilde n}-\tilde n$ and $n-\tilde{\tilde n}$. $\emptyset$ is a new standard constant meaning

---

1) We allow variable declarations $\overline{\underline{\text{ref}}\,\delta_i y_i}$, $\overline{\underline{\text{ref}}\,\delta_i y'_i}$, with shared variables for simplicity.

the empty relation $\in \mathfrak{R}^{\mu}$, := ? is random assignment [AP], {(...)} is a new standard operator to form one element relations, $\cup$ forms the union of relations and <u>while</u>* is the *-operator known from dynamic logic [Ha].

The copy rule applied to $g(\ldots,\tilde{\tilde{g}},\ldots)$ will transform a formal procedure statement x(...) resp. x in the body of g to $\tilde{\tilde{g}}(\overline{u_i},\overline{u_j''},\overline{h_1})$ resp. $\tilde{\tilde{g}}$ with non-formal actual parameters $\overline{u_i}$, $\overline{u_j''}$, $\overline{h_1}$ which is executed like a non-deterministic assignment statement. It looks for a tuple $(T,\overline{d_i},\overline{d_i'},\overline{d_j''},\overline{r_1}) \in$ the content r of $\tilde{\tilde{g}}$ such that $\overline{u_i}$ determines T and the values of $\overline{u_i},\overline{u_j''},\overline{h_1}$ are $\overline{d_i},\overline{d_j''},\overline{r_1}$. If there is one then $\overline{d_i'}$ is assigned to $\overline{u_i}$, otherwise the program aborts. Without actual parameters the determined sharing class T is $\emptyset$ and the possible contents r of $\tilde{\tilde{g}}$ are $\emptyset$ or $\{\emptyset\}$. $\tilde{\tilde{g}}$ *skips* if $r=\{\emptyset\}$ and aborts otherwise. So x acts like a value parameter of mode <u>val</u>μ.

<u>Lemma 6</u>. An ALGOL60-form program s with procedures and no sideeffects and its translated program $\tilde{s}$ without procedures as parameters, but with (even finite) relation variables, are schematically equivalent. $\tilde{s}$ has no sideeffects also and no procedures as actual parameters (no call by name).

<u>Proof</u>. [La] deals only with programs s without value parameters, but global "read only" parameters of procedures in form of global value parameters are harmless (as well as global non-formal or formal procedure identifiers are). ◊

A program s is called <u>I-divergent</u> iff $\models_I$ {<u>true</u>}s{<u>false</u>}. The following theorem answers a question in [dBCM]:

<u>Theorem</u> 1. L_{ss} has uniformly decidable divergence problems for finite interpretations I.

<u>Proof</u>. If $s \in L_{ss}$ then the translated I-interpreted $\tilde{s} \in \mathbb{L}$ can be considered to govern a <u>stack system</u> [GGH] or even a <u>regular canonical system</u> [Bü] due to implementation techniques by modified run time systems in [La]. ◊

<u>Corollary</u> 1. The emptiness problems for level-n OI-tree or OI-string languages are decidable.

<u>Proof</u>. <u>Level n-grammars</u> or <u>n-rational program schemes</u> are essentially L_{ss}-programs without assignments [Da]. ◊

Let Σ be a finite signature and L_{ss}^{det} be that sublanguage of L_{ss} without choice operator ▯. L_{ss}^{det} is <u>acceptable with recursion</u> [Li, CGH]. Due to [CGH] we may conclude from Theorem 1

<u>Theorem</u> 2. The set of valid Hoare assertions $\models_I$ {P}s{Q}, $s \in L_{ss}^{det}$, P,

Q∈LF, is recursively enumerable relative to Th(I) for all expressive Herbrand interpretations I.

As the transformed language 𝕃 has no procedures as parameters we have

<u>Theorem</u> 3: $L_{ss} \cup \mathbb{L}$ has a <u>sound and relatively complete</u> proof calculus $\mathfrak{C}$, i.e.

$$\mathbb{T}h(I) \vdash_{\mathfrak{C}} \{\mathbb{P}\}s\{\mathbb{Q}\} \text{ iff } \models_{I} \{\mathbb{P}\}s\{\mathbb{Q}\}$$

for interpretations I expressive w.r.t. formulas $\mathbb{P},\mathbb{Q} \in \mathbb{L}F$. $\mathbb{T}h(I)$ is $\{\mathbb{P}\in\mathbb{L}F \mid \models_I \mathbb{P}\}$.

<u>Proof</u>. We construct rules due to the schematical equivalence transformations above and modify the proof calculus in [Ol1] from single mode variables to many modes <u>ref</u>δ and <u>ref</u>μ.(, , , ,)∈ is a new standard operator of mode $\underline{val}\mathfrak{q}_{\tilde{n}}$, $\underline{val\delta_i}$, $\underline{val\delta_i}$, $\underline{val\delta''_j}$, $\underline{val\mu_1}$, $\underline{val}\mu \to \beta$. We mention some modified proof rules:

<u>while</u>*-rule

$$\frac{\{\mathbb{P}\}E|s\{\mathbb{Q}\}}{\{\mathbb{P}\}E|\underline{while}^{*}s\ \underline{end}^{*}\{\mathbb{Q}\}} .$$

Random assignment axiom

$$\{\mathbb{P}\}E|\overline{y_i} := ?\ \{\exists \overline{z_i}\,(\mathbb{P}[\overline{z_i}/\overline{y_i}])\} .$$

Non-deterministic assignment axiom

$$\{\mathbb{P}\}E|\tilde{\mathfrak{g}}(\overline{u_i},\overline{u''_j},\overline{h_1})\{\exists \overline{z_i}\,(\mathbb{P}[\overline{z_i}/\overline{u_i}] \wedge (T,\overline{z_i},\overline{u_i},\overline{u''_j},\overline{h_1}) \in \tilde{\mathfrak{g}})\}$$

where $\overline{u_i}$ and $\overline{z_i}$ determine sharing class $T\in\mathfrak{q}_{\tilde{n}}$.

Relation variable elimination-rule due to Lemma 6

$$\frac{\{\mathbb{P}\}E|<\underline{ref}\mu\tilde{\mathfrak{g}},\ \tilde{\mathfrak{g}}:=\emptyset;\ \overset{*}{W\tilde{\mathfrak{g}}};\ g(\ldots,\tilde{\mathfrak{g}},\ldots)>\{\mathbb{Q}\}}{\{\mathbb{P}\}E|g(\ldots,\tilde{g},\ \ldots)\{\mathbb{Q}\}} .$$

Invariance rule:

$$\frac{\{\mathbb{P}\}E|s\{\mathbb{Q}\}}{\{\mathbb{P}\wedge\mathbb{R}\}E|s\{\mathbb{Q}\wedge\mathbb{R}\}}$$

without assignments of E|s to free variables of ℝ. ◊

<u>Corollary</u> 2. The set of valid Hoare assertions $\models_I\{P\}s\{Q\}$, $s\in L_{ss}$, P, Q∈LF, is recursively enumerable relative to 𝕋h(I) for all expressive interpretations I, expressive w.r.t. 𝕃F.

<u>Problems</u>. It is still open whether determinism in Theorem 2 can be

dropped and $\mathbb{T}h(I)$, $\mathbb{L}F$ in Theorem 3 and Corollary 2 can be replaced by Th(I), LF (compare Conjecture 1 in [LO]).

V. Separation Rule

The authors of [O12, DJ] present proof calculi $\mathcal{H}'$ similar to our $\mathcal{H}$ for which, restricted to their languages, Theorem 3 holds. $\mathcal{H}'$ has a so called separation rule instead of relation variable elimination:

$$\frac{[\{\overline{y_i}=\overline{y_i'}\}E|\tilde{g}(\overline{y_i'},\overline{y_j''},\overline{g_1})\{\mathbb{G}_T\}]_{T\in\mathfrak{T}_{\tilde{n}}},\quad \{\mathbb{F}\}E|\,g(\ldots,\tilde{\tilde{g}},\ldots)\{\mathbb{Q}\}}{\{\mathbb{P}\}E|\,g(\ldots,\tilde{g},\ldots)\{\mathbb{Q}\}}$$

where

- $\mathbb{F}$ abbreviates $\mathbb{P}\wedge\bigwedge_{T\in\mathfrak{T}_{\tilde{n}}}(\forall\overline{y_i},\overline{y_i'},\overline{y_j''},\overline{g_1})((T,\overline{y_i},\overline{y_i'},\overline{y_j''},\overline{g_1})\in\tilde{\tilde{g}}\Rightarrow\mathbb{G}_T)$,
- all variables $\overline{y_i},\overline{y_i'},\overline{y_j''},\overline{g_1},\tilde{\tilde{g}}$ are "distinct" such that $\overline{y_i}$ and $\overline{y_i'}$ determine T,
- these variables do not occur in the conclusion,
- all free variables in $\mathbb{G}_T$ are among those free in $\overline{y_i}$, $E|\tilde{g}(\overline{y_i'},\overline{y_j''},\overline{g_1})$.

<u>Lemma 7</u>. The separation rule is derivable in $\mathcal{H}$.

<u>Proof</u>. There is a formal proof tree for
$\mathbb{T}h(I)\cup\{$premisses of separation rule$\}$

$$\vdash_{\mathcal{H}} \{\mathbb{P}\}E|\langle \underline{\text{ref}}\,\mu\tilde{\tilde{g}},\ \tilde{\tilde{g}}:=\emptyset;\ \overset{*}{W\tilde{g}};\ g(\ldots,\tilde{\tilde{g}},\ldots)\{\mathbb{Q}\}$$

and relation variable elimination yields

$\vdash_{\mathcal{H}}$ conclusion of separation rule.

The proof tree in intermittent assertions notation looks like

$\{\mathbb{P}\}$

$E|\langle \underline{ref}\,\mu\tilde{\tilde{g}},\ \tilde{\tilde{g}}:=\emptyset;$

$\{\mathbb{P}\wedge\tilde{\tilde{g}}=\emptyset\}$

$\mathbb{T}h(I)\ni\ \Downarrow$

$\{\mathbb{F}\}$

$\underline{while}^*$

$\Box$

$T\in\mathfrak{T}_{\tilde{n}}$

$\langle\overline{\underline{ref}\,\delta_i y_i},\ \overline{\underline{ref}\,\delta_i y_i'},\ \overline{\underline{ref}\,\delta_j'' y_j''},\ \overline{\underline{ref}\,\mu_1 g_1},$

$\overline{y_i}:=?;\ \overline{y_i'}:=\overline{y_i};\ \overline{y_j''}:=?;\ \overline{g_1}:=?;$

$\{\mathbb{F}\wedge\overline{y_i}=\overline{y_i}\}$

invar. rule
appl. upon premis $\tilde{g}(\overline{y_i'},\overline{y_j''},\overline{g_1});$

$\{\mathbb{F}\wedge\mathbb{G}_T\}$

$\tilde{\tilde{g}}:=\tilde{\tilde{g}}\cup\{(T,\overline{y_i},\overline{y_i'},\overline{y_j''},\overline{g_1})\}\rangle$

$\{\exists\tilde{\tilde{\tilde{g}}}(\mathbb{F}[\tilde{\tilde{\tilde{g}}}/\tilde{\tilde{g}}]\wedge\mathbb{G}_T\wedge\tilde{\tilde{g}}=\tilde{\tilde{\tilde{g}}}\cup\{(T,\overline{y_i},\overline{y_i'},\overline{y_j''},\overline{g_1})\})\}$

$\mathbb{T}h(I)\ni\ \Downarrow$

$\{\mathbb{F}\}$

$\underline{end}^*;$

premis $g(\ldots,\tilde{\tilde{g}},\ldots)\rangle$

$\{\mathbb{Q}\}$ ◊

Lemma 8. For every partially correct Hoare assertion

$\{\mathbb{P}\}E|g(\ldots,\tilde{g},\ldots)\{\mathbb{Q}\}$

a formal proof in $\hat{\mathfrak{R}}$ from

$\mathbb{T}h(I)\cup$ {premisses of separation rule}

can be found such that all premisses are partially correct provided I is expressive w.r.t. $\mathbb{LF}$ and $\mathbb{L}$.

Proof. For $\mathbb{G}_T$ we take formulas which are strongest postconditions - they exist due to expressivity - of $\overline{y_i}=\overline{y_i'}$ and $E|\tilde{g}(\overline{y_i'},\overline{y_j''},\overline{g_1})$ such that all boundary conditions of the separation rule hold. The strongest postcondition of $\mathbb{P}\wedge\tilde{\tilde{g}}=\emptyset$ and $W_{\tilde{g}}^{*}$ is a formula $\tilde{\mathbb{F}}\in\mathbb{L}F$ meaning

"$\mathbb{F}\wedge(\tilde{\tilde{g}}$ is finite)".

$\mathbb{F}$ is an invariant of $W_{\tilde{g}}^{*}$. So a formal proof similar to that above can be constructed where $\mathbb{F}$ is replaced by $\tilde{\mathbb{F}}$ such that all premisses - with $\mathbb{F}$ replaced by $\tilde{\mathbb{F}}$ - are partially correct. But $\tilde{\mathbb{F}}\Rightarrow\mathbb{F}$ is $\in\mathbb{T}h(I)$ and $\{\mathbb{F}\}\, E|g(\ldots,\tilde{\tilde{g}},\ldots)\{\mathbb{Q}\}$ is also partially correct since any terminating computation employs only finitely many tuples $\in\tilde{\tilde{g}}$. ◊

Remark. Our approach allows to work with finite relations $r\in\mathfrak{R}^{\mu}$ rendering an even shorter proof.

Theorem 4. Separation and relation variable elimination rule are exchangeable.

The final premis of the separation rule presented in [O12] is slightly more general than ours:

$$(*)\quad \{\mathbb{P}_1\}\, E|g(\ldots,\tilde{\tilde{g}},\ldots)\, \{\mathbb{Q}_1\}$$

where $\tilde{\tilde{g}}$ occurs freely in $\mathbb{P}_1$, $\mathbb{Q}_1$ only in the form $(T,\overline{u_i},\overline{u_i'},\overline{u_j''},\overline{h_1})\in\tilde{\tilde{g}}$ and $\mathbb{P}$, $\mathbb{Q}$ result from $\mathbb{P}_1$ and $\mathbb{Q}_1$ by substituting such expressions by $\mathbb{G}_T[\overline{u_i},\overline{u_i'},\overline{u_j''},\overline{h_1}/\overline{y_i},\overline{y_i'},\overline{y_j''},\overline{g_1}]$. Since partial correctness of (*) implies that for

$$\{\mathbb{F}\}E|g(\ldots,\tilde{\tilde{g}},\ldots)\{\mathbb{Q}\}$$

for all approximating semantics $[\![\ ]\!]_j'$, $j\in N_o$, the [O12] separation rule is also sound, even exchangeable provided we do not restrict to finite relation models.

We see the schematical equivalence transformation in Lemma 6 reveals a very natural access to $\mathcal{H}$ and $\mathcal{H}'$ and their sound- and relative completeness.

Acknowledgements: I am grateful for several discussions with C. Crasemann, Dr. W. Damm, M. Krause and Dr. E.R. Olderog.

References

[AP] K.R. Apt, G.D. Plotkin: A Cook's Tour of Countable Nondeterminism. In: S. Even, O. Kariv: Autom. Lang. Progr., 8th Coll., Acre, July 1981. Springer LNCS 115, 479-494 (1981)

[dBCM] J.W. de Bakker, J.W. Klop, J.J.Ch. Meyer: Correctness of Programs with Function Procedures. In: D. Kozen (ed.): Logics of Programs. Springer LNCS 131, 94-112 (1982)

[Bü] J.R. Büchi: Regular Canonical Systems. Arch. math. Logik Grundlagenforsch. 6, 91-111 (1964)

[CGH] E.M. Clarke, S.M. German, J.Y. Halpern: Effective Axiomatizations of Hoare Logics. Manuscript (1981); will appear in JACM

[Co] S.A. Cook: Soundness and Completeness of an Axiomatic System for Program Verification. SIAM J. Comput. 7, 70-90 (1978)

[Da] W. Damm: The IO- and OI-hierarchies. TCS 20, 95-207 (1982)

[DJ] W. Damm, B. Josko: A Sound and Relatively* Complete Hoare-Logic for a Language with Higher Type Procedures. Schriften Informatik Angew. Math. 77 (1982)

[GGH] S. Ginsburg, S.A. Greibach, M.A. Harrison: Stack Automata and Compiling. JACM 14, 172-201 (1967)

[Ha] D. Harel: First-Order Dynamic Logic. Springer LNCS 68 (1979)

[Cr] Ch. Crasemann: Darstellung und Transformation ALGOL-artiger Programmiersprachen mit endlichen Prozedurarten. Diplomarbeit, Kiel (1981)

[La] H. Langmaack: On Termination Problems for Finitely Interpreted ALGOL-like Programs. Acta Informatica 18, 79-108 (1982)

[LO] H. Langmaack, E.R. Olderog: Present-day Hoare-like Systems for Programming Languages with Procedures: Power, Limits and most likely Extensions. In: J.W. de Bakker, J. van Leeuwen: Proceed. Autom. Lang. Progr., 7th Coll., Noordwijkerhout, July 1980. Springer LNCS 85, 363-373 (1980)

[Li] R.J. Lipton: A Necessary and Sufficient Condition for the Existence of Hoare Logics. In: 18th Symp. Found. Computer Sci., Ed. IEEE Comp. Soc., IEEE 77 CH 1278-1C, 1-6 (1977)

[Ni] M. Nivat: Non-Deterministic Programs: An Algebraic overview. In: S.H. Lavington (ed.): Inform. Proc. 80. North-Holland 17-28 (1980)

[Ol1] E.R. Olderog: Sound and Complete Hoare-like Calculi Based on Copy Rules. Acta Informatica 16, 161-197 (1981)

[Ol2] E.R. Olderog: Correctness of Programs with PASCAL-like Procedures without global Variables. Inst. Inform. Prakt. Math. Bericht 8110 (1981); will appear in TCS

[vW] A. van Wijngaarden et al. (ed.): Revised Report on the Algorithmic Language ALGOL68. Acta Informatica 5, 1-236 (1975)

Estimating a Probability Using Finite Memory *

Extended Abstract

Frank Thomson Leighton and Ronald L. Rivest
Mathematics Department and Laboratory for Computer Science
Massachusetts Institute of Technology, Cambridge, Mass. 02139

Abstract: Let $\{X_i\}_{i=1}^{\infty}$ be a sequence of independent Bernoulli random variables with probability p that $X_i = 1$ and probability $q = 1 - p$ that $X_i = 0$ for all $i \geq 1$. We consider time-invariant finite-memory (i.e., finite-state) estimation procedures for the parameter p which take $X_1, \ldots$ as an input sequence. In particular, we describe an n-state deterministic estimation procedure that can estimate p with mean-square error $O(\frac{\log n}{n})$ and an n-state probabilistic estimation procedure that can estimate p with mean-square error $O(\frac{1}{n})$. We prove that the $O(\frac{1}{n})$ bound is optimal to within a constant factor. In addition, we show that linear estimation procedures are just as powerful (up to the measure of mean-square error) as arbitrary estimation procedures. The proofs are based on the Markov Chain Tree Theorem.

1. Introduction

Let $\{X_i\}_{i=1}^{\infty}$ be a sequence of independent Bernoulli random variables with probability p that $X_i = 1$ and probability $q = 1 - p$ that $X_i = 0$ for all $i \geq 1$. Estimating the value of p is a classical problem in statistics. In general, an *estimation procedure* for p consists of a sequence of estimates $\{e_t\}_{t=1}^{\infty}$ where each e_t is a function of $\{X_i\}_{i=1}^{t}$. When the form of the estimation procedure is unrestricted, it is well-known that p is best estimated by

$$e_t = \frac{1}{t} \sum_{i=1}^{t} X_i .$$

As an example, consider the problem of estimating the probability p that a coin of unknown bias will come up "heads". The optimal estimation procedure will, on the tth trial, flip the coin to determine X_t ($X_t = 1$ for "heads" and $X_t = 0$ for "tails") and then estimate the proportion of heads observed in the first t trials.

The quality of an estimation procedure may be measured by its mean-square error $\sigma^2(p)$. The *mean-square error* of an estimation procedure is defined as

$$\sigma^2(p) = \lim_{t \to \infty} \frac{1}{t} \sum_{i=1}^{t} \sigma_t^2(p),$$

where

$$\sigma_t^2(p) = E((e_t - p)^2)$$

denotes the expected square error of the tth estimate. For example, it is well-known that $\sigma_t^2(p) = \frac{pq}{t}$ and $\sigma^2(p) = 0$ when $e_t = \frac{1}{t} \sum_{i=1}^{t} X_i$.

---

* This research was supported by the Bantrell Foundation and by NSF grant MCS-8006938.

In this paper, we consider time-invariant estimation procedures which are restricted to use a finite amount of memory. A *time-invariant finite-memory estimation procedure* consists of a finite number of states $S = \{1, \ldots, n\}$, a start state $S_0 \in \{1, \ldots, n\}$, and a transition function τ which computes the state S_t at step t from the state S_{t-1} at step $t-1$ and the input X_t according to

$$S_t = \tau(S_{t-1}, X_t).$$

In addition, each state i is associated with an estimate η_i of p. The estimate after the tth transition is then given by $e_t = \eta_{S_t}$. For simplicity, we will call a finite-state estimation procedure an "FSE".

As an example, consider the FSE shown in Figure 1. This FSE has $n = \frac{(s+1)(s+2)}{2}$ states and simulates two counters: one for the number of inputs seen, and one for the number of inputs seen that are ones. Because of the finite-state restriction, the counters can count up to $s = \Theta(\sqrt{n})$ but not beyond. Hence, all inputs after the sth input are ignored. On the tth step, the FSE estimates the proportion of ones seen in the first $\min(s,t)$ inputs. This is

$$e_t = \frac{1}{\min(s,t)} \sum_{i=1}^{\min(s,t)} X_i .$$

Hence the mean-square error of the FSE is $\sigma^2(p) = \frac{pq}{s} = O(\frac{1}{\sqrt{n}})$.

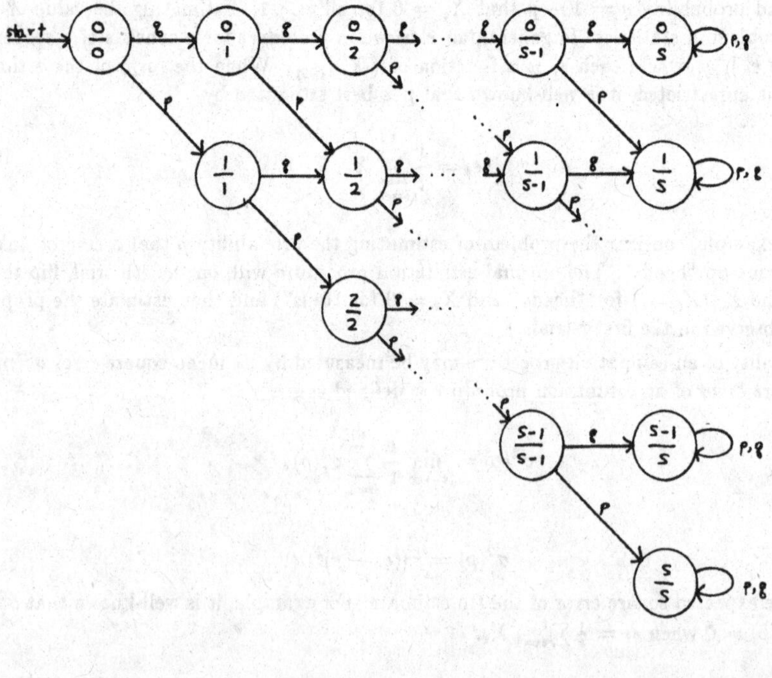

Figure 1: *An* $\frac{(s+1)(s+2)}{2}$*-state deterministic FSE with mean-square error* $\sigma^2(p) = \frac{pq}{s}$. *States are represented by circles. Arrows labeled with q denote transitions on input zero. Arrows labeled with p denote transitions on input one. Estimates are given as fractions and represent the proportion of inputs seen that are ones.*

In [23], Samaniego considered probabilistic FSEs and constructed the probabilistic FSE shown in Figure 2. *Probabilistic* FSEs are similar to nonprobabilistic (or *deterministic*) FSEs except that a probabilistic FSE allows probabilistic transitions between states. In particular, the transition function τ of a probabilistic FSE consists of probabilities τ_{ijk} that the FSE will make a transition from state i to state j on input k. For example, $\tau_{320} = \frac{2}{n-1}$ in Figure 2. So that τ is well-defined, we require that $\sum_{j=1}^{n} \tau_{ijk} = 1$ for all i and k.

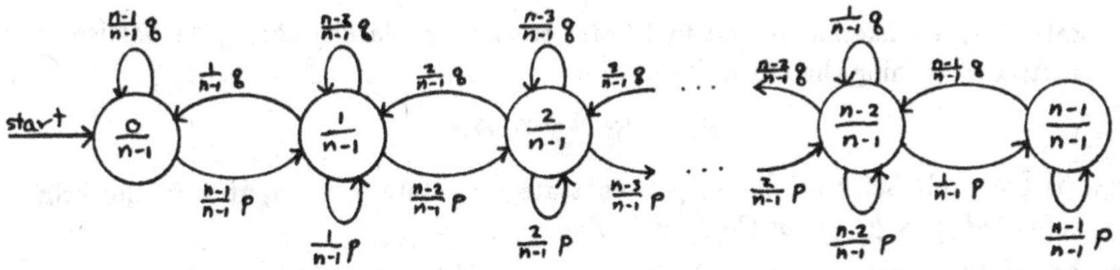

Figure 2: *A probabilistic n-state FSE with mean-square error* $\sigma^2(p) = \frac{pq}{n-1}$. *States are represented by circles in increasing order from left to right (e.g., state 1 is denoted by the leftmost circle and state n is denoted by the rightmost circle). State i estimates* $\frac{i-1}{n-1}$ *for* $1 \leq i \leq n$. *The estimates are shown as fractions within the circles. Arrows labeled with fractions of q denote probabilistic transitions on input zero. Arrows labeled with fractions of p denote probabilistic transitions on input one. For example, the probability of changing from state 2 to state 3 on input 1 is* $\frac{n-2}{n-1}$.

In this paper, we show that the mean-square error of the FSE shown in Figure 2 is $\sigma^2(p) = \frac{pq}{n-1} = O(\frac{1}{n})$, and that this is the best possible (up to a constant factor) for an n-state FSE. In particular, we will show that for any n-state FSE (probabilistic or deterministic), there is some value of p for which $\sigma^2(p) = \Omega(\frac{1}{n})$. Previously, the best lower bound known for $\sigma^2(p)$ was $\Omega(\frac{1}{n^2})$. The weaker bound is due to the "quantization problem", which provides a fundemental limitation on the achievable performance of any FSE. Since the set of estimates of an n-state FSE has size n, there is always a value of p (in fact, there are many such values) for which the difference between p and the closest estimate is at least $\frac{1}{2n}$. This means that the mean-square error for some p must be at least $\Omega(\frac{1}{n^2})$. Our result (which is based on the Markov Chain Tree Theorem [14]) proves that this bound is not achievable, thus showing that the quantization problem is not the most serious consequence of the finite-memory restriction.

It is encouraging that the nearly optimal FSE in Figure 2 has such a simple structure. This is not a coincidence. In fact, we will show that for every probabilistic FSE with mean-square error $\sigma^2(p)$, there is a linear probabilistic FSE with the same number of states and with a mean-square error that is bounded above by $\sigma^2(p)$ for all p. (An FSE is said to be *linear* if the states of the FSE can be linearly ordered so that transitions are made only between consecutive states in the ordering. Linear FSEs are the easiest FSEs to implement in practice since the state information can be stored in a counter and the transitions can be effected by a single increment or decrement of the counter.)

We also study deterministic FSEs in the paper. Although we do not know how to achieve the $\Theta(\frac{1}{n})$ lower bound for deterministic FSEs, we can come close. In fact, we will construct an n-state deterministic FSE that has mean-square error $O(\frac{\log n}{n})$. The construction uses the input to deterministically simulate the probabilistic transitions of the FSE shown in Figure 2.

The remainder of the paper is divided into five sections. In Section 2, we present some background material on Markov chains (including the Markov Chain Tree Theorem) and prove that the FSE shown in Figure 2 has mean-square error $O(\frac{1}{n})$. In Section 3, we construct an n-state deterministic FSE with mean-square error $O(\frac{\log n}{n})$. The $\Omega(\frac{1}{n})$ lower bound for n-state FSEs is proved in Section 4. In Section 5, we demonstrate the universality of linear FSEs. We conclude in Section 6 with references and open questions.

2. Theory of Markov Chains

An n-state FSE act like an n-state first-order stationary Markov chain. In particular, the transition matrix P defining the chain has entries

$$p_{ij} = \tau_{ij1}p + \tau_{ij0}q$$

where τ_{ijk} is the probability of changing from state i to state j on input k in the FSE. For example, $p_{33} = \frac{2}{n-1}p + \frac{n-3}{n-1}q$ for the FSE in Figure 2.

From the definition, we know that the mean-square error of an FSE depends on the limiting probability that the FSE is in state j given that it started in state i. (This probability is based on p and the transition probabilities τ_{ijk}.) The long-run transition matrix for the corresponding Markov chain is given by

$$\overline{P} = \lim_{t \to \infty} \frac{1}{t}(I + P + P^2 + \cdots + P^{t-1}).$$

This limit exists because P is stochastic (see Theorem 2 of [4]). The ijth entry of $\overline{P}$ is simply the long-run average probability $\overline{p}_{ij}$ that the chain will be in state j given that it started in state i.

In the case that the Markov chain defined by P is ergodic, every row of $\overline{P}$ is equal to the same probability vector $\pi = (\pi_1 \cdots \pi_n)$ which is the stationary probability vector for the chain. In the general case, the rows of $\overline{P}$ may vary and we will use π to denote the S_0-th row of $\overline{P}$. Since S_0 is the start state of the FSE, π_i is the long-run average probability that the FSE will be in state i. Using the new notation, the mean-square error of an FSE can be expressed as

$$\sigma^2(p) = \sum_{i=1}^{n} \pi_i(\eta_i - p)^2.$$

Several methods are known for calculating long-run transition probabilities. For our purposes, the method developed by Leighton and Rivest in [14] is the most useful. This method is based on sums of weighted arborescences in the underlying graph of the chain. We review the method in what follows.

Let $V = \{1, \ldots, n\}$ be the nodes of a directed graph G, with edge set $E = \{(i,j) \mid p_{ij} \neq 0\}$. This is the usual directed graph associated with a Markov chain. (Note that G may contain self-loops.) Define the *weight* of edge (i,j) to be p_{ij}. An edge set $A \subseteq E$ is an *arborescence* if A contains at most one edge out of every node, has no cycles, and has maximum possible cardinality. The *weight* of an arborescence is the product of the weights of the edges it contains. A node which has outdegree zero in A is called a *root* of the arborescence.

Clearly every arborescence contains the same number of edges. In fact, if G contains exactly k minimal closed subsets of nodes, then every arborescence has $|V| - k$ edges and contains one root in each minimal closed subset. (A subset of nodes is said to be *closed* if no edges are directed out of the subset.) In particular, if G is strongly connected (i.e., the Markov chain is irreducible), then every arborescence is a set of $|V| - 1$ edges that form a directed spanning tree with all edges flowing towards a single node (the root of the tree).

Let $\mathcal{A}(V)$ denote the set of arborescences of G, $\mathcal{A}_j(V)$ denote the set of arborescences having root j, and $\mathcal{A}_{ij}(V)$ denote the set of arborescences having root j and a directed path from i to j. (In the special case $i = j$, we define $\mathcal{A}_{jj}(V)$ to be $\mathcal{A}_j(V)$.) In addition, let $\|\mathcal{A}(V)\|$, $\|\mathcal{A}_j(V)\|$ and $\|\mathcal{A}_{ij}(V)\|$ denote the sums of the weights of the arborescences in $\mathcal{A}(V)$, $\mathcal{A}_j(V)$ and $\mathcal{A}_{ij}(V)$, respectively.

Leighton and Rivest proved the following in [14].

The Markov Chain Tree Theorem [14]: *Let the stochastic $n \times n$ matrix P define a finite Markov chain with long-run transition matrix $\overline{P}$. Then*

$$\overline{p}_{ij} = \frac{\|\mathcal{A}_{ij}(V)\|}{\|\mathcal{A}(V)\|}.$$

Corollary: *If the underlying graph is strongly connected, then*

$$\overline{p}_{ij} = \frac{\|\mathcal{A}_j(V)\|}{\|\mathcal{A}(V)\|}.$$

As an example, consider once again the probabilistic FSE displayed in Figure 2. Since the underlying graph is strongly connected, the corollary means that

$$\pi_i = \frac{\|\mathcal{A}_i(V)\|}{\|\mathcal{A}(V)\|}.$$

In addition, each $\mathcal{A}_i(V)$ consists of a single tree with weight

$$\frac{n-1}{n-1}p \cdot \frac{n-2}{n-1}p \cdots \frac{n-(i-1)}{n-1}p \cdot \frac{i}{n-1}q \cdot \frac{i+1}{n-1}q \cdots \frac{n-1}{n-1}q$$

and thus

$$\|\mathcal{A}_i(V)\| = \binom{n-1}{i-1}\frac{(n-1)!}{(n-1)^{n-1}}p^{i-1}q^{n-i}.$$

Summing over i, we find that

$$\begin{aligned}\|\mathcal{A}(V)\| &= \sum_{i=1}^{n}\binom{n-1}{i-1}\frac{(n-1)!}{(n-1)^{n-1}}p^{i-1}q^{n-i}\\ &= \frac{(n-1)!}{(n-1)^{n-1}}(p+q)^{n-1}\\ &= \frac{(n-1)!}{(n-1)^{n-1}}\end{aligned}$$

and thus that

$$\pi_i = \binom{n-1}{i-1}p^{i-1}q^{n-i}.$$

Interestingly, this is the same as the probability that $i-1$ of the first $n-1$ inputs are ones and thus the FSE in Figures 1 and 2 are equivalent (for $s = n-1$) in the long run! The FSE in Figure 2 has fewer states, however, and mean-square error $\sigma^2(p) = \frac{pq}{n-1} = O(\frac{1}{n})$.

The Markov Chain Tree Theorem will also be useful in Section 4 where we prove a lower bound on the worst-case mean-square error of an n-state FSE and in Section 5 where we establish the universality of linear FSEs.

3. An Improved Deterministic FSE

In what follows, we show how to simulate the n-state probabilistic FSE shown in Figure 2 with an $O(n \log n)$-state deterministic FSE. The resulting m-state deterministic FSE will then have mean-square error $O(\frac{\log m}{m})$. This is substantially better than the mean-square error of the FSE shown in Figure 1, and we conjecture that the bound is optimal for deterministic FSEs.

The key idea in the simulation is to use the randomness of the inputs to simulate a fixed probabilistic choice at each state. For example, consider a state i which on input one changes to state j with probability 1/2, and remains in state i with probability 1/2. (See Figure 3a.) Such a situation arises for states $i = \frac{n+1}{2}$ and $j = \frac{n+1}{2} + 1$ for odd n in the FSE of Figure 2. These transitions can be modelled by the deterministic transitions shown in Figure 3b.

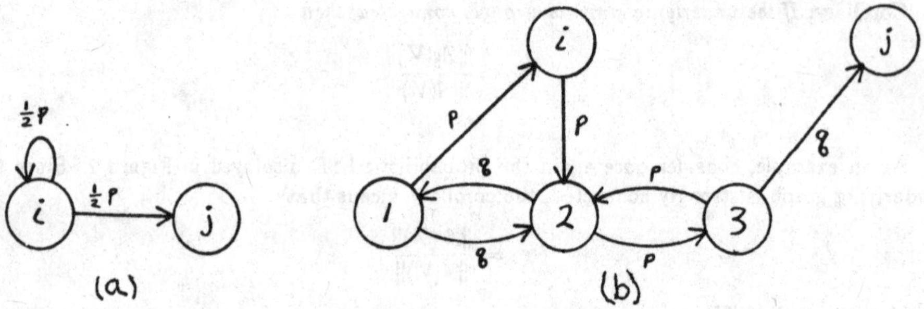

Figure 3: *Simulation of (a) probabilistic transitions by (b) deterministic transitions.*

The machine in Figure 3b starts in state i and first checks to see if the input is a one. If so, state 2 is entered. At this point, the machine examines the inputs in successive pairs. If "00" or "11" pairs are encountered, the machine remains in state 2. If a "01" pair is encountered, the machine returns to state i and if a "10" pair is encountered, the machine enters state j. Provided that $p \neq 0, 1$ (an assumption that will be made throughout the remainder of the paper), a "01" or "10" pair will (with probability 1) eventually be seen and the machine will eventually decide to stay in state i or move to state j. Note that regardless of the value of p $(0 < p < 1)$, the probability of encountering a "01" pair before a "10" pair is identical to the probability of encountering a "10" pair before a "01" pair. Hence the deterministic process in Figure 3b is equivalent to the probabilistic process in Figure 3a. (The trick of using a biased coin to simulate an unbiased coin has also been used by von Neumann in [18] and Hoeffding and Simons in [10].)

It is not difficult to generalize this technique to simulate transitions with other probabilities. For example, Figure 4b shows how to simulate a transition which has probability $\frac{3}{8}p$. As before, the simulating machine first verifies that the input is a one. If so, state a_2 is entered and remaining inputs are divided into successive pairs. As before, "00" and "11" pairs are ignored. The final state of the machine depends on the first three "01" or "10" pairs that are seen. If the first three pairs are "10" "10" "10", "10" "10" "01", or "10" "01" "10" (in those orders), then the machine moves to state j. Otherwise, the machine returns to state i. Simply speaking, the machine interprets strings of "01"s and "10"s as binary numbers formed by replacing "01" pairs by 0s and "10" pairs by 1s and decides if the resulting number is bigger than or equal to $101 = 5$. Since "01" and "10" pairs are encountered with equal probability in the input string for any p, the probability that the resulting number is 5 or bigger is precisely $\frac{3}{8}$.

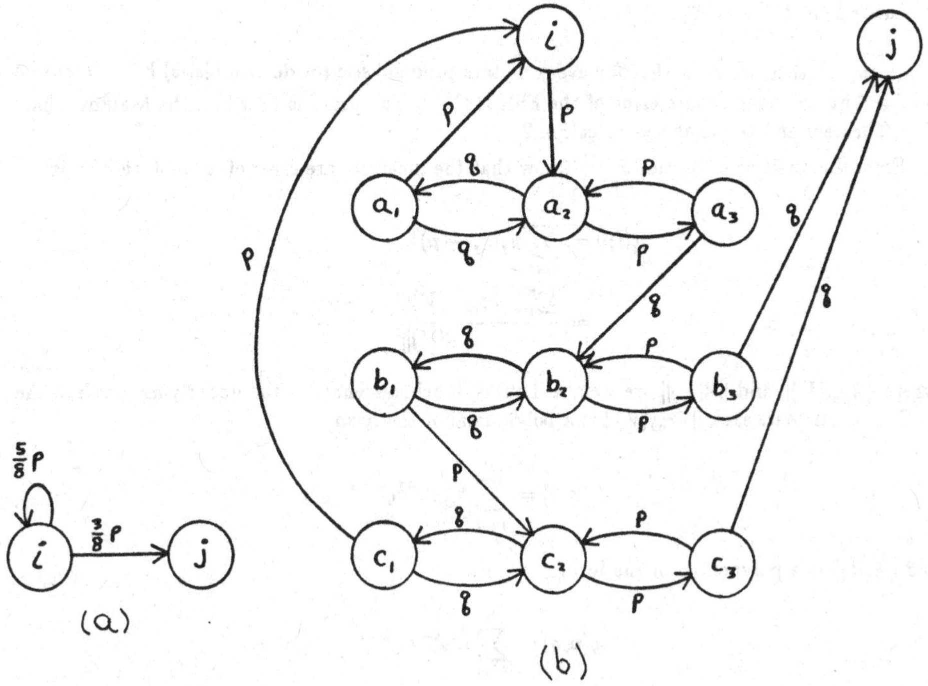

Figure 4: *Simulation of (a) probabilistic transitions by (b) deterministic transitions.*

In general, probabilistic transitions of the form shown in Figure 5 (where x is an integer) can be simulated with $3i$ extra deterministic states. Hence, when $n-1$ is a power of two, the n-state probabilistic FSE in Figure 2 can be simulated by a deterministic FSE with $6(n-1)\log(n-1) = O(n \log n)$ additional states. When n is not a power of two, the deterministic automata should simulate the next largest probabilistic automata that has 2^a states for some a. This causes at most a constant increase in the number of states needed for the simulation. Hence, for any m, there is an m-state deterministic automata with mean-square error $O(\frac{\log m}{m})$.

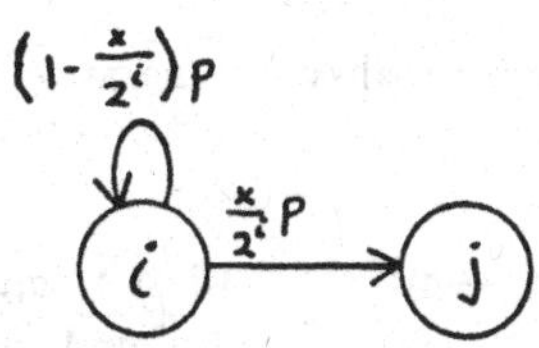

Figure 5: *General probabilistic transition.*

4. Lower Bound

In this section, we show that for every n-state probabilistic (or deterministic) FSE, there is a p such that the mean-square error of the FSE is $\Omega(\frac{1}{n})$. The proof is based on the Markov Chain Tree Theorem and the analysis of Section 2.

From the analysis of Section 2, we know that the mean-square error of an n-state FSE is

$$\sigma^2(p) = \sum_{j=1}^{n} \pi_j(\eta_j - p)^2 = \frac{\sum_{j=1}^{n} \|\mathcal{A}_{S_{0j}}(V)\|(\eta_j - p)^2}{\|\mathcal{A}(V)\|}$$

where $\|\mathcal{A}_{S_{0j}}(V)\|$ and $\|\mathcal{A}(V)\|$ are weighted sums of arborescences in the underlying graph of the FSE. In particular, each $\|\mathcal{A}_{S_{0j}}(V)\|$ is a polynomial of the form

$$f_j(p,q) = \sum_{i=1}^{n} a_{ij} p^{i-1} q^{n-i}$$

and $\|\mathcal{A}(V)\|$ is a polynomial of the form

$$g(p,q) = \sum_{i=1}^{n} a_i p^{i-1} q^{n-i}$$

where $a_i = \sum_{j=1}^{n} a_{ij}$ and $a_{ij} \geq 0$ for all $1 \leq i,j \leq n$. The nonnegativity of the a_{ij}'s follows from the fact that every edge of the graph underlying the FSE has weight $p_{ij} = \tau_{ij1}p + \tau_{ij0}q$ where τ_{ij1} and τ_{ij0} are nonnegative. Since every arborescence in the graph has $m \leq n-1$ edges, every term in the polynomial for $\|\mathcal{A}_{S_{0j}}(V)\|$ has the form $ap^r q^s$ where $r + s = m$. Multiplying by $(p+q)^{n-1-m} = 1$ then puts $f_j(p,q)$ in the desired form. The identity for $g(p,q)$ follows from the fact that $\|\mathcal{A}(V)\| = \sum_{j=1}^{n} \|\mathcal{A}_{S_{0j}}(V)\|$.

From the preceding analysis, we know that

$$\sigma^2(p) = \frac{\sum_{j=1}^{n} \sum_{i=1}^{n} a_{ij} p^{i-1} q^{n-i} (\eta_j - p)^2}{\sum_{i=1}^{n} a_i p^{i-1} q^{n-i}}$$

where $a_i = \sum_{j=1}^{n} a_{ij}$ and $a_{ij} \geq 0$ for $1 \leq i,j \leq n$. In what follows, we will show that

$$\int_{p=0}^{1} \sum_{j=1}^{n} \sum_{i=1}^{n} a_{ij} p^{n+i-1} q^{2n-i} (\eta_j - p)^2 dp \quad \geq \quad \Omega(\frac{1}{n}) \int_{p=0}^{1} \sum_{i=1}^{n} a_i p^{n+i-1} q^{2n-i} dp$$

for all $a_{ij} \geq 0$ and η_j. Since the integrands are always nonnegative, we will have thus proved the existence of a p $(0 < p < 1)$ for which

$$\sum_{j=1}^{n} \sum_{i=1}^{n} a_{ij} p^{n+i-1} q^{2n-i} (\eta_j - p)^2 \quad \geq \quad \Omega(\frac{1}{n}) \sum_{i=1}^{n} a_i p^{n+i-1} q^{2n-i}.$$

By dividing both sides by $p^n q^n$, this will prove the existence of a p for which

$$\sum_{j=1}^{n} \sum_{i=1}^{n} a_{ij} p^{i-1} q^{n-i} (\eta_j - p)^2 \quad \geq \quad \Omega(\frac{1}{n}) \sum_{i=1}^{n} a_i p^{i-1} q^{n-i}$$

and thus for which $\sigma^2(p) \geq \Omega(\frac{1}{n})$.

The proof relies heavily on the following well-known identites:

$$(*) \qquad \int_0^1 p^i(1-p)^j\,dp = \frac{i!j!}{(i+j+1)!} \qquad \text{and}$$

$$(**) \qquad \int_0^1 p^i(1-p)^j(p-\eta)^2\,dp \geq \frac{(i+1)!(j+1)!}{(i+j+3)!(i+j+2)}$$

for all η.

The proof is now a straightforward computation.

$$\begin{aligned}
&\int_{p=0}^1 \sum_{j=1}^n \sum_{i=1}^n a_{ij} p^{n+i-1} q^{2n-i} (\eta_j - p)^2\,dp \\
&= \sum_{j=1}^n \sum_{i=1}^n a_{ij} \int_0^1 p^{n+i-1}(1-p)^{2n-i}(p-\eta_j)^2\,dp \\
&\geq \sum_{j=1}^n \sum_{i=1}^n \frac{a_{ij}(n+i)!(2n-i+1)!}{(3n+2)!(3n+1)} \qquad \text{by } (**) \\
&= \sum_{i=1}^n \frac{a_i(n+i)!(2n-i+1)!}{(3n+2)!(3n+1)} \\
&= \sum_{i=1}^n \frac{(n+i)(2n-i+1)}{(3n+2)(3n+1)^2} \, \frac{a_i(n+i-1)!(2n-i)!}{(3n)!} \\
&\geq \frac{2n(n+1)}{(3n+2)(3n+1)^2} \sum_{i=1}^n \frac{a_i(n+i-1)!(2n-i)!}{(3n)!} \\
&= \Omega(\frac{1}{n}) \sum_{i=1}^n a_i \int_0^1 p^{n+i-1}(1-p)^{2n-i}\,dp \qquad \text{by } (*) \\
&= \Omega(\frac{1}{n}) \int_{p=0}^1 \sum_{i=1}^n a_i p^{n+i-1} q^{2n-i}\,dp .
\end{aligned}$$

It is worth remarking that the key fact in the preceding proof is that the long-run average transition probabilities of an n-state FSE can be expressed as ratios of $(n-1)$-degree polynomials with nonnegative coefficients. This fact comes from the Markov Chain Tree Theorem. (Although it is easily shown that the long-run probabilities can be expressed as ratios of $(n-1)$-degree polynomials, and as infinite polynomials with nonnegative coefficients, the stronger result seems to require the full use of the Markov Chain Tree Theorem.) The remainder of the proof essentially shows that functions of this restricted form cannot accurately predict p. Thus the limitations imposed by restricting the class of transition functions dominate the limitations imposed by quantization of the estimates.

5. Universality of Linear FSEs

In Section 4, we showed that the mean-square error of any n-state FSE can be expressed as

$$\sigma^2(p) = \frac{\sum_{j=1}^n \sum_{i=1}^n a_{ij} p^{i-1} q^{n-i} (\eta_j - p)^2}{\sum_{i=1}^n a_i p^{i-1} q^{n-i}}$$

where $a_i = \sum_{j=1}^{n} a_{ij}$ and $a_{ij} \geq 0$ for $1 \leq i, j \leq n$. In this section, we will use this fact to construct an n-state *linear* FSE with mean-square error at most $\sigma^2(p)$ for all p. We first prove the following simple identity.

Lemma 1: *If $a_1, \ldots, a_n$ are nonnegative, then*

$$\sum_{j=1}^{n} a_j(\eta_j - p)^2 \geq a(\eta - p)^2$$

for all p and $\eta_1, \ldots, \eta_n$ where $a = \sum_{j=1}^{n} a_j$ and $\eta = \frac{1}{a}\sum_{j=1}^{n} a_j\eta_j$.

Proof: Since $a_1, \ldots, a_n$ are nonnegative, $a = 0$ if and only if $a_j = 0$ for $1 \leq j \leq n$. Thus

$$\sum_{j=1}^{n} a_j(\eta_j - p)^2 \geq a(\eta - p)^2$$

if and only if

$$a\sum_{j=1}^{n} a_j(\eta_j - p)^2 \geq a^2(\eta - p)^2$$

which is true since

$$\begin{aligned} a\sum_{j=1}^{n} a_j(\eta_j - p)^2 - a^2(\eta - p)^2 &= a\sum_{j=1}^{n} a_j\eta_j^2 - a^2\eta^2 \\ &= \left(\sum_{i=1}^{n} a_i\right)\left(\sum_{j=1}^{n} a_j\eta_j^2\right) - \left(\sum_{i=1}^{n} a_i\eta_i\right)\left(\sum_{j=1}^{n} a_j\eta_j\right) \\ &= \sum^{1\leq i,j\leq n} a_ia_j(\eta_j^2 - \eta_i\eta_j) \\ &= \sum^{1\leq i<j\leq n} a_ia_j(\eta_j - \eta_i)^2 \end{aligned}$$

is nonnegative. ∎

Let $\eta_i' = \frac{1}{a_i}\sum_{j=1}^{n} a_{ij}\eta_j$ for $i \leq i \leq n$. From Lemma 1, we can conclude that

$$\sigma^2(p) \geq \frac{\sum_{i=1}^{n} a_i p^{i-1} q^{n-i}(p - \eta_i')^2}{\sum_{i=1}^{n} a_i p^{i-1} q^{n-i}}$$

for $0 \leq p \leq 1$. This ratio of sums is similar to the mean-square error of a linear FSE which never moves left on input one and never moves right on input zero. For example, the mean-square error of the linear FSE in Figure 6 can be written in this form by setting

$$a_i = u_1 \cdots u_{i-1} v_{i+1} \cdots v_n$$

for $1 \leq i \leq n$.

Given a nonnegative set $\{a_i\}_{i=1}^{n}$, it is not always possible to find sets $\{u_i\}_{i=1}^{n-1}$ and $\{v_i\}_{i=2}^{n}$ such that $0 \leq u_i, v_i \leq 1$ and $a_i = u_1 \cdots u_{i-1} v_{i+1} \cdots v_n$ for all i. There are two possible difficulties. The first problem is that a_i might be larger than one for some i. This would mean that some u_j or v_j must be greater than one, which is not allowed. The second problem involves values of a_i which are zero. For example, if $a_1 \neq 0$ and $a_n \neq 0$, then each u_i and v_i must be nonzero. This would not be possible if $a_i = 0$ for some $i, 1 < i < n$.

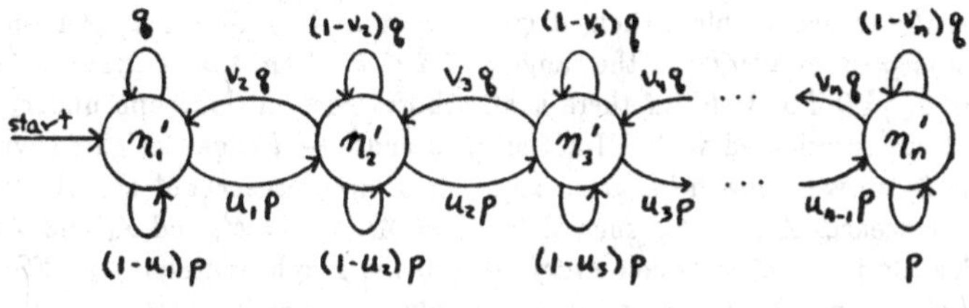

Figure 6: *Universal linear FSE.*

Fortunately, both difficulties can be overcome. The first problem is solved by observing that the mean-square error corresponding to the set $\{ca_i\}_{i=1}^n$ is the same as the mean-square error corresponding to $\{a_i\}_{i=1}^n$ for all $c > 0$. By setting

$$u_i = \frac{a_{i+1}}{a_i} \quad \text{and} \quad v_{i+1} = 1 \quad \text{if} \quad a_i \geq a_{i+1},$$

$$u_i = 1 \quad \text{and} \quad v_{i+1} = \frac{a_i}{a_{i+1}} \quad \text{if} \quad a_{i+1} \geq a_i,$$

$$\text{and} \qquad c = \frac{u_1 \cdots u_{n-1}}{a_n},$$

it can be easily verified that the mean-square error of the FSE shown in Figure 6 is

$$\frac{\sum_{i=1}^n ca_i p^{i-1} q^{n-i} (p - \eta_i')^2}{\sum_{i=1}^n ca_i p^{i-1} q^{n-i}} = \frac{\sum_{i=1}^n a_i p^{i-1} q^{n-i} (p - \eta_i')^2}{\sum_{i=1}^n a_i p^{i-1} q^{n-i}}$$

provided that $a_i > 0$ for $1 \leq i \leq n$. This is because

$$\begin{aligned} u_1 \cdots u_{i-1} v_{i+1} \cdots v_n &= \frac{ca_n}{u_i \cdots u_{n-1}} v_{i+1} \cdots v_n \\ &= ca_n \left(\frac{v_{i+1}}{u_i}\right) \cdots \left(\frac{v_n}{u_{n-1}}\right) \\ &= ca_n \left(\frac{a_i}{a_{i+1}}\right) \cdots \left(\frac{a_{n-1}}{a_n}\right) \\ &= ca_i . \end{aligned}$$

If $a_1 = \cdots = a_{j-1} = 0$ and $a_{k+1} = \cdots = a_n = 0$ but $a_i \neq 0$ for $j \leq i \leq k$, then the preceding scheme can be made to work by setting $u_1 = \cdots = u_{j-1} = 1$, $u_k = \cdots = u_{n-1} = 0$, $v_2 = \cdots = v_j = 0$, $v_{k+1} = \cdots = v_n = 1$,

$$u_i = \frac{a_{i+1}}{a_i} \quad \text{and} \quad v_{i+1} = 1 \quad \text{if} \quad a_i \geq a_{i+1} \quad \text{for} \quad j \leq i \leq k-1,$$

$$u_i = 1 \quad \text{and} \quad v_{i+1} = \frac{a_i}{a_{i+1}} \quad \text{if} \quad a_{i+1} \geq a_i \quad \text{for} \quad j \leq i \leq k-1,$$

$$\text{and} \qquad c = \frac{u_j \cdots u_{k-1}}{a_k}.$$

To overcome the second problem then, it is sufficient to show that if $a_j \neq 0$ and $a_k \neq 0$ for some FSE, then $a_i \neq 0$ for every i in the range $j \leq i \leq k$. From the analysis in Sections 2 and 4, we know that $a_i \neq 0$ if and only if there is an arborescence in the graph underlying the FSE which has $i-1$ edges weighted with a fraction of p and $n-i$ edges weighted with a fraction of q. In Lemma 2, we will show how, given any pair of arborescences A and A', to construct a sequence of arborescences $A_1, \ldots, A_m$ such that $A_1 = A$, $A_m = A'$, and A_i and A_{i+1} differ by at most one edge for $1 \leq i < m$. Since every edge of the graph underlying an FSE is weighted with a fraction of p or q or both, this result will imply that a graph containing an arborescence with $j-1$ edges weighted with a fraction of p and $n-j$ edges weighted with a fraction of q, and an arborescence with $k-1$ edges weighted with a fraction of p and $n-k$ edges weighted with a fraction of q, must also contain an arborescence with $i-1$ edges weighted with a fraction of p and $n-i$ edges weighted with a fraction of q for every i in the range $j \leq i \leq k$. This will conclude the proof that for every n-state FSE with mean-square error $\sigma^2(p)$, there is an n-state linear FSE with mean-square error at most $\sigma^2(p)$ for $0 \leq p \leq 1$.

Lemma 2: *Given a graph with arborescences A and A', there is a sequence of arborescences $A_1, \ldots, A_m$ such that $A_1 = A$, $A_m = A'$, and A_{i+1} can be formed from A_i for $1 \leq i < m$ by replacing a single edge of A_i with an edge of A'.*

Proof: The sequence of edge replacements proceeds in two phases. In the first phase, a node v in A_i is selected such that

1) v is neither a root of A_i nor a root of A',
2) the edge from v in A_i is different than the edge from v in A', and
3) the edges from all ancestors of v (if any) in A_i are edges in A'.

Then the edge from v in A_i is replaced by the edge from v in A' to form A_{i+1}.

The first phase continues until the supply of nodes that satisfy the three conditions is exhausted. At this point, every edge in A_i that is not on a path from a root of A' to a root of A_i is also in A'.

In the second phase, a root v of A_i that is not a root of A' is selected and the edge from v in A' is inserted to form A_{i+1}. In addition, the unique edge that enters v and that is descendent in A_i from a root of A' is removed in A_{i+1}. The ancestor of v in A_i that is a descendent of a root in A' then becomes a root of A_{i+1}. Note that the length of the path from the root of A' to the root of A_{i+1} is one less than the length of the path from the root of A' to v. Thus repetition of this process will eventually produce an arborescence A_m which has the same roots as A'. At this point, the procedure terminates. (For an example of this process, see Figure 7.)

Since every arborescence has exactly one root in each minimal closed subset of nodes, the preceding algorithm constructs a sequence of graphs $A_1, \ldots, A_m$ such that $A_1 = A$, $A_m = A'$, and A_i and A_{i+1} differ in at most one edge for $1 \leq i < m$. In order to complete the proof, we must show that each A_i is an arborescence. The proof is by induction, and shows that if A_i has no cycles or nodes with outdegree greater than one, then A_{i+1} has no cycles or nodes with outdegree greater than one. Since A_i and A_{i+1} have the same number of edges, we will have thus shown that A_{i+1} is an arborescence if A_i is an arborescence.

The outdegree constraint is straightforward to verify since, in the first phase, the outdegree of the nodes is not changed, and in the second phase, outgoing edges are added only to roots. It is also easy to verify that cycles are not introduced in the procedure. If a cycle were introduced in the first phase, it would have to consist of edges that are also in A' (by the third constraint on v), thus violating the acyclicity of A'. If a cycle were formed in the second phase, it could only contain edges which are not on the path from a root of A' to a root of A_i (since the last edge in this path was removed). Such edges are in A', however, again violating the acyclicity of A'. ∎

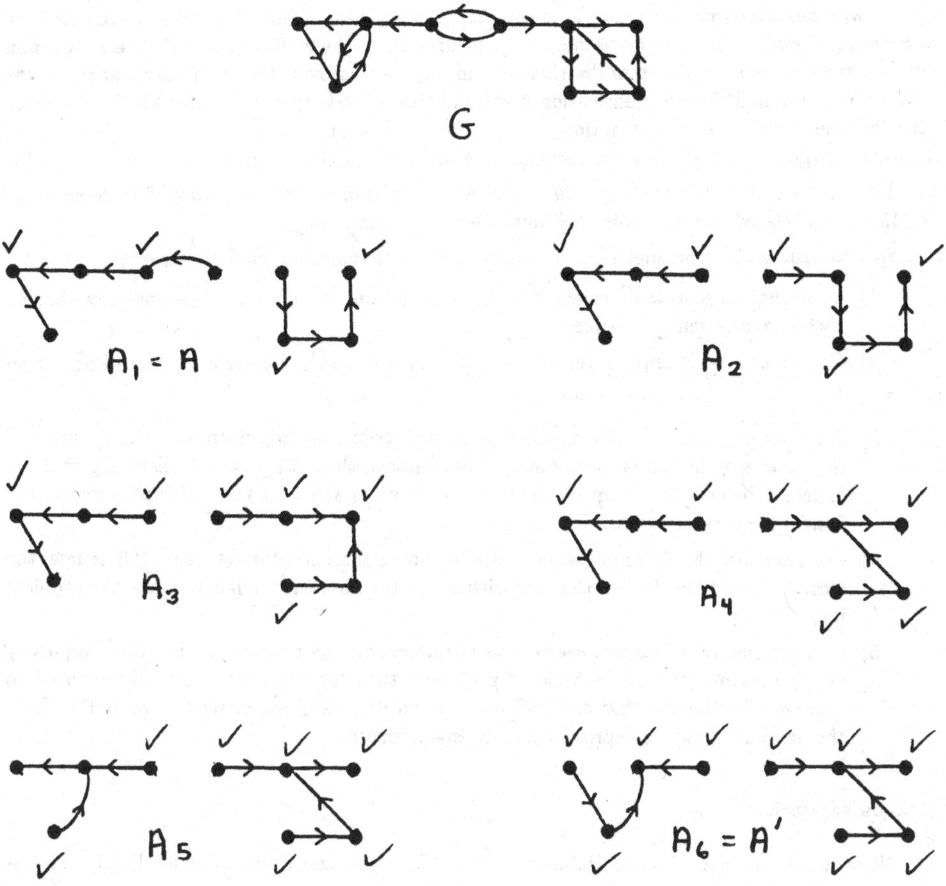

Figure 7: *Deforming A into A' by a sequence of edge replacements. Checkmarks denote nodes for which the outgoing edge is in A'. Arborescences A_2, A_3 and A_4 are formed during the first phase.*

6. Remarks

There is a large literature on problems related to estimation with finite memory. Most of the work thus far has concentrated on the *hypothesis testing problem* [1, 3, 9, 25, 26, 27]. Generally speaking, the hypothesis testing problem is more tractable than the estimation problem. For example, several constructions are known for n-state automata which can test a hypothesis with long-run error at most $O(\alpha^n)$ where α is a constant in the interval $0 < \alpha < 1$ that depends only on the hypothesis. In addition, several researchers have studied the *time-varying* hypothesis testing problem [2, 11, 12, 16, 21, 28]. Allowing transitions to be time-dependent greatly enhances the power of an automata. For example, a 4-state time-varying automata can estimate a probability with an arbitrarily small mean-square error.

As was mentioned previously, Samaniego [23] studied the problem of estimating the mean of a Bernoulli distribution using finite memory, and discovered the FSE shown in Figure 2. Hellman studied the problem for Gaussian distributions in [8], and discovered an FSE which achieves the lower bound implied by the quantization problem. (Recall that this is not possible for Bernoulli distributions.) Hellman's construction uses the fact that events at the tails of the distribution contain a large amount of information about the mean of the distribution.

The work on digital filters (e.g., [19, 20, 22]) and on approximate counting of large numbers [6, 15] is also related to the problem of finite-memory estimation.

We conclude with some questions of interest and some topics for further research.

1) Construct an n-state deterministic FSE with mean-square error $o(\frac{\log n}{n})$ or show that no such construction is possible.
2) Construct a truly optimal (in terms of worst-case mean-square error) n-state FSE for all n.
3) Consider estimation problems where a prior distribution on p is known. For example, if the prior distribution on p is known to be uniform, then the n-state FSE in Figure 2 has expected (over p) mean-square error $\Theta(\frac{1}{n})$. Prove that this is optimal (up to a constant factor) for n-state FSEs.
4) Consider models of computation that allow more than constant storage. (Of course, the storage should also be less than logarithmic in the number of trials to make the problem interesting.)
5) Can the amount of storage used for some interesting models be related to the complexity of representing p? For example, if $p = a/b$, then $\log a + \log b$ bits might be used to represent p. Suppose that the FSE may use an extra amount of storage proportional to the amount it uses to represent its current prediction.

Acknowledgements

We thank Tom Cover, Martin Hellman, Robert Gallager, and Peter Elias for helpful discussions.

References

[1] B. Chandrasekaran and C. Lam, "A Finite-Memory Deterministic Algorithm for the Symmetric Hypothesis Testing Problem," *IEEE Transactions on Information Theory*, Vol. IT-21, No. 1, January 1975, pp. 40-44.

[2] T. Cover, "Hypothesis Testing with Finite Statistics," *Annals of Mathematical Statistics*, Vol. 40, 1969, pp. 828-835.

[3] T. Cover and M. Hellman, "The Two-Armed Bandit Problem With Time-Invariant Finite Memory," *IEEE Transactions on Information Theory*, Vol. IT-16, No. 2, March 1970, pp. 185-195.

[4] J. Doob, *Stochastic Processes*, Wiley, New York, 1953.

[5] W. Feller, *An Introduction to Probability Theory and its Applications*, Wiley, New York, 1957.

[6] P. Flajolet, "On Approximate Counting," INRIA Research Report No. 153, July 1982.

[7] R. Flower and M. Hellman, "Hypothesis Testing With Finite Memory in Finite Time," *IEEE Transactions on Information Theory*, May 1972, pp. 429-431.

[8] M. Hellman, "Finite-Memory Algorithms for Estimating the Mean of a Gaussian Distribution," *IEEE Transactions on Information Theory*, Vol. IT-20, May 1974, pp. 382-384.

[9] M. Hellman and T. Cover, "Learning with Finite Memory," *Annals of Mathematical Statistics*, Vol. 41, 1970, pp. 765-782.

[10] W. Hoeffding and G. Simons, "Unbiased Coin Tossing with a Biased Coin," *Annals of Mathematical Statistics*, Vol. 41, 1970, pp. 341-352.

[11] J. Koplowitz, "Necessary and Sufficient Memory Size for m-Hypothesis Testing," *IEEE Transactions on Information Theory*, Vol. IT-21, No. 1, January 1975, pp. 44-46.

[12] J. Koplowitz and R. Roberts, "Sequential Estimation With a Finite Statistic," *IEEE Transactions on Information Theory*, Vol. IT-19, No. 5, September 1973, pp. 631-635.

[13] S. Lakshmivarahan, *Learning Algorithms – Theory and Applications*, Springer-Verlag, New York, 1981.

[14] F. Leighton and R. Rivest, "The Markov Chain Tree Theorem," to appear.

[15] F. Morris, "Counting Large Numbers of Events in Small Registers," *Communications of the ACM*, Vol. 21, No. 10, October 1978, pp. 840-842.

[16] C. Mullis and R. Roberts, "Finite-Memory Problems and Algorithms," *IEEE Transactions on Information Theory*, Vol. IT-20, No. 4, July 1974, pp. 440-455.

[17] K. Narendra and M. Thathachar, "Learning Automata – A Survey," *IEEE Transactions on Systems*, Vol. SMC-4, No. 4, July 1974, pp. 323-334.

[18] J. von Neumann, "Various Techniques Used in Connection With Random Digits," *Monte Carlo Methods*, Applied Mathematics Series, No. 12, U. S. National Bureau of Standards, Washington D. C., 1951, pp. 36-38.

[19] A. Oppenheim and R. Schafe, *Digital Signal Processing*, Prentice-Hall, Englewood Cliffs, New Jersey, 1975.

[20] L. Rabiner and B. Gold, *Theory and Application of Digital Signal Processing*, Prentice-Hall, Englewood Cliffs, New Jersey, 1975.

[21] R. Roberts and J. Tooley, "Estimation With Finite Memory," *IEEE Transactions on Information Theory*, Vol. IT-16, 1970, pp. 685-691.

[22] A. Sage and J. Melsa, *Estimation Theory With Applications to Communications and Control*, McGraw-Hill, New York, 1971.

[23] F. Samaniego, "Estimating a Binomial Parameter With Finite Memory," *IEEE Transactions on Information Theory*, Vol. IT-19, No. 5, September 1973, pp. 636-643.

[24] F. Samaniego, "On Tests With Finite Menory in Finite Time," *IEEE Transactions on Information Theory*, Vol. IT-20, May 1974, pp. 387-388.

[25] F. Samaniego, "On Testing Simple Hypothesis in Finite Time With Hellman-Cover Automata," *IEEE Transactions on Information Theory*, Vol. IT-21, No. 2, March 1975, pp. 157-162.

[26] B. Shubert, "Finite-Memory Classification of Bernoulli Sequences Using Reference Samples," *IEEE Transactions on Information Theory*, Vol. IT-20, May 1974, pp. 384-387.

[27] B. Shubert and C. Anderson, "Testing a Simple Symmetric Hypothesis by a Finite-Memory Deterministic Algorithm," *IEEE Transactions on Information Theory*, Vol. IT-19, No. 5, September 1973, pp. 644-647.

[28] T. Wagner, "Estimation of the Mean With Time-Varying Finite Memory," *IEEE Transactions on Information Theory*, Vol. IT-18, July 1972, pp. 523-525.

THE GREEDY AND DELAUNEY TRIANGULATIONS ARE NOT BAD IN THE AVERAGE CASE and MINIMUM WEIGHT GEOMETRIC TRIANGULATION OF MULTI-CONNECTED POLYGONS IS NP-COMPLETE

Andrzej Lingas
Software Systems Research Center
Linköping University
581 83 Linköping, Sweden

1. *Introduction*

Let S be a set of n points in the plane. A *triangulation* of S is a maximal set of non-intersecting straight-line segments between these points. Any triangulation of S, partitions the *convex hull* of S (see [Ll77,Sha75]) into triangles. For a set of straight-line segments in the plane, T, let $|T|$ denote the total length of the segments in T. A *minimum weight triangulation* is any triangulation which minimizes $|T|$ among all triangulations of S, T. Minimum weight triangulations have an application in interpolating values of two-argument functions [Ll77].

There are two well known triangulation algorithms: the Greedy triangulation and the Delauney triangulation (see [DG70,Ll77, MZ79]). The former inserts a segment into the plane if it is smallest among all segments between points in S not intersecting those already in the place. The latter simply constructs the dual of the Voronoi diagram for S. Manacher and Zorbist [MZ79] show that neither approximates the optimum. Let $GT(S)$ and $DT(S)$ denote the outcome of the Greedy triangulation and the Delauney triangulation of S, and let $M(S)$ stand for the total length of a minimum weight triangulation of S. Specifically, for arbitrary large n Manacher and Zorbist construct sets of n points in the plane, S', S'', such that

$$|GT(S')|/M(S') \geq \Omega(n^{1/3})$$

$$|DT(S'')|/M(S'') \geq \Omega(n/logn)$$

Kirkpatrick [Ki80] strengthens the latter result by exhibiting sets S''' for which:

$$|DT(S''')|/M(S''') \geq \Omega(n)$$

The lack of practically interesting bounds on the worst case performance of the Greedy and Delauney triangulations suggests analyzing the average case performance of these heuristics. It seems natural to assume the uniform point distribution, i.e.

if A is the finite region in the plane from which the n points of S are drawn and B is a part of A then for $i = 1, ..., n$, the probability that the $i - th$ point is in B is equal to $area(B)/area(A)$.

It turns out that the Delauney and Greedy triangulations choose only local connections inside the convex hull when S uniformly covers the sample area. In the case of the Delauney triangulation, this observation immediately follows from the definition.

Following Angluin and Valiant [AV77], let almost certainly mean with the probability of at least $1 - cn^{\alpha}$ where c, α are constants satisfying $c>0$, $\alpha>1$. The elementar outcome of the above observation and the assumption of uniform point distribution is as follows:

Let S be drawn from a square in the plane. We have $|DL(S)|/M(S) = O(logn)$, and $|GT(S)|/M(S) = O(logn)$ almost certainly (of course, these results generalize to include the case when the sample area takes any other, reasonable, fixed shape).

By virtue of this corollary, the ideas of the Delauney and Greedy triangulations seem to be not accidental. Probably, they have been raised by intuitions concerning the expected point distribution.

The status of the minimum weight triangulation problem is still unknown (see the twelfth open problem in [GJ78]). In 1977 Lloyd showed the related problem of whether a given set of edges contains a triangulation of S to be NP-complete [Ll77]. We show the NP-completeness of the following triangulation problem:

Minimum Weight Geometric Triangulation of Multi-connected Polygons (MWGTMP): Given a rational number k and a polygon with polygonal holes, partition the figure into triangles by drawing non-intersecting diagonals of the total length not exceeding k.

In contrast to the NP-completeness of MWGTMP, we observe that a minimum weight geometric triangulation of a simply connected polygon with n corners can be found in time $O(n^4)$ by dynamic programming. Moreover, in Appendix we give an evidence that the following, more closely related to MWT, triangulation problem is NP-complete.

Minimum Weight Geometric Triangulation (MWGT): Given a rational number k and a set of points in the plane S, partition the convex hull of S into triangles such that:

(a) the edges of the triangles consist of sequences of straight-line segments between points in S,
(b) none of points in S is interior to any of the triangles,
(c) the total length of the perimeters of the triangles does not exceed k.

Note that if the set of points contains triples of colinear points then a triangulation satisfying (a) and (b) might be non-maximal, i.e. a triangle edge passing through at least three points in this set may appear. Therefore, MWGT is different from the problem of finding a minimum weight triangulation.

2. *The triangulations are good in the average case*

The Greedy and Delauney triangulations

The first polynomial time heuristic for minimum weight triangulation was given by Duppe and Gottschalk in [DG70]. The heuristic of Duppe and Gottschalk is well known as the Greedy triangulation. Its simplest version is as follows:

L ← the set of all straight-line segments between points in S;
GT ← $\emptyset$;
<u>*while*</u> $L \neq \emptyset$ <u>*do*</u>
<u>*begin*</u>
  w ← a shortest edge in L ;

$GT \leftarrow GT \cup \{w\}$;
$L \leftarrow L - \{w\} - \{\, m \in L \mid w$ intersects the inside of $m \,\}$
end;
output GT

To specify the Shamos and Hoey heuristic for minimum weight triangulation [SH75], known as the Delauney triangulation, we informally introduce the concept of the *Voronoi diagram* of S (following [Ll77]).

Given a point s in S, the *Voronoi polygon* associated with s is a maximal convex polygon whose inside consists of all points in the plane such that no point in S is so close to p as s. The Voronoi polygons for points in S partitions the plane into convex polygons. The *straight-line dual* of the Voronoi diagram of S is a planar graph on S, where two points in S are connected by an edge if and only if their Voronoi polygons share an edge.

The Delauney triangulation is as follows:

construct the Voronoi diagram of S ,
$T \leftarrow$ the set of edges in the straight-line dual of the Voronoi diagram ,
extend T to a complete triangulation of S ,
output T

As, if more than three Voronoi edges may share an endpoint, the third step in the above algorithm is necessary.

Probabilistic Analysis

Let us assume the sample area from which the n points in S are drawn to be a rectangle of a constant aspect ratio. Suppose that we can partition the rectangle into rectangular cells of length l and width w. It is possible to prove that the Delauney and Greedy triangulations choose only edges of length $O(w)$ within the distance of $\Omega(w)$ from the edges of the rectangle, if every of these cells contains a point in S. On the other hand, we can set $w = O(\sqrt{logn/n} \times |CH(S)|)$ such that under the assumption of uniform point distribution all cells contains a point in S and $M(S) \geq \Omega(\sqrt{n/logn} \times |CH(S)|)$, almost certainly. Since any triangulation of S has at most $3n-9$ edges inside $CH(S)$, we conclude that $|D(S)|/M(S) \leq O(logn)$ and $|GT(S)|/M(S) \leq O(logn)$ almost certainly. In the case of the novel triangulation, we employ results from Section 2 to derive a weaker estimation. In fact, we prove a more general theorem showing the trade off between the hypothesis on the magnitude of $|T(S)|/M(S)$ and their probability for $T \in \{DT, GT\}$.

Theorem 1. Let P be a rectangle in the plane of length L and width W, where $L \geq W$. Let S be a random set of n points in P. Under the assumption of uniform point distribution, if t is a positive real number, then

$$Pr[|DT(S)|/M(S) \leq O(t \times (L/W))] \geq 1 - n \exp -t$$

$$Pr[|GT(S)|/M(S) \leq O(t \times (L/W))] \geq 1 - 2n \exp -t$$

Proof. Let $i = \lfloor \sqrt{n/t} \rfloor$ and $l = L/i$, $w = W/i$. Divide P into the grid of $i \times i$ rectangular cells, each of length l and width w. The probability that each of these rectangles contains a point in S is not less than

$$1-\sum_{k=1}^{i\times i}(1-t/n)^n \geq 1-n\exp(-t)$$

Further, we assume that each of these cells contains a point in S. Consider any triangulation of S, T. Clearly, for any boundary cell that is not on a corner, the total length of the pieces of $|T|$ lying inside it is at least w. The edges incident to any point of S lying inside $CH(S)$ divide the area around the point into angles of less than 180 degrees. Therefore, the total length of the pieces of T lying inside a given cell is greater than w provided that the cell is not a corner one. There are i^2-4 such cells. Hence $|T| \geq (i^2-4)w$ which implies $M(S) \geq (i^2-4)w$. On the other hand, we have $|CH(S)| \leq 2il+2(i-2)w$, and by the Euler formula for planar graphs, the triangulation T contains no more than $3n-9$ *inner* edges, i.e. edges inside $CH(S)$. For brevity, r will stand for $2\sqrt{l^2+w^2}$ further.

Case 1: The Delauney triangulation.
Since it is assumed that every cell contain a point in S, every point in P is in a distance of at most $r/2$ from another point in S. It follows from the definition of Delauney triangulation that each inner edge of $DT(S)$ is of length not greater than
$r \leq 2\sqrt{2}w(L/W)$. Hence, we have

$$|T|/M(S) \leq [2il+2(i-2)w)+(3n-9)\times 2\sqrt{2}w(L/W)]/(i^2-4)\times w \leq O(t\times(L/W))$$

Case 2: The Greedy triangulation.
Let us partition $GT(S)$ into the three sets of edges in $GT(S)$ defined as follows:

DL is the set of all (deep and long) edges e in $GT(S)$ such that there exists a segment of e that is of length $> 7r$ and is placed in the distance of at least r from each edge of the rectangle P,
SL is the set of all (shallow and long) edges e in $GT(S)$ such that $|e| > 7r$ and $e \notin DL$,
O is the set of all other edges in $GT(S)$, i.e. $O = GT(S) - (DL \cup SL)$.

Note that all endpoints of edges in SL are placed in 2×24 outer vertical layers, and $2\times 24\times\lceil L/W\rceil$ outer horizontal layers of the grid. These outer layers include less than $k\times i$ cells where $k=48(\lceil L/W\rceil+1)$. Under the assumption that each cell contains a point in S, by the inequality $\binom{m}{l} \leq \left(\frac{m\times e}{l}\right)^l$, where $1 \leq l \leq m$ (see [AV78]), the number of points points from S in $k\times i$ given cells is less than $2e\times t\times k\times i$ with the probability of at least:

$$1-\binom{n-i^2}{2e\times t\times k\times i-k\times i}\times\left(\frac{t\times k\times i}{t\times i^2}\right)^{2e\times t\times k\times i-k\times i} \geq 1-2^{-2e\times t\times(k-1)\times i}$$

Thus, each of the cells contains a point in S, and the number of endpoints of edges in SL is less than $2e\times k\times t\times i$ with the probability of at least:

$$(1-n\exp-t)\times(1-2^{-2e\times(k-1)\times t\times i}) \geq 1-2n\exp-t$$

Let us assume the above hypothesis. By the Euler formula for planar graphs, we have $\#SL \leq 6e\times k\times t\times i$. Clearly, any edge in $GT(S)$ is of length at most $\sqrt{2}l\times i$. Putting everything together, we have:

$$|GT(S)/M(S) \leq (|DL| + |SL| + |O|)/M(S) \leq$$

$$[(\#DL + 6e \times k \times t \times i) \times \sqrt{2}l \times i + 3n \times 7r]/(i-2)^2 \times w$$

To prove the theorem for the Greedy triangulation it is sufficient to show that $DL = \emptyset$. Let e be an edge in DL. We shall show that there exist points a and b in S such that $|(a,b)| < |e|$, (a,b) crosses e, and no edge in $GT(S)$ of length $\leq |(a,b)|$ crosses (a,b); a contradiction with the definition of $GT(S)$. To start with, we need the following definition and lemma:

An edge is said to *split* a continuous line in the form of a convex closed loop if the intersection of the edge with the line consists of at least two points.

Lemma 5. Let c be a continuous line in the form of a convex closed loop, and let e be an edge in $GT(S)$ splitting c. Let f be another edge in $GT(S)$ such that no endpoint of f lies inside c and no edge in the triangulation T of length $\leq d$ splits c between f and e. Let $c(S,f,e)$ be the collection of all points in S lying inside c or on the perimeter of c: either in the area between f and e or on f. If $c(S,f,e)$ is not empty, then assuming that edges in $GT(S)$ of length $> d$ are transparent, there exists a point in $c(S,f,e)$ that sees the whole piece of e lying within c.

Proof of the lemma. Let p be a point in $c(S,f,e)$. If it does not see the whole piece, then there exists a point q in $c(S,f,e)$ that is an end of a non-transparent edge (i.e. an edge of length $\leq d$) in T, lying between p and e. If q does not see the whole piece of e, then there exists a point in $c(S-\{p\},f,e)$ that is an end of a non-transparent edge, *etc*. The proof follows from the finiteness of S. ∎

Since $e \in DL$, there exists a continuous piece of e that is of length $> 7r$ and is placed in the distance of at least r from the edges of the rectangle P. Draw a circle c of diameter $7r$ whose center overlaps with that of the above piece of e. Let A, B be the two halves of c separated by e. It follows from the size of c that $A \cap S \neq \emptyset$ and $B \cap S \neq \emptyset$.
If no edge in $GT(S)$ of length $\leq 7r$ crosses A, then by Lemma 5 there exists a point in $A \cap S$ that sees the whole diameter of c lying on e, provided that edges in T of length $> 7r$ are transparent. Let us set a to this point. Otherwise, there exists an edge f crossing A such that $|f| \leq 7r$ and no edge of length $\leq 7r$, crosses A between f and e. Again, by Lemma 5, if $c(S,f,e)$ is not empty, then there exists a point in $A \cap S$ that sees the whole diameter of c on e, provided that edges in T of length $> 7r$ are transparent. Then, let us set a to this point. If $c(S,f,e)$ is empty, let us consider the rectangle R of length r and width r shown in Fig. 1. As the rectangle R lies inside the large rectangle P by the definition of the circle c, it includes at least one cell with a point in S. In consequence, the endpoints of f are located in the distance of at most $2.5r$ from e, and their perpendicular projections on e lie in the distance of at most $0.5r$ from the nearest crossing between e and c.
First, suppose that there exists a point b in $B \cap S$ that sees the whole diameter of c on e. If the point a has been already defined, then the edge (a,b) lies within c, crosses e and is not crossed by any edge of length $\leq 7r$. We obtain a contradiction with the definition of $GT(S)$. If the point has not been defined yet, let us pick the endpoint of f that is the closest to b. Let K be the figure outside c bounded by c, f and the segment between the chosen endpoint of f and the nearest crossing e with c. We have $K \cap S \neq \emptyset$ since the chosen endpoint of f is in S. By a geometric argument, any point in K is in the distance of at

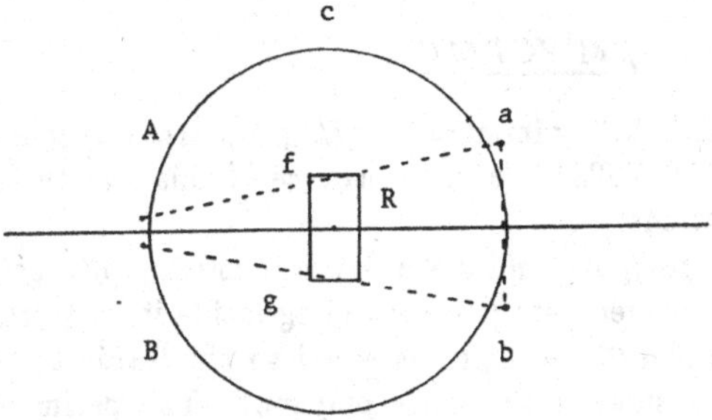

Fig. 1. A possible configuration of the circle c and the edges e, f, g.

most $6r$ from b. Since $c(S,f,e)$ is empty, no edge in $GT(S)$ of length $\leq 6r$ crosses K. The piece of A between f and e together with K forms a figure whose boundary is a convex closed loop. By Lemma 5 and the emptiness of $c(S,f,e)$ there exists a point a in $K \cap S$ that sees the whole diameter of c on e, provided that edges in T of length $> 6r$ are transparent. This contradicts the definition of $GT(S)$ since $|(a,b)| \leq 6r < |e|$ and no edge in T of length $\leq 6r$ crosses (a,b).

If such a point b does not exist and the point a has been already defined, then we proceed dually. So, we may assume without loss of generality that such a point b does not exist and the point a has not been defined yet. Then, by Lemma 5 there exists an edge g of length $\leq 7r$ crossing B such that no edge in T of length $\leq 7r$ crosses c between e and g and $c(S,g,e)$ is empty. Our observations on the endpoints of f also hold for the endpoints of g. Since $|f|,|g| \leq 7r$, the segment between the left endpoints of f and g or between the right endpoints of f and g either crosses or touches the diameter of c on e. Without loss of generality, we may assume that the segment between the left endpoints, say v, crosses or touches the diameter of c on e. Let L_f be the area outside c between f, c, and v. Analogously we define L_g. For any points $x \in L_f$, $y \in L_g$, $|(x,y)| \leq 6r$. As in the case of K, by Lemma 5 and the emptiness of $c(S,f,e)$ ($c(S,g,e)$, respectively), there exists a point a in $L_f \cap S$ (respectively, b in $L_g \cap S$) which sees the whole piece of e lying between the crossing of e with v and the distant crossing of e with c, provided that edges in T of length $> 6r$ are transparent. Since (a,b) crosses e, $|(a,b)| \leq 6r < |e|$, and no edge in T of length $\leq 6r$ crosses (a,b), we again obtain a contradiction with the definition of $GT(S)$. ∎

By substituting $logn$ for t and assuming that the sample area is a square we obtain the following corollary:

Corollary 1. Let S be a random set of n points chosen from a square. For any positive real α, we have:

$$Pr(|DT(S)|/M(S) \leq O(\alpha \times logn)) \geq 1 - n^{1-\alpha}$$

$$Pr(|GT(S)|/M(S) \leq O(\alpha \times logn)) \geq 1 - 2n^{1-\alpha}$$

3. NP — completeness of MWGTMP

In the definition of the minimum weight geometric triangulation of multi-connected polygons problem (MWGTMP) as in the course of this and the next section, we assume the following conventions:

A *polygon with polygonal holes* is a figure consisting of a polygon and a collection of non-overlapping, non-degenerate polygons lying inside it. Vertices of the figure have real coordinates. The *inside* of the figure is equal to the inside of the outer polygon minus the boundaries and insides of the inner polygons. The perimeter of the outer polygon and the contours of the inner polygons form *boundaries* of the figure enclosing its *inside*. A *diagonal* of the figure is any straight-line segment between two of its vertices, lying inside it. A *geometric triangulation* of the figure is a set of its non-intersecting diagonals partitioning its inside into triangles. Notice that a geometric triangulation of the figure is not necessarily maximal as more than two collinear vertices may appear on an edge of a triangle. MWGTMP may be defined as follows:

Given a polygon with polygonal holes and a rational number r, determine whether there exists a geometric triangulation of the figure, T, such that $|T| \leq r$.

The convex hull of a planar point set S together with the interior points of S, can be viewed as a convex polygon with degenerate holes. It will be denoted by $C(S)$ further. We may draw the distinction between MWGTMP and MWT by rephrasing the decision problem of MWT in terms of geometric triangulation as follows:

Given a set of real-coordinate points in the plane, S, and a real number r, determine whether there exists a geometric triangulation of $C(S)$, T, such that T is maximal (i.e. no new diagonal can be draw without crossing these from T) and $|T| \leq r$.

We shall reduce planar satisfiability (PLSAT), shown to be NP-complete in [Lic82], to MWGTMP.

A formula F in conjunctive normal form with exactly three literals per clause (3CNF), whose variables x_i, form the set X and clauses form the set C, is said to be *planar* if the bipartite graph $G(F) = (X \cup C,\ E)$ with $E = \{(x_j, c_j) \mid x_i \text{ or } \neg x_i \text{ is a literal in } c_j\}$ is planar. In fact, we use a slightly less restricted version of PLSAT; the version we use is to decide whether a given planar 3CNF-formula is satisfiable.

To reduce PLSAT to MWGTMP, we construct a polygon with polygonal holes , H , and a rational k such that there exists a geometric triangulation of H whose length is at most k if and only if the input formula F is satisfiable. The figure H will be also used in the hypothetical proof of the NP-completeness of MWGT in Appendix. Its general construction in part follows the constructions presented in [OS82] and [Lin82].

H consists of closed loops and junctions. Variables of F one-to-one correspond to loops, and clauses of F one-to-one correspond to junctions. A straight section of a loop is shown in Fig. 2 A . There are two ways of optimally triangulating such a section (see Fig. 2 B, C). One of them is interpreted as transmitting the 0 signal, and the other as transmitting the 1 signal. A loop corresponding to a variable x enters and leaves a junction corresponding to a clause c if and only if x or $\neg x$ is a literal in c. The straight-line loop section entering a junction is supposed to carry the truth value of the corresponding literal. Therefore, we sometimes need to install inverters at the entry to a junction.

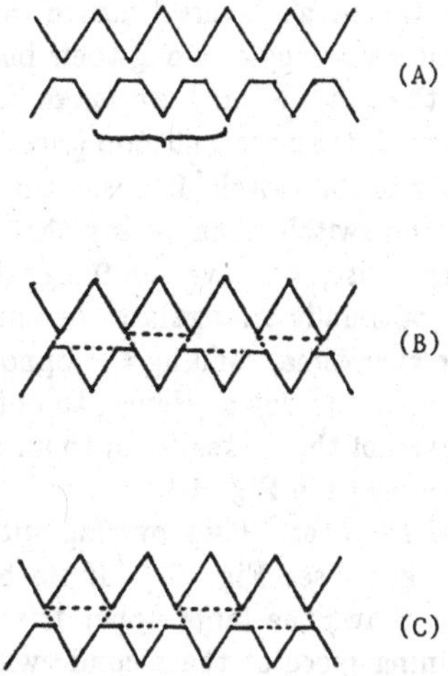

Fig. 2. An example of a straight section of a loop (A) and optimal geometric triangulations of the section (B,C).

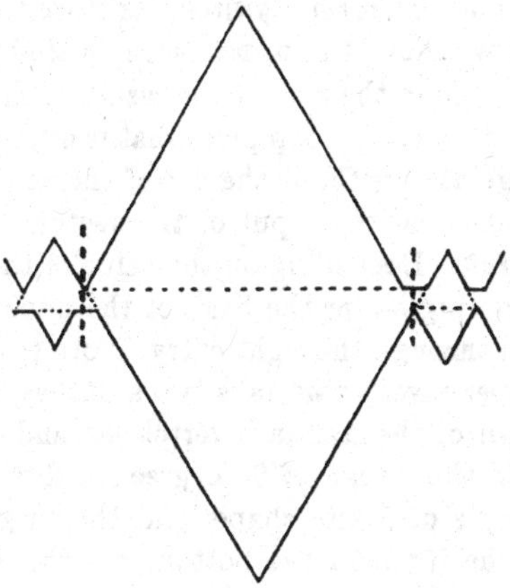

Fig. 3. An example of a switch and an optimal geometric triangulations of the switch.

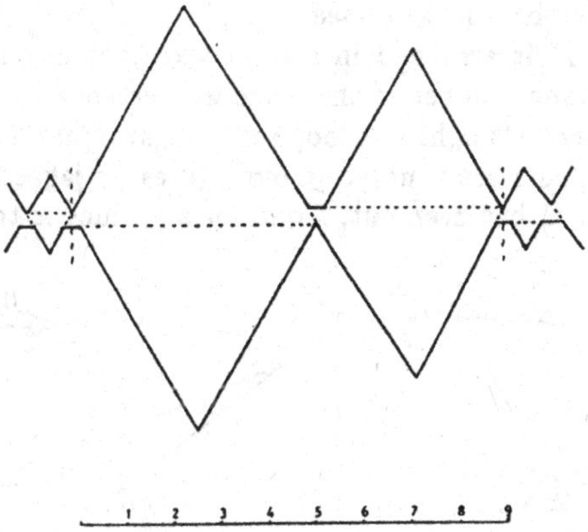

Fig. 4. An example of an inverter and an optimal geometric triangulation of the inverter.

In the design of inverters, loop bends and junctions, we use a universal device called a *switch* . To form a switch, we stick two identical, equilateral triangles along their bases. Next we move the upper triangle slightly down and to the left. Finally we make some entries along the axis of the resulting figure to connect it with the adjacent loop (see Fig. 3). Consider the loop piece that is adjacent to the left entry of the switch. If it is optimally triangulated without the use of the short diagonal inside the switch, then we say that the 1 signal is at the input of the switch (see Fig. 3). Otherwise, we have the 0 signal at the input. Depending on the value of the input signal, we optimally triangulate the switch by drawing either the basis of the upper large triangle or vice versa, sending the opposite signal through the right entry. Note that the right entry is upside down. Hence, to obtain a proper inverter we take two switches, with the total length of their axes equal to an odd number of the standard vertebrae, and connect them in series (see Fig. 4).

In the design of 60 degree bend we use two identical switches. They overlap with a rectangle of a kite shape, and their right entries are blocked (see Fig. 5). If we have 1 at the input of the bottom switch, then the best is to draw: the large upper triangle inside this switch, next the largest triangle in the remaining piece of the second switch, and finally the shortest diagonals in the resulting quadrangles (see Fig. 5 A). Hence, the signal leaving the upper switch is opposite to that entering the bottom switch. The symmetric triangulation is optimal when the 0 signal enters the bottom switch.

To form a junction, we pick three identical, very large switches. Next, we cut identical, equilateral triangles off the top and bottom of each of these switches. Then, we place these cut switches such that their tops form an equilateral triangle. Finally, we erase these tops (see Fig. 6). We shall see that clause junctions behave like three-input OR gates.

Straight-line loop pieces must enter switches and junctions with an appropriate vertebrae phase. By connecting two appropriately long switches of total length l in series, we form a *phase shifter*. In fact, an inverter is a phase shifter where l is equal to an odd multiple of the standard vertebrae length (see Fig. 4).

By applying switches, H is arranged in such a way that any maximal straight-line loop section consists of an even number of the standard vertebrae.

Let us cut H into maximal straight-line loop sections, switches, bends, inverters, phase shifters and junctions (such cuts are denoted in our figures by jagged lines). Let D be the set of all devices into which H has been cut. Consider a geometric triangulation of H, T.

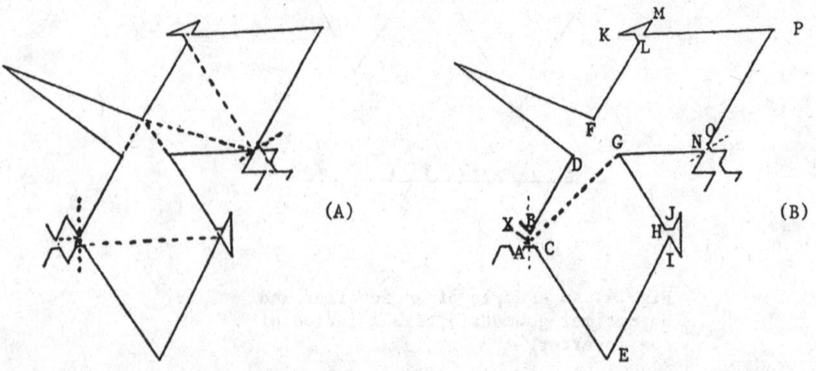

Fig. 5. An example of a bend with an optimal geometric triangulation (A), and distinguished points of the bend (B).

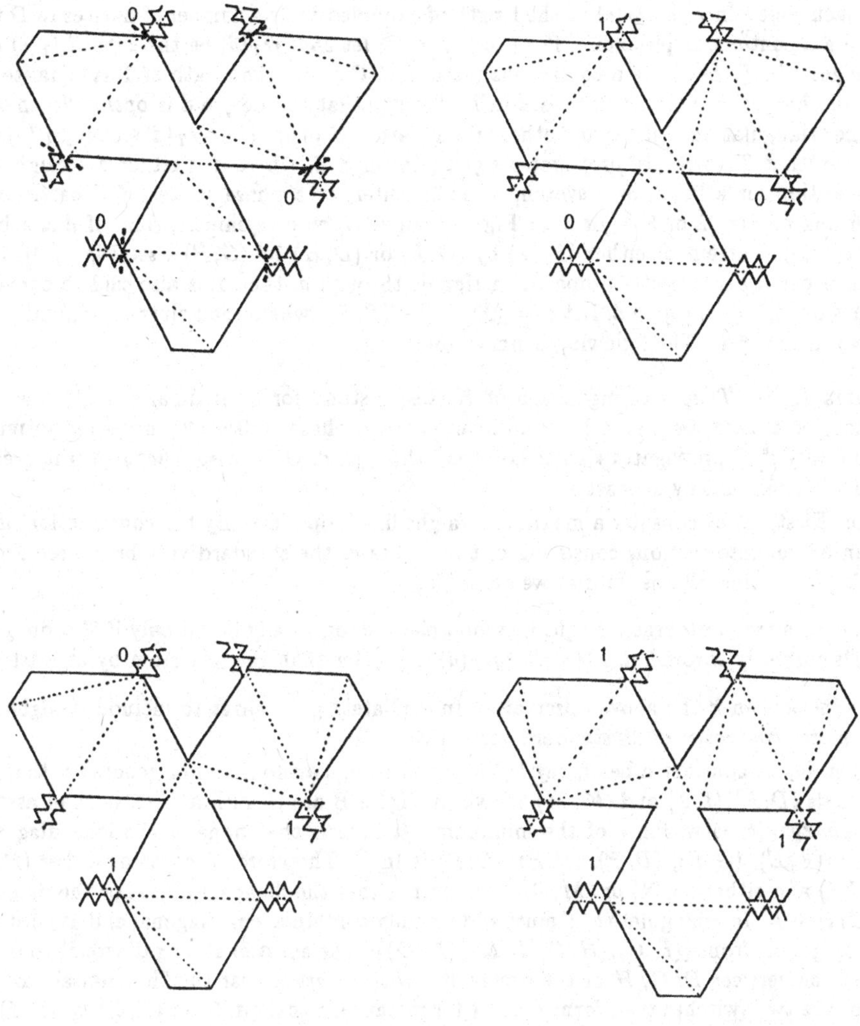

Fig. 6. An example of a junction and optimal geometric triangulations of the junction.

For each edge e in T, let $l_T(e)$ be the length of e divided by the number of devices in D that contain a continuous piece of e. For every d in D, let $charge_T(d)$ be the sum of $l_T(e)$ over all edges e in T that have a continuous piece in d. Clearly, the length of T is equal to the sum of $charge_T(d)$ over all devices d in D. We say that the device d is *optimally charged* by the triangulation T if for any other triangulation U of H, $charge_T(d) \leq charge_U(d)$. We also say that T *correctly propagates signals* through d, where d is either a straight-line loop section, or a bend, or a switch, or an inventer, or a phase shifter, if T partitions d according to Fig. 2 or 5 A, or 3, or Fig. 4, respectively, or symmetrically. If d is a bend and the replacement of either (F,N) by (G,L) or (D,H) by (G,B) (see Fig. 5 B) in T yields a partition correctly propagating signals through d, then T is also said to correctly propagate signals through d. Let $\epsilon = |(X,G)| - |(B,G)|$ where the points X, B, and G are shown in Fig. 5 B. The following lemmas hold:

Lemma 1. Let T be a triangulation of H. Let d stand for a maximal straight-line loop section, or a bend, or a switch, or an inverter, or a phase shifter. T charges d optimally if and only if T propagates signals correctly through d. Otherwise, $charge_T(d)$ is greater than the minimum by at least ϵ.

Proof. First, let us consider a maximal straight-line loop piece. By the construction of H, it can be cut into sections consisting of two copies of the standard vertebrae (see Fig. 2 A). By inspecting all possibilities we observe:

T charges a two-vertebrae straight-line loop piece, d, optimally if and only if T propagates signals correctly through d. Else, $charge_T(d)$ is greater than the minimum by at least ϵ.

By induction on k the above observation immediately generalizes to include straight-line loop pieces composed of $2k$ standard vertebrae.

In turn, let us consider a bend, say b. We may assume without loss of generality that the diagonals $(D,F),(I,J)$ and (K,M) shown in Fig. 5 B are in T. Further, we shall assume that $charge_T(b)$ is within ϵ of the minimum. It follows that none of the long diagonals (D,E), (F,E), (G,E), (D,P), (F,P), (G,P) is in T. Therefore, T contains either (B,H) or (C,I) and either (L,N) or (M,O). Moreover, either the diagonal (D,G) or the diagonal (F,G) is in T. To triangulate b, T must additionally contain a long diagonal and at least two tiny diagonals from $\{(B,C),(H,I),(L,M),(N,O)\}$. The additional long diagonal connects one of the vertices D, G, H at the center of b with a vertex near the "horizontal" axis of one of the two switches transformed to b (for instance, either (A,G) or (B,G), or (D,I), or (D,H), or (F,O), or (F,N), or (G,M), or (G,L)). If T propagates signals correctly through b (remember the definition of this phrase), then the additional long diagonal does not cross this axis and only two additional tiny diagonals are drawn. Otherwise, the long diagonal intersects the axis and still at least two tiny diagonals are drawn; hence, $charge_T(b)$ is greater than the minimum at least by ϵ.

The lemma trivially holds for switches, hence, it holds also for inverters and phase-shifters which are connections of two switches in series. ▮

Lemma 2. Let T be the triangulation of H such that for any junction j, $charge_T(j)$ is within ϵ of the minimum. T carries at least one 1 to the inputs of each junction, and charges each junction optimally.

Proof. Arguing as in the proof of Lemma 6 for bends, we conclude that T partitions any junction j into (see Fig. 6):

(a) a large triangle covering the center of the junction and half of one of the three switches transformed to the junctions,
(b) five trapezoids crossed by diagonals.

If T carries at least one 1 to the inputs of j, then there are at least three smaller trapezoids among the above five-tuple. Otherwise, there are only two smaller trapezoids. As the switches transformed to j are much larger than those transformed to a bend, the difference between the length of the former and latter triangulation within j is greater than ϵ ∎

For each device d in D, we can easily find the minimum possible value of $charge_T(d)$. Let k be the sum of the minimum charges over all devices in D. It follows from Lemma 1 and 2 and the design of H that T is a minimum weight triangulation of H and the formula F is satisfiable if and only if $|T| < k + \epsilon$. On the other hand, if F is satisfiable then we can triangulate the entries of junctions according to the values of corresponding literals in a valuation satisfying F, and then complete the partial triangulation according to the propagation rules. By Lemma 1 and 2, we obtain a triangulation of length k. Hence:

Lemma 3.
(1) F is satisfiable if and only if there exists a triangulation of H whose length is k.
(2) F is not satisfiable if and only if every triangulation of H is of length $\geq k + \epsilon$.

As H and k can be constructed in logarithmic space and MWGT is in NP, we conclude:

Theorem 2. MWGTMP is NP-complete in the strong sense (see [GJ78]).

Of course, to prove the NP-completeness of MWGTMP, it is sufficient to derive only the first part of Lemma 8. The second part, exhibiting the gap between optimal and other triangulations of H, will be used in Appendix. In contrast to the NP-completeness of MWGTMP, we have:

Fact 1. A minimum weight geometric triangulation of a simply connected polygon with n corners can be found in time $O(n^4)$.
Proof. We apply a dynamic programming procedure, similar to that for finding a minimum weight triangulation of a simply connected polygon, given in [Lin83]. Let an *intermediate polygon* mean a figure whose contour consists of a continuous piece of the contour of the original polygon and none or one of its diagonals. If an intermediate polygon is not a triangle, we split it into smaller polygons as follows. First, we define a candidate vertex: if the intermediate polygon is the original polygon then any its vertex may be chosen, otherwise we choose an arbitrary endpoint of the boundary diagonal. Now, we may split the intermediate polygon by drawing either a diagonal not adjacent to the candidate point which cuts off a triangle whose corner is the candidate point or two diagonals connecting the candidate point and the other endpoint of the boundary diagonal with another vertex. The drawn diagonals may overlap with boundary edges. The first way yields at most $\binom{n-1}{2}$ different splittings, the second at most $n - 3$ different splittings. Let us inductively assume that for each of the intermediate polygons which is a part of the given intermediate polygon, a minimum weight triangulation has been found. A minimum weight triangulation of the given intermediate polygon can be found by trying all of the at most $O(n^2)$ possible splittings and choosing that yielding a triangulation of the smallest total edge length. Because there are $O(n^2)$ intermediate polygons, the entire procedure takes $O(n^4)$ time. ∎

Acknowledgments

I would like to express my appreciation to Ron Pinter for his encouragment, and to Joseph O'Rourke for a lot of constructive comments.

References

[AV78] Angluin,D., and L.G. Valiant, *Fast probabilistic algorithms for Hamiltonian circuits and matchings*, Proc. 9th Ann. ACM Symp. on Theory of Computing, New York, 1978.
[DG70] Duppe, R.D. and Gottschalk, H.H., *Automatische Interpolation von Isolinen bei willkurlich stutzpunkten*, Allgemeine Vermessungsnachrichten, 77, 1970.
[GJ78] Garey, M.R., and D.S. Johnson, *Computers and Intractability: A Guide to the Theory of NP-completeness*, H. Freeman, San Francisco.
[Ki80] Kirkpatrick,D.G., *A Note on Delauney and Optimal Triangulations*, Information Processing Letters, Vol. 10, No.3, 1980.
[Lic82] Lichtenstein, D., *Planar Formulae and their Uses*, SIAM Journal on Computing, Vol. 11, No. 2, 1982.
[Lin82] Lingas,A., *The Power of Non-rectilinear Holes*, Proceedings of 9th ICALP, Aarhus, July 1982.
[Lin83] Lingas, A., *Advances in Minimum Weight Triangulation*, Ph.D. dissertation, Linköping University, 1983.
[Ll77] Lloyd, E.L., *On Triangulations of a Set of Points in the Plane*, Proc. 18th Annual IEEE Conference on the Foundations of Computer Science, Providence , 1977.
[MZ79] Manacher,G.K. and A.L. Zorbrist, *Neither the Greedy nor the Delauney triangulation of a planar point set approximates the optimal triangulation*, Information Processing Letters, Vol.9, No.1, 1979.
[OS82] O'Rourke J. and K. Supowit, *Some NP-hard polygon decomposition problems*, to appear.
[SH75] Shamos,M.I. and Hoey, D., *Closest Point Problems*, Proceedings of the 16th Annual Symposium on the Foundations of Computer Science, IEEE, 1975.
[Sha75] Shamos, M.I., *Geometric Complexity*, Proceedings of 7th ACM Symposium on the theory of Computing, 1975.

Appendix: NP — completenessof MWGT ?

The decision problem of minimum weight geometric triangulation for planar point sets (MWGT) may be defined in terms of geometric triangulation of multi-connected polygons as follows:

Given a set of real-coordinate points in the plane, S, and a rational r, determine whether there exists a geometric triangulation of $C(S)$ whose total length does not exceed r.

Thus, MWGT differs from MWT only in releasing the requirement of maximality for geometric triangulation (see the definition of MWT given in the previous section).

In this section, we give an idea of how to prove NP-completeness of the minimum weight geometric triangulation problem (MWGT). In fact, we prove that if the figure H from the previous section satisfies some conjecture, then MWGT is NP-complete. Although the conjecture seems intuitively obvious to the author, it probably requires a long proof. If it can be proved, then perhaps we could use the NP-completeness of MWGT in order to prove the NP-completeness of MWT.

Analogously as in the previous section, our aim is to reduce PLSAT to MWGT. Let F be a planar 3CNF formula, and let H and k respectively be the figure and the threshold number constructed in the reduction of PLSAT to MWGTMP. Let δ be a rational. Since dimensions of H are polynomially related to the size of F, in time polynomial in the length of the descriptions of F and δ, we can construct the set of points in the plane S such that:

(a) all points of S lie on boundaries of H,
(b) all vertices of H are in S,
(c) for any boundary point of H, there is a point of S within the distance $\delta/2$ at most.

Let us assume the following notations:

m = the length of a minimum weight geometric triangulation of H,
h = the total length of minimum weight geometric triangulations of the polygonal holes in H, and the polygons between the convex hull of S and H, provided that the set of vertices of these holes and polygons is extended to the set of all points in S respectively lying on their boundaries.
b = the total length of boundaries of H plus the length of the convex hull of S.

The number b can be determined in polynomial in the size of F time. We shall choose δ such that the cardinality of S will be polynomially related to the number of vertices of H, and in consequence, to the size of F. Therefore, we can also find h in polynomial time, by an obvious generalization of the cubic-time algorithm for minimum weight geometric triangulation of simply connected polygons (i.e. extending the set of polygon vertices to include all points of S lying on the perimeters of these polygons).

Consider a minimum weight geometric triangulation of S, say T. We shall show that $m+h+b-C\delta \le |T| \le m+h+b$, where C is a constant uniform in the size of F. As previously, let k be the length of a minimum weight geometric triangulation of H when F is satisfiable. By utilizing the gap between k and the length of a minimum weight triangulation of H when F is not satisfiable (see Lemma 8 in Section 3), we can choose δ so small that S has a geometric triangulation of the length not greater than $k+h+b$ if and only if F is satisfiable (i.e. $\epsilon > C\delta$. Like the gap, δ is polynomial in the size of F.

Given a polygon with polygonal holes, a $\delta-$*quadrangle* is any convex quadrangle r such that:

(1) the vertices of r lie on boundaries of the figure,
(2) the edges of r lie within the figure,
(3) at least one of the edges of r lies on a polygonal boundary and is of length not greater than δ.

A set of non-intersecting segments between points in S, lying within H, and partitioning H into triangles and δ-quadrangles is called a *δ-geometric triangulation* of H.
Analogously, given a polygonal hole in H, or a polygon between the convex hull of S and H, a set of non-intersecting segments between points in S, lying within the hole or polygon, respectively, and partitioning it into triangles and δ-quadrangles is called a *δ-geometric triangulation* of the hole or polygon, respectively.

The conjecture on H is as follows:

Conjecture 1. There exists a rational δ polynomially related to the size of F and a constant c uniform in F such that:

(a) if $m(\delta)$ stands for the minimum length of a δ-geometric triangulation of H, then $m(\delta) = m$.

(b) if $h(\delta)$ stanas for the minimum total length of δ-geometric triangulations of the holes in H and polygons between the convex hull of S and H, then $h(\delta) \geq h - c\delta$.

In other words, Conjecture 1 (a) says: for δ small enough, any minimum weight geometric triangulation of H achieves the minimum length among all δ-geometric triangulations of H. Really, if we look at the diagrams of standard parts of H, it is difficult to imagine how the use of the additional vertices on boundaries of H or δ-quadrangles, when δ is very small, could provide better solutions. Conjecture 1 (b) says: for δ small enough, the difference between the total length of minimum weight geometric triangulations of the holes in H and polygons between the convex hull of S and H, and the minimum total length of δ-geometric triangulations of the same figures is at most proportional to δ. As we do not know the exact shape of the holes in H, we cannot say that Conjecture 1 (b) is weaker than Conjecture 1 (a).

Let E be the set of all boundary edges of H and all edges of the convex hull. Next, let d be the minimum distance between two non-adjacent edges in E.

We can easily find a triangulation of S, for instance, by applying one of the polynomial-time heuristics mentioned in Introduction. We shall use its length, say M, to estimate the length of a minimum weight geometric triangulation of S.

Let us call a maximal piece of a boundary edge of H, not touching edges of T, a *window*. Any window is framed by either a vertex of H and an edge in T (see Fig. 7 A) or two edges in T (see Fig. 7 B). Each of these framing edges touches some edges over and below the crossed boundary edge. With the window, let us associate the pieces of the framing edges lying between the closest edges in E which are touched over and below. By the definition of d, each of these pieces is of length d at least. Two windows can share such a piece, two more can share the upper part of the piece, and two the lower part. It follows from the optimality of T that the total number of windows is not greater than $6M/d$. By filling them with additional diagonals, we extend the length of T by less than $(6M/d) \times \delta$, obtaining a set of edges covering all boundaries of H. The additional diagonals cut some triangles in T into δ-quadrangles and triangles. By Conjecture 1 , the length of the entire resulting δ-geometric triangulation is not less than $m+h+b-c\delta$. Thus the length of T is not less than $m+h+b-(6M/d+c) \times \delta$. By choosing δ small enough and employing the ϵ gap between the value of m when F is satisfiable, i.e. k, and not satisfiable, we obtain:

Theorem 3. If Conjecture 1 holds, then MWGT is NP-complete.

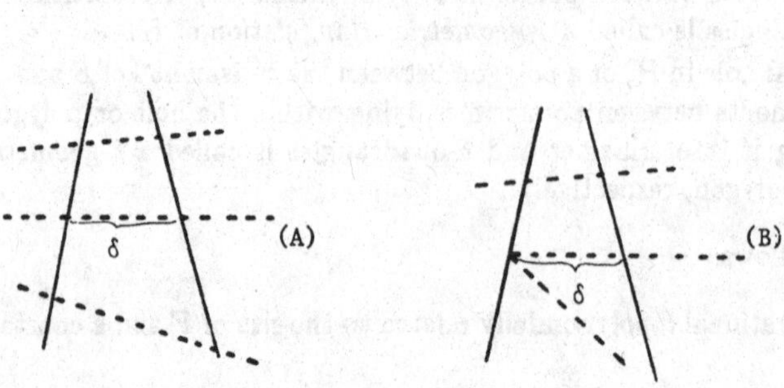

Fig. 7. Two cases of a window in a boundary edge of H. Edges in T are marked with continous lines, whereas edges of H are marked with broken lines.

Decision Problems for Exponential Rings: The p-adic case

Angus Macintyre*
Department of Mathematics
Yale University
New Haven, Connecticut 06520

§1. Exponential rings.

An exponential ring (or E-ring) is a pair (R,E), where R is a commutative ring with 1, and E is a morphism of the additive group of R into the multiplicative group of R. E-rings are an equational class, whose basic algebra is elegantly presented in [D1].

Frequently one deals with E-rings R with extra structure. If R is a field, we refer to it as an E-field. If R is an ordered ring (resp. field), we refer to it as an ordered E-ring (resp. ordered E-field). In the latter setting, an important role is played by the Dahn-Wolters axiom $E(x) \geq x+1$ [D1]. This inequality is of course inspired by the classical $e^x \geq x+1$ on $\mathbb{R}$, and its role in proving $\frac{d}{dx}e^x = e^x$.

Without doubt the most interesting E-rings are $(\mathbb{C},e^x)$ and $(\mathbb{R},e^x)$. The former is undecidable, and we hope that the latter is not. Much has been learned about both in recent years. To learn the basics, the reader should consult the admirable [D1] and [D2]. Deeper information may be glimpsed in [H].

I refer to [D1] for the basic notions on exponential polynomials. $R[X]^E$ is the E-ring of exponential polynomials over R. The reader is assumed familiar with the universal property of $R[X]^E$ (freeness), and with the completeness theorems in [D1] giving conditions under which an $f \in R[X]^E$ which is identically zero on R is the zero of $R[X]^E$. For example, this is true in $\mathbb{R}$ or $\mathbb{C}$ with the classical e^x.

§2. p-adic exponentiation.

It has proved worthwhile in model theory to look systematically for analogies between $\mathbb{R}$ and $\mathbb{Q}_p$. For example, in [M1] I gave a new quantifier-elimination for $\mathbb{Q}_p$, because the Ax-Kochen elimination was not precisely analogous to that for $\mathbb{R}$. Recently I learned of the gratifying use of this elimination by Denef [De] in connection with Poincare series.

Now, there is a p-adic e^x, defined by the usual series. But the series converges only for $v(x) > e/p-1$ [A]. So here we have a partially

*Partially supported by N.S.F. Grant

defined E on $R = \mathbb{Q}_p$. As in $\mathbb{R}$ we have $E(o) = 1$, and $E(x+y) = E(x).E(y)$, but of course only when the right hand side is defined. See [A].

There are devices for getting a totally defined E, not on $\mathbb{Q}_p$ but say on $\tilde{\mathbb{Q}}_p$, the algebraic closure of $\tilde{\mathbb{Q}}_p$. See [A]. From a logician's standpoint this move is regrettable, and for two reasons. The first is that $\tilde{\mathbb{Q}}_p$ has no analogy to $\mathbb{R}$ (for example, it is not locally compact). Secondly, I think $(\tilde{\mathbb{Q}}_p, E)$ is undecidable, for the following reason. One defines a p-adic log, and considers the equation

$$\log(1+x) = 0.$$

This has infinitely many zeros in $\tilde{\mathbb{Q}}_p$, and for each $1+x$ is a root of unity [A]. So one interprets $(\tilde{\mathbb{Q}}_p, \Gamma)$ where Γ is the group of roots of unity. I conjecture that the latter structure is undecidable.

Let us therefore stay on $\mathbb{Q}_p$. Let $\mathbb{Z}_p$ be the ring of p-adic integers. It is known that the function $(1+p)^x$ on $\mathbb{N}$ extends (uniquely) to a function $E_p : \mathbb{Z}_p \to \mathbb{Z}_p$ such that $(\mathbb{Z}_p, E_p)$ is an E-ring.

Lemma 1. E_p is analytic on $\mathbb{Z}_p$, with derivative $\frac{d}{dx}E_p(x) = \log(1+p).E_p(x)$.

Proof. $E_p(x) = e^{x \log(1+p)}$ for $x \in \mathbb{Z}_p$. ∎

From this just as in [D1,§4] one deduces:

Theorem 2. Any identity in the language of E-rings and constants from $\mathbb{Z}_p$ which holds in $(\mathbb{Z}_p, E_p)$ is derivable from the axioms of E-rings together with the diagram of $(\mathbb{Z}_p, E_p)$.

This is the precise analogue of a result about $(\mathbb{R}, e^x)$ and $(\mathbb{C}, e^x)$ [D].

There is some room for improvement. Note that $\mathbb{N}$ is closed under $+, \cdot, E_p$. Also, $\mathbb{N}$ is dense in $\mathbb{Z}_p$. So we naturally restrict to the positive language of E-rings (i.e. we drop out $-$), and have firstly:

Lemma 3. Any identity in the positive language of E-rings holds in $\mathbb{N}$ if and only if it holds in $\mathbb{Z}_p$.

Several people, notably Henson-Rubel [HR] and Wilkie [W] have provided satisfying completeness theorems for exponentiation on $\mathbb{N}$. In particular we have:

Theorem 4. An identity in the positive language of E-rings holds in $(\mathbb{N}, E_p)$ if and only if it is derivable from the following axioms:

(1) axioms for commutative semirings with 1;

(2) $E(x+y) = E(x).E(y)$

(3) $E(o) = 1$

(4) $E(1) = 1+p$.

Such a completeness theorem does not formally imply a decision procedure for identities (but in the case of the above theorem known proofs do yield decidability). Actually decidability was proved earlier, by other methods, in [M2].

Theorem 5. The set of identities in the positive language of E-rings holding in $(\mathbb{N},E_p)$ is primitive recursive.

I make a final observation about E_p. We have on $\mathbb{R}$ the function $E_p^{\mathbb{R}}(x) = (1+p)^x$. $(\mathbb{N},E_p)$ is not dense in $(\mathbb{R},E_p^{\mathbb{R}})$, but nevertheless I proved in [M2] that the positive identities of $(\mathbb{N},E_p)$ are exactly those of $(\mathbb{R},E_p^{\mathbb{R}})$. So, although we must strictly distinguish $(1+p)^x$ on $\mathbb{R}$ and $\mathbb{Z}_p$, we have:

Theorem 6. The set of identities in the positive language of E-rings holding in $(\mathbb{Z}_p,E_p)$ is the same as the set of positive identities holding in $(\mathbb{R},E_p^{\mathbb{R}})$.

Problem 1. Are the E-ring identities of $(\mathbb{Z}_p,E_p)$ the same as those of $(\mathbb{R},E_p^{\mathbb{R}})$?

§3. Finiteness Theorems.

3.1. After the identity problem is resolved, or equivalently, the free E-rings are understood, one turns to the structure of zero-sets.

Thus, let (R,E) be an E-ring, and let $f \in R[X_1,\ldots,X_{n+m}]^E$ (i.e. f is an E-polynomial over R). We analyze the sets

$$\{(x_1,\ldots,x_n) \in R^n : f(x_1,\ldots,x_n,y_1,\ldots,y_m) = 0\}$$

$$(= \mathrm{Zer}(f,y_1,\ldots,y_m))$$

as $y_1,\ldots,y_m$ vary over R.

When $n = 1$, and (R,E) is $(\mathbb{R},e^x)$ one has:

Theorem 7. There is a primitive recursive function $N_m : \mathbb{Z}[X_1,\ldots,X_{m+1}]^E \to \mathbb{N}$ such that for any $\alpha_1,\ldots,\alpha_m \in \mathbb{R}$ and any $f \in \mathbb{Z}[X_1,\ldots,X_{m+1}]^E$ either $\mathrm{Zer}(f,\alpha_1,\ldots,\alpha_m) = \mathbb{R}$ or $\mathrm{Zer}(f,\alpha_1,\ldots,\alpha_m)$ has cardinality $\le N_m(f)$.

Proof. See [R] or [M2]. ∎

The above result fails for $(\mathbb{C},e^x)$ for reasons directly connected with the undecidability of that structure.

There is much interesting work in progress concerning

(i) higher-dimensional analogues;

(ii) analogues for Pfaffian analytic functions.

For (i) the main papers are [D1] and [H]. The finiteness theorems in [D1] are not effective, but I have made them so in unpublished lectures. In the same spirit I can extend Theorem 7 to Pfaffian functions using [H].

3.2. A natural goal is to prove the analogue of Theorem 7 for $(\mathbb{Z}_p, E_p)$. The methods used in the real case fail utterly. But since $\mathbb{Z}_p$ is compact we have stronger hypotheses, and some progress has been made.

The basic point is that each $f \in \mathbb{Z}_p[X]^E$ defines a function analytic on $\mathbb{Z}_p$ [A]. Thus Strassmann's Theorem [L] applies, giving:

Lemma 8. If $f \in \mathbb{Z}_p[X]^E$ either f is identically zero on $\mathbb{Z}_p$ or f has only finitely many zeros on $\mathbb{Z}_p$.

This is far short of what we want. I believe the following:

Conjecture. There is a primitive recursive function $N_{m,p} : \mathbb{Z}[X_1,\ldots,X_{m+1}]^E \to \mathbb{N}$ such that for any $\alpha_1,\ldots,\alpha_m$ in $\mathbb{Z}_p$ and any $f \in \mathbb{Z}[X_1,\ldots,X_{m+1}]^E$ either $\mathrm{Zer}(f,\alpha_1,\ldots,\alpha_m) = \mathbb{Z}_p$ or $\mathrm{Zer}(f,\alpha_1,\ldots,\alpha_m)$ has cardinality $\leq N_{m,p}(f)$.

Note that at present we do not even have a bounding function $N_{m,p}$, far less a primitive recursive one.

3.3. We have just seen an important respect in which we know far less about $\mathbb{Z}_p$ than about $\mathbb{R}$. To finish, I shall exhibit some respects in which we know more about $\mathbb{Z}_p$ than about $\mathbb{R}$. Though we know far less globally about exponential polynomials over $\mathbb{Z}_p$, we know more locally.

$\mathbb{Q}_p$ has only finitely many field extensions of dimension n. Each is given by a polynomial over $\mathbb{Q}$, and these polynomials can be found effectively. In particular, one can effectively present, for each n, a finite extension of $\mathbb{Q}_p$ containing all extensions of $\mathbb{Q}_p$ of dimension $\leq n$.

Note that each finite extension K of $\mathbb{Q}_p$ has an appropriate E_p. This will be defined by

$$E_p(x) = e^{x \log(1+p)} \quad , \text{ for } v(x) \geq 0.$$

If O_p is the ring of integers of K, E_p maps O_p to O_p, and extends the usual E_p. O_p is a free $\mathbb{Z}_p$-module of rank $[K:\mathbb{Q}_p]$, and it is easy to see that E_p on O_p is determined by its values on a basis of O_p over $\mathbb{Z}_p$. So, the diagram of (O_p, E_p) is uniformly recursive in the diagram of $(\mathbb{Z}_p, E_p)$ and the finite data giving E_p on a basis of O_p over $\mathbb{Z}_p$.

With this hint, one can state:

Theorem 8. There is an algorithm which, given $f \in \mathbb{Z}[X]^E$ computes a finite extension K of $\mathbb{Q}_p$ with integers O_P, and then computes, recursively in the diagram of (O_P, E_P), the following:

(i) the number of roots of f in $\mathbb{Z}_p$, with multiplicities;

(ii) a bound for the valuation of any nonzero root;

(iii) the roots to any desired accuracy.

The proof is complicated, and will be given elsewhere. It involves techniques from Amice, Chapter 4, as well as [M1].

References

[A] Y. Amice, Les Nombres P-adiques, Presses Universitaires de France, 1975.

[De] J. Denef, The rationality of the Poincaré series associated to the p-adic points on a variety, preprint, Leuven, 1983.

[D1] L. van den Dries, Exponential rings, exponential polynomials and exponential functions, to appear in Pacific Journal.

[D2] ______________, Real analytic Hardy fields and exponentially definable subsets of the plane, to appear in American Journal.

[H] A.G. Hovanskii, On a class of systems of transcendental equations, translated in Soviet Math. Doklady 22 (1980), 762-765.

[HR] W. Henson and L. Rubel, preprint, Urbana 1982.

[L] D.J. Lewis, Diophantine equations: p-adic methods, 25-75 in Studies in Number Theory, (W.J. LeVeque, editor) MAA 1969.

[M1] A. Macintyre, On definable subsets of p-adic fields, J.S.L. 41 (1976), 605-610.

[M2] __________, The laws of exponentiation, Springer Lecture Notes 890 (1979), 185-198.

[R] D. Richardson, Solution of the identity problem for integral exponential functions, Zeitschr fur Math. Logik 15 (1969), 333-360.

[W] A. Wilkie, preprint, Yale, 1981.

FUNCTIONAL BEHAVIOR OF NONDETERMINISTIC PROGRAMS*

Michael G. Main
Department of Computer Science
University of Colorado
Boulder, CO 80309 USA

David B. Benson
Department of Computer Science
Washington State University
Pullman, WA 99164-1210 USA

ABSTRACT

The functional behavior of a deterministic program is a function $f:D\to D$, where D is some set of states for the computation. This notion of functional behaviors can be extended to nondeterministic programs using techniques from linear algebra. In particular, the functional behavior of a nondeterministic program is a linear transformation $f:A\to A$, where A is a free semiring module. Other notions from linear algebra carry over into this setting. For example, weakest preconditions and predicate transformers correspond to well-studied concepts in linear algebra. Finally, we consider multiple-input and multiple-output programs. The functional behavior of a nondeterministic program with multiple inputs and outputs is a linear transformation $f:\bigotimes^m A\to\bigotimes^n A$, where $\bigotimes^x A$ is an iterated tensor product of the semiring module A. This is in contrast to the deterministic case, where such a program is a function $f:D^m\to D^n$, using the Cartesian products D^m and D^n.

1. INTRODUCTION

In denotational semantics, the behavior of a deterministic program is a function $f:D\to D$, where D is a data space or set of "states" for some machine. If nonterminating computations are possible, then D may contain a special element $\perp \in D$ to represent this fact. A tuple of inputs or outputs to a program can be represented by the set $D^m = \{(d_1, \cdots d_m) \mid d_i \in D\}$. In particular, the functional behavior of a program with an m-tuple of inputs and an n-tuple of outputs is a function $f:D^m\to D^n$.

The purpose of this paper is to extend our understanding of the functional behavior of programs to nondeterministic situations. Toward this end, we advocate the use of concepts from linear algebra which encompass at least three different views of nondeterminism. In the first view, the only property of interest is what possible outputs a nondeterministic program may produce from a given input. This is the widely studied standard notion of nondeterminism [3,7,12,13,14,16]. An alternative is to record with each possible output state the number of different computation paths which lead to it [1]. Such a record may indicate the relative probability of any state occurring as an output, similar to models studied by Kozen and Saheb-Djahromi [8,15]. A third view of nondeterminism also generalizes Kozen's work. In this view, we record with each state some predicate which must hold in order for that state to be a possible output. The predicates may involve timing considerations which can affect a computation, or they may be statements about nondeterministic choices made by a program.

These three notions of nondeterminism are developed in section 2. The unifying idea behind the three models is a semiring module. In all three cases, we show how the functional behavior of a nondeterministic program is a linear transformation $f:A\to A$, where A is a free semiring module generated by a set D of states.

Semiring modules are a generalization of vector spaces. In section 3, we show how some other ideas from linear algebra generalize to our setting. In particular, we show how

*This work was supported in part by National Science Foundation Grant MCS-8003433.

elements of a semiring module A^* -- called the dual module of A -- correspond to "conditions" in the sense of Dijkstra [3,4]. Weakest preconditions are developed using kernels of linear transformations. Predicate transformers are linear functional transformers.

Programs with a tuple of inputs or outputs are considered in section 4, using a suggestion of Hennessy and Plotkin [7]. The functional behavior of a nondeterministic program with an m-tuple of inputs and an n-tuple of outputs is shown to be a linear transformation $f:\otimes^m A \to \otimes^n A$, where $\otimes^z A$ is an iterated tensor product of the module A.

Our study is limited in two ways: First, we consider mainly finite nondeterminism. For any given input, a nondeterministic program has only a finite number of possible outputs. For the most part, our results carry over to infinite nondeterminism, and occasionally we indicate how to do this. The second restriction is that at the moment we do not consider recursively defined programs. We plan to handle such programs in the future using ordered semiring modules and least fixed point techniques, extending the work of Plotkin, Smyth and others [7,12,16].

2. NONDETERMINISM, SEMIRINGS AND SEMIRING MODULES

We start from a set of possible deterministic states for a computation. The set of states is denoted by D to remind one of deterministic, domain or data. These states may have internal structure (for example, they may be continuations or infinite data streams), however we are not concerned with such structure.

2.1. Nondeterministic Distributions of States

Nondeterminism occurs when the output of a computation is not uniquely determined by its input. In this case, a record may be kept of the possible output states which could arise from a given input state. Such a record is called a ***nondeterministic distribution of states***, or simply a ***distribution***. There are a variety of notions for a nondeterministic distribution of states. Manes discusses many in his development of distributional set theories [11]. We discuss three such ideas, concentrating on *finite* nondeterminism -- i.e., each computation has only a finite number of output choices for a given input. Most of the results carry over to the infinite case and occasionally we point out how to do this.

The first possibility is to list all the different deterministic states which may arise in a nondeterministic computation starting from a given input state. In this case, a distribution consists of a finite subset of D. If infinite nondeterminism is allowed in the model, then infinite subsets of D are also suitable distributions. In either case, the collection of all distributions has set union as the semantic correspondent to the **or** operator available in some programming languages. For reasons made clear later, it is convenient to use the addition sign to represent the union of distributions: for distributions x and y, the distribution $x+y$ is read "x or y" and is the set union of x and y. The collection of all distributions has the structure of a commutative monoid with respect to +. The empty set is the identity for this monoid.

There remains the question of the meaning of the empty set of states. We take the view that the empty set is not a possible outcome of a nondeterministic computation. That is, every computation must produce some state as its output. If a computation never terminates, the "output state" may be represented by a special element $\perp \in D$. Despite the fact that the empty distribution is an impossible output, we keep it in the collection of distributions in order to answer questions such as: what inputs to a particular program give a correct output? In general, the answer to this question will be a nondeterministic distribution of states. Sometimes there may be no input which makes a program correct, in which case the answer to the above question will be "the empty distribution". Questions like these are the subject of section 3

If the issue is simply which states may be reached by a nondeterministic computation, then the subset notion of distributions suffices. Another choice is to count the number of different computation paths which give rise to each state in a final distribution [1]. In this case, we need a *multiset* of deterministic states to record the number of computation paths leading to each possible state. For example, the multiset $\{d_1, d_1, d_2\}$ represents two paths leading to state d_1 and one path leading to state d_2. A finite distribution is any finite multiset with elements from D. For infinite nondeterminism, infinite multisets are allowed.

Additive notation is a convenient way of denoting multisets. Let $\sum_{d \in D} n_d d$ be a formal sum running over all the states in D. Each term $n_d d$ consists of the count $n_d \geq 0$ associated with the state $d \in D$. Thus, $\sum_{d \in D} n_d d$ denotes the multiset containing n_d copies of d for each $d \in D$. The empty multiset, denoted by 0, represents an impossible outcome, as did the empty set in the subset version of nondeterministic distributions. We may also view a sum $\sum_{d \in D} n_d d$ as an element in a vector space with unit vectors d and coefficients n_d. This is not strictly correct, as the coefficients are natural numbers, rather than arbitrary real numbers. The correct formalism -- a semiring module -- is given later in this section.

For finite nondeterminism, each coefficient n_d in a sum $\sum_{d \in D} n_d d$ is an element of $\mathbf{N} = \{0, 1, 2, \ldots\}$. Furthermore, only a finite number of the n_d are nonzero. If infinite nondeterminism is of interest, additive notation may still be used by extending the allowable coefficients to $\mathbf{N}^\infty = \mathbf{N} \cup \{\infty\}$. Infinite nondeterminism is further developed elsewhere [1].

A third view of nondeterminism is an extension of the idea of recording the path count of a state. Indeed, it also generalizes some aspects of Kozen's work on probabilistic nondeterminism [8]. Let C be any distributive lattice with a supremum (1) and an infinum (0). The elements of C may be thought of as conditions or predicates having an effect on what outputs are possible from a nondeterministic computation. For example, the predicates could make statements about timing considerations which affect a computation. The "least upper bound" operation of the lattice corresponds to the **or** of two predicates, while "greatest lower bound" is **and**. The supremum is the always **true** predicate, and the infinum is the **false** predicate.

In this view of nondeterminism, we record the condition $c_d \in C$ which must hold for each state $d \in D$ to be a possible output. A distribution is a formal sum $\sum_{d \in D} c_d d$ with the coefficients drawn from C. For finite nondeterminism, only a finite number of the coefficients are nonzero in any sum. Results relating this view of nondeterminism to problems in concurrent computation are given elsewhere [2]. Of course, this last view includes the subset version of distributions. Let the lattice of conditions be the two-element Boolean algebra $\mathbf{B}$, so that formal sums $\sum_{d \in D} b_d d$ represent subsets of D.

The systems of coefficients mentioned above are all instances of commutative positive semirings. While specific details vary in the examples, there is a great deal of commonality best exposed in the general setting described below.

2.2. Semirings

Let k be a set with two distinguished elements 0 and 1 $(0 \neq 1)$ and two binary operations on k, denoted + and $\cdot$. The operation + is called *addition* and $\cdot$ is *multiplication*. The tuple $\langle k, +, \cdot, 0, 1 \rangle$ is a *semiring* if the following conditions hold:

(1) $\langle k,+,0\rangle$ is a commutative monoid.

(2) $\langle k,\cdot,1\rangle$ is a monoid.

(3) Multiplication distributes over addition. That is, for all $r,s,t \in k$:

$$r\cdot(s+t) = (r\cdot s)+(r\cdot t) \quad \text{and} \quad (s+t)\cdot r = (s\cdot r)+(t\cdot r).$$

(4) $r\cdot 0 = 0 = 0\cdot r$, for all $r \in k$.

We frequently write k for $\langle k,+,\cdot,0,1\rangle$. The identity for addition (0) is called the *zero* and the identity for multiplication (1) is the *unit*. A semiring is *commutative* if its multiplication is commutative. If every element has an additive inverse, then k is a *ring*. A semiring is *positive* if for all $r,s \in k$: $r+s = 0$ implies $r = s = 0$.

Examples: The natural numbers, $\mathbf{N}$, and the natural numbers extended to infinity, $\mathbf{N}^\infty$, are commutative positive semirings, with the usual operations. The set of all integers and the set of all reals are commutative semirings, but not positive. The two-element Boolean algebra $\mathbf{B} = \langle\{0,1\},\vee,\wedge,0,1\rangle$ is a commutative positive semiring, as is any distributive lattice with an infinum and supremum ($0 \neq 1$).

2.3. Semiring Modules

Let k be a semiring. A *k-module* consists of a commutative monoid $\langle M,+,0\rangle$ and a function from $k\times M$ to M (the image of $\langle r,x\rangle$ being written rx). The operations are subject to the axioms:

$$(r+s)x = (rx)+(sx)$$

$$r(x+y) = (rx)+(ry)$$

$$(r\cdot s)x = r(sx)$$

$$0x = 0$$

$$1x = x.$$

We ordinarily write M for the module $\langle M,+,0\rangle$ over the semiring k. The operation from $k\times M$ to M is called *scalar multiplication*. Note that the symbols + and 0 are each used in two different ways: the addition and zero for the semiring k and also the monoid operation and identity for M. If k is a ring, then the definition of a semiring k-module coincides with the definition of a ring k-module [9, V]. A subset X of a k-module M is called a *basis* of M provided that every element of M can be expressed as a finite sum $r_1x_1 + \cdots + r_nx_n = \sum_{i=1}^{n} r_ix_i$, where (r_i) is a sequence of elements from k and (x_i) is a sequence from X. Other authors term a "semi-module" what we have defined as a module. Since we will only consider modules over semirings, the shorter term is preferable.

Examples: Let $\langle M,+,0\rangle$ be a commutative idempotent monoid. Then M is a $\mathbf{B}$-module with scalar multiplication defined by $1x = x$ and $0x = 0$ for all $x \in M$.

Every commutative semiring $\langle k,+,\cdot,0,1\rangle$ is a commutative monoid $\langle k,+,0\rangle$. This monoid is a k-module. The scalar multiplication is just the multiplication of the semiring.

If k is a semiring and D is a set, then the collection of formal sums of the form $\sum_{d\in D} r_d d$ is a k-module. Addition and scalar multiplication are defined pointwise, so that:

$$\sum_{d\in D} r_d d + \sum_{d\in D} s_d d = \sum_{d\in D} (r_d+s_d)d$$

$$s\left(\sum_{d\in D} r_d d\right) = \sum_{d\in D} (s \cdot r_d) d$$

The collection of formal sums remains a k-module if we include only those sums where a finite number of coefficients are nonzero. In both cases, the formal sum with all zero coefficients, denoted 0, is the identity for +.

A function $f: M \to N$, from one k-module M to another N, is a *linear transformation* (or "module morphism") if it is a monoid morphism from the monoid M to the monoid N, compatible with scalar multiplication. These facts may be recorded in the single equation:

$$f(rx+sy) = r(f(x)) + s(f(y)), \text{ for all } r,s \in k \text{ and } x,y \in M.$$

2.4. Free Modules

Let k be a semiring and D be any set. As described above, the collection of formal sums of the form $\sum_{d\in D} r_d d$, with coefficients from k is a k-module. It remains a k-module if we include only those sums with a finite number of nonzero coefficients. In the following we describe the universal property of this module of finite formal sums, denoted $k^{(D)}$.

Consider the function $\varepsilon: D \to k^{(D)}$ which maps each $d \in D$ to the formal sum ε_d whose coefficient at d is 1 and all other coefficients are zero. The sums of the form ε_d form a basis for $k^{(D)}$ which is *free* in the following sense: Suppose M is a k-module and $f: D \to M$ is a function. Then there is a unique linear transformation $\bar{f}: k^{(D)} \to M$ making the following triangle commute:

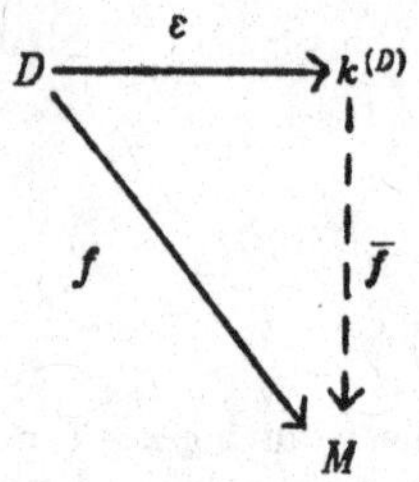

In particular, $\bar{f}\left(\sum_{d\in D} r_d d\right) = \sum_{d\in D} r_d(f(d))$. The fact that each formal sum in $k^{(D)}$ has a finite number of nonzero coefficients guarantees that the sum $\sum_{d\in D} r_d(f(d))$ in M is defined.

Because of this property, we call $k^{(D)}$ a *free* k-module over D, with *insertion* $\varepsilon: D \to k^{(D)}$. The practical significance of the universal property is that every linear transformation $g: k^{(D)} \to M$ is completely determined by its image on the basis elements ε_d. Moreover, any function from these basis elements to M extends uniquely to a linear transformation from $k^{(D)}$ to M.

2.5. Program Behaviors

At the start of this section, we gave three views of nondeterminism, starting from a set D of deterministic states. For finite nondeterminism, the collection of nondeterministic distributions was always a free k-module $k^{(D)}$ for some commutative positive semiring k (see table 1). The basis elements $\varepsilon_d \in k^{(D)}$ correspond to deterministic states. The formal sum 0, with all zero coefficients, is an impossible outcome, representing no state. The addition operation in the k-module corresponds to the **or** operator available in some programming languages.

View of Nondeterminism	Semiring of Scalars	Finite Nondeterministic Distributions
subsets	Boolean semiring, **B**	$\mathbf{B}^{(D)}$
multisets model	Natural numbers, **N**	$\mathbf{N}^{(D)}$
conditions model	Distributive lattice, C, with 0 and 1	$C^{(D)}$

Table 1. Models of Nondeterminism.

Suppose k is any commutative positive semiring and $A = k^{(D)}$ is a free k-module over D, considered as the collection of nondeterministic distributions. The functional behavior of a nondeterministic program is a linear transformation $f : A \to A$. Linearity implies that for all $r \in k$ and $x,y \in A$:

$$f(rx) = r(f(x))$$

$$f(x+y) = f(x) + f(y).$$

The first axiom means that if r is the requirement for x to be input, then r is again the requirement for $f(x)$ to be output. The second axiom means that when the input is x **or** y, then the output is $f(x)$ **or** $f(y)$.

Not all of the linear transformations on A represent program behaviors. Since zero is not a possible output, we require that $f(x) = 0$ iff $x = 0$. A linear transformation that meets this requirement is called a *positive* transformation.

If we have computations that never terminate, then A may contain a special element $\perp$ to represent such a computation. In general, we do not require $f(\perp) = \perp$, since a program may give output from exogenous events not explicitly given in its input. A linear transformation which does have $f(\perp) = \perp$ is called *strict*.

For infinite nondeterminism, a similar model arises. The main difference is that the semiring of scalars and their modules need to have countably infinite sums defined. Moreover, the infinite sum operation needs to be associative and commutative, and multiplication must distribute over infinite sums. The extended natural numbers $\mathbf{N}^{\infty}$, form such a semiring. In this infinite model, linear transformations must preserve infinite sums -- i.e., $f\left(\sum_{i \in I} x_i\right) = \sum_{i \in I} f(x_i)$, for any countable index set I.

3. DUAL MODULES, KERNELS AND WEAKEST PRECONDITIONS

Recall that every commutative semiring k is itself a k-module with scalar multiplication just the semiring multiplication (section 2.3). For any other k-module, A, the collection of all linear transformations from A to k is a k-module, denoted A^* and called the *dual module* of A. Scalar multiplication and addition are defined pointwise, so that if f and g are linear transformations from A to k, then:

$$(f+g)(x) = f(x)+g(x)$$

$$(rf)(x) = r(f(x)),$$

for all $x \in A$ and $r \in k$. If $A = k^{(D)}$ is the set of nondeterministic distributions for some set D of deterministic states, then A^* can be interpreted as "conditions" in the sense of Dijkstra [3,4]. The correspondence between conditions and A^* is given in this section.

We begin with the simple case when k is the Boolean semiring $\mathbf{B} = \{0,1\}$ and $A = \mathbf{B}^{(D)}$ is the free Boolean module over a set D of deterministic states. We will view A as the set of finite subsets of D, with set union as addition. A condition, in the sense of Dijkstra, is just a subset $R \subseteq D$ of deterministic states that are acceptable, according to some rule. Equivalently, a condition is a function $f:D \to \mathbf{B}$, where $f(d) = 0$ iff d is an acceptable state. Using 0 for an *acceptable* state may seem backwards at first. The reason for this choice becomes clear when we extend f to all of A.

Since A is free over D, there is a unique linear transformation $\bar{f}:A \to \mathbf{B}$ which makes the following triangle commute (section 2.4):

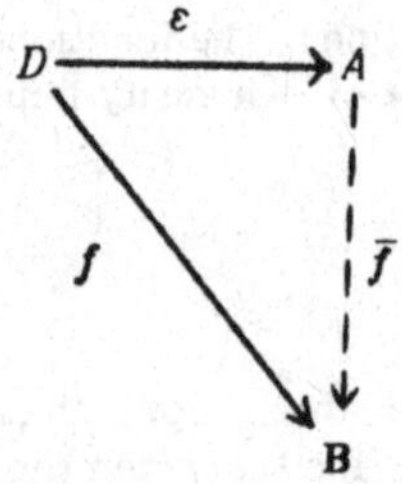

In particular, $\bar{f}:A \to \mathbf{B}$ takes a finite subset $S \subseteq D$ to $\sum_{d \in S} f(d)$. It follows that $\bar{f}(S) = 0$ iff $f(d) = 0$ for all $d \in S$. Thus, if we consider a nondeterministic distribution $S \subseteq D$ to be acceptable iff each $d \in S$ is acceptable, then the set of acceptable distributions are those elements of A which are mapped to 0 by $\bar{f}$. In linear algebra, this subset of A is called the ***kernel*** of $\bar{f}$, denoted $\mathbf{ker}(\bar{f}) = \{S \in A \mid \bar{f}(S) = 0\}$.

So, each condition is a function $f:D \to \mathbf{B}$, which extends to a unique linear transformation $\bar{f}:A \to \mathbf{B}$. In this way, a condition *is* a linear transformation from A to $\mathbf{B}$. Moreover, since A is free over D, each linear transformation $g:A \to \mathbf{B}$ is uniquely determined by its image on the basis elements ε_d ($d \in D$). The module A^*, consisting of all linear transformations from A to $\mathbf{B}$, is the collection of all possible conditions. For a condition $g:A \to \mathbf{B}$, the set of acceptable nondeterministic distributions is the kernel of g.

When $k = \mathbf{N}$ (the multiset model), the dual module A^* also corresponds to conditions, although in this case a condition $f:A \to \mathbf{N}$ records more than just the acceptability or unacceptability of each state. For $x \in A$, we interpret $f(x)$ to be a count of the number of different ways in which a state x is unacceptable. For example, we could keep track of the number of different nondeterministic computation paths that could lead to an unacceptable output with input x. The requirement that $f:A \to \mathbf{N}$ be a linear transformation formalizes the idea that the number of ways in which x **or** y is unacceptable is the sum of the number of ways that x and y are unacceptable on their own. Once again, the kernel of a condition $g:A \to \mathbf{N}$ corresponds to the set of states which are acceptable.

A third case is when k is a distributive lattice of predicates. In this case, a condition $g:A \to k$ records requirements for a state to be unacceptable. A distribution $x \in A$ is unacceptable iff the predicate $g(x) \in k$ is true. The linearity of a condition $g:A \to k$ means that

$x+y$ is acceptable iff x is acceptable and y is acceptable. The kernel of a condition corresponds to the set of states which are always acceptable.

In summary: when a k-module $A = k^{(D)}$ is considered as the set of nondeterministic distributions, then the dual module A^*, consisting of all linear transformations from A to k, is the set of "conditions" in the sense of Dijkstra [3,4]. For a condition $g:A \to k$, the kernel of g (those elements mapped to 0) corresponds to the set of those states which meet the condition. As an example, the always **true** condition (every state is acceptable) corresponds to the linear transformation $0:A \to k$ which maps every $x \in A$ to $0 \in k$. The kernel of $0:A \to k$ is all of A -- i.e., every nondeterministic distribution is acceptable. On the other hand, the linear transformation $1:A \to k$ with $1(\varepsilon_d) = 1$ for all $d \in D$ corresponds to the always **false** condition -- i.e., it is impossible to have an acceptable state. In this case, $\mathbf{ker}(1) = \{0\}$ consists of only the impossible state.

Now, a nondeterministic program is a linear transformation $t:A \to A$. If $g:A \to k$ is a condition, then the composition $g \circ t:A \to k$ is also a condition. Specifically, $g \circ t$ is the "weakest precondition" for g with program t. That is, if a distribution $x \in A$ satisfies the condition $g \circ t$ (i.e., $x \in \mathbf{ker}(g \circ t)$), then carrying out the program t on x is certain to establish the truth of condition g (i.e., $t(x) \in \mathbf{ker}(g)$). Moreover, $g \circ t$ is the "weakest" such condition, in that as many states as possible are acceptable (it has the largest possible kernel).

Dijkstra denotes this weakest precondition by $wp(t,g)$. The form $wp(t,-)$, with the post-condition left as a parameter, is called a predicate transformer. In our setting, a predicate transformer has the form $-\circ t$, called a linear functional transformer in linear algebra.

4. MULTIPLE INPUT, MULTIPLE OUTPUT PROGRAM BEHAVIORS

Programs with tuples of inputs or outputs require the use of tensor products as the appropriate algebraic structure in the face of nondeterminism. This use of tensor products is not new, but our presentation and motivation differs from previous uses [7,13,14]. Throughout this section, k is any commutative positive semiring.

4.1. Nondeterministic Pairs and Tensor Products

Suppose A is a k-module, considered as a set of nondeterministic distributions, as in section 2. The module A may be free, but we do not require this at the moment. Consider the set of all ordered pairs of distributions: $A \times A = \{(x,y) \mid x \in A \text{ and } y \in A\}$. This set is a k-module with $(x_1,y_1)+(x_2,y_2) = (x_1+x_2,y_1+y_2)$ and $r(x,y) = (rx,ry)$. For nondeterministic programs with a pair of inputs or outputs, we want an element such as $(x_1,y_1)+(x_2,y_2)$ to be the nondeterministic choice between the pairs (x_1,y_1) and (x_2,y_2). Now, $(x_1,y_1)+(x_2,y_2)$ is an element of $A \times A$, but it is not the element we want, because in $A \times A$:

$$(x_1,y_1)+(x_2,y_2) = (x_1,y_2)+(x_2,y_1).$$

In short, there is no way to tell which distributions are paired together. If we choose some other k-module P to represent nondeterministic distributions of pairs, we want each pair $(x,y) \in A \times A$ to be contained in P. This can be achieved by a *function* $\otimes:A \times A \to P$ which takes each pair $(x,y) \in A \times A$ to an element $x \otimes y$ in P (note the infix notation). Following a suggestion of Hennessy and Plotkin [7], this function should be *bilinear*; that is, for all $x,y,z \in A$ and $r \in k$:

$$x \otimes (y+z) = (x \otimes y)+(x \otimes z),$$

$$(x+y) \otimes z = (x \otimes z)+(y \otimes z),$$

$$(rx\otimes y) = r(x\otimes y) = (x\otimes ry)$$

Intuitively, the first axiom can be interpreted as follows: If a pair has x as its first component and either y or z as its second component, then that is the same as the pair (x,y) or the pair (x,z). The second axiom has a similar meaning. The third axiom means that a requirement that is necessary for one component of a pair to occur is also needed for the pair as a whole to occur.

So, what we want is a k-module representing nondeterministic pairs of states, together with a bilinear function mapping $A\times A$ into this k-module. The tensor product provides a free or universal way to achieve this. Specifically, the tensor product of A with itself is a k-module $A\otimes A$ together with a bilinear function $\otimes: A\times A \to A\otimes A$. The function $\otimes$ is universal in the following sense: suppose P is some k-module and $g: A\times A \to P$ is a bilinear function. Then there is a unique k-module morphism $h: A\otimes A \to P$ such that the following triangle commutes:

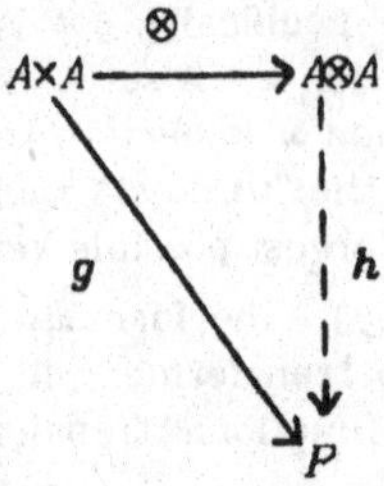

Because of this universal property among bilinear functions, we use the k-module $A\otimes A$ as the set of nondeterministic distributions of pairs of states. The element $x\otimes y$ represents the pair of distributions (x,y).

4.2. Tensor Products of Free Modules

In general, the construction of the tensor product $A\otimes A$ involves reducing the free k-module $k^{(A\times A)}$ by an appropriate quotient [5,6,10]. However, in one important case -- when A is free -- the construction of $A\otimes A$ is straightforward and sheds some more light on why we believe $A\otimes A$ is an appropriate state space for nondeterministic distributions of pairs of states. For this case, we start with a set D of deterministic states. The set of nondeterministic distributions is the free k-module $k^{(D)}$, as in section 2. Following this line of thought, a deterministic pair of states is an element of $D\times D = \{(d,e) \mid d \in D \text{ and } e \in D\}$. The set of nondeterministic distributions of pairs of states is the free k-module $k^{(D\times D)}$ over $D\times D$. The following theorem justifies our use of tensor products by showing $k^{(D)}\otimes k^{(D)} = k^{(D\times D)}$. It is a generalization of a well-known theorem for ring modules [9, IX].

Theorem 4.1. *For any set D, the free k-module $k^{(D\times D)}$ is a tensor product $k^{(D)}\otimes k^{(D)}$. The universal bilinear map $\otimes: k^{(D)}\times k^{(D)} \to k^{(D\times D)}$ is defined by*

$$\left[\sum_{d\in D} r_d d\right]\otimes\left[\sum_{e\in D} s_e e\right] = \sum_{(d,e)\in D\times D} (r_d s_e)(d,e).$$

As a concrete example, suppose $x = r_1 d_1 + r_2 d_2$ and $y = s_1 d_1 + s_2 d_2$ are distributions. From theorem 4.1, we have:

$$(x\otimes y) = (r_1 d_1 + r_2 d_2)\otimes(s_1 d_1 + s_2 d_2)$$

$$= (r_1 d_1 \otimes s_1 d_1) + (r_1 d_1 \otimes s_2 d_2) + (r_2 d_2 \otimes s_1 d_1) + (r_2 d_2 \otimes s_2 d_2)$$

This expresses all of the possible pairings of a deterministic state from the distribution x with one from y. If we have additional information that only the d_1 states are paired together, and the d_2 states are similarly paired, then we can express this knowledge as:

$$z = (r_1d_1 \otimes s_1d_1) + (r_2d_2 \otimes s_2d_2)$$

within the tensor product. Expression of such information is not possible in the Cartesian product.

4.3. Nondeterministic n-tuples

Consider programs which have an n-tuple of inputs or outputs. If A is the k-module of nondeterministic distributions then we could propose the n-fold Cartesian product $A^n = \{(x_1, \cdots, x_n) \mid x_i \in A\}$ as a state space of nondeterministic n-tuples. This is a k-module with pointwise operations, however it has the same shortcoming for n-tuples that $A \times A$ has for pairs. Namely, there is no way to express a nondeterministic choice between two n-tuples $(x_1, \cdots, x_n)$ and $(y_1, \cdots, y_n)$ without also including tuples such as $(x_1, y_2, \cdots, y_n)$ and $(y_1, x_2, \cdots, x_n)$ -- among others.

As with pairs, we can choose some other k-module P to represent nondeterministic distributions of tuples, and in this case, we require a function $\otimes: A^n \to P$ mapping each $(x_1, \cdots, x_n) \in A^n$ to an element $(x_1 \otimes \cdots \otimes x_n) \in P$. This function should be linear in each of its n components. For example, if n=3, then we require:

$$(w+x) \otimes y \otimes z = (w \otimes y \otimes z) + (x \otimes y \otimes z),$$

$$x \otimes (w+y) \otimes z = (x \otimes w \otimes z) + (x \otimes y \otimes z),$$

$$x \otimes y \otimes (w+z) = (x \otimes y \otimes w) + (x \otimes y \otimes z),$$

$$r(x \otimes y \otimes z) = (rx \otimes y \otimes z) = (x \otimes ry \otimes z) = (x \otimes y \otimes rz).$$

Such a function is called *multilinear*.

The iterated tensor product $\overset{n}{\otimes} A$ provides a universal multilinear function with domain A^n. That is, there is a universal multilinear function $\otimes: A^n \to \overset{n}{\otimes} A$, with the image of $(x_1, \cdots, x_n) \in A^n$ being written $(x_1 \otimes \cdots \otimes x_n)$. This multilinear function is universal in exactly the same way that $\otimes: A \times A \to A \otimes A$ is universal for bilinear functions. Thus, if $g: A^n \to P$ is a multilinear function, then there is a unique linear transformation $h: \overset{n}{\otimes} A \to P$ with $h(x_1 \otimes \cdots \otimes x_n) = g(x_1, \cdots, x_n)$.

Because of this universal property, we use the k-module $\overset{n}{\otimes} A$ as the set of nondeterministic distributions of n-tuples of states. In general, $\overset{n}{\otimes} A$ can be constructed as a quotient module of a free module. We omit this general construction here, but point out several important special cases: $\overset{0}{\otimes} A$ is just the k-module k; $\overset{1}{\otimes} A$ is A itself and $\overset{2}{\otimes} A$ is $A \otimes A$. The tensor product $\overset{n}{\otimes} A$ is particularly simple when $A = k^{(D)}$ is free over some set D:

Theorem 4.2. *For any set D, the free k-module $k^{(D^n)}$ is a tensor product $\overset{n}{\otimes} k^{(D)}$. The universal multilinear map $\otimes: \left[k^{(D)}\right]^n \to k^{(D^n)}$ is defined by*

$$\left[\varepsilon_{d_1} \otimes \cdots \otimes \varepsilon_{d_n}\right] = \varepsilon_{<d_1, \cdots, d_n>},$$

where the ε_s are the appropriate insertions into the free k-modules.

4.4. Program Behaviors

Given a k-module A as a set of nondeterministic distributions, the k-module $\overset{n}{\otimes} A$ is the set of nondeterministic distributions of n-tuples of states. The functional behavior of a program with an m-tuple of inputs and an n-tuple of outputs is a linear transformation $f: \overset{m}{\otimes} A \to \overset{n}{\otimes} A$. The requirement of linearity is motivated by the same reasoning used in section 2.5 for single-input, single-output programs. As with single-input single-output programs, not all linear transformations represent program behaviors. Since zero is not a possible output, a linear transformation that represents a program behavior must be positive. Notice that because of multilinearity, zero has an annihilator property in distributions of tuples. That is $x_1 \otimes \cdots \otimes 0 \otimes \cdots \otimes x_n = 0$. This means that if any one component of a tuple is impossible, then the entire tuple is impossible. The converse is not true -- that is $x_1 \otimes \cdots \otimes x_n$ may be zero even if none of the x_i are zero. In this case, $(x_1, \cdots, x_n)$ can be thought of as an inconsistent tuple. For example, suppose r and s are elements of the semiring k with $r \cdot s = 0$. This might occur if k is a distributive lattice of predicates, with r and s mutually incompatible. For any $x, y \in A$ we have

$$(rx \otimes sy) = (r \cdot s)(x \otimes y) = 0(x \otimes y) = 0.$$

This means that the distribution rx can never be paired with the distribution sy.

One advantage of this view of program behaviors is that it indicates several different methods of specifying a program $f: \otimes^m A \to \otimes^n A$ with m inputs and n outputs. These methods are listed here:

(1) **Deterministic inputs method:** If $A = k^{(D)}$ is a free k-module over D, then $\otimes^m A = k^{(D^m)}$ is free over the set D^m (theorem 4.2). Therefore, every function $f: D^m \to \otimes^n A$ determines a unique linear transformation $\bar{f}: \otimes^m A \to \otimes^n A$. Moreover, from the fact that k is positive, it can be shown that $\bar{f}$ is a positive transformation iff $f(d_1, \cdots, d_m) \neq 0$ for all m-tuples $(d_1, \cdots, d_m) \in D^m$. This method is equivalent to specifying a nondeterministic program by giving its result for any deterministic input.

(2) **Parallel method:** Suppose $f: A \to A$ and $g: A \to A$ are linear transformations. They may be combined to form a linear transformation $(f \otimes g): A \otimes A \to A \otimes A$ defined by $(f \otimes g)(x \otimes y) = f(x) \otimes g(y)$. This may be thought of as f and g acting in parallel with no communication -- *i.e.*, we have combined two single-input, single-output processes to achieve one process with two inputs and two outputs. If f and g are both positive transformations, this does not guarantee that $f \otimes g$ is also a positive transformation. In particular, suppose $f(x) = ry$ and $g(x) = sy$ for some $x, y \in A$ and $r, s \in k$. If $r \cdot s = 0$ in k, then $f \otimes g(x \otimes x) = ry \otimes sy = 0$. This indicates that the conditions under which f may accept x as input are mutually incompatible with the conditions under which g may accept x -- i.e., $r \cdot s = 0$. This parallel method can be extended to combine two linear transformations $f: \otimes^m A \to \otimes^n A$ and $g: \otimes^p A \to \otimes^q A$, yielding $f \otimes g: \otimes^{m+p} A \to \otimes^{n+q} A$.

(3) **Multilinear method:** Suppose $g: A^m \to \otimes^n A$ is a multilinear function. Then g extends to a unique linear transformation $h: \otimes^m A \to \otimes^n A$ with $h(x_1 \otimes \cdots \otimes x_m) = g(x_1, \cdots, x_m)$. Thus, we can specify a linear transformation $h: \otimes^m A \to \otimes^n A$ by giving its corresponding multilinear function $g: A^m \to \otimes^n A$. The linear transformation h is a positive transformation iff $g(x_1, \cdots, x_m) = 0$ implies $(x_1 \otimes \cdots \otimes x_m) = 0$. This follows from the fact that k is positive and $\otimes^m A$ is finitely generated by elements of the form $(x_1 \otimes \cdots \otimes x_m)$.

5. DISCUSSION

We have used techniques of linear algebra to specify the functional behavior of nondeterministic programs. If D is a set of deterministic states for a computation, then the functional behavior of a nondeterministic program is a linear transformation $f: A \to A$, where A is a free semiring module generated by D. A program with m inputs and n outputs is a linear transformation $f: \otimes^m A \to \otimes^n A$, where the domain and codomain are iterated tensor products.

A linear transformation $g: A \to k$ to the underlying semiring k corresponds to a "condition", as used by Dijkstra to formalize proofs of correctness. In this setting, the set of nondeterministic distributions which meet the condition is the kernel of g, $\mathbf{ker}(g) = \{x \in A \mid g(x)=0\}$.

In the future we plan to study recursively defined programs using ordered semiring modules and least fixed point techniques. This will be related to the powerdomains introduced by Plotkin [12] and Smyth [16] and used by Hennessy and Plotkin [7] for the semantics of nondeterministic and parallel programming languages. In essence, their powerdomains consider the case where the underlying semiring is the two-element Boolean algebra.

We are also extending our work to nondeterministic concurrent programs. The functional behavior of such a program is a linear transformation $f: A \to A$, where A is a free semiring algebra. In this case, f *may* also be an algebra morphism, which indicates that the program involves no interprocess communication.

REFERENCES

(1) D.B. Benson. Counting paths: nondeterminism as linear algebra, to appear in *IEEE Trans. Software Engineering*.

(2) D.B. Benson. Studies in fork-join parallelism, Washington State University Technical Report CS-82-101, Pullman, WA 99164 (1982).

(3) E.W. Dijkstra. Guarded commands, nondeterminacy and formal derivation of programs, *CACM* 18 (1975), 453-457.

(4) E.W. Dijkstra. *A Discipline of Programming*, (Prentice-Hall, 1976).

(5) P.A. Grillet. The tensor product of semi-groups, *Trans. Amer. Math. Soc.* 138 (1969), 267-280.

(6) P.A. Grillet. The tensor product of commutative semi-groups, *Trans. Amer. Math. Soc.* 138 (1969), 281-293.

(7) M.C.B. Hennessy and G.D. Plotkin. Full abstraction for a simple parallel programming language, in: *Mathematical Foundations of Computer Science 79*, LNCS 74, (Springer-Verlag, 1979), 108-120.

(8) D. Kozen. Semantics of probabilistic programs, *JCSS* 22 (1981), 328-350.

(9) S. MacLane and G. Birkhoff. *Algebra*, (MacMillan Publishing Co., 1979).

(10) M.G. Main and D.B. Benson. An algebra for nondeterministic distributed processes, Washington State University Technical Report CS-82-087, Pullman, WA 99164 (1982).

(11) E.G. Manes. A Class of Fuzzy Theories, *J. Math. Analysis and Applications* 85 (1982), 409-451.

(12) G.D. Plotkin. A powerdomain construction, *SIAM J. Computing* 5 (1976), 452-487.

(13) A. Poigné. Using least fixed points to characterize formal computations of nondeterminate equations, in: *Formalizations of Programming Concepts* (J. Diaz and I. Ramos, Eds.), LNCS 107, (Springer-Verlag, 1981), 447-459.

(14) A. Poigné. On effective computations of nondeterministic schemes, in: *5th International Symposium on Programming*, LNCS 137, (Springer-Verlag, 1982), 323-336.

(15) N. Saheb-Djahromi. CPO's of measures for nondeterminism, *TCS* 12 (1980), 19-37.

(16) M. Smyth. Powerdomains, *JCSS* 16 (1978),

A SINGLE SOURCE SHORTEST PATH ALGORITHM FOR GRAPHS WITH SEPARATORS

K. Mehlhorn B. H. Schmidt

Fachbereich 10 - Angewandte
Mathematik und Informatik
Universität des Saarlandes
6600 Saarbrücken/West Germany

Abstract: We show how to solve a single source shortest path problem on a planar network in time $O(n^{3/2}\log n)$. The algorithm works for arbitrary edge weights (positive and negative) and is based on the planar separator theorem. More generally, the algorithm works in time $O(n^{a+b}\log n + n^{3a} + n^{d})$ on graphs $G=(V, E)$ which have a separator of size n^a, have at most n^b edges and where the separator can be found in time n^d.

1. Introduction

A network $N = (V, E, C)$ is a directed graph $G = (V, E)$ (where $|V| = n$, $|E| = e$) together with a real-valued function $C : E \to \mathbb{R}$. The length of a path $w = v_1 \ldots v_m$ is defined

$$l(w) = \sum_{i=1}^{m-1} C(v_i, v_{i+1}).$$

Let us denote the minimal length of any path from x to y (with respect to $W \subset V$) by

$$\mathrm{Min}(x,y;W) = \inf \{ l(w) \ ;\ w=v_1 \ldots v_n \text{ is a path from } x \text{ to } y \text{ and for } 1 \leq i \leq n \text{ we have } v_i \in W \}.$$

The single source shortest path problem is defined by

(SSSP): Let $N = (V, E, C)$ be a directed network and let s be a designated vertex in V.
Compute $\mathrm{Min}(s,x;V)$ for every vertex $x \in V$.

The most popular solution to SSSP is the Bellman/Ford algorithm. It solves SSSP in time $O(n \cdot e)$.

A more efficient solution is known if edge weights are non-negative, i.e. $C(x,y)\geq 0$ for all edges (x,y). In this case Dijkstra's algorithm runs in time $O(\min(n^2, e\cdot\log n))$. Finally we should mention that the all-pair shortest path problem, i.e. compute $\text{Min}(x,y;V)$ for all $x,y\in V$, can be solved in time $O(\min(n^3, n\cdot e\cdot\log n)$; here n^3 comes from Kleene's algorithm and $n\cdot e\cdot\log n$ comes from an observation of Edmonds/Karp. They have shown that having solved SSSP once for a single source s one can transform the network N into a network N' = (V, E, C') such that N' has non-negative weights, yet the same shortest paths as N. Hence the remaining n-1 SSSP's can be solved for a cost of $O(n\cdot e\cdot\log n)$ by Dijkstra's algorithm.

In this paper we show how to solve SSSP on planar graphs in time $O(n^{3/2}\log n)$. This should be seen in contrast to the running time of the Bellman/ford algorithm. More generally we show how to improve upon the Bellman/Ford algorithm for all graphs having a separator property.

<u>Definition:</u> Let $a, b \in \mathbb{R}$, $0 < a < 1 \leq b$.
A family F of graphs has the <u>(a,b)-separator property</u> if for every $G = (V, E) \in F$, $n = |V|$, we have

(1) $|E| = O(n^b)$

(2) there is a partition of V into three pairwise disjoint sets V_1, S, V_2 such that

(2.1) $|S| = O(n^a)$

(2.2) $|V_1 \cup S| \leq 2n/3$, $|V_2 \cup S| \leq 2n/3$

(2.3) there are no edges $(v_1, v_2) \in E$ with $v_1\in V_1$, $v_2\in V_2$, i.e. S separates V_1 from V_2.

(2.4) $G_i = (V_i \cup S, E_i)$, the subgraph spanned by $V_i \cup S$, belongs to F for i=1,2.

<u>Theorem:</u> Let F be a family of graphs having an (a,b)-separator property such that separators can be found in time n^d and space n^e for a graph G in F with n nodes.

Then the single single source shortest path problem on graphs in F can be solved in time
$$O(n^{a+b}\log n + n^{3a} + n^d)$$
and space
$$O(n^{a+1} + n^e) \ .$$

Together with the planar separator theorem of Lipton/Tarjan we get the following

Corollary: SSSP on planar networks can be solved in time $O(n^{3/2}\log n)$ and space $O(n^{3/2})$.

For reasons of fairness we want to stress that our algorithm uses more space than the Bellman/Ford algorithm. Bellman/Ford uses $O(n)$.

2. The Algorithm

Let $N = (V, E, C)$ be a network out of a family F of graphs having the (a,b)-separator property. If $W \subset V$ then the network induced by W is $(W, (W \times W) \cap E, C)$.

Let us first present the following observation due to Edmonds/Karp as

Lemma 1: Let $N = (V, E, C)$ be a network, $s \in V$.
Suppose we have computed $\mathrm{Min}(s,x;V)$ for all $x \in V$.
Define $\overline{C} : E \to \mathbb{R}$ by
$\overline{C}(u,v) = C(u,v) + \mathrm{Min}(s,u;V) - \mathrm{Min}(s,v;V)$ then

a) $\overline{C}(u,v) \geq 0$ for all $(u,v) \in E$

b) if p is a path from u to v, and $l(\overline{l})$ is the length of p with respect to C $(\overline{C})$ then $\overline{l}(p) = l(p) + \mathrm{Min}(s,u;V) - \mathrm{Min}(s,v;V)$

Remark: The Lemma 1 shows that shortest paths with respect to C are identical to shortest paths with respect to $\overline{C}$.

Proof of Lemma 1:

a) $\mathrm{Min}(s,u;V) + C(u,v) < \mathrm{Min}(s,v;V)$ is a contradiction to the definition of the function "Min".

b) Let $p = v_0 \ldots v_k$, $u = v_0$, $v = v_k$ then we have

$$\overline{l}(p) = \sum_{i=o}^{k-1} \overline{l}(v_i, v_{i+1})$$

$$= \sum_{i=0}^{k-1} l(v_i, v_{i+1}) - \mathrm{Min}(s,v_{i+1};V) + \mathrm{Min}(s,v_i;V)$$

$$= l(p) - \mathrm{Min}(s,v;V) + \mathrm{Min}(s,u;V)$$

Lemma 1 above can be used to derive an efficient many source shortest path algorithm. Let $S \subset V$. Suppose that we want to compute $Min(t,v;V)$ for all $t \in S$ and $v \in V$. This can be done as follows:

(1) Choose $s \in S$ arbitrary and compute $Min(s,v;V)$ for all $v \in V$.

(2) Transform edge weights as described in Lemma 1, solve $|S| - 1$ shortest path problems with non-negative edge costs and translate back the result.

The running time of this algorithm is the running time of <u>one</u> single source problem plus $O(|S| \cdot e \cdot \log n)$.

We are now in the position to describe our new algorithm.

Let $N = (V, E, C)$ be a network belonging to a family of graphs with an (a,b)-separator property

<u>Algorithm SSSPS - Single Source Shortest Path on graphs with Separators</u>

1. Find a separator S of N, i.e. find a partition V_1, S, V_2 of V which satisfies conditions (2.1) to (2.4). Set $S := S \cup \{s\}$.
   <u>Remark:</u> By assumption this step takes time $O(n^d)$ and space $O(n^e)$.

2. Compute $Min(t,v;V_1 \cup S)$ for all $t \in S$, $v \in V_1 \cup S$ and compute $Min(t,v;V_2 \cup S)$ for all $t \in S$, $v \in V_2 \cup S$.
   <u>Remark:</u> In this step we apply the many source algorithm described above. In order to solve the required single source problems on the subnetwork spanned by $V_1 \cup S$ ($V_2 \cup S$) we use our algorithm recursively. Thus running time of this step is
   $T(|V_1 \cup S|) + T(|V_2 \cup S|) + O(n^a n^b \cdot \log n)$
   where T is the running time (yet to be determined) of our algorithm. Similarly space requirement is
   $S(|V_1 \cup S|) + S(|V_2 \cup S|) + n^a n$

3. Let $\overline{N} = (S, S \times S, \overline{C})$ where $\overline{C}(r,t) = \min\{\infty, Min(r,t,V_1 \cup S), Min(r,t,V_2 \cup S)\}$
   Solve the single source shortest path problem on $\overline{N}$ with source $s \in S$. Call the solution $\overline{Min}(s,t;S)$.

<u>Remark:</u> Because $\overline{N}$ is a complete network we need time $O(n^{3a})$ and space $O(n^{2a})$. We show in claim 1 below that: $\overline{Min}(s,t;S) = Min(s,t;V)$ for all $t \in S$.

4. For each $v \in V$ compute

$$Min(s,v;V) = \begin{cases} \min_{t \in S} \{ \overline{Min}(s,t;S) + Min(t,v;V_1 \cup S)\} & \text{if } v \in V_1 \\ \min_{t \in S} \{ \overline{Min}(s,t;S) + Min(t,v;V_2 \cup S)\} & \text{if } v \in V_2 \end{cases}$$

<u>Remark:</u> To combine the intermediate results computed so far we need time $O(n^{1+a})$. Claim 2 below shows the correctness of the result.

<u>Theorem 1:</u> Let F be a family of graphs having an (a,b)-separator property Let N = (V, E, C) be a network in F and let s be a fixed vertex of V.

Then algorithm SSSPS computes $Min(s,x;V)$ for all $x \in V$.

<u>Proof:</u>

<u>claim 1:</u> After performing step 3 we have for $t \in S$
$\overline{Min}(s,t;S) = Min(s,t;V)$

<u>Proof:</u> Let t be any vertex in S. A shortest path w from s to t in N has the form

$$s = s_o \xrightarrow[g_o^1]{} s_1 \xrightarrow[g_o^2]{} s_2 \xrightarrow[g_1^1]{} s_3 \xrightarrow[g_1^2]{} \ldots \rightarrow s_k = t$$

where g_i^j is a shortest path from vertex $s_{2i+j-1} \in S$ to vertex $s_{2i+j} \in S$ running completely within $S \cup V_j$ (j=1,2).
Hence

$$Min(s,t;V) = l(w) = \sum_{i,j} l(g_i^j) = \sum_h \overline{C}(s_h,s_{h+1})$$

$$= \overline{Min}(s,t;S)$$

The third equality follows from the fact that $l(g_i^j) = \overline{C}(s_{2i+j-1},s_{2i+j})$ by definition of $\overline{C}$.

<u>claim 2:</u> After step 4 we have computed $Min(s,x;V)$ for each $x \in V$.

<u>Proof:</u> Let x be any vertex of N, $w = sv_1 \ldots v_m x$ the shortest path to x.

<u>case 1:</u> $x \in S$: claim 1 yields the stated result.

<u>case 2:</u> $x \in V_1$

On the path from s to x there exists at least one vertex $v_i \in S$ (possibly s itself).

Break w into w = s...t...x where t is the <u>last</u> vertex lying on w with $t \in S$. Claim 1 yields that the shortest path from s to t is found. The choice of t and $x \in V_1$ yields for $tv_r \ldots v_m x$ that $v_r, \ldots, v_m \in V_1$. This part of w is computed in step 2 as $\mathrm{Min}(t,x;V_1 \cup S)$. Summing the two values gives the shortest path from s to x.

<u>case 3:</u> $x \in V_2$

The argumentation runs totally analogous to case 2 where V_1 is substituted by V_2.

We are now ready to give the main theorem

<u>Theorem 2:</u> Let F be a family of graphs having an (a,b)-separator property such that separators can be found in time $O(n^d)$ and space $O(n^e)$ for a graph G in F with n nodes. $(0<a<1\le b)$

Then the single source shortest path problem on graphs G in F can be solved in

time $O(n^{a+b}\log n + n^{3a} + n^d)$ and

space $O(n^{a+1} + n^e)$.

<u>Proof:</u> Summing the time bounds already stated at each step of the algorithm we get:

$$T(n) = \max_{\substack{n_1,n_2\le 2n/3 \\ n_1+n_2=n+n^a}} \left[T(n_1) + T(n_2) + n^{a+b}\log n + n^{3a} + n^d \right]$$

and $T(1) = 1$.

Recall that $|V_1 \cup S| \le 2n/3$, $|V_2 \cup S| \le 2n/3$ and

$|V_1 \cup S| + |V_2 \cup S| \le n + n^a$.

T(n) is clearly non-decreasing.

Let $U(n) = T(n)/n$.

Then $U(1) = 1$ and

$$U(n) = \max_{\substack{n_1,n_2\le 2n/3 \\ n_1+n_2=n+n^a}} \left[(n_1/n)U(n_1) + (n_2/n)U(n_2) + n^{a+b-1}\log n + n^{3a-1} + n^{d-1} \right]$$

$$\leq (1+n^{a-1})\ U(2n/3) + n^{a+b-1}\log n + n^{3a-1} + n^{d-1}$$

since $U(n_1) \leq U(n_2) \leq U(2n/3)$ and $n_1+n_2 = n + n^a$. Hence

$$U(n) \leq \sum_{i=0}^{(\log n)/\log(3/2)} \left[\prod_{j=0}^{i} (1+((2/3)^j n)^{a-1}) \right] \cdot f((2/3)^i n)$$

where $f(m) = m^{a+b-1}\log m + m^{3a-1} + m^{d-1}$.

$$\leq \sum_{i=0}^{(\log n)/\log(3/2)} \prod_{j=0}^{i} \left[1 + ((2/3)^j n)^{a-1}\right] \cdot (2/3)^{i\cdot c}$$

where $c = \mathrm{Max}(\ a+b-1,\ 3a-1,\ d-1) > 0$.

Next note that

$$\prod_{j=0}^{i} \left[1 + ((2/3)^j n)^{a-1} \right] = e^{\sum_{j=0}^{i} \ln(1+((2/3)^j n)^{a-1})}$$

$$\leq e^{\sum_{j=0}^{i} ((2/3)^j n)^{a-1}}$$

$$\leq e^{O(\ n^{a-1}(3/2)^{(1-a)\cdot i}\ )}$$

$$\leq e^{O(\ n^{a-1}\cdot n^{1-a})} = O(1)$$

since $i \leq (\log n)/\log(3/2)$ and hence $(3/2)^i \leq n$.

We can now finally conclude

$$U(n) = O(f(n))$$

and hence $$T(n) = O(n^{a+b}\log n + n^{3a} + n^d)$$

<u>Corollary:</u> The single source shortest path problem on planar graphs is solvable in

time $O(n^{3/2}\log n)$ and

space $O(n^{3/2})$.

<u>Proof:</u> From Lipton/Tarjan we get $d=1$, $a=1/2$ and $b=1$.

•

References:

Bellman R.E.
On a Routing Problem
Quart. Appl. Math. 16 (1958) pp. 87-90

Dijkstra E.W.
A Note on two Problems in Connection with Graphs
Num. Math. Vol. 1 (1959) pp. 269-271

Edmonds J., Karp R.M.
Theoretical Improvements in Algorithmic Efficiency for Network Flow Problems
J. ACM 5 (1962) p. 345

Lipton R., Tarjan R.E.
A Separator Theorem for Planar Graphs
Waterloo Conference on Theoretical Comp. Science Aug.77 pp. 1-10

Floyd F.W.
Algorithm 97: Shortest Path
C. ACM 5 (1962) p. 345

ISOMORPHISM TESTING AND CANONICAL FORMS FOR k-CONTRACTABLE GRAPHS
(A Generalization of Bounded Valence and Bounded Genus)

Gary L. Miller *
Department of Mathematics
Massachusetts Institute of Technology
Cambridge, MA 02139

Abstract. This paper includes polynomial time isomorphism tests and canonical forms for graphs called k-contractable graphs for fixed k. The class of k-contractable graphs includes the graphs of bounded valence and the graphs of bounded genus. The algorithm uses several new ideas including: (1) it removes portions of the graph and replaces them with groups which are used to keep track of the symmetries of these portions; (2) it maintains with each group a tower of equivalence relation which allows a decomposition of the group. These towers are called a tower of Γ_k actions. It considers the canonical intersection of groups.

1. INTRODUCTION

The author, and independently other researchers [FM80, L180, M180], have presented polynomial time algorithms for isomorphism testing of graphs of bounded genus. These algorithms are based on fairly complicated analyses of embeddings of graphs on two dimensional surfaces. Since then, Luks has presented a polynomial time algorithm for isomorphism testing of graphs of bounded valence [Lu80]. The ideas used in the bounded valence algorithm are very appealing. They showed relationships between computational group theory and graph isomorphism. The existence of a polynomial time algorithm which in a natural way tests isomorphism of graphs of bounded valence and bounded genus has been an open question [Ba81]. We show that the class of graphs, called the k-contractable graphs, contains the graphs of bounded genus. They trivially contain the graphs of bounded valence. Therefore, these graphs form a common generalization of the two classes. We give a polynomial time algorithm for testing isomorphism of these graphs.

More recently, several authors [BL83, FSS83] have shown that graphs of bounded valence have p-time constructable canonical forms. We also show how these ideas can be extended to the k-contractable graphs.

We give the first of several definitions of k-contractable graphs. Later definitions of k-contractable graphs will enlarge the class of graph which will also be called k-contractable for each k. Consider the following three operations on a graph, G.

*This work partially supported by NSF Grant MCS 800756-A01.

The first operation, removing leaves, simply removes all leaves and their associated edges. The second operation, removing multiple vertices, identifies vertices of valence two which have the same neighbors. The third operation, contracting edges of valence $\leq k$, simultaneously identifies the end points of edges common to two vertices whose valence is $\leq k + 1$. It then removes selfloops and multiple edges.

Definition 1.1. The graph G is k-contractable if the application of the above three operations eventually reduces G to a point.

The definition seems to be dependent on the order in which one applies these three operations. Nevertheless, in the last section we show that any graph which is fixed by all three operations has its genus bounded below by $\Omega(k)$. Diagram 1 describes an infinite periodic planar graph. From this graph we can construct arbitrarily large graphs of genus 1 which are not 10-contractable. These graphs are 6-contractable using a slightly stronger definition of the third operation.

The paper consists of four other sections. Section 2, the preliminaries, contains basic definition plus the notation of a tower of Γ_k actions which will be used throughout. Section 3, Canonical ordering and set of orderings, contains the basic group theoretic algorithms used in the isomorphism tests. Section 4 includes the notation of a graph where the symmetries at a vertex are not arbitrary but restricted to a group. This last notion will be used in section 5 to decompose a class of graphs where at intermediate stages the graphs are those with restricted vertex symmetries. The graph for which this contraction procedure works will be called the k-contractable graphs. Section 6 shows that the k-contractable graph contains the graphs of genus ϵk for some $\epsilon > 0$.

2. PRELIMINARIES

2.1 Graph Theoretic Preliminaries

Throughout this paper graphs will be denoted by G, H, and K; groups by A, B, and C; and sets by X, Y, and Z. Graphs may have multiple edges but no selfloops. It will be important that they are allowed to have multiple edges. The edges and vertices of G will be denoted by E(G) and V(G), respectively. The edges common to some vertex v or set of vertices will be denoted by E(v). Let ME denote the multiple edge equivalence relation on G, i.e. eMEe' if e and e' are common to the same points. The valence of a given vertex v will be the number of vertices adjacent to v, i.e. the number of edges ignoring multiplicity. Let G be a graph and $Y \subseteq V$. We say two edges e and e' of G are Y equivalent if there exists a path from e to e' avoiding points of Y.

Definition 2.1. The graph Br induced from an equivalence class of Y-equivalent edges will be called a bridge, or a bridge of the pair (G,Y). The vertex frontier of Br is the vertices of Br in Y, while the edge frontier of Br is the edges of Br common to the vertex frontier. A bridge is trivial if it is a single edge.

The main graph theoretic construction we shall use is contracting nonfrontier edges to a point.

Definition 2.2. If $Y \subseteq V$, the vertices of G, then Contract(G,Y) will be the graph obtained from G by identifying the nonfrontier (internal) vertices of Br for each bridge Br of G, and removing selfloops. If $Y = \emptyset$ then Contract(G,Y) is a single vertex.

Let Y_k be the vertices of G with valence greater than k. The intuition behind the k-contractable graphs is it is those graphs for which the successive application of Contract(G,Y_k) yields a single point. Here we keep track of the symmetries of the bridges with groups. We attempt to render this idea.

2.2 Group Theoretic Preliminaries

Let Sym(X) denote the group of all permutations of X. We let S_n denote the symmetric group on a set of size n. The group A is a permutation group on X if $A \leq \mathrm{Sym}(X)$. The degree of A is $|X|$, while the order is $|A|$. Let π be an equivalence relation on X. Let $A(\pi)$ denote the subgroup of A which stabilizes the equivalence classes X/π of π, i.e. $A(\pi) = \{\alpha \in A | x\pi\alpha(x)$ for all $x \in X\}$. If $Y \subseteq X$, we let Y denote the relation $\{xYy | x,y \not\in Y \text{ or } x = Y\}$. Thus, A(Y) is the subgroup of A which fixes Y pointwise, while A[Y] is the subgroup which stabilizes Y. We let id denote the empty relation. We say A preserves π if $x\pi y$ implies $\alpha(x)\pi\alpha(y)$ for all $\alpha \in A$. The subgroup of A preserving π we will denote by $A[\pi]$. A is primitive if it only preserves the trivial equivalence relations X and id. We say the relation π contains π' if $x\pi' y$ implies $x\pi y$ for all x and y in X, denoted by $\pi' \leq \pi$. If π is an equivalence relation then X/π denotes the equivalence classes of π. The restriction of an equivalence relation π to Y is denoted by $\pi \upharpoonright Y$. Formally, $\pi \upharpoonright Y$ is defined by $x \; \pi\upharpoonright Y y$ if $x,y \not\in Y$ or $x,y \in Y$ and $x\pi y$. If $Y \subseteq X$ then Y/π are the equivalence classes of π restricted to Y.

The equivalence classes of the relation π defined by, $x\pi y$ if for some $\alpha \in A$ $\alpha(x) = y$, are called the orbits of A. The induced action of A on some orbit Y is the image of A in Sym(Y) which we identify with the quotient group A/A(Y). In general we shall let $A \upharpoonright Y$ denote the faithful action of A[Y] on Y, i.e. A[Y]/A(Y).

An isomorphism is a surjective map which sends edges to edges and vertices to vertices, and preserves incidence and other possible structure. Groups will be permutation groups and they will act from the left.

2.3 Towers of Γ_k-Actions

Throughout this paper we shall either restrict the groups considered or the way they may act.

Definition 2.3. For $k \geq 2$, let Γ_k denote the class of groups A such that all the composition factors of A are subgroups of S_k.

We shall use the following fact about the primitive actions of Γ_k groups.

Theorem 2.4 [BCP ta]. There is a function $\lambda(k)$ such that any primitive action of $A \in \Gamma_k$ of degree n has order at most n^λ.

The main theorem seems to require that we allow all groups but restrict the way in which they can act. Even in the case of cubic graphs the edge stabilizer is a 2-group but the full group may be arbitrary.

Definition 2.5. A group A acting on a set X is a Γ_k-action if for all $x \in X$ the subgroup $A(x) \in \Gamma_k$.

We extend the notation of a Γ_k-action to a tower of such actions. The sequence $(\pi_0, \ldots, \pi_t)$ is a tower of equivalence relations on X if $X = \pi_0 \geq \ldots \geq \pi_t = id$. We shall often write a tower as $(\pi_1 \ldots, \pi_t)$ where it is understood that $\pi_0 = X$. This gives a useful generalization of Γ_k-actions.

Definition 2.6. $(A, \pi_0 \ldots, \pi_t)$ is a tower of Γ_k-actions if:

(1) the sequence $(\pi_0, \ldots, \pi_t)$ is a tower of equivalence relations on X;

(2) $A \subseteq Sym(X)$;

(3) A preserves π_i for $0 \leq i \leq t$;

(4) for each $Y \in X/\pi_i$, $0 \leq i \leq t$, the action of A[Y] on Y/π_{i+1} is a Γ_k-action.

We write (4) more formally.

(4') If $S \in X/\pi_i$ and $T \in S/\pi_{i+1}$ then $A[T]/A(\pi_{i+1} \upharpoonright S) \in \Gamma_k$.

It is easy to see that (4) and (4') are equivalent since the natural homomorphism from $A[T]$ into $\mathrm{Sym}(S/\pi_{i+1})$ has kernal $A(\pi_{i+1} \upharpoonright S)$.

We shall prove some simple closure properties about towers of Γ_k actions. We state them as lemmas.

Lemma 2.7. If $(A,\pi_0,\ldots,\pi_t)$ is a tower of Γ_k actions and $B \subseteq A$ then $(B,\pi_0,\ldots,\pi_t)$ is a tower of Γ_k actions.

Proof. It is clear that $(B,\pi_0,\ldots,\pi_t)$ satisfies the first three conditions. We show it satisfies (4'). Let $S \in X/\pi_i$ and $T \in S/\pi_{i+1}$. We must show that $B[T]/B(\pi_{i+1} \upharpoonright S) \in \Gamma_k$. But, $B[T] \subseteq A[T]$ and $B(\pi_{i+1} \upharpoonright S) = B[T] \cap A(\pi_{i+1} \upharpoonright S)$. So by the Second Isomorphism Theorem and the Correspondence Theorem $B[T]/A(\pi_{i+1} \upharpoonright S) \cap B[T]$ is isomorphic to a subgroup of $A[T]/A(\pi_{i+1} \upharpoonright S)$. The latter quotient group is in Γ_k. Therefore, the first quotient group is in Γ_k, since Γ_k is closed under taking subgroups.

Lemma 2.8. If $(A,\pi_0,\ldots\pi_t)$ is a tower of Γ_k actions and $Y \subseteq X = \pi_0$ then $(A \upharpoonright Y, \pi_0 \upharpoonright Y, \ldots, \pi_t \upharpoonright Y)$ is a tower of Γ_k actions.

Proof. Since $A \upharpoonright Y = A[Y] \upharpoonright Y$ and by the previous lemma, towers of Γ_k actions are closed under taking subgroup. We may assume that $A = A[Y]$. Let $S' \in Y/\pi_i$, $0 \le i \le t$, and $T' \in S'/\pi_{i+1}$. Since $S',T' \neq \phi$ and they are subsets of equivalence classes of π_i and π_{i+1} respectively, there exists unique elements $S \in X/\pi_i$ and $T \in S/\pi_{i+1}$ containing S' and T', respectively. We must show that $A[T']/A(\pi_i \upharpoonright S') \in \Gamma_k$. We have the following chain of inclusions

$$A[T] = A[T'] \supseteq A(\pi_i \upharpoonright S') \supseteq A(\pi_i \upharpoonright S) .$$

So our quotient is a section of a Γ_k group and thus Γ_k.

3. CANONICAL ORDERING OF SETS AND SET OF ORDERINGS

3.1 Canonical Forms

As in [BL83, FSS83] we say a function $CF:K \to K$, where K is a class of graphs, is a canonical form for K if:

(i) for G in K, $CF(G) \approx G$

(ii) for G,H in K, $G \approx H$ if and only if $CF(G) = CF(H)$.

In the previous papers, they considered linearly ordering the vertices as a canonical form or presentation. We shall order edges. For each edge e we shall consider it as oriented, i.e. e^{-1}, the reverse of e, is distinct from e. Formally, a canonical form of a graph G will be a linear ordering of the oriented edges of G which satisfies conditions (i) and (ii). We shall often let I,J be maps from $\{1,\ldots,|E|\}$ to E. In general, I will be a map from $\{1,\ldots,|X|\}$ to X, in which case we will call I an ordering of X. If $A \subseteq \mathrm{Sym}(X)$ then the pair (I,A) determines the set of ordering $\{aI \mid a \in A\}$. The algorithms considered will return all equivalent ordering, i.e. pairs (I,A). We consider several canonization problems.

Problem 3.1. String canonical forms for towers of Γ_k-actions.

Input: A colored set X with orderings (I,A) where A is given as a tower of Γ_k-actions, $(A,\pi_0,\ldots,\pi_t)$.

Find:

(1) $\alpha \in A$ such that αI is canonical;

(2) group $B \subseteq A$ of elements which preserve coloring.

Formally, an algorithm CF satisfies condition (1) if whenever CF on $(I,A,\pi_0,\ldots,\pi_t)$ returns αI and CF on $(\beta I,A,\pi_0,\ldots,\pi_t)$ returns γI for $\beta \in A$ then $\alpha\gamma^{-1} \in B$. Thus the canonical form may be a function of $(\pi_0,\ldots,\pi_t)$. The ordering I is said to be $\leq$ the order J if (X with ordering I) is lexigraphically before (X with ordering J).

Problem 3.2. Graph canonical forms restricted to a tower of Γ_k-actions.

Input: A graph G with ordering I of V(G) and a tower of Γ_k-actions $(A,\pi_0,\ldots,\pi_t)$ on V(G).

Find: (1) $\alpha \in A$ such that αI is a canonical ordering of V(G);

(2) group $B \subseteq A$ of automorphisms of G in A.

We list a third problem which we will not use in this paper but whose polynomial time solution will follow easily from the ideas in this paper and the ideas in [M1ta] and may have application elsewhere.

Problem 3.3. Hypergraph canonical forms restricted to tower of Γ_k-actions.

In problem 3.3 the graph in problem 3.2 is replaced by a hypergraph.

Before presenting the fourth problem of this section we give a polynomial time solution to problem 3.1. This algorithm gives:

Theorem 3.4. String canonical forms for towers of Γ_k-actions is polynomial time constructable for fixed k.

Let $(A,\pi_0,\ldots,\pi_t)$ be a tower of Γ_k-actions on a colored set X. Further, let I be an ordering of X.

We consider two procedures, CF which returns the canonical ordering and C which returns the group of symmetries. If $S \subseteq X$ we define C and CF as follows:

(i) $C_S(A) = \{\alpha \in A | \alpha$ preserves color on $S\}$;

(ii) $CF_S(I,A)$ = canonical αI, $\alpha \in A$, for coloring on S only.

Space does not permit giving the procedure for C but it follows easily from that of CF.

The algorithm will have a recursive form similar to [Lu80, BL83]. The procedure has two phases. The first phase is used to reduce the group's action on S/π_i to a Γ_k group. While the second phase just applies an algorithm similar to the color canonialization algorithm of [BL83] to an action which is Γ_k. In the procedure X, I, $\pi_0, \ldots, \pi_t$, and t will be global variables and S will be an A-stable subset of X.

<u>Procedure</u>: $CF_S(I,A,i)$.

<u>Begin</u>: (1) <u>If</u> $S = \{x\}$ for some $x \in X$ <u>then return</u> I;

(2) <u>If</u> A is not transitive on S <u>then</u>

(a) "Canonically" pick an A-stable partition of S w.r.t. I, say, S_1, S_2;

(b) <u>Return</u> $CF_{S_2}(CF_{S_1}(I,A,i), C_{S_1}(A), i)$;

(3) If $S \subseteq T \in X/\pi_i$ for some T <u>then</u>

(a) "Canonically" pick $S' \in S/\pi_{i+1}$ w.r.t. I;

(b) Compute $A' = A[S']$ and right coset representatives of A' in A, say, $\{\sigma_1, \ldots, \sigma_\ell\}$;

(c) <u>Return</u> $\operatorname{Min}_j\{CF_S(\sigma_j I, A', i+1)\}$;

(4) (a) Find a canonical primitive block system w.r.t. I on S, say, $\pi \geq \pi_i \mid S$;

(b) Compute $A' = A(\pi)$ and right coset representatives $\{\sigma_1, \ldots, \sigma_\ell\}$ of A' in A;

(c) <u>Return</u> $\operatorname{Min}_j\{CF_S(\sigma_j I, A', i)\}$.

<u>End</u>

Since the algorithm parallels earlier algorithms it follows that $CF_X(I,A,0)$ will compute a string canonical form.

To see that CF runs in polynomial time we must bound the size of ℓ whenever step (4) is implemented. We state three facts which follow for any recursive call of CF, say, $CF(\sigma,A,i)$ by lemmas 2.7 and 2.8.

(i) $(A \restriction S, \pi_0 \restriction S, \ldots, \pi_t \restriction S)$ is a tower of Γ_k-actions;

(ii) If $|S/\pi_i| > 1$ then $A \restriction S/\pi_i$ is in Γ_k;

(iii) If $|S/\pi_i| = 1$ then $A \restriction S/\pi_{i+1}$ is a Γ_k-action.

By a straightforward calculation one can show that the number of recursive calls is bounded by $n^{\lambda+2}$, where λ is the constant from theorem 2.4. This completes the proof of theorem 3.4.

To apply the solution to the string canonical forms to the graph canonical forms, we simply consider the group as acting on pairs of vertices. Since edges are pairs of vertices we color these pairs according to whether they are edges or nonedges. But this is the string canonical form problem. We need only show that a tower of Γ_k-actions on X can be "lifted" to a tower of Γ_k-actions on X^2.

We state this lifting in a slightly stronger form which we will need later. If π is a relation on X and τ is a relation of Y then define $\pi\cdot\tau$ on $X\times Y$ by $(x,y)\pi\cdot\tau(x',y')$ if $x\pi x'$ and $y\tau y'$. Thus, a polynomial time algorithm follows for problem 3.2 from the following lemma.

Lemma 3.5. If $(A,X,\pi_1,\ldots,\pi_t)$ and $(B,Y,\pi_1,\ldots,\pi_t)$ are towers of Γ_k-actions then so is $(A\times B, X\times Y, \pi_1\cdot\tau_1,\ldots,\pi_t\cdot\tau_t)$.

3.2 Canonical Group Intersection

In this section we consider the problem of canonically intersecting two permutation groups. The solution again will parallel the work of [Lu80, BL83]. In practice the two groups may not be acting on the same set. Thus, we consider a slight generalization of the problem.

Let A act on X and B act on Y. The amalgamated intersection of A and B or simply the intersection of A and B, $A \cap B$, is the group of elements in $\mathrm{Sym}(X \cup Y)$ which stabilizes X and Y and whose action on X is in A and on Y is in B.

We shall say a function CIN is canonical form for $A \cap B$ if it returns ordering satisfying condition (1).

(1) $\mathrm{CIN}(I,J,A,B) = (\alpha I, \beta J)$ and $\mathrm{CIN}(aI,bJ,A,B) = (\alpha' I, \beta' J)$ implies $\alpha'\alpha^{-1} \in A$ and $\beta'\beta^{-1} \in B$ for $a \in A$ and $b \in B$.

This gives the fourth problem.

Problem 3.6. Canonical intersection of an arbitrary group with a tower of Γ_k-actions.

Input: Two orderings (I,A) and (J,B) where A is given as a tower of Γ_k-actions.

Find: $\alpha \in A$ and $\beta \in B$ such that $(\alpha I, \beta J)$ is canonical.

We do not require solutions to canonical intersections to return a linear ordering of $X \cup Y$. But, there are many natural orderings of $X \cup Y$ determined by αI and βJ. For the applications here we find the two orderings more natural.

The algorithm for problem 3.6 will be a combination of the group intersection algorithm in [Lu80] and the canonization algorithms of [BL83, FSS83].

We say $(I,J) \leq (I_1,J_1)$ if I and I_1 first enumerate $X \wedge Y$ and $J^{-1}I$ is lexographically before $J_1^{-1}I_1$.

The problem of simply computing the intersection of A and B when A is a tower of Γ_k-actions is also polynomial computable. The algorithm proposed is a natural combination of the algorithm for color symmetries in a tower of Γ_k-actions and the group intersection algorithm in [Lu80] for Γ_k groups. Due to space constraints we will not present it here. The canonization procedure will call this algorithm.

Let C be a subgroup of $A \times B$ acting on $X \times Y$. Let $Pr_1(C)$ $Pr_2(C)$ be the projections of C on X and Y, respectively. Consider the following function on C for subsets Z of $X \cap Y$.

$$IN_Z(C) = \{(\alpha,\beta) \in C | \alpha \restriction Z = \beta \restriction Z\} .$$

Similar to IN_Z we extend CIN. We have $CIN_Z(I,J,C)$ return $(\alpha I, \beta J) \in C$ which is canonical w.r.t. $C_Z = \{(a,b) \in C | a \restriction Z = b \restriction Z\}$. We give a list of recursive properties of CIN_Z which easily produces the desired polynomial time algorithm.

(3.7). If $Pr_1(C)$ is not transitive on Z with stable canonical partition Z_1, Z_2, then:

$$CIN_Z(I,J,C) = CIN_{Z_2}(CIN_{Z_1}(I,J,C), IN_{Z_1}(C)) .$$

(3.8). If $A^* \subseteq Pr_1(C)$ with right coset representatives $\{\alpha_1,\ldots,\alpha_\ell\}$ in $Pr_1(C)$ then:

$$CIN_Z(I,J,C) = \text{Min}\{CIN_Z(\alpha_i I, \beta_i J, C^*)\}$$

where $(\alpha_i,\beta_i) \in C$ and $C^* = \{(\alpha,\beta) \in C | \alpha \in A^*\}$.

(3.9). If $Z = \{z\}$ then:

$$CIN_Z(I,J,C) = \text{Min}\{(\alpha_i I, \beta_i J)\}$$

where (α_i,β_j) are right coset representatives of $C((z,z))$ in C.

Using these three identities about CIN and the recursive control structure of the color canonicalization algorithm we can compute the intersection and the canonical intersection in $n^{\lambda+2}$ recursive calls of identity (3.9). The stabilizer of (z,z) in C can be computed using Sim's algorithm as analyzed in [FHL].

In the case that B is also a tower of Γ_k-actions then we can return not only the intersection but a tower of Γ_k-actions. The following lemma will suffice.

Lemma 3.10. If $(A,X,\pi_1,\ldots,\pi_t)$ and $(B,Y,\tau_1,\ldots,\tau_t)$ are towers of Γ_k-actions then $(A \cap B,\ X \cap Y,\ \pi_1 \cap \tau_1,\ldots,\pi_k \cap \tau_k)$ is a tower of Γ_k-actions.

4. SYMMETRIES OF A VERTEX GIVEN BY A GROUP

In [MI79] we discussed gadgets — graphs which were used to denote symmetries or as a data structure for symmetries. Here we reverse those ideas and replace bridges or gadgets of a graph by a group or coset which will represent the symmetries of the frontier of a bridge. We shall apply these ideas to isomorphism testing and canonical forms for k-contractable graphs. Here, we present an algorithm which under certain conditions tests isomorphism of graphs where the vertices have specified symmetries. We make these notations precise in what follows. It seems crucial that the graphs considered have multiple edges. Throughout this section the graphs are assumed to have multiple edges.

Definition 4.1. A graph with specified symmetry is a graph $G = (V,E)$, a set of ordering (I_v,A_v) for each set $E(v)$, $v \in V$, and a consistent partition P of the vertices G. The partition P is consistent if vPw implies that $I_w^{-1}A_wI_w = I_v^{-1}A_vI_v$.

We next consider restriction on the way the group at each vertex can act.

Definition 4.2. A graph G has its vertex symmetries given by towers of Γ_k-actions if G has specified symmetry where A_v is given in the form $(A_v,\pi_1,\ldots,\pi_t)$, a tower of Γ_k-actions, and the partition P is consistent with this structure. We shall say the symmetries are Γ_k on the multiple edges if for every vertex $v \in V(G)$ the induced action of A_v on $E(v)/ME$ is a Γ_k-action. We shall often refer to these graphs as simply Γ_k-graphs. An ismorphism of G must preserve this structure.

Theorem 4.3. Isomorphism and canonical form for Γ_k graphs are polynomial time constructable for fixed k.

The assumption that the symmetries are Γ_k-actions on the multiple edge relation will insure that the induced action on vertices will be tractable. It would be interesting to know if this constraint can be dropped. By identifying multiple edges the symmetries become Γ_k-actions. In this case, the edge stabilizer of a connected graph is a group in Γ_k. We state this well-known fact as a lemma.

Lemma 4.4. If G is connected with specified symmetries which are Γ_k-actions then the automorphisms of G which stabilize an edge form a group in Γ_k.

We explain the canonical form algorithm here. It will use the leveling idea. By standard techniques we may assume the graph G is connected. For each edge e in E(G) we compute the canonical form from e. We shall level the edges and vertices by their distance from e. Using this leveling we shall inductively construct the partial automorphisms from edges to edges and from vertices to vertices. We begin the formal construction.

Label the edge e' of G with the integer which is the distance (the number of vertices in a shortest path) from e to the edge e', e.g. e is labeled 0. Vertices of G are labeled with the integer which is the number of edges they are from e, the end points of e are labeled 1. An edge is even if both end points are labeled the same, otherwise it is odd.

Let G_i be the induced graph on edges labeled $\leq i$. That is, G_i is the graph on vertices labeled $\leq i + 1$ and edges labeled $\leq i$. The graph $\bar{G}_i$ consists of: (1) G_i; (2) all odd edges labeled i + 1 where the end-point labeled i + 2 has been replaced with a new distinct vertex for each edge; (3) two copies of each even edge labeled i + 1 where one copy is attached to one end point labeled i + 1 and the other copy is attached to the other end point labeled i + 1. Again, the other end-point of these even edges is a new vertex. The vertex symmetries for vertices labeled $\leq i$ of G_i will be those of G while the vertices labelled i + 1 will have no restriction on symmetries. The vertex symmetries of $\bar{G}_i$ for vertices labeled $\leq i + 1$ will be those of G. Again, the symmetries of vertices labeled i + 2 will not be constrained.

Let Auto(G_i) be the automorphisms of G_i which fix e. Similarly, Auto($\bar{G}_i$) are the automorphisms of $\bar{G}_i$ which fix e.

We shall need inductively two conditions or facts concerning the isomorphism. First, that the automorphisms of G_i and $\bar{G}_i$ which fix e acting on the edges are written as a tower of Γ_k-actions. Second, the automorphism of G_i leaving e fixed acting on the vertices is in Γ_k. We consider the second condition first. If we identify multiple edges of $\bar{G}_{i-1}$ but not multiple copies of the vertices and the symmetries are those induced from the vertices of $\bar{G}_{i-1}$, then the new graph satisfies the hypothesis of lemma 7. Therefore, the automorphism of the graph fixing the edge e are in Γ_k. Now, any automorphism of $\bar{G}_{i-1}$ induces an automorphism on this graph. Since the action on the vertex is unchanged by identifying multiple edges we have the second condition for $\bar{G}_{i-1}$. If we now also identify the multiple vertices of $\bar{G}_{i-1}$, the automorphism fixing e will still be in Γ_k. But this is the same graph we obtain by identifying the multiple edges of G_i. This proves the second condition. We shall maintain the first condition throughout the construct.

We need only give a polynomial time algorithm for constructing $\text{Auto}(\bar{G}_i)$ from $\text{Auto}(G_i)$ and constructing $\text{Auto}(G_{i+1})$ from $\text{Auto}(\bar{G}_i)$ where the groups are given as towers of Γ_k-actions. We consider the latter case first.

The elements of $\text{Auto}(G_{i+1})$ are simply those elements of $\text{Auto}(\bar{G}_i)$ which preserve multiple copies of vertices and edges. That is, they preserve the relation $a \equiv b$, a and b are copies of the same edge or vertex. We obtain the canonical form for this relation by applying the graph canonical form restricted to a tower of Γ_k-actions algorithm (3.2). Here the graph has vertices consisting of the vertices and edges of $\bar{G}_i$ and the edges are the multiple copies relation. Since towers of Γ_k-action are closed under taking subgroups the first condition is inductively satisfied for $\text{Auto}(G_{i+1})$.

We have left the construction of $\text{Auto}(\bar{G}_i)$ from $\text{Auto}(G_i)$ which we must show is a tower of Γ_k-actions. Let $(A,\pi_1,\ldots,\pi_t) = \text{Auto}(G_i)$, a tower of Γ_k-actions. Let E_i be the edges of $\bar{G}_i$ which are common to a vertex labeled i. The maps on E_i which preserve the symmetry of vertices labeled i can be written as a direct product of wreath products since the symmetries are consistent. That is, it will be of form $\Pi A_{ij} \text{Wr} S$. Let B be this group. The group $\text{Auto}(\bar{G}_i)$ will be the amalgamated intersection of A and B. By (3.6) this intersection and its canonical form are constructable in polynomial time. To show that the intersection can be written as a tower of Γ_k-actions we note the following. Let π_{ij} be the ith equivalence relation of vertex j. We claim that $\tau_i = \bigcap_j \pi_{ij}$, where V_j has label $\le i + 1$, form a tower for $A \cap B$. By induction, assume it is true for A where the intersection is taken over vertices labeled $\le i$. In the construction of B we used the symmetric group in the wreath product. But we know that the induced action on the vertices labeled $i + 1$ given by A is in Γ_k. So we may restrict the wreath product to this Γ_k group. Let B' be this smaller wreath product. Now, $(B', \tau_1', \ldots, \tau_t')$ is a tower of Γ_k-actions where $\tau_i' = \bigcap_j \tau_{ij}$, V_j has label $i + 1$. This proves the theorem.

We shall need that the full group of automorphisms of G can be written as a tower of Γ_k-actions.

Let G be a graph whose vertex symmetries are given by towers of Γ_k-actions and these symmetries are Γ_k on the multiple edges. Suppose the vertex symmetries of G are $(A_i, \pi_{1i}, \ldots, \pi_{ti})$ for vertex V_i. Let ME be the multiple edge relation on G. In this case the automorphisms of G are a tower of Γ_k-actions.

Lemma 4.5. If G and $(A_i, \pi_{1i}, \ldots, \pi_{ti})$, are as above and A is the group of automorphisms of G acting on the edges, then $(A, ME, \tau_1, \ldots, \tau_t)$, where $\tau_i = (\bigcap_j \pi_{ij}) \cap ME$ for $v_i \in V(G)$, is a tower of Γ_k-actions.

5. k-CONTRACTABLE GRAPHS

In this section we simultaneously define the valence k-contractable graphs and present a polynomial time algorithm for testing isomorphisms of these graphs. We define the valence k-contractable graphs via a decomposition algorithm. The definition is unsatisfactory since small perturbations may result in a different class of graphs. We leave it as an open problem to find a satisfactory definition. The definition is sufficient enough so that any perturbation will still contain the graphs of bounded genus and bounded valence. Let G be a graph with prescribed symmetries either given by towers of Γ_k-actions or unconstrained. We shall assume that two unconstrained vertices have at most one edge between them. We shall call these graphs Γ_k-contractable graphs.

We shall say a vertex v is Γ_k if the symmetries of v induce a Γ_k-action on the multiple edge relation ME; otherwise it is not Γ_k. Br is a Γ_k-bridge if it is a bridge of (G,Y) where Y is the set of vertices which are not Γ_k in G. A Γ_k-bridge is not formally a Γ_k-graph for two reasons. First, the unconstrained vertices have no associated tower of relations. This problem is remedied by allowing these unconstrained vertices to "inherit" the symmetries from their neighbors. Note that each neighbor v' of an unconstrained vertex v either shares only a single edge with v' or else its symmetries are a tower of Γ_k-

actions. Thus, the symmetries of an unconstrained vertex can be restricted to a product of wreath products where the wreath products are of the form $AW_rS_{k'}$, where A is the inherited symmetry from a neighboring vertex and $k' \leq k$. Second, we have not specified the symmetry of frontier vertices. We transform Br into a modified bridge so that it has the form of a Γ_k-graph. For each vertex v of Br common to a frontier vertex v' of Br, we introduce a new copy of the frontier vertex $\bar{v}'$ and have edges between v and v' go between v and $\bar{v}'$. We now view these new frontier vertices as unconstrained vertices and allow them to inherit the symmetries of their neighbor. Let $\bar{B}r$ be the bridge obtained from Br by the above construction.

Given any Γ_k-bridge Br, we can compute the automorphisms and canonical form by first constructing $\bar{B}r$ and applying the isomorphism test for Γ_k-graphs. This procedure will return with a group in the form of a tower of Γ_k-actions. Applying (3.2) we can compute the subgroup and canonical form of Auto($\bar{B}r$) which sends multiple copies of vertices to corresponding multiple copies of vertices. This will be Auto(Br) and its canonical form.

Lemma 5.1. The automorphism and canonical form for a Γ_k-bridge is polynomial time constructable and the automorphisms can be written as a tower of Γ_k-actions.

This gives a natural decomposition of Γ_k-contractable graphs, say G. For each Γ_k-bridge Br of G we identify the internal vertices of Br and remove selfloops. We denote this graph by Contract(G).

The vertex symmetries of this new vertex will be the induced action of Auto(Br) on the frontier edges. This will be a tower of Γ_k-actions. We call this graph $\text{Contract}_k(G)$ which is a Γ_k-contractable graph. By standard argument $\text{Contract}_k(G)$ is a canonical operation on G.

If we apply Contract_k to a tree of valence $> k + 1$ then the procedure will simply return the original graph. Graphs that are sent to themselves under a procedure will be called fixed points. We introduce a decomposition procedure analogous to the tree isomorphism algorithm. The procedure Remove Leaves will remove leaves and let their neighbors "inherit" their symmetries. The details will appear in the final paper.

We introduce a third reduction which corresponds to a generalized 3-connected decomposition.

Two vertices of valence 2, ignoring multiple edges, are multilpe if their neighboring vertices are the same. This gives a natural equivalence relation on valence 2 vertices. An equivalence class will simply be called a set of multiple vertices. Let $v_1,\ldots,v_\ell$ be a set of multiple vertices of G. Multiple vertices can be identified with the new vertex "inheriting" the symmetries of the multiple vertices and their common neighbors. The third reduction is called Remove Multiple Vertices. Again, the details will appear in the final paper.

The graph G is a fixed point of these three reductions if it is a fixed point of each reduction. Note that we may arrive at a different fixed point depending on the order which we apply these reductions. For specificity's sake, suppose we consider fixed points of the following procedure.

Procedure: $\text{Reduction}_k(G)$.

> If G = Remove Leaves(G) then
> G ← Remove Leaves(G)
> else if G ≠ Remove Multiple Vertices(G) then
> G ← Remove Multiple Vertices(G)
> else G ← $\text{Contract}_k(G)$.

Definition 5.2. G is a k-contractable graph if successive application of reduction applied to G yields a singleton.

From the discussion above we get

Theorem 5.3. Isomorphism for k-contractable graphs is polynomial time testable for fixed k.

6. THE BOUNDED GENUS CASE

Here we shall show that graphs of bounded genus are k-contractable graphs. Thus, demonstrating that the k-contractable graphs form a class of graphs which is a common generalization of the bounded valence and the bounded genus graphs. The containment will follow by showing that the fixed graphs under the reduction operation have the property that their genus grows linearly in k. Throughout the rest of the discussion let G be a fixed point. Since neither the genus nor the fact that G is a fixed point is effected by multiple edges, we may assume without loss of generality that G has no multiple edges. Similarly, we may assume that G has no vertices of valence 2. Not all vertices of G will have valence $\geq k + 1$. Let S be the set of vertices of G with valence $\leq k$. Then, S will be an independent set. Let v' denote the number of vertices of G in V-S. We first state a relationship between genus and k-contractable graphs as defined in the previous sections. We shall actually prove a slightly stronger result for a stronger notion of k-contractable.

Theorem 6.1. If G is a fixed point of Reduction_{k-1} then the genus of G,g satisfies

$$2g \geq ((k/2 - 6)/6)v' + 2 .$$

To see that such a large value of k is necessary consider the infinite tiling of the plane in diagram 1. Since this tiling is periodic we can construct arbitrarily large graphs of genus 1 which are fixed points of Reduction_{11}.

Let V' denote the vertices V-S. We distinguish two types of edges of G. The edges between points of V' will be called type A edges and those between V' and S will be called type B. Since we can easily distinguish these two types we can include in Reduction a procedure which restricts the symmetries at each vertex to the coset which preserves type. Call this new reduction procedure Reduction'. For $\text{Reduction}'_6$ the example from diagram 1 will contract to a point. For Reduction' we get the following result.

Theorem 6.2. If G is a fixed point of $\text{Reduction}'_k$ then the genus of G,g satisfies

$$2g \geq ((k - 6)/6)V' + 2 .$$

Note that we are using $\text{Reduction}'_k$ since fixing one edge at a vertex will only in general effect one of the two types of edges at that point. This gives the following corollary for k-contractable graphs with respect to Reduction'.

Corollary 6.3. If $k > 4g + 2$ and $g \geq 1$ then the k-contractable graphs include the graphs of genus g. For $g = 0$ (the planar case) $k = 5$ will suffice.

To see the corollary we simply note that $v' \geq 3$ since a fixed point can have no multiple valence 2 vertices.

Proof of Theorem 6.2. The proof uses standard counting argument based on Euler's formula $2g = 3 - f - v + 2$ where g is the genus of some embedding and e, f, and v are the numbers of edges, faces, and vertices, respectively.

Let G be a graph with some fixed embedding. Further assume G is fixed by $\text{Reduction}'_k$. Without loss of generality we may add new vertices of type S and new edges of type A as long as the genus is unchanged If any vertex in V' has two consecutive edges of type A we may add to this face a valence 3 vertex of type S. On the other hand, if a vertex $v \in V'$ has two consecutive type B edges, then we may add a type A edge across this face common to v. Here we use the fact that S is an independent set. Without loss of generality we may assume that the edges at each vertex of V' are alternately of type A and then type B. So, if a equals the number of type A edges and b equals the number of type B edges then $2a = b$. Using this fact one can show:

Lemma 6.4. $f \le a + b/2 = 3a$.

Using the following facts: (1) $|V'| + |S| = V$, (2) $|S| \le b/3$, (3) $e = b + a$, (4) $b \ge k|V'|$, we get theorem 6.2.

ACKNOWLEDGEMENTS

I would like to thank Tom Leighton for most helpful discussions especially in the last section. I would also like to thank Laslo Babai, Eugene Luks, and Jeff Kahn. This work was supported by the National Science Foundation.

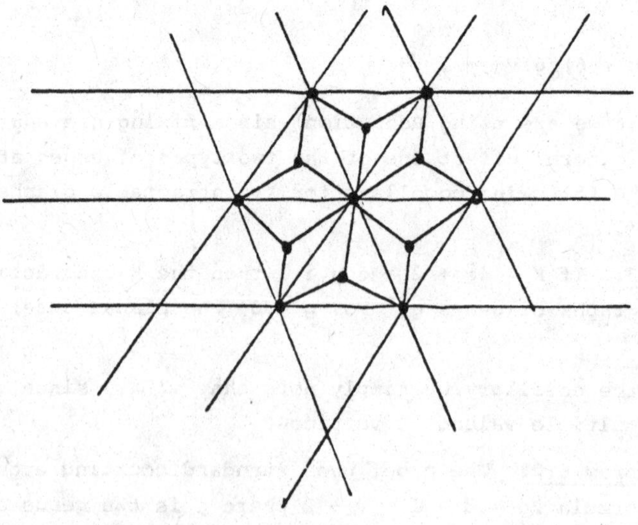

Diagram 1.

Bibliography

[Ba 81] L. Babai, "Moderately Exponential Bound for Graph Isomorphism", Proc. Conf. on Foundation of Computation Theory, Szeget (1981).

[BCP ta] L. Babai, P.J. Cameron, P.P. Palfy, "On the Order of Primitive Permutation Groups with Bounded Nonabelian Composition Factors", in preparation.

[BL 83] L. Babai, E. Luks, "Canonical Labeling of Graphs", STOC 83.

[Ca 81] P.J. Cameron, "Finite Permutation Groups and Finite Simple Groups", Bull. London Math. Soc. 13, 1981, pp. 1-22.

[FM 80] I.S. Filotti, J.N. Mayer, "A Polynomial-time Algorithm for Determining the Isomorphism of Graphs of Fixed Genus", Proc. 12th ACM Symp. Th. Comp. (1980), pp. 236-243.

[FMR 79] I.S. Filotti, G.L. Miller and J. Reif, "On Determining the Genus of a Graph in $0(V^{0(g)})$ Steps".

[FSS 83] Furer, Schnyder, Specker, "Normal Forms for Frivalent Graphs", STOC 83.

[HT 73] J.E. Hopcroft, R.E. Tarjan, "Dividing a Graph into Triconnected Components", SIAM J. Comput., Vol. 2, No. 3, Sept. 1973, pp. 294-303.

[Li 80] D. Lichtenstein, "Isomorphism for Graphs Embeddable on the Projective Plane", Proc. 12th ACM Symp. Th. Symp. (1980), pp. 218-224.

[Lu 80] E.M. Luks, "Isomorphism of Bounded Valence can be Tested in Polynomial Time", in Proc. 21st Annual Symposium of Foundations of Computer Science, IEEE (1980).

[Ml 79] G.L. Miller, "Graph Isomorphism, General Remarks", JCSS, Vol. 18, No. 2, April 1979, pp. 128-141.

[Ml 80] G.L. Miller, "Isomorphism Testing for Graphs of Bounded Genus" (working paper), Proc. 12th ACM Symp. Th. Comp. (1980), pp. 225-235.

[Ml ta1] G.L. Miller, "Isomorphism of Graphs which are Pairwise k-Separable", submitted to Information and Control.

[Ml ta2] G.L. Miller, "Isomorphism of k-Contractable Graphs (a generalization of bounded valence and bounded genus)", submitted to Information and Control.

FINDING DOMINATORS

Renata Ochranová
Computing Science Department, Faculty of Science
J.E. Purkyně University
Janáčkovo nám. 2a, 662 95 Brno
Czechoslovakia

Abstract: Algorithm for the construction of the dominator tree for reducible control flow graphs working in time $O(r)$ (r is the number of arcs of the graph), is presented.

1. Introduction

Dominance relation is an important tool for program structure analysis, optimization and verification. Its significance and the scope of possible applications are ever increasing. In paper [1], a fast algorithm for finding dominators in a flowgraph is presented. The algorithm uses depth-first search as well as an efficient method of computing functions defined on paths in trees. A simple implementation of the algorithm runs in $O(r \log n)$ time, where r is the number of ares and n is the number of nodes in the graph. A more sophisticated implementation runs in $O(r\alpha(r, n))$ time, where $\alpha(r, n)$ is a functional inverse of Ackermann's function.

This algorithm is faster than a straightforward algorithm for finding dominators suggested by Purdom and Moore [2], the running time of which is $O(rn)$ and is faster than the algorithm given in Aho and Ullman [3], which works with bit vectors of length n. Each node v has a bit vector which encodes a superset of the dominators of v. The algorithm makes several passes over the graph, updating the bit vectors during each pass, until no further changes to the bit vector occur. The bit vector for each node v then encodes the dominators of v. This algorithm requires $O(r)$ bit vector operations per pass for $O(n)$ passes, or $O(nr)$ bit vector operations total. Since each bit vector operation requires $O(n)$ time, the running time of the algorithm is $O(n^2 r)$ on general flowgraph, while on reducible flowgraph it requires $O(r)$, because only two passes are needed. There are two disadvantages of this approach: first, the space complexity is $O(n^2)$ and, second, computing the tree from bit vectors encoding the relation requires $O(n^2)$ time in the worst case. It is just the dominator tree which is required for many kinds of global flow analysis [4].

The algorithm finding the dominator tree of a given reducible control flow graph (RFG), presented in this paper, uses the fact that RFG and its maximal acyclic subgraph have the same dominator tree; further, it utilizes the possibility of transforming the original graph to other graphs which reduce the problem of the detection of the pair 'node-its immediate dominator' to the detection of the pair 'node- its immediate successor'.

It is easy to prove that the algorithm described bellow runs in $O(r)$ for control flow graphs (CFG) of class of programs which satisfy the so called condition of branch isolation (see par. 2 of this paper). This result follows from the fact that the leafs of dominator tree for CFG of programs of this class have a unique immediate successor in a maximal acyclic subgraph of the original graph so that each of transformations over given RFG requires just one step.

The concept of condition of branch isolation was introduced by A. Moravec and further investigated in [5] where it was proved that above mentioned class comprises the class CFG of programs with **if-the-else** and loops of Modula and BJ_n-loops (and of course the **while** and **repeat** construct).

The time complexity of our algorithm is surely not worse $O(n^2)$ and a detailed analysis indicates that it equals $O(r)$. At least, no counterexample was found.

2. Basis notions

A *directed graph* (or graph) G is a pair $G = (N,A)$, where N is a finite nonempty set of nodes and A is a mapping $A : N \to 2^N$ which assigns to every node $x \in N$ the set $A(x)$ of all immediate successors of x.

An ordered $(n + 1)$-tuple of nodes of G $(x_0, x_1, \ldots, x_n)$, $n \geq 0$ such that $x_i \in A(x_{i-1})$ $(1 \leq i \leq n)$ is called a *path from* x_0 *to* x_n *through* $x_1, \ldots, x_{n-1}$ with length n. A path of length 1 is called an *arc*. If there is a path from x to y, we say that the node y is accessible from the node x (in G).

We say that $y \in N$ is an *immediate successor* (*immediate predecessor*) of $x \in N$ iff $y \in A(x)$ $(y \in A^{-1}(x))$, where the mapping $A^{-1}: N \to 2^N$ is defined by $A^{-1}(x)$ $\{z \in N: x \in A(z)\}$. The node y is a *successor* (*predecessor*) of x iff y is accessible from x (x is accessible from y).

The *inverse graph* is the same as the given one except that all arcs have opposite orientation, i.e. the sets of successors and predecessors of a given node are interchanged.

The control *flow graph* (CFG) is a triple $G = (N,A,b)$, where (N,A) is a directed graph, $b \in N$, and every node $x \in N$ is accessible from the *initial node* $b \in N$; $|N|$ is the number of elements of N.

By *terminal node* we understand any node with no successors. If a given CFG G has the only terminal node $e \in N$ and if, moreover, e is accessible from all nodes of G, we use for the CFG the notation $G = (N,A,b,e)$.

Let $G = (N,A,b)$ be a CFG, $x,y \in N$. The node x *dominates* (is a *dominator* of) the node y (written as $x \doteq y$) iff every path from b to y goes through x. If, moreover, $x \neq y$, we say that x properly dominates y $(x \leftharpoondown y)$. The node x is an *immediate dominator* of y $(x = y_{-1})$ iff

a) x is a proper dominator of y

b) if z is a proper dominator of y and $z \neq y$, then z is a dominator of x.

In what follows by a dominator always a proper dominator is meant. All concepts we have just defined concern the *dominance with respect to the initial node* b. However, in the case of the CFG with the only terminal node e, dual concepts relating to the dominance with respect to the terminal node can be defined and utilized. The node y *dominates the node* x *with respect to the terminal node* e $(x \risingdotseq y)$ iff every path from x to e goes through y; the variants of the notions are defined analogously.

By a *dominator tree* (dominator tree w.r.t. terminal node) of a CFG $G = (N,A,b)$ $(G = (N,A,b,e))$ we understand the Hasse diagram of the poset $(N,\doteq)$ $((N,\risingdotseq))$ its root is b (e).

We call a node $x \in N$ the *pure predessor* of the node y iff $y \in A(x)$ and, simultaneously, $y \not\risingdotseq x$; x_{+1} is the *immediate dominator of* x *with respect to the terminal node* e.

We say that the CFG G fulfils *the condition of branch isolation* iff for every node q the following holds: if q has at least two distinct pure predecessors in G then $(q_{-1})_{+1} = q$.

3. A dominator algorithm for reducible control flow graph (RFG)

Here it is convenient to utilize the following property of RFG:

$\overline{G}$ is a RFG iff both $\overline{G}$ and its maximal acyclic subgraph G have the same dominator tree (w.r.t. initial node).

The maximal acyclic subgraph G of an RFG $\overline{G}$ is obtained from $\overline{G}$ by deleting backward arcs. An arc (x,y) is backward iff rPOSTORDER$[x] \geq r$POSTORDER$[y]$.

(We assume a numbering of the nodes (of $\overline{G}$) from 1 to $|N|$, in array rPOSTORDER, indicating the reverse order in which each node was visited last (see [6]).

The following algorithm finding the dominator tree of a given RFG utilizes the possibility of transforming the original graph to other graphs which reduce the problem of the detection of the pair 'node-its immediate dominator' to the detection of the pair 'node- its immediate successor'.

Let $\overline{G} = (N,\overline{A},b)$ be a RFG and $G = (N,A,b)$ its maximal acyclic subgraph.

To construct the dominator tree of G means to find for every node $x \in N$ the set of all nodes in N which are immediately dominated by x in G. One of such nodes, y say, can be easily found: it is the immediate successor of x in G, its only immediate predecessor in G is the node x, i.e. $A^{-1}(y) = \{x\}$.

LEMMA 3.1: *Let* $G = (N,A,b), x \in N$. *If the set* M *of all the nodes that are immediately dominated by* x *is not empty, then it contains at least one node* $y \in M$ *such that* $A^{-1}(y) = \{x\}$.

LEMMA 3.2: *Let* $G = (N,A,b), x,y_1,y_2,\ldots y_n \in N, A(x) = \{y_1,\ldots,y_n\}, n \geq 1$. *If* $|A^{-1}(y_i)| > 1, 1 \leq i \leq n$ *then there exist no* $z \in N$ *such that* $x \leftarrow z$.

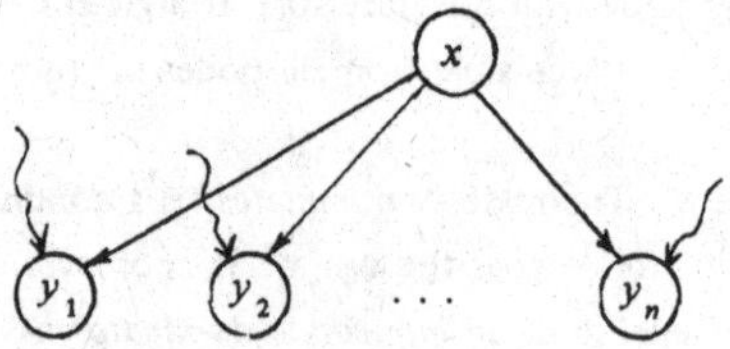

Proof of 3.2: Let us suppose that there exists a node $z \in U$ such that $x \leftarrow z$. Then every path from b to z going through the node x is going also through one of the nodes y_i, $i = 1,\ldots,n$ and because G is CFG, there exists in G a path frôm the node b into the node z, which does not go through the node x and so $x \not\leftarrow z$. A contradiction. □

Proof of 3.1: If such a node y, $H^{-1}(y) = \{x\}$ had not exist, it would mean that $|H^{-1}(z)| > 1$ holds for each node $z \in H(x)$ and according to lemma 3.2 the node x would not dominate to any node in G. □

But not every node immediately dominated in G by x must be connected with x by an arc. E.g., in the graph G, Fig. 1, we have not only $d = e_{-1}$ and $d = f_{-1}$, but also $d = g_{-1}$. The node g is not immediate successor of d, but it is 'near by' - it is an immediate successor of immediate successors (e and f) of d. Actually, the following lemma shows that whenever the immediate successors $y_1,\ldots,y_n$ of the given node x have the property $A^{-1}(y_i) = \{x\}$ $(1 \leq i \leq n)$ while they themselves are not the dominators (and this is the case of the nodes e and f according to the lemma 3.2), we can find among their immediate successors a node y such that $x = y_{-1}$.

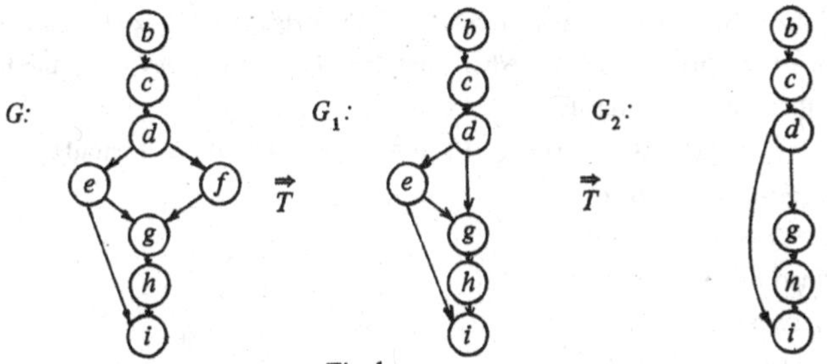

Fig. 1

LEMMA 3.3: *Let* $G = (N,A,b)$, $x, y_1, \ldots, y_n \in N$, $n \geq 1$. *Let* $A^{-1}(y_i) = \{x\}$, $1 \leq i \leq n$, $|A^{-1}(y')| > 1$ *for all* $y' \in A(y_i)$ $(1 \leq i \leq n)$ *and* $|A^{-1}(z)| > 1$ *for all* $z \in A(x) - \{y_1, y_2, \ldots, y_n\}$ *(whenever this set is nonempty). Further, let* $D(x)$ *be the set of nodes immediately dominated by the node* x, *and* $D(x) - \{y_1, \ldots, y_n\} \neq \phi$ *Then there exists a node* $y \in \bigcup_{i=1}^{n} A(y_i) \cup (A(x) - \{y_1, y_2, \ldots, y_n\})$ *such that* $y \in D(x)$.

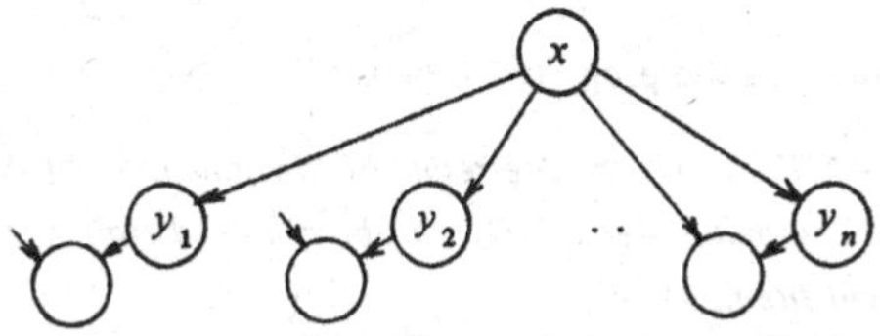

Proof. For the node y, $H^{-1}(y) \subseteq \{y_1, \ldots, y_n, x\}$ holds. If such a node y had not exist, then on each path from the initial node, going through the node x and its successor in G, there would have been a node, through which a path would have been going from the node b and such, that the node x would not have lied thereon. Then, however, the node x, except the nodes $y_1, \ldots, y_n$, would not immediately have dominated any node of the graph G, which is a contradiction with the assumption $D(x) - \{y_1, \ldots, y_n\} \neq \phi$ □

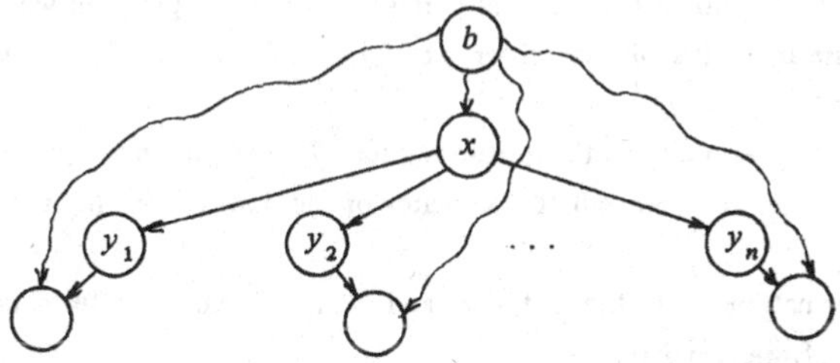

The nodes which do not dominate any node from G (e.g. the nodes $y_1, y_2, \ldots, y_n$ from preceding lemma) and for which the immediate dominator is known are of no more interest from the point of view of the dominator tree construction. It would be therefore suitable 'to get rid' of them, of course in such a way that the dominance relation is preserved. The following transformation T will do this job:

DEFINITION 3.4: Let $G = (N,A,b)$ be an acyclic CFG, $x,y \in N$ nodes such that $A^{-1}(y) = \{x\}$. Further, let the set of all immediate successors of y be empty or every immediate successor of y have more than one immediate predecessors. By the *transformation* T we understand the replacement of the nodes x,y as well as the arc (x,y) by the node x. The predecessors of the original node x

become the predecessors of the 'new' node x; the successors of the original node x (except y) or y become the successors of the 'new' node x. When applying T to the nodes x,y, the node y is said to be *attached* to the node x. Formally,

if $G = (N,A,b)$, $x,y \in N$, $A^{-1}(y) = \{x\}$, $A(y) = \phi$ or for all $u \in A(y)$ $|A^{-1}(u)| > 1$ holds,

then $G \underset{T}{\Rightarrow} G'$ (G is transformed by T to G')

where $G' = (N', A', b')$, $N' = N - \{y\}$, $b' = b$

$A': N' \rightarrow 2^{N'}$ is defined by

$A'(w) = A(w)$ for every node $w \in N - \{x,y\}$

$A(x) = (A(x) - \{y\}) \cup A(y)$.

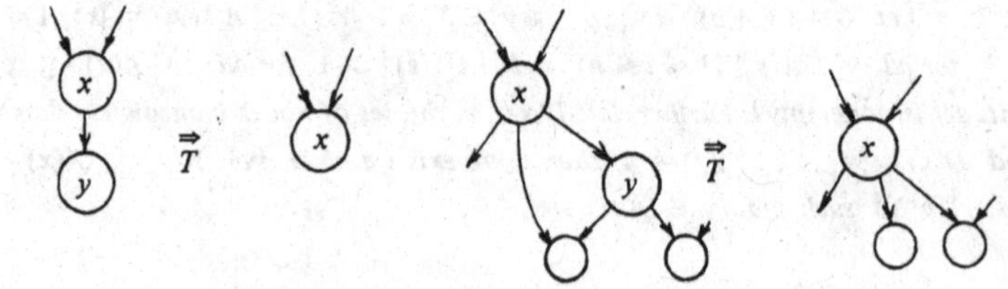

Note. Evidently, the transformation T preserves the property 'to be CFG'.

LEMMA 3.5: *Let* $G = (N,A,b)$, $G' = (N', A', b')$ *be the result of the aplication of the transformation* T *to the nodes* $x,y \in N$. *Then the dominator tree of* G' *can be obtained from the dominator tree of* G *by deletion of the arc* (x,y) *and the node* y.

Proof. It is sufficient to show that if $D(x) = \{d_1, \ldots, d_n, y\}$ is a set of nodes, which are immediately dominated by x in G, then the set of nodes immediately dominated by x in G' is $D'(x) = D(x) - \{y\}$. For each node $d_i \in D(x)$, $i = 1, \ldots, n$ it holds either

a) no path in G leading from b and going through x into d_i goes through y and in this case every path leading from b into d_i in G' will go through the node x,

b) in G there exists a path leading from the node b into d_i going through the node x and such, that it contains the node y. To this path there will correspond in G' a path, on which the node y will be missing, otherwise the paths will not differ. Totally, it holds for $i = 1, \ldots, n$: if $x = (d_i)_{-1}$ in G, then $x = (d_i)_{-1}$ in G'.

If the nodes x and y fulfil the assumptions for transformation T, then the node y is a leaf of the dominator tree and it holds that x is an immediate dominator of the node y in G, i.e. the arc (x,y) belongs to the dominator tree.

The application of transformation T to the nodes x and y in G has the effect that the arc (x,y) and the node y is cut of the dominator tree. □

COROLLARY 3.6: *Under the assumption of lemma 3.3 let further* $y \in D(x)$, $y \notin A(x)$, $A^{-1}(y) \subseteq \{y_1, \ldots, y_n, x\}$. *Let* $G' = (N', A', b')$ *be the result of the application of the transformation* T *to the pairs* $x,y_1; x,y_2; \ldots; x,y_n$. *Then* $A^{-1}(y) = \{x\}$ *in* G'.

Proof. As it holds $H^{-1}(y) \subseteq \{y_1, \ldots, y_n, x\}$ and because by repeating applications of T we actually 'attache' the nodes $y_1, \ldots, y_n$ to the node x, the node y in G will have the only immediate predecessor x. □

Thus, e.g., by applying T to the pairs d,e and d,f in the graph G (Fig. 1) we get the graph G_1 in which it is easy to find another node dominated by d, namely the node g. There is, however, one more dominator of d in G, namely the node i, which cannot be obtained by the described procedure. The node d does not - even in the graph G_2 - satisfy the assumptions of lemma 3.3: the node $g \in A(d)$ is not a leaf of the dominator trees, neither of the graph G nor of the graph G_2. It can become such a leaf by suitable applications of T.

LEMMA 3.7: *Let* $G = (N,A,b)$ *be an acyclic CFG. Then there exists the sequence of CFG's* $G_0, G_1, \ldots, G_k$, $k \geq 0$ *such that for all* $i = 1, 2, \ldots, k$ *it is* $G_{i-1} \underset{T}{\Rightarrow} G_i$, $G_0 = G$ *and* G_k *is the trivial graph.*

Proof.: follows from the lemma 3.5. □

THEOREM 3.8: *Let* $G = (N,A,b)$ *be an acyclic CFG,* $G_0, G_1, \ldots, G_k$ *a sequence of CFG's such that for all* i, $1 \leq i \leq k$, *it is* $G_{i-1} \underset{T}{\Rightarrow} G_i$, $G_0 = G$ *and* G_k *is the trivial graph. Let* $x,y \in N$. *Then* x *is the immediate dominator of* y *iff it is* $A^{-1}(y) = \{x\}$ *in some of the graphs* $G_0, G_1, \ldots, G_k$.

Proof.: follows from the preceding results. □

ALGORITHM 3.9: Construction of dominator tree

Input: An acyclic CFG $G = (N,A,b)$ represented by a list of nodes and their immediate successors and immediate predecessors

Output: The dominator tree of G

```
procedure ATTACH y TO x ;
   begin U:=U − {y} ;
         A(x):=(A(x) − {y})∪A(y);
         for each immediate successor of y succ(y) do
             A⁻¹(succ(y)) := (A⁻¹(succ(y)) − {y})∪{x}
   end;
begin x:=b;add x to the dominator tree;
      {x is either a dominator or the only node of the graph}
      while there exists a node y such that A⁻¹(y)= {x} do
          begin if the node y and the arc (x,y) are not
                    in the dominator tree
                then add y to the dominator tree
                     as a successor of the node x;
                if y is not a dominator of any node then
                   begin ATTACH y TO x;
                         if x is not a dominator and x≠b
                         then x := pred(x)
                         {x has now exactly one immediate
                         predecessor pred(x) in CFG, na-
                         mely its immediate dominator}
                   end
                                                   else
                {y is a dominator}
                x :=y
          end
end.
```

It seems that algorithm 3.9 runs in $O(r)$ time, where r is the number of arcs of the input CFG. The construction of a maximal acyclic subgraph requires preliminary processing of the given RFG by the reverse POSTORDER algorithm, which takes $O(r)$ steps, too.

There are several interesting applications of the dominance relation, e.g. in program testing, where besides the dominator tree w.r. t. initial node, also the dominator tree w.r.t. terminal node are used (see [7]). The idea of getting the last mentioned tree by applying the discussed algorithm 3.9 to the inverse graph, need not work, because the inverse graph of a given RFG need not generally be reducible. Therefore direct construction of the dominator tree w.r.t. terminal node, of a given RFG can be tried.

The algorithm can be based on the idea of finding an acyclic graph having the same dominator tree w.r.t. terminal node as the original graph.

Its time complexity is $O(cr)$, where c is maximum of the numbers, indicating the depth from which a nested loop is being left.

The complexity $O(cr)$ is achieved by constructing acyclic graph separately for every loop, starting from inner loops and proceeding to outer ones.; algorithm 3.9 is thereby utilized.

The obtained algorithm is at the same time a solution of the problem of finding dominator tree for nonreducible CFG with reducible inverse graph.

References

[1] Lengauer,T., and Tarjan,R.E.: A Fast Algorithm for Finding Dominators in a Flowgraph. ACM Transactions on Programming Languages and Systems, Vol. 1, No. 1, July 1979, 121-141

[2] Purdom,P.W., and Moore,E.F. Algorithm 43o: Immediate predominators in a directed graph. Comm. ACM, Vol. 15, No. 8, Aug. 1972, 777-778

[3] Aho, A.V., and Ullman,J.D.: Principles of Compiler Design. Addison-Wesley, Reading, Mass., 1977

[4] Tarjan,R.E.: Fast Algorithms for Solving Path Problems JACM, Vol. 28, No. 3, July 1981, 594-614

[5] Kohoutková-Nováková,J.: The Conditions of BJ_n-structuredness, Scripta Fac. Sci. Nat. Univ. Purk. Brun., Vol. 12, No. 10, 1982, 471-480

[6] Hecht,M.S.: Flow Analysis of Computer Programs. Elsevier North-Holland, Inc., 1977

[7] Moravec,A.: The Base of Control Flow Graph. Scripta Fac. Sci. Nat. Univ. Purk. Brun., Vol. 8, No. 10, 1978, 27-40

CHARACTERIZING COMPOSABILITY OF ABSTRACT IMPLEMENTATIONS

F. Orejas
Facultat d'Informàtica
Universitat Politècnica
Barcelona, SPAIN

In programming by stepwise refinement, every abstraction level is supported by an abstract data type, i.e. at every level the program text designed up to this level is a program written in terms of (and only of) data and operations of a given abstract data type. Then, an implementation just defines the relation between two levels, or better, between the abstract data types supporting these levels.

The intuition for the concept of implementation seems very simple. An implementation of an a.d.t. T0 by T1 consists, basically, in giving T1 the look of T0 by deriving in T1 the operations and, in some sense, the structure of T0. However, quite a number of approaches have been proposed to describe (more or less) formally this concept. Since the pioneering work of Hoare (HOA72), we may cite, without pretending to be exhaustive, ADJ78, GHM76, PAI80, ORE81, GAN81, EHR82, EKMP82, GM82, SW82 and EK82. Some of these approaches are "abstract", in the sense that the operations to be derived are just added to the signature and their behaviour is specified using equations.

One of the key problems of implementations is composability, i.e. if I1 is an implementation of T0 by T1 and I2 is an implementation of T1 by T2, is the composition of I1 and I2 an implementation of T0 by T2? or, in which conditions may we compose implementations? The importance of composability comes from the application of abstract data types to program design by stepwise refinement: composability of implementations guarantees the correctness of the whole design process.

Abstract implementation in general do not compose, moreover the problem lies, usually, on the relation between syntax and semantics of implementations. To be more precise, the semantics of syntactic composition do not correspond, in general, to composition of the semantic constructs (see the remark after counter-example 2.3).

In this paper we characterize composability for EKMP's implementations. The reason for this choice is the following, from the approaches known to me, this is the one that makes a clear distinction between syntax and semantics of implementations, allowing to study the composability problem on the appropiate setting.

The paper is organized as follows, in section 1 we review the concepts of implementation and implementation correctness due to EKMP; in section 2, we define two kinds of composition (also due to EKMP) and show counter-examples for both; section 3 is the core of the paper, results are obtained characterizing composability completely; finally, in section 4, some conclusions are proposed, comparing the results obtained here with related work done by EKMP. Because of space restrictions, most proofs have been omitted or are just sketched, detailed proofs may be found in the full version of this paper (ORE82).

1. Preliminaries

Familiarity with the usual notions on algebraic specification of abstract data types is assumed. For detail see ADJ78 and EKMP82.

Definition 1.1

Given specifications SP0 = SP+(S0,Σ0,E0) and SP1 = SP+(S1,Σ1,E1), both persistent with respect to SP, a weak implementation I of SP0 by SP1, written I: SP1 ==>SP0, is a triple I = (ΣSORT,EOP,HID), where ΣSORT is a signature called sorts implementing operations, EOP is a set of equations called operations implementing equations, and HID is the hidden component, HID = (SHID, ΣHID,EHID), consisting of hidden sorts, SHID, a hidden signature, ΣHID, and a set of hidden equations EHID; such that the following syntactic requirements are satisfied:

SORTI = SP1+(S0+SHID,ΣSORT,∅) and
OPI = SORTI+(∅,ΣHID,EHID)+(∅,Σ0,EOP)

are combinations, and for every $\sigma \epsilon \Sigma SORT_{w,s}$, $s \epsilon S0+SHID$.

Definition 1.2

Given a weak implementation I of SP0 by SP1, the semantical functor SEM_I associated to I is defined as the composition of the following three functors:

$$SEM_I = Alg_{\Sigma 1} \xrightarrow{SYNT} Alg_{OPI'} \xrightarrow{REST} Alg_{\Sigma 0} \xrightarrow{ID} Alg_{SP0}$$

where OPI' = OPI-E1, SYNT is the free functor from $Alg_{\Sigma 1}$ to $Alg_{OPI'}$, ID is the free functor from $Alg_{\Sigma 0}$ to Alg_{SP0}, and REST is the composition of the forgetful functor FORG from $Alg_{OPI'}$ to $Alg_{\Sigma 0}$, the reachability functor REACH from $Alg_{\Sigma 0}$ to $RAlg_{\Sigma 0}$ ($RAlg_{\Sigma 0}$ is the category of of reachable $\Sigma 0$-algebras), and the inclusion functor INC from $RAlg_{\Sigma 0}$ to $Alg_{\Sigma 0}$.

Definition 1.3

A weak implementation I: SP1 ⟹ SP0 is OP-complete iff for each term t in $T_{\Sigma+\Sigma 0}$ there is a t' in $T_{\Sigma(SORT1)}$ such that $t \equiv_{OPI} t'$.

I is RI-correct iff $SEM_I(T_{SP1}) \simeq T_{SP0}$. I is an implementation iff it is OP-complete and RI-correct.

2. Composition and strong composition of implementations

As we have seen, implementations have syntax and semantics. The syntax of an implementation is a (sort of) enrichment, the semantics is its associated functor SEM_I. Thus, to define composition of implementations we must remain at the syntactic level, the semantics shall always be the associated functor.

Given implementations I2: SP2 ⟹ SP1 and I1: SP1 ⟹ SP0 (from now on, we shall consider SP=(S,Σ,E), SPi=SP+(Si,Σi,Ei)(i=0-2), all of them persistent w.r.t. SP, and Ij=(ΣSORTj,EOPj,HIDj), with HIDj=(SHIDj,ΣHIDj, EHIDj) (j=1,2)), the most natural idea to define composition I12 would be to put together I1 and I2, i.e. I12=I1+I2, but then we may have that OPI12 is not a specification (violating the syntactic requirements), because if S1 is not empty, we may have operations in ΣSORTI12 acting upon or producing results on a sort in S1. Thus, it seems reasonable to add to the hidden component of I12 S1 and Σ1, but what about E1?

EKMP define two classes of composition: composition, in which E1 is added to the hidden component of I12, and strong composition in which E1 is not added. It seems that EKMP prefer (at least terminologically) to have E1 in the hidden component. Personally, I think that strong composition is more natural. The reason for EKMP's choice is probably that composition preserve OP-completeness (see proposition 2.4), while strong composition, in general, does not (see counter-example 2.3). However, it will be proved (corollary 3.9) that the condition for preservation of RI-correctness is simpler for strong composition.

Definition 2.1

Given implementations I2: SP2 ⟹SP1 and I1: SP1 ⟹SP0, the composition of I1 and I2, $\bar{I}12$:SP2 ⟹SP0, is defined:

ΣSORT12 = ΣSORT1+ΣSORT2   EOP12 = EOP1+EOP2

SHID12 = SHID1+SHID2+S1   ΣHID12 = ΣHID1+ΣHID2+Σ2

EHID12 = EHID1+EHID2+E1

We also define strong composition of I1 and I2, SI12, in the same way, but with:

EHID12 = EHID1+EHID2

It is easy to see that if I1 and I2 satisfy the syntactic requirements, so do I12 and SI12. However, if I1 and I2 are OP-complete and RI-corect I12 need not to be RI-correct and SI12 need not to be neither OP-complete, nor RI-correct.

Counter-example 2.2 (EKMP)

Let SP2, SP1 and SP0 be, respectively, the integers, the naturals and the boolean specifications (in this case, SP is empty), i.e.

	S	Σ	E
SP2 =	S2	Σ2	E2
	int	0: → int	i1) s(p(x)) = x
		s: int → int	i2) p(s(x)) = x
		p: int → int	
SP1 =	S1	Σ1	E1
	nat	z: → nat	∅
		n: nat → nat	
SP0 =	S0	Σ0	E0
	bool	true: → bool	∅
		false: → bool	

and let I2: SP2 ⟹ SP1 and I1: SP1 ⟹ SP0 be the following implementations:

	ΣSORT	EOPS
I2 =		
	c2: int → nat	imp1) c2(0) = z
		imp2) c2(s(x)) = n(c2(x))
I1 =		
	c1: nat → bool	imp3) c1(z) = true
		imp4) c1(n(x)) = false

It can be easily proved that both I2 and I1 are correct implementations. However, neither I12, nor SI12 are RI-correct (in fact, in this example I12 and SI12 coincide, since E1 is empty):

$$\text{true}\equiv c1(z)\equiv c1(c2(0))\equiv c1(c2(s(p(0))))\equiv c1(n(c2(p(0))))\equiv \text{false}$$

□

Counter-example 2.3

Let SP, SP0, SP1, SP2, I1 and I2 be:

SP =

S	Σ	E
bool	true: → bool	e1) not(true)=false
	false: → bool	e2) not(not(x))=x
	not: bool → bool	

SP0 = SP +

S0	Σ0	E0
int0	zero0: → int0	e3) succ0(pred0(x))=x
	succ0: int0 → int0	e4) pred0(succ0(x))=x
	pred0: int0 → int0	e5) even?(zero0)=true
	even?: int0 → bool	e6) even?(succ0(x))= not(even?(x))

SP1 = SP +

S1	Σ1	E1
int1	zero1: → int1	f3) succ1(pred1(x))=x
	succ1: int1 → int1	f4) pred1(succ1(x))=x
	pred1: int1 → int1	

SP2 = SP +

S2	Σ2	E2
int2	zero2: → int2	∅
	succ2: int2 → int2	
	pred2: int2 → int2	

I1 =

ΣSORT1	EOP1
c1: int1 → int0	g1) zero0 = c1(zero1)
	g2) succ0(c1(x)) = c1(succ1(x))
	g3) pred0(c1(x)) = c1(pred1(x))
	g4) even?(zero0) = true
	g5) even?(succ0(x)) = not(even?(x))

I2 =

ΣSORT2	EOP2
c2: int2 → int1	h1) zero1 = c2(zero2)
	h2) succ1(c2(x)) = c2(succ2(x))
	h3) pred1(c2(x)) = c2(pred2(x))

I1 and I2 are correct implementations of SP1 by SP0, and of SP2 by SP1, respectively, but SI12 is not OP-complete since the term:

even?(pred0(zero0))

is not OPSI12-congruent with any term in $T_{\Sigma(SORTSI12)}$.□

Remark

As it was said in the introduction, the fact that the composition of two correct implementations may not be correct comes from the fact that the semantics of syntactic composition may not coincide with composition of semantic constructs, i.e. in our case, composition of the semantical functors.

It could be said that this composition problem is only on EKMP's approach (and, so, deduce that it is a wrong approach); but, indeed, other approaches share the same problem, although it may be hidden.

It is specially interesting to study the case of the approaches that do not consider the enrichment step as part of the implementations (for example, PAI80, GM82, SW82).

Suppose we have specifications SP0,...,SPn, and we want to implement every SPi by SPi+1 ($0\leq i<n$), and then obtain the composition. But assume that the enrichment step has not been done yet. The first problem is that, for every $i\leq n$, we should enrich SPi with <u>all</u> the sorts and operations of SP0,..., SPi-1 (except with those already present in SPi. Clearly, this would be absolutely against the principles of stepwise refinement (separation of concerns), unless we can do those enrichments in a systematic way: by defining parameterized enrichments *E*1,...,*E*n, such that, for every i, *E*i applied to SPi yields an implementation of SPi-1. Now the question would be: shall *E*1(...*E*n(SPn)...) be an implementation of SP0? For any of those approaches, the answer is: in general, <u>no</u>. Appropiate adaptations of counter-examples 2.2 and 2.3 would serve to prove it. □

The only positive result about composition is the following:

<u>Proposition 2.4</u> (EKMP)

If I2: SP2 ==>SP1 and I1: SP1 ==>SP0 are OP-complete, so is I12.

3. Composability and strong composability of implementations

As it was said in the introduction, to guarantee the correctness of a stepwise refinement design, the correctness of the composition of implementations used in the design must be achieved. It is my feeling that the best way to solve this problem consists in asking implementations to verify stronger conditions which guarantee composability, that is, which guarantee composition of a given implementation with <u>any</u> other implementation.

Definition 3.1

An implementation I1:SP1 ⟹SP0 is composable (resp. strongly composable) iff for every implementation I2: SP2 ⟹SP1, the composition I12 (resp. the strong composition SI12) is an implementation.

Definition 3.2

An implementation I: SP1 ⟹SP0 is strongly OP-complete iff for every ($\Sigma+\Sigma 0$)-term t0 there is a Σ(SORTI1)-term t1 such that $t0 \equiv_{E(OPI1^*)} t1$, where $E(OPI1^*)$ = E+EHID+EOP+{<t=t'>/$t \equiv_{SP1} t'$ and their sort is in S}.

Theorem 3.3 (Characterization of strong composability)

Let I1: SP1 ⟹SP0 be an implementation, then the following statements are equivalent:

1) I1 is strongly composable.

2) I1 is strong OP-complete and for every $\Sigma+\Sigma 1$-algebra A, such that there exists a homomorphism from REACH(A) to T_{SP1}, it holds:

$$SEM_{I1}(A) \simeq T_{SP0}$$

3) I1 is strong OP-complete and for every $\Sigma+\Sigma 1$-algebra A, such that $T_{SP1} \subsetneqq A$, it holds:

$$SEM_{I1}(A) \simeq T_{SP0}$$

We shall prove 2) ⇒ 1) ⇒ 3) ⇒ 2), with the help of the following lemma:

Lemma 3.4

If I1: SP1 ⟹SP0 is strong OP-complete, then for every implementation I2: SP2 ⟹SP1, SI12 is OP-complete.

Sketch of the proof

It is enough to see that for every $\Sigma+\Sigma 1$-terms t1 and t2 with sort in S, if $t1 \equiv_{SP} t2$ then $t1 \equiv_{OPI2} t2$. By OP-completeness of I2, there are terms t1' and t2' in $T_{\Sigma(SORTI2)}$ such that $t1' \equiv_{OPI2} t1$ and $t2' \equiv_{OPI2} t2$, but by RI-correctness of I2 and persistency of SP1 and SORTI2 w.r.t SP, $t1 \equiv_{SP1} t2 \Rightarrow t1 \equiv_{OPI2} t1' \equiv_{OPI2} t2' \equiv_{OPI2} t2$.□

Proof of the theorem

2) ⇒ 1) If SI12 is not OP-complete, then by lemma 3.4, I1 is not strong OP-complete. Suppose SI12 is not RI-correct, it may be proved that:

$$T_{SP0} \neq SEM_{SI12}(T_{SP2}) \simeq SEM_{I1}(FORG_{I2} \cdot SYNT_{I2}(T_{SP2}))$$

but if I2 is RI-correct, there is a morphism from

$REACH(FORG_{I2} \cdot SYNT_{I2}(T_{SP2}))$ to T_{SP0}.

1) ⇒ 3) If I1 is not strong OP-complete, then let SP2 be $SP+(S2,\Sigma2,\emptyset)$ with

$$S2 = \{s'/s\varepsilon S1\}$$

$$\Sigma2_{w',s'} = \{\sigma'/\sigma\varepsilon\Sigma1_{w,s}\} \quad \text{if } s\varepsilon S1$$

$$\Sigma2_{w',s'} = \emptyset \quad \text{if } s\varepsilon S$$

i.e. S2 and Σ2 are just renamings of S1 and of some operations of Σ1. Now, let I2 be:

$$\Sigma SORT2 = \{c_s : s' \rightarrow s/s\varepsilon S1\}$$

$$EOP2 = \{<t=t'>/\ t\equiv_{SP1}t' \text{ and their sort is in } S\} \cup$$

$$\cup \{<\sigma(c_{s1}(x1),\dots,c_{si}(xi),xi+1,\dots,xn)=c_s(\sigma'(x1,\dots,xn)>/$$

$$\sigma\varepsilon\Sigma1_{s1\dots sn,s},\ s,s1,\dots,si\varepsilon S1 \text{ and } si+1,\dots,sn\varepsilon S\}$$

It may be proved (ORE82) that SP2 is persistent w.r.t. SP, I2 is an implementation of SP1 by SP, but SI12 is not OP-complete.

Suppose that A is such that $T_{SP1} \subseteq A$ and $SEM_{I1}(A) \neq T_{SP0}$. Let $SP2=SP+(S2,\Sigma2,E2)$, with:

$$S2 = \{s'/\ s\varepsilon S1\}$$

$$\Sigma2_{\lambda,s'} = \{\underline{a}/\ a\varepsilon A_s\} \cup \{\sigma'/\ \sigma\varepsilon\Sigma1_{\lambda,s}\} \quad s\varepsilon S1$$

$$\Sigma2_{w',s'} = \{\sigma'/\sigma\varepsilon\Sigma1_{w,s}\} \quad s\varepsilon S1$$

$$E2 = \{<t1'=t2'>/\ t1\equiv_A t2\}$$

and let I2 be:

$$\Sigma SORT2 = \{c_s : s' \rightarrow s/\ s\varepsilon S1\}$$

$$EOP2 = \{<\sigma(c_{s1}(x1),\dots,c_{si}(xi),xi+1,\dots,xn)=c_s(\sigma'(x1,\dots,xn)>/$$

$$\sigma\varepsilon\Sigma1_{s1\dots sn,s},\ s,s1,\dots,si\varepsilon S1 \text{ and } si+1,\dots,sn\varepsilon S\} \cup$$

$$\cup \{<t1=t2>/\ t1,t2\varepsilon T_{\Sigma+\Sigma1_s},\ s\varepsilon S \text{ and } t1\equiv_{SP1}t2\}$$

$$SHID2 = \{s'/\ s\varepsilon S\}$$

$$\Sigma HID2_{\lambda,s'} = \{\underline{a}/\ a\varepsilon A_s\} \quad s\varepsilon S$$

$$\Sigma HID2_{s',s} = \{c_s\} \quad s\varepsilon S$$

$$EHID2 = \{<c_s(\underline{a})=t>/t\varepsilon T_{\Sigma\ \Sigma1}(A) \text{ and } t^A=a\}$$

(we assume, without loss of generality, that operations in Σ1 have their first parameters of sorts in S1, and the rest with sorts in S).

Again, it may be proved that SP2 is persistent w.r.t. SP, I2 is an implementation of SP1 by SP2, but SI12 is not RI-correct.

3) ⇒ 2) Suppose there exists a Σ+Σ1-algebra A, such that there exists a morphism $h: REACH(A) \rightarrow T_{SP1}$ and $SEM_{I1}(A) \neq T_{SP0}$. Then, let $B = A/\equiv_{ES}$ with $ES = \{<t1=t2>/\ t1,t2\ T_{\Sigma+\Sigma1} \text{ and } t1\equiv_{SP1}t2\}$.

It can be easily proved that $T_{SP1} \subseteq B$ and $SEM_{I1}(B) \neq T_{SP0}$.□

Corollary 3.6

If I2: SP2 ⟹SP1 and I1: SP1 ⟹SP0 are strongly composable, then SI12 is strongly composable.

Theorem 3.7 (Characterization of composability)

If I1: SP1 ⟹SP0 is an implementation, then the following statements are equivalent:

1) I1 is composable
2) For every Σ+Σ1-algebra A such that there exists a homomorphism from REACH(A) to T_{SP1}, it holds:

$$SEM_{I1}(A/\equiv_{E1}) \simeq T_{SP0}$$

3) For every Σ+Σ1-algebra A such that $T_{SP1} \subsetneq A$, it holds:

$$SEM_{I1}(A/\equiv_{E1}) \simeq T_{SP0}$$

The proof is almost identical to that of theorem 3.5.

Corollary 3.8

If I2: SP2 ⟹SP1 and I1: SP1 ⟹SP0 are composable, then so is I12.

Corollary 3.9

If I1 is strongly OP-complete, I1 is composable implies that I1 is strongly composable.

Example 3.10

Implementation I1 of counter-example 2.2 is not composable or strongly composable, because if we define the algebra A:

$$A_{nat} = \{-1,0,1,2,\ldots\}$$
$$z^A = 0$$
$$n^A(i) = i+1$$

then $SEM_{I1}(A)$ is a one-point algebra non-isomorphic to booleans.

We may arrange I1 simply by changing the equation imp4) into:

imp4') cl(n(z)) = false

However, if we want a composable (strongly composable) implementation closer to the old one, we may add a hidden component:

SHID1 = {nat1}

ΣHID1 = z1: → nat1
n1: nat1 → nat1

c: nat1 → nat

EHID1 = eh1) c(z1) = z

eh2) c(n1(x)) = n(c(x))

and change the equation imp4 by the new equation:

imp4") false = c1(c(n1(x))) □

Example 3.11

Implementation I1 of counter-example 2.3 is not strongly composable, because it is not strongly OP-complete. We can make it strongly OP-complete by adding the equation:

g6) even?(pred0(x)) = not(even?(x))

□

4. Conclusion

Abstract implementations should compose because, in practice, concrete implementations do compose. Therefore, an implementation, to be considered correct, should be composable. Then, what we have obtained are (semantical) characterizations of properties that should be achieved by implementations.

Although this characterization applies only to EKMP's approach, similar results could be obtained for other approaches (in ORE82, results are presented for IR-implementations, viz. EHR82, EK82). However, for those approaches not considering the enrichment step, the characterization would be difficult because of its hiding of the problem (see the remark after counter-example 2.3).

EKMP do also present some results about composition of implementations. However, instead of studying composability as a property that should be achieved by implementations, they have been dealing, mainly, with the problem of studying under which circumstances may we compose two implementations in order to obtain a new correct implementation. In this sense, they have obtained some sufficient conditions to guarantee the correctness of composition. It is my feeling that this is not the correct approach. We may see the reason by looking at the problem of iterated composition: suppose we have to compose implementations I1,... ..,In, using their approach we would have to check composition of I1 with I(2,...,n). But, first of all, this is something against the spirit of design by stepwise refinement: at once, we would have to check the correctness of the whole design process. Also, suppose we find the composition incorrect, with our approach we would be able to determine which implementations are problematic (i.e. non composable), with EKMP's we would not have a hint (except, perhaps, our intuition) of which implementations would have to be changed.

Finally, it is clear that syntactic characterizations (or, at least, sufficient conditions) are needed in order to simplify proofs. Some results have been obtained, although they are not given here (they will be in a longer version of ORE82).

ACKNOWLEDGEMENTS

This paper was started during a stay in Paris invited by M. Nivat, with financial support from INRIA. A lecture of M.C. Gaudel gave me the first hints to the problem. I am most grateful to J. Goguen, H. Ehrig, M. Wirsing and R. Burstall for very valuable discussions. Also to Quim Gabarró and Jose Luis Balcazar for patient listening. This work is partially supported by the Comisión Asesora de Investigación del Ministerio de Educación (ref. 3866-79).

6. References

ADJ78 Goguen, J.A.; Thatcher, J.W.; Wagner, E.G.
"An initial algebra approach to the specification, correctness and implementation of abstract data types", in 'Current Trends in Programming Methodology, Vol. IV: Data Structuring', R. T. Yeh (ed.), Prentice-Hall 1978, pp. 80-149.

EHR82 Ehrich, H.-D.
"On the theory of specification, implementation and parameterization of abstract data types", JACM 29,1 (Jan. 1982), pp. 206-227.

EKMP82 Ehrig, H.; Kreowski, H.-J.; Mahr, B.; Padawitz, P.
"Algebraic implementations of abstract data types", TCS 20,3 (July 1982), pp. 209-263.

EK82 Ehrig, H.; Kreowski, H.-J.
"Parameter passing commutes with implementation of parameterized data types", Proc. 9th. ICALP Aarhus, 1982, LNCS 140, pp. 197-211.

GAN81 Ganzinger, H.
"Parameterized specifications: parameter passing and optimizing implementations", Tech. Rep., TU Munich- 18110, 1981.

GHM76 Guttag, J.V.; Horowitz, E.; Musser, D.R.
"Abstract data types and software validation", USC Res. Rep. ISI/RR-76-48, 1976.

GM82 Goguen, J.A.; Meseguer, J.
"Universal realization, persistent interconnection and implementation of abstract modules", Proc. 9th. ICALP, Aarhus, 1982 LNCS 140, pp. 265-281.

HOA72 Hoare, C.A.R.
"Proof of correctness of data representations", Acta Informatica 1 (1972), pp. 271-281.

ORE81 Orejas, F.
"On the representation of data types", Proc. ICFPC, Peñíscola, 1981, LNCS 107, pp. 419-431.

ORE82 "Characterizing composability of abstract implementations", Fac. d'Informàtica de Barcelona, Report de Recerca RR 82/08, 1982.

PAI80 Pair, C.
"Sur les modèles des types abstraits algébriques", C.R.I. Nancy Res. Rep. 80 P 052, 1980.

SW82 Sannella, D.; Wirsing, M.
"Implementations of parameterised implementations", Proc. 9th. ICALP Aarhus, 1982, LNCS 140, pp. 473-488.

Propositional Logics of Programs: New Directions

Rohit Parikh
Department of Computer Science
Brooklyn College
Brooklyn, NY, 11210

Abstract: We discuss new developments in Propositional Logic of Programs, specifically the μ-calculus, and Game Logic. While this paper is intended largely as a survey, some new results are stated.

Introduction: Since the introduction of Propositional Dynamic Logic (PDL) by Fischer and Ladner, many developments have taken place. Completenss proofs for the new logic have been provided in [P1], [KP] and other places. Extensions of the logic have been considered, with converse operator and the loop construct [P1], [St], and there have been side trips into Process Logic, Temporal Logic, etc. Many of these have already been reported in the survey paper [P2]. In this paper we want to discuss some developments during the last two years, specifically in the μ-calculus and Game Logic.

Most of these propositional logics are decidable, with the exception of CFPDL, the extension of PDL which allows recursive calls. The last has been shown to be π^1_1 complete in [HPS], The decidability of those logics which *are* decidable can always be proved by reduction to SnS, but sometimes there is a finite model property which gives a direct decidability proof and a much better complexity bound. A natural question to ask is: what is the largest propositional logic in this general area which is decidable? The μ-calculus and Game Logic are two quite natural candidates and are studied in sections 3 and 4 respectively. In section 5 we give an application of many-person Game Logic to proving the correctness of a cake cutting algorithm.

§2:*Preliminaries*: We assume that the reader has some familiarity with Dynamic Logic. However, just for the sake of completeness we give a few definitions. We have a state space W and a language L^- which can be used to make statements about individual states. Thus the notion $s \models A$ where s is a state and A is a formula of L^-, is assumed to be defined, and means intuitively: the formula A is true at the state s. We assume also that we have some actions on W which may take us from one state to another, usually in a non-deterministic way.

Now we augment the language L^- to a larger language L which is closed under the operations of L^- and also under the modalities $\langle\alpha\rangle$ and $[\alpha]$ where α is any action. Thus if A is a formula of L then $s\models\langle\alpha\rangle A$ means that there is a t such that the action α *may* take us from s to t and $t\models A$. Similarly, $s\models[\alpha]A$ iff for all t such that α can take us from s to t, $t\models A$. For example, if a cake is being cut between two people by the action c, F_1 means that the first piece is fair (one person's fair share) and F_2 means that the second piece is fair. Then we have $[c](F_1\vee F_2)$ and also $\langle c\rangle(F_1\wedge F_2)$ I.e. no matter how the cake is cut, at least one piece is fair, and it is possible to cut it so that both pieces are fair.

The various actions are closed under certain operations like (We shall use the convention of using letters a,b,c for atomic actions or programs and α, β etc for complex ones):

$(\alpha;\beta)$: first do α and then β.
α^*: do α some finite number of times (maybe 0)
if A then α else β
$\alpha\cup\beta$: Do either α or β non-deterministically.

etc. See [FL] or [P1] or [KP] for a fuller discussion.

§3: *The μ-calculus*: A very natural way to arrive at the μ-calculus is to look at some of the axioms for PDL. The following are easily seen to be valid.

(1) $\langle\alpha;\beta\rangle A \equiv \langle\alpha\rangle\langle\beta\rangle A$
(2) $\langle\alpha\cup\beta\rangle A \equiv \langle\alpha\rangle A\vee\langle\beta\rangle A$
(3) $\langle\alpha^*\rangle A \equiv A\vee\langle\alpha\rangle\langle\alpha^*\rangle A$

Notice that axioms 1 and 2 allow us to eliminate the program connectives ; and ∪. However, the connective * cannot be eliminated so easily since it appears on both sides of its own definition. But if we write X for $\langle\alpha^*\rangle A$, then X satisfies:

(4) $X \equiv A\vee\langle\alpha\rangle X$

Unfortunately, (4) does not have a unique solution. E.g. W (the space of *all* states) may be a solution. What characterises $\langle\alpha^*\rangle A$ among all solutions is that it is the least, i.e. it holds of a state only when it *has* to, by (4). Thus we can write

$\langle\alpha^*\rangle A \equiv \mu X(X \equiv A \vee \langle\alpha\rangle X)$

or, with a small abuse of notation,

$\langle\alpha^*\rangle A \equiv \mu X(A \vee \langle\alpha\rangle X)$

It turns out that the notion of "least set satisfying a condition" is strong enough for us to define all program connectives of PDL and more.

Actually, not every condition defines a least set satisfying it. E.g. there is no least infinite subset of a given set. We need to say that the condition we are looking at is special in some way, and it is sufficient that the condition be monotonic. Specifically, we have the theorem:

Theorem: (Tarski-Knaster) let ϕ be a monotonic operator on some set W. I.e. for $X, Y \subseteq W$, if $X \subseteq Y$ then $\phi(X) \subseteq \phi(Y)$. Then there is a smallest subset X_o of W such that $\phi(X_o) = X_o$.

This allows us to define the language of the μ-calculus as follows (see [Pr] for a related but slightly different treatment of the μ-calculus. Our version is taken from [K])

atomic formulae: $P_1, \ldots, P_n$

Set parameters: $X_1, \ldots, X_i, \ldots$

atomic programs: $a_1, \ldots, a_m$

Formulae: Each atomic formula is a formula

Each set parameter is a formula

If A, B are formulae, so are $\neg A$ and $A \vee B$

If A is a formula and a is an atomic program, then $\langle a\rangle A$ is a formula

If A is a formula with parameter X and all occurrences of X in A are positive, then $\mu X(A(X))$ is a formula.

Semantics: A model M gives a universe W together with extensions $\pi(P) \subseteq W$ for all atomic formulae P and $\rho(a) \subseteq W \times W$ for all atomic programs a. Suppose that the formula A contains (at most) the parameters $X_1, \ldots, X_k$ and $U_1, \ldots, U_k$ is a sequence of subsets of W. Then we define $\pi((M, U_1, \ldots, U_k), A)$ by induction on the complexity of A as follows:

$\pi((M, U_1, \ldots, U_k), P_i) = \pi(P_i)$

$\pi((M, U_1, \ldots, U_k), X_i) = U_i$

$\pi((M, U_1, \ldots, U_k), \neg A) = W - \pi((M, U_1, \ldots, U_k), A)$

$\pi((M,U_1,...,U_k),\ A\vee B)$

$= \pi((M,U_1,...,U_k),\ A) \cup \pi((M,U_1,...,U_k),\ A)$

$\pi((M,U_1,...,U_k),\langle a\rangle A)$

$= \{s \mid \exists t,\ t\in \pi((M,U_1,...,U_k),A) \wedge (s,t) \in \rho(a)\}$

$\pi((M,U_1,...,U_{k-1}),\mu X_k(A(X_k))$ = least U_k such that

$\pi((M,U_1,...,U_k),\ A) = U_k$

If A has no parameters, then A is closed and we write $M,s\models A$ to indicate that $s\in\pi(M,A)$, or A is true at s in M. A is satisfiable if there is an M,s such that $M,s\models A$ and valid if for all M,s, $M,s\models A$.

It is shown in [KP2] that the validity problem for the μ-calculus is decidable. However, the decision procedure is not elementary. It is shown in [K] that there is an exponential time decision procedure for a *restricted* version of the μ-calculus, but the question for the full version is open.

The μ-calculus contains the propositional Game Logic which we shall discuss next. Now the μ-calculus includes Game Logic which includes $PDL^{\triangleright}$ which *properly* includes PDL. Thus all of these logics are proper extensions of PDL. It would be very nice to be able to show that the μ-calculus is the *maximal* logic satisfying certain conditions, rather like Lindstrom's characterisation of first order logic.

§4.*Game Logic*: In this section we describe a Propositional Logic of Games which lies in expressive power between PDL and the μ-calculus. It is stronger than the first, but *might* be equal in expressive power to the second.

If we think of $\langle\alpha\rangle$ and $[\alpha]$ of PDL as predicate transformers, they are rather similar to the quantifiers ∃ and ∀ of First Order Logic. Indeed, the quantifiers can be reduced to the two modalities if random assignments are available, see [MP]. Following Ehrenfeucht, we can think of the modalities $\langle\alpha\rangle$ and $[\alpha]$ as (one or more) moves by players I and II respectively. Thus the modalities of PDL become simple games and just as we can combine programs using the constructs ∪, ; and *, games can also be combined in the same way. With this preamble we proceed to a detailed discussion.

We assume that the reader is familiar with the syntax and

semantics of PDL and the μ-calculus. (See [FL], [KP1], [P] for the first and [K] for the second.) However, those for Game Logic *can* be defined independently. We have a finite supply $g_1,\ldots,g_n$ of atomic games and a finite supply $P_1,\ldots,P_m$ of atomic formulae. Then we define games α and formulae A by induction.

1. Each P_i is a formula.
2. If A and B are formulae, then so are $A \vee B$, $\neg A$.
3. If A is a formula and α is a game, then $(\alpha)A$ is a formula.

4. Each g_i is a game.
5. If α and β are games, then so are $\alpha;\beta$ (or simply $\alpha\beta$), $\alpha\vee\beta$, $\alpha\wedge\beta$, $\langle\alpha*\rangle$, $[\alpha*]$ and α^d.
6. If A is a formula then $\langle A\rangle$ and $[A]$ are games.

Intuitively, the games can be explained as follows. $\alpha;\beta$ is the game: play α and then β. The game $\alpha\vee\beta$ is: player I decides whether α or β is to be played, and then the chosen game is played. The game $\alpha\wedge\beta$ is similar except that player II makes the decision. In $\langle\alpha*\rangle$, the game α is played repeatedly (perhaps zero times) until player I decides to stop. If he never says "stop" then he loses. He may not stop in the middle of some play of α. Similarly with $[\alpha*]$ and player II. If during any of these games, a player whose move it is finds he cannot play, then he loses automatically. Thus a stalemate is not a draw. In α^d, the two players interchange roles. Finally, with $\langle A\rangle$, the formula A is evaluated. If A is false, then I loses, otherwise we go on. (Thus $\langle A\rangle B$ is equivalent to $A\wedge B$.) Similarly with $[A]$ and II.

Formally, a model for game logic consists of a set W of worlds, for each P a subset $\pi(P)$ of W and for each primitive game g a subset $\rho(g)$ of $W\times P(W)$, where $P(W)$ is the power set of W. $\rho(g)$ must satisfy the monotonicity condition: if $(s,X) \in \rho(g)$ and $X \subseteq Y$, then $(s,Y) \in \rho(g)$. In other words, $\rho(g)$ thought of as an operator $\rho(g)(X) = \{s \mid (s,X)\in\rho(g)\}$ is monotonic in X. We define $\pi(A)$ and $\rho(\alpha)$ for more complex formulae and games as follows:

2'. $\pi(A\vee B) = \pi(A)\cup\pi(B)$

$\pi(\neg A) = W-\pi(A)$

3'. $\pi((\alpha)A) = \{s \mid (s,\pi(A))\in\rho(\alpha)\}$

and

5'. $\rho(\alpha;\beta) = \{(s,X) \mid \exists Y\ (s,Y)\in\rho(\alpha)$ and $\forall t\in Y,\ (t,X)\in\rho(\beta)\}$

$\rho(\alpha\vee\beta) = \rho(\alpha)\cup\rho(\beta)$

similarly for conjunction with $\cap$.

$\rho(\langle\alpha^*\rangle) = \{(s,X) | s \in \mu Y(X \subseteq Y \wedge (\forall t)((t,Y) \in \rho(\alpha) \Rightarrow t \in Y)\}$

$\rho([\alpha^*]) = \{(s,X) | s \in \nu Y(Y \subseteq X \wedge (\forall t)(t \in Y \Rightarrow (t,Y) \in \rho(\alpha))\}$

where νY means: the largest Y such that...

$\rho(\alpha^d) = \{(s,W-X) | (s,X) \notin \rho(\alpha)\}$

6'. $\rho(\langle A\rangle) = \{(s,X) | s \in \pi(A) \cap X\}$

and $\rho([A]) = \{(s,X) | s \in X - \pi(A)\}$

These conditions can be written equivalently as follows:

$\rho(\alpha;\beta)(X) = \rho(\alpha)(\rho(\beta)(X))$

$\rho(skip)(X) = X$

$\rho(\alpha \vee \beta)(X) = \rho(\alpha)(X) \cup \rho(\beta)(X)$

$\rho(\alpha \wedge \beta)(X) = \rho(\alpha)(X) \cap \rho(\beta)(X)$

$\rho(\langle\alpha^*\rangle)(X) = \mu Y(X \subseteq Y \wedge Y \supseteq \rho(\alpha)(Y))$

$\rho([\alpha^*])(X) = \nu Y(Y \subseteq X \wedge Y \subseteq \rho(\alpha)(Y))$

$\rho(\alpha^d)(X) = W - \rho(\alpha)(W-X)$

$\rho(\langle A\rangle)(X) = \pi(A) \cap X$

$\rho([A])(X) = X \cup (W - \pi(A))$

So far we have made no connection with PDL. However, given a language of PDL we can associate with it a Game Logic where to each program a_i of PDL we associate two games $\langle a_i\rangle$ and $[a_i]$. We take

$\rho(\langle a\rangle) = \{(s,X) | \exists t\ (s,t) \in R_a \text{ and } t \in X\}$

and

$\rho([a]) = \{(s,X) | \forall t\ (s,t) \in R_a \text{ implies } t \in X\}$

and the formulae of PDL can be translated easily into those of game logic. However, Game Logic is more expressive. The formula $\langle[b]^*\rangle$false of game logic says that there is no infinite sequence of states $s_1,...,s_i,..$ such that b can take us from s_i to s_{i+1} for all i. This notion can be expressed in Streett's PDL but not in PDL. We suspect that the formula $\langle(\langle a\rangle;[b])^*\rangle$false, which says that player I can make "a" moves to player II's "b" moves in such a way that eventually player II will be deadlocked, cannot be expressed in PDL either. Finally, let us show how well-foundedness can be defined in Game Logic. Given a linear ordering R over a set W, consider the model of Game Logic where $\rho(g)$ denotes [a] and R_a is the inverse relation of R. Then R is well-founded over W iff the formula $\langle g^*\rangle$false is true. Since player I cannot terminate the game without losing, and he also loses if he never terminates, the only way he can win is to keep saying to player II, keep playing, and hope that player II will sooner or later be deadlocked. (the subgame [a] of $\langle[a]^*\rangle$ is a game where player II moves, and in the main game $\langle[a]^*\rangle$, player I is only responsible for deciding how many times is [a] played). Thus I wins iff there are no infinite descending sequences of R on W.

However, game logic can be easily translated into the μ-calculus of [K] and by the decision procedure of [KP2], is decidable. We do not know if there is an elementary decision procedure.

Completeness: the following axioms and rules are complete for the "dual-free" part of game logic.
The axioms of game logic:
1) All tautologies
2) $(\alpha)(A \Rightarrow B) \Rightarrow ((\alpha)A \Rightarrow (\alpha)B)$
3) $(\alpha;\beta)A \Leftrightarrow (\alpha)(\beta)A$
4) $(\alpha \vee \beta)A \Leftrightarrow (\alpha)A \vee (\beta)A$
5) $(\langle\alpha^*\rangle)A \Leftrightarrow A \vee (\alpha)(\langle\alpha^*\rangle)A$
6) $(\langle A?\rangle)B \Leftrightarrow A \& B$
Rules of Inference:
1) Modus Ponens
2) $\dfrac{A \Rightarrow B}{(\alpha)A \Rightarrow (\alpha)B}$
3) $\dfrac{(\alpha)A \Rightarrow A}{(\langle\alpha^*\rangle)A \Rightarrow A}$ (Bar Induction)

The soundness of these axioms and rules is quite straightforward. The completeness proof is similar to that in [KP1]. The details will appear elsewhere.

§5 *A cake cutting algorithm*: A fairly common method used by children for sharing something fairly is: "you divide and I will pick". The person dividing has then a strong incentive to make the pieces as equal as possible. A more general algorithm that works for n people dividing something, say a cake, goes as follows:

The first person cuts out a piece which he claims is his fair share. Then the piece goes around being inspected, in turn, by persons p_2, p_3, ... etc. Anyone who thinks the piece is not too large just passes it. Anyone who thinks it is too big, may reduce it, putting some back into the main part. After the piece has been inspected by p_n, the *last* person who reduced the piece, takes it. If there is no such person, i.e., no one challenged p_1, then the piece is taken by p_1. In any case, one person now has a piece, and the algorithm continues with n-1 participants. Note incidentally that the algorithm described above for two people is not the special case n=2 of this more general algorithm.

A question recently raised by Even, Paz and Rabin is: what is the minimum number of cuts needed by an algorithm that works? They have shown that the algorithm described above can take $O(n^2)$ cuts, but that there is another algorithm that needs only $O(n\log(n))$ cuts. However, no good lower bound is known.

We are not here interested in the complexity issue, but just to enter into the spirit of the thing we raise the following question: the algorithm described above works only if all the participants involved are greedy.-i.e. they will take more than their share if we don't watch out. However, adults dividing food often are in a polite mood and try to take *less* than their fair share. Now the algorithm described above can easily be adapted to polite people by changing each reducing action to an increasing action when $p_2,...,p_n$ inspect the piece cut out by p_1. Thus p_3 might say, "no, no, that is too little, let me give you more", etc., and the last person to increase the piece would get it. This modified algorithm will then work for polite people. A similar observation applies to the $n\log(n)$ algorithm. However, it is not clear that this must be true in general, that greedy algorithms and polite algorithms come in pairs. Thus we could ask if the complexities are the same in both cases and also if there are algorithms that work if some people are polite and others are greedy. The solution to this last problem is easy if we know which are which. Then an algorithm that works would be one that gives *nothing* to the polite people and uses a "greedy" algorithm to divide the cake between the rest.

In any case, what we are actually going to be concerned with here is the question: what does it mean to say that either of these two algorithms *works*? And how do we prove its correctness? We show how to solve both these questions in the context of Dynamic Logic and many-person Game Logic.

As the reader may recall, in Dynamic Logic we have a state space W and a language L which can be used to make statements about individual states. Thus the notion $s \models A$ where s is a state and A is a formula of L, is assumed to be defined, and means intuitively: the formula A is true at the state s. We assume also that we have some actions on W which may take us from one state to another, usually in a non-deterministic way. In the example above, a typical action may be a cutting action, or a reducing action, both of which are non-deterministic.

L is closed under the modalities $\langle a\rangle$ and $[a]$ where a is any action. Thus if A is a formula of L then $s\models\langle a\rangle A$ means that there is a t such that the action a *may* take us from s to t and $t\models A$. Similarly, $s\models[a]A$ iff for all t such that a can take us from s to t, $t\models A$. For example, if a cake is being cut between two people by the action c, say F_1 means that the first piece is fair (one person's fair share) and F_2 means that the second piece is fair. Then we have $[c](F_1 \vee F_2)$ and also $\langle c\rangle(F_1 \wedge F_2)$ I.e. no matter how the cake is cut, at least one piece is fair, and it is possible to cut it so that both pieces are fair. Note that both participants must agree to these two statements though they need not agree on which particular pieces are fair.

Now we are ready to state one sense in which the cake cutting algorithm is correct. Suppose that at some point in the algorithm some person p accepts $[a]A$ where a is a formula and action a is just about to be performed. Then afterwards, p must accept A. Also if p accepts $\langle a\rangle B$ and *p herself performs action a and the algorithm calls for B to be realised* then p must accept B after a is done. However, another person p' who also accepted both $[a]A$ and $\langle a\rangle B$ before a was done need not accept B after, though he must also accept A.

The correctness of the algorithm then consists in the fact that after the algorithm is finished, each person p_i must accept the proposition F_i which states that the piece received by p_i is fair.

An alternative, game theoretic interpretation will be given later.

The Proof: Now we proceed to a semi-formal proof of the correctness of the algorithm described before.

A state will consist of the values of n+2 variables. The variable m has as its value the main part of the cake. The variable x is the piece under consideration. For i=1 to n, the variable x_i has as its value the piece, if any, assigned to the person p_i. The variables $m, x, x_1, .., x_n$ range over subsets of the cake.

The algorithm uses three basic actions.

c cuts a piece from m and assigns it to x. c works only if x is 0.

r (reduce) transfers some (non-zero) portion from x back to m.

a_i (assign) assigns the piece x to person p_i. Thus a_i is simply, $(x_i,x):=(x,0)$.

The basic predicates are $F(u,k)$ where u is some piece and $k < n$, and means: the piece u is big enough for k people. $F(u)$ abbreviates $F(u,1)$ and F_i abbreviates $F(x_i)$.

We assume that everyone always accepts the following propositions for all $k \leqslant n$.

(1) $F(m,k) \Rightarrow \langle c\rangle(F(m,k-1)\wedge F(x))$

If the main piece is big enough for k people, it is possible to cut out a fair piece, leaving enough for k-1 people.

(2) $F(m,k) \Rightarrow [r^*]F(m,k)$

If the main piece is big enough for k people, it remains so when more is added to it.

(3) $F(m,k) \Rightarrow [c][r^*](F(m,k-1)\vee\langle r\rangle(F(m,k-1)\wedge F(x)))$

If the main piece was big enough for k people, then after cutting and several reductions, either it is big enough for k-1 people, or else a reduction will make m big enough for k-1 people and leave x fair.

(4) $F(x) \Rightarrow [a_i]F_i$ Obvious.

There are tacit assumptions of relevance, e.g. that r and c can only affect statements in which m or x occurs. We assume moreover that everyone accepts $F(m,n)$ at the beginning.

The main algorithm consists of n cycles during each of which one person is assigned a piece. We show now that after the kth cycle, the people still in the game accept $F(m,n-k)$ and each p_i who is assigned a piece, accepts F_i. This is true at start since k=0, everyone accepts $F(m,n)$ and no one yet has a piece. We now consider the inductive step from k to k+1. We assume that everyone in the game accepts $F(m,n-k)$ at this stage.

Since p_1 (or whoever does the cutting) *does* the cutting, by (1) she must accept $F(m,n-k-1)\wedge F(x)$. If no one does an r, she gets x, and she must accept this as fair since x did not change. If someone does do an r she must (by (2) still accept $F(m,n-k-1)$ and this is OK since she will then be participating at the next stage.

Let us now consider the other people.

The last person to do r (if there is someone who does r) must (by (3) accept F(x) and therefore accept x when it is assigned to him.

A person who refrains from doing r must accept F(m,n-k-1) because of (3) and will be in the next cycle with n-k-1 participants.

A person who does do r but is not the last such person, must accept F(m,n-k-1) at the time of doing r and hence also after more r's are done. Hence he will accept F(m,n-k-1) at the next cycle.

Thus we have shown that if p_i is assigned the piece during that cycle, then p_i accepts F_i and the other people still in the game accept F(m,n-k-1) at the next stage. This finishes the inductive step and we are done.

It is also possible to give a game-theoretic analysis of this problem. Namely, if we think of the algorithm as an n-person game, then every participant p_i has a strategy for ensuring that F_i holds when the game is over.

We notice first that each move of game α consists of two things. First we have an execution of some atomic program a by some person p. Moreover, the game α is replaced by a new game α' which is just the *rest of* α. Let A be some property that some player q wants to have holding at the end of the game (q may or may not equal p) and let $(q,\alpha)A$ mean that player q has a winning strategy, playing α to achieve A. (In two person games we did not need to mention q explicitly, since everything could be seen from player I's point of view.)

Then if q is the same as p then $(q,\alpha)A$ is equivalent to $(p,\alpha)A$ which is equivalent to $\langle a\rangle(p,\alpha')A$. For player p can achieve A after α iff she can achieve A after a and α' iff $\langle a\rangle(p,\alpha')A$ is true.

If q is not p, then he can be sure of achieving A after α iff he can be sure of achieving A after a play of a by p and then α'. And thus $(q,\alpha)A$ is equivalent to $[a](q,\alpha')A$.

Finally, when the game is *over*, then A can be achieved iff A is true.

These three observations taken together allow us to show that the proof we gave before can be put in terms of winning strategies in an n-person game. We leave the details to the reader.

Yet another way to look at this problem is measure theoretically. Given n probability measures $\mu_1,\ldots,\mu_n$ on a space X, the algorithm shows the existence of a partition $\{X_1,\ldots,X_n\}$ such that $\mu_i(X_i) \geqslant 1/n$. However, it is in fact true that there can be a partition with $\mu_i(X_i) = 1/n$. Can we find an algorithm that will achieve this latter property? Or at least to within ϵ?

Finally, we point out that there is a clear sense in which none of the algorithms described above are fair since they allow something very like gerrymandering. Suppose, for example, that there are two participants p and q. p loves icing, but q likes both cake and icing equally. Thus if we represent the cake by the interval [0,2] where [0,1] is the cake, and [1,2] is the icing, then we might have $\mu_1([0,1]) = 1/10$ and $\mu_1([1,2]) = 9/10$. On the other hand, $\mu_2([0,1]) = \mu_2([1,2]) = 1/2$. Now the wily player p divides the cake into two pieces X and Y where X = [0,1.1] and Y = [1.1,2]. Since $\mu_2(X) = .55$, q will choose X and leave Y to p. However $\mu_1(Y) = .81$ so that player p has got much the better bargain. Is it possible to define a notion of fairness that will get around this problem and find an algorithm that is fairer than the ones we have described?

References

[CKS] Chandra, A., Kozen, D., and Stockmeyer, L.,"Alternation", *J. ACM* 28, (1981) 114-133.

[E] Ehrenfeucht, A., " An Application of Games to to the Completeness Problem for Formalised Theories", *Fund. Math.*, 49 (1961) 129-141.

[EPR] S. Even, A. Paz and M. Rabin, oral communication.

[FL] M. Fischer and R. Ladner, "Propositional Dynamic Logic of Regular Programs", *J. Comp. and System Science* 18 (1979) 194-211.

[GH] Gurevich, Y., and Harrington, L., "Trees, Automata, and Games", *Proc. 14th STOC Symposium*, 1982, 60-65.

[K] Kozen, D., "Results on the Propositional μ-calculus", *Proc 9th ICALP* (1982) Springer LNCS vol 348-359

[KP1] D. Kozen and R. Parikh, "An Elementary Proof of the Completeness of PDL", *Theor. Comp. Sci.* 14 (1981) 113-118.

[KP2] Kozen, D., and Parikh, R., "A Decision Procedure for the Propositional μ-calculus", Typescript, April 1983.

[MP] A. Meyer and R. Parikh, "Definability in Dynamic Logic", *JCSS* 23 (1981) 271-298.

[MS] Mycielski, J., and Steinhaus, H., "A Mathematical Axiom Contradicting the Axiom of Choice", *Bull. Acad. Pol. Sci.*, 10, (1962) 1-3.

[P1] R. Parikh, "The Completeness of Propositional Dynamic Logic", *Proc. 7th Symp. on Math. Found. Comp. Sci*, Springer LNCS 64 403-415.

[P2] R. Parikh, "Propositional Dynamic Logics of Programs: A Survey", *Logics of Programs* Ed. E. Engeler, Springer LNCS 125 102-144.

[P3] R. Parikh, "A Completeness Result for a Propositional Game Logic", Manuscript, Nov. 1982.

[Pr] V. Pratt, "A Decidable mu-calculus (Preliminary report)" IEEE-FOCS 22 (1981) 421-428.

[Ra] Rabin, M., "Decidability of Second Order Theories and Automata on Infinite Trees", *Tran. AMS*, 141 (1969) 1-35.

[St] Streett, R., "Propositional Dynamic Logic of Looping and Converse", *Proc. 13th STOC* (1981) 375-383.

[vNM] von Neumann, J., and Morgenstern, O., *the Theory of Games and Economic Behavior*, Princeton Univ. Press, 1944.

A NEW PROBABILISTIC MODEL FOR THE STUDY OF ALGORITHMIC PROPERTIES OF RANDOM GRAPH PROBLEMS

Marco Protasi - Istituto di Matematica,
Università dell'Aquila,
Via Roma 33, L'Aquila, Italy.

Maurizio Talamo - IASI - CNR,
Via Buonarroti 12, Roma, Italy.

1. *Introduction*

In the probabilistic analysis of algorithms for solving random graph problems one of the most controversial and crucial points is given by the choice of the probability distribution that we assume on the set of the inputs before performing the analysis.

Until now the models proposed in the literature are of the following type. Given a graph of n nodes, we assume that every pair of nodes is an edge with fixed probability p $(0 < p < 1)$ independently from the presence or the absence of any other edges; p can be a constant (the socalled constant density model) (see for istance [ER] , [K] , [GM] , [BE]) and examples of problems analyzed in this way are Max-clique and Min chromatic number; or p can be depending on n ([AV] , [KS] , [ER]); for istance $p = a \log n/(n-1)$, where a is a suitably chosen constant, in the case of matching problems. Assuming the costant density model, since the analysis is asymptotic, in practice we only describe probabilistic properties of dense random graphs; in fact the graph $G = (V,E)$ has, in this model, $\theta(n^2)$ edges, that is there exist two positive constants c_1, c_2 such that $c_1 n^2 \leqslant |E| \leqslant c_2 n^2$. This implies that the constant density model is able to deal with particular types of graphs. On the other hand, assuming p as a function of n, we can describe sparse graphs, but the rate of sparsity is fixed. So in the case $p(n) = a \log n/(n-1)$, because of the asymptoticity, $|E| = \theta(n \cdot \log n)$. Therefore in every case, we are restricted to particular types of graphs. We note that, therefore the known models determine graphs always having substantially the same number of edges and this fact clearly is not a realistic assumption.

Instead, a good model should be, at least, sufficient powerful to describe the evolution of the random graphs while the sparsity of the graph is varying since the sparsity is one of the most important properties for the characterization of a random graph problem.

To obtain this condition the model has to be parametric but this fact is necessary but not sufficient to assure the goodness of a general model. A way to reach the goal of showing that the model is satisfactory consists in studying the performance of an algorithm over a problem and seeing if the algorithm behaves as we would expect intuitively. Generally it is very difficult to forecast, a priori, what will be the performance of an algorithm. However if we consider random graph problems, we reach our aim using a greedy algorithm. In fact, because of the characteristics of the greedy, increasing the sparsity of the graph, we naturally expect that the solution achieved by the greedy has a value nearer and nearer to the value of the optimal solution, and when the graph is sufficiently sparse, the greedy reaches the optimum.

Before presenting this new model some final considerations must be done. As we said the model has to be parametric, i.e. if two probability values p_1 and p_2 on the existence of an edge are substantially different then the corresponding optimal solutions are two different functions; this condition allows to overcome partially the problem of the asymptoticity because if the solutions are given by different functions, the asymptotic analysis will not destroy this difference.

The parametricity has changed remarkably the mathematical proofs with respect to the classical ones. Even exploiting the standard probabilistic techniques, the combinatorial part of the proofs is quite different from the techniques used in the literature. Finally, in our study we found two threshold values of the optimal solution, after which the analysis changes abruptly. On one hand this result is a bit surprising but on the other hand it can be framed in the environment of the theory of random graphs, where threshold points in some important problems are already known ([BE], [Ko], [P], [B]).

2. *The new model*

First of all, we give the definition of the new model.

Definition 1. Given a graph $G = (V,E)$ of n nodes, every pair (i, j), with $i, j \in V$, is an edge with probability $1- n^{-c/n}$, independently from the presence or absence of any other edges, where c can assume every value between n/log n and 1/n.

We call this model "parametric density model".

When the base of the logarithm is not specified, every integer greater than 1 can be assumed as base.

It is immediate to show that

Proposition 1. When $c = n/\log_b n$, for every integer b the parametric density model coincides with the constant density model ($p = 1 - 1/b$). When c tends to 1/n, the parametric density model describes almost null graphs.

Therefore proposition 1 assures that in this parametric model we are able to deal with dense and very sparse graphs, passing through any possible intermediate situation.

In the following we will study two random graph problems: MAX-INDEPENDENT SET and MIN–CHROMATIC NUMBER (see [GJ] for the definitions). We note that the results of the MAX INDEPENDENT SET problem can be trivially extended to MAX-CLIQUE problem.

Other random graph problems could be analyzed, but we will present the results for these two problems because of their relevance and paradigmaticity in the theory of random graphs.

As we said in the introduction we will test the significativity of the model using a greedy algorithm. For the description of this type of algorithm see, for example, [PS].

The greedy algorithm for the problems that we will consider has already been studied from a probabilistic point of view in the constant density model ([BE], [GM]). It has been shown that the greedy algorithm achieves a solution having value which is half of the value of the optimal solution almost surely.

3 *Probabilistic evaluation of the optimal solution*

In this paragraph we want to calculate the value of the optimal solution in our model. First of all we consider the MAX-INDEPENDENT SET problem.

Let I (n) be the random variable that denotes the value of the maximum independent set of a graph of n nodes. Then we can state the following theorem.

Theorem 1

If $4 \leq c \leq \dfrac{n}{\log n}$

$$\lim_{n \to \infty} \frac{I(n)}{n} = \frac{2}{c} \quad \text{almost surely}$$

Proof Firstly we prove that

$$\text{Prob}\left(I(n) \geq \frac{2n}{c}\right) = o \text{ as } n \to \infty \quad \text{fast enough}$$

Let $d = d(n) = \dfrac{2n}{c}$

$$\text{Prob}(I(n) \geq d) \leq \binom{n}{d} \left(n^{-\frac{c}{n}}\right)^{\frac{d(d-1)}{2}}$$

$$\leq \frac{n^d}{d!} \left(n^{-\frac{c}{n}}\right)^{\frac{d(d-1)}{2}}$$

(by simple algebraic steps)

$$\leq \frac{n}{d!}$$

$$= o\left(n^{-i}\right) \qquad \text{for every integer } i > 1$$

The Borel Cantelli Lemma [C] assures the almost sure convergence.

In order to prove that

$\text{Prob}(I(n) < d) = o$ as $n \to \infty$ fast enough

it is sufficient to show that

$\text{Prob}(Y_d = o) = o$ as $n \to \infty$ fast enough where Y_d is the random variable that denotes the number of the independent sets of size d.

We have that

$$\text{Prob}(Y_d = o) \leq \frac{\sigma^2(n,d)}{E^2(n,d)}$$

where σ^2 is the variance, and E is the expectation of Y_d.

The second part of the thesis follows if we are able to prove that $\dfrac{\sigma^2(n,d)}{E^2(n,d)} = 0$ as $n \to \infty$ fast enough.

For $d < n/2$

$$\frac{\sigma^2(n,d)}{E^2(n,d)} = \sum_{l=2}^{d} \frac{\binom{d}{l}\binom{n-d}{d-l}}{\binom{n}{d}} \cdot \left(n^{\frac{c}{n}\binom{l}{2}} - 1\right)$$

To prove that this formula tends to zero, the dissecting technique is used. So the proof is divided in three subcases

a) When $c = n/\log n$

b) When the value of l is such that $n^{\frac{c}{2}\cdot\binom{l}{2}} \to \infty$ as $n \to \infty$

c) When the value of l is such that $n^{\frac{c}{2}\cdot\binom{l}{2}}$ tends to a finite quantity as $n \to \infty$

The standard technique consists in bounding $\frac{\sigma^2}{E^2}$ from above by $\frac{d^4}{n^2}$ which is sufficient in case a) but not in cases b) and c).

A more refined analysis shows that there exists a constant $h_c \geq 1$ such that we can bound $\frac{\sigma^2}{E^2}$ from above by $\frac{d^4}{n} h_c^{-d}$ which is sufficient to prove the convergence in cases b) and c)

QED

Some remarkable observations have to be done on Theorem 1. First of all, if c = n/log n, by Proposition 1, the model coincides with the constant density model and in fact we find again the same value discovered in [GM] for the maximum independent set using the constant density model. Furthermore, Theorem 1 holds at most when c = 4. In this case I (n) is about n/2; it is natural to ask what happens when the value of the optimal solution is greater than n/2. Finally we note that the proof cannot be applied beyond n/2 because in this case the approximation of the binomial changes. So we discover that n/2 is a threshold value by the following theorem

Theorem 2

If $\frac{1}{n} \leq c \leq 4$

$$\lim_{n\to\infty} \frac{I(n)}{n} = \frac{1+\sqrt{1+2c}}{c+1+\sqrt{1+2c}} \quad \text{almost surely}$$

Proof. Since $\binom{n}{d} = \binom{n}{n-d}$ putting

$d = d(n) = \left(1-\frac{1}{K}\right)n, \; K > 2$ we have

$$\binom{n}{n-d} n^{-\frac{c}{n}\frac{d(d-1)}{2}} = \binom{n}{n/K} n^{-\frac{c}{2}\left(1-\frac{1}{K}\right)\left(\left(1-\frac{1}{K}\right)n-1\right)}$$

It is easy to prove that in order to have
Prob (I (n) $\geq$ d) = o as $n \to \infty$ fast enough

it must be $1-\frac{1}{K} = \frac{1+\sqrt{1+2c}}{c+1+\sqrt{1+2c}}$

The second part of the thesis can be proved analogously to the second part of Theorem 1, obviously changing the approximation of the binomial

QED

Theorem 2 shows that for c decreasing from 4 towards 1/n, the value of the optimal solution is increasing from n/2 to n. This means that in our model for the maximum independent set we are able to capture all the possible values of the optimal solution from the case in which the graph is dense until the case in which practically every node belongs to the optimal solution.

At this point to validate the parametric model, we have to analyze the probabilistic performance of the greedy algorithm.

In the constant density model it has been shown that the greedy algorithm achieves a solution having value which is the half of the value of the optimal solution, while in the case of very sparse graphs, it is natural to expect that the values achieved by the greedy and the optimal value tend to coincide. These results will be proved in the following paragraph, so showing that the parametric model succeeds in approximating the real situation pretty well.

4 *Probabilistic evaluation of the greedy algorithm*

Let $I^{GR}(n)$ the random variable that denotes the value of the largest independent set achieved by the greedy algorithm on a graph of n nodes

Theorem 3:

If $\frac{1}{n} \leq c \leq \frac{n}{\log n}$

$$\lim_{n\to\infty} \frac{I^{GR}(n)}{n} = \frac{1}{c} \qquad \text{almost surely}$$

Proof. Also in this case the proof is divided in two parts.

Let $d^{GR}(n) = \theta I(n)$ with $\theta \leq 1$

and $m = m(n) = o(n)$

$$1) \ \mathrm{Prob}\,(I^{GR}(n) \geq d^{GR}(n)) \leq \prod_{i=d^{GR}-m}^{d^{GR}-1} \left(1-\left(1-n^{-\frac{c}{n}i}\right)^{n}\right)$$

By a sequence of algebraic inequalities it is possible to show that

$\mathrm{Prob}\,(I^{GR}(n) \geq d^{GR}(n)) = o$ as $n\to\infty$ fast enough

if, given $I(n) = Tn$, $\quad \theta = \frac{1}{cT}$

$$\text{where} \begin{cases} T = \dfrac{2}{c} & \text{if } \dfrac{n}{\log n} \geq c \geq 4 \\[2ex] T = \dfrac{1+\sqrt{1+2c}}{c+1+\sqrt{1+2c}} & \text{if } \dfrac{1}{n} \leq c \leq 4 \end{cases}$$

2) $\text{Prob}\,(I^{GR}(n) < d^{GR}(n)) \leq \prod_{i=1}^{d^{GR}(n)} \left(1 - n^{-\frac{c}{n} i}\right)^{\alpha_i - 1}$

with $\sum_{i=1}^{d^{GR}(n)} = n$ where a_i is the number of nodes that the greedy algorithms examines in order to add the i - th node to the solution

Again it is possible to prove that $\theta = \frac{1}{cT}$

By 1) and 2) we obtain $\frac{I^{GR}(n)}{n} \to \frac{1}{c}$

since $I(n) = T \cdot n$ and $\theta = \frac{1}{cT}$

QED

Note that for $c = \frac{3}{2}$, $\theta = 1$ hence for $c < \frac{3}{2}$, $I^{GR}(n)$ tends to $I(n)$

Corollary 1: 1) If $4 \leqslant c \leqslant \frac{n}{\log n}$

$$\lim_{n \to \infty} \frac{I^{GR}(n)}{I(n)} = \frac{1}{2} \quad \text{almost surely}$$

2) If $\frac{3}{2} \leqslant c \leqslant 4$

$$\frac{1}{2} \leqslant \lim_{n \to \infty} \frac{I^{GR}(n)}{I(n)} \leqslant 1 \quad \text{almost surely}$$

3) If $\frac{1}{n} \leqslant c \leqslant \frac{3}{2}$

$$\lim_{n \to \infty} \frac{I^{GR}(n)}{I(n)} = 1 \quad \text{almost surely}$$

The corollary describes all the performance of the greedy algorithm. Until $c = 4$ or equivalently until the value of the optimal solution is about n/2, the greedy always achieves the half of the value of the optimal solution ; after n/2 the sparsity of the graph begins to be sufficient to improve the performance of the greedy; when we arrive at $c = 3/2$ or the value of the optimal solution is about 2/3 n, the graph is sufficiently sparse to allow the greedy to reach the optimum value; of course after 2/3 n until n the greedy continues to reach the optimum. It is interesting to note that 2/3 n is the second threshold point.

We have therefore proved that the performance of the greedy is as it had to be and this shows that our claim on the validity of the model was right. The parametric model enjoys the properties that a good and honest probabilistic model must have.

As regards the MIN-CHROMATIC NUMBER, similar results can be shown.

Let C (n) be the random variable that denotes the value of the minimum chromatic number of a graph of n nodes

Theorem 4

1) If $4 \leq c \leq \frac{n}{\log n}$

$$\liminf_{n \to \infty} C(n) = \frac{c}{2}$$ almost surely

2) If $\frac{1}{n} \leq c \leq 4$

$$\liminf_{n \to \infty} C(n) = \frac{c + 1 + \sqrt{1 + 2c}}{1 + \sqrt{1 + 2c}}$$ almost surely

Let $C^{GR}(n)$ be the random variable that denotes the value of the chromatic number achieved by the greedy algorithm on a graph of n nodes.

Theorem 5

If $\frac{1}{n} \leq c \leq \frac{n}{\log n}$

$$\liminf_{n \to \infty} C^{GR}(n) = c$$ almost surely

Also in this case, the ratio between the values of the optimal solution and the solution achieved by the greedy is between 1/2 and 1. It is interesting, anyhow, to observe that for this problem, probabilistically, the solution furnished by the greedy begins to be near to the optimum when the corresponding deterministic input can be solved in polynomial time, unlike what happens for MAX-INDEPENDENT SET.

References

(AV) D. Angluin, L.G. Valiant "Fast probabilistic algorithms for hamiltonian paths and matchings", J. Comp. Syst. Sci, Vol. 18 (1979)

(B) B. Bollobas "Graph theory. An Introductory course" Springer Verlag, New York (1979)

(BE) B. Bollobas, P. Erdös "Cliques in random graphs" Math. Proc. Camb. Phil. Soc., Vol. 80 (1976)

(C) V.L. Chung "A course in probability theory "Academic Press (1974)

(ER) P. Erdös, A. Renyi "On the evolution of random graphs" Publ. Math. Inst. Hungar. Acad. Sci., Vol. 5 (1960)

(GJ) M. R. Garey, D. S. Johnson "Computers and intractability. A guide o the theory of NP - completeness", Freeman, San Francisco, 1978).

(GM) G. R. Grimmett, C. J. H. Mc Diarmid "On colouring random graphs" Math. Proc. Camb. Phil. Soc. Vol 77, (1975).

(K) R. M. Karp "The probabilistic analysis of some combinatorial search algorithms" In J. F. Tranb (ed.) "Algorithms and complexity: New directions and recent results", Academic Press, New York (1976)

(Ko) A.D. Korshunov "Solution of a problem of Erdös and Renyi on Hamiltonian cycles in nonoriented graphs" Soviet. Mat. Doklady, Vol. 17 (1976)

(KS) R.M. Karp, M. Sipser "Maximum matchings in sparse random graphs" Proc. 22th Ann. Symp. on Foundations of Computer Science, I EEE Computer Society (1981)

(P) L. Posa "Hamiltonian circuits in random graphs" Discr. Math., Vol. 14, (1976)

(PS) C. Papadimitriou, D. Steiglitz "Combinatorial optimization. Algorithms and complexity" Prentice Hall (1982)

ON DIAGONALIZATION METHODS AND THE STRUCTURE OF LANGUAGE CLASSES

Kenneth W. Regan
Merton College
Oxford, OX1-4JD U.K.

1. Introduction

The first purpose of this paper is to popularize an "automatic" diagonalization technique that seems custom-tailored for the study of subrecursive reducibilities and language classes. The basic method has roots in the work of Ladner [Lad75] and Landweber, Lipton, and Robertson [LLR81], while the key theorem appears in slightly different forms in the papers of Schöning ([Sö81],[Sö82]) and Chew and Machtey ([CM81]). We present another version of the theorem here.

Second, we illustrate the power and sharpness of this "out-running" technique by simultaneously proving analogues for other equivalence classes or reducibility relations of the following result announced by P. Young in the extended abstract [Yg83].

Theorem 1: Every polynomial many-one degree either consists of a single p-isomorphism class, or else allows the order-embedding of any countable partially-ordered set into it, with "size-increasing polynomial-time computable-and-invertible reducibility" as the order relation.

Several other results of independent interest are proved along the way.

Third, we attempt to boil all this down to its essential mathematical content (which we suspect may prove to be the same for the "out-gunning" [our terms] methods of [Yg83] when the full version of it [joint with S. Mahaney] appears.) The question is how "effective" diagonalization must be to be useful. We observe that the known methods have an essential element of asymmetry which renders them "one-way" tools only: they are excellent for generating desired mathematical structures, but not very good for preventing undesired ones.

2. Preliminaries and Polynomial Reducibilities

We carry over the order relation and arithmetical operations on N to Σ^*, where $\Sigma = \{0,1\}$, by associating to each string x the natural number having binary representation 1x. The empty string λ corresponds to 1. Here $|x|$ denotes the length of x as a string rather than its absolute value as a number. For all $x,y \in \Sigma^*$ we set $\langle x,y \rangle := a^2 - 2(a-b) + (x<y)$, where $a = \max(x,y)$, $b = \min(x,y)$, and $(x<y)$ is 1 if $x<y$ and 0 otherwise. This gives us a polynomial-time computable bijection from $\Sigma^* \times \Sigma^*$ to Σ^* which also satisfies $|x| + |y| \leq |\langle x,y \rangle|$ for all $x,y \in \Sigma^*$ and is length-nondecreasing in each argument. We iterate $\langle\, , \rangle$ from the right, so that e.g. $\langle x,y,z \rangle$ stands for $\langle x,\langle y,z \rangle\rangle$.

Fixed "acceptable" (see [Rog67]) recursive enumerations of off-line deterministic language-acceptors and transducers are respectively denoted by $[M_i]_{i=1}^{\infty}$ and $[T_j]_{j=1}^{\infty}$ throughout. $L(M_i)$ denotes the language accepted by M_i, and $\Phi(T_j)$ or simply Φ_j the function computed by T_j. For short we write $T_j(x)$ for $\Phi(T_j)(x)$. A standard reference for Turing Machines and definitions of complexity is [HU79].

If $f: \Sigma^* \rightarrow \Sigma^*$ is total, we define $\underline{f^*}$ to be the equivalence class $\{g \mid g \text{ is total } \& \ g(x) = f(x) \text{ for all but finitely many } x\}$. Similarly for a language A, $\underline{A^*}$ denotes $\{B \mid A \triangle B \text{ is finite}\}$, where $A \triangle B$ stands for $(A - B) \cup (B - A)$, and is called the <u>*-type</u> of A. A language class $\mathcal{C}$ is <u>closed under finite variations</u> (f.v.'s) if $A \in \mathcal{C} \Rightarrow A^* \subseteq \mathcal{C}$ for all $A \subseteq \Sigma^*$, and similarly for function classes.

The <u>direct sum</u> $A \oplus B$ of languages A and B is defined to be the union of $\{0x \mid x \in A\}$ and $\{1y \mid y \in B\}$; $\underline{\oplus}$ is also iterated from the right. For any language A we define inductively $S_0(A) := \{A\}$, and for $n \geq 1$, $S_n(A) := \{\emptyset \oplus B, B \oplus B \mid B \in S_{n-1}(A)\}$. We let <u>#</u> denote the symmetric closure of the relation given for all languages A and B by: for some $A' \subseteq \Sigma^*$ and $n \in N$, $B \in S_n(A')$ and $A' \in A^*$. The equivalence class of A modulo # is written $A^{\#}$ and called A's <u>#-type</u>. A useful note: $\emptyset^{\#} = \emptyset^*$. For any (recursive) A all languages in $A^{\#}$ have the same asymptotic time or space complexity, and except for the trivial cases $A = \emptyset$, $A = \Sigma^*$ are equivalent under polynomial-time many-one reducibility. We justify working with #-types, as opposed to languages themselves, below.

<u>FP</u> denotes the class of polynomial-time computable functions on Σ^*. Where intent is clear we allow FP functions to have the extended range $\Sigma^* \cup \{\text{Error}\}$, where <u>Error</u> is a fixed word outside Σ^*. If f is 1-1 we let $\underline{f^{-1}}$ denote its <u>total left inverse</u>, given for all $x \in \Sigma^*$ by

$$f^{-1}(x) := \begin{cases} y & \text{if } y \text{ such that } f(x) = y \text{ exists,} \\ \text{Error} & \text{otherwise.} \end{cases}$$

Asserting $f^{-1} \in FP$ is stronger than saying the inverse is polynomial-time computable where defined, since we require f^{-1} to <u>recognize</u> where the inverse is not defined.

<u>Definition</u> 1: <u>LIFP</u> is the class of functions $f: \Sigma^* \rightarrow \Sigma^*$ such that (a) f is 1-1, (b) $f \in FP$, $f^{-1} \in FP$, and (c) $\forall x \in \Sigma^*$, $|f(x)| > |x|$.

We write $A \leq^p_{li} B$ if for some $f \in$ LIFP, $f(A) \subseteq B$ and $f(\overline{A}) \subseteq \overline{B}$. The subscript _li_ stands for both "left-invertible" and "length-increasing".

A prime motivation for studying this reducibility is a theorem of L. Berman and J. Hartmanis [BH77]: If $A \leq^p_{li} B$ and $B \leq^p_{li} A$, then A and B are polynomial-time _isomorphic_ in the sense that for some permutation g of Σ^*, with g and g^{-1} polynomial-time computable, we have $g(A) = B$. Then we write $A \equiv^p B$. Defining $B \times \Sigma^*$ to be $\{<x,y> \mid x \in B, y \in \Sigma^*\}$ we obtain

Proposition 2: For all $A,B,C \subseteq \Sigma^*$, (a) $A \leq^p_m B \Rightarrow A \leq^p_{li} B \times \Sigma^*$, (b) $B \times \Sigma^* \leq^p_m B$, and (c) $A \leq^p_m C$ & $C \equiv^p B \times \Sigma^* \Rightarrow A \oplus C \equiv^p B \times \Sigma^*$. Therefore the p-isomorphism class of $B \times \Sigma^*$ is maximal for $\{L \mid L \equiv^p_m B\}$ with respect to $\leq^p_{li}$. _Also_: $\{L \mid L \equiv^p B \times \Sigma^*\}$ $(B \neq \Sigma^*)$ is closed under _#_.

The proof may be obtained via padding-function arguments. The authors of [BH77], drawing on the proven analogous case of r.e.-complete sets and recursive isomorphism, conjecture that for NP-complete sets the $\equiv^p_m$-degree and the maximal p-isomorphism type coincide. We will show that if this conjecture fails then the structure of #-types of NP-complete sets is universal for countable partial orders, and hence that the B-H conjecture for languages fails by as much as it conceivably can.

To extend $\leq^p_{li}$ and similar reducibility relations to classes we make the following convention: $\mathcal{C} \leq^p_{li} \mathcal{D}$ means $(\forall A \in \mathcal{C})(\exists B \in \mathcal{D})\, A \leq^p_{li} B$.

Lemma 3: For all languages A,B,C, (a) $A \leq^p_{li} A \oplus B$

(b) $B \oplus C \leq^p_{li} A \Rightarrow B \leq^p_{li} A$ & $C \leq^p_{li} A$

(c) $B \leq^p_{li} A$ & $C \leq^p_{li} A \Rightarrow B \oplus C \leq^p_{li} A \oplus A$

(d) (for some $X \in A^\#$, $Y \in B^\#$, $X \leq^p_{li} Y$) $\Leftrightarrow A^\# \leq^p_{li} B^\#$

(e) $A^\# \leq^p_{li} A^\#$, and $\emptyset^\# \leq^p_{li} A^\#$ (since $A^\# = (\emptyset \oplus A)^\# = (A \oplus A)^\#$)

(f) $(A \oplus B)^\#$ is a least-upper-bound for $A^\#$ and $B^\#$ in the $\leq^p_{li}$-ordering.

The proof is direct in all cases. Although as (e) states $\leq^p_{li}$ is reflexive on #-types this is not true of languages: if $L = \{0^{2\uparrow n} \mid n \in N\}$, where $2\uparrow n$ is the iterated exponential of n 2's, then for all $x,y \in L$ $y > x \Rightarrow |y| \geq 2^{|x|}$, and so no length-increasing reduction of L to itself can be computable in polynomial time. The least-upper-bound property of (f) fails to hold for languages for the same reason.

For all languages A and B we define $A^\# \oplus B^\# := (A \oplus B)^\#$. While it is possible to have $A' \in A^\#$ for which $(A' \oplus B)^\# \neq (A \oplus B)^\#$, and $\oplus$ is generally not commutative or associative on #-types, we can observe:

Lemma 4: For all languages A, B, and C,

(a) $(A \oplus B) \leq^p_{li} \emptyset \oplus (B \oplus A)$

(b) $[(A \oplus B) \oplus C] \leq^p_{li} \emptyset \oplus (\emptyset \oplus [A \oplus (B \oplus C)])$

(c) $[(A \oplus A) \oplus B] \leq^p_{li} \emptyset \oplus [(A \oplus B) \oplus (A \oplus B)]$.

Combined, these imply by induction that $\{X^\# \oplus Y^\# \mid X \in A^\#, Y \in B^\#\}$ has its members all equivalent under $\leq^p_{1i}$, as are expressions of the form $\oplus_{i=1}^m D_i^\#$ $(m \in N)$ no matter which order the binary $\oplus$ operations are taken in. Working modulo this equivalence we shall feel free to use such expressions as a notational convenience. To obtain a true partial order we define $A \underline{p^\#} B$ if $A^\# \leq^p_{1i} B^\#$ and $B^\# \leq^p_{1i} A^\#$. This gives us

Corollary 5: The equivalence classes of languages modulo $p^\#$ form an upper semilattice with sup operation $\oplus$ (and zero-element $\emptyset^\#$).

3. Recursively Presentable Classes

A class $\mathcal{C}$ of recursive languages is recursively presentable (r.p.) if there exists a recursive universal language for $\mathcal{C}$, i.e. a language U such that $\mathcal{C} = \{U_k \mid k \in N\}$, where $U_k := \{x \mid \langle x,k\rangle \in U\}$ for all k. Equivalently, there exists a recursively enumerated list $[Q_k]_{k=1}^\infty$ of deterministic acceptors such that for each k Q_k halts on all inputs and $\mathcal{C} = \{L(Q_k) \mid k \in N\}$. The same criteria apply to classes $\mathfrak{F}$ of total recursive functions: $\mathfrak{F}$ is recursively presentable if there exists a total recursive function u such that $\mathfrak{F} = \{\lambda x.u(\langle x,k\rangle) \mid k \in N\}$.

A witness function for a language L with respect to a universal language U (such that $L \neq U_k$ for all k) is a map f giving $f(k) \in L \,\Delta\, U_k$ for all k. The following criterion and theorem capture the essence of recursive presentability and the concomitant availability of recursive witness functions. Here we let F be a sound recursively axiomatized formal system strong enough to represent all recursive predicates. It does not matter much which one we choose; Peano Arithmetic will do.

Definition 2: A class $\mathcal{C}$ of languages has the recursive refutability (r.r.) property (w.r. to F) if for some predicate S in the language of F

(a) for all i: $L(M_i) \in \mathcal{C} \Leftrightarrow (\exists j)\, S(i,j)$

(b) for all i,j: M_i total & $\neg S(i,j) \Rightarrow$ '$\neg S(i,j)$' is provable in F.

Theorem 6 ([Re83]): Let $\mathcal{C}$ be a class of languages containing L^* for some L. Then $\mathcal{C}$ is recursively presentable iff $\mathcal{C}$ has the r.r. property and is contained in DTIME[t] for some nondecreasing recursive function t.

Any other Blum complexity measure can be substituted for time without changing Theorem 6. The proof is largely a matter of taking a recursive presentation $[Q_k]_{k=1}^\infty \supseteq$ DTIME[t] by halting machines (obtainable by a lemma) and for all j,k accepting strings iff Q_k does unless for some n the nth derivation of F in some enumeration is a proof of $\neg S(i_k,j)$, where i_k is the index of Q_k in $[M_i]_{i=1}^\infty$; if so strings of length $\geq$ n are accepted iff they are in L. Virtually the same definition and theorem using instead the reference list $[T_j]_{j=1}^{\infty}$ of transducers apply to classes $\mathfrak{F}$ of functions. The extra hypotheses of Theorem 6 are needed because the null class $\emptyset$ and the class REC of all recursive languages both have the r.r. property but are not recursively presentable. If we define #Steps(i,x) to be the (possibly infinite) number of steps M_i takes on input x, we can state a "recursively refutable" predicate for REC as:

$$S_R(i,\langle k,c\rangle) \;:=\; \text{"}L(M_k) = L(M_i) \;\&\; M_k \text{ halts for all inputs } \& \\ \forall x,m,n : [\#Steps(k,x) = m \;\&\; \sum_{y\leq x} \#Steps(i,y) = n] \Rightarrow m \leq c\cdot n\text{"}.$$

The last bit is superfluous for defining REC but needed for the r.r. property. The "effective falsifiability" criterion of (b), which guarantees the presence of "witnesses" whenever conditions S(i,j) defining $\mathcal{C}$ fail, seems to be the key to obtaining an intuitive grasp of the class $\mathcal{C}$. (See comments at the end of [LLR81] about non-r.p. classes.) Practically all complexity classes in the literature thus far considered tractable for study have been shown to be r.r.; see e.g. [Sö82], [Re82].

An r.r. predicate for the function class FP may be informally stated with $j = \langle k,m\rangle$ as "T_k runs in time $n^m + m$ and computes the same function as T_i." We use a presentation $[X_k]_{k=1}^{\infty}$ of FP functions (with extended range $\Sigma^* \cup \{\text{Error}\}$) then obtainable from Thm. 6 to devise one for LIFP.

Lemma 7: LIFP is recursively presentable.

Proof: LIFP is contained in DTIME$[2^n]$, but as LIFP itself does not satisfy the first hypothesis of Theorem 6 we start with LIFP $\cup\, c_\lambda^*$ instead, where c_λ is the constant-λ function. Then (informally) for all $i \in N$, $\phi(T_i) \in \text{LIFP} \cup c_\lambda^* \Leftrightarrow \exists j = \langle k,m,n\rangle$ such that:

$$\phi(T_i) = \phi(X_k) \;\;\&\;\; \{(\forall y\colon |y| > n \Rightarrow X_k(y) = \lambda) \;\;\underline{\text{or}} \\ [\,(\phi(X_k) \text{ is 1-1}) \;\&\; (X_k(y) \neq \text{Error for all } y \in \Sigma^*) \;\&\; (\forall x\colon |X_k(x)| > |x|) \;\& \\ (\forall y\colon X_m(X_k(y)) = y) \;\&\; (\forall y\colon X_m(y) = \text{Error} \Leftrightarrow y \notin \text{Range}[\phi(X_k)])\,]\,\}\,.$$

This does the trick. If the last clause fails for some y but everything before it in the [ ]-brackets holds then either $X_m(y)$ = Error & y is in Range$[\phi(X_k)]$, which is checkable, or $X_m(y) \neq$ Error & $y \notin$ Range$[\phi(X_k)]$, which can also be proved owing to the length-increasing property of $\phi(X_k)$, as one need only check $X_k(z) \neq y$ for strings z of length $< |y|$.

Then, letting $[Y_k]_{k=1}^{\infty}$ be the presentation of LIFP $\cup\, c_\lambda^*$ obtained from the theorem, we replace the f.v.'s of c_λ by LIFP functions in a new presentation. For all k let Z_k be a halting transducer computing:

$$Z_k(x) \;:=\; \begin{cases} Y_k(x) & \text{if for all } y \leq x,\ Y_k(y) \neq \lambda \\ x + a & \text{otherwise, where } a = \max\{Y_k(y) \mid y < x\}\,. \end{cases}$$

Then each Z_k computes a function in LIFP and for all k, $\Phi(Y_k) \in$ LIFP $\Rightarrow$ $\lambda \notin$ Range$[\Phi(Y_k)]$ $\Rightarrow$ $\Phi(Z_k) = \Phi(Y_k)$. ⁞⁞

We fix the presentation $[Z_k]_{k=1}^{\infty}$ for use below; that no Z_k itself runs in polynomial time is not important. The group G_p of p-isomorphisms (see [BH77]) may be shown to be r.p. in a similar manner.

The following result is stated for $\leq_{1i}^{p}$, but it holds quite generally for reducibilities arising from recursively presentable function classes and also for polynomial bounded Turing and truth-table reducibilities.

Proposition 8: For any recursive languages A, B, and C,
(a) $\{L \mid L \leq_{1i}^{p} A\}$ is recursively presentable
(b) $\{L \mid A \leq_{1i}^{p} L\}$ has the r.r. property
(c) $\{L \mid B \leq_{1i}^{p} A \oplus L\}$ has the r.r. property
(d) $\{L \mid B \leq_{1i}^{p} C \oplus (A \oplus L)\}$ has the r.r. property. (Etc.)

Proof: (a) If $[Q_k]_{k=1}^{\infty}$ is to be the desired presentation, then for each k and all x let Q_k accept x iff $Z_k(x) \in A$. (b) For all i, $A \leq_{1i}^{p} L(M_i)$ $\Leftrightarrow$ $\exists j,k,c$: $S_R(i,\langle j,c\rangle)$ & $[(\forall x)\ x \in A \Leftrightarrow Z_k(x) \in L(M_j)]$. This works because if the first part holds M_j is total and so any failure of the second part can be checked. (c) and (d) are similar to (b). ⁞⁞

The family of classes having the r.r. property is closed under finite unions and intersections, and the same goes for r.p. classes if their intersection contains L^* for some L. We say an infinite list $[\mathcal{C}_m]_{m=1}^{\infty}$ of (necessarily r.p.) classes is recursively presented if there is a recursive universal language U of triples $\langle x,k,m\rangle$ such that for all m, $\mathcal{C}_m = \{\{x \mid \langle x,k,m\rangle \in U\} \mid k \in N\}$. It follows that $\bigcup_{m=1}^{\infty} \mathcal{C}_m$ is also recursively presentable. Hence, combining this with the observation that L^*, $L^{\#}$, and $\{X \mid X\ p^{\#}\ L\}$ are r.p. for any recursive L, we have

Proposition 9: (a) If $\mathcal{C}$ is r.p. then the closures of $\mathcal{C}$ under $*$, $\#$, and $p^{\#}$ are also r.p. The same goes for the r.r. property.
(b) Proposition 8 holds with all languages involved replaced by their respective #- or $p^{\#}$-types on the r.h. side of the set definitions.

This is what we need in the next two sections. Additionally, for any recursive A and B, $\{L \mid A^{\#} \leq_{1i}^{p} L^{\#} \leq_{1i}^{p} B^{\#}\}$ is r.p. if nonempty, and $\{L \mid A^{\#} \sim_{1i}^{p} L^{\#}\}$ has the r.r. property. Taking finite or recursively presented unions of the above classes does not alter these properties.

From now on we make the conventions that $A^{\#} \sim_{1i}^{p} L^{\#}$ means $A^{\#} \leq_{1i}^{p} L^{\#}$ or $L^{\#} \leq_{1i}^{p} A^{\#}$, and that $A^{\#} \not\sim_{1i}^{p} L^{\#}$ means $A^{\#}$ and $L^{\#}$ are incomparable under the LIFP reducibility ordering. Additionally, if $A^{\#} \leq_{1i}^{p} B^{\#}$ but $B^{\#} \not\leq_{1i}^{p} A^{\#}$ we write $A^{\#} <_{1i}^{p} B^{\#}$ for short.

4. Uniform Diagonalization Methods

The answer to the Existential Question for these and other recursively presentable classes is that they exist to be diagonalized out of. The following result, independently discovered in slightly different forms by U. Schöning and P. Chew & M. Machtey and dubbed the "uniform diagonalization theorem" (UDT), provides an elegant, efficient way of accomplishing this automatically. We state the former's version.

Theorem 10 ([Sö81]): Suppose $\mathcal{C}_1$ and $\mathcal{C}_2$ are recursively presentable classes closed under finite variations, and A_1, A_2 are recursive languages such that $A_1 \notin \mathcal{C}_1$, $A_2 \notin \mathcal{C}_2$, and furthermore, $A_1 \in P$, $A_2 \notin \{\emptyset, \Sigma^*\}$. Then we can construct E such that $E \notin \mathcal{C}_1$, $E \notin \mathcal{C}_2$, and yet $E \leq_m^p A_2$.

$\mathcal{C}_1$ may be thought of as the "high" class and $\mathcal{C}_2$ as the "low" class. Example: $\mathcal{C}_1 = \{L \mid L \equiv_m^p L_{SAT}\}$, $\mathcal{C}_2 = P$, $A_1 = \emptyset$, $A_2 = L_{SAT}$; if $NP \neq P$ the hypotheses are satisfied and we have Ladner's result that there are sets in NP which are neither NP-complete nor in P. In most cases one can take $A_1 = \emptyset$, which [CM81] assumes to allow a weaker condition on $\mathcal{C}_1$.

The proof actually only requires that $\mathcal{C}_1$ contain no f.v.'s of A_1 and $\mathcal{C}_2$ no f.v.'s of A_2. It also suffices for $\mathcal{C}_1, \mathcal{C}_2$ merely to have the r.r. property, since we can first intersect both with $\{L \mid L \leq_m^p A_2\}$.

We would like the conclusion of Theorem 10 to say $E \leq_{li}^p A_2$, but whether we can get this in general seems moot. In applying it for languages we would also encounter the difficulty that the classes of Prop. 8 are not in general closed under f.v.'s. Working with #-types, however, removes these problems and lets us craft a special version of the UDT.

Theorem 11: Let B be a recursive language and $\mathcal{C}_1, \mathcal{C}_2$ r.r. classes such that $\emptyset^\# \cap \mathcal{C}_1 = \emptyset$ and $B^\# \cap \mathcal{C}_2 = \emptyset$. Then we can construct E s.t. (a) $E^\# \cap (\mathcal{C}_1 \cup \mathcal{C}_2) = \emptyset$ and (b) $E \leq_{li}^p \emptyset \oplus B$ (so $E^\# \leq_{li}^p B^\#$).

Proof: Aside from modifications for LIFP reducibility and the stylistic change of mixing numbers and strings, the proof basically follows [Sö81].

By the remarks above and Proposition 9 the construction can only be helped by taking the #-closures of $\mathcal{C}_1$ and $\mathcal{C}_2$, and then working with recursive presentations $[P_k]_{k=1}^\infty$ of $\{L \mid L^\# \leq_{li}^p B^\#\} \cap \mathcal{C}_1^\#$ and $[Q_k]_{k=1}^\infty$ of $\{L \mid L^\# \leq_{li}^p B^\#\} \cap \mathcal{C}_2^\#$ instead. Since the latter contains no finite variations of B there must for each $k \in N$ be infinitely many strings in $L(Q_k) \triangle B$. Therefore the functions $q_k: \Sigma^* \to \Sigma^*$ sending strings x to $\min\{z \mid z > x \;\&\; z \in L(Q_k) \triangle B\}$ are recursive for each k, though they need not all be primitive recursive. Since $[Q_k]_{k=1}^\infty$ is recursively enumerated we can majorize them all by a recursive function r_2 given by

$$r_2(a) := \max\{q_k(x) \mid x,k \leq a\} \qquad (a \in \Sigma^*).$$

Similarly, in the case of $\mathcal{C}_1^{\#}$ and $\emptyset$ we obtain recursive functions $p_k: x \mapsto \min\{z \mid z \;\; x \;\&\; z \in L(P_k) \,\Delta\, \emptyset\}$, and subsequently r_1 given by

$$r_1(a) := \max\{p_k(x) \mid x,k \leq a\} \qquad (a \in \Sigma^*).$$

Here r_1 and r_2 are recursive witness functions certifying that $\emptyset \notin \mathcal{C}_1^{\#}$ and $B \notin \mathcal{C}_2^{\#}$. It is possible (see [LLR81]) to find a recursive function s which "out-runs" both of them, and whose <u>gap language</u>, defined to be

$$\underline{G[s]} := \{x \mid s^m(\lambda) < x \leq s^{m+1}(\lambda) \text{ for some even number } m\},$$

is an infinite-coinfinite language <u>in P</u>. (NB: the standard definition of G[s] uses $|x|$ in place of x and 0 for λ.) Now for form's sake we set

$$E := (G[s] \cap B) \cup (\overline{G[s]} \cap \emptyset) \qquad (\text{i.e. } E = G[s] \cap B).$$

First we observe that $E \leq_{1i}^{p} \emptyset \oplus B$ via the LIFP function f defined by

$$f(x) := \begin{cases} 0x & \text{if } x \in \overline{G[s]}, \\ 1x & \text{if } x \in G[s]. \end{cases} \qquad (x \in \Sigma^*).$$

E is in fact nothing but a very "gappy" subset of B. We show that E cannot be in $\mathcal{C}_2^{\#}$; that $E \notin \mathcal{C}_1^{\#}$ follows similarly.

Suppose $E \in \mathcal{C}_2^{\#}$; then by the above we can find k such that $E = L(Q_k)$. Take any even m such that $s^m(\lambda) \geq k$. By the definition of q_k the string $z := q_k(s^m(\lambda))$ is in $B \,\Delta\, L(Q_k) = B \,\Delta\, E$. Observe $s^m(\lambda) < z \leq q_k(s^m(\lambda))$ because q_k is increasing. Since $k \leq s^m(\lambda)$ we have $r_2(s^m(\lambda)) \geq q_k(s^m(\lambda))$, and since s was chosen to majorize r_2, $s(s^m(\lambda)) \geq r_2(s^m(\lambda))$. Therefore $s^m(\lambda) < z \leq s^{m+1}(\lambda)$, and so $z \in G[s]$.

However, any string in G[s] is either in both E and B or in neither, and this contradicts $z \in B \,\Delta\, E$. Hence $E \notin \mathcal{C}_2^{\#}$, and the same for $\mathcal{C}_1^{\#}$. ▦

This is all the diagonalization one need consciously think about in this paper. The same result holds if one replaces # by $p^{\#}$ or any other equivalence extending $\underline{*}$ whose types are r.p. Before delving into applications, however, we pause to consider a consequence of the UDT.

<u>Corollary</u> 12 ([Sö81],[CM81]): Let $\mathcal{D}$ be a class closed under $\leq_m^p$, and suppose $\mathcal{C}$ is a nonempty r.p. class closed under f.v.'s and properly contained in $\mathcal{D}$. Then $\mathcal{D} - \mathcal{C}$ is NOT recursively presentable, (and if $\emptyset^* \cap (\mathcal{D} - \mathcal{C}) = \emptyset$ not presentable by r.e. indices either—[CM81].)

For example, EXPTIME - P is not r.p., and neither is NP - P if NP $\neq$ P. Intuitively speaking, this means it is easy to jump out of an r.p. class $\mathcal{C}$ yet stay within a larger class $\mathcal{D}$ closed under $\leq_m^p$, but not at all easy to jump from the complement of $\mathcal{C}$ in $\mathcal{D}$ back into $\mathcal{C}$. Therein consists the asymmetry between r.p. classes and their complements, which is also reflected in the asymmetrical roles of '$S(i,j)$' and '$\neg S(i,j)$' in Theorem 6. If r.p. classes represent "order" (at least to one's imagination—see [LLR81] and earlier remarks), then non-r.p. classes represent "chaos". In the next section we will show that <u>difference classes</u> such as the following, when nonempty, are so chaotic as to contain any countable poset under the $\leq^p_{1i}$-ordering of their #-types.

<u>Definition</u> 3: For $C \subseteq \Sigma^*$, $\mathcal{D}_C := \{L \mid L \equiv^p_m C\} - \{L \mid L \equiv^p C \times \Sigma^*\}$.

<u>Proposition</u> 13: Let C be recursive, and suppose $\mathcal{D}_C$ is nonempty. Then $\mathcal{D}_C$ is not recursively presentable.

<u>Proof</u>: We point out facts and techniques glossed over later on. Let A be some set in $\mathcal{D}_C$ and put $B = C \times \Sigma^*$. Take $\mathcal{C}_1 = \{L \mid A \oplus L \equiv^p B\}$ and $\mathcal{C}_2 = \{L \mid A \oplus L \in \mathcal{D}_C\}$. $\mathcal{C}_1$ is r.p. because the group G_p of p-isomorphisms is, and the initial assumption that $\mathcal{D}_C$ is r.p. may be seen to imply that $\mathcal{C}_2$ is r.p. as well. Then $\emptyset^\# \cap \mathcal{C}_1 = \emptyset$ and also $B^\# \cap \mathcal{C}_2 = \emptyset$ because $\mathcal{D}_C$ and $\{L \mid L \equiv^p C \times \Sigma^*\}$ are closed under #.

Applying Theorem 11 then gives us a language E such that $E \notin \mathcal{C}_1$, $E \notin \mathcal{C}_2$, and yet $E \leq^p_{1i} \emptyset \oplus B$. (Prop. 2(a) gives $E \leq^p_{1i} B$.) Set $D = A \oplus E$; doing this makes up for $\{L \mid L \equiv^p_m C\}$ not being closed under $\leq^p_m$. As $A \equiv^p_m C$ and $E \leq^p_m B \leq^p_m C$ we have $A \oplus E \equiv^p_m C$, so D is in one of $\mathcal{D}_C$ and $\{L \mid L \equiv^p B\}$. However, either possibility contradicts one of the conditions on E. Therefore $\mathcal{D}_C$, and in fact any superset of $\mathcal{D}_C$ omitting B* for some B s.t. $B \equiv^p C \times \Sigma^*$, cannot be recursively presentable. ⁞⁞⁞

5. <u>Embedding Structures Into Nonempty Difference Classes</u>

We exploit the fact that $\mathcal{D}_A$ when nonempty is not recursively presentable to embed any countable partial order into $\mathcal{D}_A/\#$ (and $\mathcal{D}_A/p^\#$), thereby proving analogues of Young's result. The symbols L and P do double-duty. A poset P is <u>finite-downward</u> if $\forall x \in P$, $\{y \mid y <_P x\}$ is finite. We prove the main theorem after stating three lemmas; we omit the proofs of the first two as they are straightforwardly algorithmic.

<u>Theorem</u> 14: If X and Y are recursive languages such that $X^\# <^p_{1i} Y^\#$ then every countable poset P can be embedded (properly) between $X^\#$ and $Y^\#$ under $\leq^p_{1i}$. If P is finite-downward then existing sups can be preserved.

<u>Lemma</u> 15: Every countable poset P can be extended to a countable lower semilattice L so that existing infs and sups are preserved. L can be chosen to match finiteness or finite-downwardness of P.

Lemma 16: Every countable lower semilattice L admits a bijection $\theta: L \to N$ s.t. for all $x \in L$, $\{y \mid y >_L x \ \& \ \theta(y) < \theta(x)\}$ is a lower semi-sublattice of L (and hence possesses a least element). If L is finite downward, also $\theta(x \vee y) \geq \max\{\theta(x), \theta(y)\}$ for all $x, y \in L$ whose sup exists.

Remarks: Infinite subsets of L need not have infs; for P = the rationals under $\leq$ no countable extension having this property exists. We query whether Lemma 16 holds for any cardinal and the ordinals below it.

Lemma 17: Let A, B, and $C_1, \ldots, C_m$ ($m \in N$) be recursive languages such that $A^\# <^p_{1i} B^\#$ strictly. Then we can construct a recursive D such that

(a) $A^\# <^p_{1i} D^\# <^p_{1i} B^\#$

(b) for each i, if $C_i^\# \not\leq^p_{1i} A^\#$ and $B^\# \not\leq^p_{1i} C_i^\#$, then $D^\# \not\sim^p_{1i} C_i^\#$

(c) for each pair i,j, if $C_j^\# \not\leq^p_{1i} C_i^\# \oplus A^\#$, then $C_j^\# \not\leq^p_{1i} C_i^\# \oplus D^\#$.

Proof: Define three relevant subsets of $\{1 \ldots m\}$: $\underline{R} := \{i \mid C_i^\# \not\leq^p_{1i} A^\#\}$, $\underline{S} := \{i \mid B^\# \not\leq^p_{1i} C_i^\#\}$, and $\underline{T} := \{(i,j) \mid C_j^\# \not\leq^p_{1i} C_i^\# \oplus A^\#\}$. Here R and S correspond to the conditions of (b), and T to those of (c). Then set

$$\mathcal{C}_1 = \{L \mid B^\# \leq^p_{1i} A^\# \oplus L^\#\} \cup \Big(\bigcup_{i \in R} \{L \mid C_i^\# \leq^p_{1i} A^\# \oplus L^\#\}\Big) \cup \Big(\bigcup_{i,j \in T} \{L \mid C_j^\# \leq^p_{1i} C_i^\# \oplus (A^\# \oplus L^\#)\}\Big);$$

$$\mathcal{C}_2 = \{L \mid L^\# \leq^p_{1i} A^\#\} \cup \Big(\bigcup_{i \in S} \{L \mid L^\# \leq^p_{1i} C_i^\#\}\Big).$$

By earlier results, $\mathcal{C}_1$ and $\mathcal{C}_2$ are #-closed classes having the r.r. property ($\mathcal{C}_2$ is r.p.), and the conditions on R, S, and T ensure that $\emptyset \notin \mathcal{C}_1$ and $B \notin \mathcal{C}_2$. The UDT then yields E s.t. $E \notin \mathcal{C}_1$, $E \in \mathcal{C}_2$, and $E^\# \leq^p_{1i} B^\#$. Then taking $D = A \oplus E$ satisfies (a), (b), and (c). ∎

Remark: The lemma holds even with infinitely many C_i's so long as the sublists determined by R, S, and T are recursively presentable.

Proof of Theorem 14: Embed P in L using Lemma 15, and let $[x_i]_{i=1}^\infty$ be the enumeration of L obtained from Lemma 16. Let X and Y correspond to extra least and greatest elements x_0 and y respectively attached to L. For Stage 0 map x_0 to X, also calling the latter D_0, and map y to Y.

At Stage n, $n \geq 1$, let $D_0, \ldots, D_{n-1}$ be the already-constructed images of $x_0, \ldots, x_{n-1}$ respectively. Define $\underline{J} := \{i \mid x_i <_L x_n,\ i \leq n-1\}$, and set $A = \oplus_{i \in J} D_i$. If $x_n = \sup_L \{x_i \mid i \in J\}$ then take $D_n = A$ and go on to Stage n+1. If not, then take B to be Y or D_k according to whether $\{x_i \mid x_i >_L x_n \ \& \ i \leq n-1\}$ is empty or not, where in the latter case k is the index of the least element promised by Lemma 16. For the C-list in Lemma 17 take $D_0,\ldots,D_{n-1}$ and $\oplus_{i\in I} D_i$ for all $I \subseteq \{0,\ldots,n-1\}$. Use the lemma to construct D_n and proceed to the next stage.

Clearly $x_i <_L x_n \Rightarrow D_i^{\#} <^p_{1i} D_n^{\#}$ and $x_n <_L x_j \Rightarrow D_n^{\#} <^p_{1i} D_j^{\#}$ for all i,j. For all j, $x_j \not<_L x_n \Rightarrow D_j^{\#} \not<^p_{1i} D_n^{\#}$ so long as $D_j \not\leq^p_{1i} A^{\#}$. Therefore the entire lower semilattice can be order-embedded (in a sup-preserving way if $[x_i]_{i=1}^{\infty}$ from Lemma 16 allows it) so long as the last bit always holds.

Suppose it doesn't, so that for some minimal index j, $D_j^{\#} \leq^p_{1i} A^{\#}$ but $x_j \not<_L x_n$. Note: $j \notin J$. Say a subset J' of J has Property Z if we have $D_j^{\#} \leq^p_{1i} \oplus_{i\in J'} D_i^{\#}$. We filter the set $\{D_i \mid x_i <_L x_n \ \&\ i \leq n-1\}$ by first removing any language which is the $\oplus$ of two-or-more others in the set, and second, by considering leftover elements in nondecreasing order under $\leq^p_{1i}$ and removing them if doing so does not destroy Property Z. Represent the final set so obtained as $\{D_{i_1},\ldots,D_{i_k}\}$, in order of increasing indices. Last, put $Z := D_{i_1} \oplus \ldots \oplus D_{i_k}$, so that $D_j^{\#} \leq^p_{1i} Z^{\#} \leq^p_{1i} A^{\#}$.

If $j > i_k$, first suppose that D_j was chosen as the $\oplus$ of earlier-constructed languages. By minimality of the index j the elements of L corresponding to th se languages all lie below x_n in L, and since x_j was meant to be their sup in L, $x_j <_L x_n$, contradicting $x_j \not<_L x_n$. Else, some language A_j and an earlier-constructed $B_j \in \{D_0,\ldots,D_{j-1}\}$ were used as "A" and "B" in applying Lemma 17 at Stage j. By the minimality of j we must have $B_j^{\#} \not\leq^p_{1i} A^{\#}$, so $B_j^{\#} \not\leq^p_{1i} Z^{\#}$ and clearly $Z^{\#} \not\leq^p_{1i} A_j^{\#}$. However, since $D_{i_1},\ldots,D_{i_k}$ were all constructed by Stage j their $\oplus$, namely Z, was on the C-list in the application of Lemma 17 at that stage, and so by (b) D_j was constructed s.t. $D_j^{\#} \not<^p_{1i} Z^{\#}$. This contradicts $D_j \leq^p_{1i} Z^{\#}$.

For the case $j < i_k$, we use (c) of Lemma 17 to derive a similar contradiction. Let A_k be the language that was chosen as "A" at Stage i_k. If D_{i_k} was chosen equal to A_k then D_{i_k} is the $\oplus$ of two or more languages with indices in J, contradicting the way $\{D_{i_1},\ldots,D_{i_k}\}$ was produced above. Else, we know that $A_k^{\#} <^p_{1i} D_{i_k}^{\#}$ and hence, as we can verify, that $D_j^{\#} \leq^p_{1i} D_{i_1}^{\#} \oplus \ldots \oplus D_{i_{k-1}}^{\#} \oplus A_k^{\#}$ cannot hold. For if it did, then A_k could be written as the $\oplus$ of languages in $\{D_i \mid x_i <_L x_n \ \&\ i \leq n-1\}$ which survive the first round of filtering, and which by the order in which the second round is taken are still there when D_{i_k} comes up for removal; but then D_{i_k} would already have been removed. Therefore, setting $C_i := D_{i_1} \oplus \ldots \oplus D_{i_{k-1}}$ we have $D_j^{\#} \not\leq^p_{1i} C_i^{\#} \oplus A_k^{\#}$, and so by (c) of Lemma 17, D_{i_k} was constructed at Stage i_k to satisfy $D_j^{\#} \not\leq^p_{1i} C_i^{\#} \oplus D_{i_k}^{\#} = Z^{\#}$. This also contradicts $D_j^{\#} \leq^p_{1i} Z^{\#}$, completing the proof of the theorem. ▪

Remarks: The embedding does not necessarily preserve infs, not even of two elements. We do not know whether finite-downwardness is needed for the preservation of all sups. Whether and which lattices can be embedded as lattices makes an interesting question in conjunction with known recursion-theoretic results. If L and the set of pairs in L possessing sups are recursive, the embedding can be done recursively by keeping track of the sets R, S, and T at each stage. In particular, $[D_i]_{i=1}^{\infty}$ will be recursively presented and usable as an adjunct to the C-list, so that the embedding can be repeated afresh by #-types incomparable with everything in the original—and as often as desired.

Choosing representatives tells us that languages pairwise incomparable under $\leq_{1i}^{p}$ exist, indeed infinitely many of them. We query whether denseness under $\leq_{1i}^{p}$ holds for languages in general. For size-<u>nondecreasing</u> invertible p-reducibility [Yg83] shows dense language chains do exist.

Since $\mathcal{D}_C$ nonempty implies $\neg(A\ p^{\#}\ C \times \Sigma^*)$ for any $A \in \mathcal{D}_C$, and Lemma 17 works just as well when stated for $p^{\#}$-types, the embedding can be done with $p^{\#}$-types as elements so that the image is a sub-partial-order of $(\mathcal{D}_C / p^{\#}, \leq_{1i}^{p})$. It is a sub-upper-semilattice if the original poset is an upper semilattice that is finite downward. Similar things can be done for weaker reducibilities such as $\leq_1^p$ and $\leq_m^p$. Since (REC, $\leq_m^p$) is already an upper semilattice and the required classes are automatically closed under f.v.'s, a simpler version of Lemma 17 suffices to embed any countable poset into, say, NP - P if nonempty. We remark, however, that if nonempty (NP - P, $\leq_m^p$) is not a lattice (see [LLR81]), and this hints at the unlikelihood of getting lattice-embeddings in general.

6. <u>Concluding Remarks About Diagonalization</u>

Suppose a heavenly messenger reliable for speaking truths provable in set theory were to announce, "All NP-complete sets are p-isomorphic, and so P $\neq$ NP (etc.) But it will not stop raining until you prove it." How would we go about it? We have seen that diagonalization is a felicitous tool for generating complex mathematical structures, but here we would have to show that the structures of the last section do <u>not</u> exist. This puts the task at hand on the wrong side of the asymmetries observed in conjunction with Theorem 6 and Corollary 12. The familiar notion of diagonalization as discussed here is not on the side of the angels.

D. Kozen in [Kz80], observing the recursiveness of the witness functions for any r.p. class, uses this to advance a notion for which "If NP $\neq$ P is provable at all, then it is provable by diagonalization." Since witness functions such as those of Theorem 11 need not be primitive recursive even when the presentation is, there is in general no way of predicting when the required witnesses will appear, and the round lot of theorists seem not to accept this notion as "effective". In the most familiar cases the identity pops up as the required witness function.

The natural meeting ground, then, might be "primitive recursive diagonalization." However, we can hint that this notion is still too strong.

Proposition 18: Given any recursive universal language U for P we can, under the assumption NP $\neq$ P, construct a language E $\in$ NP - P such that no witness function for E with respect to U is primitive recursive.

Proof: PRIM is itself r.p.; let $[Z_k]_{k=1}^{\infty}$ present it and $[Q_k]_{k=1}^{\infty}$, NP. Then for each j,k let R_{jk} be a machine that mimics Q_k on input x if for all $m \leq x$, $Z_j(m) \in L(Q_k) \Delta U_m$, and otherwise accepts x iff $x \in L_{SAT}$. Using the UDT with P and whatever class is presented by $[R_{jk}]_{j,k=1}^{\infty}$ yields E. ▒

There is nothing special about P or NP here, or even PRIM; DTIME[t] would serve as well for any recursive t. The result may not say much about e.g. the fixed case $E = L_{SAT}$, but it supports our final point: if we restrict ourselves to such a notion of "effective" diagonalization we can probably prove only the opposite kinds of results from the ones we desire.

Acknowledgements: The author wishes to thank Dr. Uwe Schöning for suggestions and comments helpful in preparing this work, and the anonymous referees for suggestions on how to tighten the final draft.

References

[BH77] L. Berman and J. Hartmanis. On isomorphisms and density of NP and other complete sets. SIAM J. Comp. 6, 1977, pp 305-321.

[CM81] P. Chew and M. Machtey. A note on structure and looking-back (...) J. Comp. Sys. Sci. 22, 1981, pp 53-59.

[HU79] J. Hopcroft and J. Ullman. Introduction to Automata Theory, Languages, And Computation. (Reading, Mass: Addison-Wesley 1979)

[Kz80] D. Kozen. Indexings of subrecursive classes. Theoretical Computer Science 11, 1980, pp 277-301.

[Lad75] R. Ladner. On the structure of polynomial-time reducibility. J. ACM 22, 1975, pp 155-171.

[LLR81] L. Landweber, R. Lipton, and E. Robertson. On the structure of sets in NP and other classes. TCS 15, 1981, pp 181-200.

[Re82] K. Regan. Computability, enumerability, and the polynomial hierarchy. M.Sc. qualifying dissertation, Oxford, 1982.

[Re83] K. Regan. Arithmetical degrees of index sets for complexity classes. Draft, in preparation for submission to TCS in 1983.

[Rog67] H. Rogers. Theory of Recursive Functions and Effective Computability. (New York: McGraw-Hill, 1967).

[Sö81] U. Schöning. Untersuchungen zur Struktur von NP... Ph.D. dissertation, Stuttgart, 1981.

[Sö82] U. Schöning. A uniform approach to obtaining diagonal sets in complexity classes. Theor. Comp. Sci. 18, 1982, pp 95-103.

[Yg83] P. Young. Some structural properties of polynomial reducibilities and sets in NP. Proc. 15th ACM Symp., 1983.

A NEW SOLUTION FOR THE BYZANTINE GENERALS PROBLEM+

(extended abstract)

Rüdiger K. Reischuk *
Fachbereich Informatik
Universität des Saarlandes
6600 Saarbrücken
West-Germany

ABSTRACT: We define a new model for algorithms to reach Byzantine Agreement. It allows to measure the complexity more accurately, to differentiate between processor faults and to include communication link failures. A deterministic algorithm is presented that exhibits early stopping by phase $2f+4$ in the worst case, where f is the actual number of faults, under less stringent conditions than the ones of previous algorithms. Also its average performance can easily be analysed making realistic assumptions on random distributions of faults. We show that it stops with high probability after a small number of phases.

1. Introduction

The Byzantine Generals Problem has first been studied in [PSL]. It serves as a model for a distributed system of n completely interconnected processors of which some may be faulty. They want to reach a type of agreement called Byzantine Agreement on a value which one of them, the transmitter, holds.

Byzantine Agreement (BA) is achieved when:

(I) all correctly operating processors agree on the same value, and
(II) if the transmitter is correct, then all correctly operating processors agree on its value.

This problem seems to be basic for reliable distributed computation. We would like to refer the reader to [PSL] and papers appeared later [LF, Da, DLM, DSa, DSb, DSc, DSd, FFL, DFFLS, DR, DRS] for detailed discussion.

These papers prove lower bounds for algorithms to reach BA for various complexity measures as the time or the amount of information exchange and also give several deterministic algorithms for it. We assume that information exchange always takes place in synchronous phases. An algorithm may either be authenticated or nonauthenticated. In the first case the processors share a signature scheme which allows each one to sign messages, such that nobody else can alter a signed message or forge a signature. The only assumption in the nonauthenticated case is that each processor can uniquely identify the sender of a message. Here we will only consider nonauthenticated algorithms.

It has been observed that one should distinguish between two different kinds of agreement: Immediate and Eventual Byzantine Agreement (IBA and EBA). IBA also requires that the correct processors unanimously agree on the time when the agreement is achieved. See [DRS] for further details.

+ Research was done while visiting the IBM Research Laboratory, San Jose, California

* New Address: Fakultät für Mathematik, Universität Bielefeld, 4800 Bielefeld 1

The main results relevant to this paper can be summarized by the following:

(1.1) To reach Byzantine Agreement by a nonnauthenticated algorithm the number of faulty processors must be less than 1/3 of the total number of processors [PSL].

(1.2) If t is a bound for the maximum number of faults an algorithm is supposed to handle and $f < t$ is the actual number of faults then in no case IBA can be reached before phase $t + 1$ and in the worst case EBA not before phase $f + 2$ [LF, DSb, DSd].

Four different types of nonauthenticated algorithms are known. The first three work for any ratio between correct and incorrect processors as long as (1.1) is satisfied. The algorithm in [PSL] reaching IBA matches the lower bound of $t+1$ phases, but requires exchanging an amount of information which is exponential in t. The others only send a small number of messages polynomial in n and t. The algorithm presented in [DDFLS] runs $2t+3$ phases and achieves IBA. Both algorithms in [DRS] reach EBA and have a worst case time bound of $\min\{2f+5, 2t+3\}$, resp. $\min\{f+2, t+1\}$. The last algorithm is optimal with respect to time, but it can be used only if the number of faults is relatively small $(n > 2t^2 + O(t))$.

For a distributed system it may be unlikely, but not absolutely impossible that a certain percentage of processors (for example 1 percent) becomes faulty. Then a large system (let's say 10,000 processors) may not reach BA in t (= 100) phases. To guarantee IBA in any circumstances the system always has to wait more than that number of phases even in situations when there are no faults at all.

The (worst-case) time-bound $f+2$ for EBA should be expected significantly smaller in general, but for every large system this number may still be much bigger than let's say 5 or 10, in most cases. Thus one would like to have algorithms which for large f reach EBA considerably faster than $f+2$ in most cases where the system contains f faulty processors. The algorithms in [DRS] do not seem to possess this property unless one makes very stringent assumptions on the behavior of faulty processors. This problem is not shared by the algorithm below. Other improvements will be discussed in the following.

The performance of algorithms to reach BA has been evaluated so far only by their time complexity and the amount of information the processors are required to exchange. We think that it is also important to measure how much internal computation each processor has to do, in particular how much memory space it needs to store the current state of the algorithm from its point of view. For example, the algorithm in [PSL] does not only require to exchange an exponential number of messages, each processor also has to store all the incoming information till phase $t+1$ when it is able to decide on the value. This is necessary because the decision function heavily depends on every single message ever received, and there seems to be no way to simplify the evaluation of this particular function.

In section 2 we generalize and at the same time simplify the notion of agreement algorithm as defined in [DSd, DRS]. The behavior of a processor at a given phase does no longer depend on all the messages received so far, rather each processor makes transitions between states which only depend on the messages of the current phase.

We also consider the problem which processors have to be considered faulty and for which period of time. Let us call a run of a BA algorithm a history. The known algorithms require to count a processor as a faulty one for the whole history whenever it made a single mistake at some point of time. For a large distributed system performing extended computation this may not be very satisfying, because during a long history almost all processors might be down at least for a little while.

Therefore it would be of interest to have a notion of incorrectness that better differenciates between different kinds of faulty behavior. We would like to have algorithms that reach agreement for any number of faulty processors as long as only a small number of faults occurs within each phase. This does not contradict (1.1), since in our present context that result should be stated more precisely:

(1.3) Byzantine Agreement cannot be achieved for histories for which in each phase 1/3 or more processors may be faulty.

An algorithm that handles more faults spreaded over the time has to reintegrate processors that temporarily went down. For this purpose the complexity of the internal computation is also an important factor. If during the time a processor was incorrect the algorithm changed into a different and complex state, it may not be possible or involve too much work to provide it with the information needed to continue correct computation.

Finally we also want to include communication link failures as possible faults. In [DSc] it is shown how to convert a convential algorithm that can stand t faulty processors into an algorithm that also handles some communications link failures. The modified algorithm achieves BA for all histories for which there exists a set of at most t processors, that include all processors ever faulty in that history, and the sender or the receiver of a link that ever failed. All the remaining processors (and also other correct processors with not too many faulty links) will agree on the same value.

However a simple analysis shows that, if in practice the probability of a link failure is fixed or more likely increases with the size n of the distributed system, then for any $\alpha > 0$ with probability tending to 1 there is no set of processors of size αn without any link failures between processors in it. Thus a set which covers all the link failures has to include almost all processors, but such a situation cannot be handled by any nonauthenticated algorithm (1.1).

In section 3 we describe the algorithm. Its worst case time complexity is $2f+4$ and it works for any number of faults if one of the following conditions holds:

(1.4) There are no communication link failures and for each three consecutive phases less than 1/6 of the total number of processors behave faulty.

(1.5) Within each phase the ratio between the number of processors, that are faulty or have more than a certain number Γ (to be defined later) of faulty communication links, and the total number of processors is less than 1/20.

Section 4 contains some comments on reintegration and synchronization. Finally we analyse the expected run-time of the algorithm and estimate the probability that condition (1.4) or (1.5) stay true for a long time interval.

2. A Model for Agreement Algorithms

Let $PR = \{p_1,\dots,p_n\}$ be a set of n processors. For $1 \le i, j \le n$ there is a communication link from p_i to p_j, this means we assume complete interconnection between processors. p_1 is a distinguished processor called <u>transmitter</u>. Let ST_p be a set of states for $p \in PR$, V be the set of values the transmitter may possibly hold, and let MSG denote a set of messages the processors may send to each other. We think of MSG as the powerset of some set of <u>atomic</u> messages.

An agreement algorithm for PR is defined by a set of functions $\{F_p, M_p | p \in PR\}$ with

$$F_p : MSG^n \times ST_p \to ST_p \quad \text{and}$$

$$M_p : ST_p \to MSG^n \quad .$$

The algorithm consists of running synchronous phases of message sending, message receiving and internal computation (state transition). Such a sequence of phases is called a history. According to the message sending function M_p which depends on its current state processor p is supposed to send messages to other processors at the beginning of a phase. At the end of a phase processor p will receive the messages sent to it by other processors during that phase and depending on this information and its current state change into a new state as specified by the state transition function F_p . This state will also be the state of p at the beginning of the next phase.

For receiving as for sending messages the i-th element of a sequence from MSG^n when applied to F_p , resp. produced by M_p denotes the information transfer between p and processor p_i . (We make the technical assumption that each processor also sends a message to itself.)

For the transmitter ST_p includes states σ_v for $v \in V$ corresponding to the values it may hold, while for other processors there is just one state σ_0 in which p starts. Each ST_p also includes a final state τ_A for each subset A of V . We require that for a final state s $M_p(s)$ equals the sequence of empty messages. Notice that we do not necessarily exclude transitions from final states back into nonfinal states.

The algorithm is uniform if the pairs of functions are the same for all processors and if the message sending function always produces a sequence of equal messages. All the known algorithms are almost completely uniform. The algorithm which will be presented below has this property to a much less extent.

In each phase each processor p and each communication link (p,q) from p to a processor q is either in the faulty or nonfaulty mode. Assume that we are given an agreement algorithm and in a history H processor p is in state s at the end of phase $k-1$. If in phase k of H p is in the nonfaulty mode it sends out the sequence of messages $M_p(s)$ at the beginning of that phase, otherwise it may send anything. If q and edge (p,q) are nonfaulty q at the end of phase k actually receives the message sent by p , otherwise q may receive anything. Let Y be the sequence of messages p received at phase k . In the nonfaulty mode p goes into the new state $F_p(Y,s)$. Otherwise it may also enter other states, such a transition will be called <u>incorrect</u> .

For $0 \le \gamma \le 1$ a processor p is <u>γ-correct</u> at a given phase if p, at least γn of the n edges with target p and at least γn edges leaving from p are in the nonfaulty mode during that phase.

Let Q be a condition on the set of histories for processors PR and j be a natural number including infinity. We say that under condition Q an agreement algorithm $\{(F_p, M_p) | p \in PR\}$ <u>reaches Eventual Byzantine Agreement for j-finally γ-correct processors by phase k</u> if, for each k phase history H on PR which satisfies Q, the following conditions hold:

(I) There exist $1 \le \ell \le k$ such that all processors, which are γ-correct from phase $\ell - j + 1$ to phase ℓ have reached the same final state by phase ℓ and don't change it anymore unless they become faulty.

(II) If p is γ-correct from phase $\ell - j + 1$ to phase ℓ and the transmitter is γ-correct at the first phase, then the final state of p at phase ℓ corresponds to the value of the transmitter.

If in addition holds:

(III) All processors, which are γ-correct from phase $\ell - j + 1$ to ℓ, reach their final state <u>at</u> phase ℓ,

then we call this agreement <u>immediate</u>.

j measures how much time we are willing to spend till a once faulty processor has to be reintegrated and to agree with the other correct processors. The previously known algorithms reach agreement for j equal infinity and $\gamma = 1$. We would like to reach agreement with j as small as possible and some $\gamma < 1$.

It also depends on condition Q how fast fault recovery has to be achieved. Previous paper always required that within the whole algorithm at most $t < n/3$ processors ever behave faulty, this means no fault recovery was necessary, but the set of admitted histories was rather limited. An algorithm with good fault recovery might work correct on less stringent conditions.

Similar to (1.1) it can easily be shown that for a set of histories, in which at each phase up to ρn processors may be faulty, BA can be achieved only if $\gamma + \rho < 1/3$. Also, if one wants to reach EBA before phase $t+1$, from (1.2) follows that no algorithm can guarantee that every processor stops at the same time (immediately). This indicates that in general $j = 1$ might not be achievable.

3. The Algorithm

In this section we will present the basic algorithm for reaching Eventual Byzantine Agreement. Assume that n equals $\delta m+1$ for some natural numbers δ and m. We require that during the algorithm one of the following conditions hold:

(3.1) $\delta=6$ and for each three consecutive phases at most m processors are not 1-correct within one of these phases.

(3.2) $\delta=20$ and within each phase less than εn processors are not γ-correct, where $\varepsilon=1/20$ and $\gamma=19/20$ . .

We will use two other parameters α and β and chose $\alpha=1$ and $\beta=0$ in case of (3.1) and $\alpha=3$ and $\beta=1$ for (3.2) . As atomic messages only v and v_* for $v \in V$ will be needed, where $*$ is one of the following tags: "low" or "high" . In order to present the algorithm we must specify functions F_p and M_p . The sending of messages will not depend on the receiver, therefore we regard the value of M_p as a single element, the message that p will send to every processor.

At some phase k during the algorithm it may happen that a processor p has not yet reached a final state, but there are no values (atomic messages) p has to send at that phase. Since other processor must be able to distinguish this case from the one, in which p does not send messages anymore, because it has reached a final state, we make the following convention: in the first case we write $M_p = \emptyset$ (p sends a message, but it does not contain any values), while $M_p = \lambda$ means that p does not send any message.

The set ST_p of states for p includes elements (A,B,k) from $[2^V] \times [2^V] \times \{1,2,\ldots\}$ with the following interpretation: A is the set of values which have high support, while B contains values with low support. k is a counter for the current phase.

We require that the system is completely synchronized and that an incorrect transition of a processor may only influence the first two segments of its state. This means even during phases in which a processor is in the faulty mode it has to stay synchronized with the other processors. Later we will show how these conditions can be relaxed.

In the model of section 2 final states don't have a counter for the current phase. If the state transition function excludes leaving a final state this is obviously not necessary. But the algorithm below will force a (correct) processor p to return back from a final state into a nonfinal state, if p entered the final state by an incorrect transition. In this case p had to know the current phase number.

Since in any case we will drop the conditions on synchronization later, we omit to attach phase numbers also to final states when describing the basic algorithm below.

Let $k \geq 1$ and $f(k) = \lfloor k'/2 \rfloor$ where $k' \equiv k \bmod (2n)$ and $1 \leq k' \leq 2n$. We will use the auxiliary functions

$$W_{low}, W_{high}, W_k : V \times MSG^n \rightarrow \{1,\ldots,n\}$$

W_k will be used to lay importance on the special processor for phase k which will be $p_{f(k)}$. For $v \in V$ and $X \in MSG^n$ $W_{low}(v,X)$ counts how many elements of X include either v_{low} or v_{high}.
$W_{high}(v,X)$ counts only elements that include v_{high}.
$W_k(v,X)$ equals $W_{low}(v,X)$ if the $f(k)$-th element of X includes v_{high}, otherwise it equals $W_{high}(v,X)$.

For a set $Y \in 2^V$ $[Y]_{high}$ denotes the set $\{y_{high} | y \in Y\}$. The same notation will be used for the tag "low".

Let $A \in 2^V$ and $X = (X_1,\ldots,X_n) \in MSG^n$. We say that predicate FINAL(A,X) holds iff besides $(\alpha+\beta)m$ all the remaining X_i equal either $[A]_{high}$ or λ.
This predicate expresses a condition for a processor to enter a final state: a vast majority of processors either has stopped or sends the same set of values with high support and supports no other values.

Rule 1. (Initialization)

If v is the transmitter's value then p_1 is in state σ_v at the beginning of the first phase, every other processor is in state σ_0.

Rule 2. (Definition of M)

$M_p(\sigma_v) = \{v\}$, $M_p(\sigma_0) = \lambda$.
If $s = (A,B,k)$ with $A,B \in 2^V$ and $k \geq 1$ then $M_p(s) = [A]_{high} \cup [B]_{low}$.
For any other state s $M_p(s) = \lambda$.

(Notice that by convention in case 2 for $A = B = \emptyset$ processor p sends the empty set as its message, while for a final state it sends no message at all. This will become important for the evaluation of predicate FINAL.)

Rule 3. (Definition of F)

Phase 1: Let $x \in MSG$, $y \in MSG^{n-1}$ and $s \in \{\sigma_0\} \cup \{\sigma_v | v \in V\}$.
If $x = \{v\}$ with $v \in V$ then $F_p(x,y,s) = (x,\emptyset,1)$,
else $F_p(x,y,s) = (\emptyset,\emptyset,1)$.

Phase k > 1: Assume that at the beginning of phase k p is in state s and receives messages $X \in MSG^n$. Define $A,B \in 2^V$ by:

For $p \neq p_{f(k)}$ $v \in V$ belongs to A iff $W_k(v,X) > (4\alpha+\beta)m$,
otherwise it belongs to B iff $W_k(v,X) > (2\alpha+\beta)m$.
For $p_{f(k)}$ v belongs to A iff $W_k(v,X) > (3\alpha+\beta)m$ and B is empty.

If $s = (C,D,k-1)$ with $C,D \in 2^V$ and FINAL(C,X) holds then $F_p(s,X) = \tau_C$.
If $s = \tau_C$ for $C \in 2^V$ and FINAL(C,X) holds then $F_p(s,X) = s$.
In any other case $F_p(s,X) = (A,B,k)$.

Theorem 1: For $n = 6m+1$ the algorithm above reaches EBA for 2-finally correct processors by phase $k+2$ for all histories, in which no link failures occur, at each consecutive three phases at most m processors are faulty within these phases and the special processor of phase $k-1$ and k is the same and in both phases correct. If the transmitter is correct at phase 1, then this is already achieved at phase 3 .

In particular, if we do not differenciate between temporary and permanent faults and do not require reintegration (j equals infinity), we get

Theroem 2: The above algorithm reaches EBA by phase $2f+4$ for histories, in which at most f processors are ever faulty.

Theorem 3: For $n = 20m+1$ and $\gamma = 19/20$ the algorithm above reaches EBA for 2-finally γ-correct processors by phase $k+2$ for all histories that satisfy the following condition: at each phase at most m processors are either faulty or have more than m faulty outgoing or more than m faulty incoming links, and the special processor of phase $k-1$ and k is the same and γ-correct in both phases.

These Theorems can be proved by a series of Lemmata stating several properties of the algorithm. We won't give a proof here, a complete version can be found in [R] .

4. Complexity Analysis, Reintegration and Synchronization

In the definition of the state transition function F one can add the constraint that each element of the sequence X of messages received at phase 2 has to be a single value, otherwise it is replaced by the empty set. This prevents a faulty processor from introducing more than one value at phase 2 and implies:

(4.1) For each history that satisfies either (3.1) or (3.2) there is a set W of at most 5 values with the property: If p made a correct transition into state (A,B,k) and $k > 1$, then the sets A and B contain only elements from W.

Thus the number of atomic messages correct processors have to exchange in each phase is bounded by $O(n^2)$.

If within a given history at most f processors are faulty we get a worst case upper bound $O(n^2+n^2*f)$ for the total number of messages, which is better by roughly a factor n compared to the algorithms in [DRS]. From (4.1) follows that at phase k every correct processors can specify its actual state by $\log k + O(\log|V|)$ bits. If V contains many elements each processor might encode the actual values it has to consider after the first phase by short strings and store this encoding in memory.

Changing states requires only very simple computation. In addition, for all but final states a current state s of a processor p is almost independent of the former state s'. s is influenced only indirectly by s' through the message p sends to itself. For large n one could almost neglect such kind of messages. In particular, assume that a processor was down for a while and comes up again without any knowledge about the present state of the algorithm except the number of the current phase. After receiving and correctly processing the messages of one phase it can immediately continue its part in the algorithm as if it had been correct all the time.

Finally we want to weaken the condition on synchronization. So far we required that the correct processors are completely synchronized and that even a faulty processor stays synchronized with the correct processors. What we actually need is that its clock shows the correct time at the moment when it goes back into the nonfaulty mode.

Instead of complete synchronization it is sufficient that the individual clocks differ by only a small amount δ, which is considerably smaller that the length of a phase Δ, and that the system peridiodically updates the individual clocks, for example by running another EBA algorithm.

For the purpose of reintegration let each processor include in its messages the current phase number. If a processor p has lost synchronization during the time it was faulty and wants to return into the correct mode at a certain point, within time 2Δ it will receive at least $n-m$ messages carrying the same phase number, assume this number is k. Let p chop off the first m and the last m messages with time stamp k, since they might have been sent by faulty processors either too early or too late and take for example the average of the time when the remaining messages were received. This approximately gives the point of time in phase k, when every processor expects the incoming messages. Till a new clock synchronization algorithm is finished p can set its clock according to this value and it will deviate from the others by only a small amount.

5. Probabilistic Analysis

In the preceeding sections we analysed the worst-case behavior of the new algorithm. We now want to evaluate the performance under the assumption that faults are distributed in some random way. Only the question whether a processor or a communication link is in the faulty or nonfaulty mode will be determined by a random variable. If a fault actually occurs we don't make any assumptions on what kind of fault it is. The analysis will cover the worst things that may happen, like sending wrong information on purpose and forming collusions with other faulty processors.

Let S be either a processor or a communication link, $k \geq 1$ and $R(S,k)$ a random variable with values 0 or 1. S is in the nonfaulty mode at phase k if $R(S,k) = 1$, otherwise it is faulty. We require that $R(S,k)$ and $R(S',k')$ are independent for $S \neq S'$. For a distributed system one can assume that a failure of one processor does not influence the correct behavior of anybody else. Also a communication link can be considered as consisting of three parts, the communication channel itself and the connections of the channel to the two parties. If we count a failure of a connection as a fault of the corresponding processor, the independence of processors and communication channels can be justified.

Let $p(S,k)$ be the probability that $R(S,k)$ equals 0 and p (resp. q) be the maximum of $p(S,k)$ for $k \geq 1$ and all processors S (resp. links S). We can assume

(5.1) the probability for the event $\{R(S,k-1) = 0 \text{ or } R(S,k) = 0\}$ does not exceed $2p$,

since a failure of S at phase $k-1$ is more likely to induce also a failure at phase k.

For $j \geq 1$ let $A(j)$ be the event:

$$\{R(p_1,1) = 0 \text{ and for all } 2 \leq \ell \leq j \text{ holds: } R(p_\ell,2\ell-1) = 0 \text{ or } R(p_\ell,2\ell) = 0\}$$

It follows

$$\text{Prob}(A(j)) \leq p*(2p)^j \quad .$$

If for a history H satisfying (3.1) the algorithm has not reached EBA by phase k, then by Theorem 1 H must belong to $A(j)$ for $j = \lfloor k/2 \rfloor - 1$.

<u>Theorem 4:</u> Let H be a history that satisfies condition (3.1) and the above assumption on the probability distribution of processor faults. Then the algorithm described in section 3 reaches EBA for 2-finally correct processors by phase k with probability at least

$1-p$ for $k = 3$ and
$1-p\,(2p)^j$ for $k > 3$ and $j = \lfloor k/2 \rfloor - 2$.

For example, for $p = 5\,\%$ the algorithm will reach agreement within 6 phases with probability at least 0,995 and its average runtime is smaller than 4 .

We now consider the case where communication links may also be faulty. The probability p' that a given processor S is not γ-correct at a given phase can be bounded by the probability p that S is not correct plus the probability that at least $\rho n = (1-\gamma)n$ of its links are incorrect, which does not exceed

$$\sum_{j=\rho n}^{n} \binom{n}{i} q^{i} (1-q)^{n-1} \quad .$$

For $q < \rho$ this expression decreases exponentially with n . For example, for $n = 100$, $\gamma = 19/20$ and $q = 2\,\%$ the sum is less than $1\,\%$. If we replace p by p' the analysis above applies directly for histories that satisfy condition (3.2), and for the probability that the algorithm terminates fast we get the same bounds.

Finally we want to estimate the probability that the conditions (3.1) and (3.2) hold for a sequence of phases of length L . In practice, having only estimations for the probability of faults in the distributed system we cannot guarantee that these conditions hold for every history. But if we know that with high probability they stay true for quite a long time, then, even when repeatedly running this algorithm, we have to expect only very few inconsistent agreements.

Condition (3.1) (resp. (3.2)) are obviously satisfied if at each phase

(5.2) less than $\zeta = 1/18$ of the total number of processors are faulty,

resp.

(5.3) less than $\zeta' = 1/20$ of all processors are not γ-correct.

The probability, that at a given phase (5.2) or (5.3) does not hold, can be estimated as above by summing up the tail of the binomial distribution and for $p < \zeta$ (resp. $p' < \zeta'$) decreases exponentially fast in n . Let us assume that it is bounded by $O(\alpha^n)$ for some $\alpha < 1$ (α can be chosen as $(p/\zeta)^{\zeta}\ ((1-p)/(1-\zeta))^{1-\zeta}$) .

Similar to the argument for (5.1) we may assume that the probability that (5.2), resp. (5.3) stays true for a sequence of L consecutive phases is at least $(1-\alpha^n)^L$. If L is bounded by a polynomial in n it is easy to see that this expression still converges to 1 exponentially fast.

References:

[Da] D. Dolev, "The Byzantine Generals Strike Again", Journal of Algorithm, vol. 3, no. 1, 1982 .

[Db] D. Dolev, "Unanimity in an Unknown and Unreliable Environment", 22nd Annual Symposium on Foundations of Computer Science, pp. 159 - 168, 1981 .

[DFFLS] D. Dolev, M. Fischer, R. Fowler, N. Lynch and R. Strong, "Efficient Byzantine Agreement Without Authentication", IBM Research Report RJ3428, 1982 .

[DR] D. Dolev and R. Reischuk, "Bounds on Information Exchange for Byzantine Agreement", Proceedings, ACM SIGACT-SIGOPS Symposium on Principles of Distributed Computing, Ottawa, August 1982, IBM Research Report, RJ3587, 1982 .

[DRS] D. Dolev, R. Reischuk and H.R. Strong, "'Eventual' is earlier than 'Immediate'", 23rd IEEE-FOCS Conference, Chicago, November 1982, IBM Resarch Report RJ3632, 1982 .

[DSa] D. Dolev and H.R. Strong, "Polynomial algorithms for multiple processor agreement", Proceedings, the 14th ACM SIGACT Symposium on Theory of Computing, May 1982, IBM Research Report RJ3342, 1981 .

[DSb] D. Dolev and H.R. Strong; "Authenticated Algorithms for Byzantine Agreement", IBM Research Report RJ3416, 1982 .

[DSc] D. Dolev and H.R. Strong, "Distributed Commit with Bounded Waiting", Proceedings, Second Symposium on Reliability in Distributed Software and Database Systems, Pittsburgh, July 1982, IBM Research Report RJ3417, 1982 .

[DSd] D. Dolve and H.R. Strong, "Requirements for Agreement in a Distributed System", Proceedings, the Second International Symposium on Distributed Data Bases, Berlin, Sep. 1982, IBM Research Report RJ3418, 1982 .

[FFL] M. Fischer, R. Fowler and N. Lynch, "A Simple and Efficient Byzantine Generals Algorithm", Proceedings, Second Symposium on Reliability in Distributed Software and Database Systems, Pittsburgh, July 1982 .

[FLy] M. Fischer and N. Lynch, "A lower Bound for the Time to Assure Interactive Consistency", Information Processing Letters, to appear.

[LM] L. Lamport and P.M. Melliar-Smith, "Synchronizing Clocks in the Presence of Faults", Technical Report, Computer Science Laboratory, March 1982 .

[PSL] M. Pease, R. Shostak and L. Lamport, "Reaching Agreement in the Presence of Faults", JACM 27, 1980, 228 - 234 .

[R] R. Reischuk, "A New Solution for the Byzantine Generals Problem", IBM Research Report RJ3673, 1982 .

MODULAR DECOMPOSITION OF AUTOMATA (SURVEY)

D. Rödding

Institut für mathematische
Logik und Grundlagenforschung
D-4400 Münster

In this paper we present an introductory survey about a modular decomposition theory of finite automata which has mainly been developed by a team at the universities of Münster and Dortmund (FRG). A fundamental concept of this theory is that of a Normed Network of Mealy-automata, for the following reasons: 1. It is simple enough for a lucid mathematical treatment. 2. It is rich enough to provide some very difficult combinatorial problems. 3. It is flexible enough to be useful in more general investigations. We therefore first give a survey about Normed Networks:

1. Theory of Normed Networks

Let us start with the well-known concept of a Mealy-automaton $A=(X_A, Y_A, Z_A, \delta_A, \lambda_A)$

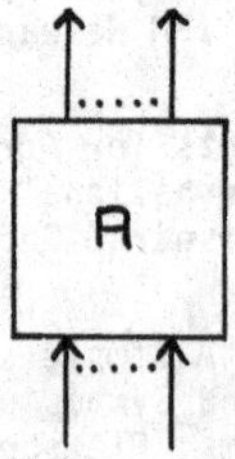

consisting of finite, nonempty sets X_A (the set of input-lines), Y_A (the set of output-lines, Z_A (the set of internal states), the transition-function $\delta_A: X\times Z \to Z$ and the output-function $\lambda_A: X\times Z \to Y$.
A Normed Network over Mealy-automata $A_1,\ldots,A_n$ will consist of copies $B_1,\ldots,B_m$ of $A_1,\ldots,A_n$ (the components of the network) and interconnections according to the following restrictions:

1. Each output-line of B_i is connected with at most one input-line of some B_j.
2. There are input-lines of some B_i, that aren't connected with any output-line (the input lines of the network).

3. There are output-lines of some B_i, that aren't connected with any input-line (the output-lines of the network).

Normed Networks are represented by pictures like this:

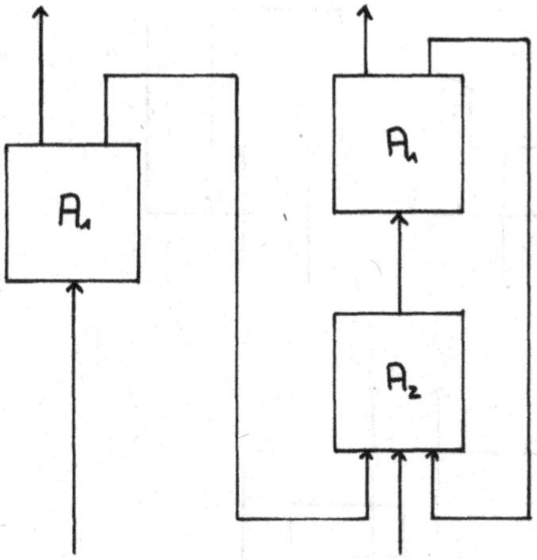

We now describe the behaviour of a Normed Network: The internal state of a network is given by the internal states of its components. A signal entering the network by an input-line belonging to the component C_1 of the network will change the state of C_1 according to δ_{C_1} and appear on an output-line of C_1 according to λ_{C_1}. This output-line is an output-line of the net or connected to an input-line of a component C_2. In the second case the signal changes the state of C_2 according δ_{C_2} and reaches an output-line of C_2 according to λ_{C_2}, and so on. Finally the signal will appear on an output-line of the net, or it will get into an infinite loop. From this description one can see how to interpret a network over Mealy-automata as a partial Mealy-automaton, where δ and λ are allowed to be simultanously undefined (in the following partial Mealy-automata are simply called automata).

Further it is easy to see that every Normed Network can be built up by iteration of the two processes

parallel composition

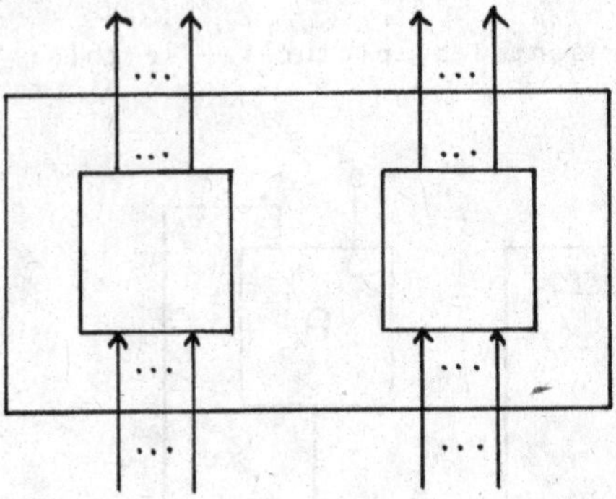

and feedback

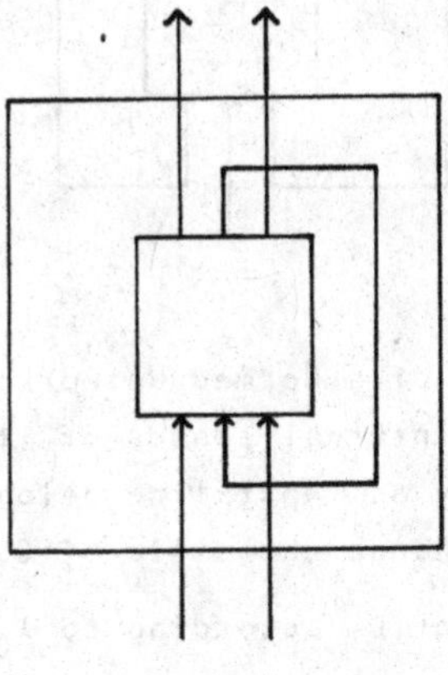

Mathematically precise definitions of the above sketched concepts can be found, for example, in [Ott73], [PrRö 74], [Mü81a].

For a given class K of automata let be NN(K) (Normed Networks of K) the closure of K with respect to

(1) parallel composition

(2) feedback

(3) isomorphic representatives.

The central idea of modular decomposition is to find finite classes K of simple automata which form a "basis" in the following sense: For all automata A there exists N∈NN(K) such that N simulates A. We understand "simulation" in the sense of one of the following concepts, listed with record to decreasing strength of concept:

(1) isomorphic embedding (of course it is not reasonable to postulate that N and A are isomorphic),
(2) realization in the sense of Hartmannis and Stearns via appropriate partition of the set of states of the simulating automaton,
(3) behaviouristic simulation (with respect to I/O-behaviour).

For précise definitions see, for example, [Ott 73], [PrRö 74], [RöRö 79], [Mü81a].

To give an example of a basis look at the following special automata H,E and K:

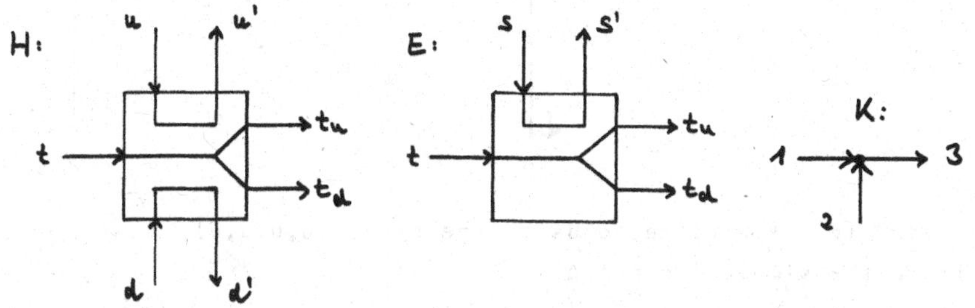

H has two internal states u (up) and d (down). A signal entering H by t (test) leaves H by the output-line t_u resp. t_d according to the actual state u or d of H without changing the state. A signal on input-line u (resp. d) forces the state u (resp. d) and uses output-line u' (resp. d'). E has two internal states u and d, the t-device works like that of H and a signal on input-line s alters the state and uses output-line s'. K is a "union of wires" having only one state, and input-signals 1 or 2 leave K by output 3.

We have the following results: {H,K} and {E,K} are bases with respect to isomorphic embedding.

For exact definitions of H,E and K and proofs of further basis results see, for example [Ott 73], [PrRö 74], [Mü81a].

To give an illustration for the handling of Normed Networks and an example for simulation we simulate H with a network over E and K in the sense of (1):

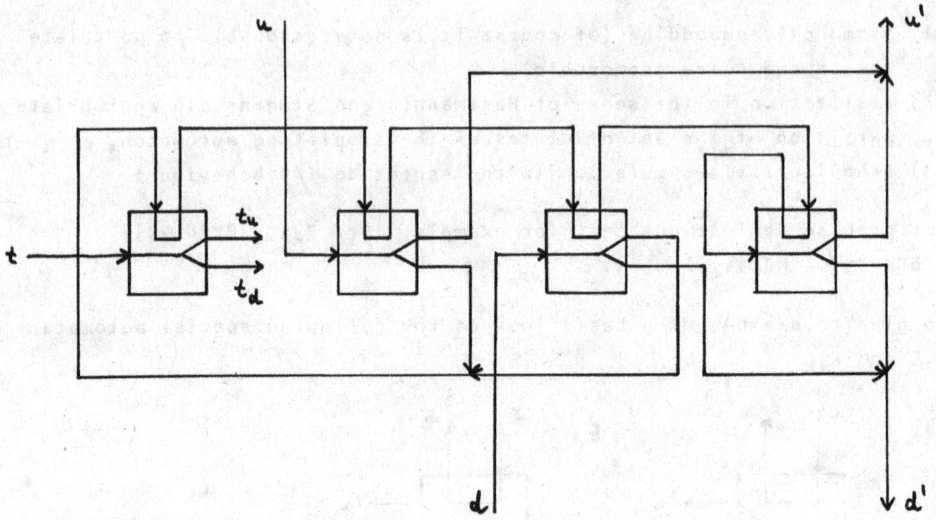

Here the state u(d) of H corresponds to the state (u,u,u,u) ((d,d,d,d)) of the simulating network.

After having some positive basis results, immediately the question arises how complicated a class *K* must be to form a basis. In this context [Kö 76] has introduced a monotony-property about which [Kö 76] and [Vo 80] have proved the following results.

(1) "To be monotone" is a decidable property of automata.
(2) All automata with only one input, one output or one internal state are monotone.
(3) Each basis *K* (with respect to behaviouristic simulation) contains an automaton which is not monotone.
(4) There exists an automaton F with one input, two states and two outputs, acting like a "flip-flop", such that the following equivalence holds for all totally defined Mealy-automata A:{A,F,K} is a basis with respect to isomorphic embedding iff A is not monotone.

These results may be regarded as an approximative answer to the (still open) decision problem, whether a given finite set *K* of automata forms a basis or not. For a short survey cf. [Rö 83].

In the context of Normed Networks there have been examined complexity questions of various kinds:

[Ott 73], for example, has investigated the question, how many H-components are needed for simulation of automata by networks over H and the simple (see above) F und K. He has proved that the number of H-components depends linearly on the number of outputs of the simulated automaton only, and that one needs only three H-components to simulate an automaton with two outputs.

[KB 75] has investigated networks built up by the two processes serial connection

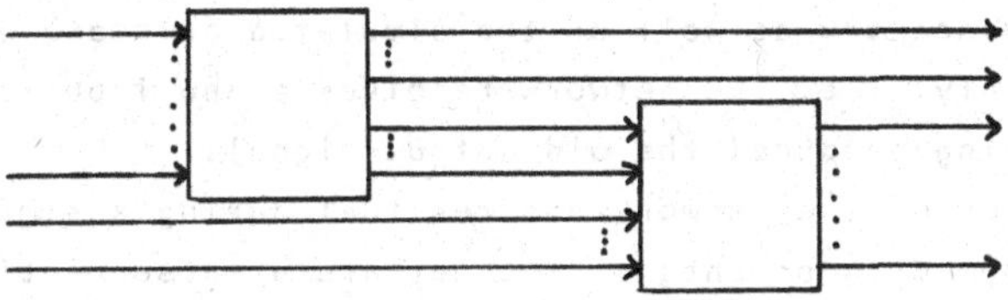

and feedback. His considerations have a hardware-oriented background: Realizising a network as an electronic circuit one has to regard the fact that a component of the net in general is able to process a new input signal correctly only after a certain recovery time. So in order to avoid "delay-circuits" it is very useful to have networks built up by a small number of feedback-operations. [KB 75] has proved that one cannot totally avoid feedback, but that one feedback-loop is sufficient for some universal bases. For a more detailed survey see [Rö 83].

[Kö 76] has reduced the conceptual freedom of arbitrary network-constructions to some special types allowing a more algebraic treatment. For a presentation of his results see [Rö 83].

Recently some investigations have been made about computing time, i.e. the number of components of a network that are used during a simulation period. The standard proofs for the basis-property of a class K give const.$|X|.|Z|$ as an upper estimate for the computing time of a network over K simulating $A=(X,Y,Z,\delta,\lambda)$. [Schä 82] has improved this result to const.$\log|X|.\log|Z|$ as an upper bound for computing time. One can improve this even to const.$(\log|X| + \log|Z|)$ ([PrRöSchäBr 83]) if one allows "parallel computation" by introducing two new modules V and W which work in the following way: V (one input, two outputs) produces two output-signals (namely: one signal on each of its two output-channels), if it has got an input-signal. W (two inputs, one output) produces one output-signal after having got an input-signal on each of its input-lines. The mathematical framework for these automata ($\alpha\beta\gamma$-automata or APA-nets, alternatively) shall be sketched later.

Due to the fact that we are simulating here Mealy-automata only and that a simulating network shall remain a simulating network also if one replaces a normed component by a simulating network ("transitivity" of simulation), the network of $K\cup\{V,W\}$ simulating A will obey the following restrictions:

(1) The simulating network as well as the simulated automata are used sequentially only, i.e. the network receives a new input-signal only after having produced the old output-signal.
(2) The construction of the network ensures that during a simulation process all normed components of the net are used sequentially. All components receive new input-signals only if their output-channels are free.
(3) The simulations are hang-up-free and prompt.

These conditions guarantee that for the single components no concurrency problems arise and that all wires are 1-safe.

As the last topic in this section let us treat the problem of self-correcting networks. A possible interpretation of a fault in a network is a spontaneous change of the state of one of it's components. There should be no restrictions according to the possible location of such a fault, but there should be, of course, restrictions concerning the number of faults that a network cen tolerate.

For Normed Networks we define "period of using" to be the "time interval" between a signal entering the network and the next signal entering the network, and "resting interval" the "time interval" between an output signal leaving the network and the next input signal entering the network. We distinguish between two kinds of self-correcting simulation: A network N simulates an automaton A k-self-correcting ($k \in N_+$) iff N acts like A even if in every resting interval at most k faults occur in N. N simulates A stable-k-self-correcting iff N acts like A even if in every period of using at most k faults occur in N. Thereby k-self-correcting networks are thought to model systems which are used rarely and have long resting intervals, whereas stable-k-self-correcting networks fit to systems which are used often and have short resting intervals.

Clearly one must define self-correction in connection with simulation for if one would define a network N to be self-correcting iff it would behave correctly started in an arbitrary state even if in every resting interval one fault would occur, this condition would force the states of N all to be equivalent and therefore N to be trivial. In a network N, however, which simulates an automaton A, a faulty simulation state is not necessary a simulation state again, and therefore in this case the self-correction condition does not force states of A to be equivalent.

Let's now turn to the question whether there exists a basis with self-correcting properties. In fact every automaton can be simulated stable-k-self-correcting by a network of H and K([PrRö 74]).The proof bases on two principles:

(1) In a network N∈NN(H,K) simulating a given automaton A all H-components are replaced by networks H* over H and K (with the same input-and output-lines as H) that acts in the following way:
  (a) A test-input for H* tests 2k+1 H-components of H* and recognizes per majority the right state (only k faults are allowed to occur!).
  (b) A signal on input-line u or d for H* corrects all faults in the network.

(2) There are networks N∈NN(H,K) simulating A that ensure that in each simulation process every H-automaton will be used at least once by an input-line u or d.

On the other hand by [Pr 75] bases have been found which are not sufficient for self-correction.

Finally some investigations have been made about self-correcting networks built up by serial composition and a single feedback-loop and about computing time in self-correcting networks. For a survey see [PrRöSchäBr 83], for special literature [PrRö 74], [Pr 75], [Pr 79c].

In the next section we consider (partial) Mealy-automata with special designed input and output devices and adequately normed construction principles that lead to some applications to logic (like some very small computation-universal systems).

2. Normed constructions and applications to logic

For a technical realization of automata it can be useful to connect basis automata not in an arbitrary way but only like "plugs". Therefore, we divide the input and output lines of a (partial) Mealy-automaton in left ones and right ones, and receive an automaton of the type $\begin{pmatrix} k & l \\ m & n \end{pmatrix}$ which has

k left output lines <1<,...,<k<,
l right input lines <1<,...,<l<,
m left input lines >1>,...,>m>,
n right output lines >1>,...,>n>

and is represented by a picture like this:

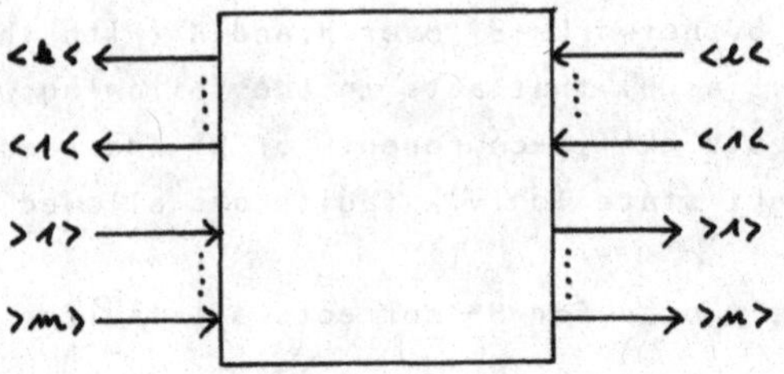

Two automata A of the type $\begin{pmatrix} k & l \\ m & n \end{pmatrix}$ and B of the type $\begin{pmatrix} l & r \\ n & s \end{pmatrix}$ may be concatenated to an automaton C=AB of the type $\begin{pmatrix} k & r \\ m & s \end{pmatrix}$ according to the following sketch:

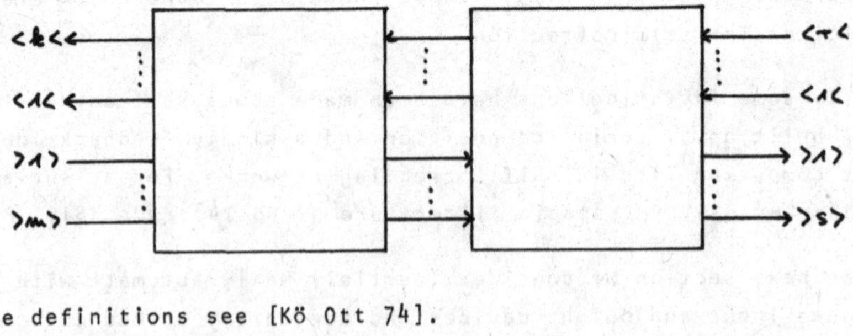

For precise definitions see [Kö Ott 74].

[Kö Ott 74] has solved the basis problem for chains of automata by specifying "basic"-automata, each of which has type $\begin{pmatrix} 2 & 2 \\ 2 & 2 \end{pmatrix}$ and for each type $\begin{pmatrix} k & l \\ m & n \end{pmatrix}$ left and right end-automata L(k,m) and R(l,n) with type $\begin{pmatrix} k & 2 \\ m & 2 \end{pmatrix}$ resp. $\begin{pmatrix} 2 & 1 \\ 2 & n \end{pmatrix}$ and max(k, m) resp. max(l,n) states which are universal in the following sense: Every automaton A of type $\begin{pmatrix} k & l \\ m & n \end{pmatrix}$ can be simulated by a chain $L(k,m)\ B_1,\dots,B_t\ R(l,n)$ built up from basic-automata $B_1,\dots,B_t$ and appropriate end-automata by concatenation.

Their method is first to simulate A by a Normed Network of simple basis automata, then to distort this network to a chain and then to simulate the resulting connection bulks of arbitrary breadth by automata-chains again.

[Kö 76] has improved this result by sequentially simulating channel bulks to a specification of 19 basic-automata, each of them with 2 states only and type $\begin{pmatrix} 2 & 2 \\ 2 & 2 \end{pmatrix}$. This result is optimal in the following sense:

(1) One can't have a basis consisting only of automata with one state (see above).

(2) One can't have a basis consisting only of automata of the type $\begin{pmatrix} 1 & 1 \\ m & m \end{pmatrix}$ (resp. $\begin{pmatrix} k & k \\ 1 & 1 \end{pmatrix}$), see [Kö Ott 74].

Let's consider now two logical problems connected with chain constructions, called the "decision problem" and the axiomatisation-problem for chains: One can define a (standard interpreted) first order language with constants and variables for type $\begin{pmatrix} 2 & 2 \\ 2 & 2 \end{pmatrix}$-automata, a function symbol for concatenation and a binary predicate symbol for equivalence of automata (instead of "=" to avoid a trivial reduction of the decision problem of this language to the well-known unsolvable problem for the language of concatenation of finite symbol-strings) and one can investigate the decision problem of this language. [Ott 74] has proved that a slightly extended language has the full complexity of the arithmetical predicates.

The axiomatisation-problem concerns the axiomatisation of the equivalence of two chains. [Kö 76] has found a first (approximative) solution of this problem: He has specified 6 automata of the type $\begin{pmatrix} 3 & 3 \\ 3 & 3 \end{pmatrix}$ which are sufficient for simulating each type $\begin{pmatrix} 2 & 2 \\ 2 & 2 \end{pmatrix}$ - automaton via concatenation in a special sense and some simple (!) axioms and rules to axiomatize the equivalence of chains built up from these 6 automata.

[KB 77] gives the two-dimensional generalization of the concept presented above: He considers cells A

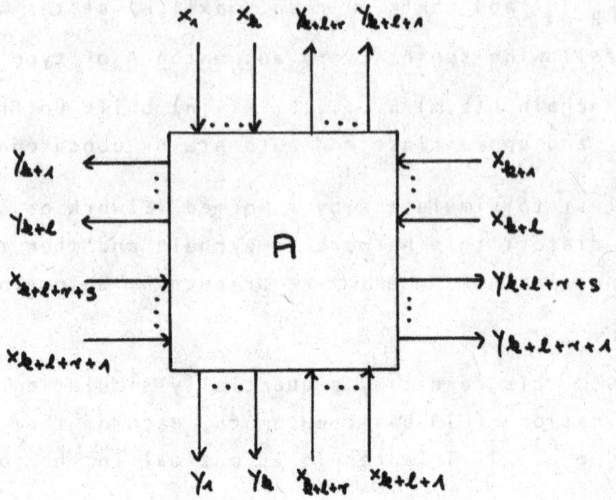

and rectangles F(a,b,A) of length a and breadth b, consisting of a·b copies of A:

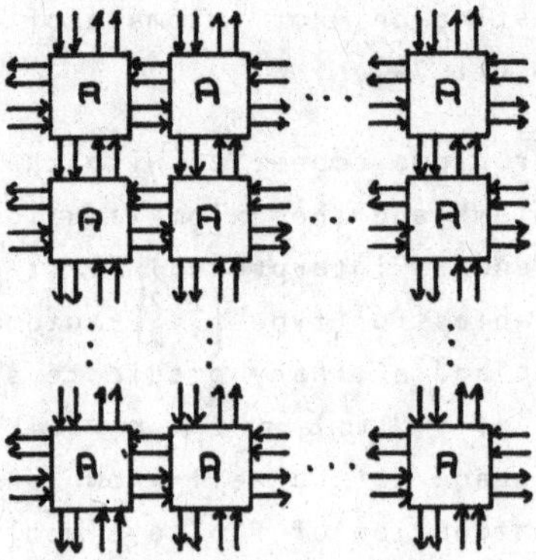

After having made precise the concept of simulation of cells by such arrays (concerning an appropriate handling of inputs and outputs to ensure transitivity of simulation), he defines a cell with 4 inputs and 2 states which is sufficient to simulate all cells and is minimal with respect to the number of inputs and states.

[KB 77] also has investigated infinite iterative arrays built up from one cell A. In this concept every point of the Gaussian plane gets a copy of a fixed cell A, and these copies are connected as in the finite case to an infinite cellular space F(A):

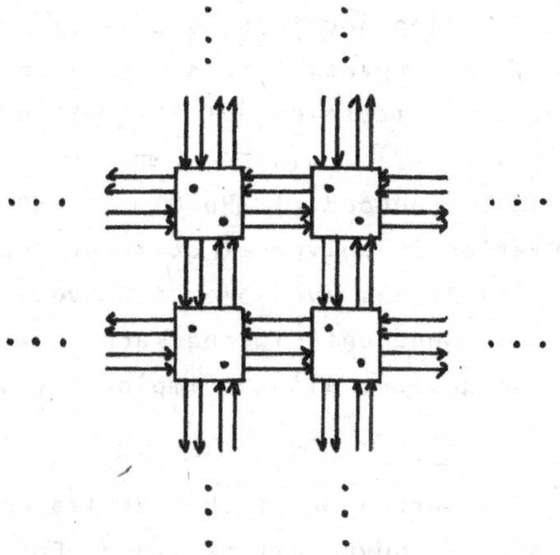

To enable an interaction of these cellular spaces with the environment (especially for START- and STOP-signals) each cell has an additional free input x_o and output y_o, as indicated in the above figure by dots.

With respect to the fact that the program of a register machine is a finite automaton and registers may be realized as infinite chains of finite automata, it is clear that there exist computational-universal cellular spaces F(A) simulating a universal register maschine.

Universality here includes a start|stop-standardization (i.e. there are fixed cells to receive the start-inpuls and to produce the stop-inpuls of a computation), and a finite initial plane-inscription (i.e. at the beginning of a computation all but a finite number of cells are in a fixed "quiescent" state).

But [KB 77] has succeeded to find some very small cells A with computational-universal corresponding cellular space F(A), namely one cell with 4 lateral input-lines (minimal!) and 4 states, and one cell with 10 lateral input-lines and 2 states (minimal!). In the proofs for the universality of a cell A first the program of a register machine is simulated by a Normed Network. Then the components of this network and the connection lines between them are simulated by finite arrays F(a,b,A), which fit to each another, and the natural numbers in the registers are represented by special state strings of corresponding length in the plane F(A). Similar technics have been used earlier also by [Pr 76b] and [Ott 75].

It is easy to see how to translate universal cellular spaces in universal two-dimensional Turing machines, states translating in letters, wires in states, cells processing a signal in working fields, signal directions in movement directions of the Turing head. The results of [Wa 73] and [KB Ott 77] could be strengthened with respect to the complexity measure introduced by [Ho 63] in [KB 77] by a slightly modified translation of universal cellular spaces in Turing machines. The result of [KB 77] has even been improved by [Pr 79a], who specified a universal two-dimensional Turing machine with 2 states, 4 letters and dynamic stop-device, also by implementing a Normed Network in the plane.

The following table gives a survey about the results concerning universal Turing machines of the above sketched type. For a complete survey also about other types of universality see [KB 77], [KB Ott.77], [Pr 79a], [Mü 81a].

Author	Year	States	Letters	Tape dimension	Heads	Complexity
Wagner	1973	8	4	2	1	$3\cdot 10^{67}$
Kleine Büning Ottmann	1977	3	6	2	1	$5\cdot 10^{44}$
Kleine Büning	1977	2	5	2	1	2^{16}
Kleine Büning	1977	10	2	2	1	10^{38}
Priese	1979	2	4	2	1	10^{12}

It should be remarked that no two-dimensional Turing machine with 1 state or with 2 states and 2 letters can be universal in the way sketched above ([He 68], [Wa 73]). Therefore only the case "2 states, 3 letters" still remains open.

[Pr 76b] uses another framework for investigating simple combinatorial structures, namely two-dimensional Thue systems (in the following shortly called Thue systems). Thue systems work on the Gaussian plane covered with the letters of a finite alphabet, but almost everywhere with blanks. The (finitely many) rules r=s of the Thue system allow to replace any finite subpattern r of such an inscription (which may contain the blank symbol) by the equally shaped pattern s, and vice versa, independently from the four orientations in the plane.

Now one can start from the concept of normed networks and generalize it by making all micro-procedures reversible. Because the activities in a Normed Network are determined, one has an embedding of the network in its reversible closure. The reversibility is introduced on the one hand to obtain Thue systems rather than Semi Thue systems, and on the other hand to receive an especially simple basis (using reversibility for avoiding hang up's, for example). One can simulate now such reversible nets by Thue systems, can represent natural numbers in the plane and implement the processes "+1", "-1" and "test" by Thue systems. This work has been done by [Pr 76b], and he has proved the computational universality of the following very small system:

alphabet: {a,c,e}, blank symbol e,
rules: aaea=ccaa
eaca=aece
ccac=eace .

The results of Priese concerning Thue systems involve a new solution of the synchronization problem. In the definition of the Thue systems synchronization problems are avoided by sequential application of rules. But even if the systems of Priese run concurrently or synchronously, during a task-oriented behaviour (simulating a register machine) no configurations arise which could involve overlapping problems.

For an extensive discussion of this question see [Pr 76a]. In this paper also a simple computational-and constructional-universal Thue system supplying nontrivial self-reproduction can be found.

Later investigations about Thue systems in [Pr 79b] have shown that the process of replacing a word by its reflected image involves a very simple computational universal Thue system, and that there exists a computational universal Thue system with two rules only.

[Pr 78] regards computational-universal Semi Thue systems which can be interpreted as cellular spaces. Parallel computations are implemented and overlapping problems avoided in a similar way as in [Pr 76a].

We want to conclude this section with two further remarks on "applications to logic":

(1) There have been made some approximative investigations about functionals of finite type that are representable by finite

automata. For an introductory survey see [Rö Rö 79].

(2) There has been found another NP-complete problem in the area of the question whether a signal entering a network in a special state produces an output-signal or not ("loop-problem", [KB 83]).

In the last section we will refer some generalizations of the concept of Normed Networks:

3. Further automata concepts

The most simple generalization of (partial) Mealy-automata is the concept of indeterminate Mealy-automata $A=(X,Y,Z,\Omega)$, $\Omega \subseteq X \times Z \times Z \times Y$, whereby $(x,z,z',y) \in \Omega$ means that A, having the internal state z, may react to an input x by changing its state to z' and giving the output y. Such indeterminate Mealy-automata are used sequentially by the environment and connected to networks like Mealy-automata. With respect to the basis question we have the result that one can achieve a basis for indeterminate Mealy-automata (which ensures prompt and hang-up-free simulation) by adding a single automaton I (indeterminator) to an arbitrary basis for (partial) Mealy-automata. I has 1 input-line, 1 state, 2 output-lines and reacts to an input indeterminately by giving an output on its first or second output-line. For a proof see [PrRöSchäBr 83].

Furthermore some investigations have been made about indeterminate Mealy-automata orienting their behaviour according to a preference ordering of their states. This concept can be regarded as a first approximative access for the modelling and theoretical treatment of mutual interactions between acting units in society. For a survey see [Rö Rö 79], for results see [Na Rö 78], [Kn 77].

A further generalization of the concept of indetermined Mealy-automata is that of $\alpha\beta\gamma$-automata. An $\alpha\beta\gamma$-automaton $A=(X,Y,Z,\alpha,\beta,\gamma)$ acts no longer sequentially (like a Mealy-automaton), but makes its transitions according to the relations $\alpha \subseteq X \times Z \times Z$, $\beta \subseteq Z \times Z$, $\gamma \subseteq Z \times Z \times Y$. Thereby $(x,z,z') \in \alpha$ means that A having the internal state z may absorb an input x and pass into the state z', $(z,z') \in \beta$ means that A having the internal state z may pass into the state z' without changing the inscription of the external lines, $(z,z',y) \in \gamma$ means that A having the internal state z may produce an output-signal y and pass into the state z'.

A simulation concept for $\alpha\beta\gamma$-automata must take into account that the environment of an $\alpha\beta\gamma$-automaton is allowed to put an input-signal on each free input-line during a computation and to take off an output-signal from each output-line which carries a signal.

A network N over αβγ-automata $A_1,\ldots,A_n$ consists of copies $B_1,\ldots B_m$ of $A_1,\ldots,A_n$ and connections between them which obey the same restrictions as connections between Mealy-automata. But the internal state of such a network is given now by the internal states of its components and a declaration of those internal wires of the network which carry a signal. If one interprets β-transitions of a component and α- or γ-transitions concerning an internal wire of the net to be β-transitions of the network, and α- resp. γ-transitions of a component concerning external wires of the net to be α- resp. γ-transitions of the network, it is easy to see that networks over αβγ-automata are αβγ-automata again.

In this context the basis problem is reformulated again and solved positively with respect to a simulation concept that does not involve promptness, but negatively with respect to a very restrictive simulation concept involving promptness. This work has been done by [Kn 77]. For an survey also see [Rö Rö 79], for results [Mü 81a].

It should be remarked that the very heart of the mentioned basis construction consists of a Normed Network of Mealy-automata, and that αβγ-automata are used only to handle the peripherie. So the positive basis result never could have been proved without an extensive investigation of Normed Networks.

If one regards αβγ-automata orienting their behaviour according to a preference ordering of their states the above sketched basis result can be sharpened: There exists a very simple set of αβγ-automata with preferences which form a basis for αβγ-automata (even for a much richer class of automata) with respect to a strong simulation concept involving promptness. αβγ-automata with preferences and related concepts have been examined by [Mü 81b].

[Pr 83] deals with a slightly modified concept of concurrent networks over indeterminated automata, namely with APA-nets. An APA (asynchronous parallel automaton) $A=(X,Y,Z,\rightarrow)$, $\rightarrow \subseteq P(X)\times Z\times Z\times P(Y)$, specifies elementary transitions $(M,z)\rightarrow(z',N)$ with the following meaning: A, having the internal state z and at least one input-signal on each input-line $x\in M$, removes one input-signal from each input-line $x\in M$, passes into the state z' and puts an output-signal on each output-line $y\in N$. The concepts of simulation and constructing networks in

[Pr 83] involve infinite wire capicity, but after having restricted the wire capicity to a natural number n there don't remain essential differences between $\alpha\beta\gamma$-automata and APA's.

[Pr 83] has developed a mathematically precise concept of simulation for concurrent systems to study the relations between modular concurrent systems (like APA-nets) and non-persistent concurrent systems which involve conflicts. With this formal tool he succeeded in proving a hierarchy theorem about Petri-net classes in a mathematically precise manner, and he could represent these Petri-net classes as network classes over some special APA's. The former results essentially base on the theory of Normed Networks and lead to a modular decomposition theory for Petri-nets.

Finally we give a short list of current investigations: fast computations, pipelining, self-correction with respect to the probability of faults, self-reduplication in graph-systems and trade-processes.

We hope to have convinced the reader that the theory of modular decomposition of finite automata is not only an interesting mathematical object by itself but also a very subtle and powerful tool for the analysis of combinatorial and logical problems just as it provides suitable models in data processing, economics and social sciences.

For her engaged help in the preparation of this paper I would like to thank Frau Anne Brüggemann of the university of Münster.

4. References

[He 68] Herman, G.T.: The Halting Problem of One State Turing-Machines with n-Dimensional Tape. ZmLG 14 (1968).

[Ho 63] Hooper, PH.K.: Some Small, Multi-Tape Universal Turing-Machines. Notices AMS Vol. 10 (1963), 63T359

[KB 75] Kleine Büning, H.: Netzwerke endlicher Automaten für Potentialautomaten. Diplomarbeit, Inst. für math. Logik und Grundlagenforschung, Münster 1975

[KB 77] Kleine Büning, H.: Über Probleme bei homogener Parkettierung von Z×Z durch Mealy-Automaten bei normierter Verwendung. Dissertation, Inst. für math. Logik und Grundlagenforschung, Münster 1977

[KB Ott 77] Kleine Büning, H./Ottmann, Th.: Kleine universelle mehrdimensionale Turingmaschinen. EIK 13 (1977)

[KB 83] Kleine Büning, H.: Complexity of Loop-Problems in Normed Networks. In: Börger, E./Hasenjäger, G./Rödding, D. (eds.), Proceedings of the Symposium "Rekursive Kombinatorik", Münster 1983. To appear in LNCS

[Kn 77] Kniza, K.-P.: Endliche Automaten mit Präferenzen. Diplomarbeit, Inst. für math. Logik und Grundlagenforschung, Münster 1977

[KöOtt 74] Körber, P./Ottmann, Th.: Simulation endlicher Automaten durch Ketten aus einfachen Bausteinautomaten. EIK 10 (1974)

[Kö 76] Körber, P.: Untersuchungen an sequentiellen, durch normierte Konstruktionen gewonnenen Netzwerken endlicher Automaten. Dissertation, Inst. für math. Logik und Grundlagenforschung, Münster 1976

[Mü 81a] Müller, J.: Netzwerke endlicher Automaten - eine modulare Zerlegungstheorie für Automaten. Ausarbeitung am Inst. für math. Logik und Grundlagenforschung, Münster 1981

[Mü 81b] Müller, J.: Die mathematische Behandlung von Präferenz und Tausch unter Zugrundelegung des Automatenbegriffes. Dissertation, Inst. für math. Logik und Grundlagenforschung, Münster 1981

[NaRö 78] Nachtkamp, H.H./Rödding, W.: On the Aggregation of Preferences to Form a Preference of a System. Nav. Res. Log. Quaterly 25 (1978)

[Ott 73] Ottmann, Th.: Über Möglichkeiten zur Simulation endlicher Automaten durch eine Art sequentieller Netzwerke aus einfachen Bausteinen. ZmLG 19 (1973)

[Ott 74] Ottmann, Th.: Arithmetische Prädikate über einem Bereich endlicher Automaten. Arch. math. Log. 16 (1974)

[Ott 75] Ottmann, Th.: Eine universelle Turingmaschine mit zweidimensionalem Band, 7 Buchstaben und 2 Zuständen. EIK 11 (1975)

[PrRö 74] Priese, L./Rödding, D.: A Combinatorial Approach to Self-Correction. J. Cybern. 4 (1974)

[Pr 75] Priese, L.: On the Minimal Complexity of Component-Machines for Self-Correcting Networks. J. Cybern. 5 (1975)

[Pr 76a] Priese, L.: On a simple Combinatorial Structure Sufficient for Supplying Nontrivial Self-Reproduction. J. Cybern. 6 (1976)

[Pr 76b] Priese, L.: Reversible Automaten und einfache universelle 2-dimensionale Thue-Systeme. ZmLG 22 (1976)

[Pr 78] Priese, L.: A Note on Asynchronous Cellular Automata. JCSS 17 (1978)

[Pr 79a] Priese, L.: Towards a Precise Characterization of the Complexity of Universal and Nonuniversal Turing Machines. SIAM J. Comput. (1979)

[Pr 79b] Priese, L.: Über ein 2-dimensionales Thue-System mit zwei Regeln und unentscheidbarem Wortproblem. ZmLG 25 (1979)

[Pr 79c] Priese, L.: On Stable Organisations of Normed Networks. In: Pichler, F. (ed.), Progress in Cybernetics and Systems Research. Hemisphere Publ. Comp. (1979)

[Pr 83] Priese, L.: Automata and Concurrency. To appear in Theoretical Computer Science

[PrRöSchäBr 83] Priese, L./Rödding, D./Schätz, R./Brüggemann, A.: Modular Decomposition of Automata. In: Börger, E./ Hasenjäger, G./Rödding, D. (eds.), Proceedings of the Symposium "Rekursive Kombinatorik", Münster 1983. To appear in LNCS

[RöRö 79] Rödding, D./Rödding, W.: Networks of Finite Automata. In: Pichler, F. (ed.), Progress in Cybernetics and Systems Research. Hemisphere Publ. Comp. (1979)

[Rö 83] Rödding, D.: Networks of Finite Automata I. In: Priese, L. (ed.), Report on the 1st GTI-Workshop, Universität Paderborn, Bericht Nr. 13, Reihe Theoretische Informatik (1983)

[Schä 82] Schätz, R.: Basissatz für Mealy-Automaten bei schneller, sequentieller Simulation, Arbeitspapier Nr. 3, Inst. für math. Logik und Grundlagenforschung, Münster (1982)

[Vo 80] Vobl, R.: Komplexitätsuntersuchungen an Basisdarstellungen endlicher Automaten. Diplomarbeit, Inst. f. math. Logik und Grundlagenforschung, Münster 1980

[Wa 73] Wagner, K.: Universelle Turingmaschinen mit n-dimensionalem Band. EIK 9 (1973)

A KERNEL LANGUAGE FOR ALGEBRAIC SPECIFICATION AND IMPLEMENTATION -- EXTENDED ABSTRACT* --

Donald Sannella
Department of Computer Science
University of Edinburgh

Martin Wirsing
Fakultät für Informatik
Universität Passau

Abstract

A kernel specification language called ASL is presented. ASL comprises five fundamental but powerful specification-building operations and has a simple semantics. Behavioural abstraction with respect to a set of observable sorts can be expressed, and (recursive) parameterised specifications can be defined using a more powerful and more expressive parameterisation mechanism than usual. A simple notion of implementation permitting vertical and horizontal composition (i.e. it is transitive and monotonic) is adopted and compared with previous more elaborate notions. A collection of identities is given which can provide a foundation for the development of programs by transformation.

1 Introduction

In recent years there has been a great deal of work on developing the algebraic approach to specification of data types and programs. Guttag [Gut 75] and others began by viewing an abstract data type as a class of heterogeneous algebras and showing how such a type can be specified by a signature (a collection of sorts and operators) together with a set of axioms. For quite simple data types (e.g. natural numbers) such an approach can be used without problems. But it is more convenient to build large algebraic specifications in a structured fashion by combining and modifying smaller specifications. Several specification languages have been developed to support this structured approach, including Clear [BG 77, 80] (cf. [HKR 80]), CIP-L [Bau 81] and LOOK [ZLT 82, ETLZ 82]. Each language provides a certain set of operations for use in building specifications together with a convenient syntax and a formal semantics.

We describe here (section 3) a kernel language for algebraic specification called ASL (a significantly revised version of the ASL in [Wir 82]). This language is nothing more than a collection of five fundamental but powerful specification-building operations. It has a simple semantics in comparison with high-level specification languages like Clear, CIP-L and LOOK. ASL is intended mainly as a kernel language rather than for writing specifications. That is, it provides a solid foundation on top of which high-level specification languages can be built. The semantics of the constructs of such a language would then be expressed by mapping them into ASL expressions.

ASL differs from previous specification languages in a number of important respects:

- ASL is a language for describing classes of *algebras* rather than for building sets of *axioms* (theories) like most other specification languages. Some of the operations of ASL (e.g. **abstract**) cannot be viewed as simple operations on theories.
- An ASL specification may be *loose* (i.e. it may possess non-isomorphic models). Loose specifications are also allowed by Clear, CIP-L and LOOK but not by some previous approaches (e.g. the initial algebra approach [ADJ 76, 78]). Loose specifications can be precise while leaving some freedom of choice (e.g. to the implementator).
- ASL is oriented toward a 'behavioural' approach to specification rather than toward an initial or final algebra approach. Along with [GGM 76] and others, we argue that it is usually irrelevant how values of a sort are represented in an algebra as long as the desired input/output relation is satisfied. ASL includes a very general abstraction operation which can be used to behaviourally abstract from a specification, relaxing interpretation to those algebras which are behaviourally equivalent to a model. This can be used to write 'abstract model' specifications as in [LB 77].

---

*The full version of this paper is available as Report CSR-131-83, Dept. of Computer Science, Univ. of Edinburgh.

- The approach to parameterisation in ASL (section 5) is more general and flexible than in other languages. The main difference is that the signature of the result of applying a parameterised specification may depend on the signature of the actual parameter in a more flexible way than before. Since parameterised specifications may be recursive we can write 'abstract domain equations' as in [HR 80] and [EL 81].

Since ASL is a powerful specification language it is possible to adopt a simple notion of the implementation of one specification by another ($T \rightsquigarrow T'$) which can easily be extended to the case of parameterised specifications. Then the transitivity of implementations (vertical composition -- if $T \rightsquigarrow T'$ and $T' \rightsquigarrow T''$ then $T \rightsquigarrow T''$) follows immediately and the monotonicity of ASL's operations gives horizontal composition (specification-building operations preserve implementations, e.g. if $P \rightsquigarrow P'$ and $A \rightsquigarrow A'$ then $P(A) \rightsquigarrow P'(A')$). These results permit the development of programs from ASL specifications in a gradual and modular fashion. A number of more elaborate notions of implementation can be expressed using ASL, including notions which coincide with or approximate most previously proposed definitions.

An advantage of the kernel language approach is that facts about the basic operations (easy to prove because of the simple semantics) automatically extend to facts concerning the high-level constructs of any language built on top of the kernel. Thus the ASL identities and relations given in section 7 extend to identities and relations on any language built on top of ASL. These could be used as the basis for a methodology of program development by transformation of specifications.

2 Algebraic background

In this section the algebraic definitions which will be needed throughout the rest of the paper are presented.

2.1 Signatures

In order to get a clean mathematical semantics of parameterisation with fixed points of recursive parameterised specifications (see section 5) we need a more elaborate definition of signatures and signature morphisms than the standard one (as in e.g. [BG 80]). First, we need to fix the set of possible sorts and operators to ensure that the possible signatures and signature morphisms form sets rather than classes. Then we extend the usual definition of a signature morphism -- as a total function from one (finite) signature to another -- to a partial function from the (infinite) set of all sorts and operators into that set. Since we think that signature morphisms should be computable we require them to be partial recursive functions. Formally:

Fix arbitrary countably infinite sets Λ of sorts and Γ of operators.

Def: A *signature* Σ is a pair $<S,\Omega>$ where $S \subseteq \Lambda$ is a set (of *sorts*) and Ω is a family of subsets of Γ (*operators*) indexed by $S^* \times S$. The index of a set $O \in \Omega$ is the *type* of every element of O. Let the *universal signature* Σ_{univ} be $<S_{univ},\Omega_{univ}>$ where $S_{univ} = \Lambda$ and Ω_{univ} is the family $(\Gamma)_{us \in \Lambda^* \times \Lambda}$.

Def: A *signature morphism* σ is a pair $<f,g>$ where $f: S_{univ} \rightarrow S_{univ}$ is a partial recursive function and g is a family of partial recursive functions $g_{us}: (\Omega_{univ})_{us} \rightarrow (\Omega_{univ})_{f^*(u)f(s)}$, where $u \in S^*_{univ}$, $s \in S_{univ}$ and $f^*: S^*_{univ} \rightarrow S^*_{univ}$ is the extension of f to strings of sorts. We write $\sigma: \Sigma \rightarrow \Sigma'$ if $\Sigma = \sigma^{-1}(\Sigma')$ (i.e. Σ is the inverse image of Σ'). Then $\sigma: \Sigma \rightarrow \Sigma'$ implies that $\sigma|_\Sigma$ (σ restricted to the domain Σ) is a total function into Σ'. Furthermore, we write $\sigma(s)$ for $f(s)$ and $\sigma(\omega)$ for $g_{us}(\omega)$, where $\omega \in \Omega_{us}$.

Note that infinite signatures are permitted; for examples showing how this could be useful see [Wir 82]. Moreover, the definition of signature permits overloading (i.e. several operators having the same name but different types) as does the definition in [BG 80].

According to the above definition, a signature morphism $\sigma: \Sigma \rightarrow \Sigma'$ is almost the same as in [BG 80]; the difference is that a signature morphism σ can simultaneously be $\sigma: \Sigma A \rightarrow \Sigma A'$ and $\sigma: \Sigma B \rightarrow \Sigma B'$ for $\Sigma A \neq \Sigma B$ and $\Sigma A' \neq \Sigma B'$. This difference is important. Signature morphisms are used for renaming the sorts and operators of a specification (via the derive operation); since it is possible to define signature morphisms which 'make sense' over a range of signatures, we can (for example) write a parameterised specification which systematically renames the sorts and operators of any specification it is given as an actual parameter, which is impossible in Clear, CIP-L, LOOK, or the ADJ approach to parameterisation [ADJ 78, 80]. This point is discussed at greater length in section 5.

2.2 Algebras

The definitions of a (total) Σ-algebra A with carriers $|A|$ and of a Σ-homomorphism are as usual, except that the carrier $|A|_s$ is required to be non-empty for every $s \in sorts(\Sigma)$. The reason for this requirement is that permitting such degenerate algebras would give rise to problems in later definitions (see the definitions of reachable and $\equiv_W$ in section 2.4). The class of all Σ-algebras will be denoted $Alg(\Sigma)$.

Given a Σ'-algebra A' and an injective signature morphism $\sigma:\Sigma \to \Sigma'$, we can recover the Σ-algebra buried inside A' (since A' is just an extension of this algebra). The definition extends without modification to the case in which σ is not injective, where the Σ-algebra will contain multiple copies of some of the carriers and operations of A'.

Def: If $\sigma=\langle f,g \rangle$ is a signature morphism $\sigma:\Sigma \to \Sigma'$ and A' is a Σ'-algebra, then the *σ-restriction* of A', written $A'|_\sigma$ is the Σ-algebra with carrier $|A|_s=|A'|_{f(s)}$ for each $s \in sorts(\Sigma)$, and $\omega_A=g(\omega)_{A'}$ for each $\omega \in opns(\Sigma)$. When σ is obvious we sometimes use the notation $A'|_\Sigma$.

2.3 Terms and the term algebra

Σ-terms, the translation $\sigma(t)$ of a Σ-term t by a signature morphism $\sigma:\Sigma \to \Sigma'$, and the term algebra $W_\Sigma(X)$ are defined as usual. For some choices of Σ and X, $W_\Sigma(X)$ will have an empty carrier for some sort $s \in sorts(\Sigma)$ (in this case $W_\Sigma(X)$ is not an algebra, strictly speaking). We then say that $W_\Sigma(X)$ is *empty* in s. If we have a Σ-term t and an assignment $\phi:X \to |A|$ of values in A to variables then the value of t in A under ϕ is denoted $\phi^\#(t)$ (i.e. $\phi^\#:W_\Sigma(X) \to A$ is the unique homomorphism extending ϕ).

Def: If Σ is a signature then let X_Σ be a $sorts(\Sigma)$-indexed set of variables with $(X_\Sigma)_s=\mathbb{N}$ for each $s \in sorts(\Sigma)$. If Σ is obvious we will write X instead of X_Σ. We write x_1, x_2, y, a etc. instead of 1_s, 2_s etc. $\in (X_\Sigma)_s$.

Notation: If Z is an S-indexed set and $S' \subseteq S$, then $Z_{S'}$ denotes the restriction of Z to S'. For example, the notation $|W_\Sigma(X_S)|_{S'}$ refers to the (S'-indexed) set of Σ-terms of sorts in S' containing variables of sorts in S.

2.4 Properties of algebras and W-equivalence

Def: If A is a Σ-algebra and $S \subseteq sorts(\Sigma)$ is a set of sorts, then A is *reachable* on S if for every sort $s \in S$ and every carrier element $a \in |A|_s$ there is a term $t \in |W_\Sigma(X_{S'})|_s$ and assignment $\phi:X_\Sigma \to |A|$ such that $\phi^\#(t)=a$, where $S'=sorts(\Sigma)-S$. Unreachable carrier elements are called *junk*. If an algebra is reachable on all sorts then it is *finitely generated*.

Equivalently, A is reachable on S iff there exists a surjective homomorphism $f:W_\Sigma(X_{S'}) \to A$.

Def: A *Σ-formula* is a first-order equational formula on Σ; that is, a formula built from Σ-terms using = (term equality), the logical connectives $\neg$, $\wedge$, $\vee$ and $\Rightarrow$ and the quantifiers $\forall$ and $\exists$. Satisfaction of a Σ-formula e by a Σ-algebra A ($A \models e$) is defined as usual.

In fact, any notion of Σ-formula will do; we only need to know when a Σ-formula is satisfied by a Σ-algebra. The definition above gives one example of such a notion. The semantics of ASL can thus be viewed as parameterised by the notions of formula and satisfaction. The semantics of Clear [BG 80] is parameterised by an *institution* [GB 83] -- i.e. by notions of signature, algebra, formula and satisfaction which must satisfy certain properties. The semantics of ASL can be made independent of the notion of algebra and (to some extent) of the notion of signature as well, but the properties which the notions must satisfy are different (see [SW 83] for details).

Def: If A,A' are Σ-algebras and $W \subseteq |W_\Sigma(X)|$ then A and A' are *W-equivalent* ($A \equiv_W A'$) if there are surjective assignments $\phi:X \to |A|$ and $\phi':X \to |A'|$ such that $\forall t,t' \in W.\ (\phi^\#(t)=\phi^\#(t') \Leftrightarrow \phi'^\#(t)=\phi'^\#(t'))$.

This definition generalises the various notions of *behavioural equivalence* in the literature. If OBS$\subseteq$sorts(Σ) is a set of *observable sorts* then two Σ-algebras are considered to be behaviourally equivalent with respect to OBS if all computations yielding a result of observable sort give the same result in both algebras. There is some disagreement over which class of inputs to these computations should be considered: $|W_\Sigma(X)|_{OBS}$-equivalence (all inputs) is behavioural equivalence according to [Rei 81] and [GM 82]; $|W_\Sigma(X_{OBS})|_{OBS}$-equivalence (inputs of observable sorts) is behavioural equivalence in the sense of [Sch 82] and [GM 83]; and $|W_\Sigma(\phi)|_{OBS}$-equivalence (no inputs) is the same as behavioural (or I/O) equivalence in [BM 81] and [Kam 83] (and implied by [GGM 76]) except that in these three papers only finitely generated algebras are considered. There are other choices for W which yield interesting equivalences; one of these (used to define the junk operation) is given in the next section.

3 The language ASL and its semantics

ASL is a language for describing classes of algebras. It contains five constructs, each construct embodying a primitive operation on classes of algebras. These are:

- Form a *basic specification* having a given signature Σ and given axioms E. This specifies the class of all Σ-algebras satisfying E.
- Take the *sum* T+T' of two specifications, specifying the class of algebras obtained by combining a model of T with a model of T'. This allows large specifications to be built from smaller specifications.
- Restrict interpretation to those models which are *reachable* on certain sorts. Requiring reachability is the same as restricting by a certain second-order principle which is equivalent to structural induction.
- *Derive* a specification from a richer specification by renaming or forgetting some sorts and operators but otherwise retaining the class of models. This can be used to hide the details of a constructive specification to give a more abstract result.
- *Abstract* away from certain details of the specification, relaxing interpretation to those algebras which are the same as a model with respect to some observability criterion. With an appropriate observability criterion this amounts to *behavioural abstraction* with respect to a set of observable sorts.

These fundamental and mutually independent operations can be composed to give higher-level operations for building specifications in a wide variety of ways. ASL is a *kernel* language which provides a foundation on top of which high-level specification languages such as Clear, CIP-L and LOOK can be built. The semantics of the specification-building constructs of these languages can be expressed by mapping them into ASL expressions. A specification language has been defined on top of a previous version of ASL [Gau 83] and we have informally redefined the specification part of CIP-L on top of ASL (see [Wir 82] for the basic idea). We do not intend that ASL itself be used directly for writing specifications, although in the next section examples are given showing that this is possible.

<u>Syntax</u>

Expr	::=	Basic-Spec | Sum | Reachable | Derive | Abstract
Basic-Spec	::=	< signature, set of formulas >
Sum	::=	Expr + Expr
Reachable	::=	**reachable** Expr **on** set of sorts
Derive	::=	**derive from** Expr **by** signature morphism
Abstract	::=	**abstract** Expr **wrt** set of terms

No special syntax is provided for signatures, sets, formulas or signature morphisms; the usual mathematical notation will be used in examples.

<u>Semantics</u>

The semantics of ASL is defined by two functions

Sig: Expr → signature
Mod: Expr → class of algebras

such that for any expression T, Mod⟦T⟧ is a class of Sig⟦T⟧-algebras. We use square brackets [ ] to denote classes. The definition of Sig below includes context conditions for each construct; if these are not satisfied then the expression is invalid. It is easy to prove that for any specification T, Mod⟦T⟧ is closed under isomorphism.

$Sig[\![<\Sigma,E>]\!] = \Sigma$ — the operators and sorts used in E are in Σ

$Sig[\![T+T']\!] = Sig[\![T]\!] \cup Sig[\![T']\!]$

$Sig[\![$**reachable** T **on** $S]\!] = Sig[\![T]\!]$ — $S \subseteq sorts(Sig[\![T]\!])$

$Sig[\![$**derive from** T **by** $\sigma]\!] = \Sigma$ — $\sigma:\Sigma \rightarrow Sig[\![T]\!]$ (recall that $\Sigma = \sigma^{-1}(Sig[\![T]\!])$)

$Sig[\![$**abstract** T **wrt** $W]\!] = Sig[\![T]\!]$ — $W \subseteq |W_\Sigma(X)|$, where $\Sigma = Sig[\![T]\!]$

$Mod[\![<\Sigma,E>]\!] = \{ A \in Alg(\Sigma) \mid A \models E \}$

$Mod[\![T+T']\!] = \{ A \in Alg(Sig[\![T+T']\!]) \mid A|_{Sig[\![T]\!]} \in Mod[\![T]\!] \text{ and } A|_{Sig[\![T']\!]} \in Mod[\![T']\!] \}$

$Mod[\![$**reachable** T **on** $S]\!] = \{ A \in Mod[\![T]\!] \mid A \text{ is reachable on } S \}$

$Mod[\![$**derive from** T **by** $\sigma]\!] = \{ A|_\sigma \mid A \in Mod[\![T]\!] \}$

$Mod[\![$**abstract** T **wrt** $W]\!] = \{ A \in Alg(Sig[\![T]\!]) \mid \exists A_0 \in Mod[\![T]\!].(A_0 \equiv_W A) \}$

The + operation is not quite the same as + in Clear, since no account is taken of shared subspecifications. This feature of Clear is designed to make it easy to build specifications without worrying about the names of sorts and operators. Such high-level features have no place in a kernel language like ASL. The same effect can be achieved manually by use of + in conjunction with the **derive** operation.

The **reachable** construct restricts interpretation to models which are reachable on the given set of sorts S. It can be used to express the **data** operation in 'hierarchical' Clear [SW 82] and the **based on** construct of CIP-L. The **data** operation of 'ordinary' Clear [BG 80] and the **constraining** operation of LOOK [ETLZ 82] cannot be fully expressed in ASL because they restrict to the class of *initial* models. We do not view this as a disadvantage. In our opinion the initial algebra approach to specification [ADJ 76] adopted by Clear and LOOK has more problems than advantages; this view seems to be shared by others, e.g. [GGM 76], [Wand 79] and [Bau 81]. Some of these problems are: initial models do not always exist for specifications having axioms which include ∨ or ∃; to prove that an inequality $t \neq t'$ holds, one must in general prove that the equality $t = t'$ is not provable; implementations have unpleasant properties in the presence of an operation for restricting to initial models [SW 82]; and in the stepwise development of specifications and programs, the set of constructors for a data type is often fixed at an early stage, whereas the inequalities satisfied by the type are only established once all design decisions have been made. No power is lost by abandoning the initial algebra approach [BBTW 81].

The **derive** operation corresponds to **derive** in Clear. This already gives a hint of abstraction because it is possible to construct a specification which employs auxiliary sorts and operators and then use the **derive** operation to forget them, retaining only the semantics of the remaining sorts and operators. But this is not real abstraction, because the structure induced by the auxiliary operators remains (compare the examples List and Impoverished-List in the next section). The real abstraction is done by the **abstract** operation which ignores invisible structure (compare the examples Impoverished-List and Behavioural-Set). The result of abstracting from T with respect to a set W of visible terms is the class of algebras which are W-equivalent to a model of T. No similar operation is found in any other specification language, so far as we are aware.

An interesting use of **abstract** is to express behavioural abstraction with respect to a set of observable sorts:

behaviour T **wrt** $OBS =_{def}$ **abstract** T **wrt** $|W_\Sigma(X_{OBS})|_{OBS}$ where $\Sigma = sig[\![T]\!]$ and $OBS \subseteq sorts(\Sigma)$

(Please note that **behaviour** is only an abbreviation for a special case of **abstract**; it is not a new operation of ASL.) This gives the class of all algebras which are behaviourally equivalent (with respect to OBS) to a model of T, using a notion of behavioural equivalence due to [Sch 82] and [GM 83] (this is the notion which seems to fit most gracefully with our notion of implementation). This operation can be used to abstract from a concretely-specified input/output behaviour as in the 'abstract model specifications' of [LB 77]. It also allows us to adopt a very simple notion of implementation, as discussed in section 6.

Another use of **abstract** is to express the **junk** operation:

junk T **on** S $=_{def}$ **abstract** T **wrt** $|W_\Sigma(X_{S'})|$ where Σ=sig⟦T⟧, S⊆sorts(Σ) and S'=sorts(Σ)-S

This gives those algebras which are the same as models of T except that they may contain arbitrary junk (non-reachable values) in sorts S. It can be seen as a kind of dual to the **reachable** operation. Note that some of the models of **junk** T **on** S will be reachable on S even if none of the models of T are. We can select these by applying the **reachable** operation. This particular combination occurs often so we give it a name:

restrict T **on** S $=_{def}$ **reachable** (**junk** T **on** S) **on** S where S⊆sorts(T)

This gives the class of reachable (on S) subalgebras of models of T which are unchanged for sorts not in S.

The following abbreviations will be convenient in the sequel:

reachable T	$=_{def}$	**reachable** T **on** sorts(T)	restrict to the finitely generated models of T
junk T	$=_{def}$	**junk** T **on** sorts(T)	allow arbitrary junk in all sorts
restrict T	$=_{def}$	**restrict** T **on** sorts(T)	finitely generated subalgebras of models of T

Clear's **enrich** operation (add some sorts, operators and axioms to a specification) can be expressed using the + and basic-spec operations:

enrich T **by sorts** S **opns** F **axioms** E $=_{def}$ T + < < sorts(T) ∪ S, opns(T) ∪ F >, E >

The notation T=T' (where T and T' are ASL expressions) will be used to abbreviate Mod⟦T⟧=Mod⟦T'⟧; similarly, T⊆T' means Sig⟦T⟧=Sig⟦T'⟧ and Mod⟦T⟧⊆Mod⟦T'⟧.

4 Examples

The specifications of booleans, natural numbers, and lists of natural numbers in ASL are much the same (except for syntax) as they would be in CIP-L:

```
Bool =def reachable
            enrich ∅ by
              sorts  bool
              opns   true, false : bool
              axioms true ≠ false

Nat =def reachable
            enrich ∅ by
              sorts  nat
              opns   0 : nat
                     succ : nat → nat
              axioms 0 ≠ succ(x)
                     succ(x) = succ(y)  ⟺  x = y

List =def reachable
            enrich Bool + Nat by
              sorts  list
              opns   nil : list
                     cons : nat, list → list
                     head : list → nat
                     tail : list → list
                     ∈ : nat, list → bool
              axioms head(cons(a,l)) = a
                     tail(cons(a,l)) = l
                     a ∈ nil = false
                     a ∈ cons(a,l) = true
                     a ≠ b  ⟹  a ∈ cons(b,l) = a ∈ l
```

All models of each of these specifications are isomorphic to the standard model. The axioms in Bool and Nat are required to avoid trivial models, in contrast to Clear and LOOK. The inequations in Bool and Nat together with the axioms of List induce inequations like cons(a,cons(a,l))≠cons(a,l) so it is not necessary to state them explicitly.

Suppose ΣSet denotes the following signature:

```
Sig⟦Bool⟧ ∪ Sig⟦Nat⟧ ∪ ( sorts  set
                           opns   ∅ : set
                                  add : nat, set → set
                                  ∈ : nat, set → bool )
```

and σ:ΣSet→sig⟦List⟧ is the signature morphism with σ(*set*)=*list*, σ(∅)=*nil*, σ(*add*)=*cons* and σ(*x*)=*x* for all other sorts and operators *x* in ΣSet. Then the specification

Impoverished-List $=_{def}$ **derive from** List **by** σ

has exactly the same class of models as List except for the absence of *head* and *tail* and the renaming of the sort *list* and some of the remaining operators. The formulas add(a,add(a,S))≠add(a,S) and a≠b ⟹ add(a,add(b,S))≠add(b,add(a,S)) still hold in every model of Impoverished-List, although there is no longer any context in which values like [1,2], [2,1] and [2,2,1] can be distinguished.

Behavioural abstraction results in a broader class of models:

Behavioural-Set $=_{def}$ **behaviour** Impoverished-List **wrt** {nat, bool}

Models of Behavioural-Set include the models of Impoverished-List as well as the algebra with a carrier consisting of the set of *bags* of natural numbers (satisfying add(a,add(b,S))=add(b,add(a,S)) and add(a,add(a,S))≠add(a,S)) and the standard model of finite sets with carrier $\mathcal{P}(\mathbb{N})$ (where add(a,add(b,S))=add(b,add(a,S)) and add(a,add(a,S))=add(a,S)) and all algebras isomorphic to them. All models may include arbitrary junk for the sort *set*. Trivial models (satisfying e.g. add(a,∅)=∅) are still excluded. If we form a specification from List which is similar to Behavioural-Set but with the order of **derive** and **behaviour** reversed, the result is identical to Impoverished-List except that its models may contain junk (and different from Behavioural-Set):

junk Impoverished-List **on** {set} = **derive from** (**behaviour** List **wrt** {bool, nat}) **by** σ ⊂ Behavioural-Set

Behavioural-Set has almost the same class of models as the following more direct specification of sets:

Loose-Set $=_{def}$ **enrich** Bool + Nat **by**
  sorts set
  opns ∅ : set
    add : nat, set → set
    ∈ : nat, set → bool
  axioms a ∈ ∅ = false
    a ∈ add(a,S) = true
    a ≠ b ⟹ a ∈ add(b,S) = a ∈ S

The only difference between the models of Behavioural-Set and Loose-Set is that models of Behavioural-Set may contain arbitrary junk of sort *set*, while any junk in models of Loose-Set must satisfy the axioms of Loose-Set:

Behavioural-Set = **junk** Loose-Set **on** {set} = **behaviour** Loose-Set **wrt** {nat, bool}

In order to restrict interpretation to the standard model of sets we must add more information to Loose-Set:

Set $=_{def}$ **enrich reachable** Loose-Set **on** {set} **by**
  axioms add(a,add(b,S)) = add(b,add(a,S))
    add(a,add(a,S)) = add(a,S)

The only model of Set (up to isomorphism) is the standard model. The same class of models results if the order of **enrich** and **reachable** is switched. Now

Behavioural-Set = **behaviour** Set **wrt** {bool, nat} = **behaviour** (**junk** Set **on** {set}) **wrt** {bool, nat}

In fact, if Set is **enrich** Loose-Set **by axioms** E or **enrich reachable** Loose-Set **on** {set} **by axioms** E where E is any set of axioms consistent with those in Loose-Set, then these identities still hold.

Set can be extended by adding a new value, an 'infinite set' which contains every natural number:

Infinite-Set $=_{def}$ **reachable enrich junk** Set **on** {set} **by**
  opns infset : set
  axioms add(a, infset) = infset
    a ∈ infset = true
  on {set}

In every model of Infinite-Set the value of *infset* will be different from every other value of sort *set*. Apart from this new value, the models of Infinite-Set are exactly the models of Set. This kind of extension (in which a new constructor is added to a previously **reachable**-restricted sort) is not possible in Clear, CIP-L or LOOK.

If we use **derive** to forget the operator *infset* the result is almost the same as Set; the only difference is that every model will contain a single junk element. We can apply **restrict** to obtain their reachable subalgebras:

Set = **restrict** (**derive from** Infinite-Set **by** σ) **on** {set}

where σ:Sig⟦Set⟧↪Sig⟦Infinite-Set⟧ is the inclusion.

Suppose that Loose-Set is enriched as follows:

Loose-Bag $=_{def}$ **enrich** Loose-Set **by**
opns howmany : nat, set → nat
axioms howmany(a, $\emptyset$) = 0
howmany(a, add(a, S)) = succ(howmany(a, S))
a ≠ b ⟹ howmany(a, add(b, S)) = howmany(a, S)

Recall that the models of Loose-Set included the standard model where add(a, add(a, S))=add(a, S) as well as models where add(a, add(a, S))≠add(a, S). The models of Loose-Set in which repeated elements are ignored cannot be extended to give models of Loose-Bag; if {a, a}={a} then howmany(a, {a, a})=howmany(a, {a}) so 2=1. The other models of Loose-Set (extended by *howmany*) remain. The original models of Loose-Set (along with models containing arbitrary junk of sort *set*) can be regained by forgetting *howmany* and applying behavioural abstraction:

behaviour (**derive from** Loose-Bag **by** σ) **wrt** {nat, bool} = **junk** Loose-Set **on** {set}

where σ: Sig⟦ Loose-Set ⟧ ↪ Sig⟦ Loose-Bag ⟧ is the inclusion.

Although the examples in this section are very small, they illustrate some of the things which can be accomplished using ASL. Some of these things are impossible in any other algebraic specification language, viz behavioural abstraction (as in the construction of Behavioural-Set from List) and the addition of a new element to a reachable-restricted sort (as in the construction of Infinite-Set from Set).

5 Parameterised specifications with recursion

The semantics of a nonparameterised specification consists (as described in section 3) of a signature Σ together with a class M of Σ-algebras, that is:

⟦ T ⟧ = < Σ, M> where $\Sigma \subseteq \Sigma_{univ}$ and M ⊆ Alg(Σ) such that M is closed under isomorphism

The collection of isomorphism classes of (countable) Σ-algebras forms a set for any Σ. Therefore the collection of possible pairs < Σ, M> forms a set, which we will call SEM. If < Σ, M> ∈ SEM, then Sig< Σ, M>=Σ and Mod< Σ, M>=M. We will refer to classes of Σ-algebras which are closed under isomorphism as *Σ-model classes*.

The semantics of a parameterised specification is a function taking a member of SEM together with a signature morphism as argument and giving a member of SEM as a result (similar to Clear):

f : SEM X signature morphism → SEM

The generalisation to multiple parameters is not difficult but this presentation will be confined to the 1-parameter case. A parameterised specification is written λX:R[σ].B where X is the *formal parameter*, R is the *parameter requirement* (itself a specification), σ is the *formal fitting morphism* and B is the *body* (a specification which normally contains X, may contain σ, and may refer to the sorts and operators of R). Application is written (λX:R[σ].B)(ARG[ρ]) where ρ:Sig⟦ R ⟧→Sig⟦ ARG ⟧ is the *fitting morphism* which matches the *actual parameter* ARG with R. In contrast to Clear, the fitting morphism ρ is available for use in the body B via the formal fitting morphism σ. The semantics of application is as follows (where B_ρ[ARG/X] is an abbreviation for B[ARG/X, ρ/σ, $\rho(\omega)/\omega$ for all $\omega \in$ Sig⟦ R ⟧] -- the substitution into the body B of ARG for X and ρ for σ, and of $\rho(\omega)$ for ω for every sort or operator ω in Sig⟦ R ⟧):

Sig⟦ (λX:R[σ].B)(ARG[ρ]) ⟧ = Sig⟦ B_ρ[ARG/X] ⟧

$$\mathrm{Mod}[\![(\lambda X{:}R[\sigma].B)(ARG[\rho])]\!] = \begin{cases} \mathrm{Mod}[\![B_\rho[ARG/X]]\!] & \text{if } [\ A|_\rho \mid A \in \mathrm{Mod}(ARG)\ ] \subseteq \mathrm{Mod}[\![R]\!] \\ \mathrm{Alg}(\mathrm{Sig}[\![B_\rho[ARG/X]]\!]) & \text{otherwise} \end{cases}$$

Note that ARG is a semantic object from SEM, not a specification; this is necessary for the semantics of recursion.

This semantics describes a parameterisation mechanism which is more powerful and more expressive than in other languages. Using this we can define parameterised specifications in which the signature of the result depends on the signature of the actual parameter in a more flexible way than previously possible. For example, suppose we want to write a parameterised specification called Copy which produces a specification containing two copies of its actual parameter (i.e. two copies of all its sorts and operators). In Clear, CIP-L, LOOK and the ADJ approach to parameterisation this is impossible; the parameterised specification can only transform the part of the actual parameter which corresponds to the formal parameter. The best we could do is to make two copies of this part of the actual parameter, leaving the rest of the actual parameter alone. We can write Copy in ASL as follows:

$$\begin{aligned}
\text{Copy} \;&=_{def}\; \lambda X{:}\phi[\sigma].\; X + \textbf{derive from } X \textbf{ by } \rho \\
&\text{where } \rho: \Sigma_{univ} \to \Sigma_{univ} \text{ is defined by} \\
&\quad \rho(s') = s \quad \text{for } s' \in \Lambda \\
&\quad \rho(\omega') = \omega \in \Gamma_{s1\ldots sn \to s} \quad \text{for } \omega' \in \Gamma_{s1'\ldots sn' \to s'}
\end{aligned}$$

(this assumes that Λ and Γ are closed under 'priming': $s \in \Lambda \Rightarrow s' \in \Lambda$ and $\omega \in \Gamma_{us} \Rightarrow \omega' \in \Gamma_{u's'}$). Copy(Nat[$\phi$]) then has the sorts *nat* and *nat'* and operators *0: nat*, *0': nat'*, *succ: nat→ nat* and *succ': nat'→ nat'*. Note how heavily this specification relies on the definition of signature morphisms in section 2.1.

But this specification is not quite correct; suppose T contains *f: s→s* and *f': s'→s'*. Then Copy(T[ϕ]) will include the operators *f: s→s*, *f': s'→s'* and *f'': s''→s''*. In order to get two copies of each sort and operator, Copy has to take account of the signature of the actual parameter. So in fact we need ρ in Copy to be parameterised by the signature of the actual parameter:

$$\begin{aligned}
\text{Copy} \;&=_{def}\; \lambda X{:}\phi[\sigma].\; X + \textbf{derive from } X \textbf{ by } \rho(\text{Sig}(X)) \\
&\text{where } \rho: \text{signature} \to \text{signature morphism} \quad \text{is defined by } \rho(\Sigma) = \rho_\Sigma \\
&\text{where } \rho_\Sigma: \Sigma_{univ} \to \Sigma_{univ} \text{ is in turn defined by} \\
&\quad \rho_\Sigma(s\underbrace{'\cdots'}_{n+1}) = s \qquad \text{where n is the maximum number of} \\
&\quad \rho_\Sigma(\omega\underbrace{'\cdots'}_{n+1}) = \omega \qquad \text{primes on a sort or operator in } \Sigma
\end{aligned}$$

In order to define the semantics of recursive parameterised specifications we need orderings on signatures, on Σ-model classes and on signature morphisms. For these we use signature inclusion, set containment and the 'less defined' relation ($\sqsubseteq$) on partial functions respectively.

Theorem: All operators are monotonic with respect to signature inclusion and containment of model classes.

Note that the operations are also continuous for signatures and (except **reachable**) for model classes.

The monotonicity of the operations implies that every fixed-point equation for signatures or for model classes (on the same signature) has a least solution (taking the usual pointwise extension of an ordering on a set to an ordering on functions on the set). Therefore we define the semantics of recursive parameterised specifications (written $Yt(\lambda X{:}R[\sigma].B)$ where B may contain t) as the least fixed point of the equation $t = \lambda X{:}R[\sigma].B$; that is:

$\text{Sig}[\![Yt(\lambda X{:}R[\sigma].B)]\!]$ = the function (of type SEM × signature morphism → signature)

which is the least solution of $\quad \text{Sig}[\![t]\!](\text{ARG},\rho) = \text{Sig}[\![(\lambda X{:}R[\sigma].B)(\text{ARG}[\rho])]\!]$

$\text{Mod}[\![Yt(\lambda X{:}R[\sigma].B)]\!]$ = the function (: SEM × signature morphism → model class)

which is the least solution (i.e. the 'least' according to $\supseteq$, which is actually the greatest) of

$$\text{Mod}[\![t]\!](\text{ARG},\rho) = \text{Mod}[\![(\lambda X{:}R[\sigma].B)(\text{ARG}[\rho])]\!]$$

in the class of functions taking a SEM-object ARG with signature Σ and a signature morphism $\rho: \text{Sig}[\![R]\!] \to \Sigma$ and giving a $\text{Sig}[\![Yt(\lambda X{:}R[\sigma].B)]\!](\text{ARG},\rho)$ -model class as result.

Then applying a recursive parameterised specification to an argument is just function application:

$$\text{Sig}[\![Yt(\lambda X{:}R[\sigma].B)(\text{ARG}[\rho])]\!] = \text{Sig}[\![Yt(\lambda X{:}R[\sigma].B)]\!](\text{ARG},\rho)$$

$$\text{Mod}[\![Yt(\lambda X{:}R[\sigma].B)(\text{ARG}[\rho])]\!] = \text{Mod}[\![Yt(\lambda X{:}R[\sigma].B)]\!](\text{ARG},\rho)$$

Generalisation to mutually recursive definitions is possible (see [Wir 82]).

Recursive parameterised specifications can be used to write 'abstract domain equations' as in [HR 80] and

[EL 81]. By monotonicity, every such equation has a solution which can be computed within a finite number of iterations (if specifications are finite and every signature morphism has finite domain).

6 Implementation of specifications

The programming discipline of stepwise refinement advocated by Wirth and Dijkstra suggests that a program be evolved by working gradually via a series of successively lower-level refinements of the specification toward a specification which is so low-level that it can be regarded as a program. This approach guarantees the correctness of the resulting program, provided that each refinement step can be proved correct. A formalisation of this approach requires a definition of the concept of refinement, i.e. of the *implementation* of one specification by another.

In programming practice, proceeding from a specification to a program (by stepwise refinement or by any other method) means making a series of design decisions. These will include decisions concerning the concrete representation of abstractly defined data types, decisions about how to compute abstractly specified functions (choice of algorithm) and decisions which select between the various possibilities which the high-level specification leaves open. The following very simple formal notion of implementation captures this idea; a specification T is implemented by another specification T' if T' incorporates more design decisions than T:

Def: If T and T' are specifications, then T is *implemented* by T', written $T \rightsquigarrow T'$, if $\emptyset \neq T' \subseteq T$.

For example, suppose SetChoose specifies the standard model of sets of natural numbers (like Set in section 4) together with an operator *choose*: *set* → *nat* constrained only by the following axiom:

choose(add(x,S)) ∈ add(x,S) = true

That is, *choose* will select some arbitrary element of any non-empty set. And suppose SetChoose' is SetChoose augmented by axioms which further constrain *choose* to always select the minimal element. Then Mod⟦SetChoose'⟧ ⊆ Mod⟦SetChoose⟧ and so SetChoose ⇝ SetChoose' (since SetChoose' is satisfiable).

As another example, Behavioural-Set from section 4 (recall Behavioural-Set = **behaviour** Set **wrt** {bool, nat}, where Set specifies the standard model of sets) is implemented by List (lists of natural numbers together with the operator ∈) once the 'auxiliary' operators *head* and *tail* have been forgotten and the sort *list* and operators *nil* and *cons* renamed as *set*, ∅ and *add*:

Behavioural-Set ⇝ **derive from** List **by** σ

where σ: Sig⟦Behavioural-Set⟧ → sig⟦List⟧ is a signature morphism with σ(*set*)=*list*, σ(∅)=*nil*, σ(*add*)=*cons* and σ(*x*)=*x* for all other sorts and operators *x* in Behavioural-Set. But note:

Set ⇝̸ **derive from** List **by** σ

since Set itself (before behavioural abstraction) is satisfied only by algebras isomorphic to the standard model. Under most previous notions of implementation (see below) Set ⇝ **derive from** List **by** σ is a proper implementation. This was necessary because previous specification languages did not permit behavioural abstraction, so the notion of implementation had to capture it.

This notion of implementation extends to give a notion of the implementation of parameterised specifications:

Def: If P=λX:R[σ].B and P'=λX:R[σ].B' are parameterised specifications, then P is *implemented* by P', written P ⇝ P', if for all actual parameters ARG∈SEM with fitting morphism ρ: Sig⟦R⟧ → Sig(ARG) such that $\{A|_\rho \mid A \in Mod(ARG)\} \subseteq$ Mod⟦R⟧, P(ARG[ρ]) ⇝ P'(ARG[ρ]).

This definition can easily be generalised to parameterised specifications with multiple parameters.

An important issue for any notion of implementation is whether implementations can be composed *vertically* and *horizontally* [GB 80]. Implementations can be vertically composed if the implementation relation is transitive (T ⇝ T' and T'$\rightsquigarrow$T'' implies T$\rightsquigarrow$T'') and they can be horizontally composed if the specification-building operations preserve implementations (i.e. P$\rightsquigarrow$P' and A$\rightsquigarrow$A' implies P(A) $\rightsquigarrow$ P'(A'); A$\rightsquigarrow$A' and B$\rightsquigarrow$B' implies A+B $\rightsquigarrow$ A'+B'; and a similar rule holds for each of the remaining operations). Our notion of implementation has both these properties (the proofs are immediate by transitivity of $\subseteq$ and monotonicity of ASL's operations):

Theorem (vertical composition): If T$\rightsquigarrow$T' and T'$\rightsquigarrow$T'' then T$\rightsquigarrow$T''.

Theorem (horizontal composition): If A$\rightsquigarrow$A', B$\rightsquigarrow$B' and P=λX:R[σ].C $\rightsquigarrow$ P'=λX:R[σ].C', then:

1. A + B $\rightsquigarrow$ A' + B' iff A' + B' is satisfiable
2. For any S$\subseteq$sorts(A), **reachable** A **on** S $\rightsquigarrow$ **reachable** A' **on** S iff **reachable** A' **on** S is satisfiable
3. For any $\sigma:\Sigma\rightarrow$Sig$[\![$A$]\!]$, **derive from** A **by** σ $\rightsquigarrow$ **derive from** A' **by** σ
4. For any W$\subseteq|W_\Sigma(X)|$, **abstract** A **wrt** W $\rightsquigarrow$ **abstract** A' **wrt** W
5. If ρ:Sig$[\![$R$]\!]\rightarrow$Sig$[\![$A$]\!]$ is a fitting morphism such that $\{M|_\rho$ | M$\in$Mod$[\![$A$]\!]\}\subseteq$ Mod$[\![$R$]\!]$ and $\{M|_\rho$ | M$\in$Mod$[\![$A'$]\!]\}\subseteq$ Mod$[\![$R$]\!]$, then P(A[ρ]) $\rightsquigarrow$ P'(A'[ρ])

These two results allow large structured specifications to be refined in a gradual and modular fashion. All of the individual small specifications which make up a large specification can be separately refined in several stages to give a collection of lower-level specifications (this is easy because of their small size). When the low-level specifications are put back together, the result is guaranteed to be an implementation of the original specification.

ASL can be used to express a number of other concepts of implementation as well, including notions which coincide with or approximate most previously proposed definitions such as [EKMP 82], [EK 82], [GM 82] and [SW 82]. Only one of these is given below; see [SW 83] for some others.

Def: If A and A' are Σ-algebras, then A$\geqslant$A' if there exists a surjective homomorphism f:A$\rightarrow$A'. If T and T' are specifications with Sig$[\![$T$]\!]$=Sig$[\![$T'$]\!]$, then T' is a *homomorphic image* of T (T$\geqslant$T') if for every A$\in$Mod$[\![$T$]\!]$ there exists an A'$\in$Mod$[\![$T'$]\!]$ such that A$\geqslant$A'.

Def: If T and T' are specifications, σ:Sig$[\![$T$]\!]\rightarrow$Sig$[\![$T'$]\!]$ is a signature morphism, OBS$\subseteq$ sorts(T) and **reachable** T = T then T $\underset{FIR}{\overset{\sigma}{\Rightarrow}}$ T' if $\emptyset\neq$ **derive from** T' **by** $\sigma\geqslant$ **junk** T.

This corresponds to the notion of implementation in [Ehr 79], and is a simplified version of the notion in [EK 82]. Observe that Set $\underset{FIR}{\overset{\sigma}{\Rightarrow}}$ List where σ is an appropriate signature morphism, and note that this notion may be extended to give a notion of the implementation of parameterised specifications.

When using a powerful specification language one can adopt a simple notion of implementation. Previous languages and specification methods were less powerful (lacking operations like **behaviour**) so a more complex notion of implementation was necessary to handle cases like the implementation of sets by lists above. With ASL such complexity is not required because all such cases can be handled by explicit use of the **behaviour** operation.

One benefit of such a simple notion of implementation is that one can reason about implementations in a formal way using the specification language itself rather than at a metalevel using a metalanguage. For example, the identities in the next section can be used to prove the transitivity of $\underset{FIR}{\Rightarrow}$ (see [SW 83]). A second benefit is that with this simple notion the specifier has more freedom to say exactly what is required. For example, in some situations we might really want sets to be implemented only using a representation isomorphic to the standard model (e.g. in cases where the choice of data representation influences the complexity of an algorithm). In ASL one has the freedom not to apply behavioural abstraction in cases such as these. Finally, the simple notion of implementation permits vertical and horizontal composition of implementations, but this is generally not the case for the more complicated notions unless rather strong conditions are imposed (see e.g. [EKMP 82], [SW 82] and [GM 82]).

7 Identities and transformation of specifications

Because the semantics of ASL is simple, it is easy to prove that certain identities and relations between specifications hold. For example (see [SW 83] for some others):

Theorem: 1. **reachable (reachable T on S) on S' = reachable (reachable T on S') on S ⊇ reachable T on S ∪ S'**

2. W' ⊆ W implies **abstract (abstract T wrt W) wrt W' = abstract T wrt W'**
   = abstract (abstract T wrt W') wrt W

   so a. **behaviour (junk T on S) wrt OBS = behaviour T wrt OBS** if S ∩ OBS = ∅
   b. **junk (junk T on S') on S = junk T on S = junk (junk T on S) on S'** if S' ⊆ S
   c. **behaviour (behaviour T wrt OBS') wrt OBS = behaviour T wrt OBS** if OBS ⊆ OBS'
   d. **junk (behaviour T wrt OBS) on S = behaviour T wrt OBS** if S ∩ OBS = ∅

3. **derive from (derive from T by σ) by σ' = derive from T by σ'•σ**

4. **behaviour (restrict T on S) wrt OBS = behaviour T wrt OBS**
   if S ∩ OBS = ∅ and $W_{\Sigma}(X_{S'})$ is non-empty in all sorts of S, where Σ=Sig⟦T⟧, S'=sorts(Σ)-S

5. **abstract (derive from T by σ) wrt W ⊇ derive from (abstract T wrt σ(W)) by σ**

6. **abstract (abstract T wrt W) wrt W' ⊆ abstract T wrt W ∩ W'**

   so a. **junk (junk T on S) on S' ⊆ junk T on S ∪ S'**
   b. **behaviour (behaviour T wrt OBS) wrt OBS' ⊆ behaviour T wrt OBS ∩ OBS'**

7. **reachable (T + reachable T' on S) on S' = T + reachable T' on S** if S' ⊆ S

8. **reachable (enrich T by axioms E) on S = enrich reachable T on S by axioms E**

9. T ⩾ T' implies **junk T on S ⩾ junk T' on S**

10. T ⩾ T' implies **derive from T by σ ⩾ derive from T' by σ**

11. ∀t.(λX:R[σ].B)(ARG[ρ]) = B_{ρ}[ARG/X][∀t.(λX:R[σ].B)/t]
    if $[A|_{\rho}$ | A∈Mod(ARG)] ⊆ Mod⟦R⟧

But it is possible to find counterexamples showing that the following inequations hold:

Fact: 1'. **abstract (derive from T by σ) wrt W ≠ derive from (abstract T wrt σ(W)) by σ**

2'. **reachable (reachable T on S) on S' ≠ reachable T on S ∪ S'**

3'. **abstract (abstract T wrt W) wrt W' ≠ abstract T wrt W ∩ W'**

4'. **behaviour (behaviour T wrt OBS) wrt OBS' ≠ behaviour (behaviour T wrt OBS') wrt OBS**
    ≠ behaviour T wrt OBS ∪ OBS'

These properties can be useful for understanding the effects of ASL's operations. For example, properties 2a and 4 together indicate that the behaviour operation disregards any junk of invisible sorts.

It is possible to carry out proofs concerning specifications using the above properties. For example, solutions of domain equations can be computed. The following theorem can be proved in this way.

Theorem (vertical composition for $\xrightarrow[FIR]{}$): $T \xrightarrow[FIR]{\sigma} T'$ and $T' \xrightarrow[FIR]{\sigma'} T''$ implies $T \xrightarrow[FIR]{\sigma \bullet \sigma'} T''$.

These rules provide transformations for changing one specification into another specification which is equivalent (or an implementation, using the rules containing ⊆). Therefore they could be used as the basis of a method for developing data structures and programs from specifications (see e.g. [Bau 81a]).

8 Concluding remarks

The small set of operations in ASL seems to provide a powerful means for writing specifications. But some of the operations we decided not to include are interesting as well. Here are two which together could replace abstract:

Def: If A, A' are Σ-algebras and $W \subseteq |W_\Sigma(X)|$ then A is *W-finer* then A' ($A \leq_W A'$) if there are surjective assignments $\phi: X \to |A|$ and $\phi': X \to |A'|$ such that $\forall t, t' \in W.\ (\phi^\#(t) = \phi^\#(t') \implies \phi'^\#(t) = \phi'^\#(t'))$.

The *W-coarser* relation $\geq_W$ is obtained by replacing $\implies$ in this definition by $\impliedby$.

$$\mathrm{Sig}[\![T\Delta W]\!] = \mathrm{Sig}[\![T\nabla W]\!] = \mathrm{Sig}[\![T]\!] \qquad \text{if } W \subseteq |W_\Sigma(X)| \text{ where } \Sigma = \mathrm{Sig}[\![T]\!]$$
$$\mathrm{Mod}[\![T\Delta W]\!] = \{ A \in \mathrm{Alg}(\mathrm{Sig}[\![T]\!]) \mid \exists A_0 \in \mathrm{Mod}[\![T]\!].\ (A \leq_W A_0) \}$$
$$\mathrm{Mod}[\![T\nabla W]\!] = \{ A \in \mathrm{Alg}(\mathrm{Sig}[\![T]\!]) \mid \exists A_0 \in \mathrm{Mod}[\![T]\!].\ (A \geq_W A_0) \}$$

Then **abstract** T **wrt** W $=_{def}$ $T\Delta W + T\nabla W$
hom T **wrt** S $=_{def}$ **behaviour** T **wrt** S + $T\nabla|W_\Sigma(X)|$ where $\Sigma = \mathrm{Sig}[\![T]\!]$
T/eqns $=_{def}$ $\langle \mathrm{Sig}[\![T]\!], \mathrm{eqns}\rangle + T\nabla|W_\Sigma(X)|$ where $\Sigma = \mathrm{Sig}[\![T]\!]$

The **hom** operation is the same as behavioural abstraction except that it only permits models which are coarser than models of T (i.e. in which more terms are identified). An operation permitting only finer models can be defined similarly. T/E is the quotient of T by the equations E as defined in [Wir 82] (not exactly the usual quotient, since everything coarser than the quotient is included as well). Other interesting possibilities are:

$$\mathrm{Sig}[\![T \cup T']\!] = \mathrm{Sig}[\![T \cap T']\!] = \mathrm{Sig}[\![T]\!] \qquad \text{if } \mathrm{Sig}[\![T]\!] = \mathrm{Sig}[\![T']\!]$$
$$\mathrm{Mod}[\![T \cup T']\!] = \{ A \in \mathrm{Alg}(\mathrm{Sig}[\![T]\!]) \mid \exists A_0 \in \mathrm{Mod}[\![T]\!], A'_0 \in \mathrm{Mod}[\![T']\!].\ (A \text{ is the glb of } A_0 \text{ and } A'_0) \}$$
$$\mathrm{Mod}[\![T \cap T']\!] = \{ A \in \mathrm{Alg}(\mathrm{Sig}[\![T]\!]) \mid \exists A_0 \in \mathrm{Mod}[\![T]\!], A'_0 \in \mathrm{Mod}[\![T']\!].\ (A \text{ is the lub of } A_0 \text{ and } A'_0) \}$$

The lub (least upper bound) and glb (greatest lower bound) are with respect to the homomorphic image relation $\geq$ defined in section 6. Note that the lub and glb are not defined uniquely but only up to isomorphism.

Then $T\Delta$ $=_{def}$ $\langle \mathrm{Sig}[\![T]\!], \emptyset\rangle \cap T$ (i.e. $T\Delta|W_\Sigma(X)|$)
$T\nabla$ $=_{def}$ $\langle \mathrm{Sig}[\![T]\!], \emptyset\rangle \cup T$ (i.e. $T\nabla|W_\Sigma(X)|$)
hom T **wrt** S $=_{def}$ **behaviour** T **wrt** S + $T\nabla$
T/eqns $=_{def}$ $\langle \mathrm{Sig}[\![T]\!], \mathrm{eqns}\rangle + T\nabla$

Parameterised specifications with signature morphisms as parameters are a special case of parameterised specifications as defined here. This allows the expression of e.g. Clear-style procedure application with avoidance of name clashes. But signature morphisms are not yet 'first class citizens'; it is not possible to specify 'requirements' for signature morphism parameters. For example, it should be possible to require that a signature morphism be defined at least (or at most) on a particular domain, or that it extends a given signature morphism. This should be a straightforward extension. Another interesting generalisation would be to allow (recursive) higher-order parameterised specifications.

Inference in ASL specifications is more complex than in a 'flat' equational specification or in an ordinary structured theory as in LCF [GMW 79] or Clear. Besides the usual inference rules which allow theorems to be derived by combining axioms, inference rules are needed which allow theorems in a specification (say T) to be converted to theorems in a larger specification built from T (say T + T') as in [SB 83]. For example:

thm **in** T $\implies$ thm **in** T + T'
σ(thm) **in** T $\implies$ thm **in derive from** T **by** σ
thm **in** T and $\forall t \in \mathrm{terms}(\mathrm{thm}).[t \in W \text{ and } \forall x \in FV(t)_s.\forall y \in X_s.t[y/x] \in W]$ $\implies$ thm **in abstract** T **wrt** W

The last of these implies the following rule:

thm **in** T and thm contains only terms of sorts in OBS with variables of OBS sorts
$\implies$ thm **in behaviour** T **wrt** OBS

The **reachable** operation gives rise to an induction principle.

Finally, it would be interesting to build a new high-level specification language on top of ASL, trying to make available most of the power of ASL (e.g. behavioural abstraction) in higher-level specification-building operations while hiding some of the sharp edges (e.g. it probably should not be possible to get the effect of **abstract** T **wrt** W for arbitrary W). The result should be more versatile and expressive than any present specification language.

To avoid confusion, it is important to point out the differences between the present paper and [Wir 82] which also defined a language called ASL (we will refer to the two languages as new ASL and old ASL respectively). Apart from details of syntax, the differences between the two languages are as follows:

- New ASL contains an important new operation (**abstract**) which allows the expression of behavioural abstraction. Old ASL includes a 'quotient' operation which is not provided in new ASL. This change gives a language which is more oriented toward a behavioural approach to specification. The quotient operation was difficult to use in writing specifications [Gau 83] and did not easily extend from equational axioms to general first-order axioms.
- New ASL includes a more general and flexible parameterisation mechanism than old ASL.
- Old ASL is a language for specifying partial algebras, while new ASL (as described here) is for specifying total algebras. There is no difficulty in changing new ASL to specify partial algebras; we restricted attention to total algebras only for simplicity of presentation.

Furthermore, the present paper develops and justifies an elegant and simple notion of implementation of ASL specifications. This notion was mentioned briefly in [Wir 82], but here it is more appropriate because new ASL can express behavioural abstraction.

Acknowledgements

Thanks for useful discussions and helpful comments: from DS to Rocco de Nicola, David Rydeheard, Oliver Schoett and (especially) Rod Burstall; and from MW to Manfred Broy and Marie-Claude Gaudel. This work was supported by the Science and Engineering Research Council and the Sonderforschungsbereich 49, Programmiertechnik, München.

9 References

Note: LNCS n denotes Springer Lecture Notes in Computer Science, Vol. n

[ADJ 76] Goguen, J.A., Thatcher, J.W. and Wagner, E.G. An initial algebra approach to the specification, correctness, and implementation of abstract data types. IBM research report RC6487. Also in: Current Trends in Programming Methodology, Vol. 4: Data Structuring (R.T. Yeh, ed.), Prentice-Hall, pp. 80-149 (1978).

[ADJ 78] Thatcher, J.W., Wagner, E.G. and Wright, J.B. Data type specification: parameterization and the power of specification techniques. SIGACT 10th Annual Symp. on the Theory of Computing, San Diego, California.

[ADJ 80] Ehrig, H., Kreowski, H.-J., Thatcher, J.W., Wagner, E.G. and Wright, J.B. Parameterized data types in algebraic specification languages (short version). Proc. 7th ICALP, Noordwijkerhout, Netherlands. LNCS 85, pp. 157-168.

[Bau 81] Bauer, F.L. *et al* (the CIP Language Group) Report on a wide spectrum language for program specification and development (tentative version). Report TUM-I8104, Technische Univ. München.

[Bau 81a] Bauer, F.L. *et al* (the CIP Language Group) Programming in a wide spectrum language: a collection of examples. Science of Computer Programming 1, pp. 73-114.

[BBTW 81] Bergstra, J.A., Broy, M., Tucker, J.V. and Wirsing, M. On the power of algebraic specifications. Proc. 10th MFCS, Strbske Pleso, Czechoslovakia. LNCS 118, pp. 193-204.

[BG 77] Burstall, R.M. and Goguen, J.A. Putting theories together to make specifications. Proc. 5th IJCAI, Cambridge, Massachusetts, pp. 1045-1058.

[BG 80] Burstall, R.M. and Goguen, J.A. The semantics of Clear, a specification language. Proc. of Advanced Course on Abstract Software Specifications, Copenhagen. LNCS 86, pp. 292-332.

[BM 81] Bergstra, J.A. and Meyer, J.J. I/O computable data structures. SIGPLAN Notices 16, 4 pp. 27-32.

[Ehr 79] Ehrich, H.-D. On the theory of specification, implementation, and parametrization of abstract data types. Report 82, Univ. of Dortmund. Also in: JACM 29, 1 pp. 206-227 (1982).

[EK 82] Ehrig, H. and Kreowski, H.-J. (1982) Parameter passing commutes with implementation of parameterized data types. Proc. 9th ICALP, Aarhus, Denmark. LNCS 140, pp. 197-211.

[EKMP 82] Ehrig, H., Kreowski, H.-J., Mahr, B. and Padawitz, P. Algebraic implementation of abstract data types. Theoretical Computer Science 20, pp. 209-263.

[EL 81] Ehrich, H.-D. and Lipeck, U. Algebraic domain equations. Report 125, Univ. of Dortmund.

[ETLZ 82] Ehrig, H., Thatcher, J.W., Lucas, P. and Zilles, S.N. Denotational and initial algebra semantics of the algebraic specification language LOOK. Draft report, IBM research.

[Gau 83] Gaudel, M.-C. Persònal communication with M. Wirsing.

[GB 80] Goguen, J.A. and Burstall, R.M. CAT, a system for the structured elaboration of correct programs from structured specifications. Technical report CSL-118, Computer Science Laboratory, SRI International.

[GB 83] Goguen, J.A. and Burstall, R.M. Institutions: logic and specification. Draft report, SRI International.

[GGM 76] Giarratana, V., Gimona, F. and Montanari, U. Observability concepts in abstract data type specification. Proc. 5th MFCS, Gdansk. LNCS 45, pp. 576-587.

[GM 82] Goguen, J.A. and Meseguer, J. Universal realization, persistent interconnection and implementation of abstract modules. Proc. 9th ICALP, Aarhus, Denmark. LNCS 140, pp. 310-323.

[GM 83] Goguen, J.A. and Meseguer, J. An initiality primer. Draft report, SRI International.

[GMW 79] Gordon, M.J., Milner, A.J.R. and Wadsworth, C.P. Edinburgh LCF. LNCS 78.

[Gut 75] Guttag, J.V. The specification and application to programming of abstract data types. Ph.D. thesis, Univ. of Toronto.

[HKR 80] Hupbach, U.L., Kaphengst, H. and Reichel, H. Initial algebraic specification of data types, parameterized data types, and algorithms. VEB Robotron, Zentrum für Forschung und Technik, Dresden.

[HR 80] Hornung, G. and Raulefs, P. Terminal algebra semantics and retractions for abstract data types. Proc. 7th ICALP, Noordwijkerhout, Netherlands. LNCS 85, pp. 310-323.

[Kam 83] Kamin, S. Final data types and their specification. TOPLAS 5, 1 pp. 97-121.

[LB 77] Liskov, B.H. and Berzins, V. An appraisal of program specifications. Computation Structures Group memo 141-1, Laboratory for Computer Science, MIT.

[Rei 81] Reichel, H. Behavioural equivalence -- a unifying concept for initial and final specification methods. Proc. 3rd Hungarian Computer Science Conf., Budapest, pp. 27-39.

[SB 83] Sannella, D.T. and Burstall, R.M. Structured theories in LCF. Proc. 8th CAAP, L'Aquila, Italy. LNCS, to appear.

[SW 82] Sannella, D.T. and Wirsing, M. Implementation of parameterised specifications. Report CSR-103-82, Dept. of Computer Science, Univ. of Edinburgh; extended abstract in: Proc. 9th ICALP, Aarhus, Denmark. LNCS 140, pp. 473-488.

[SW 83] Sannella, D.T. and Wirsing, M. A kernel language for algebraic specification and implementation. Report CSR-131-83, Dept. of Computer Science, Univ. of Edinburgh.

[Sch 82] Schoett, O. A theory of program modules, their specification and implementation. Draft report, Univ. of Edinburgh.

[Wand 79] Wand, M. Final algebra semantics and data type extensions. JCSS 19 pp. 27-44.

[Wir 82] Wirsing, M. Structured algebraic specifications. Proc. AFCET Symp. on Mathematics for Computer Science, Paris, pp. 93-107.

[ZLT 82] Zilles, S.N., Lucas, P. and Thatcher, J.W. A look at algebraic specifications. Draft report, IBM research.

A FAST CONSTRUCTION OF DISJOINT PATHS IN COMMUNICATION NETWORKS

by

ELI SHAMIR and ELI UPFAL

Institute of Mathematics and Computer Science

The Hebrew University, Jerusalem, ISRAEL

Abstract An incremental connection problem is to add k disjoint paths from s_i to t_i, $1 \le i \le k$, in an operating network. A parallel distributed algorithm is presented, which solves the problem efficiently in a general situation. Its probable performance is analyzed in a random graph setup.

1. INTRODUCTION

Let a graph G and a set R of k disjoint pairs be given. Does G contain k vertex disjoint paths, connecting v to u for each pair $(v,u) \in R$, and how to construct them?

This algorithmic problem is NP-complete, even for planar graphs [3]. Its relevance to routing in interconnection network is clear. However, most of the studies of such networks (a recent account is given in [1]) were devoted to complexity lower bounds or to constructing special convenient and economic networks. Our approach is different. To motivate it consider an operation of a large and extended network which over a time interval $[t-\Delta t, t]$ accumulates a set R of *incremental connection requests*. These requests require routing via disjoint paths which are also disjoint from busy paths established for previous requests. The resources available to compute and switch a routing for R are the free vertices and edges at time t. These constitute a dynamic graph G_t, which clearly change with t and has a random character.

We are led to search for a good routing algorithm for incremental requests R, where "good" stands for:

(1) **General:** It applies to most graphs and requests, within reasonable limitation. Spaces for random graphs parametrized by edge density seem suitable input spaces.

(2) **Flexible and Dynamic:** The algorithm adjusts to partial fulfillment and handles easily restarts of the program, responding to dynamic changes of G_t and R.

(3) **Parallel and Distributed:** Clearly, a parallel construction of disjoint paths which is based on local computation is highly desirable.

We adopt the following computation model. Each vertex v is identified with a processor labeled by v. Each v receives as input a list of neighbors (edges), an upper estimate of n (the size of the graph) and further specific data detailed below. There is no common memory. Messages between neighbors are sent and received. For convenience only, we take a common clock to synchronize the steps of all vertices. At each clock cycle, v first receive a message from some w and then sends a message to some w', (messages can be empty). Synchronization by a central clock is convenient but not essential - in any case it can be simulated by local clocks which keep the step count of a processor in pace with its neighbors.

This model can be used for various graph-problems, e.g. matching, as done in [4]. For the present problem the specific data is (for each v) the Boolean function end_point(v) (=1 if v is an endpoint of a path) and the partial function other_end_point (v) (the destination).

(4) **Performance** Good performance is expressed in routing large $|R|$, a low edge density for G_t and a quick parallel algorithm. Our algorithm is based on growing in parallel of vertex-disjoint trees from all end-points of the request R. A branch of a tree is a possible path. Let n be the size (number of vertices) of G_t. To have a fair chance of meeting, a typical pair of trees Γ_v, Γ_u, $(v,u) \in R$ requires size $O(n^{1/2}/\alpha)$. Hence $|R|$ is limited to $\alpha n^{1/2}$. The density of edges required is $O(\alpha \log n)$ neighbors per vertex of G_t (quite low). The speed (number of parallel steps) is $O(\alpha^2 \log^2 n)$ - quite fast.

The limitation $\alpha n^{1/2}$ on the size of R is method-dependent, but we believe it is inherent in the problem of satisfying in parallel connection requests for *general* graphs. The role of the constant α is analyzed at the end of section 5. To multiply the size of R by α for a fixed n, we have to multiply the number of phases (so the total time) of the algorithm by α^2.

2. THE ALGORITHM AND ANALYSIS - INFORMAL DESCRIPTION

A full formal presentation is given in section 3. The algorithm starts or restarts by a call to Direct_Edges(v). This procedure, which contains random choices (a ballot), is designed to give direction to the edges in a distributed but non-conflicting manner. It succeeds with probability $1 - o(1)$.

Making G_t into a digraph and using Random_Edge(v) for pick-ups of a neighbor (see the discussion in section 5) facilitates the probability analysis, which is otherwise very cumbersome or even impossible for distributed processes.

Each execution of the pair of procedures (Build_Tree(v), Mark_Path(v)), in this order, is called a *phase*. One phase is the core of the Algorithm and its analysis. Its two procedures are parallel one, executed by all vertices in parallel.

Build_Tree. A vertex is *free* in a phase if it does not belong to paths created in previous phases. Each free vertex x which is an endpoint, after choosing a random order between 1 to n, starts to build a tree $\Gamma(x)$: the root is x, and x sends messages to two random neighbors. Thereafter for $2\log_2 n$ steps (the main loop of Build_Tree(v)), each free vertex v receiving the first connect message from w (consisting of 3 values: x - the tree root, destination of x and order(x)) joins the tree by setting the identifier father(v):=w. Then v sends connect messages to two random neighbors. If a vertex v receiving a connect message with root x belongs to the tree rooted at z - the destination of x, a message "found" is created.

Mark_Path This is designed to select a unique path (once a "found" is created) and mark it. A "found" created at a meeting of trees $\Gamma(x)$, $\Gamma(z)$ travels up one tree ($\Gamma(x)$ where order(x) > order(z)). The first "found" message to reach x travels back to z and marks a unique path. Since tree heights are bounded by $\log_2 n$, Mark_Path takes at most $3\log_2 n$ steps.

A phase creates a several new disjoint paths, *using at most two new edges and five messages per vertex*. The crucial Lemma in section 5 proves that there is a $d > 0$ such that executing a phase gives any free pair $(v,u) \in R$ a probability $> d$ to connect, independent of what happened at other phases.

Thus globally we have to assure (with $1 - o(1)$ probability) that $r = D\log n$ phases can run (without emptying a list of neighbors), for suitable $D(d)$. Then we quit and state that all pairs are connected with probability $1 - o(1)$. This is the way our main theorem is stated and proved. In practice, it may make more sense to restart after r phases (even $r = 1$) at time $t' > t$, if busy resources are freed, the dynamic graph changes and the request set R is updated.

3. Parallel Disjoint Paths Algorithm

```
Program Disjoint_Paths(r);

input  for each v∈V a set of neighbors adj_list(v).
       if v is an end-point of a required path,
       end_point(v)=true and other_end_point(v) contains the
       other end-point of the required path.

begin
  pardo for each v∈V
    begin
      status(v):=free;
      Direct_Edges(v);
      repeat r times do
        Build_Tree(v);
        Mark_Path(v);
      od
    end
  od
end Disjoint_Paths Algorithm

procedure Direct_Edges(v);
begin
  new_edges(v):=ϕ;
  for each u∈ adj_list(v) do
    order(v,u):=Random({1, . . . ,n^3});
    send order(v,u) to u;
  od
  for each u∈ adj_list(v) do
    if order(v,u)<order(u,v) then
      new-edges(v):=new_edges(v)∪{u};
  od
end Direct_Edges;

procedure Build_Tree(v);
begin
  father(v):=ϕ;
  son(v):=ϕ;
  order(v):=Random({1, . . . ,n});
  if end_point(v) and status(v)=free then
    repeat 2 times do
      son(v):=Random_Edge(used_edges(v),new_edges(v));
      send link(v,other_end_point(v),order(v)) message to son(v);
    od
    son(v):=ϕ;
  else
    repeat 2log_2 n times do
      if receive link(origin,destination,order) message from w then
        used_edges(v):=used_edges(v)∪{w};
        if father(v)=ϕ and status(v)=free then
          father(v):=w;
          origin(v):=origin;
          destination(v):=destination;
          order(v):=order;
```

```
            repeat 2 times do
              son(v):=Random_Edge(used_edges(v),new_edges(v));
              send link(origin,destination,order) message to son(v);
            od
            son(v):=φ
            else if status(v)=free and origin(v)=destination then
            if order(v)<order then
              send found message to w
            else send found message to father(v);

     od
end Build_Tree;

Function Random_Edge(used_edges(v),new_edges(v));
begin
   choice:=Random({1, . . . ,n-1});
   if choice ≤ |used_edges(v)| then
     return Random(used_edges(v));
   else
     edge:=Random(new_edges(v));
     used_edges(v):=used_edges(v) ∪ edge;
     new_edges(v):=new_edges(v)-edge;
    return edge;
end Random_Edge;

Procedure Mark_Path(v);
begin
   repeat 3log2n times do
     if receive a found message from w then
        if not end_point(v) and son(v)=φ then
          son(v):=w;
          send found message to father(v);
        else if end_point(v) and son(v)=φ then
          status(v):=connect;
          path_neighbor1(v):=w;
          send mark message to w;
     if receive a mark message from w then
       status(v):=connect;
       path_neighbor1(v):=father(v);
        if not end_point(v) then
          if father(v)=w then
            path_neighbor2(v):=son(v);
            send mark message to son(v);
          else
            path_neighbor2(v):=w;
            send mark message to father(v);
   od
end Mark_Path;

Procedure Random(A);
  returns a random element from the set A;
```

4. THE MAIN THEOREM - THE PROBABILITY SETUP

For the input graph G_t we use standard random graph spaces over n labeled vertices (cf. Erdös - Rényi papers in [2]). The space $G_{n,p}$ is defined by an independent edge probability p, while $G_{n,N}$ is defined by having N random edges. We require

$$(4.1) \qquad p \geq C\log\frac{n}{n} \text{ or } N \geq Cn\log n,\ n \to \infty$$

for a suitable C. In both cases the average degree is at least $C\log n$. But C should be taken sufficiently large so that with probability $1-o(1)$, the minimal degree of G_t is $\geq 4D\log n$, so that $r = D\log n$ phases run through without emptying an adjacency list.

THEOREM *Let $G_t \in G_{n,p}$ or $G_{n,N}$ with p or N satisfying (4.1). Let $R = \{(v_i, u_i)\}$ be a set of interconnection requests, $|R| \leq \alpha n^{1/2}$. Then the algorithm Disjoint_Paths(r) presented in section 3, running $r = D\log n$ phases, produces disjoint paths for all $(v,u) \in R$ with probability* $1-o(1)$.

The probability is a product of two factors. One is the probability of the set of inputs G_t. The other factor is the probability of the set of choices attached to the various random steps of the algorithm.

In the discussion at section 2 we have in fact reduced the proof of the theorem to the analysis of one phase.

5. ANALYSIS OF ONE PHASE

Random_Edge(v) is a handy procedure for various random graph algorithms, implementing the instruction "pick another neighbor for v" (and send it a link message in our case).

Usually, this pick-up is interesting only when "another" makes sense, i.e. the set new-edges(v) of yet unknown neighbors of v is not empty.

Random_Edge(v) is designed to obtain independence of the pick-up result from other steps of the algorithm, and distribute the probability that u is picked-up evenly among all candidates, old and new. this probability would be uniformly $\frac{1}{n-1}$ for each $u \neq v$ if v picked up alone at this step (e.g. in sequential programs). For parallel algorithms it is not hard to see that if u does not pick-up at the same step (e.g. if u is new) then (for a graph with n vertices)

$$\text{Prob}\{ v \text{ pick-up } u \} \geq \frac{1}{n-1}$$

Recall that $|R| \leq \alpha n^{1/2}$. We take $\alpha = 1$ and then treat the effect of α. Thus at worst, $n^{1/2}$ paths of length $2\log n$ exists in G_t at a start of a phase. This assumption and the use of Random_Edge(v) to pick from partly used links, makes each phase analysis completely independent of other phases.

For a pair $(v,u) \in I$ free at the start of a phase, we need an estimate of the joint probability that Γ_v and Γ_u grow to a "fair" size during the phase, then there is a fair chance to connect them. It seems that the only way to achieve such an estimate is to study the growth of one tree under an arbitrary condition $\mathcal{B}$. Let

(5.1) $F(\Gamma, \mathcal{B}, C) = \{$ the tree Γ grows to size $\geq Cn^{1/2}$ in the phase $| \mathcal{B} \}$.

Where $\mathcal{B}$ is any feasible event involving the other trees.

LEMMA *For suitable positive constants* C, d', d,

(5.2) $\quad Prob\{ F(\Gamma, \mathcal{B}, C) \} \geq d'$.

$$\mathcal{E} = \{ \text{the free pair } (v,u) \in R \text{ is path connected in a phase} \}$$

(5.3) $\quad Prob(\mathcal{E}) \geq d$.

Proof The conditioned growth of a tree is a complicated branching process of unknown and varying birthrate. Its estimate becomes possible after we introduce a branching process $Y = \{Y(j)\}$ which serves as a stochastic lower bound to all the conditioned tree processes. Let the distribution of

$Y(j)$ = number of sons of an element in generation j of Y.

be computed under the worst possible assumption across the board: all the trees had maximal growth (i.e. full binary trees) up to the point under consideration. This strikes out vertices, at most

(5.4) $\quad n^{1/2}2^{j+3}$ at generation j, $2n^{1/2}\log n$ at generation 0,

(the 0 - generation misses the vertices on at most $\sqrt{n}$ old paths created at previous phases). This leaves Y with some number of candidates for linking to an element in generation j, where this number for Y is smaller than the corresponding number for any tree process conditioned upon $\mathcal{B}$. All other factors being equal, we see that the distribution $Y(j)$ gives smaller probability to l sons ($l \geq 1$) compared to any conditioned tree process at generation j. Thus $Y(j)$ is a stochastic lower bound to all these processes, as claimed.

In the branching process Y, birthrate slows down with increasing j. The distribution $Y(j)$ are explicitly computable from (5.4). For the first moments, we have

$$m_j = E(Y(j)) = 2P_j = 2(1 - \frac{2n^{1/2}\log n}{n})(1 - \frac{n^{1/2}2^{j+3}}{n})$$

(5.5)

$$\sigma_j = VAR(Y(j)) = 2P_j(1 - P_j)$$

Let X_h be the size of the h generation of Y. By simple recursion formulas (cf. [4]) we get

$$E(X_h) = \prod_{j=1}^{h} m_j\,, \qquad VAR(X_h) = \prod_{j=1}^{h} m_j (\sum_{j=1}^{h} \frac{\sigma_j^2}{m_j} \prod_{s=j+1}^{h} m_s).$$

Substitution from (5.5) and doing simple estimates one can easily show that for suitable h^* (an integer near $\frac{1}{2}\log n - 2$) the product giving $E(X_{h^*})$ is at least $an^{1/2}$ and the $VAR(X_{h^*})$ is a small fraction of this, so by Chebyshev:

(5.6) $\quad Prob\{X_{h^*} \geq Cn^{1/2}\} \geq d'$

for suitable positives C and d'. This estimate for Y proves (5.2) for the conditioned tree growth.

If two trees grow to have front $Cn^{1/2}$ at generation h^* (the probability for this is at least $(d')^2$), then the probability that no connection between these trees occurs at generation $h^* + 1$ is estimated by

(5.7) $\quad (1 - \frac{Cn^{1/2}}{n-1})^{4Cn^{1/2}} \approx e^{-4C^2}$

Hence

(5.8) $\quad Prob(\mathcal{E}) \geq (d')^2(1 - e^{-4C^2}) = d$

This proves (5.3)

Now if the request is to route $\alpha n^{1/2}$ paths in parallel, then we consider trees of size $\frac{Cn^{1/2}}{\alpha}$ in (5.1). The probability d' in (5.2) is uneffected, but instead of (5.8) we have

$$prob(\mathcal{E}) \geq (d')^2(1 - e^{-4\frac{c^2}{\alpha^2}}) \approx 4(d')^2 \frac{C^2}{\alpha^2},$$

so if α grows, the basic pair-connected probability of a phase is proportional to α^{-2}, the expected number of phases to run is multiplied by α^2.

Concluding Remark. Networks are designed for the function of connection, which we studied here, or for the function of concentration [1]. The graph-theoretic paradigm for concentration is perfect matching, which we analyzed in a similar way in [4].

References

1. S.N. Bhatt, On concentration and connection networks, *TM 196/1981, M.I.T.* Cambridge, Mass. 1981.

2 P. Erdös, *The Art of Counting - Selected Writings*. J. Spencer Ed., The M.I.T. Press, Cambridge 1973.

3. M.R. Garey and D.S. Johnson, *Computers and Intractability A Guide to the Theory of NP-Completeness*. W.H. Freeman and Company, San Francisco, 1979.

4. E. Shamir and E. Upfal, N - processors graphs distributively achieve perfect matchings in $O(\log^2 N)$ beats. *Proc. of Annual ACM Sym. on Principles of Distributed Computing*, 1982, 238-241.

A TIGHT Ω(loglog n)-BOUND ON THE TIME FOR PARALLEL RAM'S TO COMPUTE NONDEGENERATED BOOLEAN FUNCTIONS

Hans-Ulrich Simon
Institut für angewandte Mathematik und Informatik
der Universität des Saarlandes
D-6600 Saarbrücken
W.-Germany

Abstract:

A function $f:\{0,1\}^n \to \{0,1\}$ is said to depend on dimension i iff there exists an input vector x such that f(x) differs from $f(x^i)$, where x^i agrees with x in every dimension except i. In this case x is said to be critical for f with respect to i. f is called nondegenerated iff it depends on all n dimensions.

The main result of this paper is that for each nondegenerated function $f: \{0,1\}^n \to \{0,1\}$ there exists an input vector x which is critical with respect to at least $\Omega(\log n)$ dimensions. A function achieving this bound is presented.

Together with earlier results from Cook,Dwork [2] and Reischuk [3] we can conclude that a parallel RAM requires at least $\Omega(\log\log n)$ steps to compute f.

1. Notations and Main Theorem

Let us define a PRAM (= Parallel RAM) to consist of a collection of processors which compute synchronously in parallel and which communicate with a common global random access memory. At each step each processor can read from one global memory cell, do some computing and write into one global memory cell. Any number of processors can read a given global memory cell at once, but we allow at most one processor to attempt to write into a given memory cell in one step. At the beginning of the computation of a function $f(x_1,\dots,x_n)$ the values $x_1,\dots,x_n$ are stored in the global memory cells $C_1,\dots,C_n$. At the end of the computation $f(x_1,\dots,x_n)$ has to be stored in C_1 (compare the definitions in [1],[2] and [3]).

Let $B = \{0,1\}$. For each Boolean function $f:B^n \to B$ and for each input vector x let c(f,x) denote the number of dimensions i such that x is critical for f with respect to i. Let $c(f) := \max \{c(f,x) \mid x \in B^n\}$. In [2] and [3] it is shown that a PRAM requires at least $\Omega(\log(c(f)))$ steps to compute f.

F_n denotes the set of nondegenerated Boolean functions of n variables. Let $c_n := \min \{c(f) \mid f \in F_n\}$.

Theorem: Let $n \geq 2$.

$$\frac{1}{2}\log(n) - \frac{1}{2}\log\log(n) + \frac{1}{2} < c_n < \log(n) + 2 .$$

Corollary:

Let $f \in F_n$. Then a PRAM requires at least $\Omega(\log\log n)$ steps to compute f.

2. Proof of the Theorem

The upper bound for c_n is shown by the following

Example 1:

For $x=(x_1,\ldots,x_n) \in B^n$ let $v(x) := \sum_{i=1}^{n} x_i 2^{n-i}$. For $n=m+2^m$ let

$$f_n(x_1,\ldots,x_m,y_0,\ldots,y_{2^m-1}) := y_{v(x)} .$$

f_n has the following properties:

(i) $f_n \in F_n$.

(ii) $c(f_n) = m+1$.

(iii) A PRAM (with m processors only) can compute f_n in $\lceil \log m \rceil + 2$ steps.

To prove the lower bound for c_n some additional notations are required. Let $G = (V,E)$ be an undirected graph. The minimum degree $md(G)$ is defined by $md(G) := \min \{\text{degree}(v) \mid v \in V\}$. Any not empty, finite sequence $p=(v_1,\ldots,v_r)$ of vertices such that

$$\forall i \in [1:r-1]: \quad \{v_i,v_{i+1}\} \in E$$

is called a path in G. p is called a cycle iff in addition $v_1=v_r$. For each function $f:E \rightarrow B$, labeling the edges of G by 0 or 1, the weight $W_f(p)$ of p with respect to f is defined by

$$W_f(p) := \sum_{i=1}^{r-1} f(\{v_i,v_{i+1}\}) \quad , \text{ where } \Sigma \text{ denotes the integer sum.}$$

Let $E_n := \{\{x,y\} \mid x,y \in B^n$ and x,y differ in exactly one dimension$\}$.
The undirected graph $C_n := (B^n, E_n)$ is called the <u>n-dimensional cube</u>. For every function $f\colon B^n \to B$ let Δ_f denote a function from E_n to B defined by

$$\Delta_f(\{x,y\}) = \begin{cases} 1 & \text{if } f(x) \neq f(y) \\ 0 & \text{if } f(x) = f(y) \end{cases}$$

<u>Example 1 (continued):</u>

$$f_3(x_1,y_0,y_1) = \begin{cases} y_0 & \text{if } x_1 = 0 \\ y_1 & \text{if } x_1 = 1 \end{cases}$$

and Δ_{f_3}, regarded as functions which label the vertices and the edges of C_3, can be drawn as

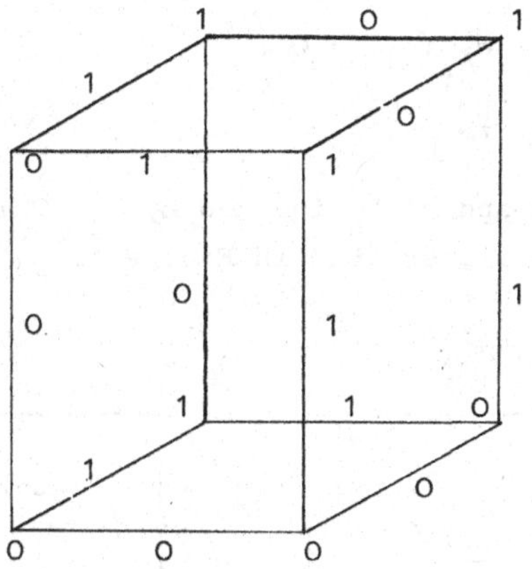

The following Lemmata are obvious but important.

<u>Lemma 1:</u>

Let $G=(V,E)$ be a not empty, partial subgraph of C_n, i.e. $\phi \subsetneqq V \subset B^n$, $E \subset E_n$. Then $|V| \geq 2^{md(G)}$.

<u>Lemma 2:</u>

Let f be a function from B^n to B and let c be a cycle in C_n. Then the weight of c with respect to Δ_f is even.

Let $f \in F_n$ be arbitrary but fixed. From now on we regard the vertices and the edges of C_n as labeled by f and Δ_f. Let $c := c(f)$.

Observation:

For each vertex x of C_n there are $c(f,x) \leq c$ edges labeled 1 incident on x.

For every vertex $x \in B^n$ let x_i denote the i'th component of x. Let $i \in [1:n]$ an arbitrary but fixed dimension. Since f is nondegenerated there exists an edge $\{x,x^i\}$ labeled 1. W.l.o.g. $x_i=0$ and $x^i_i=1$. For $j=0,1$ let $V_j := \{y \in B^n \mid y_i=j\}$. C^j_n denotes the (n-1)-dimensional subcube induced by V_j. We define subsets $U_j \subset V_j$ in the following way:

a) $y \in U_0$ iff there exist paths p_j in C^j_n such that

(i) p_0 starts in x and ends in y.

(ii) p_1 starts in x^i and ends in y^i.

(iii) $W_{\Delta_f}(p_0) = W_{\Delta_f}(p_1) = 0$.

b) $y \in U_1$ iff $y^i \in U_0$.

G_j denotes the subgraph of C^j_n induced by U_j. This construction and the following claim are illustrated in Figure 1.

Figure 1:

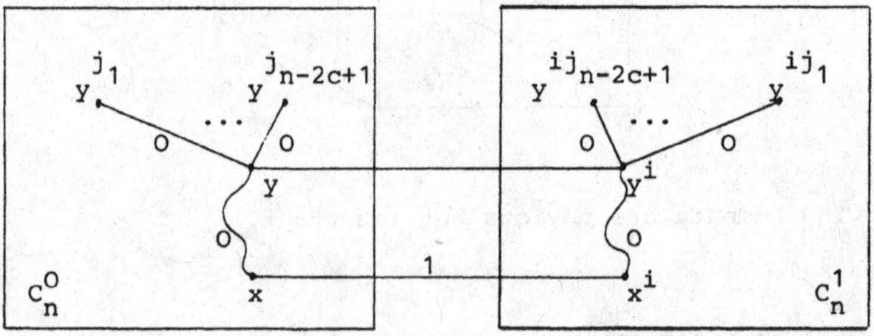

Claim:

1) $x \in U_0$ and $x^i \in U_1$.

2) $\forall y \in U_0$: $\{y,y^i\}$ is labeled 1 .

3) $md(G_0) = md(G_1) \geq n-2c+1$.

Proof of the claim:

1) The paths $p_0=(x)$ and $p_1=(x^i)$ fulfil the conditions (i),(ii) and (iii) above.

2) Let $y \in U_0$, $y^i \in U_1$, p_0 a path weighted 0 from x to y and p_1 a path

weighted 0 from x^i to y^i. Let us assume for the sake of contradiction that $\{y,y^i\}$ is labeled 0. Then

$$p_0 \cdot (y,y^i) \cdot p_1^{-1} \cdot (x^i,x) \ ,$$

where "$\cdot$" denotes the composition and " $^{-1}$ " the reversal of paths, is a cycle weighted 1 in contradiction to Lemma 2. Thus $\{y,y^i\}$ is labeled 1.

3) Let $y \in U_0$ and $D_i := [1:n] \setminus \{i\}$. From the observation above and from the fact that $\{y,y^i\}$ is labeled 1 it follows:

(1) There are at most c-1 dimensions $j \in D_i$ such that $\{y,y^j\}$ is labeled 1. There are at most c-1 dimensions $j \in D_i$ such that $\{y^i,y^{ij}\}$ is labeled 1, where y^{ij} agrees with y in every dimension except i and j.

(2) There are at most 2(c-1) dimensions $j \in D_i$ such that $\{y,y^j\}$ is labeled 1 or $\{y^i,y^{ij}\}$ is labeled 1.

(3) There are at least $n-1-2(c-1)=n-2c+1$ dimensions $j \in D_i$ such that $\{y,y^j\}$ is labeled 0 and $\{y^i,y^{ij}\}$ is labeled 0.

Thus $md(G_0) = md(G_1) \geq n-2c+1$.

By the claim and Lemma 1: $|U_0| = |U_1| \geq 2^{n-2c+1}$. Thus there are at least 2^{n-2c+1} edges labeled 1 in dimension i. Summing over all dimensions we observe that at least $n2^{n-2c+1}$ edges are labeled 1. On the other hand this number cannot exceed $c2^{n-1}$. Setting

$$n2^{n-2c+1} \leq c2^{n-1}$$

a straightforward computation shows that

$$c > \frac{1}{2}\log(n) - \frac{1}{2}\log\log(n) + \frac{1}{2} \ ,$$

provided that $n \geq 2$. This proves the Theorem.

3. Conclusions

What are the corresponding results in the case of nondegenerated functions $f: S_1 \times \ldots \times S_n \rightarrow S$, where $S_1,\ldots,S_n$ are arbitrary finite sets with at least two elements ? The following example shows that there exist nondegenerated functions which are computable by a single processor in constant time.

Example 2:

For every $n \in \mathbb{N}$ let f_n^ε be the function from $[1:n] \times B^n$ to B given by $f_n(i, x_1, \ldots, x_n) := x_i$.

With a straightforward modification of this example one can show that for every $\varepsilon > 0$ there exists a family f_n^ε of functions of n variables $x_1, \ldots, x_n$ such that

(1) For every $i \in [1:n]$ at most $O(n^\varepsilon)$ values can be assigned to x_i.

(2) A single processor can compute f_n^ε in constant time.

On the other hand one can show by the main theorem of this paper and an easy binary coding argument the

Corollary:

Let f_n be a family of nondegenerated functions of n variables $x_1, \ldots, x_n$ such that at most $O(\log n)$ values can be assigned to x_i for every $i \in [1:n]$. Then a PRAM requires at least $\Omega(\log\log n)$ steps to compute f_n.

Acknowledgements:

I am grateful to Rüdiger Reischuk for many helpful discussions and for pointing me to the family f_n in example 1, and to Helmut Alt and Kurt Mehlhorn for suggestions to simplify the original proof.

References:

[1] A.Borodin, J.Hopcroft. Routing and Merging on Parallel Models of Computation. Proc. 14'th annual ACM, 5/1982. pp.338-344.

[2] S.Cook, C.Dwork. Bounds on the Time for Parallel RAM's to Compute Simple Functions. Proc. 14'th annual ACM, 5/1982. pp.231-233.

[3] R.Reischuk. A Lower Time Bound for Parallel RAM's without Simultaneous Writes. IBM Research Report RJ3431 (40917), 3/1982.

THE IDENTIFICATION OF PROPOSITIONS AND TYPES IN MARTIN-LÖF'S TYPE THEORY: A PROGRAMMING EXAMPLE

Jan Smith

Department of Computer Science
University of Göteborg
Chalmers University of Technology
S-412 96 Göteborg, Sweden

INTRODUCTION.

Bishop's book Foundations of Constructive Analysis [1] shows that practically all of classical analysis can be rebuilt constructively. Its appearance in 1967 gave rise to a number of formalizations of constructive mathematics. Per Martin-Löf proposed that his formalization, intuitionistic type theory, may also be used as a programming language. His ideas are unfolded in [11]. Viewed as a programming language, type theory is a functional language with a very rich type structure. Compared with other functional languages, like Hope [3], ML [5] or SASL [14], one of the main differences is that general recursion is not allowed in type theory. The use of general recursion equations is replaced by primitive recursion. For natural numbers, this means that the only recursive definitions allowed are of the form

$$\begin{cases} f(0) = c \\ f(s(n)) = g(n,f(n)) \end{cases}$$

where $s(n)$ denotes the successor of n; and correspondingly for lists

$$\begin{cases} f(nil) = c \\ f(a.l) = g(a,l,f(l)) \end{cases}$$

where $a.l$ denotes the list obtained by adding the object a to the left of the list l. The use of this restrictive form of recursion makes it possible to give a very simple and coherent semantics for type theory, the one developed in [11]. It also makes it easier to reason about programs; for example, the rule of type theory involving primitive recursion for natural numbers corresponds closely to the induction rule for natural numbers. This correspondance is explained below in connection with the formulation of the rules for natural numbers.

At first sight, it may seem like a severe limitation not to have general recursion available. But this is not so, because definition by primitive recursion may involve functions of higher type. For instance, all the recursive functions that are provably total in first order arithmetic are definable in type theory. One way of seeing this is to note that the theory of primitive recursive functionals of finite type in Gödel [6] is a subtheory of type theory, and then use the theorem that all recursive functions provably total in first order arithmetic are definable in Gödel's theory. Of course, a metamathematical result like this may not be of much use in actually constructing workable programs.

Many algorithms used in programming are directly definable by primitive recursion, but there are important exceptions, for example the program quicksort, which sorts a list s in the following way:

If s = nil then quicksort of s is nil. If s = a.l, partition l into two lists $l_{\leq}$ and $l_{>}$, where $l_{\leq}$ consists of those elements of l that are smaller than or equal to a and $l_{>}$ of those that are greater than a. Apply quicksort to $l_{\leq}$ and $l_{>}$ and concatenate the resulting lists with a in between; this list is the value of quicksort on s.

Quicksort is clearly a program that cannot be defined directly by primitive recursion on lists, because at least one of the lists $l_{\leq}$ and $l_{>}$ must have a length less than that of l. Moreover, neither $l_{\leq}$ nor $l_{>}$ need be an initial segment of l. However, quicksort satisfies a course-of-values recursion of the form

$$\begin{cases} f(nil) = c \\ f(a.l) = g(a,l,f(d_1(a,l)),f(d_2(a,l))) \end{cases}$$

where

$$length(d_1(a,l)) \leq length(l) \quad \text{and} \quad length(d_2(a,l)) \leq length(l)$$

For natural numbers there is a well-known method from recursion theory for reducing course-of-values recursion in general to primitive recursion by introducing an auxiliary function $\tilde{f}(n)$, which stores all the values f(m) for m < n on a list; for the details, I refer to [8]. This method clearly does not work for lists, because, in general, if l is a list with length greater than one, there may be infinitely many lists with length smaller than the length of l.

In the explanation of intuitionistic predicate logic given by Heyting [7], the logical constants are explained in terms of constructions. Martin-Löf's type theory is a theory of constructions with such a strong type system that each proposition can be expressed as a type, namely the type of constructions, expressing proofs of the proposition, using Heyting's explanation. The purpose of this paper is to solve, in type theory, the course-of-values equations

$$\begin{cases} f(nil) = c \\ f(a.l) = g(a,l,f(d_1(a,l)),\ldots,f(d_k(a,l))) \end{cases}$$

where

$$length(d_i(a,l)) \leq length(l) \qquad (i = 1,\ldots,k)$$

and thereby using a method which will illustrate the identification of propositions and types. The idea is to give an informal proof of a natural course-of-values induction rule. This proof is just a few lines long and, when formalized in type theory, a program will be obtained which solves the equations.

It should be noted that the use of intuitionistic, or constructive, logic is here not motivated by any philosophical argument. If we use non-constructive reasoning when proving the existence of a program, it is in general no longer possible to obtain the program from the proof. The idea of using a formalization of constructive mathematics for programming is not new; it was already suggested by Bishop [2] and also by Constable [4]. Constructive proofs are also used in the quite different context of automatic program synthesis, see e.g. [9].

The program for the solution will be written in a completely formal notation, but the correctness proof, i.e., the proof that the solution really satisfies the equations, will be given by informal mathematics. However, in the proof, all steps are straightforward applications of rules of type theory. So, there are no problems in formalizing the correctness proof and having it checked by a computer. This has actually been done, using the implementation of type theory given by Petersson [13].

Finally, I will construct a program for quicksort in type theory, as an example of the method.

SOME RULES OF TYPE THEORY.

The program for the solution of the course-of-values equations and the proof that it satisfies the equations, only involve a tiny part of type theory. However, since the method I use for obtaining the solution involves the identification of propositions and types, more rules of type theory are needed.

If we regard a type A as a proposition and we have $a \in A$ then we may read this as "a is a proof of A" and since we are often not concerned with the details of the construction of that proof, we may suppress the object a and write "A is true" or just "A". If, in the rules of type theory, we read some of the types as propositions and suppress the explicit proof-objects, all the rules of intuitionistic arithmetic may be obtained, formulated in natural deduction. A proof of a proposition A in this formalization of arithmetic can be mechanically transformed back into a proof in type theory, thereby giving an object a and a derivation of $a \in A$. I will only give those rules which we actually are going to use. In terms of propositions, these rules involve implication, universal quantification and induction on natural numbers and lists. For further details of type theory, I refer to Martin-Löf [10,11] and, for some programming examples, to Nordström [12].

The objects of the types do not only form proof-objects, but they are also the programs of type theory. Expressions for the objects are built up from variables by means of various primitive forms, which will be given in connection with the rules, and by means of abstraction $(x_1,\ldots,x_k)b$ and application $b(a_1,\ldots,a_k)$. We do not use the more common lambda-notation for abstraction, because we want to reserve the lambda for the objects in the function types. For abstraction and application, the rules of β- and η-reduction hold, i.e., $((x_1,\ldots,x_n)b)(a_1,\ldots,a_k) \equiv b(a_1,\ldots,a_k/x_1,\ldots,x_k)$, where $b(a_1,\ldots,a_k/x_1,\ldots,x_k)$ denotes the result of substituting $a_1,\ldots,a_k$ for $x_1,\ldots,x_k$ in b, and $(x_1,\ldots,x_k)(b(x_1,\ldots,x_k)) \equiv b$ provided that $x_1,\ldots,x_k$ does not occur free in b. The programs of type theory are always evaluated outermost first , i.e., lazy evaluation is used, corresponding to "call by need" in a conventional programming language.

The rules are formulated in natural deduction and assumptions are written within square brackets.

<u>Natural numbers</u>. We let N denote the type of natural numbers. The objects of type N

are 0 and s(a) provided $a \in N$, where s denotes the successor function. So, we have

N-introduction: $0 \in N$ $\qquad \dfrac{a \in N}{s(a) \in N}$

We want to define functions on the natural numbers by primitive recursion and we therefore introduce the constant rec, which is computed according to the rules

$$\begin{cases} rec(0,c,e) = c \\ rec(s(a),c,e) = e(a,rec(a,c,e)) \end{cases}$$

So, defining f by $f(n) \equiv rec(n,c,e)$ corresponds to the introduction of f by the primitive recursion

$$\begin{cases} f(0) = c \\ f(s(a)) = e(a,f(a)) \end{cases}$$

Let C(x) be a type for $x \in N$. We then have the following rule, which should be obvious from the computation rules for rec,

N-elimination: $\dfrac{n \in N \qquad c \in C(0) \qquad e(x,y) \in C(s(x)) \;\; [x \in N,\; y \in C(x)]}{rec(n,c,e) \in C(n)}$

For instance, defining plus by $plus(m,n) \equiv rec(n,m,(x,y)s(y))$ we can use N-elimination, by putting $C(x) \equiv N$ and $e(x,y) \equiv s(y)$, to get $plus(m,n) \in N$ $[m \in N,\; n \in N]$.

By regarding C(n) as a proposition and leaving out its proof-objects in the N-elimination rule, we get the induction rule for natural numbers:

$$\frac{n \in N \qquad C(0) \qquad C(s(x)) \;\; [x \in N,\; C(x)]}{C(n)} .$$

The correspondence between the N-elimination rule and the induction rule can be explained as follows. According to Heyting, a proposition is proved by giving a proof-construction for it. In the antecedent of the N-elimination rule, we have $c \in C(0)$, so C(0) is true. We also have $e(x,y) \in C(s(x))$ provided that $x \in N$ and $y \in C(x)$, so C(s(x)) is true provided that $x \in N$ and C(x) is true. Hence, by induction, C(n) is true for all natural numbers n.

We can also get the N-elimination rule from the induction rule. That C(0) is true, means, according to Heyting's explanation, that we have a proof-object c and $c \in C(0)$. That C(s(x)) is true under the assumptions $x \in N$ and C(x), means that we must have a proof-object e(x,y) and $e(x,y) \in C(s(x))$ under the assumptions $x \in N$ and $y \in C(x)$. So, by primitive recursion, we have an object of type C(n) for each natural number n, and the constant rec is introduced to express this object, i.e., $rec(n,c,e) \in C(n)$.

Lists. We let List(A) denote the type of lists whose elements are objects of type A.

List-introduction: $nil \in List(A)$ $\qquad \dfrac{a \in A \qquad l \in List(A)}{a.l \in List(A)}$

As for natural numbers, we want to introduce functions on lists by primitive recursion. Hence, we introduce the constant listrec, which is computed according to the rules

$$\begin{cases} \text{listrec}(\text{nil},c,e) = c \\ \text{listrec}(a.l,c,e) = e(a,l,\text{listrec}(l,c,e)) \end{cases}$$

So, defining f by $f(l) \equiv \text{listrec}(l,c,e)$ corresponds to the introduction of f by the primitive list recursion

$$\begin{cases} f(\text{nil}) = c \\ f(a.l) = e(a,l,f(l)) \end{cases}$$

Let $C(l)$ be a type for $l \in \text{List}(A)$. We then have the following rule, which should be obvious from the computation rules for listrec,

List-elimination:

$$\frac{\begin{array}{l} l \in \text{List}(A) \\ c \in C(\text{nil}) \\ e(x,y,z) \in C(x.y) \quad [x \in A,\ y \in \text{List}(A),\ z \in C(y)] \end{array}}{\text{listrec}(l,c,e) \in C(l)}$$

For instance, defining length by $\text{length}(l) \equiv \text{listrec}(l,0,(x,y,z)s(z))$ we can use List-elimination, by putting $C(l) \equiv N$ and $e(x,y,z) \equiv s(z)$, to get $\text{length}(l) \in N \quad [l \in \text{List}(A)]$.

As for natural numbers, we can obtain an induction rule for lists from the elimination rule:

$$\frac{l \in \text{List}(A) \qquad C(\text{nil}) \qquad C(x.y) \quad [x \in A,\ y \in \text{List}(A),\ C(y)]}{C(l)}$$

Cartesian product of a family of types. This type is introduced in order to allow us to reason about functions and to introduce the universal quantifier and implication. If A is a type and $B(x)$ is a type under the assumption $x \in A$, then we may introduce the Cartesian product $(\Pi x \in A)B(x)$. An object of this type is a function which, when applied to an object a of type A, gives an object of type $B(a)$. The functions are formed by means of lambda-abstraction.

Π-introduction:

$$\frac{b(x) \in B(x) \quad [x \in A]}{(\lambda x)b(x) \in (\Pi x \in A)B(x)}$$

Function application is expressed by the constant ap, which is computed in the usual way:

$$\text{ap}((\lambda x)b(x),a) = b(a)$$

From this computation rule, we get the elimination rule for Π:

Π-elimination:

$$\frac{a \in A \qquad c \in (\Pi x \in A)B(x)}{\text{ap}(c,a) \in B(a)}$$

Heyting's explanation of the universal quantifier is that $(\forall x \in A)B(x)$ is true if we can give a function which, when applied to an object a of type A, gives a proof of the proposition $B(a)$. Reading "proof of the proposition $B(a)$" as "object of the type $B(a)$", we see that the proposition $(\forall x \in A)B(x)$ corresponds to the type $(\Pi x \in A)B(x)$. As before, if we suppress some of the explicit constructions in the Π-rules, we obtain the natural deduction rules for the universal quantifier.

$\forall$-introduction: $\dfrac{B(x) \quad [x \in A]}{(\forall x \in A)B(x)}$ $\forall$-elimination: $\dfrac{a \in A \qquad (\forall x \in A)B(x)}{B(a)}$

If B does not depend on x, we define the <u>function type</u> from A to B by

$$A \to B \equiv (\Pi x \in A)B$$

From the rules for Π, we get, as special cases,

$\to$-introduction: $\dfrac{b(x) \in B \quad [x \in A]}{(\lambda x)b(x) \in A \to B}$ $\to$-elimination: $\dfrac{a \in A \qquad c \in A \to B}{ap(c,a) \in B}$

Heyting's explanation of the implication is that $A \supset B$ is true provided we can give a function which, when applied to a proof of the proposition A, gives a proof of the proposition B. Reading "proposition" as "type", we see that $A \supset B$ corresponds to $A \to B$. We get the natural deduction rules for $\supset$ from the rules for $\to$:

$\supset$-introduction: $\dfrac{B \quad [A]}{A \supset B}$ $\supset$-elimination: $\dfrac{A \qquad A \supset B}{B}$

<u>Boolean</u>. The type Boolean has two objects, true and false.

Boolean-introduction: $\text{true} \in \text{Boolean}$ $\qquad \text{false} \in \text{Boolean}$

The expression (if b then c else d) is computed in the usual way, which gives

Boolean-elimination: $\dfrac{b \in \text{Boolean} \qquad c \in C(\text{true}) \qquad d \in C(\text{false})}{(\text{if } b \text{ then } c \text{ else } d) \in C(b)}$

COURSE-OF-VALUES RECURSION ON LISTS.

Let A and C be types and assume that we have

$$c \in C$$

$$g(a,l,y_1,\ldots,y_k) \in C \quad [a \in A,\ l \in \text{List}(A),\ y_1 \in C,\ldots,\ y_k \in C]$$

and

$$d_i(a,l) \in \text{List}(A) \quad [a \in A,\ l \in \text{List}(A)] \qquad (i = 1,\ldots,k)$$

where

$$\text{length}(d_i(a,l)) \leq \text{length}(l) \quad [a \in A,\ l \in \text{List}(A)]$$

The course-of-values equations to be solved are

$$\begin{cases} f(nil) = c \\ f(a.l) = g(a,l,f(d_1(a,l)),\ldots,f(d_k(a,l))) \end{cases}$$

In order to solve these equations, I will give an informal proof of the course-of-values induction rule

$$\frac{\begin{array}{l} l \in List(A) \\ C(nil) \\ C(a.s) \quad [a \in A,\ s \in List(A),\ C(d_1(a,s)),\ldots,\ C(d_k(a,s))] \\ length(d_i(a,s)) \leq length(s) \quad [a \in A,\ s \in List(A)] \qquad (i=1,\ldots,k) \end{array}}{C(l)}$$

where $C(l)$ is a proposition depending on $l \in List(A)$. Since propositions and types are identified in type theory, we know that for each proposition in the antecedents of the course-of-values induction rule there must exist an explicit construction of an object of the corresponding type. A proof of this induction rule is a method of going from proofs of the antecedents to a proof of $C(l)$. Hence, given a proof of this induction rule, we can give a corresponding recursion rule in type theory, giving an object $f(l)$ of type $C(l)$:

$$\frac{\begin{array}{l} l \in List(A) \\ c \in C(nil) \\ g(a,s,y_1,\ldots,y_k) \in C(a.s) \quad [a \in A,\ s \in List(A),\ y_1 \in C(d_1(a,s)),\ldots,\ y_k \in C(d_k(a,s))] \\ length(d_i(a,s)) \leq length(s) \quad [a \in A,\ s \in List(A)] \qquad (i=1,\ldots,k) \end{array}}{f(l) \in C(l)}$$

When we have constructed this function f, it is possible to see that it satisfies the course-of-values equations above in the more general case when the type C depends on $l \in List(A)$. Since I do not know of any interesting applications of this more general situation, I will carry out the simplifications of f that are possible when C does not depend on $l \in List(A)$, and then show that the function so obtained satisfies our original equations. In order to simplify the notation, I assume that we only have one function d_1, which I write d. The arguments will be valid for the cases of several functions $d_1,\ldots,d_k$ without any changes.

The identification of propositions and types means that we can work most of the time using propositions, and then in the final stage, we can introduce the explicit constructions, which will give us programs. The course-of-values induction rule has a very short and simple proof. To get a program from this proof is a tedious task of transforming the details of the proof to type theory. This could, however, be automated; it is the proof of the induction rule that is the creative part of the construction of the program.

The course-of-values induction rule will be proved by proving

$$P(n) \equiv (\forall l \in List(A))(length(l) \leq n \supset C(l)) \qquad (1)$$

by induction on $n \in N$. $P(0)$ is obviously true, since $length(l) \leq 0$ implies $l = nil$ and we know that $C(nil)$ is true. Assume that $P(x)$ is true. We then have to show that

$$\text{length}(l) \leq s(x) \supset C(l) \qquad (2)$$

holds for all $l \in \text{List}(A)$. This will be done by list induction. The case of $l = \text{nil}$ is trivial since $C(\text{nil})$ is true. Let $l = u.v$ and assume

$$\text{length}(u.v) \leq s(x)$$

from which we get

$$\text{length}(d(u,v)) \leq x \qquad (3)$$

because d is a length decreasing function and $\leq$ is transitive. As induction hypothesis, we have assumed that $P(x)$ is true, which, together with (3), gives

$$C(d(u,v))$$

From this and the third premiss of the induction rule we are about to prove, we get

$$C(u.v)$$

and thereby (1) is proved. Hence, by putting $n = \text{length}(l)$ in (1), the course-of-values induction rule is proved.

We now have to repeat this proof in type theory in order to get the program for the solution. From the proof of (1) we will get a function F and a derivation of

$$F(n) \in (\Pi l \in \text{List}(A))(\text{length}(l) \leq n \to C(l))$$

remembering that the Π- and $\to$-types interpret the universal quantifier and implication, respectively. The solution f can then be defined by

$$f(l) \equiv \text{ap}(\text{ap}(F(\text{length}(l)),l),\ldots)$$

where the dots denote a proof, or construction, of the proposition $\text{length}(l) \leq \text{length}(l)$, i.e., $\ldots \in \text{length}(l) \leq \text{length}(l)$. What construction the dots denote depends on the particular definition we have chosen of the proposition $m \leq n$. When we have obtained F, it is easy to see that the construction denoted by the dots never will be used in the computation of $F(n)$; it is only the existence of a construction that is needed. So, there is no reason for defining $\leq$ and then construct the object denoted by the dots. I will use the dot notation in similar situations below.

We proved $P(n)$ by induction and the corresponding rule of type theory is N-elimination, so $F(n)$ will be constructed by recursion. Since $c \in C(\text{nil})$ we clearly have, by $\to$- and Π-introduction,

$$(\lambda l)(\lambda p)c \in (\Pi l \in \text{List}(A))(\text{length}(l) \leq 0 \to C(l)) \qquad (1)$$

Assume

$$x \in N \quad (2) \qquad \text{and} \qquad y \in (\Pi l \in \text{List}(A))(\text{length}(l) \leq x \to C(l)) \quad (3)$$

We now have to construct an object of type $(\Pi x \in \text{List}(A))(\text{length}(l) \leq s(x) \to C(l))$ and this will be done by list recursion. Clearly

$$(\lambda p)c \in \text{length}(\text{nil}) \leq s(x) \to C(\text{nil}) \qquad (4)$$

Assume

$u \in A$ (5), $v \in List(A)$ (6) and $p \in length(u.v) \leq s(x)$ (7)

Since $length(u.v) = s(length(v))$, there obviously exists a construction of the proposition $length(v) \leq x$ under the assumption (7):

$$\ldots \in length(v) \leq x \qquad (8)$$

From (8) and the premiss $length(d(u,v)) \leq length(v)$, we get, by the transitivity of $\leq$,

$$\ldots \in length(d(u,v)) \leq x$$

which, together with the induction hypothesis (3), gives

$$ap(ap(y,d(u,v)),\ldots) \in C(d(u,v))$$

Substituting this into the third premiss of the recursion rule we are proving gives

$$g(u,v,ap(ap(y,d(u,v)),\ldots)) \in C(u.v) \qquad (9)$$

$\rightarrow$ -introduction on (9) gives

$$(\lambda p)g(u,v,ap(ap(y,d(u,v)),\ldots)) \in length(u.v) \leq s(x) \rightarrow C(u.v) \qquad (10)$$

whereby the assumption (7) is discharged. Since we have (4) and a derivation of (10) from (5) and (6), we can use List-elimination to get

$$listrec(l,(\lambda p)c,(u,v,w)(\lambda p)g(u,v,ap(ap(y,d(u,v)),\ldots))) \in$$
$$length(l) \leq s(x) \rightarrow C(l) \quad [l \in List(l)] \qquad (11)$$

Π -introduction on (11) gives

$$(\lambda l)listrec(l,(\lambda p)c,(u,v,w)(\lambda p)g(u,v,ap(ap(y,d(u,v)),\ldots))) \in$$
$$(\Pi l \in List(A))(length(l) \leq s(x) \rightarrow C(l)) \qquad (12)$$

We can now define F by

$$F(n) \equiv$$
$$rec(n,$$
$$(\lambda l)(\lambda p)c,$$
$$(x,y)(\lambda l)listrec(l,(\lambda p)c,(u,v,w)(\lambda p)g(u,v,ap(ap(y,d(u,v)),\ldots))))$$

We then get, by N-elimination,

$$F(n) \in (\Pi l \in List(A))(length(l) \leq n \rightarrow C(l)) \quad [n \in N]$$

since we have (1) and a derivation of (12) from the assumptions (2) and (3).

If the type C does not depend on $l \in List(A)$, we can simply take away the dependence on the proof of $length(l) \leq n$ and change the definition of F to

$$F(n) \equiv rec(n,(\lambda l)c,(x,y)(\lambda l)listrec(l,c,(u,v,w)g(u,v,ap(y,d(u,v)))))$$

or, in the case of several functions $d_1,\ldots,d_d$,

$$F(n) \equiv$$
$$rec(n,$$
$$(\lambda l)c,$$
$$(x,y)(\lambda l)listrec(l,c,(u,v,w)g(u,v,ap(y,d_1(u,v)),\ldots,ap(y,d_k(u,v)))))$$

It now remains to show that f defined by $f(l) \equiv ap(F(length(l)),l)$ satisfies the course-of-values equations; but, before we enter the details of this, let us see how the method works in a simple example. The solution to the equations

$$\begin{cases} h(nil) = 0 \\ h(a.l) = s(h(tail(l))) \end{cases}$$

where $tail \equiv listrec(l,nil,(u,v,w)v)$, is obtained by defining $h(l) \equiv ap(H(length(l)),l)$ where

$$H(n) \equiv rec(n,(\lambda l)0,(x,y)(\lambda l)listrec(l,0,(u,v,w)s(ap(y,tail(v)))))$$

The computation of $h(3.2.4.5.nil)$ goes as follows:

$$h(3.2.4.5.nil) = ap(H(4),3.2.4.5.nil) = s(ap(H(3),4.5.nil)) = s(s(ap(H(2),nil))) = s(s(0)) \equiv 2$$

To show that the method of solving the course-of-values equations is correct, the following theorem has to be proved:

<u>Theorem</u>. Let F be defined as above. Then $F(n) \in List(A) \to C \quad [n \in N]$ and $f(l)$ defined by

$$f(l) \equiv ap(F(length(l)),l)$$

solves the course-of-values equations.

I leave out the simple proof that $F(n)$ is of type $List(A) \to C$ when $n \in N$. The proof that f solves the equations is based on the lemma:

<u>Lemma</u>. If $n \in N$ and $l \in List(A)$ then

$$length(l) \leq n \quad \text{implies} \quad ap(F(n),l) = ap(F(length(l)),l)$$

We will prove the lemma by proving

$$(\forall l \in List(A))(length(l) \leq n \supset ap(F(n),l) = ap(F(n+1),l)) \qquad (1)$$

by induction on $n \in N$. Since $length(l) \leq 0$ implies $l=nil$ and, by the definition of F, $ap(F(0),nil) = c = ap(F(1),nil)$, (1) holds for $n = 0$. As induction hypothesis, assume that (1) is true. We then have to show that

$$length(l) \leq n+1 \supset ap(F(n+1),l) = ap(F(n+2),l)$$

holds for all $l \in List(A)$. This will be done by list induction. By the definition of F, we have $ap(F(n+1),nil) = c = ap(F(n+2),nil)$ which takes care of the case $l=nil$. Let $l = a.s$ and assume that $length(l) \leq n+1$. The definition of F gives

$$ap(F(n+1),l) = g(a,s,ap(F(n),d(a,s))) \qquad (2)$$

and

$$ap(F(n+2),l) = g(a,s,ap(F(n+1),d(a,s))) \qquad (3)$$

Since $length(d(a,s)) \leq length(s) \leq n$ we can use the induction hypothesis to get

$$ap(F(n),d(a,s)) = ap(F(n+1),d(a,s))$$

which, together with (2) and (3), gives

$$ap(F(n+1),l) = ap(F(n+2),l)$$

and thereby the lemma is proved.

We can now prove that $f(l) \equiv ap(F(length(l),l)$ satisfies the course-of-values equations

$$\begin{cases} f(nil) = c \\ f(a.l) = g(a,l,f(d(a,l))) \end{cases}$$

The first equation is an immediate consequence of the definition of F. The definition of F also gives

$$f(a.l) \equiv ap(F(length(a.l)),a.l) =$$
$$listrec(a.l,c,(u,v,w)g(u,v,ap(F(length(l)),d(u,v)))) = g(a,l,ap(F(length(l)),d(a,l))) \quad (1)$$

Because $length(d(a,l)) \leq length(l)$, we can apply the lemma to get

$$ap(F(length(l)),d(a,l)) = ap(F(length(d(a,l))),d(a,l)) \equiv f(d(a,l)) \quad (2)$$

(1) and (2) give $f(a.l) = g(a,l,f(d(a,l)))$, i.e., the second equation is satisfied.

Remark. The proof of the course-of-values induction rule determines the solution of the equations. So, if we choose another proof, we will get a different program. We proved the induction rule by proving $(\forall l \in List(A))(length(l) \leq n \supset C(l))$ by induction on $n \in N$ and in the induction step, we used list induction. But this list induction can be replaced by a separation into two cases: $length(l) \leq n$ and $length(l) \leq n+1$. If we work out the details of this proof, we will get the following definition of F:

```
F(n) ≡
 rec(n,
     (λl)c,
     (x,y)(λl)(if length(l)≤x then ap(y,l) else listrec(l,c,(u,v,w)g(u,v,ap(y,d(u,v))))))
```

This program is somewhat longer than the one we obtained above and there will also occur superfluous steps in the computation of $f(l)$. However, this definition of F has one advantage; it is easier to see that f is a solution to the course-of-values equations, because the lemma now becomes trivial.

QUICKSORT.

Let A be a type and $\leq$ a Boolean valued function of two arguments defined on A, i.e., $a \leq b \in Boolean\ [a \in A,\ b \in A]$. In order to give the course-of-values equations for quicksort, we have to define some functions:

$$concat(l,s) \equiv listrec(l,s,(x,y,z)(x.z))$$

$$filter_{\leq}(a,l) \equiv listrec(l,nil,(x,y,z)(\text{if } x \leq a \text{ then } x.z \text{ else } z))$$

and

$$filter_{>}(a,l) \equiv listrec(l,nil,(x,y,z)(\text{if } x \leq a \text{ then } z \text{ else } x.z))$$

The equations for quicksort are

$$\begin{cases} quicksort(nil) = nil \\ quicksort(a.l) = concat(quicksort(filter_{\leq}(a,l)),\ a.quicksort(filter_{>}(a,l))) \end{cases}$$

We must show that these equations satisfy the requirements on course-of-values equations, i.e. that

$nil \in List(A)$ (1), $concat(y_1,a.y_2) \in List(A)\ [a \in A,\ y_1 \in List(A),\ y_2 \in List(A)]$ (2)

$length(filter_{\leq}(a,l)) \leq length(l)\ [a \in A,\ l \in List(A)]$ (3)

and
$$\text{length}(\text{filter}_>(a,l)) \leq \text{length}(l) \qquad (4)$$

I leave out the simple proofs of (1) and (2). We prove (3) by list induction. By definition, we have $\text{filter}_\leq(a,\text{nil}) = \text{nil}$. Assume that (3) holds for $v \in \text{List}(A)$. For $l = u.v$, where $u \in A$, we get two cases:

1) $u \leq a = \text{true}$

$\text{length}(\text{filter}_\leq(a,u.v)) = \text{length}(u.\text{filter}_\leq(a,v)) \leq \text{length}(v) + 1 = \text{length}(u.v)$

2) $u \leq a = \text{false}$

$\text{length}(\text{filter}_\leq(a,u.v)) = \text{length}(\text{filter}_\leq(a,v)) \leq \text{length}(v) < \text{length}(u.v)$

(4) is proved in a similar way.

Now we can apply our method of solving course-of-values equations and define quicksort by
$$\text{quicksort}(l) \equiv \text{ap}(Q(\text{length}(l),l)$$
where

```
 Q(n) ≡
   rec(n,
      (λl)nil,
      (x,y)(λl)listrec(l,nil,(u,v,w)concat(ap(y,filter≤(u,v),u.ap(y,filter>(u,v)))))
```

By the theorem, we know that our way of defining quicksort in type theory gives a function from List(A) to List(A), satisfying the claimed equations.

Acknowledgements. I am very greatful to Per Martin-Löf for many helpful suggestions. I also would like to thank Bengt Nordström and Kent Petersson for many discussions on type theory and programming.

References.

1. E.Bishop, Foundations of Constructive Analysis (McGraw-Hill 1967).
2. E.Bishop, Mathematics as a numerical language, Myhill, Kino and Vesley, eds., Intuitionism and Proof Theory pp.53-71 (North-Holland 1970).
3. R.M.Burstall, D.B.McQueen and D.T.Sanella, Hope: An experimental applicative language, Proceedings of the 1980 LISP conference, pp.136-143.
4. R.Constable, Constructive Mathematics and Automatic Program Writers, Information Processing 71 (North-Holland 1972).
5. M.J.Gordon, A.J.Milner and C.P.Wadsworth, Edinburgh LCF, Lecture Notes in Computer Science 78 (Springer-Verlag 1979).
6. K.Gödel, Über eine bisher noch nicht benütze Erweiterung des finiten Standpunktes, Dialectica, Vol. 12, 1958, pp.280-287.
7. A.Heyting, Intuitionism, an introduction (North-Holland 1956).
8. S.C.Kleene, Introduction to Metamathematics (North-Holland 1952).
9. Z.Manna and R.Waldinger, A deductive approach to program synthesis, ACM Transactions on Programming Languages and Systems, Vol.2, No.1, pp.92-121, 1980.
10. P.Martin-Löf, An Intuitionistic Theory of Types: Predicative Part, Logic Colloquium 73, Rose and Shepardson, eds., pp.73-118 (North-Holland 1975).
11. P.Martin-Löf, Constructive Mathematics and Computer Programming, Logic, Methodology and Philosophy of Science VI, pp.153-175 (North-Holland 1982).
12. B.Nordström, Programming in Constructive Set Theory, Some Examples, Proceedings of the Conference on Functional Programming Languages and Computer Architecture, ACM, Portsmouth, New Hampshire 1981.
13. K.Petersson, A programming system for type theory, LPM Memo 21,1982, Dept. of Computer Science, Chalmers Univ. of Technology, Göteborg, Sweden.
14. D.Turner, SASL Language Manual, St.Andrews University, Technical report 1976.

REMARKS ON SEARCHING LABYRINTHS BY AUTOMATA

Andrzej Szepietowski

Mathematical Institute, Technical University
of Gdańsk, Gdańsk, Majakowskiego 11/12, Poland

Introduction

A labyrinth is a 2-dimensional checkboard with some cells forbidden. For any component of connectedness of forbidden cells a set of adjacent accessible cells is called a shore of this component. Cells having only one point on common are connected but not adjacent. A cell belongs to a northern (southern) shore if its southern (northern) neighbour is forbidden.

To search a labyrinth, a finite automaton, started in any accessible cell, must visit every reachable cell without passing through any forbidden cells. In each step, the automaton can identify which of its neighbour cells are accessible and then, depending on its state, moves north, east, south or west by one cell. An automaton may be equipped with a finite number of distinguishable pebbles or with a counter, or a push-down store. A labyrinth may be also searchable by a finite set of finite automata (for definitions see [1,4,5]). An automaton masters a labyrinth if it visits infinitely many cells.

Budach [3] has proved that there is no finite automaton which can search (master) each finite (cofinite) labyrinth. He has shown that for every finite automaton there is a cofinite trap. Muller [7] has proved that for every finite automaton there is a cofinite trap, the set of the forbidden cells of which has no more than three components of connectedness. Blum and Kozen [1] have proved that there exists a finite 2-pebble-automaton (or 1-counter-automaton, or a set of two finite automata) searching each finite labyrinth. Blum and Sakoda [2] have proved that there exists a 7-pebble-automaton which can search every labyrinth. Hoffmann [6] has proved that there is no 1-pebble-automaton which can search (master) every finite (cofinite) labyrinth.

We claim that :

1. A finite 5-pebble-automaton and a set of 5 finite automata can search every labyrinth.
2. A push-down-automaton with one pebble can search every labyrinth, the set of the forbidden cells of which has not components with infinite shore.
3. A finite 1-pebble-automaton can serch (master) each finite (infinite) labyrinth, the set of the forbidden cells of which has no more than three components of connectedness.
4. There exists a set of labyrinths searchable by one push-down-automaton and not searchable by any counter-automaton.

From point no. 3. and from Muller's theorem [7] it follows that the finite 1-pebble-automaton is more powerful than the finite automaton, and from point no. 4. it follows that the push-down-automaton is more powerful than the counter-automaton.

We have prowed in [10] that a finite 5-pebble-automaton can search every labyrinth, i.e. the first part of point no. 1. Since the proof of this theorem will be used in the sequel, we present the abridgement of this proof:

The finite automaton with 5 pebbles O, C_1, C_2, E, F simulates the 2-counter-automaton M which is capable of searching every labyrinth (see [2,5]). Pebble O marks the position of the automaton M. The contents of i-th counter is stored as the distance properly defined between O and C_i $(i = 1,2)$. The automaton with E, F moves between O, C_1, and C_2 to increment or decrement the counters. From Blum-Kozen's theorem [1] it follows that a 2-pebble-automaton can find an infinite path in every infinite labyrinth and it can walk along this path up and down, so there is a 2-pebble-automaton, which can make a potentialy infinite distance between O and C_i.

From Hoffmann's theorem [6] it follows that 1-pebble-automaton is not capable of finding an infinite path in every infinite labyrinth.

Results.

Blum and Kozen [1] have proved that a set of two finite automata (as well as an automaton with two pebbles) can search every finite labyrinth and master every infinite labyrinth. Hence in the proof that 5-pebble-automaton can search every labyrinth we may substitute a second automaton for two pebbles, and we have:

Corollary. There exist two finite automata, one with three pebbles and the other without pebbles (as well as five finite automata), which can search every labyrinth.

Theorem 1. There exists a push-down-automaton A with one pebble which can search each labyrinth, the set of the forbidden cells of which has not any components with infinite shore.

Proof :

Blum and Kozen [1] have proved that an automaton can search every finite labyrinth if it can verify whether a cell of a finite shore is unique or not, i.e. whether this cell is the westernmost of all southernmost cells of the shore. Such an automaton can also find an infinite path in every infinite labyrinth and it can walk along this path up and down.

They have also proved that a counter-automaton can verify whether a cell of a finite shore is unique.

The push-down-automaton A with one pebble can simulate the 2-counter-automaton M in every infinite labyrinth without infinite shores.

The push-down store of A holds only words in the form:

bjj...jii...i , where b is the symbol of the bottom of the push-down store.

The pebble marks the position of the 2-counter-automaton and is moved as it is. The contents of first counter of M is stored as the number of j's on the push-down store, and it may be changed if there are no i's . The contents of the second counter of M is stored as the distance between the pebble and A . To increase the second counter A walks one step by Blum-Kozen's algorithm of searching finite labyrinth. When A must verify whether a cell is unique it constructs an additional counter of i's on the top of the push-down store. During verification contents of the first and the second counters of M are not changed.

__Theorem 2__. There exists a finite 1-pebble-automaton B which can search (master) each finite (infinite) labyrinth, the set of the forbidden cells of which has no more than three components of connectedness.

Proof :

The automaton B works as follows :

1° First it goes with the pebble south down to a shore, of a first component of the set of the forbidden cells.

2° Next B drops the pebble and walks by r-h-r (right hand rule) around the first component. B interrupts walking around on each cell of the northern shore, goes north up to the obstacle, comes back south and continiues walking around. It finishes its walking around if it finds the pebble.

3° Then B walks by r-h-r along the shore of the first component with the pebble up to such a cell P which stays on the northern shore between two different components. To verify whether P stays between two different components B drops the pebble on P , goes north up to the obstacle, cell R , and walks around the component which stays above R . B finishes walking around if it finds R second time (R is the only cell of the southern shore, which stays above the pebble). If B does not find the pebble during walking around this component it means that P stays between two different components.

4° Then B drops the pebble on R and walks once around the second component (i.e. the component which stays above R) as in stage 2°.

5° Next B with the pebble walks along the shore of both, the first and the second, components looking for the third component :

First B goes with the pebble by l-h-r (left hand rule) along the shore of the second component from R to a next cell S which stays on the southern shore between two different components. While walking from R to S B stops on every cell of the northern shore, and walks once around the component which stays above this cell (as in stage 2°).

When B finds S it walks once around the component which stays below S (as in stage 2°) and comes back with the pebble to R and next to P and iterates its work from stage 3°.

Let us notice that B with the pebble systematicaly walks along both components, so it finds the third component and walks once around it (as in stage 2°), and visits the remaining cells of the labyrinth.

The same automaton B can master every infinite labyrinth with no more than three components of the forbidden cells.

<u>Theorem 3</u>. There exists a set of labyrinths M searchable by some push-down-automaton and not searchable by any counter-automaton.

Proof :

In order to describe the labyrinths of set M we will treat the chackboard as the set Z^2 , where Z is the set of integers.

Let $L \subset Z^2$ be a finite set of forbidden cells. There exists such a number d that for all $(x,y) \in L$ $|x| + |y| < d-1$.

Let us add a "frame" to L , so that we obtain the set :

$$FL = \Big\{(x,y) \in Z^2 : |x| = d \;\&\; |y| \leqslant d \text{ or } y = -d \;\&\; |x| \leqslant d \text{ or } y = d \;\&\; 0 < |x| \leqslant d\Big\} \cup L .$$

We will call this set the "box". The cell $(0,d)$ which does not belong to the box we will call the exit of the box.

Let the set $Ln = \Big\{(x,y) \in Z^2 : (x-2nd,y) \in FL\Big\}$ for $n \in Z$ be the n-th box.

The set $GL = \bigcup_{n \in Z} Ln \cup \Big\{(x,y) \in Z^2 : y \leqslant -d\Big\}$ is the set of forbidden cells of a new labyrinth SL .

The set of the forbidden cells of the labyrinth SL consists of an unbounded in two directions row of identical boxes. Each of neighouring boxes have a common wall, and the exits of all boxes are placed on level $y = d$.

The set M consists of all labyrinths constructed as described.

In order to prove theorem 3, we will show that there exists a push-down-automaton C which can search every labyrinth $SL \in M$, and that for every counter-automaton there exists a labyrinth $SL \in M$ not searchable by this automaton.

The push-down store of the automaton C holds only words in the form: $bk_1 \dots k_1 k_2 \dots k_2 k_3 \dots k_3$. Automaton C can construct three counters. The contents of i-th counter is stored as the number of k_i's on the push-down store, for $i = 1,2,3$. The second counter may be used if the third counter is empty, and the first counter may be used if both, the second and the third counters, are empty.

Let SL be an arbitrary labyrinth of the set M . In order to simplyfy the proof, let us assume that C starts above the boxes. First C goes down to the shore on the level $y = d+1$, and goes one step north. Next C goes southwest down to the level $y = d+1$ increasing the first counter by one after each step. Then C returns northeast decreasing the first counter up to emptying it, and in the same way goes southeast to the level $y = d+1$ and returns northwest. Now C goes one step north, and iterates its work.

The second and third counters are empty when C is above the level $y = d$. When C finds the exit of a box on the level $y = d$, it enters the box, and searches the interior of the box by the algorithm of Blum and Kozen [1]. While searching C stores in the second counter the depth of its position under the top of the box. The third counter is used for verification whether a cell is unique.

Now we will prove that for every counter-automaton D there exists a labyrinth $SL \in M$ not searchable by this automaton. If the counter of D is not empty, then D works as the finite automaton. From Budach's theorem [3] it follows that for every finite automaton there is a labyrinth, which satisfies the following conditions: - the set of forbidden cells L of the labyrinth is finite, - the cell $(0,0)$ is accessible (i.e. $(0,0) \notin L$) and there is the infinite path of cells, which are reachable from the cell $(0,0)$, - if the finite automaton starts on cell $(0,0)$ it visits only finite set of cells. Hence there exists a labyrinth SL which satisfies the condition: if D stays on cell $(2nd,0)$, for any $n \in Z$, it must empty its counter befor it leaves the n-th box.

Let us assume that D searches labyrinth SL. Since D must visits all cells of infinite set $\{(2nd,0): n \in Z\}$ it must empty its counter in each box. But the set of states of D and the set of cells of the interior of each box are finite, hance there exist numbers $p,q > 0$ that in the step p and $p+q$ D stays inside a box in the same state with the empty counter, and the distance between the position of D and the corners of the occupied box are the same, though the indices of the boxes may be different.

In that case the behaviour of D after step $p+q$ is the same as the behaviour after step p. Hence there is the minimal or maximal index in the set of indices of searched boxes, and we have contradiction with our assumption that D searches SL .

References.

1. Blum,M.,D.Kozen, On the power of the compass. Proc. 19th IEEE FOCS Conf. (1978), 132-142.
2. Blum,M.,W.Sakoda, On the capability of finite automata in 2 and 3 dimensional space. Proc. 17th IEEE FOCS Conf.(1977), 147-161.
3. Budach,L., Automata and labyrinths. Math. Nachr. 86 (1978), 195-283.
4. Coy,W., Of Mice and Maze. EIK 14 (1978)5, 227-232.
5. Habasiński,Z.,M.Karpiński, A Codification of Blum-Sakoda 7 Pebbles Algorithm. ICS PAS Repts. 448, Warszawa, 1981.
6. Hoffmann,F., One pebble does not suffice to search plane labyrinths. In: Fundamentals of Computation Theory; 1981 International FCT - Conference, Szeged 1981 (Ed. F. Geczeg); Lecture Notes in Computer Science, 117; Berlin - Heidelberg - New-York 1981; pp. 433-444.
7. Muller,H., Automata Catching Labyrinths with at most Three Components. EIK 15 (1979) 1/2, 3-9.
8. Szepietowski,A., Remarks on Searching Plane Labyrinths by 1-pebble-automata. Proc. of Workshop on Algorithms and Comp. Theory, Poznań 1981, pp. 49-50.
9. Szepietowski,A., On Searching Plane Labyrinths by 1-Pebble-Automata. EIK 19 (1983) 1/2, 79-84.
10. Szepietowski,A., A Finite 5-Pebble-Automaton Can Search Every Maze. IPL 15/5 (1982), 199-204.

METRICAL AND ORDERED PROPERTIES OF POWERDOMAINS

S. TISON
M. DAUCHET
G. COMYN

UNIVERSITY OF LILLE (France)

ABSTRACT.- *Many papers have been devoted to the study of the semantics of nondeterminism and proposed domains inside a powerset* $P(D)$ *which inherit their properties from the domain* D *. We try to put together order and metric approaches to powerdomains and prove eventually that both constructions induce in fact the same (metrical) properties in a wide class of SFP structures.*

The study of powerdomain constructions came from the need for defining a neat semantics for programming languages with non deterministic or parallel features. In this paper, we do not develop the semantical aspect, but only the formal one.

Two approaches are mainly followed :

- CPO approach : Plotkin [11] defined a class of domains called S.F.P. - which are particular ω-algebraic CPO's - to get a "good" category (i.e. closed under powerdomain constructors). Furthermore Smyth [13] proved that D is a S.F.P. iff D and $[D \to D]$ are ω-algebraic.
- Metric approach : Arnold and Nivat [1] gave a metric point of view of the nondeterminism; they worked on sets of trees they equipped with Painlevé's limits deduced from the metrical structure of the complete free magma.

In both cases we have to deal with ordered (resp. metrical) extensions of an ordered (resp. metrical) domain D to a given subset of $P(D)$ whose order (resp. metric) properties are conserved : Let $P_<$ (resp. P_d) those extensions. The aim of this paper is to prove that, for various ordered extensions (Smyth order and its dual, Egli-Milner order), the following commutative diagram can be constructed from a S.F.P. D :

$$\begin{array}{rcccl} & (D,<) & \xrightarrow[M]{} & (D,d) & \\ \text{CPO approach } P_< & \downarrow & & \downarrow & P_d \text{ metric approach (Hausdorf metric)} \\ & P_<(D) & \xrightarrow[M]{} & (P_<(D),\delta) & \end{array}$$

where M constructs a metrical space from an ordered one [4] and replaces lubs of increasing sequences by limits of Cauchy sequences : It consists in going from a

Scott to a Lawson topology [6].

A practical interest of this diagram is that it enables to substitute to the some complicated metric obtained via the natural powerdomain approach, a pointwise defined metric. Besides, for our part, we have introduced this diagram to facilitate our investigation on metric and order properties of trees and words non-deterministic automata or transducers.

Unfortunately, the diagram does not commute for every S.F.P.. We introduce a sufficient condition - the (P) condition - which is illustrated in the paper. This property is verified by usual trees and words structures (on finite alphabets); consequently the results we obtained enable to put together ordered and metrical approaches in these domains.

It can be easily verified that this property (P) is preserved by powerdomain construction. but not by functional construction (Consider the functions defined by :

$$f_n(x) = \text{if } x > a^n \text{ then } b \text{ else } \varepsilon$$

$$g_n(x) = \text{if } x > a^n \text{ then } c \text{ else } \varepsilon \qquad n \in \mathbb{N})$$

Nevertheless, an interesting extension of this work is the study of this problem in the area of continuous algebras where the property (P) should be formulated in a neater way and be kept by continuous homomorphisms.

I. POWERSET CONSTRUCTIONS IN DOMAINS AND METRIC SPACES

In this section we recall various ways of extending order (resp. metric) properties from a given domain to its powerset. We make explicit the definition of the corresponding operators $\mathcal{P}_<$ (resp. $\mathcal{P}_d$).

I.A.- POWERDOMAINS : THE OPERATOR $\mathcal{P}_<$ ON S.F.P.

From now on we will work only on S.F.P. objects : For more details about S.F.P.'s, the reader can refer to [10,11].

D being an S.F.P., we study three orderings on the powerset $\mathcal{P}(D)$ and use every time the same procedure we sum up in the following way :

Let $(D,<)$ be an S.F.P. . We define a quasi-order (also denoted $<$) on the powerset $\mathcal{P}(D)$ [we exclude the empty set]. Then, $\mathcal{P}_<(D)$ denotes the p.o. of equivalence classes for the canonical equivalence associated to the quasi-order. It can be proved that each $\mathcal{P}_<(D)$ is an S.F.P. [11,12] ; we explain every time the corresponding finitary basis.

Canonical representatives of equivalence classes will be described by means of Lawson topology in section II.

a) The "naïve" ordering

Let $(B^{\infty},<)$ be an S.F.P. (B its finitary basis). We denote $<_I$ the quasi-order defined on $P(B^{\infty})$ in the following way :

$$X <_I Y \iff \forall x \in X , \forall b \in B \ (b < x \Rightarrow \exists y \in Y , b < y) \quad \text{for any } X,Y \in P(B^{\infty}).$$

$\simeq_I$ denotes the canonical equivalence associated with $<_I$.

Let us define now the ideal for subsets of B^{∞} :

$$\forall X \neq \emptyset , X \in P(B^{\infty}) , I(X) \underset{def}{=} \{y \in B^{\infty} \mid x \in X \cdot y < x\}$$

Plotkin proved in [11] the following results :

PROPOSITION 1.- *i)* $X \underset{I}{\simeq} Y \iff I(X) \cap B = I(Y) \cap B$

ii) $P_<(B^{\infty})$ *is an S.F.P. Its finitary basis* B_I *in the set of ideals of non-empty finite subsets of* B.

b) The Smyth ordering

Let $(B^{\infty},<)$ be an S.F.P.; let $S(B)$ be the set of finite subsets of B . First, we define a relation on $(S(B) \times P(B^{\infty}))$ by :

$$\left.\begin{array}{l}\forall X \in S(B) \\ \forall Y \in P(B^{\infty})\end{array}\right\}, \ X <_F Y \iff \forall y \in Y , \exists x \in X \cdot x < y$$

Now we can define the quasi order $<_F$ on $P(B^{\infty})$ by :

$$X <_F Y \iff \forall A \in S(B) , A <_F X \Rightarrow A <_F Y .$$

Let us define the notion of filter as follows :

$$\forall X \in P(B^{\infty}) , X \neq \emptyset , F(X) \underset{def}{=} \{y \in B^{\infty} / \exists x \in X \cdot x < y\}$$

Then it can be proved :

PROPOSITION 2.- $P_{<_F}(B^{\infty})$ *is an S.F.P. Its finitary basis* B_F *is the set of filters of non-empty finite subsets of* B .

c) The Egli-Milner ordering

Plotkin used in [11] the following ordering :

$$X <_{EM} Y \underset{def}{\iff} X < Y \text{ and } X <_I Y$$

and proved the following :

PROPOSITION 3.- $P_{<_{EM}}(B^{\infty})$ *is an S.F.P. whose finitary basis* B_F *is the set of convex finite subsets of* B *where any* $X \in P(B^{\infty})$ *is said convex iff* $con(X) = X$ *with* $con(X) \underset{def}{=} I(X) \cap F(X)$.

I.B.- POWERSETS AS METRIC SPACES : $\mathcal{P}_d(E)$

a) The Hausdorff metric

Let (E,d) be a metric psace. For any $X,Y \in \mathcal{P}(E)$, let

$$h(A,B) = \sup\{d(a,B) \mid a \in A\} \text{ with } d(a,B) = \inf\{d(a,b) \mid b \in A\}$$

$$d(X,Y) \underset{def}{=} \sup(h(A,B),h(B,A))$$

(for sake of simplicity we denote also d the Hausdorffmetric).

PROPOSITION 4.- d *is a metric on the closed, non-empty and bounded subsets of* E.

$\mathcal{P}_d(E)$ denotes the corresponding space.

b) Painelvé's limits.

Arnold and Nivat [1] consider on $\mathcal{P}(T^{\infty}_{\Omega}(\Sigma))$ Painlevé's limits. In this case, it is easy to prove that : $A_n \xrightarrow[\text{Painlevé}]{} A \iff \bar{A}_n \xrightarrow[\text{Hausdorff}]{} \bar{A}$ with $\bar{A}$ the closure of A.

II. METRIZATION OF S.F.P.

II.A.- FROM SCOTT TOPOLOGY TO LAWSON TOPOLOGY.

The Scott topology [6] is the topology "associated to an ordering" (i.e. such that each increasing sequence converges). A subbasis of this topology is the set of filters of finite elements : i.e. the sets $P_b = \{x \mid x > b\}$ with b finite. This topology is not metrizable (since T_0 , so not separated).

The metrizable topology on S.F.P. introduced by Plotkin in [10] was named Lawson topology in [6] and has, as a sub-basis, the sets P_b and $N_b = \{x \mid \text{not } x > b\}$ for any finite b . Every S.F.P. is compact (for this topology). From now on we shall denote M this metrization.

II.B.- AN EXPLICIT METRIC ON S.F.P.

Comyn and Dauchet defined in [4] an ultra metric associated with the Lawson topology on infinitary CPO's; this metric can be easily extended to S.F.P. in the following way :

Let $\nu : \mathbb{N} \to B$ be a numbering (i.e. surjective mapping) of the finitary basis B of an S.F.P. B^{∞}. Let us define the symmetrical difference between infinitary elements of B^{∞} by :

$$x \,\Delta\, x' = \{b \in B \mid (b < x \;\&\; \text{not } b < x') \text{ or } (b < x' \;\&\; \text{not } b < x)$$

Let d_{ν} be defined by : $d_{\nu}(x,y) = \dfrac{1}{1+\mu n[\nu(n) \in x\Delta y]}$ $\quad x,y \in B^{\infty}$
with $\mu n[\nu(n) \in x\Delta y] = \inf\{n \mid \nu(n) \in x\Delta y\} = +\infty$ iff $x = y$.

It is proved in [5] that d_{ν} is an ultrametric which do not depend on the choice of the numbering ν .

II.C.- TRUNCATION IN S.F.P. [11]

Let us define now, for any $n \in \mathbb{N}$:

$$D_n = U^*(\nu\{1,2,\dots,n\}) \text{ and } \forall x \in B,\ x[n] \underset{\text{def}}{=} \sup\{b \in D_n \mid b < x\}$$

Then an ultrametric d'_ν also associated to the Lawson topology can be defined by :

$$d'_\nu(x,y) = \frac{1}{1+\mu n[x[n] \neq y[n]]}$$

Examples : If Σ is a finite alphabet, the metrics usually defined on Σ^∞ - the set of words on Σ -[3,7] or on $T^\infty(\Sigma)$ - the set of trees - [1,2,9] are uniformly equivalent to the general metrics defined before on S.F.P.'s. Usual truncations in words or trees are intuitively particular cases of general truncations in S.F.P.

III. COMMUTATION PROPERTIES

Let us now construct, for the three orderings of § I.A.2, a diagram which illustrates the commutativity of metrization M and of powerset constructions in convenient structures.

First we characterize maximal (with regard to the inclusion) elements of the equivalence classes, defined before for our three quasi orders, by means of the Lawson topology :

III.A.- CANONICAL REPRESENTATIVES

LEMMA : *For any* $A \subseteq B^\infty (A \neq \emptyset)$, $I(\bar{A})$ *(resp* $F(\bar{A})$, $\mathrm{con}(\bar{A})$) *is maximal in the* $\simeq_I$ *(resp.* $\simeq_F$, $\simeq_{EM}$) *equivalence class containing* A.
(where $\bar{A}$ denotes the closure of A in the Lawson topology).

Furthermore, we can describe $(P<_I(B^\infty),<_I)$ as the set of non-empty closed ideals of B^∞ equipped with the set inclusion, $(P<_\nu(B^\infty),<_\nu)$ as the set of non-empty closed filters with the reverse inclusion, $(P<_{EM}(B^\infty),<_{EM})$ as the set of non-empty convex closed subsets.

Let us now establish the promised diagrams.

III.B.- COMMUTATION OF M AND P.

Since we have chosen Lawson closed canonical representatives for each of the three orderings, we can now consider P_d as the Hausdorff metrization of the set canonical representatives.

1) The "naïve" ordering

Two ways of metrizing $P<_I(B^\infty)$ can now be compared : The first one consists in using P_d ; the second one in viewing first $P<_I(B^\infty)$ as an S.F.P. and applying M :

$$(B^\infty,<) \xrightarrow{M} (B^\infty,d) \xrightarrow{P_d} (P<_I(B^\infty),d_1)$$

$$(B^\infty,<) \xrightarrow{P<_I} (P<_I,(B^\infty),<_I) \xrightarrow{M} (P<_I(B^\infty),d_2)$$

Then we can establish, for any S.F.P. B^∞ the following :

LEMMA 3 : d_1 *is uniformly equivalent to* d_2 .

2) The Smyth ordering

In the same way, we have :

$$(B^\infty,<) \xrightarrow{M} (B^\infty,d) \xrightarrow{P_d} (P<_F(B^\infty),\delta_1)$$

$$(B^\infty,<) \xrightarrow{P<_F} (P<_F(B^\infty),<_F) \xrightarrow{M} (P<_F(B^\infty),\delta_2)$$

But both metrics δ_1 and δ_2 are not uniformly equivalent for every S.F.P. (Consider the flat ordering, $A_n = \{x_1,x_n\}$, $A_\infty = \{x_1\}$) . Nevertheless, both metrics are uniformly equivalent when B^∞ is $T^\infty_\Omega(\Sigma)$. More generally, let us denote (P) the following property :

$$(P) : F(A[n]) = F(B[n]) \Longrightarrow (F(A))[n] = (F(B))[n]$$

Then :

PROPOSITION : *The metrics* δ_1 *and* δ_2 *are uniformly equivalent whenever* $(B^\infty,<)$ *verifies* (P).

In $T^\infty_\Omega(\Sigma)$, the intuitive underlying meaning of (P) is : we can extend any branch up to the length n without modifying the deeper branches.

We can remark that for any S.F.P. the canonical injection $((P<_F(B^\infty),\delta_1) \xrightarrow{i} (P<_F(B^\infty),\delta_2))$ is continuous.

3) The Egli-Milner ordering.

Unfortunately, in this case, both predefined ways of metrizing $P<_{EM}(B^\infty)$ are not uniformly equivalent, even if B^∞ is $T^\infty_\Omega(\Sigma)$, as shown by :

$A_n =$ 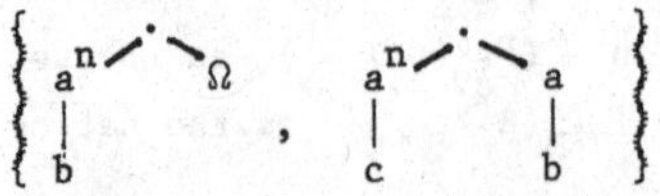 $d_1(A_n,B_n) = \frac{1}{2}$

$B_n =$ 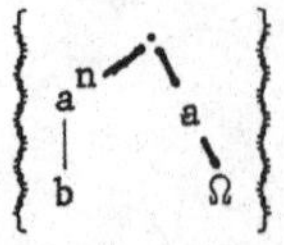 $\cup$ A_n $d_A(A_n,B_n) = \frac{1}{n+2}$

[if d_1 (resp. d_2) is the metric obtained by the first (resp. the second) way]

But, we can view the Egli-Milner quasi-order as the "product" of the naïve and Smyth quasi-order, i.e.

$$\forall X, Y, Z, T \in P(B^\infty) , (X,Y) < (Z,T) \underset{def}{\Longleftrightarrow} \begin{array}{c} X <_I Z \\ \text{and} \\ Y <_F T \end{array}$$

We define so, for any S.F.P. B^∞, a new S.F.P. - which we call $C(B^\infty)$ - by the cartesian product of the S.F.P's $P<_I(B^\infty)$, $P<_F(B^\infty)$. This S.F.P. can be metrized as any S.F.P. by $\mathcal{M}$. The metric obtained will be uniformly equivalent to any classical metric obtained on the cartesian product of the two metric spaces $P<_{I}(B^{\infty})$, $P<_{F}(B^{\infty})$, i.e. :

$$\begin{array}{rccc} & P<_{I}(B^{\infty}) & \xrightarrow{\mathcal{M}} & (P<_{I}(B^{\infty}),d') \\ & P<_{F}(B^{\infty}) & \xrightarrow{\mathcal{M}} & (P<_{F}(B^{\infty}),d'') \\ \text{Cartesian product of S.F.P.'s} & \downarrow & & \downarrow \quad \text{Cartesian product of metric spaces} \\ & C(B^{\infty}) & \xrightarrow{\mathcal{M}} & (C(B^{\infty}),\delta) \end{array}$$

$$X <_{EM} Y \iff (I(\bar{X}),\ F(\bar{X})) < (I(\bar{Y}),F(\bar{Y}))$$

So $(P <_{EM}(B^{\infty}),<_{EM})$ can be viewed as a subset of $(C(B^{\infty}),<)$.

Let us define i the canonical injection of $(P<_{EM}(B^{\infty}),<_{EM})$ in $(C(B^{\infty}),<)$, j the canonical injection of $(P <_{EM}(B^{\infty}),d)$ $(= \mathcal{M}(P<_{EM}(B^{\infty},<_{EM}))$ in $(C(B^{\infty}),\delta)$, i.e. :

$$\begin{array}{ccc} (P<_{EM}(B^{\infty}),<_{EM}) & \xrightarrow{i} & (C(B^{\infty}),<) \\ \mathcal{M}\downarrow & & \downarrow\mathcal{M} \\ (P<_{EM}(B^{\infty}),d) & \xrightarrow{j} & (C(B^{\infty}),\delta) \end{array}$$

It remains to study the relationship between d and δ , i.e. the properties of continuity for j ; we prove for any S.F.P. B^{∞} :

<u>LEMMA 4</u> : j *is uniformly continuous.*

<u>III.C.- RESULTING DIAGRAMS</u>

To sum up we know up to now (see preceding lemmas) :

- From sections III.B.1 ans III.B.2 : if an S.F.P. B^{∞} verifies (P) , the metrics obtained by P_d on $P<_{I}(B^{\infty})$ and $P<_{F}(B^{\infty})$ are uniformly equivalent to those obtained by $\mathcal{M}$.
- From this section, for any S.F.P. B^{∞} , the metric obtained by $\mathcal{M}$ on $P<_{EM}(B^{\infty})$ is uniformly equivalent to that obtained by the restriction of δ .

Thus we have an uniform equivalence between the metric obtained by $\mathcal{M}$ on $P<_{EM}(B^{\infty})$ and the metric $d_p = \sup(d(I(\bar{X}),I(\bar{Y}))\ ,\ d(F(\bar{X}),F(\bar{Y}))$ (d denotes the Hausdorff metric obtained from any canonical metric defined on B^{∞} (Cf. § II).

Finally our main result is given by the following commutative diagrams :

1) For any S.F.P. B^{∞} :

$$\begin{array}{ccc}
(B^{\infty},<) & \xrightarrow{M} & (B^{\infty},d) \\
\downarrow{\scriptstyle P<_I} & & \downarrow{\scriptstyle P_d} \\
(P<_I(B^{\infty}),<_I) & \xrightarrow[M]{} & (P<_I(B^{\infty}),d_I)
\end{array}
\qquad \text{for any S.F.P. } B^{\infty}$$

2) For any S.F.P. B^{∞} vérifying (P)

$$\begin{array}{ccc}
(B^{\infty},<) & \xrightarrow{M} & (B^{\infty},d) \\
\downarrow{\scriptstyle P<_F} & & \downarrow{\scriptstyle P_d} \\
(P<_F(B^{\infty}),<_F) & \xrightarrow[M]{} & (P<_F(B^{\infty}),d_F)
\end{array}$$

3) For any S.F.P. B^{∞} satisfying (P) :

$$\begin{array}{ccc}
(B^{\infty},<) & \xrightarrow{M} & (B^{\infty},d) \\
\downarrow{\scriptstyle P<_I}\ \downarrow{\scriptstyle P<_F} & & \downarrow{\scriptstyle P_d}\ \downarrow{\scriptstyle P_d} \\
(P<_{EM}(B^{\infty}),<_{EM}) & \xrightarrow[M]{} & (P<_{EM}(B^{\infty}),d_{EM})
\end{array}$$

In fact the third diagram can commute for an S.F.P. which does not verify the second commutative diagram, and therefore which does not verify the property (P) : It is the case of the flat ordering.

Nevertheless, some S.F.P.'s - which obviously do not satisfy (P) - nor verify the third diagram as shown by :

.../...

B^{∞} :

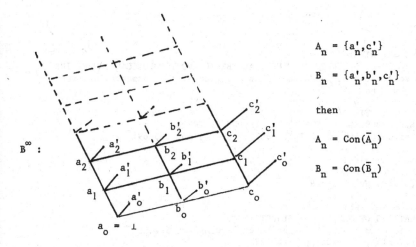

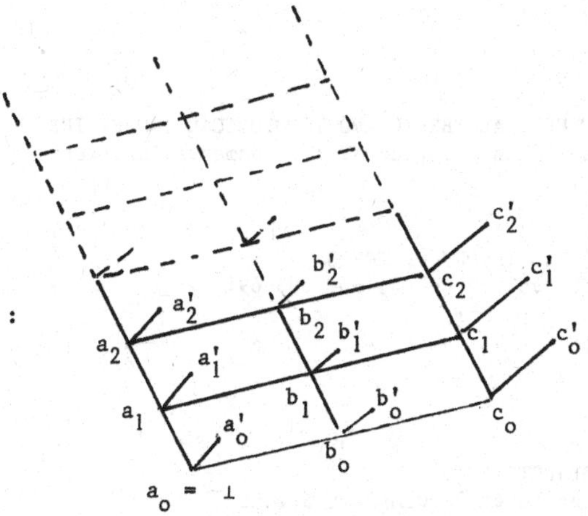

$A_n = \{a'_n, c'_n\}$

$B_n = \{a'_n, b'_n, c'_n\}$

then

$A_n = \mathrm{Con}(\bar{A}_n)$

$B_n = \mathrm{Con}(\bar{B}_n)$

Then we can easily choose numberings of the basis of B^{∞} and $P<_{EM}(B^{\infty})$ such that :

$$\delta_1(A_n, B_n) = \frac{1}{3}$$

δ_1 the metric obtained by the Hausdorff metrization $\delta_2(A_n, B_n) < 2^{-n}$, δ_2 being obtained by the metrization M on the S.F.P. $P<_{EM}(B^{\infty})$.

<u>REMARK</u> : $F(A_n[1]) = F(B_n[1]) = \{a_o, b_o, c_o\}$ but

$F(A_n)[1] = \{a_o, c_o\} \neq F(B_n)[1] = \{a_o, b_o, c_o\}$: (P) is not satisfied.

REFERENCES

[1] A. ARNOLD, M. NIVAT
THE METRIC SPACE OF INFINITE TREES; ALGEBRAIC AND TOPOLOGICAL PROPERTIES
Annales societatis mathematicae polonae Series IV : Fundamenta Informaticae
III-4, 1980 , pp. 445-476

[2] S.L. BLOOM, R. TINDELL
COMPATIBLE ORDERINGS ON THE METRIC THEORY OF TREES
SIAM J. of Computing, Nov. 1980, vol. 9, n° 4, pp. 683-691

[3] L. BOASSON, M. NIVAT
ADHERENCES OF LANGUAGES
JCSS 20, 1980, pp. 285-309

[4] G. COMYN, M. DAUCHET
APPROXIMATIONS OF INFINITARY OBJECTS
Ninth Colloquium ICALP, Lectures Notes in Computer Science,
Springer Verlag, n° 140, pp. 116-127

[5] G. COMYN
OBJETS INFINIS CALCULABLES
Thèse d'Etat, LILLE, Mars 1982

[6] G. GIERZ, K.H. HOFMANN, K. KEIMEL, J.D. LAWSON, M. MISLOVE, D. SCOTT
A COMPENDIUM OF CONTINUOUS LATTICES
Springer Verlag, 1980.

[7] F. GIRE
UNE EXTENSION AUX MOTS INFINIS DE LA NOTION DE TRANSDUCTION RATIONNELLE
Colloquium G.I., 1982, pp. 123-139

[8] J.A. GOGUEN, J. THATCHER, E. WAGNER, J. WRIGHT
INITIAL ALGEBRA SEMANTICS AND CONTINUOUS ALGEBRAS
J.A.C.M., Vol. 24, 1977, pp. 68-95

[9] M. NIVAT
INFINITE WORDS, INFINITE TREES, INFINITE COMPUTATIONS
Reprint from : Foundations of Computer cience III, Part 2 : Languages, logic
and semantics. Ed J.W. BAKKER, J. VAN LEUWEN Mathematical Centre Tract 109
1979, pp. 1-52

[10] G. PLOTKIN
T^{ω} AS A UNIVERSAL DOMAIN
JCSS 17, 1978, pp. 209-236

[11] G. PLOTKIN
A POWERDOMAIN CONSTRUCTION
SIAM J. Comput. 5, Sept. 1976, pp. 452-487

[12] M. SMYTH
POWERDOMAINS
JCSS 16, 1978, pp. 23-36

[13] M. SMYTH
THE LARGEST CARTESIAN CLOSED CATEGORY OF DOMAINS
Comp. SCI. Report, Univ. of Edinburgh, March 1982.

Economy of Description for Program Schemes
- Extended Abstract -

Peter Trum *
Detlef Wotschke *

Computer Science Department
University of Frankfurt

I. Introduction

One of the main incentives to do research in Program Schemes has always been the interest in the control-structure of a program rather than in its particular meaning.

In the past, research in this area has primarily concerned itself with questions such as whether certain control-structures can or cannot be simulated by other control-structures regardless of how expensive, awkward or how clumsy such a simulation might turn out to be. We believe that such research was extremely important to develop a feeling for which control-structures are more general or can do more than others.

We also believe that it is very important to determine whether a control-structure A, if it encompasses another control-structure B, can express or describe certain tasks much better, more economically, more efficiently, more elegantly, or just shorter than B can, provided of course that B can describe this task to begin with.

We will use the concepts of program schemes | Ianov 60, Luckham et al. 70, Manna 73, Greibach 74, Engelfriet 74 | to model control-structures. It is in this framework that we will show how some control-structures outdo others and to what degree.

We will study the economy of description between the following types of program schemes: Deterministic Ianov-Schemes (IAN), Nondeterministic Ianov-Schemes (NIAN), and both with and without auxiliary variables. For reasons of brevity we assume that the reader is familiar with these concepts and with the concepts of L-Schemes, Interpretation,

---

* Mailing Address: Fachbereich Informatik, Johann Wolfgang Goethe-Universität, Postfach 111932, 6000 Frankfurt/Main, West-Germany

Equivalence, Standard Mapping and syntdet languages. We adopt the notation used in | Engelfriet 74 |.

We also adopt the concept of nondeterministic (deterministic) Ianov-Schemes with an auxiliary variable and extend it, in the obvious way, to nondeterministic (deterministic) Ianov-Schemes with finitely many auxiliary variables ($NIAN^{HK}$, IAN^{HK} respectively) where H is the finite set of variables and K is the finite set of markers. We define the language $L_M(P)$ characterized by an $NIAN^{HK}$ or IAN^{HK} as follows:

Definition 1.1:

a) Let $\Sigma = F_\Sigma \cup P_\Sigma \cup \bar{P}_\Sigma$ be an alphabet of instruction symbols, H be a set of variables, K be a set of markers and v a variable in H. For an initial assignment a_0 to v we will denote by C_{vK} the language of all words which can be"executed"on v such that the initial value a_0 is transformed into a final value $a_j \in K$.

b) Let $H=\{v_1,\ldots,v_n\}$ be a set of variables. The language C_{HK} is defined as $C_{HK} = \bigcap_{v_i \in H} C_{v_i K}$.

c) Let $P=(\Sigma,H,K,k_0,V)$ be a $NIAN^{HK}$ or IAN^{HK}, and let s_{HK} be the following substitution:

1) $s_{HK}(\sigma)=\sigma$ for $\sigma \in \Sigma$ and

2) $s_{HK}(v_i \leftarrow a_j)=s_{HK}(v_i \neq a_j)=s_{HK}(v_i = a_j)=\varepsilon$ for $v_i \in H$, $a_j \in K$.

The language $L_M(P)$ is then defined as $L_M(P)=s_{HK}(L(V)\cap C_{HK})$.

Note that $L_M(P)$ is a regular language.

For the equivalence of two $NIAN^{HK}$'s we get the following theorem.

Theorem 1.2:

Let P_1 and P_2 be two nondeterministic or deterministic Ianov-Schemes with auxiliary variables.

Then $P_1 \equiv P_2$ if and only if $S(L_M(P_1)) = S(L_M(P_2))$, where $S(L_M(P_1))$ and $S(L_M(P_2))$ are regular languages and S is the standard mapping.

For the translatability we get the following theorem.

Theorem 1.3:

Let P_1 be a NIAN, P_2 be a IAN^{HK}, and P_3 be a $NIAN^{HK}$.

Then

1) P_1 is translatable into an equivalent IAN P if and only if $S(L(P_1))$ is syntdet.

2) P_2 is always translatable into an equivalent IAN P.

3) P_3 is translatable into an equivalent IAN P if and only if $S(L_M(P_3))$ is syntdet.

II. Economy of description for deterministic and nondeterministic Ianov-Schemes

Before we exhibit upper and lower bounds for the tradeoff in economy of description between the various classes of program schemes, let us briefly introduce our measures of size on which we will base our investigations.

Clearly, many measures of size are possible. The measures we want to choose here are designed to resemble the following complexities:

- v-size, to measure the space which a compiler has to allocate in order to store the values of the variables,
- d-size, to measure the descriptive complexity of a program, i.e., the space necessary to store the program,
- size, to measure the complexity of understanding the control flow in a program scheme.

Our measure size will be defined as the product of the two measures v-size and d-size. We believe that this product captures the number of important instantaneous descriptions necessary to get a good idea of all possible execution sequences which could occur in connection with some interpretation. It goes without saying that several other measures are possible which, for the purpose of this paper, we will not consider.

Definition 2.1:

1) Let $U = (N,\Sigma,n_0,F,\delta)$ be an IAN or a NIAN.

   Then we define:

   d-size $(U) = |N|$, v-size $(U) = 1$ and size $(U) = |N|$.

2) Let $U = (\Sigma,H,K,k_0,V)$ be a IAN^{HK} or a $NIAN^{HK}$ with $V = (N,\Sigma_{HK},n_0,F,\delta)$. Then we define:

   d-size $(U) = |N|$, v-size $(U) = |H|$ and size $(U) = |N|\cdot|H|$.

In the following definition we will explain the notion of <u>succinctness</u>.

<u>Definition 2.2:</u>

Let K_1 and K_2 be two classes of program schemes with complexity measures $size_1$ for K_1 and $size_2$ for K_2. By $(K_1, size_1) \xrightarrow{f(n)} (K_2, size_2)$ we will denote the <u>f(n)-succinctness</u> of $(K_1, size_1)$ over $(K_2, size_2)$ if and only if there exists a sequence of program schemes $U_n^1 \in K_1$ for $n \in N$ such that for every program scheme $U_n^2 \in K_2$ with $U_n^1 \equiv U_n^2$:

$size_2 \, (U_n^2) \geq f(size_1(U_n^1))$ almost everywhere.

Sometimes we say for $(K_1, size_1) \xrightarrow{f(n)} (K_2, size_2)$ that $(K_1, size_1)$ can be f(n) - <u>more succinct</u> or <u>more economical</u> than $(K_2, size_2)$.

Theorem 1.3 is our key to proving the f(n) -succinctness of (NIAN, size) over (IAN, size). Based on this theorem we will try to do two things:

1) Find a sequence P_n of nondeterministic Ianov-Schemes such that $S(L(P_n))$ is a syntdet language.
   This would imply that P_n is translatable into an equivalent deterministic Ianov-Scheme.

2) Show that for any P_n of the above sequence, <u>every</u> language L_n with $S(L_n) = S(L(P_n))$ can only be accepted by deterministic finite automata which have at least $f(size(P_n))$ states. This would imply that every IAN (deterministic Ianov-Schemes are deterministic finite automata) needs at least $f(size(P_n))$ nodes.

<u>Theorem 2.3:</u>

Let P_n be the following sequence of nondeterministic Ianov-Schemes over the alphabet $\Sigma = F_\Sigma \cup P_\Sigma \cup \bar{P}_\Sigma$ with $F_\Sigma = \{f,g\}$, $P_\Sigma = \{p,q\}$, $\bar{P}_\Sigma = \{\bar{p},\bar{q}\}$ and

P_n:

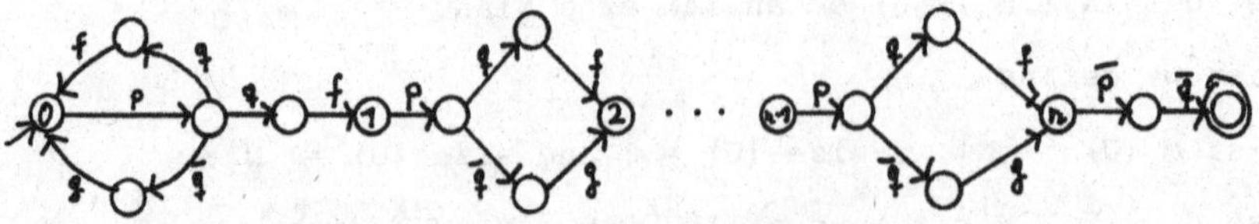

Then the following statements holds:

1) $L(P_n) = S(L(P_n))$ is syntdet,
2) size $(P_n) = 4 \cdot (n+1)$,

3) for every deterministic Ianov-Scheme P'_n such that $P'_n \equiv P_n$: size $(P'_n) \geq 2^n$.

Proof: It is easy to see that

$L_n = L(P_n) = \{pqf, p\bar{q}g\}^* . \{pqf\} \cdot \{pqf, p\bar{q}g\}^{n-1} \cdot \{\bar{p}\bar{q}\}$.

Moreover , we have $S(L(P_n)) = L_n$ and L_n syntdet. Simple counting will yield that P_n has $4 \cdot (n+1)$ nodes.

Now we want to show 3).

Let $W_n = \{pqf, p\bar{q}g\}^n$. Let $\bar{L}_n$ be a language such that $S(\bar{L}_n) = L_n$, and let $U = (N, \Sigma, n_0, \delta, F)$ be a deterministic finite automaton which accepts $\bar{L}_n$. We will prove that for any two words $w_1, w_2 \varepsilon W_n$ with $w_1 \neq w_2$ there exist two words $\bar{w}_1$ and $\bar{w}_2$ such that $w_1 \neq w_2$ and $\delta(n_0, \bar{w}_1) \neq \delta(n_0, \bar{w}_2)$. In other words, U will need at least as many states as there are words in W_n. Since W_n consists of 2^n words, U will need at least 2^n states.

Let w_1 and w_2 be two words in W_n with $w_1 \neq w_2$. Let k be the smallest index such that

$w_1 = t_1 h_1 \ldots t_{k-1} h_{k-1} pqf t_{k+1} \ldots t_n h_n$ and

$w_2 = t_1 h_1 \ldots t_{k-1} h_{k-1} p\bar{q}g t'_{k+1} \ldots t'_n h'_n$, where

$t_i, t'_i \in \{pq, p\bar{q}\}$; $h_i, h'_i \in \{f, g\}$.

Let us consider $u_1 = w_1 \ (pqf)^{k-1} \bar{p}\bar{q} \in L(P_n)$.

From $S(\overline{L_n}) = L_n$ it follows that there exists at least 1 word $\bar{u}_1$ with $u_1 \in S(\bar{u}_1)$. By the definition of S, $\bar{u}_1$ is of the following form:

$\bar{u}_1 = \bar{t}_1 h_1 \bar{t}_2 h_2 \ldots \bar{t}_k f \bar{t}_{k+1} \ldots \bar{t}_n h_n \bar{y}_1 = \bar{w}_1 \bar{y}_1$.

Similarly, for w_2 there exists y such that $w_2 y \in L(P_n)$.

Hence there exists a word $\bar{u}_2 = \bar{w}_2 \bar{y}$ such that $w_2 y \in S(\bar{w}_2 \bar{y})$.

Because of the definition of S, $\bar{u}_2$ has the form:

$$\bar{u}_2 = \bar{r}_1 h_1 \bar{r}_2 h_2 \ldots \bar{r}_k g \bar{r}_{k+1} h'_{k+1} \ldots \bar{r}_n \bar{y} = \bar{w}_2 \bar{y}.$$

Assume now that, in U, $\delta(n_0, \bar{w}_1) = \delta(n_0, \bar{w}_2)$. Since U is deterministic, it will then also accept $\bar{w}_2 \bar{y}_1$. However, since $w_2 (pqf)^{k-1} \bar{p}\bar{q} \in S(\bar{w}_2 \bar{y}_1)$ and since $w_2 (pqf)^{k-1} \bar{p}\bar{q} \notin L_n$, we obtain a contradiction to the fact that $S(\bar{L}_n) = S(L_n)$.

Consequently, $\delta(n_0, \bar{w}_1) \neq \delta(n_0, \bar{w}_2)$.

Theorem 2.3. leads us to the next theorem:

Theorem 2.4:

$$(\text{NIAN, d-size}) \xrightarrow{2^{c\,n}} (\text{IAN, d-size}) \text{ and}$$

$$(\text{NIAN, size}) \xrightarrow{2^{c\,n}} (\text{IAN, size}).$$

In our next theorem we will exhibit an upper bound for the succinctness between deterministic Ianov-Schemes and nondeterministic Ianov-Schemes.

For any nondeterministic Ianov-Scheme P we will construct a deterministic finite automaton U such that the language accepted by U equals the standard form of L(P).

We then show that, if P is translatable into a deterministic Ianov-Scheme (i.e. S(L(P)) is syntdet), we can construct a IAN P' from U with the following properties:

a) L(P')=S(L(P)), which implies that P' ≡ P, and

b) size (P') ≤ number of states in U.

Theorem 2.5:

Let $\Sigma = F_\Sigma \cup P_\Sigma \cup \bar{P}_\Sigma$ be an alphabet of instruction symbols with $P_\Sigma = \{p_1,\dots,p_k\}$, and let $P = (N,\Sigma,n_0,F,\delta)$ be a NIAN with S(L(P)) syntdet. Then there exists an equivalent IAN P' with

$$\text{size }(P') \leq 2^{\text{size }(P)\ +\ k+1}.$$

Proof: We first construct a deterministic finite automaton $U = (N_u,\Sigma,n_{0_u},\delta_u,F_u)$ accepting the language S(L(P)).

The states of U consist of all pairs (m,t) where m is an element of P(N) and t is a word in the language $T = \bigcup_{j=0}^{k} T_j$, $T_0 = \{\varepsilon\}$ and $T_j=\{p_1,\bar{p}_1\}\cdot\{p_2,\bar{p}_2\}\cdots\{p_j,\bar{p}_j\}$ for $1 \leq j \leq k$.

The start node $n_{0_u} = (n_0,\varepsilon)$ and the final states are given by $F_u = \{(m,t_k) \mid t_k \quad T_k$ and $m \cap F \neq \emptyset\}$.

In order to accept S(L(P)), U has two types of transitions:

1) Whenever U is in a state (m,ε), then U makes a sequence of moves such that all possible standard-tests can be accepted as the next input sequence. This is accomplished by the following transitions:

For all $(m,t) \in N_u$ with $t \in T_j$, $0 \leq j < k-1$:

$\delta_u((m,t),p_{j+1}) = (m,t\cdot p_{j+1})$ and

$\delta_u((m,t),\bar{p}_{j+1}) = (m,t\cdot\bar{p}_{j+1})$.

For all $(m,t) \in N_U$ with $t \in T_{k-1}$ and $\bar{p}_k \in \{p_k, \bar{p}_k\}$:
$\delta_U((m,t),\hat{p}_k) = (m', t\cdot\hat{p}_k)$ with $m' = \{m_i' \in N \mid \exists\ m_i \in m, \exists t \in (P_\Sigma \cup \bar{P}_\Sigma)^*$ such that $m_i' \in \delta(m_i,t)$ and $t\cdot\hat{p}_k \in S(t)\}$.

Whenever U is in a state (m,t_k) where t_k is a standard test, the next input symbol has to be a function symbol. In order to accept S(L(P)) deterministically we will use the standard subset construction:

For all $(m,t_k) \in N_u$, $t_k \in T_k$ and $f \in F_\Sigma$:

$\delta_u\ (m,t_k),f) = (m',\varepsilon)$ with
$m' = \{m_i' \in N \mid \exists m_i \in m$, such that
$m_i' \in \delta(m_i,f)\}$.

By induction on the number of function symbols in a word $w \in \Sigma^*$ it is easy to show that:

$\delta_u\ (n_{0_u},w) = (m,t_k)$ with $t_k \in T_k$ if and only if there exists a word $w' \in \Sigma^*$ and a state $n \in m$ such that $n \in \delta(n_0,w')$ and $w \in S(w')$.

By the construction of F_u this implies that S(L(P)) is the language accepted by U.

If we finally delete all the states that cannot be reached from the start state or cannot lead to a final state we have constructed a IAN P' with L(P') = S(L(P)). We then get the upper bound:

size $(P') \leq 2^{\text{size}(P)+k+1}$.

III. Economy of description for Ianov-Schemes with auxiliary variables

In this section we will investigate the descriptive complexity for Ianov-Schemes with auxiliary variables.

According to theorem 3.3, Ianov-Schemes with auxiliary variables are not more powerful than Ianov-Schemes without auxiliary variables. However, as we will show, infinitely often Ianov-Schemes with auxiliary variables can describe certain control-structures much more (i.e., exponentially more) economically than Ianov-Schemes without auxiliary variables.

Theorem 3.1:

Let P_n, $n \geq 1$, be the following sequence of deterministic Ianov-Schemes with auxiliary-variables:

$P_n = (\Sigma,H,K,k_0,V)$ with
$F_\Sigma = \{f_1,f_2\}$, $P_\Sigma = \{p\}$, $\bar{P}_\Sigma = \{\bar{p}\}$, $H = \{v_1,v_2,\ldots,v_n\}$, $K = \{F_1,F_2\}$ and $k_0 = (F_1,\ldots,F_1)$.

Let V be defined as:

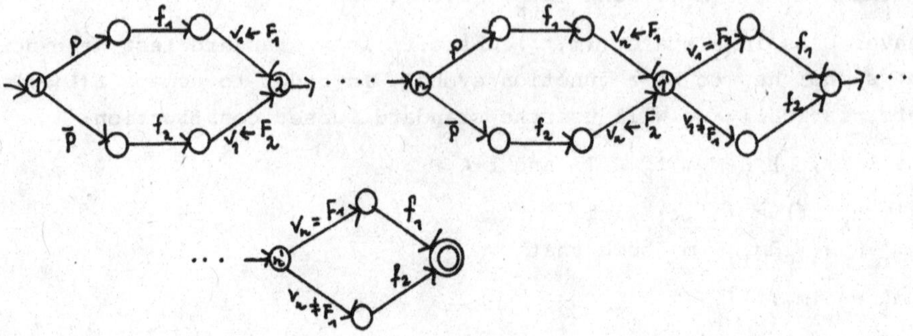

Then it holds that every deterministic Ianov-Scheme $\bar{P}_n$ with $\bar{P}_n \equiv P_n$ needs at least 2^n nodes.

<u>Proof</u>: It is easy to see that

$L_M(P) = \{wh(w) \mid w \varepsilon \{pf_1\bar{p}f_2\}^n,\ h(f_i) = f_i,\ h(\bar{p}) = h(p) = \varepsilon\}$
and that $S(L_M(P_n))$ syntdet.

Let $\bar{L}_n$ be an arbitrary language with $S(\bar{L}_n) = S(L_M(P_n))$ and let $U = (N, \Sigma, n_0, \delta, F)$ be a deterministic finite automaton which accepts $\bar{L}_n$.

We define: $W_n = \{w \mid w \varepsilon \{pf_1\bar{p}f_2\}^n\}$. In a way similar to the proof of theorem 2.3 one can show that for any two distinct words w_1 and w_2 in W_n there exist two <u>distinct</u> words $\bar{w}_1, \bar{w}_2$ such that $\delta(n_0, \bar{w}_1) \neq \delta(n_0, \bar{w}_2)$. Since W_n consists of 2^n elements, U has to have at least 2^n states and every deterministic Ianov-Schemes $\bar{P}_n$ with $\bar{P}_n \equiv P_n$ needs at least 2^n nodes. We omit the details.

Since P_n in the above proof consists of (8n+1) nodes and n variables, we obtain the following theorem:

<u>Theorem 3.2</u>:

1) $(\mathrm{IAN}^{HK}, \text{(d-size)}) \xrightarrow{2^{c \cdot n}} > (\mathrm{IAN}, \text{d-size})$

2) $(\mathrm{IAN}^{HK}, \text{size}) \xrightarrow{2^{c\sqrt{n}}} > (\mathrm{IAN}, \text{size})$

This last theorem leads us to the question whether the complexity gap between deterministic Ianov-Schemes with and without auxiliary variables will be reduced if we compare nondeterm. Ianov-Schemes without auxiliary variables. Possibly nondeterminism can simulate the use of auxiliary variables more economically than determinism. As the next theorem will express, infinitely often nondeterminism will have just as difficult a time as determinism had to simulate the use of auxiliary variables.

Theorem 3.3:

1) $(\mathrm{IAN}^{HK}, \text{d-size}) \xrightarrow{\;2^{c\cdot n}\;} (\mathrm{NIAN}, \text{d-size})$

2) $(\mathrm{IAN}^{HK}, \text{size}) \xrightarrow{\;2^{c\sqrt{n}}\;} (\mathrm{NIAN}, \text{size})$

Proof: We will use the same sequence of program-schemes which we used in the proof of theorem 3.1. Then one can show that, for every language $\bar{L}_n$ with $S(\bar{L}_n) = S(L_M(P_n))$, any nondeterministic finite automaton accepting $\bar{L}_n$ needs at least 2^n states. However, in contrast to the proof of theorem 3.1 it is essential here that for every $w \varepsilon W_n$ there exists exactly one w' such that $ww' \varepsilon L_M(P_n)$.

Our next step will be to prove an upper bound for the succinctness of deterministic Ianov-Schemes without auxiliary variables.

Theorem 3.4:

Let $P = (\Sigma, H, K, k_0, V)$ be an IAN^{HK} with $H = \{v_1, \ldots, v_n\}$, $K = \{a_1, \ldots, a_m\}$ and $V = (N, \Sigma_{HK}, n_0, \delta, F)$. Then there exists a IAN P' with $P' \equiv P$ and size $(P') \leq$ d-size $(P) \cdot m^n = |N| \cdot m^n$.

Proof: From the definition of $L_M(P)$ it follows that $L_M(P)$ can be accepted by a deterministic finite automaton U with $|N| \cdot m^n$ states. Since $L_M(P)$ is syntdet one can show (-in a way similar to the proof of theorem 3.5 -) that there exists a deterministic Ianov-Scheme P' such that size $(P') \leq |N| \cdot m^n$. Again, we omit the details.

Finally, we want to study how much more economical nondeterministic Ianov-Schemes with auxiliary viariables can be than deterministic Ianov-Schemes without auxiliary variables.

Definition 3.1:

Let $\Sigma = F_\Sigma \cup P_\Sigma \cup \bar{P}_\Sigma$ an alphabet of instruction-symbols with $P_\Sigma = \{q_1, \ldots, q_n\}$ and $F_\Sigma = \{f_0, f_1, \ldots, f_n, h_0, h_1\}$.
Let A_n be the language defined by the following context-free grammar:

$$S \longrightarrow S_1 S_1 f_0$$

$$S_k \longrightarrow S_{k+1}\ S_{k+1}\ f_k \quad \text{for } k=1,\ldots,n-1$$

$$S_n \longrightarrow S_{n+1}\ f_n$$

$S_{n+1} \longrightarrow q_1h_1 | \bar{q}_1h_2$

where S is the start symbol. Let $w \in A_n$. We than can associate w with a binary tree of height (n+1) whose leaves are labelled by q_1h_1 or $\bar{q}_1h_2$. Each leaf can be characterized by a word y of length n where

$y \in \{q_1, \bar{q}_1\} \cdot \{q_2, \bar{q}_2\} \ldots \{q_n, \bar{q}_n\} = T$. The word y describes a path through the tree where q_i indicates that, on level i of the tree, the path goes to the right. Likewise, $\bar{q}_i$ indicates that, on level i of the tree, the path goes to the left. Let L_n be defined as follows:

$L_n = \{xy \mid x \in A_n,\ y \in T$ and the leaf reached by path y is labelled $q_1h\}$.

<u>Theorem 3.5</u>:

Let L_n be as defined in definition 3.1. Then the following holds:

1) $S(L_n)$ is syntdet,
2) for every Ianov-Scheme P_n with $S(L(P_n)) = S(L_n)$:
   size $(P_n) \geq 2^{2^n}$

<u>Proof</u>: 1) Follows from the definition of L_n:

2) Let $\bar{L}_n$ be a language with $S(\bar{L}_n) = S(L_n)$ and let $U = (N, \Sigma, n_0, \delta, F)$ be a deterministic finite automaton which accepts $\bar{L}_n$. We can show that for any two distinct words w_1 and $w_2 \varepsilon A_n$ there exists two distinct words $\bar{w}_1$ and $\bar{w}_2$ such that $\delta(n_o, \bar{w}_1) \neq \delta(n_0, \bar{w}_2)$.

Since A_n contains 2^{2^n} words we obtain that size $(P_n) \geq 2^{2^n}$ for any Ianov-Scheme P_n with $S(L(P_n)) = S(L_n)$. We omit the details.

<u>Theorem 3.6</u>:

Let L_n be defined as in definition 3.1. Then there exists a nondeterministic Ianov-Scheme P_n with auxiliary variables such that

a) $L_M(P_n) = L_n$,
b) d-size $(P_n) \leq c_1 \cdot n^2$,
c) v-size $(P_n) \leq c_2 \cdot n$ and
d) size $(P_n) \leq c_3 \cdot n^3$.

The example for P_n is rather complicated. We therefore, for the purpose of this extended abstract, will not present any details here.

Combining theorem 3.6 and 3.7 we obtain:

Theorem 3.7:

1) $(\mathrm{NIAN}^{HK}, \text{d-size}) \xrightarrow{2^{c\cdot\sqrt{n}}} (\mathrm{IAN}, \text{d-size})$

2) $(\mathrm{NIAN}^{HK}, \text{size}) \xrightarrow{2^{2^{c\cdot\sqrt[3]{n}}}} (\mathrm{IAN}, \text{size})$

IV. Conclusion

As we mentioned in the introduction we believe that the results presented in this paper demonstrate how fruitful an investigation of the economy of description of program schemes turns out to be. Several other classes of program schemes and various other measures of descriptive complexity merit attention.

References:

Brown, Gries, Szymanski |1972|: S.Brown, D.Gries, T.Szymanski, "Program-Schemes with Pushdown Stores", SIAM Journal on Computing 1, 1972, pp. 242-268.

Constable, Gries, |1972|: R.L.Constable, D.Gries, "On Classes of Program Schemata", SIAM Journal on Computing 1, 1972, pp. 66-118.

Engelfriet|1974|: J.Engelfriet, "Simple Program Schemes and Formal Languages", Lecture Notes in Computer Science 20, Springer Verlag, 1974.

Garland, Luckham |1973| : S.J.Garland, D.C.Luckham, "Program Schemes, Recursion Schemes and Formal Languages", JCSS 7, 1973, pp. 119-160.

Greibach |1975|: S.A.Greibach, "Theory of Program Structures: Schemes, Semantics, Verification", Lecture Notes in Computer Science 36, Springer Verlag, 1975.

Hopcroft, Ullmann |1979|: J.E.Hopcroft, J.D.Ullmann, "Introduction to Automata Theory, Languages and Computation", Addison Wesley Publishing Company, 1979.

Ianov |1960|: I.Ianov, "On the Logical Schemes of Algorithms", Problems of Cybernetics 1, 1960, pp.82-140.

Kaplan |1969|: D.M.Kaplan, "Regular Expressions and the Equivalence of Programs", JCSS 3, 1969, pp.361-386.

Knuth, Floyd |1971|: D.E.Knuth, R.W.Floyd, "Notes on avoiding "go to" Statements", Information Processing Letters 1, 1971, pp.23-31.

Manna |1973|: Z.Manna: "Program Schemes", Currents in the Theory of Computing (A. Aho ed.), Prentice Hall, 1973, pp.90-142.

Meyer, Fisher |1971|: A.R.Meyer, M.J.Fisher, "Economy of Description by Automata, Grammars and Formal Systems", 12-th Annual Symposium on Switching and Automata Theory, 1971, pp. 188-191.

Strong |1971|: H.R.Strong, "Translating Recursion Equations into Flowcharts", JCSS 5, 1971, pp.254-285.

Valiant |1975|: L.G.Valiant, "Regularity and Related Problems for Deterministic Pushdown Automata", JACM 22,1, 1975 pp. 1-10.

ON APPROXIMATE STRING MATCHING

Esko Ukkonen

Department of Computer Science
University of Helsinki
Tukholmankatu 2
SF-00250 Helsinki 25, Finland

Abstract. An algorithm is given for computing the edit distance as well as the corresponding sequence of editing steps (insertions, deletions, changes, transpositions of adjacent symbols) between two strings $a_1a_2\ldots a_m$ and $b_1b_2\ldots b_n$. The algorithm needs time $O(s\cdot\min(m,n))$ and space $O(s^2)$ where s is the edit distance, that is, the minimum number of editing steps needed to transform $a_1a_2\ldots a_m$ to $b_1b_2\ldots b_n$. For small s this is a considerable improvement over the best previously known algorithm that needs time and space $O(mn)$. If the editing sequence is not required, the space complexity of our algorithm reduces to $O(s)$. Given a threshold value t, the algorithm can also be modified to test in time $O(t\cdot\min(m,n))$ and space $O(t)$ whether the edit distance of the two strings is at most t.

1. INTRODUCTION

The *edit distance* between two strings is usually measured as the minimum cost sequence of deletions, insertions and changes of symbols needed to transform one string into the other. Also some more general operations such as transposition of two adjacent symbols are sometimes included in the allowed editing operations. Being able to compute the edit distance as well as the corresponding sequence of editing steps has applications in several string matching problems arising in areas such as information retrieval, pattern recognition, error correction and molecular genetics.

In this paper we give an improved algorithm for computing the edit distance. For two strings $a_1a_2\ldots a_m$ and $b_1b_2\ldots b_n$ the algorithm computes the edit distance s as well as the corresponding sequence of editing steps (insertions, deletions, changes, transpositions) in time $O(s\cdot\min(m,n))$ and space $O(s^2)$. If the editing sequence is not needed, the space requirement reduces to $O(s)$. For simplicity, we will assume in this paper, that each editing operation has the same cost equal to 1; essentially the same results are true also for more general costs [8].

For small s our algorithm significantly improves the best previously known algorithm [1], [2], [4], [6], [9], whose time requirement is always $O(mn)$ and space requirement is $O(mn)$ or $O(\min(m,n))$ depending on whether or not the editing sequence is needed. In fact, the discovery of the new method was stimulated by the apparent inefficiency of the $O(mn)$ algorithm in genetic applications where m and n can be more than 10^4, c.f. [5].

Our algorithm can also be used in testing whether or not the edit distance is at most t for any fixed threshold value t. The test requires time $O(t \cdot \min(m,n))$ and space $O(t)$. This kind of a test with a relatively small t is exactly what is needed in some applications where one wants to determine from a larger set of strings all strings whose distance from a given string is at most t. In such cases the new algorithm can be considerably faster than the $O(mn)$ algorithm.

2. BASIC METHOD

Given a string $A = a_1 a_2 \ldots a_m$ from some alphabet, the possible *editing operations* on A are:

(i) *deleting* a symbol from any position, say i, to give $a_1 \ldots a_{i-1} a_{i+1} \ldots a_m$;
(ii) *inserting* a symbol, say b, at position i to give $a_1 \ldots a_i b a_{i+1} \ldots a_m$;
(iii) *changing* a symbol at position i to a new symbol b to give $a_1 \ldots a_{i-1} b a_{i+1} \ldots a_m$.

With positive costs c_D, c_I, c_C associated with deleting, inserting and changing any symbol, and strings $A = a_1 \ldots a_m$ and $B = b_1 \ldots b_n$ given, the problem is to determine a sequence of editing operations which, when applied on A, produces B so that the sum of individual costs is minimized. The minimum cost is denoted by $d(A,B)$ and called the *edit distance* from A to B.

The well-known dynamic programming method for computing $d(A,B)$ works as follows: Let $d_{ij} = d(a_1 \ldots a_i, b_1 \ldots b_j)$ for $0 \leq i \leq m$, $0 \leq j \leq n$. Hence d_{ij} denotes the edit distance from $a_1 \ldots a_i$ to $b_1 \ldots b_j$. Then the $(m+1) \times (n+1)$ matrix (d_{ij}) can be computed from the recurrence

$$(1) \quad \begin{cases} d_{oo} = 0, \\ d_{ij} = \min(d_{i-1,j-1} + (\underline{\text{if}}\ a_i = b_j\ \underline{\text{then}}\ 0\ \underline{\text{else}}\ c_C), \\ \qquad\qquad d_{i-1,j} + c_D, \\ \qquad\qquad d_{i,j-1} + c_I),\ i > 0 \text{ or } j > 0. \end{cases}$$

Clearly, matrix (d_{ij}) can be evaluated starting from d_{oo} and proceeding row-by-row or column-by-column. This takes time $O(mn)$. Finally, d_{mn} equals $d(A,B)$. Moreover, the sequence of edit operations that give $d(A,B)$ can be recovered from the matrix (d_{ij}) by following some "minimizing path" backwards from d_{mn} to d_{oo}. For computing only d_{mn} without the editing sequence it suffices to save one row or column of (d_{ij}) from which the next row or column can be generated. Hence the space requirement reduces to $O(\min(m,n))$. Different variations of this basic method have been invented and analyzed several times in various contexts, e.g. [1], [2], [4], [6], [7], [9].

The method can be extended in several directions. For example, [2] gives an extension to allow general reversals of order as an editing operation. Transposition of adjacent symbols is a special case. This operation is useful in spelling correction and genetic applications, and we analyze it in more detail. Formally, we adopt the following additional editing operation on $A = a_1a_2 \dots a_m$:

(iv) *transposing* of two adjacent symbols at position i to give $a_1 \dots a_{i-1}a_{i+1}a_ia_{i+2} \dots a_m$.

The recurrence (1) is quite easily extended to cope with this. Denote by c_T the cost associated with transposing. It follows from [2] that if $2c_T \geq c_I + c_D$ then it suffices to add to the minimization in (1) the term

$$\underline{\text{if}}\ a_{i-1}a_i = b_jb_{j-1}\ \underline{\text{then}}\ d_{i-2,j-2} + c_T$$

and the resulting recurrence correctly determines values d_{ij} when all edit operations (i) - (iv) are present. For the special case (to be assumed in the sequel) $c_D = c_I = c_C = c_T = 1$ we get

$$(2) \quad \begin{cases} d_{oo} = 0 \\ d_{ij} = \min(\ d_{i-1,j-1} + (\underline{\text{if}}\ a_i = b_j\ \underline{\text{then}}\ 0\ \underline{\text{else}}\ 1), \\ \qquad\qquad d_{i-1,j} + 1, \\ \qquad\qquad d_{i,j-1} + 1, \\ \qquad\qquad \underline{\text{if}}\ a_{i-1}a_i = b_jb_{j-1}\ \underline{\text{then}}\ d_{i-2,j-2} + 1\ ), \quad i > 0 \text{ or } j > 0. \end{cases}$$

The matrix (d_{ij}) defined by (2) can again be evaluated in time and space $O(mn)$ by the straightforward method. For computing only d_{mn} without the editing sequence, it is now necessary to save two rows or columns from which the next row or column can be generated. Thus the space requirement remains $O(\min(m,n))$.

3. NEW ALGORITHM

Let us assume that all editing operations (i) - (iv) are available. To simplify the presentation we also assume in the sequel that each operation has the unit cost, that is, $c_D = c_I = c_C = c_T = 1$. Hence the edit distance $d(A,B)$ is simply the minimum number of editing steps that transform A into B, and matrix (d_{ij}) is correctly defined by (2). We emphasize, however, that the results to be presented are valid for more general costs [8].

Graphically, the dependencies between different values d_{ij} can be illustrated by drawing a directed arc from $d_{i'j'}$ to d_{ij} if and only if the minimization step in (2) gives d_{ij} from $d_{i'j'}$. An example matrix (d_{ij}) is illustrated in Figure 1. Vertical arcs correspond to deletions, horizontal arcs correspond to insertions, short diagonal arcs correspond to changes or matches and longer diagonal arcs correspond to transpositions. It should be clear, that only those d_{ij} that are on some path from d_{oo} to d_{mn} are relevant for the value d_{mn}. If d_{mn} is small as compared to m and n, the relevant entries d_{ij} form only a small subset of the whole matrix. This suggests that a more efficient algorithm can be found by somehow limiting the scope of the evaluation of (d_{ij}).

$$B$$

		a	b	a	c	b	c
		0 → 1	2	3	4	5	6
	b	1	1	1	2	3	4	5
	a	2	1	1	1 → 2	3	4
A	b	3	2	1	2	2	2	3
	c	4	3	2	2	2	2	2
	a	5	4	3	2	2	3	3

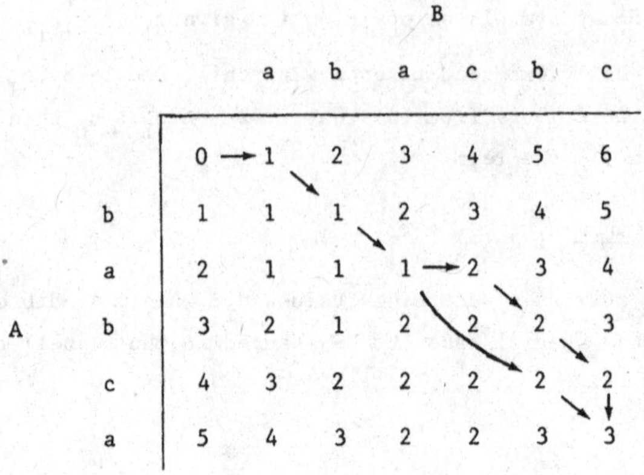

<u>Figure 1</u>. Matrix (d_{ij}) computed from (2) for strings A = babca and B = abacbc; all
arcs on paths from d_{oo} to d_{56} are also shown.

Rather than with rows or columns, our algorithm will operate with the *diagonals* of the matrix (d_{ij}). The basic Lemma 1 shows that the values d_{ij} on the same diagonal (i.e., j-i is constant) form a non-decreasing sequence which increases in unit steps.

<u>Lemma 1</u>. For every d_{ij}, $d_{ij} - 1 \leq d_{i-1,j-1} \leq d_{ij}$.

<u>Proof</u>. The minimization step in (2) directly implies that d_{ij} cannot be larger than $d_{i-1,j-1} + 1$. Hence $d_{ij} - 1 \leq d_{i-1,j-1}$.
As regards the second inequality, it is trivially true for d_{oo}. We proceed by induction on i + j. Assume first that the minimizing path to d_{ij} comes from $d_{i-1,j-1}$. Then (2) implies that $d_{ij} = d_{i-1,j-1}$ or $d_{ij} = d_{i-1,j-1} + 1$, hence $d_{ij} \geq d_{i-1,j-1}$, as required. Assume then that the minimizing path to d_{ij} comes from $d_{i-1,j}$; the symmetric case where the path comes from $d_{i,j-1}$ is similar. Then again by (2), $d_{ij} = d_{i-1,j} + 1$. By induction hypothesis $d_{i-1,j} \geq d_{i-2,j-1}$. Hence $d_{ij} \geq d_{i-2,j-1} + 1$. Since $d_{i-1,j-1} \leq d_{i-2,j-1} + 1$ by (2), this immediately implies that $d_{ij} \geq d_{i-1,j-1}$, as required. Finally, assume that the minimizing path to d_{ij} comes from $d_{i-2,j-2}$. By (2), $d_{ij} = d_{i-2,j-2} + 1$. Noting that $d_{i-2,j-2} \geq d_{i-1,j-1} - 1$ by induction hypothesis, we obtain $d_{ij} \geq d_{i-1,j-1} - 1 + 1 = d_{i-1,j-1}$, as required. □

Lemma 1 suggests an alternative way of storing matrix (d_{ij}): For each diagonal of (d_{ij}), it suffices to store information which tells the points on the diagonal where the value increases. In more detail, denote the diagonals with integers -m, -m+1, ..., 0, 1, ...,n such that the diagonal denoted by k consists of those entries d_{ij} for which j-i = k.

Let

f_{kp} = the largest index i such that $d_{ij} = p$ and d_{ij} is on diagonal k.

Since all values on diagonal k are $\geq |k|$, values f_{kp} are defined for $p = |k|, |k| + 1 \dots, p_{max}$ where p_{max} is the largest value on the diagonal k. In addition, it is convenient to define

$$f_{k,|k|-1} = \begin{cases} |k| - 1, & \text{if } k < 0; \\ -1, & \text{otherwise,} \end{cases}$$

and $f_{kp} = -\infty$ for the remaining values f_{kp} possibly referred to in the algorithms to be presented. For example, the diagonal 1 of the matrix in Figure 1 contains values 1, 1, 1, 2, 2, 3. Hence according to our definitions, $f_{1,-1} = -\infty$, $f_{10} = -1$, $f_{11} = 2$, $f_{12} = 4$, $f_{13} = 5$.

Recovering values d_{ij} from (f_{kp}) is simple: Find p such that $f_{k,p-1} < i \leq f_{kp}$ where $k = j-i$. Then $d_{ij} = p$. In particular, $d_{mn} = d(a_1 \dots a_m, b_1 \dots b_n)$ equals p so that

(3) $\qquad f_{n-m,p} = m.$

Assume that $p \geq |k|$ and that for all k', $f_{k',p-1}$ has been correctly computed. Then Algorithm A computes f_{kp}.

A0. $t := f_{k,p-1} + 1$;
A1. $t := \max(t, f_{k-1,p-1}, f_{k+1,p-1} + 1,$ <u>if</u> $a_t a_{t+1} = b_{k+t+1} b_{k+t}$ <u>then</u> $t+1)$;
A2. <u>while</u> $a_{t+1} = b_{t+1+k}$ <u>do</u> $t := t+1$;
A3. $f_{kp} :=$ <u>if</u> $t > m$ <u>or</u> $t+k > n$ <u>then</u> undefined <u>else</u> t;

<u>Algorithm A</u>.

To delineate a correctness proof for Algorithm A, note first, that in matrix (d_{ij}) the block of values $p - 1$ reaches row $f_{k,p-1}$ on diagonal k, row $f_{k-1,p-1}$ on diagonal $k - 1$ and row $f_{k+1,p-1}$ on diagonal $k + 1$. Then by (2) and by Lemma 1, the block of values p must reach at least row $t' = \max(t, f_{k-1,p-1}, f_{k+1,p-1} + 1,$ <u>if</u> $a_t a_{t+1} = b_{k+t+1} b_{k+t}$ <u>then</u> $t+1)$ on diagonal k (here $t = f_{k,p-1} + 1$). Hence $f_{kp} \geq t'$. On the other hand, the correct value $f_{kp} = t''$ is greater than t' only if $a_{t'+1} = b_{t'+1+k}$, $\dots$, $a_{t''} = b_{t''+k}$. Otherwise some of values $f_{k,p-1}$, $f_{k-1,p-1}$, $f_{k+1,p-1}$ should be larger.

To compute the edit distance $s = d(a_1 \dots a_m, b_1 \dots b_n)$, we must find p such that (3) is true. This can be done by Algorithm B.

Although Algorithm B correctly computes s, it asks Algorithm A to evaluate unnecessarily many f_{kp}'s whose value is actually undefined. This is because the range of values assigned for k in step (*) is too large. Since there are only diagonals

```
B0.  p := -1;
B1.  do
       begin
         p := p + 1;
(*)      for k := -p, -p+1, ... , p do evaluate f_kp with Algorithm A
       end
     until f_{n-m,p} = m;
B2.  s := p;
```

Algorithm B.

$-m, \ldots, n$ in matrix (d_{ij}), it follows that k can be restricted to $-m \leq k \leq n$. Moreover, each diagonal contains at most min(m,n)+1 elements. Hence for at most min(m,n) + 1 different p, f_{kp} may have a nontrivial value. Therefore it suffices that k has the same value in different executions of (*) at most min(m,n)+1 times. Hence k must in (*) satisfy the condition

$$-m \leq k \leq n \text{ and } (-p \leq k \leq -p + \min(m,n) \text{ or } p - \min(m,n) \leq k \leq p).$$

This can be further simplified such that we arrive at Algorithm B'.

```
B'0.  p := -1;
B'1.  do
        begin
          p := p + 1;
          r := p - min(m,n);
(**)      if r ≤ 0 then for k := -p, -p+1, ... , p do
              evaluate f_kp with Algorithm A
          else for k := max(-m,-p), ... , -r, r, ... , min(n,p) do
              evaluate f_kp with Algorithm A
        end
      until f_{n-m,p} = m;
B'2.  s := p;
```

Algorithm B'.

Some additional improvements are still possible based on the observation that in matrix (d_{ij}), entry $d_{i'j'}$ can be on a minimizing path leading from d_{oo} to d_{ij} only if $d_{i'j'} \leq d_{ij} - |i-j-i'+j'|$. Incorporating this in Algorithm B' reduces the number of values f_{kp} that must be evaluated to find s. However, this does not improve asymptotic efficiency of the algorithm.

To analyze the time requirement of Algorithm B', let $s = d(a_1 \ldots a_m, b_1 \ldots b_n)$. The values assigned for k in the innermost loop (**) are in the range $-s, -s+1, \ldots, s$ and each value can occur at most $\min(m,n)+1$ times. Hence Algorithm B' takes time $O(s \cdot \min(m,n))$ without counting the time needed by Algorithm A. The running time of Algorithm A is dominated by the time of loop A2. Obviously, for a fixed k, test $a_{t+1} = b_{t+1+k}$ is performed at most once for each t. Therefore, for a fixed k again, step A2 needs time $O(\min(m,n))$. This is the total time needed by all executions of step A2 with this k. There are $O(s)$ different values k, hence the total time for Algorithm A is $O(s \cdot \min(m,n))$. So also the whole method runs in time $O(s \cdot \min(m,n))$.

As regards space, Algorithm B' computes at most $O(s^2)$ (actually only $O(s \cdot \min(s,m,n))$) different f_{kp}'s, and hence $O(s^2)$ space suffices. (The simple address transformations needed in representing the relevant values f_{kp} in a one-dimensional dynamically growing vector are left to the reader.)

Using the stored values f_{kp}, the edit operation sequence corresponding to the minimum edit distance s can be found in time $O(s + \min(m,n))$ with Algorithm C. The algorithm can be understood as a simple "reversal" of Algorithm A.

```
C0.  Let p be such that f_{n-m,p} = m, that is, p := s;
     k := n-m; t := m;
C1.  while k > 0 and p > 0 do
          begin
               while a_t = b_{t+k} do t := t-1;
               Let i, 1 ≤ i ≤ 4, be such that E_i = max(E_1,E_2,E_3,E_4) where
                    E_1 = f_{k,p-1} + 1,
                    E_2 = f_{k-1,p-1},
                    E_3 = f_{k+1,p-1} + 1,
                    E_4 = if a_{t-1}a_t = b_{k+t}b_{k+t-1} then f_{k,p-1} + 2;
               if i = 1 then
                    begin announce edit operation: "change a_t to b_{t+k}";
                         t := t-1 end
               else if i = 2 then
                    begin announce edit operation: "insert b_{t+k} between a_t and a_{t+1}";
                         k := k-1 end
               else if i = 3 then
                    begin announce edit operation: "delete a_t";
                         k := k+1; t := t-1 end
               else begin announce edit operation: "transpose a_{t-1}a_t"; t := t-2 end;
          end while;
```

Algorithm C.

If the editing sequence is not needed, step A1 of Algorithm A reveals that only values $f_{k,p-1}$ for all k are needed to evaluate values f_{kp}. Since $|k| \leq s$, the space requirement reduces to O(s). So we have completed the proof of Theorem 1.

Theorem 1. Let the edit operations be deletion, insertion, change, and transposition, and let the cost of each operation be equal to 1. Then the edit distance s as well as the corresponding sequence of editing steps between strings $a_1 a_2 \ldots a_m$ and $b_1 b_2 \ldots b_n$ can be computed in time $O(s \cdot \min(m,n))$ and space $O(s^2)$. If the editing sequence is not needed, the space requirement reduces to O(s). □

Note that in the best case the running time of Algorithm B' can be considerably smaller than $O(s \cdot \min(m,n))$. This is in contrast with the basic algorithm of Section 2 that always needs time O(mn). At its best, Algorithm B' needs time $O(s^2 + \min(m,n))$. For example, the time requirement is of this form for strings $(a^r b)^s$ and $(a^r c)^s$ whose edit distance is s. Algorithm B' computes s in time $O(s^2 + s(r+1))$.

Consider then the problem of testing whether the edit distance of two strings is at most t where the threshold value t is given a priori. Clearly, this can be done with a slightly modified Algorithm B': If p grows in Algorithm B' larger than t, then announce that the edit distance is larger than t. Otherwise it is at most t. This method needs time $O(t \cdot \min(m,n))$ and space O(t).

Finally we note that Theorem 1 remains true also for reduced edit operation sets. For example, if insertion and deletion are the only operations, the corresponding algorithm is as Algorithm B' with Algorithm A as a subroutine but in the maximization step A1 of Algorithm A it suffices now to take the maximum of the second expression and the third expression.

4. CONCLUSION

We presented an $O(s \cdot \min(m,n))$ algorithm for computing the edit distance. Since $s = O(\max(m,n))$, the algorithm is always asymptotically as fast as the well-known dynamic programming method whose time complexity is O(mn).

The derivation of the algorithm was based on a careful analysis of the O(mn) method. It turned out that this method often evaluates unnecessary values and stores them inefficiently. Similar ideas can possibly be used in improving also some other dynamic programming algorithms.

Computing the edit distance is closely related to finding the longest common subsequence (LCS). In fact, let s' be the edit distance of $a_1 \ldots a_m$ and $b_1 \ldots b_n$ when the allowed edit operations include only deletion and insertion. Then the length of the LCS of these strings is $r = (m + n - s')/2$, c.f. [9]. As already mentioned, Algorithm B' after minor modifications computes s' from which we get r. The actual LCS can be found by performing on $a_1 \ldots a_m$ all deletions in the editing sequence that corresponds to s'.

For strings of approximately equal length, this method of computing the LCS seems as efficient as the recent algorithm in [3].

Acknowledgment. The author is indebted to Hannu Peltola and Jorma Tarhio for useful remarks concerning this research.

REFERENCES

1. Levenshtein,V.I.: Binary codes capable of correcting deletions, insertions and reversals. Sov. Phys. Dokl. 10 (1966), 707-710.
2. Lowrance,R. and R.A.Wagner: An extension of the string-to-string correction problem. J. ACM 22 (1975), 177-183.
3. Nakatsu,N., Y.Kambayashi and S.Yajima: A longest common subsequence algorithm suitable for similar text strings. Acta Informatica 18 (1982), 171-179.
4. Needleman,S.B. and C.D.Wunsch: A general method applicable to the search for similarities in the amino acid sequence of two proteins. J. Mol. Biol. 48 (1970), 443-453.
5. Peltola,H. & al.: SEQAID - A program package to support biopolymer sequencing. Department of Computer Science and Recombinant DNA Laboratory, University of Helsinki, 1983 (in preparation).
6. Sankoff,D.: Matching sequences under deletion/insertion constraints. Proc. Nat. Acad. Sci. 69 (1972), 4-6.
7. Sellers,P.H.: The theory and computation of evolutionary distances: Pattern recognition. J. Alg. 1 (1980), 359-373.
8. Ukkonen,E.: An algorithm for approximate string matching. In preparation.
9. Wagner,R. and M.Fisher: The string-to-string correction problem. J. ACM 21 (1974), 168-178.

DETERMINISTIC CONTEXT-FREE DYNAMIC LOGIC IS MORE EXPRESSIVE THAN DETERMINISTIC DYNAMIC LOGIC OF REGULAR PROGRAMS

Paweł Urzyczyn
Institute of Mathematics, University of Warsaw
PKiN, 00-901 Warszawa / Poland

Abstract: We show an example of an algebra $\underline{T}$, such that every deterministic regular /flow-chart/ program is equivalent in $\underline{T}$ to a loop-free approximation of itself, while a program augmented by one binary push-down store is not equivalent in $\underline{T}$ to any loop-free program. From this we deduce that the Deterministic Dynamic Logic of regular programs is strictly weaker than the Deterministic Context-Free Dynamic Logic.

1. Introduction

The aim of this paper is to compare the expressive power of programming logics based on regular /flow-chart/ programs and programs allowing parameterless recursive procedures, or cooperation with a binary push-down store /i.e. a push-down store storing only 0's and 1's/. We prove that there is an algebra $\underline{T}$ with two unary operations and one constant, such that

- $\underline{T}$ has the unwind property for all regular programs, i.e. every regular program is equivalent in $\underline{T}$ to a loop-free approximation of itself;
- there is a context-free program /i.e. a program allowing parameterless recursive calls/, total in $\underline{T}$, and not equivalent in $\underline{T}$ to any loop-free program.

The domain of $\underline{T}$ is the set of nodes in an infinite binary tree. The operations are the left and the right successors. The root is a constant.

If only loop-free programs occur in a formula of a programming logic, then the formula expresses a first-order property. Thus, the result mentioned above leads to the following comparative result. Let DDL denote the Dynamic Logic of regular programs, and let CF-DDL denote the Dynamic Logic of deterministic context-free programs, as defined in [H] by D.Harel, both with the assumption that only quantifier-free formulas can occur in tests. We prove that DDL $<$ CF-DDL, i.e. there exists a formula φ of CF-DDL, not equivalent to any formula of DDL /Theorem 4.4./. This result implies, in case of determinism, the results of Erimbetov

([E]) and Tiuryn ([T]), who proved in particular that DDL is weaker than a logic based on recursive programs.

However, the question whether DL $<$ CF-DL, where the logics under consideration allow nondeterminism, remain open. This is a non-trivial question, since, by Berman, Halpern and Tiuryn ([BHT]), we have DDL $<$ DL. /The latter can be also obtained as an easy consequence of Theorem 4.4. or even Theorem 3.2./ In addition, it can be proved, that DL is as powerful over infinite binary trees, as any reasonable logic based on programs with recursion and counters, so the question mentioned above seems to require an essentially new method. (On the other hand, A.P. Stolboushkin ([S]) has proved recently that CF-DDL $<$ CF-DL.)

The proof of the main theorem is based on a result contained in [U] and quoted here as Theorem 3.2. This is an example of an infinite binary tree with the unwind property for all flow-charts. We conjecture that the tree constructed in [U] has a similar property for all programs with binary push-down stores, and therefore it cannot be used directly for our purpose. However, finite fragments of this tree are used in the construction of $\underline{T}$.

2. Basic definitions

Throughout the paper we consider algebras of the following two similarity types:

$\mathcal{L}$ - consisting of two unary function symbols L,R and the symbol = of equality;

$\underline{\mathcal{L}}$ - being the extension of $\mathcal{L}$ by a constant symbol λ.

Thus, all the definitions below refer only to $\mathcal{L}$ and $\underline{\mathcal{L}}$.

We keep the following notational conventions. If $\underline{a}$ is a vector, say $\underline{a} \in A^k$, where A is an arbitrary set, then we assume $\underline{a} = (a_0, \ldots a_{k-1})$, if not defined otherwise. If A is an algebra and τ is a term, then $\tau_A(\underline{a})$ denotes the value of τ in A, for the valuation $\underline{a}$. The symbol ω stands for the set of nonnegative integers.

If A is a finite or infinite alphabet then A^* denotes the set of all words over A, w·v or wv is the concatenation of the words w and v, and λ is the empty word. If $u,v,w \in A^*$, and w = uv then we say that v /not u !/ is a <u>subword</u> of w, and write $v \subseteq w$. If $w \in A^*$, $e \in A$ then head(ew) = e and tail(ew) = w. The length of a word w is denoted $|w|$. For $i < |w|$, by w(i) we denote the i+1-th symbol in w, counted <u>from right to left</u> /!/, i.e. $w(i) = \text{head}(\text{tail}^{|w|-i-1}(w))$.

We remind briefly the main notions concerning DDL and CF-DDL.

The set of <u>regular programs</u> is the least set RG, satisfying the following conditions:

- if x is an individual variable and τ is a term, then $(x := \tau) \in$ RG;
- if φ is a quantifier-free formula of predicate calculus with equality, then $(\varphi?) \in$ RG;
- if $\alpha_1, \alpha_2 \in$ RG, then $(\alpha_1; \alpha_2)$, $(\alpha_1 \cup \alpha_2)$, $(\alpha_1^*) \in$ RG.

Let α be a regular program such that all the variables in α are among $\{x_1, \ldots, x_{k-1}\}$. If A is an algebra then the input/output relation $\varrho_A(\alpha)$, defined by α in A, is a binary relation in A^k such that:

- $\varrho_A(x := \tau) = \{(\underline{a}, \underline{a}') : a_j' = a_j, \text{ for } j \neq i, \text{ and } a_i' = \tau_A(\underline{a})\}$;
- $\varrho_A(\varphi?) = \{(\underline{a}, \underline{a}) : A, \underline{a} \models \varphi\}$;
- $\varrho_A(\alpha_1; \alpha_2) = \{(\underline{a}, \underline{c}) : \exists \underline{b}((\underline{a}, \underline{b}) \in \varrho_A(\alpha_1) \wedge (\underline{b}, \underline{c}) \in \varrho_A(\alpha_2))\}$;
- $\varrho_A(\alpha_1 \cup \alpha_2) = \varrho_A(\alpha_1) \cup \varrho_A(\alpha_2)$;
- $\varrho_A(\alpha_1^*) = \bigcup\{\varrho_A(\alpha_1^n) : n \in \omega\}$, where $\alpha_1^0 = \text{true?}$ and $\alpha_1^{i+1} = (\alpha; \alpha_1^i)$.

Let PV be a set of symbols, called <u>program variables,</u> and not used elsewhere. We define the set PT of <u>program terms</u> as follows:

- PV $\subseteq$ PT ;
- every assignment $(x := \tau)$ and test $(\varphi?)$ are in PT ;
- if $t_1, t_2 \in$ PT then $(t_1; t_2)$ and $(t_1 \cup t_2) \in$ PT ;
- if $t \in$ PT and Y $\in$ PV then $\mu Y(t) \in$ PT.

An occurrence of a program variable Y in a program term t is <u>bound</u> iff it is in scope of an operator μ /in a subterm of the form $\mu Y(\ldots Y \ldots)$/. A <u>context-free program</u> is a program term t, such that

- any occurrence of a program variable in t is bound ;
- if $\mu Y(t')$ is a subterm of t then Y is the only program variable that may occur free in t'.

The set of all context-free programs is denoted by CF.

For a given term $t \in$ PT with one free variable Y, and for a given $\alpha \in$ CF, we define $t^0(\alpha) = \alpha$ and $t^{i+1}(\alpha) = t(t^i(\alpha))$, where $t(t^i(\alpha))$ denotes the result of replacing Y in t by $t^i(\alpha)$. The relation $\varrho_A(\alpha)$ for $\alpha \in$ CF is defined by induction, as for $\alpha \in$ RG, but

- $\varrho_A(\mu Y(t(Y))) = \bigcup\{\varrho_A(t^i(\text{false?})) : i \in \omega\}$.

Thus, the expression $\mu Y(t)$ represents a procedure containing parameterless recursive calls of itself.

A program $\alpha \in$ RG $\cup$ CF is said to be <u>deterministic</u> iff the constructs $\cup$ and $*$ can occur in α only in the contexts:

- $(\varphi?; \alpha_1) \cup (\neg \varphi?; \alpha_2)$, abbreviated "<u>if</u> φ <u>then</u> α_1 <u>else</u> α_2 <u>fi</u>":
- $(\varphi?; \alpha_1)^*; \neg \varphi?$, abbreviated "<u>while</u> φ <u>do</u> α_1 <u>od</u>".

The set of all deterministic regular /context-free/ programs is denoted DRG /resp. DCF/.

A loop-free program is a program $\alpha \in$ DRG such that $*$ does not occur in α. For $i \in \omega$, and $\alpha \in$ DRG, let $\alpha^{(i)}$ /called the i-th approximation of α / be a loop-free program defined inductively as follows:

- $(x := \tau)^{(i)} = (x := \tau)$ and $(\varphi?)^{(i)} = (\varphi?)$, for all $i \in \omega$;
- $(\alpha_1 ; \alpha_2)^{(i)} = (\alpha_1^{(i)} ; \alpha_2^{(i)})$ and $(\alpha_1 \cup \alpha_2)^{(i)} = (\alpha_1^{(i)} \cup \alpha_2^{(i)})$, for all i ;
- $(\alpha^*)^{(0)} = \alpha^0 =$ true? and $(\alpha^*)^{(i+1)} = ((\alpha^*)^{(i)} \cup \alpha^{i+1})$.

It should be obvious that $\varrho_A(\alpha) = \bigcup\{\varrho_A(\alpha^{(i)}) : i \in \omega\}$, for any A, α . We say that α can be unwound in A , if $\varrho_A(\alpha) = \varrho_A(\alpha^{(i)})$, for some i. The algebra A has the unwind property for DRG iff every $\alpha \in$ DRG can be unwound in A.

Formulas of Deterministic Dynamic Logic /DDL/ are defined inductively as follows:

- any formula of classical predicate calculus is a formula of DDL :
- if φ , ψ are formulas of DDL and x is an individual variable then $\varphi \wedge \psi$, $\varphi \vee \psi$, $\neg\varphi$, $\exists x \varphi$, $\forall x \varphi$ are formulas of DDL :
- if $\alpha \in$ DRG and φ is a formula of DDL then $\langle\alpha\rangle\varphi$ is a formula of DDL.

Formulas of Deterministic Context-Free Dynamic Logic /CF-DDL/ are defined as above, but the construct $\langle\ \ \rangle$ applies to context-free programs.

Let α be a program with all variables among $\{x_0, \ldots x_{k-1}\}$ and let φ be a formula with all free variables among $\{x_0, \ldots, x_{k-1}, y_0, \ldots, y_{l-1}\}$. Then, for any algebra A and any $\underline{a} \in A^k$, $\underline{b} \in A^l$, we have

$A, \underline{a}, \underline{b} \models \langle\alpha\rangle\varphi$ iff there is $\underline{a}'$ such that $(\underline{a}, \underline{a}') \in \varrho_A(\alpha)$ and $A, \underline{a}', \underline{b} \models \varphi$.

The logical symbols other than $\langle\ \ \rangle$ are understood as in classical predicate calculus.

For more informations about Dynamic Logic, the reader is referred to the book [H] by D.Harel.

3. Technical background

A tree is an arbitrary set $T \subseteq \{L,R\}^*$ such that, for all $w, a \in \{L,R\}^*$, if $wa \in T$ then $a \in T$. The elements of T are called nodes or vertices of the tree. A node a is a leaf iff neither La nor Ra is in T. For any $a \in T$, the set $T(a,n) = \{w \in \{L,R\}^* : |w| \leqslant n \text{ and } wa \in T\}$ is called the n-fragment of T with the root a.

Any tree can be considered as an $\mathcal{L}$ -algebra, as well as an $\underline{\mathcal{L}}$-algebra, where λ is interpreted as the empty word, and $L(a) = La$, $R(a) = Ra$, provided the right-hand sides of the equations are elements of T.

If La or Ra is not in T then L(a) /resp. R(a)/ is equal to a. We identify any tree T with the $\mathcal{L}$-algebra T = (T,L,R). To denote the $\mathcal{L}$-extension (T,L,R,λ) we use the symbol $\underline{T}$, and such an algebra is called a <u>rooted tree</u>.

3.1. <u>Lemma</u>

Let T be an arbitrary tree. Then T has the unwind property for DRG iff $\underline{T}$ has the property.

The proof of our main theorem is based on the following fact:

3.2. <u>Theorem</u> ([U])

There exists an infinite rooted tree $\underline{T}_\omega$, which has the unwind property for DRG.

We are going to change $\underline{T}_\omega$ so that the unwind property for DRG is preserved while not all context-free programs are equivalent to loop--free programs.

3.3. <u>Definition</u>

A tree T is <u>locally similar</u> to another tree T′ iff there exists a map $F: T \to T' \times \omega$, satisfying the following conditions. /For F(a) = = (c,n), we write $F_0(a) = c$, $F_1(a) = n$./

a/ For all $a \in T$, $T(a,F_1(a)) = T'(F_0(a),F_1(a))$.

b/ If $wa \in T$ and $|w| \leqslant F_1(a)$ then $F_0(wa) = wF_0(a)$, $F_1(wa) \geqslant F_1(a) - |w|$.

c/ For any m, there is a q such that, if $a \in T$, $|w| = q$ and $wa \in T$,

d/ If $a,b \in T$ and $a \neq b$ then $F_0(a) \neq F_0(b)$.

That is, T is locally similar to T′ iff one can always reach a root of a fragment of T identical to a fragment of T′ of any required size, and this can be done in a bounded number of steps up the tree. Conditions /b/ and /d/ ensure that no troubles occur in case two such fragments overlap.

The next theorem is crucial for the considerations in Section 4.

3.4. <u>Theorem</u>

Let T′ be a tree with the unwind property for DRG and let a tree T be locally similar to T′. Then T has the unwind property for DRG.

The main idea of the proof of Theorem 3.4. is that if a computation in T of a program $\alpha \in$ DRG is sufficiently long then it must be performed /except a finite number of steps/ "within" large fragments of T, identical to certain fragments of T′. Thus, it can be simulated by a computation in T′.

Now we define a tree T, locally similar to T_ω, and such that there exists an /informal/ program cooperating with a push-down store /storing 0's and 1's/ which provides arbitrarily long computations. The key role in the construction of T will be played by an infinite sequence $H : \omega \rightarrow \{U,D\}$, where U and D are new symbols, not occuring elsewhere. This sequence is a limit of an increasing sequence of words H_n, for $n \in \omega$, defined inductively as follows:

$$H_0 = U, \quad \text{and} \quad H_{n+1} = DH_nH_n .$$

Since $H_n \subseteq H_{n+1}$, for all n, we can define H by $H(n) = H_m(n)$, for any m satisfying $|H_m| > n$.

The sequence H can be seen as a description of a behaviour of a push-down store in a certain computation. The symbol U /"up"/ indicates putting an element on the top of the stack, while D /"down"/ denotes removing the top element from the stack. For any n, H(n) is the stack operation executed in the n+1-th step of the computation. It is easily seen that the symbol U prevails over D in any initial segment of H, so the intuition is correct - the stack is always of a nonnegative height. We describe the intuition more formally. The function STACK : $\omega \rightarrow \omega^*$ is defined inductively by $\mathrm{STACK}(0) = \lambda$ and

$$\mathrm{STACK}(n+1) = \begin{cases} \mathrm{tail}(\mathrm{STACK}(n)), & \text{if } H(n) = D ; \\ n \cdot \mathrm{STACK}(n), & \text{if } H(n) = U . \end{cases}$$

We define also a function $\mathrm{TOP} : \omega - \{0\} \rightarrow \omega$ by $\mathrm{TOP}(n) = \mathrm{head}(\mathrm{STACK}(n))$.

The sequence STACK(n) describes the content of the stack in the n+1-th state of the computation /after n steps/. Any number j occuring in STACK(n) indicates an element pushed on the stack in the j+1-th step. Observe that, for all $n > 0$, $H(\mathrm{TOP}(n)) = U$.

Now return to the tree T_ω from Theorem 3.2. This is an infinite tree, so it has an infinite branch. That is, there are words $W_n \in T_\omega$ such that $|W_n| = n$ and $W_n \subseteq W_{n+1}$, for all n. Let $W : \omega \rightarrow \{L,R\}$ be defined by $W(n) = W_{n+1}(n)$. Then W represents the infinite branch.

We define a new sequence $V : \omega \rightarrow \{L,R\}$ to represent an infinite branch in the tree T we construct.

$$V(n) = \begin{cases} W(n), & \text{if } H(n) = D ; \\ W(m), & \text{if } H(n) = U,\ H(m) = D, \text{ and } n = \mathrm{TOP}(m) ; \\ L, & \text{otherwise.} \end{cases}$$

By an analogy to W_n, we define $V_0 = \lambda$, $V_{n+1} = V(n)V_n$.

For $n \in \omega$, let d(n) be the least number i such that $H(n+i) = U$.

At last we define the tree T, by

$$T = \{ wV_n : n \in \omega \text{ and } w \in T_\omega(W_n, d(n)) \} .$$

3.5. Lemma

T is a tree locally similar to T_ω.

From 3.1., 3.2., and 3.5., we obtain

3.6. Theorem

The algebra T, as well as $\underline{T}$, has the unwind property for DRG.

4. Main result

We are going to prove that DDL $<$ CF-DDL. We start with the following easy lemma:

4.1. Lemma

Assume that a regular program α with k variables can be unwound in an algebra A. Then there exists a quantifier-free formula φ of predicate calculus, such that, if B is elementarily equivalent to A then, for all $\underline{a},\underline{b} \in B^k$,

$$B,(\underline{a},\underline{b}) \models \varphi \quad \text{iff} \quad (\underline{a},\underline{b}) \in \rho_B(\alpha).$$

The meaning of a DDL-formula is determined by the input/output relations of programs occuring in the formula. Thus, by the above, we obtain:

4.2. Lemma

For any formula φ of DDL, there exists a formula ψ of classical predicate calculus, such that $Th(\underline{T}) \models \varphi \leftrightarrow \psi$, where $Th(\underline{T})$ denotes the set of all classical first-order formulas valid in $\underline{T}$.

Let τ^n, for $n \in \omega$, denote the term such that $V_n = \tau^n_{\underline{T}}(\lambda)$. If A is an algebra elementarily equivalent to $\underline{T}$, then the symbol V_n stands also for the element $\tau^n_A(\lambda) \in A$.

Now we prove that context-free programs can define non-trivial relations in $\underline{T}$.

4.3. Lemma

There exists a deterministic context-free program α with two variables x_1, x_2, such that, for every algebra A elementarily equivalent to $\underline{T}$, and for arbitrary $a_1, a_2 \in A$,

$$A,(a_1,a_2) \models \langle\alpha\rangle\text{true} \quad \text{iff} \quad \exists n \in \omega (\, a_2 = V_n \,).$$

Remark: It follows that α is not equivalent in $\underline{T}$ to any loop-free program, since the set $\{V_n : n \in \omega\}$ cannot be defined in $\underline{T}$ by a quantifier-free first-order formula.

Proof

Let α be the following program in DCF:

$x_1 := \lambda ; \mu Y($<u>if</u> $x_1 = x_2$ <u>then</u> $x_1 := x_1$ <u>else</u> <u>if</u> $x_1 = L(x_1) \vee x_1 = R(x_1)$ <u>then</u>
<u>if</u> $x_1 = L(x_1)$ <u>then</u> $x_1 := R(x_1) ; Y ;$ <u>if</u> $x_1 = x_2$ <u>then</u> $x_1 := x_1$ <u>else</u> $x_1 := R(x_1)$ <u>fi</u>
<u>else</u> $x_1 := L(x_1) ; Y ;$ <u>if</u> $x_1 = x_2$ <u>then</u> $x_1 := x_1$ <u>else</u> $x_1 := L(x_1)$ <u>fi</u> <u>fi</u>
<u>else</u> $x_1 := x_1$ <u>fi</u> <u>fi</u> .

To show that α has the desired property, we "translate" it into an informal program S, using a binary push-down store (i.e. a push-down store storing only 0's and 1's). The instructions to cooperate with the store will be the following:

- push(i) , for i = 0,1, "place the Boolean value i on the top of the stack":
- pop:<u>if</u> 0 <u>then</u> α_1 <u>else</u> α_2 <u>fi</u>, "remove the top element i from the stack, and execute α_1 or α_2 according to whether i = 0 or i = 1".

The program S has the following form:

<u>begin</u> $x_1 := \lambda$; <u>while</u> $x_1 \neq x_2$ <u>do</u>
<u>if</u> $x_1 = L(x_1)$ <u>then</u> push(1); $x_1 := R(x_1)$ <u>else</u>
<u>if</u> $x_1 = R(x_1)$ <u>then</u> push(0); $x_1 := L(x_1)$ <u>else</u>
pop:<u>if</u> 0 <u>then</u> $x_1 := L(x_1)$ <u>else</u> $x_1 := R(x_1)$ <u>fi</u> <u>fi</u> <u>od</u> <u>end</u>

Let A be elementarily equivalent to <u>T</u>, and let $a_1, a_2 \in A$. Suppose that the test $x_1 \neq x_2$ occurs in the computation of S, for the input (a_1, a_2), at least n+1 times. One can prove by induction, that the valuation of the variables x_1, x_2 is V_n, a_2 , when $x_1 \neq x_2$ is executed for the n+1-th time. At this step of computation, the push-down store contains the word stack(n) obtained from STACK(n) by replacing any m with V(m) = L by 0, and any m with V(m) = R by 1.

Thus, the computation of S for the input (a_1, a_2) converges in A if and only if $a_2 = V_n$, for some n. The verification that

$A, (a_1, a_2) \models \langle\alpha\rangle$true iff S converges in A for input (a_1, a_2)

is left to the reader, and this completes the proof.

At last we can state our main result.

4.4. <u>Theorem</u>

DDL $<$ CF-DDL, that is, there exists a formula φ of CF-DDL, not equivalent to any formula of DDL.

Proof

By Lemma 4.2., it suffices to prove that there is a formula φ of CF-DDL, such that $Th(\underline{T}) \not\models \varphi \leftrightarrow \psi$, for any formula ψ of classical predicate calculus. Let α be the context-free program constructed in Lemma 4.3., and let φ be the formula $\exists x_1(\langle \alpha \rangle true)$. By Lemma 4.3, φ defines the set $\{V_n : n \in \omega\}$ in any algebra A, elementarily equivalent to $\underline{T}$. Suppose that $Th(\underline{T}) \models \varphi \leftrightarrow \psi$, for some formula ψ of classical predicate calculus. By the Compactness Theorem, there is a model A of $Th(\underline{T})$, and an element $a \in A$, different than any V_n, and satisfying the formula ψ. This contradicts our assumption.

Acknowledgment: I wish to thank Jerzy Tiuryn for his critical remarks.

References:

[BHT] Berman,P.,Halpern,J.Y.,Tiuryn,J., On the power of nondeterminism in Dynamic Logic, in: Proc. of 9th ICALP,/M.Nielsen and E.M.Schmidt,eds./,Lecture Notes in Comp.Sci., vol.140, Springer Verlag, Berlin, 1982, 48-60.

[E] Erimbetov,M.M., Model-theoretic properties of languages of algorithmic logics /in Russian/, in:"Teorija modelej i ee primenenija", University of Alma-Ata, 1980.

[H] Harel,D., First-order Dynamic Logic, Lecture Notes in Comp.Sci. vol.68, Springer Verlag, Berlin,1979.

[S] Stolboushkin,A.P., private letter.

[T] Tiuryn,J., Unbounded program memory adds to the expressive power of first-order Dynamic Logic, in: Proc. of 22nd IEEE Symp. on FOCS, 1981.

[U] Urzyczyn,P., Non-trivial definability by iterative and recursive programs, to appear in Information and Control.

A NOTE ON POWERDOMAINS AND MODALITY

by
Glynn Winskel
Department of Computer Science
Carnegie-Mellon University
Pittsburgh, Pennsylvania 15213

Abstract

This note shows a simple connection between powerdomains and modal assertions that can be made about nondeterministic computations. We consider three kinds of powerdomains, the Plotkin powerdomain, the Smyth powerdomain and one Christened the Hoare powerdomain by Plotkin because it captures the partial correctness of a nondeterministic program. The modal operators are $\Box$ *for "inevitably" and* $\Diamond$ *for "possibly". It is shown in a precise sense how the Smyth powerdomain is built up from assertions about the inevitable behaviour of a process, the Hoare powerdomain is built up from assertions about the possible behaviour of a process while Plotkin powerdomain is built up from from both kinds of assertions taken together.*

0. Introduction.

Powerdomains are the complete partial orders (c.p.o.'s, which here we call domains) in which to denote nondeterministic computations. They can be regarded as the domain analogues of powerset with elements which represent the "sets" of different courses a nondeterministic computation can follow. Simple forms of powerdomains were first introduced independently by Egli and Milner but their constructions only worked correctly for powerdomains of flat , or discrete, domains. A breakthrough was made by Gordon Plotkin when he gave a construction of a powerdomain for a rather general class of domains. His construction works well for those domains which are algebraic *i.e.*domains which have a basis of isolated or finite elements [P1]. Although the Plotkin powerdomain construction produces an algebraic domain from an algebraic domain it is not the case that algebraic domains in general are closed under exponentiation, or function space, a vital construction in denotational semantics. However Plotkin was able to show how by restricting constructions to a slightly smaller class of domains, those algebraic domains which are SFP, one obtained a category closed simultaneously under his powerdomain construction and function space. His powerdomain construction could be used in the recursive definition of domains, justifying the recursive definition of domains like that of resumptions which have been used to give denotational semantics to some parallel programming languages in which atomic actions are interleaved—see [P1] and [HP] for details.

The original presentation of powerdomains in [P1] was hard to follow and the construction was streamlined by Mike Smyth in [Smy] which also introduced a new powerdomain subsequently called the Smyth powerdomain. The Smyth powerdomain identifies more processes than Plotkin's when one uses it to give a denotational semantics. However it has the technical advantage that the very pleasant category of consistently complete algebraic domains are closed under the Smyth powerdomain construction. The consistently complete algebraic domains are those represented in [S]; they can be thought of algebraic lattices with isolated top-elements removed. The work of Dana Scott has shown the nice properties of this category. In particular it is closed under function space. Unfortunately it is not closed under the Plotkin powerdomain.

To secure the work that follows we present the main results on powerdomains. The reader should have few problems filling in the proofs. For the full details the reader can refer to [Smy], though to be honest, here in the introduction we follow the lines suggested by Smyth—and earlier by Plotkin in [P1]—rather than the lines Smyth actually follows, using generating trees and finitely generable sets. (We use generating trees in the next section.)

Recall a *directed set* of a partial order $(D, \sqsubseteq)$ is a non-null subset $S \subseteq D$ such that $\forall s, t \in S \exists u \in S.\ s \sqsubseteq u \ \&\ t \sqsubseteq u$. A *complete partial order*, a c.p.o., is a partial order $(D, \sqsubseteq)$ which has a least element $\perp$ and all least upper bounds of directed subsets. An *isolated (or finite)* element of a c.p.o. $(D, \sqsubseteq)$ is an element $x \in D$ such that for any directed subset $S \subseteq D$ when $x \sqsubseteq \bigsqcup S$ there is $s \in S$ such that $x \sqsubseteq s$. We write D^0 for the set of isolated elements of D. Intuitively the isolated elements are that information which a computation can realise in finite time. When there are enough isolated elements to form a basis the c.p.o. is said to be *algebraic i.e.*a c.p.o. $(D, \sqsubseteq)$ is *algebraic* iff for all $x \in D$ we have $x = \bigsqcup\{e \sqsubseteq x \mid e \in D^0\}$. When $(D, \sqsubseteq)$ is algebraic and D^0 is countable, D is said to *countably algebraic* or simply ω-algebraic.

Smyth showed easy constructions of the powerdomains of ω-algebraic domains D. They were built from finite, non-null sets of isolated elements of D, which we call $M[D]$. Given an ordered set there are three natural ways to pre-order its subsets. Let us list the pre-orders: For A, B in $M[D]$, write

$$A \preceq_0 B \Leftrightarrow \forall b \in B \exists a \in A.\ a \sqsubseteq b$$
$$A \preceq_1 B \Leftrightarrow \forall a \in A \exists b \in B.\ a \sqsubseteq b$$
$$A \preceq_2 B \Leftrightarrow A \preceq_0 B \ \&\ A \preceq_1 B.$$

Smyth only considered two, the preorder $\preceq_2$, called the *Egli-Milner ordering*, and the preorder $\preceq_0$ from which he obtained the Plotkin and Smyth powerdomains respectively. However a similar treatment also yields a powerdomain associated with the pre-order $\preceq_1$. This powerdomain has been called the Hoare powerdomain by Plotkin because of its relation with C. A. R. Hoare's work on partial correctness. To be fair this powerdomain has been invented independently by many people, Plotkin and David Park to name two while the "Traces model" for a version of CSP [Ho] provides an instance of this powerdomain. The Hoare powerdomain ignores the divergence of computations completely but like the Smyth powerdomain works smoothly within the category of consistently complete algebraic domains.

There is a standard way to get an algebraic domain from a preorder with a least element, often called *completion by ideals*—see *e.g.* Scott's work, and [Gue]. The method is to take ideals(=left-closed, directed subsets) of the preorder and order them by inclusion to obtain an algebraic domain with isolated elements which correspond to equivalence classes of elements of the preorder under the preorder's natural equivalence. More formally,

0.1 Proposition. *Let $(P, \preceq)$ be a preorder with a least element $\perp \preceq p$ for all p in P. Define the ideals $I(P)$ by*

$$X \in I(P) \Leftrightarrow \emptyset \neq X \subseteq P \ \&\forall p, q.\ q \preceq p \in X \Rightarrow q \in X \ \&$$
$$\forall p, q \in X \exists r \in X.\ p \preceq r \ \&\ q \preceq r.$$

Then $(I(D), \subseteq)$ is an algebraic domain, with isolated elements $\{q \in P \mid q \preceq p\}$ for $p \in P$.

The three different powerdomains of D are obtained by completing by ideals the three preorders $\preceq_0$, $\preceq_1$, $\preceq_2$ on $M[D]$. As one would expect they carry natural notions of union induced by the union operation on the sets $M[D]$.

0.2 Proposition.
The Smyth powerdomain of D, written $P_0[D]$, is the completion by ideals of the preorder $(M[D], \preceq_0)$ i.e.$(P_0[D], \sqsubseteq_0) = (\mathcal{I}(M[D], \preceq_0), \subseteq)$; it carries a natural continuous union operation

$$X \cup_0 Y =_{def} \{A \cup B \mid A \in X \,\&\, B \in Y\}$$

which is associative, commutative, idempotent (i.e.$X \cup_0 X = X$) and satisfies the law $X \cup_0 Y \sqsubseteq X$.

The Hoare powerdomain of D, written $P_1[D]$, is the completion by ideals of the preorder $(M[D], \preceq_1)$ i.e.$(P_1[D], \sqsubseteq_1) = (\mathcal{I}(M[D], \preceq_1), \subseteq)$; it carries a natural continuous union operation

$$X \cup_1 Y =_{def} \{A \cup B \mid A \in X \,\&\, B \in Y\}$$

which is associative, commutative, idempotent and satisfies the law $X \sqsubseteq X \cup_0 Y$.

The Plotkin powerdomain of D, written $P_2[D]$, is the completion by ideals of the preorder $(M[D], \preceq_2)$ i.e.$(P_2[D], \sqsubseteq_2) = (\mathcal{I}(M[D], \preceq_2), \subseteq)$; it carries a natural continuous union operation

$$X \cup_2 Y =_{def} \{A \cup B \mid A \in X \,\&\, B \in Y\}$$

which is associative, commutative and idempotent.

It is easily verified that the union operations are well defined. For the Hoare powerdomain there is an even simpler construction. The Hoare powerdomain of an algebraic domain is isomorphic to the non-null left-closed subsets of its isolated elements, ordered by inclusion.

0.3 Proposition. *Let $\mathcal{L}(D^0)$ consist of the non-null, left-closed subsets of D^0 i.e.$X \in \mathcal{L}(D^0) \Leftrightarrow \emptyset \neq X \subseteq D^0 \,\&\, \forall d, e.\, d \sqsubseteq e \in X \Rightarrow d \in X$. Then $\mathcal{L}(D^0) \cong P_1[D]$, the Hoare powerdomain.*

Thus powerdomains of algebraic domains have a very simple construction. They can be looked on as kinds of algebras with a binary union operation over a domain as carrier. This approach led to a very pleasing characterisation of powerdomains due to Matthew Hennessy and Gordon Plotkin which in fact establishes the existence of powerdomains of arbitrary c.p.o.'s—see [HP]. Define a nondeterministic algebra to be a domain with a continuous binary "union" operation which is associative, commutative and idempotent. Define a homomorphism of such algebras to be a continuous function which preserves the "union" operation. The Plotkin powerdomain is the free algebra with respect to the obvious forgetful functor from algebras to domains. Similarly the Smyth powerdomain is the free algebra amongst those algebras which in addition satisfy $X \cup Y \sqsubseteq X$ and Hoare powerdomain is the free algebra amongst those satisfying $X \sqsubseteq X \cup Y$.

This completes our summary of the properties of powerdomains. In the following we show another way to view powerdomains as consisting of sets of modal assertions that can be made about nondeterministic computations. This indicates a relation between the denotational semantics of nondeterminism and work in the temporal logic of programs, for example [LO].

1. Nondeterministic computations.

Throughout let $(D, \sqsubseteq)$ be an ω–algebraic domain with isolated elements D^0.

We imagine a nondeterministic computation which at each state determines an element of D^0. The element could be for example a finite sequence of values which the computation extends as it progresses. Assume that the nondeterminism is bounded so that each state has only a finite number of next states and for simplicity that the states form a tree with respect to the next–state relation.

1.1 Definition. A *nondeterministic D–computation* has the form $(T, \longrightarrow, val)$ where $(T, \longrightarrow)$ is a finitely branching tree and *val* is a map to D^0 such that

$$\forall t, t' \in T. t \longrightarrow t' \Rightarrow val(t) \sqsubseteq val(t').$$

1.2 Notation. Let $(T, \longrightarrow)$ be a tree.

Let $t \in T$. Write $t \rightarrow$ for $\exists t' \in T. t \longrightarrow t'$ and $t \not\rightarrow$ for $\not\exists t' \in T. t \longrightarrow t'$.

A *branch* is a sequence $t_0, t_1, \ldots, t_n, \ldots$ where t_0 is the root node and $t_n \longrightarrow t_{n+1}$ for each $n+1$ at which the sequence is defined. By a *maximal branch* of $(T, \longrightarrow)$ we mean a branch which is either infinite, or finite of the form $t_0, t_1, \ldots, t_n$ with $t_n \not\rightarrow$.

In [Smy], Smyth extracts the finitely generable sets from labelled trees like those above; for convenience he requires they satisfy the additional axiom $\forall t \in T \exists t' \in T. t \longrightarrow t'$.

2. The Smyth powerdomain.

We now make a little language to talk about nondeterministic D–computations. The atomic statements are just elements of D^0. To get Smyth's powerdomain we include disjunction "$\vee$" and the "inevitably" modality "$\Box$" in the language.

2.1 Definition. Let the language L_0 be the least set including D^0 and such that

$$s \in L_0 \Rightarrow \Box s \in L_0 \quad \text{and,}$$
$$s, s' \in L_0 \Rightarrow (s \vee s') \in L_0.$$

2.2 Definition. (The satisfaction relation)

Let $(T, \longrightarrow, val)$ be a nondeterministic D–computation. Define $\models_T$ to be the least relation included in $T \times L_0$ such that

$$a \sqsubseteq val(t) \Rightarrow t \models_T a \quad \text{for } a \in D^0,$$
$$t \models_T s \text{ or } t \models_T s' \Rightarrow t \models_T (s \vee s') \quad \text{and,}$$
$$t \models_T s \text{ or } (t \rightarrow \& \ \forall t'. t \longrightarrow t' \Rightarrow t' \models_T \Box s) \Rightarrow t \models_T \Box s.$$

Alternatively $\models$ can be constructed inductively as the union of a chain of relations got by starting at the null relation and at each stage growing the relation in accord with the three clauses above. Because T is finitely–branching the closure ordinal of this associated inductive definition will be ω.

Another way to define satisfaction for $\Box$-statements is to say $t \models_T \Box s$ iff every maximal branch in the subtree out of t has a node which satisfies s. In a picture:

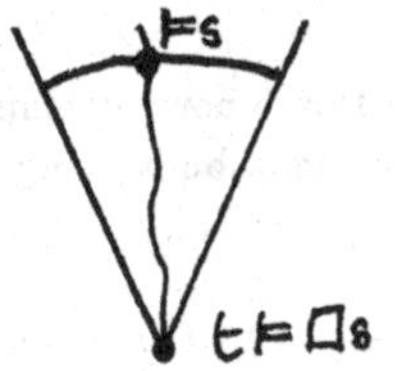

This means our satisfaction relation for statements $\Box(s \vee s')$ is the same as that for statements $(s \vee s')$ in Beth trees—see [D].

Suppose we are not interested in the statements which are initially true (at the root node) of a nondeterministic computation but in those statements which are inevitably true. Then it is natural to associate the following set of assertions with a nondeterministic computation.

2.3 Definition. Let $T = (T, \to, val)$ be a nondeterministic D-computation with root node t. Write $\models_T s$ for $t \models_T s$. Define

$$V_0(T) = \{\Box s \in L_0 \,|\models_T \Box s\}.$$

Such sets of assertions induce an obvious preorder on nondeterministic D-computations.

2.4 Definition. Let T and T' be nondeterministic D-computations. Define

$$T \preceq_0 T' \Leftrightarrow V_0(T) \subseteq V_0(T').$$

Quotienting the preorder $\preceq_0$ on nondeterministic computations by the equivalence $\simeq_0 =_{def} \preceq_0 \cap \preceq_0^{-1}$ we obtain the Smyth powerdomain (see [Smy]).

2.5 Theorem. *Let $\mathcal{T}$ be the class of nondeterministic D-computations. The Smyth powerdomain $P_0[D]$ is isomorphic to the quotient $(\mathcal{T}/\simeq_0, \preceq_0/\simeq_0)$.*

Proof. (sketched) Write $s \equiv s'$ iff $\forall T.(\models_T s \Leftrightarrow \models_T s')$. Clearly $s \vee (s' \vee s'') \equiv (s \vee s') \vee s''$ and $s \vee s' \equiv s' \vee s$ so we need not trouble ourselves over the order of disjunctions. It is easy to check that $\Box(\Box s) \equiv \Box s$ and $\Box(s \vee \Box s') \equiv \Box(s \vee s')$. A simple induction shows that each each $\Box s \in L_0$ is $\equiv$-equivalent to a normal form $\Box(a_0 \vee \cdots \vee a_n)$ for some $a_0, \ldots, a_n \in D^0$. Thus the statements $V_0(T)$, satisfied by T, are equivalent to those of a simpler form. Now, to each computation T we associate a subset of $M[D]$ given by $I(T) = \{\{a_0, \ldots, a_n\} \,|\models_T \Box(a_0 \vee \cdots a_n)\}$. From the properties of $\Box$-statements it follows that $I(T)$ is an ideal w.r.t. $\preceq_0$ and so an element of $P_0[D]$. Conversely any element x of $P[D]$ can be obtained as $x = I(T)$ for some computation T constructed as follows : The ideal x is generated by an ω-chain $X_0 \preceq_0 \cdots X_n \preceq_0 \cdots$; inductively construct T so that the labels of its nodes at height n form the set X_n. It follows that there is a 1-1, $\subseteq$-preserving correspondence between sets $V_0(T)$ and the elements of $P_0[D]$. This implies the result. ∎

Remark. Clearly from the above proof, the result holds if we restrict the statements to those of the form $\Box(a_0 \vee \cdots \vee a_n)$ where $a_0, \ldots, a_n \in D^0$.

3. The Hoare powerdomain.

To get another powerdomain, the Hoare powerdomain—sometimes called the upside-down-Smyth powerdomain—we look at assertions built using the modal operator $\Diamond$ standing for "possibly".

3.1 Definition. Define the language L_1 to be the language which is the least set including the atomic statements D^0 such that

$$s \in L_1 \Rightarrow \Diamond s \in L_1.$$

3.2 Definition. (The satisfaction relation)
Let $(T, \longrightarrow, val)$ be a nondeterministic D-computation. Define $\models_T$ to be the least relation included in $T \times L_1$ such that

$$a \sqsubseteq val(t) \Rightarrow t \models_T a \quad \text{and,}$$
$$t \models_T s \text{ or } \exists t'.t \longrightarrow t' \;\&\; t' \models_T \Diamond s \Rightarrow t \models_T \Diamond s.$$

Alternatively satisfaction for $\Diamond$-statements could be defined by saying $t \models_T \Diamond s$ iff there is a branch out of t which has a node which satisfies s. In a picture:

As before we can preorder nondeterministic computations by the statements they satisfy. This time we are interested in their possibilities.

3.3 Definition. Let $T = (T, \rightarrow, val)$ be a nondeterministic D-computation with root node t. Write $\models_T s$ for $t \models_T s$. Define

$$V_1(T) = \{\Diamond s \in L_1 \mid \models_T s\}.$$

For nondeterministic D-computations, T and T' define

$$T \preceq_1 T' \Leftrightarrow V_1(T) \subseteq V_1(T').$$

The preorder $\preceq_1$, when quotiented by the equivalence $\simeq_1 =_{def} \preceq_1 \cap \preceq_1^{-1}$, gives a powerdomain associated with the other half of the Egli–Milner ordering to Smyth's—called the upside-down-Smyth powerdomain or Hoare powerdomain.

3.4 Theorem. *Let $\mathcal{T}$ be the class of nondeterministic D-computations. The Hoare powerdomain $P_1[D]$ is isomorphic to the quotient $(\mathcal{T}/\simeq_1, \preceq/\simeq_1)$.*

Proof. Write $s \equiv s'$ iff $\forall T.(\models_T s \Leftrightarrow \models_T s')$. Each statement $\Diamond s \in L_1$ is $\equiv$-equivalent to a normal form $\Diamond a$ for some $a \in D^0$. For a computation T, define $I(T) = \{a \in D^0 \mid \models_T \Diamond s\}$. Then $I(T) \in \mathcal{L}(D^0)$, the non-null, left-closed subsets of D^0. Because each statement has a normal form it is clear that $T \preceq_1 T' \Leftrightarrow I(T) \subseteq I(T')$. However I is onto $\mathcal{L}(D^0)$ (Given $x \in \mathcal{L}(D^0)$, the reader is invited to construct T so $I(T) = x$). But $\mathcal{L}(D^0) \cong P_1[D]$, establishing the result. ∎

Remark. The same result would hold if L_1 was restricted to sentences of the form $\Diamond a$ for $a \in D^0$ or expanded to include sentences of the form $\Diamond(s \vee s')$.

4. The Plotkin powerdomain.

Finally the Plotkin powerdomain is obtained by considering information about both the inevitable and possible behaviour of a computation.

4.1 Definition. Let L_2 be the least language containing the elements D^0 as atoms and such that

$$s, s' \in L_2 \Rightarrow (s \vee s') \in L_2,$$
$$s \in L_2 \Rightarrow \Box s \in L_2,$$
$$s \in L_2 \Rightarrow \Diamond s \in L_2.$$

4.2 Definition. (The satisfaction relation.)
Let $(T, \longrightarrow, val)$ be a nondeterministic D-computation. Let $\models_T$ be the least relation included in $T \times L_2$ which satisfies:

$$a \sqsubseteq val(t) \Rightarrow t \models_T a \quad \text{for } a \in D^0,$$
$$t \models_T s \text{ or } t \models_T s' \Rightarrow t \models_T s \vee s',$$
$$t \models_T s \text{ or } (t \rightarrow \& \ \forall t'.t \longrightarrow t' \Rightarrow t' \models_T \Box s) \Rightarrow t \models_T \Box s,$$
$$t \models_T s \text{ or } \exists t'.t \longrightarrow t' \ \& \ t' \models_T \Diamond s \Rightarrow t \models_T \Diamond s.$$

Again, equivalently, one has $t \models_T \Box s$ iff all maximal branches from t meet a node satisfying s and $t \models_T \Diamond s$ iff there is a branch from t with a node satisfying s.

Again assume we are only interested in that information which holds inevitably, including statements like $\Box((\Diamond a) \vee b)$.

4.3 Definition. Let $(T, \longrightarrow, val)$ be a nondeterministic D-computation with root node t. Write $\models_T s$ for $t \models_T s$. Define

$$V_2(T) = \{\Box s \in L_2 \mid \models_T \Box s\}.$$

Let T and T' be nondeterministic D-computations. Define

$$T \preceq_2 T' \Leftrightarrow V_2(T) \subseteq V_2(T').$$

Define

$$\simeq_2 = \preceq_2 \cap \preceq_2^{-1}.$$

4.4 Theorem. *Let T be the class of nondeterministic D-computations. The Plotkin powerdomain $P_2[D]$ is isomorphic to the quotient $(\mathcal{T}/\simeq_2, \preceq_2/\simeq_2)$.*

Proof. (sketched) Again write $s \equiv s'$ iff $\forall T.\ \models_T s \equiv \models_T s'$. We have the following equivalences: $\Diamond(\Diamond s) \equiv \Diamond(\Box s) \equiv \Box(\Diamond s) \equiv \Diamond s$; $\Box(\Box s) \equiv \Box s$; $\Diamond(s \vee s') \equiv (\Diamond s) \vee (\Diamond s')$; $\Box(s \vee (\Box s')) \equiv \Box(s \vee s')$; $\Box(s \vee (\Diamond s')) \equiv (\Box s) \vee (\Diamond s')$. Using these facts, a simple induction shows each sentence s of L_2 is equivalent to one s^* in normal form as shown:

$$a_0 \vee \cdots \vee a_{n-1} \vee (\Diamond b_0) \vee \cdots \vee (\Diamond b_{m-1}) \vee \Box(c_0{}^0 \vee \cdots \vee c^0{}_{p_0-1}) \vee \cdots$$
$$\vee \Box(c_0{}^{q-1} \vee \cdots \vee c^{q-1}{}_{p_{q-1}-1}).$$

We use the convention that null sequences of statements represent $\bot \in D^0$. Observe in particular statements $\Box s$ have a normal form

$$\Box s \equiv \Box(a_0 \vee \cdots \vee a_{n-1}) \vee \Diamond b_0 \vee \cdots \vee \Diamond b_{m-1}.$$

Observe too that if $s \vee s' \in V_2(T)$ then $s \in V_2(T)$ or $s' \in V_2(T)$. From these two observations we obtain

$$T \preceq_2 T' \Leftrightarrow V_0(T) \subseteq V_0(T') \;\&\; V_1(T) \subseteq V_1(T').$$

The proof of "$\Rightarrow$" is clear. The proof of "$\Leftarrow$" follows from the two observations. Consequently, by theorems 2.5 and 3.4, we have $(\mathcal{T}/\simeq_2, \preceq_2/\simeq_2) \cong P_2[D]$. ∎

Remark. It is clear from the proof that the result also holds if we restrict the language to sentences of the form $\Diamond a$ and $\Box(a_0 \vee \cdots \vee a_n)$ where $a, a_0, \ldots, a_n \in D^0$.

The next example shows the above results do not hold if one expands the language L_2 to include conjunction, with the obvious definition of satisfaction. A domain based on this expanded set of assertions must have a more complicated domain construction than that of a simple powerdomain, quite probably as a combination of powerdomain and product constructions.

4.5 Example. Assume N is the flat domain of integers with elements $\{\bot\} \cup \omega$ ordered by $x \sqsubseteq x$ and $\bot \sqsubseteq n$ for $n \in \omega$. Extend the language L_2 to include statements of the form $s \wedge s'$ and the satisfaction relation so $t \models_T s \wedge s'$ iff $t \models_T s$ and $t \models_T s'$. Let T and T' be the nondeterministic N-computations shown:

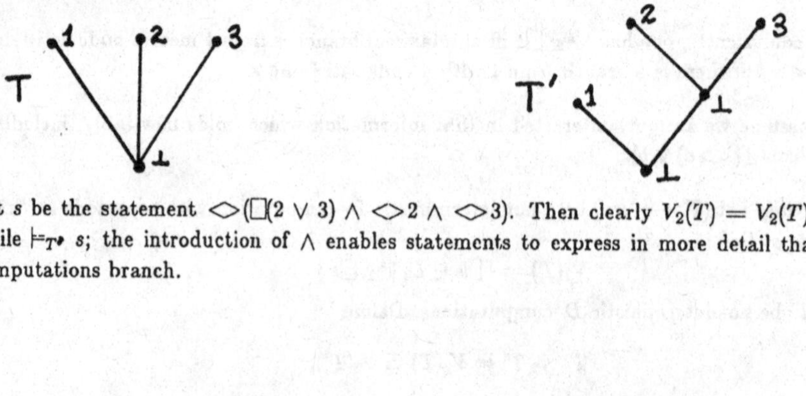

Let s be the statement $\Diamond(\Box(2 \vee 3) \wedge \Diamond 2 \wedge \Diamond 3)$. Then clearly $V_2(T) = V_2(T)$ but $\not\models_T s$ while $\models_{T'} s$; the introduction of $\wedge$ enables statements to express in more detail than L_2 how computations branch.

5. Generalisations.

It is not necessary to model the nondeterministic computations as trees. The above results would also hold if instead of trees we used transition systems. One could also allow states to be only partially defined to cope with divergence—see [HN]—provided one modified the definition of satisfaction for statements of the form $\Box s$. Such ideas are used in [HN] and [HM] to induce natural equivalences on communicating processes. It might be interesting to study the relation between domains of computations, like trees, and domains of sets of statements induced by satisfaction relations.

It would be interesting to relax the finitely-branching condition to allow ω-branching trees and in addition to the binary disjunction $\vee$ allow an infinitary disjunction $\bigvee$ over countable sets of assertions. It should be the case that one obtains versions of the Hoare and Plotkin powerdomains generalised to countable nondeterminism. The Plotkin powerdomain has been generalised to countable nondeterminism in [P2] using rather nonconstructive means, so a characterisaion based on modal assertions would provide a useful intuitive construction. Of course, if one follows the approach above and takes atomic statements to be the isolated or finite elements of a domain this construction would be of limited use because the resulting powerdomain would most likely not be algebraic, and so not amenable to the same construction itself. However, following this line may suggest a notion generalising that of isolated or finite element. Note that by the example of [AP] the obvious generalisation of section 2 to countable disjunction $\bigvee$ will not in general yield a c.p.o., so it can not directly yield a generalisation of the Smyth powerdomain to countable nondeterminism.

There are strong links with the idea of information systems a suggestive way of representing consistently complete algebraic c.p.o.'s presented by Dana Scott in [S]; elements of a domain are represented by consistent, deductively-closed sets of statements. However note until that framework is generalised to represent at least the SFP objects it will not support the Plotkin powerdomain construction. Still, it is an attractive idea, that the Scott-information denoting a computation can be regarded as the set of statements it satisfies. It invites us to look at domain constructions in a new way, as accompanying extensions to the languages with which we describe computations.

Acknowledgements.

This work was supported in part by Carnegie-Mellon University and in part by a postdoctoral fellowship from the Royal Society of Great Britain, to work at the Computer Science Department, Aarhus University, Denmark.

References

[AP] Apt, K.R. and Plotkin, G.D. A Cook's tour of Countable Nondeterminism. Lecture Notes in Comp. Sc. Vol.115, ICALP 1981.

[D] Dummett, M., Elements of Intuitionism. Oxford University Press (1977).

[Gue] Guessarian, I., Algebraic Semantics. Springer–Verlag LNCS Vol.99 (1981).

[HM] Hennessy, M.C.B. and Milner, R., On observing nondeterminism and concurrency, Springer LNCS Vol. 85. (1979).

[HN] Hennessy, M.C.B., and de Nicola, R., Testing Equivalences for Processes, Internal Report, University of Edinburgh, (July 1982).

[HP] Hennessy, M.C.B. and Plotkin, G., Full Abstraction for a Simple Parallel Programming Languages, LNCS Vol 74 (1979).

[Ho] Hoare, C. A. R., A Model for Communicating Sequential Processes, Technical Report PRG–22, Programming Research Group, Oxford University Computing Lab. (1981).

[LO] Lamport, L., and Owicki, S., Proving Liveness Properties of Concurrent Programs, Technical Report, SRI International (1980).

[P1] Plotkin, G., A powerdomain construction, SIAM J. on computing, 5, pp.452–486, 1976.

[P2] Plotkin, G., A Powerdomain for countable non–determinism, Springer–Verlag Lecture Notes in Comp. Sc. 140 (1982).

[Smy] Smyth, M., Powerdomains. JCSS Vol.16 No.1 (1978).

[S] Scott, D., Domains for Denotational Semantics, Springer–Verlag Lecture Notes in Comp. Sc. 140 (1982).

LATE ARRIVALS

REASONING WITH FAIRNESS CONSTRAINTS

David Park
Department of Computer Science
Warwick University
Coventry CV4 7AL
ENGLAND

ABSTRACT

1. In addition to the standard guarded iteration construct

$$\text{DO:}\quad \underline{\text{do}}\ B_1\text{->}\ C_1\ \Box\ldots\ldots\Box\ B_n\text{->}\ C_n\ \underline{\text{od}}$$

consider the constructs with fairness constraints:

$$\text{WDO:}\quad \underline{\text{wdo}}\ B_1\text{->}\ C_1\Box\ldots\ldots\Box\ B_n\text{->}\ C_n\ \text{od}$$

$$\text{SDO:}\quad \underline{\text{sdo}}\ B_1\text{->}\ C_1\Box\ldots\ldots\Box\ B_n\text{->}\ C_n\ \text{od}$$

with the following conditions on diverging computations:

(a) <u>weak fairness</u> : WDO may only result in a divergent computation if each C_i whose corresponding guard B_i is true at all iterations from some point on is executed at infinitely many iterations.

(b) <u>strong fairness</u>: SDO may only result in a divergent computation if each C_i whose corresponding guard B_i is true at infinitely many iterations is executed at infinitely many iterations.

2. Predicate transformers for DO, WDO are definable using fixpoint operators.

NOTATION: $\mu X.R(X)$ is the strongest predicate X such that $X = R(X)$.

$\nu X.R(X)$ is the weakest predicate x such that $X = R(X)$.

REMARK: provided $R(X)$ is monotone (i.e. provided that $(X \Rightarrow Y) \vdash (R(X) \Rightarrow R(Y))$) then both $\mu X.R(X)$ $\nu X.R(X)$ are well-defined. In accepted terminology these are respectively the minimal and maximal fixpoints of $R(X)$.

Predicate transformers for DO, WDO are then defined by

$$wp(DO, R) = \mu X.((\bigwedge_i \neg B_i \Rightarrow R) \wedge \bigwedge_i (B_i \Rightarrow wp(C_i, X)))$$

$$G_i(X) = \nu Y.((B_i \wedge wp(C_i, X)) \wedge \bigwedge_i (B_i \Rightarrow wp(C_i, X \vee Y)))$$

$$wp(WDO, R) = \mu X.((\bigwedge_i \neg B_i \wedge R) \vee \bigvee_i G_i(X))$$

3. wdo, sdo are features which admit unbounded nondeterminism. A nondeterministic integer assignement

$$x := ?$$

may be programmed using eith feature. Indeed all three features, wdo, sdo, the use of '?', are interderivable. The predicate transformers defined in (2) are valid regardless of the unbounded nondeterminism -- in contrast to the definition of wp(DO, R) by Dijkstra.

4. Reasoning for programs involving do, wdo may be formalised using fixpoint rules corresponding to the μ, ν operators for monotone functionals.

5. DEFINITION: A scheduler for the iterations DO, WDO, SDO is a deterministic transducer with

INPUT ALPHABET: subsets $I \subseteq \{1,2,\ldots.n\}$, $I \neq \phi$ (corresponding to the sets of guards true at iterations).

OUTPUT ALPABET: elements $C \in \{1,2,\ldots n\}$ (corresponding to scheduling choices at iterations).

Inputs I and corresponding outputs C must satisfy

$$C \in I$$

for each transition of the scheduler.

The scheduler is valid for DO, WDO, SDO respectively, if its repeated use to resolve nondeterminsitic choices results in a correct computation.

OBSERVATION: There are valid finite-state schedulers with the following numbers of states:

DO:	1 state
WDO:	n states
SDO:	n! states

THEOREM [Fischer, Paterson]: there exist DO, WDO, SDO such that the sizes of the schedulers observed above are in each case minimal.

[NOTE: proofs , by induction on n in the case of SDO, are elementary.]

REFERENCES:

Dijkstra, E W: A Discipline of Programming, Prentice-Hall (1976).

Park, D: A Predicate Transformer for Weak Fair Iteration; pp 259-275, Proc 6th IBM Symposium on Mathematical Foundations of Computer Science, IBM Japan (1981)

Fischer, M J, Paterson, M S: Storage Requirements for Fair Scheduling; to appear in Information Processing Letters.

Vol. 107: International Colloquium on Formalization of Programming Concepts. Proceedings. Edited by J. Diaz and I. Ramos. VII, 478 pages. 1981.

Vol. 108: Graph Theory and Algorithms. Edited by N. Saito and T. Nishizeki. VI, 216 pages. 1981.

Vol. 109: Digital Image Processing Systems. Edited by L. Bolc and Zenon Kulpa. V, 353 pages. 1981.

Vol. 110: W. Dehning, H. Essig, S. Maass, The Adaptation of Virtual Man-Computer Interfaces to User Requirements in Dialogs. X, 142 pages. 1981.

Vol. 111: CONPAR 81. Edited by W. Händler. XI, 508 pages. 1981.

Vol. 112: CAAP '81. Proceedings. Edited by G. Astesiano and C. Böhm. VI, 364 pages. 1981.

Vol. 113: E.-E. Doberkat, Stochastic Automata: Stability, Nondeterminism, and Prediction. IX, 135 pages. 1981.

Vol. 114: B. Liskov, CLU, Reference Manual. VIII, 190 pages. 1981.

Vol. 115: Automata, Languages and Programming. Edited by S. Even and O. Kariv. VIII, 552 pages. 1981.

Vol. 116: M. A. Casanova, The Concurrency Control Problem for Database Systems. VII, 175 pages. 1981.

Vol. 117: Fundamentals of Computation Theory. Proceedings, 1981. Edited by F. Gécseg. XI, 471 pages. 1981.

Vol. 118: Mathematical Foundations of Computer Science 1981. Proceedings, 1981. Edited by J. Gruska and M. Chytil. XI, 589 pages. 1981.

Vol. 119: G. Hirst, Anaphora in Natural Language Understanding: A Survey. XIII, 128 pages. 1981.

Vol. 120: L. B. Rall, Automatic Differentiation: Techniques and Applications. VIII, 165 pages. 1981.

Vol. 121: Z. Zlatev, J. Wasniewski, and K. Schaumburg, Y12M Solution of Large and Sparse Systems of Linear Algebraic Equations. IX, 128 pages. 1981.

Vol. 122: Algorithms in Modern Mathematics and Computer Science. Proceedings, 1979. Edited by A. P. Ershov and D. E. Knuth. XI, 487 pages. 1981.

Vol. 123: Trends in Information Processing Systems. Proceedings, 1981. Edited by A. J. W. Duijvestijn and P. C. Lockemann. XI, 349 pages. 1981.

Vol. 124: W. Polak, Compiler Specification and Verification. XIII, 269 pages. 1981.

Vol. 125: Logic of Programs. Proceedings, 1979. Edited by E. Engeler. V, 245 pages. 1981.

Vol. 126: Microcomputer System Design. Proceedings, 1981. Edited by M. J. Flynn, N. R. Harris, and D. P. McCarthy. VII, 397 pages. 1982.

Voll. 127: Y.Wallach, Alternating Sequential/Parallel Processing. X, 329 pages. 1982.

Vol. 128: P. Branquart, G. Louis, P. Wodon, An Analytical Description of CHILL, the CCITT High Level Language. VI, 277 pages. 1982.

Vol. 129: B. T. Hailpern, Verifying Concurrent Processes Using Temporal Logic. VIII, 208 pages. 1982.

Vol. 130: R. Goldblatt, Axiomatising the Logic of Computer Programming. XI, 304 pages. 1982.

Vol. 131: Logics of Programs. Proceedings, 1981. Edited by D. Kozen. VI, 429 pages. 1982.

Vol. 132: Data Base Design Techniques I: Requirements and Logical Structures. Proceedings, 1978. Edited by S.B. Yao, S.B. Navathe, J.L. Weldon, and T.L. Kunii. V, 227 pages. 1982.

Vol. 133: Data Base Design Techniques II: Proceedings, 1979. Edited by S.B. Yao and T.L. Kunii. V, 229–399 pages. 1982.

Vol. 134: Program Specification. Proceedings, 1981. Edited by J. Staunstrup. IV, 426 pages. 1982.

Vol. 135: R.L. Constable, S.D. Johnson, and C.D. Eichenlaub, An Introduction to the PL/CV2 Programming Logic. X, 292 pages. 1982.

Vol. 136: Ch. M. Hoffmann, Group-Theoretic Algorithms and Graph Isomorphism. VIII, 311 pages. 1982.

Vol. 137: International Symposium on Programming. Proceedings, 1982. Edited by M. Dezani-Ciancaglini and M. Montanari. VI, 406 pages. 1982.

Vol. 138: 6th Conference on Automated Deduction. Proceedings, 1982. Edited by D.W. Loveland. VII, 389 pages. 1982.

Vol. 139: J. Uhl, S. Drossopoulou, G. Persch, G. Goos, M. Dausmann, G. Winterstein, W. Kirchgässner, An Attribute Grammar for the Semantic Analysis of Ada. IX, 511 pages. 1982.

Vol. 140: Automata, Languages and programming. Edited by M. Nielsen and E.M. Schmidt. VII, 614 pages. 1982.

Vol. 141: U. Kastens, B. Hutt, E. Zimmermann, GAG: A Practical Compiler Generator. IV, 156 pages. 1982.

Vol. 142: Problems and Methodologies in Mathematical Software Production. Proceedings, 1980. Edited by P.C. Messina and A. Murli. VII, 271 pages. 1982.

Vol. 143: Operating Systems Engineering. Proceedings, 1980. Edited by M. Maekawa and L.A. Belady. VII, 465 pages. 1982.

Vol. 144: Computer Algebra. Proceedings, 1982. Edited by J. Calmet. XIV, 301 pages. 1982.

Vol. 145: Theoretical Computer Science. Proceedings, 1983. Edited by A.B. Cremers and H.P. Kriegel. X, 367 pages. 1982.

Vol. 146: Research and Development in Information Retrieval. Proceedings, 1982. Edited by G. Salton and H.-J. Schneider. IX, 311 pages. 1983.

Vol. 147: RIMS Symposia on Software Science and Engineering. Proceedings, 1982. Edited by E. Goto, I. Nakata, K. Furukawa, R. Nakajima, and A. Yonezawa. V. 232 pages. 1983.

Vol. 148: Logics of Programs and Their Applications. Proceedings, 1980. Edited by A. Salwicki. VI, 324 pages. 1983.

Vol. 149: Cryptography. Proceedings, 1982. Edited by T. Beth. VIII, 402 pages. 1983.

Vol. 150: Enduser Systems and Their Human Factors. Proceedings, 1983. Edited by A. Blaser and M. Zoeppritz. III, 138 pages. 1983.

Vol. 151: R. Piloty, M. Barbacci, D. Borrione, D. Dietmeyer, F. Hill, and P. Skelly, CONLAN Report. XII, 174 pages. 1983.

Vol. 152: Specification and Design of Software Systems. Proceedings, 1982. Edited by E. Knuth and E. J. Neuhold. V, 152 pages. 1983.

Vol. 153: Graph-Grammars and Their Application to Computer Science. Proceedings, 1982. Edited by H. Ehrig, M. Nagl, and G. Rozenberg. VII, 452 pages. 1983.

Vol. 154: Automata, Languages and Programming. Proceedings, 1983. Edited by J. Díaz. VIII, 734 pages. 1983.

Vol. 155: The Programming Language Ada. Reference Manual. Approved 17 February 1983. American National Standards Institute, Inc. ANSI/MIL-STD-1815A-1983. IX, 331 pages. 1983.

Vol. 156: M. H. Overmars, The Design of Dynamic Data Structures. VII, 181 pages. 1983.

Vol. 157: O. Østerby, Z. Zlatev, Direct Methods for Sparse Matrices. VIII, 127 pages. 1983.

Vol. 158: Foundations of Computation Theory. Proceedings, 1983. Edited by M. Karpinski, XI, 517 pages. 1983.